MARCUS AURELIUS
ANTONINUS

RECEIVING GERMAN PRISONERS IN THE FIELD
PANEL FROM TRIUMPHAL ARCH.

NOTE ON ILLUSTRATION

   This is one of twelve panels from the Triumphal Arch of Marcus, erected on the Capitol in 176 in honour of the double conquest of Germans and Sarmatians. It represents two German captives brought in by a praetorian guard. They are begging the Emperor's mercy, which the protective gesture of his hand shews is being granted. The face of Marcus is grave and sad. Behind him appears the praetorian prefect, Bassaeus Rufus. The composition of the work is fine and effective. This panel with others was taken from the Church of Santa Martina on the Capitol in 1525 and is now preserved on the first landing of the Palace of the Conservatori at Rome.

THE COMMUNINGS WITH HIMSELF OF

MARCUS AURELIUS ANTONINUS

EMPEROR OF ROME

TOGETHER WITH HIS SPEECHES AND SAYINGS

A REVISED TEXT AND A TRANSLATION
INTO ENGLISH BY

C. R. HAINES, M.A., F.S.A.

CAMBRIDGE, MASSACHUSETTS
HARVARD UNIVERSITY PRESS
LONDON
WILLIAM HEINEMANN LTD
MCMLIII

First printed 1916
Reprinted 1924
Reprinted and revised 1930
Reprinted 1953

Printed in Great Britain

ΕΙΣ ΒΙΒΛΟΝ ΜΑΡΚΟΥ [1]

Εἰ λύπης κρατέειν ἐθέλεις,
τήνδε μάκαιραν ἀναπτύσσων
βίβλον ἐπέρχεο ἐνδυκέως,
ἧς ὑπὸ γνώμην ὀλβίστην
ῥεῖά κεν ὄψεαι ἐσσομένων
ὄντων τ' ἠδὲ παροιχομένων
τερπωλήν τ' ἀνίην τε < λέγων >
καπνοῦ μηδὲν ἀρειοτέρην.

If thou would'st master care and pain,
Unfold this book and read and read again
Its blessed leaves, whereby thou soon shalt see
The past, the present, and the days to be
With opened eyes ; and all delight, all grief,
Shall be like smoke, as empty and as brief.

C. R. H.

Μόνος βασιλέων φιλοσοφίαν οὐ λόγοις οὔτε δογμάτων γνώσεσι, σεμνῷ δὲ ἤθει καὶ σωφρόνι βίῳ ἐπιστώσατο.—HERODIAN, i. 2, § 4

Οὐδὲν αὐτὸν ἐξεβιάσατο ἔξω τι τῶν ἑαυτοῦ ἠθῶν πρᾶξαι.—DIO CASSIUS 71. 30, § 2.

Ὁ λογισμὸς αὐτοῦ θεῖος καὶ ὡς ἀληθῶς ἄνωθεν ἔχων τὸ παράδειγμα καὶ πρὸς ἐκείνην ὁρῶν τὴν πολιτείαν.—ARISTIDES, Paneg in Cyz. § 427 (Jebb).

---

[1] This epigram is found at the end of the Vatican MS. and also in the *Anthologia Palatina*, ii. p. 603 (Jacobs). Possibly by Arethas (see P. Maas in *Hermes* xlviii. p. 295 ff.).

v

PREFACE

THE Greek text of this book is often difficult and in many places corrupt beyond cure, but no trouble has been spared to make the translation as accurate and idiomatic as possible. I have preferred to err, if error it be, on the side of over-faithfulness, because the physiognomy of the book owes so much to the method and style in which it is written. Its homeliness, abruptness, and want of literary finish (though it does not lack rhetoric) are part of the character of the work, and we alter this character by rewriting it into the terse, epigrammatic, staccato style so much in vogue at the present day. Another reason for literalness is that it makes a comparison with the Greek, printed beside it, easier for the unlearned. When a work has been translated so often as this one, it is difficult to be original without deviating further from the text, but I have not borrowed a phrase, scarcely a word, from any of my predecessors. If unconscious coincidences appear, it remains only to say *Pereant*

PREFACE

qui ante nos nostra dixerint! Numerous references
(such as have proved so invaluable for the due
understanding of the Bible) and good indices have
always been greatly wanted in the translations of
this work, and I have taken pains to supply the
want. For a better understanding of the character of
Marcus I have added to the *Thoughts* translations of
his *Speeches* and *Sayings,* with a Note on his attitude
towards the Christians (in which I am glad to find
myself in complete agreement with M. Lemercier).
A companion volume on the Correspondence with
Fronto will contain all his extant Letters. In conclusion my best thanks are due to Messrs. Teubner
for permission to use their text as the basis of the
revised one here printed, to Professors Leopold and
Schenkl for advice and help on various points,
and, last but not least, to my predecessors in the
translation of this " Golden Book."

C. R. HAINES.

Godalming, 1915.

CONTENTS

INTRODUCTION

It is not known how this small but priceless book of private devotional memoranda[1] came to be preserved for posterity. But the writer that in it puts away all desire for after-fame has by means of it attained to imperishable remembrance. As Renan has said, "tous, tant que nous sommes, nous portons au cœur le deuil de Marc Aurèle comme s'il était mort d'hier." Internal evidence proves that the author was Marcus Antoninus, emperor of Rome 7 March 161 to 17 March 180, and notes added in one MS between Books I and II and II and III shew that the second Book was composed when the writer was among the Quadi on the Gran, and the third at Carnuntum (Haimburg). The headquarters of Marcus in the war against the barbarians were at Carnuntum 171–173, and we know that the so-called "miraculous victory" against the Quadi was in 174.[2] But Professor Schenkl has given good reasons for thinking that the first book was really written last and prefixed as a sort of introduction to the rest of the work.[3] It was probably written as a whole, while the other books consist mostly of disconnected jottings. The style

[1] Marcus may be referring in Bk. III. 14 to this his own work as ὑπομνημάτια.

[2] See Dio, 71. 8.

[3] For a discussion of the chronology of the work, see *Journal of Philology*, vol. xxiii., No. 66, 1914.

throughout is abrupt and concise, and words have
occasionally to be supplied to complete the sense.
There is here no reasoned treatise on Ethics, no
exposition of Stoic Philosophy, such as the *sectarum
ardua ac perocculta*[1] or the *ordo praeceptionum*,[2] on
which Marcus is said to have discoursed before he set
out the last time for the war in 178, but we have a
man and a ruler taking counsel with himself, noting
his own shortcomings, excusing those of others, and
" whatsoever things are true, whatsoever things are
honourable, whatsoever things are lovely, whatsoever
things are pure," exhorting his soul to think on
these things. Never were words written more
transparently single-hearted and sincere. They
were not merely written, they were lived. Those
who accuse Marcus of pharisaism wilfully mistake
his character and betray their own. Very noticeable
is the delicacy of the author's mind and the
restrained energy of his style. He eschews all the
' windflowers ' of speech, but the simplicity, straight-
forwardness, and dignity of his thoughts lend an
imperial nobility to his expression of them. There
is a certain choiceness and even poetry in his words
which amply condone an occasional roughness and
technicality of phrase. Striking images are not
infrequent, and such a passage as Book II, 2 is
unique in ancient literature. This is not a book of
confessions, and comparatively few allusions to
personal incidents are to be found except in the
first book, while an air of complete aloofness and
detachment pervades the whole. The author expressly disclaims all δριμύτης or originality and

[1] Victor *de Caes.* xvi. 9.
[2] Vulc. Gallicanus *Vit. Av. Cass.* iii. 7.

acuteness of intellect, and there is a good deal of repetition unavoidable in the nature of the work, for "line upon line" and "precept upon precept" are required in all moral teaching.

Of his two great Stoic predecessors Marcus has no affinity with Seneca. He certainly knew all about him and they have many thoughts[1] in common, but Seneca's rhetorical flamboyance, his bewildering contradictions, the glaring divergence between his profession and his practice have no counterpart in Marcus. Epictetus the Phrygian slave was his true spiritual father, but we do not find in the Emperor the somewhat rigid didacticism and spiritual dogmatism of his predecessor. Marcus is humbler and not so confident. The hardness and arrogance of Stoicism are softened in him by an infusion of Platonism and other philosophies.[2] With the Peripatetics he admits the inequality of faults. His humanity will not cast out compassion as an emotion of the heart.[3] His is no cut and dried creed, for he often wavers and is inconsistent. Call not his teaching ineffectual. He is not trying to teach anyone. He is reasoning with his own soul and championing its cause against the persuasions and impulses of the flesh. How far did he succeed? "By nature a good man," says Dio, "his education and the moral training he imposed upon himself

[1] Marcus never quotes him by name, and though there are plenty of similarities between the two writers in thought, and even in expression, it is not certain that there is a single case of borrowing. Most of the resemblances are based on commonplaces; see, however, Sen. *Ep.* 77 = vi. 2; *Ep.* 65 = xi. 10; *de Prov.* 4 = iv. 1; *Ep.* 36 = v. 18; *de Ben.* vii. 31 = xi. 18, § 9; *Ep.* 74 = v. 8, § 3; *Ep.* 28 = v. 16.

[2] Even Epicurus is mentioned with approval, as he is also by Seneca. [3] *cp.* Epict. iii. 24, 43; *Man.* 16, etc.

INTRODUCTION

made him a far better one.[1]" " As was natural to
one who had beautified his soul with every virtuous
quality he was innocent of all wrong-doing." [2] The
wonderful revelation here given of the ἄσκησις of
the spiritual athlete in the contests of life is full
of inspiration still even for the modern world. It
has been and is a source of solace and strength to
thousands, and has helped to mould the characters
of more than one leader of men, such as Frederick
the Great,[3] Maximilian of Bavaria, Captain John
Smith, the 'saviour of Virginia,' and that noble
Christian soldier, General Gordon. It was but the
other day, on the fiftieth anniversary of Italian Unity,
that the King of Italy, speaking [4] on the Capitol,
referred to Marcus " as the sacred and propitiatory
image of that cult of moral and civil law which our
Fatherland wishes to follow," a reference received
with particular applause by those who heard it.

Whoever rescued the MS of the "Thoughts" on
the death of their author in 180, whether it was
that noble Roman, Pompeianus, the son-in-law of
Marcus, or the high-minded Victorinus, his lifelong
friend, we seem to hear an echo of its teaching in
the dying words of Cornificia, his possibly last
surviving daughter, when put to death by Caracalla
in 215 : " O wretched little soul of mine, imprisoned
in an unworthy body, go forth, be free!" [5] It was
doubtless known to Chryseros the freedman and
nomenclator of Marcus who wrote a history of Rome
to the death of his patron,[6] and to the Emperor

[1] Dio 71. 35, § 6.   [2] Aristides *ad Reg.* § 106 (Jebb).
[3] Who, however, in the field of morality cannot be said to
have profited by its lessons.
[4] March, 1911.   [5] See Dio, *Fragm.* Dindorf v. 214.
[6] Theoph. *ad Autol.* iii. 27.

Gordian I., for the latter in his youth, soon after the Emperor's death, wrote an epic poem on Pius and Marcus. He also married Fabia Orestilla, the latter's granddaughter through Fadilla (probably) and Claudius Severus. As their eldest son Gordian II. had sixty children, the blood of Marcus was soon widely diffused.

The first direct mention of the work is about 350 A.D. in the Orations of the pagan philosopher Themistius, who speaks of the παραγγέλματα (precepts) of Marcus. Then for 550 years we lose sight of the book entirely, until, about 900, the compiler of the dictionary, which goes by the name of Suidas, reveals the existence of a MS of it by making some thirty quotations, taken from books I, III, IV, V, IX, and XI.[1] He calls the book (συγγραφή) an "ἀγωγή (a directing) of his own life by Marcus the Emperor in twelve books." About the same time Arethas, a Cappadocian bishop, writing to his metropolitan, speaks of the scarcity of this μεγαλωφελέστατον βιβλίον, and apparently sends him a copy of it.[2] He also refers to it three times in scholia to Lucian, calling it τὰ εἰς ἑαυτὸν ἠθικά. Two similar references are found in the scholia to Dio Chrysostom, possibly by the same Arethas.

Again a silence of 250 years, after which Tzetzes, a grammarian of Constantinople, quotes passages from Books IV. and V. attributing them to Marcus. About 150 years later (1300 A.D.) the ecclesiastical historian, Nicephorus Callistus (iii. 31) writes that Marcus "composed a book of instruction for his son, full of universal (κοσμικῆς, ? secular) experience and wisdom."[3] About this very time Planudes, a monk

[1] See Index, under "Suidas."   [2] See A. Sonny in Philol. 54. 182f.   [3] See below, p. 63, n. 3.

of Constantinople, may have been engaged in com-
piling the anthology of extracts from various authors,
including Marcus and Aelian, which has come down
to us in twenty-five or more MSS dating from the
fourteenth to the sixteenth century.[1] They contain
in all forty-four extracts from books IV.–XII., but
are practically of no help in re-establishing the text.[2]

Our present text is based almost entirely upon two
MSS, the Codex Palatinus (P) first printed in 1558
by Xylander but now lost, which contains the whole
work, and the Codex Vaticanus 1950 (A) from which
about forty-two lines have dropped out by accidental
omissions here and there.[3] Two other MSS give some
independent help to the text, but they are incom-
plete, the Codex Darmstadtinus 2773 (D) with 112
extracts from books I.–IX. and Codex Parisinus 319
(C) with twenty-nine extracts from Books I.–IV.,
with seven other MSS derived from it or from the same
source. Apart from all these there is but one other
MS (Monacensis 323) which contains only fourteen
very short fragments from Books II., III.,IV., and VII.

Translations of this Book have been made into
Latin, English, French, Italian, German, Spanish,
Norse, Russian, Czech, Polish and Persian. In
England alone twenty-six editions of the work
appeared in the seventeenth century, fifty-eight in the
eighteenth, eighty-one in the nineteenth, and in the
twentieth up to 1908 thirty more.[4]

The English translations are as follows.—

1. *Meric Casaubon.*—" Marcus Aurelius Antoninus.
His Meditations concerning himselfe : Treating of a

---

[1] One (Vat. 2231) has just come to light.

[2] Except Cod. Monacensis 2 = C. Hoeschelianus.

[3] Guevara, in his *Dial. of Princes*, 1529, claims to have
received from Florence a Greek MS. of *The Thoughts.*

[4] See J. W. Legg, *A Bibliography of Marcus Aurelius*, 1908.

Naturall Man's Happinesse; wherein it consisteth, and of the Meanes to attain unto it. Translated out of the original Greeke with Notes by Meric Casaubon B.D., London, 1634."

This, the first English translation, albeit involved and periphrastic, is not without dignity or scholarship, though James Thomson in 1747 says that "it is everywhere rude and unpolished and often mistakes the author's meaning," while the Foulis Press Translators of 1742 find fault with its "intricate and antiquated style." It may be conveniently read in Dr. Rouse's new edition of 1900, which also contains some excellent translations of letters between Fronto and Marcus.

2. *Jeremy Collier.*—"The Emperor Marcus Antoninus His Conversation with Himself. Translated into English by Jeremy Collier M.A., London 1701." A recent edition of it by Alice Zimmern is in the Camelot Series, but it hardly deserved the honour. We may fairly say of it that it is too colloquial. James Thomson in 1747 speaks of it as "a very coarse copy of an excellent original," and as "bearing so faint a resemblance to the original in a great many places as scarcely to seem taken from it." R. Graves in 1792 remarks that it "abounds with so many vulgarities, anilities and even ludicrous expressions . . . that one cannot now read it with any patience." The comment of G. Long in 1862 is much the same, but it called forth an unexpected champion of the older translator in Matthew Arnold, who says: "Most English people, who knew Marcus Aurelius before Mr. Long appeared as his introducer, knew him through Jeremy Collier. And the acquaintance of a man like Marcus Aurelius is such an imperishable

benefit that one can never lose a peculiar sense of obligation towards the man who confers it. Apart from this however, Jeremy Collier's version deserves respect for its genuine spirit and vigour, the spirit and vigour of the age of Dryden. His warmth of feeling gave to his style an impetuosity and rhythm which from Mr. Long's style are absent." The real defect of Collier as a translator, adds Arnold, is his imperfect acquaintance with Greek.

3. *James Moor* and *Thomas Hutcheson.*—" The Meditations of the Emperor Marcus Aurelius Antoninus. Newly translated from the Greek with notes." Glasgow : The Foulis Press, 1742. Certainly the best translation, previous to Long's, for accuracy and diction, and superior to that in spirit. Dr. Rendall (1898) praises it as " the choicest alike in form and contents." R. Graves, however, in 1792, while allowing its fidelity, had pronounced it " unnecessarily literal," and shewing a " total neglect of elegance and harmony of style." A very satisfactory revision of this translation appeared in 1902, made by G. W. Chrystal.

4. *Richard Graves.*—" The Meditations of the Emperor Marcus Aurelius Antoninus. A New Translation from the Greek Original, with notes." By R. Graves, M.A., Rector of Claverton, Somerset. Bath, 1792.

A fairly accurate and smooth version of no especial distinction, but superior to most of its predecessors. An abbreviated edition of this was published at Stourport without any date by N. Swaine with the title : " The Meditations of the Emperor Marcus Aurelius Antoninus Philosophus collated with and abridged from the best translations."

INTRODUCTION

5. *George Long.*—" The Thoughts of the Emperor Marcus Aurelius Antoninus." Translated by George Long. London, 1862. This may be looked upon as in some sense the "authorized version," and it is from it that most people know their Marcus Aurelius. For nearly forty years it was master of the field. M. Arnold, though finding fault with the translator as not idiomatic or simple enough and even pedantic, yet gives him full credit for soundness, precision, and general excellence in his translation. The author tells us that he deliberately chose a ruder style as better suited, in his opinion, to express the character of the original, which is distinctive, for in spite of Arnold's dictum to the contrary the book of Marcus has a " distinct physiognomy," and here, more than is usually the case, *le style c'est l'homme.*

6. *Hastings Crossley.*—" The Fourth Book of the Meditations of Marcus Aurelius." A revised text with Translation and commentary by Hastings Crossley, M.A., London, 1882. This specimen makes us regret that the author did not publish the whole version which he tells us was in MS. The book contains an interesting appendix on the relations of Fronto and Marcus.

7. *G. H. Rendall.*—" Marcus Aurelius Antoninus to Himself: An English Translation with Introductory Study on Stoicism and the Last of the Stoics." By Gerald H. Rendall, M.A., Litt.D., London, 1898. A second edition with a different introduction was published in 1901.

This version has been pronounced by many critics the best rendering of the *Thoughts*. Its accuracy, ability, and liveliness are unquestionable.

8. *John Jackson.*—" The Meditations of Marcus

Aurelius Antoninus." Translated by John Jackson.
With an introduction by Charles Bigg. Oxford,
1906.

This version is the newest comer, and is a worthy
presentment of the *Thoughts*. There are useful
notes, but some very bold alterations of the text
have been followed in the English version. The
book would have been more acceptable without
the introduction by Dr. Bigg, which gives a most
unfair and wholly inaccurate view of the life and
character of Marcus.

Besides the above versions there are several
abridged translations of the *Thoughts*, which need
not be enumerated here. But the two chief ones
seem to be by B. E. Smith, published by the Century
Company, New York, 1899, and by J. E. Wilson,
London, 1902.

STOICISM

Stoicism was so called from the Colonnade[1] at
Athens, where Zeno about 300 B.C. first taught its
doctrines. More religious in character than any
other Greek philosophy, it brought a new moral
force into the world. It put intellectual speculation
more into the background, and carried the moral
attitude of the Cynics further into the domain of
right conduct. Oriental fervour was in it grafted
on Greek acumen, for Zeno was a Phoenician Greek
of Cyprus, and Chrysippus, the St. Paul who defined
and established[2] Stoicism, a Cilician like the Apostle.

In spite of its origin Stoicism proved wonderfully
adapted to the practical Roman character, and under
the tyranny of the early Caesars it formed the only
impregnable fortress[3] of liberty for the noblest
Romans. It reached its culmination, and found its
highest exponents as a living creed in the courtier
Seneca, the Phrygian slave Epictetus, and the
emperor Marcus Antoninus.

Stoic philosophy consisted of Logic, Physics, and
Ethics.[4] Logic, which comprised Dialectics and

[1] Στοὰ ποικίλη.
[2] εἰ μὴ γὰρ ἦν Χρύσιππος, οὐκ ἂν ἦν Στοά, an anonymous
verse quoted by Diog. Laert. *Chrys.* 5.
[3] viii. 41, 48.   [4] viii. 13.

Rhetoric, was the necessary instrument of all speculation;[1] but Marcus found no satisfaction in either branch of it, nor in such Physics as dealt with Meteorology.[2]

The key-note of Stoicism was *Life according to Nature,* and Marcus was converted to the pursuit of this possibly by Sextus the Boeotian.[3] By "Nature" was meant the controlling Reason of the Universe.[4] A study of Physics was necessary for a proper understanding of the Cosmos and our position in it, and thus formed the scientific basis of philosophy; but it was regarded as strictly subordinate, and merely a means to an end.

Though he confesses to some disappointment in his progress therein,[5] there is no doubt that Marcus was well versed in Stoic Physics. Fully recognizing the value of a scientific spirit of enquiry,[6] he describes it as a characteristic of the rational soul to "go the whole Universe through and grasp its plan,"[7] affirming that "no man can be good without correct notions as to the Nature of the Whole and his own constitution."[8]

To the Stoics the Universe—God and Matter[9]—was One, all Substance, unified by the close 'sympathy'[10] and interdependence of the parts, forming with the rational Power, that was co-extensive with it, a single entity. The Primary Being, by means of its inform-

---

[1] See Epict. i. 17.
[2] i. 7, 17, § 4; vii. 67; viii. 1.
[3] i. 9, § 1, 17, § 5. But Rusticus (i. 7) and Maximus (i. 15) were his chief instructors in Stoicism.
[4] vii. 11.　　　　　　[5] vii. 67.
[6] x. 11.　　　　　　[7] xi. 1, § 2.
[8] viii 52; xi. 5.　　　[9] αἴτιον and ὕλη.
[10] iv. 27; v. 26; ix. 9, § 3.

ing Force,[1] acting as igneous or atmospheric current[2] upon inert matter, evolved out of itself a Cosmos, subsequent modifications being by way of consequence.[3] This Universe is periodically destroyed by fire,[4] thus returning again to its pristine Being, only however to be created anew[5] on the same plan even to the smallest details; and so on for ever.

God and Matter being thus indistinguishable, for all that was not God in its original form was God in an indirect sense as a manifestation of him, the Stoic creed was inevitably pantheistic. It was also materialistic; for the Stoics, allowing existence to nothing incorporeal, by means of their strange theory of air-currents[6] inherent even in abstract things such as virtue, rendered not only them but God himself corporeal, terming him the "perfect living Being."[7] But their conceptions on this point seem to be really irreconcilable, for while on the one hand they speak of the Supreme Power by such names as Zeus, Cause or Force, Soul, Mind, or Reason of the Universe, Law or Truth, Destiny, Necessity, Providence, or Nature of the Whole, on the other they identify it with such terms as Fiery Fluid, or Heat, Ether (warm air) or Pneuma (atmospheric current).

---

[1] σπερματικὸς λόγος (used by Justin of Christ), iv. 14, 21; vi. 24; ix. 1 *ad fin.*

[2] πνεῦμα. This set up tension (τόνος), resulting in expansion and contraction (*cp.* our attraction and repulsion) and gave to things shape, quality, and relation.

[3] vi. 36, § 2; ix. 1, § 4.

[4] v. 13, 32; x. 7. The doctrine of ἐκπύρωσις was Heraclitan. *cp.* St. Peter, Ep ii. 3, 7; Justin, *Apol.* i. 20; ii. 7.

[5] παλιγγενεσία, vii. 19; xi. 1. *cp.* St. Matt. xix. 28.

[6] πνεύματα.   [7] iv. 40; x. 1.

STOICISM

Other physical theories were borrowed from Heraclitus, and Marcus constantly alludes to these, such as the "downward and upward" round of the elements[1] as they emanate from the primary Fire, air passing into fire, fire into earth, earth into water and so back again,[2] and the famous doctrine that all things are in flux.[3]

Man consists of Body, Soul, Intelligence, or Flesh, Pneuma, and the Ruling Reason.[4] But the ψυχή (soul) can be looked upon in two ways, as πνευμάτιον, an exhalation from blood,[5] and as ἡ νοερά, ἡ λογικὴ ψυχή, i.e. the ruling Reason. It is the latter, a "morsel" or "efflux"[6] from the Divine, which constitutes the real man. Marcus often speaks of this rational nature[7] of a man as his daemon, or genius enthroned within him,[8] and makes the whole problem of life depend upon how this Reason treats itself. As all that is rational is akin, we are formed for fellowship with others and, the universe being one, what affects a part of it affects the whole. Reason is as a Law to all rational creatures, and so we are all citizens of a World-state.[9] In this cosmopolitanism the Stoics approached the Christian view, ethics being divorced from national politics and made of universal application. It was no cloistered virtue the Stoics preached, showing how a man can save his own soul, but a practical positive goodness;[10] though it cannot be denied that the claims of αὐτάρκεια

[1] ἄνω κάτω. vi. 17; ix. 28.   [2] iv. 46.
[3] ἄπαντα ῥεῖ, ii. 17; iv. 3 ad fin., 36; v. 10; vi. 15; vii. 25; ix. 19; x. 7.   [4] iii. 16; xii. 3.
[5] v. 33; vi. 15, or ζωή, an inhalation from the air.
[6] ii. 1; ii. 4; v. 27.   [7] xi. 1.
[8] ii. 17; iii. 7, 16; v. 27, etc., and he calls this God, iii. 5; v. 10; xii. 26.   [9] iv. 4.   [10] vi. 30.

(the self-sufficiency of the Inner Self) and κοινωνία
(social interdependence of parts of a common whole)
are not easy to reconcile. It is certain, however,
that the Stoic admission of slaves into the brother-
hood of man had an ameliorating effect upon slavery,
and the well-known bias of Marcus in favour of
enfranchisement may well have been due to his
creed.[1]

From virtue alone can happiness and peace of
mind result, and virtue consists in submission to the
higher Power and all that he sends us, in mastery over
our animal nature, in freedom from all perturbation,[2]
and in the entire independence of the Inner Self. Since
life is Opinion[3] and everything but what we think
it, the vital question is what assent we give to the
impressions of our senses. "Wipe out imagination,"
says Marcus, time after time, "and you are saved."[4]
"Do not think yourself hurt and you remain
unhurt."[5] He longs for the day when he shall
cease to be duped by his impressions and pulled like
a puppet by his passions,[6] and his soul shall be in a
great calm. But virtue must also show itself, like
faith, in right actions. It means not only self-
control but justice and benevolence to others and
piety towards the Gods.

By the Gods Marcus sometimes means the controlling Reason,[7] sometimes, apparently, Gods in a
more popular sense, such as are even visible to the

---

[1] See *Digest*, xxviii. 4. 3.   [2] ἀταραξία, ix. 31.
[3] iv. 3; vii. 17; xi. 18, § 7, etc.
[4] xii. 25.   [5] iv. 7.
[6] ii. 2; iii. 16; vi. 16, etc.
[7] xii. 5; vi. 44; viii. 17; iii. 3; ix. 1. He even calls the
Supreme Nature πρεσβυτάτη τῶν θεῶν, ix. 1.

eyes.[1] He often puts the alternative God (or Gods) and Atoms,[2] but himself firmly believes that there are immortal Gods[3] who care for mankind, live with them, and help even bad men.[4] He bids himself call upon them, follow them,[5] be their minister, live with them and be likened to them.[6] They too are part of the Cosmos and subject to its limitations, and by our own loyalty to Destiny we contribute to the welfare and permanence of God himself. But a predestined Order of things involved fatalism, and the Stoics were hard put to it to maintain the complete freedom of the will.

Unfortunately the Stoic scheme left no room for Immortality. At most a soul could only exist till the next conflagration, when it must be absorbed again into the Primary Being. Seneca indeed, who was no true Stoic, speaks in almost Christian terms of a new and blissful life to come,[7] but Epictetus turns resolutely, and Marcus with evident reluctance, from a hope so dear to the human heart. In one place the latter even uses the expression "another life," [8] and finds it a hard saying that the souls of those who were in closest communion with God should die for ever when they die.[9] But he does not repine. He is ready for either fate, extinction or transference elsewhere.[10]

One more question remains, that of Suicide. The Stoics allowed this, if circumstances made it im-

---

[1] xii. 28 ; iii. 16; viii. 19: ὁ ἥλιος καὶ οἱ λοιποὶ θεοί.
[2] iv. 3, § 2 ; viii. 17 ; xi. 18, § 1.
[3] ii. 11 ; vii. 70.   [4] ix. 11, 27, 40.
[5] A Stoic precept.   [6] cp. Julian, Conv. 421.
[7] Ep. 54, 102 ; Polyb. Consol. 28 ; ad Marciam, 25.
[8] iii. 3.   [9] xii. 5.
[10] iv. 21 ; xi. 3 ; xii. 31.

possible for a man to maintain his moral standard.[1] The door is open, but the call must be very clear.[2] Still the act seems quite inconsistent with the doctrine of submission to Destiny, and the classing of things external as indifferent.

In this brief sketch of Stoicism much has perforce been omitted, and much may seem obscure, but Marcus confesses that "things are in a manner so wrapped up in mystery that even the Stoics have found them difficult to apprehend."[3] This at least we know, that Stoicism inspired some of the noblest lives ever lived, left its humanizing impress upon the Roman Law, which we have inherited, and appeals in an especial way to some of the higher instincts of our nature.

[1] v. 29 ; ix. 2.
[2] xi. 3 ; Epict. i. 29, § 28 ; i. 24 *ad fin.* ; iii. 13, § 14.
[3] v. 10.

BIBLIOGRAPHY

Of the chief editions and commentaries referred to in the critical notes.

Xyl.—The premier edition from the lost Palatine MS., issued in 1558, with a Latin translation by Xylander (*i.e.* W. Holzmann of Augsburg).

Cas.—Meric Casaubon's first edition of the original Greek in 1643. Reprinted 1680.

Gat.—Thomas Gataker's edition, published in 1652 at Cambridge with a new Latin version and voluminous notes including contributions from *Saumaise* (*Salm.*), *Boot*, and *Junius*. Reprinted 1696, 1704, 1707, 1729 (*Wolle* and *Buddeus*), 1744, 1751, 1775 (*Morus*).

Sch.—Jo. Matth. Schultz. Editions 1802 (Sleswig), 1820 (Leipzig), 1842 (Paris). *Menagius* and *Reiske* supplied notes to Schultz.

Cor.—A. Coraes, in vol. iv. : πάρεργα τῆς βιβλιοθήκης Ἑλληνικῆς. Paris, 1816. This editor has made more successful emendations of the text than any other.

Bach.—Nicholas Bach, "De Marco Aurelio Antonino," Lipsiae, 1826.

Pierron.—Alexis Pierron, "Pensées de l'Empereur Marc Aurèle Antonin." Paris, 1843 (with introduction and notes).

Lofft.—Edition by C. L. Porcher (=Capel Lofft). New York, 1863. Proof-sheets of this, with additional notes, are in the British Museum.

Scaph.—Panag. Schaphidiotes, "Κριτικαὶ Παρατηρήσεις ἐπὶ τῶν εἰς ἑαυτὸν ιβ´ βιβλίων Μάρκου Ἀντωνίνου." Athens, 1881.

Stich.—Jo. Stich, "Adnotationes criticae ad M. Antoninum," *Programm der K. Studienanstatt, Zweibrücken,* 1880/1. The same editor brought out an edition for the Teubner Series in 1882, and a second revised edition in 1903, with valuable introductions and index.

BIBLIOGRAPHY

Nauck.—August Nauck, "De M. Antonini Commentariis," 1882, *Bulletin de l'Académie impériale des Sciences de St. Petersbourg* (28), pp. 196–210. See also "Mélanges Gréco-Romains" ii. 743-5.

Pol.—Hermann J. Polak, "In Marci Antonini Commentarios analecta critica," *Hermes* xxi. (1886), pp. 321–356, and *Sylloge commentationum quam C. Conto obtulerunt philologi Batavi*, Lugd. Bat., 1894, pp. 85–94.

Rend.—G. H. Rendall, "On the text of M. Aurelius Antoninus τὰ εἰς ἑαυτόν," *Journal of Philology*, xxiii., pp. 116–160.

Wilam.—Ulrich de Wilamowitz-Moellendorf, Griechisches Lesebuch ii., pp. 311–320. Berlin, 1902.

Hoffm.—P. Hoffmann, "Notes critiques sur Marc Aurèle," *Revue de l'Instruction publique en Belgique*, xlvii., 1904, pp. 11–23.

Sonny.—Adolf Sonny, "Zur Ueberlieferung Geschichte von M. A.," *Philologus* 54, pp. 181–3.

Leop.—J. H. Leopold, "Ad M. Antonini commentarios," *Mnemosyne* xxxi., 1902, pp. 341–364; xxxiv., 1907, pp. 63–82. He also brought out a new edition of the Greek text for the Clarendon Press in 1911.

Fourn.—Paul Fournier, "Pensées de Marc Aurèle." Traduction d'Auguste Couat éditée par P. Fournier. Paris, 1904. There are numerous notes.

Rich.—Herbert Richards, "Notes on Marcus Aurelius," *Classical Quarterly*, xix., Feb., 1905, pp. 18–21.

Kron.—A. J. Kronenberg, "Ad M. Antoninum," *Classical Review*, xix., July, 1905, pp. 301–3.

Schmidt.—Karl Fr. W. Schmidt, "Textkritische Bemerkungen zu Mark Aurel," *Hermes*, xlii. 1907, pp. 595–607.

Lemerc.—A. P. Lemercier, "Les Pensées de Marc Aurèle," Paris, 1910, with notes and a good introduction.

Schenkl.—Heinrich Schenkl, a new edition of the *Thoughts* for the Teubner Press, 1913. The latest and most complete edition with valuable introductions and full indices. The same Editor has also published "Zur handscriftlichen Ueberlieferung von Marcus Antoninus" (*Eranos Vindobonensis*, 1893), and "Zum erste Buche des Selbstbetrachtungen des Kaisers Marcus Antoninus" (Wiener Studien, 1912).

BIBLIOGRAPHY

Haines.—C. R. Haines, "The Composition and Chronology of the *Thoughts* of Marcus Aurelius," *Journal of Philology,* vol. xxxiii., No. 66, pp. 278–295.

For the history and doctrines of Stoicism besides the standard work of Zeller and the recent treatise on "Roman Stoicism" by E. V. Arnold, the following will be found useful :—N. Bach (mentioned above) 1826 ; H. Doergens, "de comparatione Antoninianae philosophiae cum L. Annaei Senecae," 1816 ; the admirable essay on Stoicism by G. H. Rendall prefixed to his edition of 1898 ; " Greek and Roman Stoicism " by C. H. S. Davis, 1903 ; and " Stoic and Christian " by Leonard Alston, 1906.

P = Codex Palatinus (Xylander), = T (Schenkl).
A = Codex Vaticanus 1950.
C = Codex Parisinus 319.
D = Codex Darmstadtinus 2773.
Mo² = Codex Monachensis (Munich) 529.

< > Words thus enclosed are inserted by conjecture.
[ ] Words in the text which should probably be omitted.
†   Doubtful readings in the text.
" " mark quotations or words of a speaker.
' ' mark proverbial, colloquial, or poetical expressions.

MARCUS AURELIUS
ANTONINUS

ΜΑΡΚΟΥ ΑΥΡΗΛΙΟΥ ΑΝΤΩΝΙΝΟΥ

ΑΥΤΟΚΡΑΤΟΡΟΣ

ΤΩΝ ΕΙΣ ΕΑΥΤΟΝ

ΒΙΒΛΙΟΝ Α

αʹ. Παρὰ τοῦ πάππου Οὐήρου, τὸ καλόηθες καὶ ἀόργητον.

βʹ. Παρὰ τῆς δόξης καὶ μνήμης τῆς περὶ τοῦ γεννήσαντος, τὸ αἰδῆμον καὶ ἀρρενικόν.

γʹ. Παρὰ τῆς μητρός, τὸ θεοσεβὲς καὶ μεταδοτικόν· καὶ ἀφεκτικὸν οὐ μόνον τοῦ κακοποιεῖν, ἀλλὰ καὶ τοῦ ἐπὶ ἐννοίας γίνεσθαι τοιαύτης· ἔτι δὲ τὸ λιτὸν κατὰ τὴν δίαιταν καὶ πόρρω τῆς πλουσιακῆς διαγωγῆς.

δʹ. Παρὰ τοῦ προπάππου, τὸ μὴ εἰς δημοσίας διατριβὰς φοιτῆσαι, καὶ τὸ ἀγαθοῖς διδασκάλοις κατ᾽ οἶκον χρήσασθαι, καὶ τὸ γνῶναι, ὅτι εἰς τὰ τοιαῦτα δεῖ ἐκτενῶς ἀναλίσκειν.

---

[1] sc. " I had an example of," " was in the way to learn." But the construction varies and sometimes a direct statement of characteristics is given. It is obvious that Marcus does *not* claim to possess all the good qualities enumerated.

[2] Died before 136. The grandfather of M. (§ 1) died

MARCUS AURELIUS ANTONINUS

THE EMPEROR

TO HIMSELF

BOOK I

1. FROM MY GRANDFATHER VERUS,[1] a kindly disposition and sweetness of temper.

2. FROM WHAT I HEARD OF MY FATHER[2] AND MY MEMORY OF HIM, modesty and manliness.

3. FROM MY MOTHER, the fear of God, and generosity; and abstention not only from doing ill but even from the very thought of doing it; and furthermore to live the simple life,[3] far removed from the habits of the rich.

4. FROM MY GRANDFATHER'S FATHER,[4] to dispense with attendance at public schools, and to enjoy good teachers at home,[5] and to recognize that on such things money should be eagerly spent.

aged nearly 90 in 138 (Capit. *Vit. Mar.* vi. 1; *Vit. Pii* iv. 2).

[3] *cp.* Aristides, *ad Reg.* § 115 (Jebb) διαίτης εὐτέλεια (of Marcus).

[4] Catilius Severus, *praef. urbi*, who hoped to succeed Hadrian (Spart. *Vit. Hadr.* v. 10; xxiv. 6).

[5] Capit. *Vit. Mar.* (ii. 3–iii. 4) gives a list of these.

MARCUS AURELIUS

έ. Παρὰ τοῦ τροφέως, τὸ μήτε Πρασιανὸς μήτε Βενετιανός, μήτε Παλμουλάριος ἢ Σκουτάριος γενέσθαι· καὶ τὸ φερέπονον καὶ ὀλιγοδεές, καὶ τὸ αὐτουργικὸν καὶ ἀπολύπραγμον· καὶ τὸ δυσπρόσδεκτον διαβολῆς.

ϛ. Παρὰ Διογνήτου, τὸ ἀκενόσπουδον· καὶ τὸ ἀπιστητικὸν τοῖς ὑπὸ τῶν τερατευομένων καὶ γοήτων περὶ ἐπῳδῶν καὶ περὶ δαιμόνων ἀποπομπῆς καὶ τῶν τοιούτων λεγομένοις· καὶ τὸ μὴ ὀρτυγοτροφεῖν, μηδὲ περὶ τὰ τοιαῦτα ἐπτοῆσθαι· καὶ τὸ ἀνέχεσθαι παρρησίας· καὶ τὸ οἰκειωθῆναι φιλοσοφίᾳ καὶ τὸ ἀκοῦσαι πρῶτον μὲν Βακχείου, εἶτα Τανδάσιδος καὶ Μαρκιανοῦ†· καὶ τὸ γράψαι διαλόγους ἐν παιδί· καὶ τὸ σκίμποδος καὶ δορᾶς ἐπιθυμῆσαι καὶ ὅσα τοιαῦτα τῆς Ἑλληνικῆς ἀγωγῆς ἐχόμενα.

ζ. Παρὰ Ῥουστίκου, τὸ λαβεῖν φαντασίαν τοῦ χρῄζειν διορθώσεως καὶ θεραπείας τοῦ ἤθους· καὶ τὸ μὴ ἐκτραπῆναι εἰς ζῆλον σοφιστικόν, μηδὲ τὸ συγγράφειν περὶ τῶν θεωρημάτων, ἢ προτρεπτικὰ λογάρια διαλέγεσθαι, ἢ φαντασιοπλήκτως τὸν ἀσκητικὸν ἢ τὸν εὐεργετικὸν ἄνδρα ἐπιδείκνυσθαι· καὶ τὸ ἀποστῆναι ῥητορικῆς καὶ ποιητικῆς καὶ ἀστειολογίας· κ.ιὶ τὸ μὴ ἐν στολῇ κατ᾽ οἶκον

---

[1] The name has perhaps dropped out. Capit. *Vit. Pii* x. 5 has an anecdote of the death of the *educator* of Marcus, but Aristides in his funeral oration on Alexander of Cotiaeum calls the latter not only διδάσκαλος but τροφεὺς to Marcus and Verus (Jebb's Ed. § 149). But he is mentioned below § 10.

[2] Capit. *Vit. Ver.* vi. 2 ; Malalas xi. *ad fin.*

[3] Dio (71. 6, § 2) calls M. φιλόπονος.

[4] A Diognetus taught M. painting (Capit. iv. 9).

[5] *cp.* Capit. xiii. 6 ; Dio 71. 9, § 2 (Xiphilinus).

4

BOOK I

5. FROM MY TUTOR,[1] not to side with the Green Jacket or the Blue[2] at the races, or to back the Light-Shield Champion or the Heavy-Shield in the lists; not to shirk toil,[3] and to have few wants, and to do my own work, and mind my own concerns; and to turn a deaf ear to slander.

6. FROM DIOGNETUS,[4] not to be taken up with trifles; and not to give credence to the statements of miracle-mongers and wizards[5] about incantations and the exorcizing of demons,[6] and such-like marvels; and not to keep quails, nor to be excited about such things: not to resent plain speaking; and to become familiar with philosophy and be a hearer first of Baccheius, then of Tandasis and Marcianus; and to write dialogues as a boy; and to set my heart on a pallet-bed and a pelt[7] and whatever else tallied with the Greek regimen.

7. FROM RUSTICUS,[8] to become aware of the fact that I needed amendment and training for my character; and not to be led aside into an argumentative sophistry; nor compose treatises on speculative subjects, or deliver little homilies,[9] or pose ostentatiously as the moral athlete or unselfish man; and to eschew rhetoric,[10] poetry, and fine language; and not to go

---

[6] Undoubtedly refers to the Christians, see *Digest* L. 13. 1, § 3, and *cp.* Justin, *Apol.* ii. 6 of Rome itself. The Christians constantly boasted of their power to exorcize: Tert. *Apol.* 23; Iren. ii. 6, § 2; Lact. v. 21. *cp.* also the legend ot Abercius and his visit to Rome to cure Lucilla.

[7] Capit. *Vit. Mar.* ii. 6

[8] i. 17, §§ 4, 6. *cp. Digest.* xlix. 1. 1, § 3 "Rusticus, our friend"; Capit. iii. 3; Them. *Orat.* xiii. 173 c; Fronto, *ad Ant.* 1. 2. [9] λογάρια (*ratiunculae*). *cp.* Epict. i. 29. 55.

[10] i. 17, § 4. *cp.* Fronto, *ad Ant.* i. 2 (Nab. p. 96); *de Eloqu.* 3 (Nab. p. 150). Dio (71. 35, § 1) says M. was ἀσκηθεὶς ἐν τοῖς ῥητορικοῖς λόγοις.

περιπατεῖν, μηδὲ τὰ τοιαῦτα ποιεῖν· καὶ τὸ τὰ
ἐπιστόλια ἀφελῶς γράφειν, οἷον τὸ ὑπ' αὐτοῦ
τούτου ἀπὸ Σινοέσσης τῇ μητρί μου γραφέν·
καὶ τὸ πρὸς τοὺς χαλεπήναντας καὶ πλημμελή-
σαντας εὐανακλήτως καὶ εὐδιαλλάκτως, ἐπειδὰν
τάχιστα αὐτοὶ ἐπανελθεῖν ἐθελήσωσι, δια-
κεῖσθαι· καὶ τὸ ἀκριβῶς ἀναγινώσκειν καὶ μὴ
ἀρκεῖσθαι περινοοῦντα ὁλοσχερῶς· μηδὲ τοῖς
περιλαλοῦσι ταχέως συγκατατίθεσθαι· καὶ τὸ
ἐντυχεῖν τοῖς Ἐπικτητείοις ὑπομνήμασιν, ὧν
οἴκοθεν μετέδωκεν.

η΄. Παρὰ Ἀπολλωνίου, τὸ ἐλεύθερον καὶ
ἀναμφιβόλως ἀκύβευτον· καὶ πρὸς μηδὲν ἄλλο
ἀποβλέπειν μηδὲ ἐπ' ὀλίγον ἢ πρὸς τὸν λόγον·
καὶ τὸ ἀεὶ ὅμοιον, ἐν ἀλγηδόσιν ὀξείαις, ἐν ἀπο-
βολῇ τέκνου, ἐν μακραῖς νόσοις· καὶ τὸ ἐπὶ
παραδείγματος ζῶντος ἰδεῖν ἐναργῶς, ὅτι δύναται
ὁ αὐτὸς σφοδρότατος εἶναι καὶ ἀνειμένος· καὶ
τὸ ἐν ταῖς ἐξηγήσεσι μὴ δυσχεραντικόν· καὶ
τὸ ἰδεῖν ἄνθρωπον σαφῶς ἐλάχιστον τῶν ἑαυτοῦ
καλῶν ἡγούμενον τὴν ἐμπειρίαν καὶ τὴν ἐντρέχ-
ειαν τὴν περὶ τὸ παραδιδόναι τὰ θεωρήματα·
καὶ τὸ μαθεῖν, πῶς δεῖ λαμβάνειν τὰς δοκούσας
χάριτας παρὰ φίλων, μήτε ἐξηττώμενον διὰ
ταῦτα μήτε ἀναισθήτως παραπέμποντα.

θ΄. Παρὰ Σέξτου, τὸ εὐμενές· καὶ τὸ παρά-

---

[1] As Marcus in the case of Herodes, see Philost. *Vit. Soph.*
ii. 12 (Kayser's ed. p. 243).

[2] *cp.* Fronto, *ad Caes.* v. 36. Capit. (*Vit. Pii* x. 4) and
Lucian (*Demonax* 31) shew him in a different light, as
ill-mannered and avaricious. He is mentioned as Ἀντωνίνου
ἑταῖρος by Epiphanius.

[3] See the behaviour of Marcus on the death of M. Annius

about the house in my robes, nor commit any such breach of good taste; and to write letters without affectation, like his own letter written to my mother from Sinuessa; to shew oneself ready to be reconciled to those who have lost their temper and trespassed against one, and ready to meet them halfway as soon as ever they seem to be willing to retrace their steps[1]; to read with minute care and not to be content with a superficial bird's-eye view; nor to be too quick in agreeing with every voluble talker; and to make the acquaintance of the *Memoirs of Epictetus*, which he supplied me with out of his own library.

8. FROM APOLLONIUS,[2] self-reliance and an unequivocal determination not to leave anything to chance; and to look to nothing else even for a moment save Reason alone; and to remain ever the same, in the throes of pain, on the loss of a child,[3] during a lingering illness; and to see plainly from a living example that one and the same man can be very vehement and yet gentle: not to be impatient in instructing others; and to see in him a man who obviously counted as the least among his gifts his practical experience and facility in imparting philosophic truths; and to learn in accepting seeming favours from friends[4] not to give up our independence for such things nor take them callously as a matter of course.

9. FROM SEXTUS,[5] kindliness, and the example of a

Verus, aged 7, at Praeneste in 169 (Capit. xxi. 3), and on the death of his first-born son T. Aelius Antoninus soon after birth in 147. (*Corp. Inscrip. Graec.* Boeckh 3176.) *cp.* Dio 71. 34, § 5.

[4] *cp.* Fronto, *ad Appian.* (Nab. p. 246).

[5] Capit. iii. 1. He was of Chaeronea and grandson of Plutarch. *cp.* Suidas *sub voce*: "He was held in such honour by the Emperor as to act as his assessor on the bench."

δεῖγμα τοῦ οἴκου τοῦ πατρονομουμένου· καὶ τὴν
ἔννοιαν τοῦ κατὰ φύσιν ζῆν· καὶ τὸ σεμνὸν
ἀπλάστως· καὶ τὸ στοχαστικὸν τῶν φίλων
κηδεμονικῶς· καὶ τὸ ἀνεκτικὸν τῶν ἰδιωτῶν καὶ
†τὸ ἀθεώρητον οἰομένων.†

2 Καὶ τὸ πρὸς πάντας εὐάρμοστον, ὥστε κολακείας μὲν πάσης προσηνεστέραν εἶναι τὴν
ὁμιλίαν αὐτοῦ, αἰδεσιμώτατον δὲ αὐτοῖς ἐκείνοις
παρ' αὐτὸν ἐκεῖνον τὸν καιρὸν εἶναι· καὶ τὸ καταληπτικῶς καὶ ὁδῷ ἐξευρετικόν τε καὶ τακτικὸν
τῶν εἰς βίον ἀναγκαίων δογμάτων.

3 Καὶ τὸ μηδὲ ἔμφασίν ποτε ὀργῆς ἢ ἄλλου τινὸς
πάθους παρασχεῖν, ἀλλὰ ἅμα μὲν ἀπαθέστατον
εἶναι, ἅμα δὲ φιλοστοργότατον· καὶ τὸ εὔφημον
καὶ τοῦτο ἀψοφητί· καὶ τὸ πολυμαθὲς ἀνεπι-
φάντως.

ι'. Παρὰ Ἀλεξάνδρου τοῦ γραμματικοῦ, τὸ
ἀνεπίπληκτον· καὶ τὸ μὴ ὀνειδιστικῶς ἐπιλαμβάν-
εσθαι τῶν βάρβαρον ἢ σόλοικόν τι ἢ ἀπηχὲς
προενεγκαμένων, ἀλλ' ἐπιδεξίως αὐτὸ μόνον ἐκεῖνο,
ὃ ἔδει εἰρῆσθαι, προφέρεσθαι, ἐν τρόπῳ ἀποκρίσ-
εως ἢ συνεπιμαρτυρήσεως ἢ συνδιαλήψεως περὶ
αὐτοῦ τοῦ πράγματος, οὐχὶ περὶ τοῦ ῥήματος,
ἢ δι' ἑτέρας τινὸς τοιαύτης ἐμμελοῦς παρυπο-
μνήσεως.

ια'. Παρὰ Φρόντωνος,[1] τὸ ἐπιστῆσαι, οἷα ἡ
τυραννικὴ βασκανία καὶ ποικιλία καὶ ὑπόκρισις,
καὶ ὅτι ὡς ἐπίπαν οἱ καλούμενοι οὗτοι παρ'
ἡμῖν εὐπατρίδαι ἀστοργότεροί πως εἰσίν.

[1] ad Caes. iii. 2.

---

[1] Of Cotiaeum, see Aristides, *Orat.* xii. 142 ff. (Jebb's Ed.).
He lived to a great age. He was in Rome in 145 (see *ibid.* § 159)
and resided at the palace (§§ 148, 154). See above on i. 5.

BOOK I

household patriarchally governed ; and the conception of life in accordance with Nature ; and dignity without affectation ; and an intuitive consideration for friends ; and a toleration of the unlearned and the unreasoning.

And his tactful treatment of all his friends, so that simply to be with him was more delightful than any flattery, while at the same time those who enjoyed this privilege looked up to him with the utmost reverence ; and the grasp and method which he shewed in discovering and marshalling the essential axioms of life.

And never to exhibit any symptom of anger or any other passion, but to be at the same time utterly impervious to all passions and full of natural affection ; and to praise without noisy obtrusiveness, and to possess great learning but make no parade of it.

10. From Alexander the Grammarian,[1] not to be captious ; nor in a carping spirit find fault with those who import into their conversation any expression which is barbarous or ungrammatical or mispronounced, but tactfully to bring in the very expression, that ought to have been used, by way of answer, or as it were in joint support of the assertion, or as a joint consideration of the thing itself and not of the language, or by some such graceful [2] reminder.

11. From Fronto, to note the envy, the subtlety, and the dissimulation which are habitual to a tyrant ; and that, as a general rule, those amongst us who rank as patricians are somewhat wanting in natural affection.[3]

---

[2] Or, *relevant*.

[3] See Fronto, *ad Ver.* ii. 7 (Fronto ii. 154). Marcus acknowledges greater debts to Fronto elsewhere, e.g. *ad Caes.* iii. 12, *Verum dicere ex te disco. Ea re prosum dis hominibusque ardua.* Justinian, *Inst.* ii. 18. Pr.

ιβ΄. Παρὰ Ἀλεξάνδρου τοῦ Πλατωνικοῦ, τὸ μὴ πολλάκις μηδὲ χωρὶς ἀνάγκης λέγειν πρός τινα ἢ ἐν ἐπιστολῇ γράφειν, ὅτι ἄσχολός εἰμι· μηδὲ διὰ τούτου τοῦ τρόπου συνεχῶς παραιτεῖσθαι τὰ κατὰ τὰς πρὸς τοὺς συμβιοῦντας σχέσεις καθήκοντα προβαλλόμενον τὰ περιεστῶτα πράγματα.

ιγ΄. Παρὰ Κατούλου, τὸ μὴ ὀλιγώρως ἔχειν φίλου αἰτιωμένου τι, κἂν τύχῃ ἀλόγως αἰτιώμενος, ἀλλὰ πειρᾶσθαι καὶ[1] ἀποκαθιστάναι ἐπὶ τὸ σύνηθες· καὶ τὸ περὶ τῶν διδασκάλων ἐκθύμως εὔφημον, οἷα τὰ περὶ Δομετίου[2] καὶ Ἀθηνοδότου ἀπομνημονευόμενα· καὶ τὸ περὶ τὰ τέκνα ἀληθινῶς ἀγαπητικόν.

ιδ΄. Παρὰ τοῦ ἀδελφοῦ μου Σεουήρου, τὸ φιλοίκειον καὶ φιλάληθες καὶ φιλοδίκαιον· καὶ τὸ δι᾽ αὐτὸν γνῶναι Θρασέαν, Ἐλβίδιον, Κάτωνα, Δίωνα, Βροῦτον· καὶ φαντασίαν λαβεῖν πολιτείας ἰσονόμου, κατ᾽ ἰσότητα καὶ ἰσηγορίαν διοικουμένης, καὶ βασιλείας τιμώσης πάντων μάλιστα τὴν ἐλευθερίαν τῶν ἀρχομένων· καὶ ἔτι παρὰ τοῦ αὐτοῦ τὸ ὁμαλὲς[3] καὶ ὁμότονον ἐν τῇ τιμῇ τῆς φιλοσοφίας· καὶ τὸ εὐποιητικόν, καὶ τὸ εὐμετάδοτον ἐκτενῶς, καὶ τὸ εὔελπι, καὶ τὸ πιστευτικὸν περὶ τοῦ ὑπὸ τῶν φίλων φιλεῖσθαι· καὶ τὸ ἀνεπίκρυπτον πρὸς τοὺς καταγνώσεως ὑπ᾽ αὐτοῦ τυγχάνοντας· καὶ τὸ μὴ δεῖσθαι στοχασμοῦ τοὺς φίλους αὐτοῦ περὶ τοῦ, τί θέλει ἢ τί οὐ θέλει, ἀλλὰ δῆλον εἶναι.

---

[1] This seems at first sight like our inaccurate "try and," but καὶ must mean *even*.

[2] Δομητίου PAD. For Δομετίου *cp.* Herodian i. 3, § 4; *C.I.G.* 4154, etc.   [3] ἀμελὲς PAD : ὁμαλὲς Cor.

BOOK I

12. FROM ALEXANDER THE PLATONIST,[1] not to say to anyone often or without necessity, nor write in a letter, *I am too busy,* nor in this fashion constantly plead urgent affairs as an excuse for evading the obligations entailed upon us by our relations towards those around us.

13. FROM CATULUS,[2] not to disregard a friend's expostulation even when it is unreasonable, but to try to bring him back to his usual friendliness; and to speak with whole-hearted good-will of one's teachers, as it is recorded that Domitius[3] did of Athenodotus; and to be genuinely fond of one's children.

14. FROM MY 'BROTHER' SEVERUS,[4] love of family, love of truth, love of justice, and (thanks to him!) to know Thrasea, Helvidius, Cato, Dion, Brutus; and the conception of a state with one law for all, based upon individual equality and freedom of speech, and of a sovranty which prizes above all things the liberty of the subject; and furthermore from him also to set a well-balanced and unvarying value on philosophy; and readiness to do others a kindness, and eager generosity, and optimism, and confidence in the love of friends; and perfect openness in the case of those that came in for his censure; and the absence of any need for his friends to surmise what he did or did not wish, so plain was it.

---

[1] See Phil. *Vit. Soph.* ii. 5, p.247 Kays. He was summoned by Marcus to Pannonia about 174 and made his Greek secretary.

[2] A Stoic, see Capit. iii. 2.

[3] Domitii were among the maternal ancestors of Marcus, and an Athenodotus was Fronto's teacher (*ad Caes.* iv. 12; Nab. p. 73).

[4] See Index II. He was father of the son-in-law of Marcus.

ιε′. Παρὰ Μαξίμου, τὸ κρατεῖν ἑαυτοῦ καὶ
κατὰ μηδὲν περίφορον εἶναι· καὶ τὸ εὔθυμον ἔν τε
ταῖς ἄλλαις περιστάσεσι καὶ ἐν ταῖς νόσοις· καὶ
τὸ εὔκρατον τοῦ ἤθους καὶ μειλίχιον καὶ γεραρόν·
καὶ τὸ οὐ σχετλίως κατεργαστικὸν τῶν προ-
κειμένων.

2　Καὶ τὸ πάντας αὐτῷ πιστεύειν, περὶ ὧν λέγοι,
ὅτι οὕτως φρονεῖ, καὶ περὶ ὧν πράττοι, ὅτι
οὐ κακῶς πράττει. καὶ τὸ ἀθαύμαστον καὶ ἀν-
έκπληκτον, καὶ μηδαμοῦ ἐπειγόμενον ἢ ὀκνοῦν ἢ
ἀμηχανοῦν ἢ κατηφὲς ἢ προσεσηρός, ἢ πάλιν
θυμούμενον ἢ ὑφορώμενον.

3　Καὶ τὸ εὐεργετικὸν καὶ **τὸ** συγγνωμονικὸν
καὶ τὸ ἀψευδές· καὶ τὸ ἀδιαστρόφου μᾶλλον ἢ
διορθουμένου φαντασίαν παρέχειν· καὶ ὅτι οὔτε
ᾠήθη ἄν ποτέ τις ὑπερορᾶσθαι ὑπ' αὐτοῦ, οὔτε
ὑπέμεινεν ἂν κρείττονα αὐτοῦ αὑτὸν ὑπολαβεῖν·
καὶ τὸ εὐχαριεντίζεσθαι.†[1]

ιϛ′. Παρὰ τοῦ πατρός, τὸ ἥμερον, καὶ μενετικὸν
ἀσαλεύτως ἐπὶ τῶν ἐξητασμένως κριθέντων· καὶ
τὸ ἀκενόδοξον περὶ τὰς δοκούσας τιμάς· καὶ τὸ
φιλόπονον καὶ ἐνδελεχές· καὶ τὸ ἀκουστικὸν τῶν
ἐχόντων τι κοινωφελὲς εἰσφέρειν· καὶ τὸ ἀπαρα-
τρέπτως [εἰς] τὸ[2] κατ' ἀξίαν ἀπονεμητικὸν
ἑκάστῳ· καὶ τὸ ἔμπειρον, ποῦ μὲν χρεία ἐντάσεως,
ποῦ δὲ ἀνέσεως· καὶ τὸ παῦσαι τὰ περὶ τοὺς
ἔρωτας τῶν μειρακίων.

---

[1] εὖ χαριεντίζεσθαι Menag. : εὔχαρι ἐν ταῖς ὁμιλίαις Leop. :
εὔχαρι ἐν τ . . . . ίζεσθαι Schenkl.　[2] ἀεὶ τοῦ Schenkl.

---

[1] i. 16, § 9 ; viii. 25.　See Capit. iii. 2 ; Index II.
[2] Marcus raised a temple to Εὐεργεσία, a new deity.　See
Dio 71. 34, § 3.　[3] cp. iii. 5.

BOOK I

15. FROM MAXIMUS,[1] self-mastery and stability of purpose; and cheeriness in sickness as well as in all other circumstances; and a character justly proportioned of sweetness and gravity; and to perform without grumbling the task that lies to one's hand.

And the confidence of every one in him that what he said was also what he thought, and that what he did was done with no ill intent. And not to shew surprise, and not to be daunted; never to be hurried, or hold back, or be at a loss, or downcast, or smile a forced smile, or, again, be ill-tempered or suspicious.

And beneficence[2] and placability and veracity; and to give the impression of a man who cannot deviate from the right way rather than of one who is kept in it[3]; and that no one could have thought himself looked down upon by him, or could go so far as to imagine himself a better man than he; and to keep pleasantry within due bounds.

16. FROM MY FATHER,[4] mildness, and an unshakable adherence to decisions deliberately come to; and no empty vanity in respect to so-called honours; and a love of work and thoroughness; and a readiness to hear any suggestions for the common good; and an inflexible determination to give every man his due; and to know by experience when is the time to insist and when to desist; and to suppress all passion for boys.[5]

[4] Here Pius, his adoptive father, is meant, not as above (i. 2) his father Verus. For a first sketch of this eulogy of Pius see below vi. 30.

[5] It is not quite clear whether this means that Pius had put away this vice from himself or others, but the active verb seems rather to favour the latter view. Capit. *Vit. Pii* ii. 1, calls him *clarus moribus* (*cp.* also Aur. Vict. *de Caes.* xv.), but Julian says he was σώφρων οὐ τὰ ἐς Ἀφροδίτην.

2 Καὶ ἡ κοινονοημοσύνη, καὶ τὸ ἐφεῖσθαι τοῖς
φίλοις μήτε συνδειπνεῖν αὐτῷ πάντως μήτε
συναποδημεῖν ἐπάναγκες· ἀεὶ δὲ ὅμοιον αὐτὸν
καταλαμβάνεσθαι ὑπὸ τῶν διὰ χρείας τινὰς
ἀπολειφθέντων· καὶ τὸ ζητητικὸν ἀκριβῶς ἐν
τοῖς συμβουλίοις, καὶ ἐπίμονον, ἀλλ' † οὗτοι¹
προαπέστη † τῆς ἐρεύνης ἀρκεσθεὶς ταῖς προ-
χείροις φαντασίαις· καὶ τὸ διατηρητικὸν τῶν
φίλων καὶ μηδαμοῦ ἀψίκορον μηδὲ ἐπιμανές·
καὶ τὸ αὔταρκες ἐν παντί, καὶ τὸ φαιδρόν· καὶ τὸ
πόρρωθεν προνοητικόν, καὶ τῶν ἐλαχίστων προ-
διοικητικὸν ἀτραγῴδως.

3 Καὶ τὸ τὰς ἐπιβοήσεις καὶ πᾶσαν κολακείαν
ἐπ' αὐτοῦ σταλῆναι· καὶ τὸ φυλακτικὸν ἀεὶ τῶν
ἀναγκαίων τῇ ἀρχῇ, καὶ ταμιευτικὸν τῆς χορηγ-
ίας, καὶ ὑπομενετικὸν τῆς ἐπὶ τῶν τοιούτων
τινῶν καταιτιάσεως· καὶ τὸ μήτε περὶ θεοὺς
δεισίδαιμον, μήτε περὶ ἀνθρώπους δημοκοπικὸν
ἢ ἀρεσκευτικὸν ἢ ὀχλοχαρές, ἀλλὰ νῆφον ἐν
πᾶσι, καὶ βέβαιον, καὶ μηδαμοῦ ἀπειρόκαλον
μηδὲ καινοτόμον.

4 Καὶ τὸ τοῖς εἰς εὐμάρειαν βίου φέρουσί τι,
ὧν ἡ τύχη παρέχει δαψίλειαν, χρηστικὸν ἀτύφως
ἅμα καὶ ἀπροφασίστως, ὥστε παρόντων μὲν
ἀνεπιτηδεύτως ἅπτεσθαι, ἀπόντων δὲ μὴ δεῖσθαι·
καὶ τὸ μηδὲ ἄν τινα εἰπεῖν μήτε ὅτι σοφιστής,
μήτε ὅτι οὐερνάκλος μήτε ὅτι σχολαστικός,
ἀλλ' ὅτι ἀνὴρ πέπειρος, τέλειος, ἀκολάκευτος,

¹ οὐ τὸ PA : οὗτοι Stich : ὅτι οὐ Gat. : οὔποτε Cor.

14

BOOK I

And his public spirit, and his not at all requiring his friends to sup with him or necessarily attend him abroad,[1] and their always finding him the same when any urgent affairs had kept them away; and the spirit of thorough investigation which he shewed in the meetings of his Council, and his perseverance; nay his never desisting prematurely from an enquiry on the strength of off-hand impressions; and his faculty for keeping his friends and never being bored with them or infatuated about them; and his self-reliance in every emergency, and his good humour; and his habit of looking ahead and making provision for the smallest details without any heroics.

And his restricting in his reign public acclamations and every sort of adulation; and his unsleeping attention to the needs of the empire, and his wise stewardship of its resources, and his patient tolerance of the censure that all this entailed; and his freedom from superstition with respect to the Gods and from hunting for popularity with respect to men by pandering to their desires or by courting the mob: yea his soberness in all things[2] and stedfastness; and the absence in him of all vulgar tastes and any craze for novelty.

And the example that he gave of utilizing without pride, and at the same without any apology, all the lavish gifts of Fortune that contribute towards the comfort of life, so as to enjoy them when present as a matter of course, and, when absent, not to miss them: and no one could charge him with sophistry, flippancy,[3] or pedantry; but he was a man mature,

[1] *cp.* Fronto, *ad Caes.* iii. 20; v. 44.
[2] *cp.* St. Paul, Tim. ii. 4. 5.
[3] *lit.* that he was a " home-bred slave," *i.e.* impudent.

προεστάναι δυνάμενος, καὶ τῶν ἑαυτοῦ καὶ ἄλλων.

5 Πρὸς τούτοις δὲ καὶ τὸ τιμητικὸν τῶν ἀληθῶς φιλοσοφούντων, τοῖς δὲ ἄλλοις οὐκ ἐξονειδιστ-ικὸν οὐδὲ μὴν εὐπαράγωγον ὑπ' αὐτῶν· ἔτι δὲ τὸ εὐόμιλον καὶ εὔχαρι οὐ κατακόρως· καὶ τὸ τοῦ ἰδίου σώματος ἐπιμελητικὸν ἐμμέτρως, οὔτε ὡς ἄν τις φιλόζωος οὔτε πρὸς καλλωπ-ισμὸν οὔτε μὴν ὀλιγώρως, ἀλλ' ὥστε διὰ τὴν ἰδίαν προσοχὴν εἰς ὀλίγιστα ἰατρικῆς χρῄζ-ειν ἢ φαρμάκων καὶ ἐπιθεμάτων ἐκτός.

6 Μάλιστα δὲ τὸ παραχωρητικὸν ἀβασκάνως τοῖς δύναμίν τινα κεκτημένοις, οἷον τὴν φραστικὴν ἢ τὴν ἐξ ἱστορίας νόμων ἢ ἐθῶν ἢ ἄλλων τινῶν πραγμάτων· καὶ συσπουδαστικὸν αὐτοῖς, ἵνα ἕκαστοι κατὰ τὰ ἴδια προτερήματα εὐδοκιμῶσι· πάντα δὲ κατὰ τὰ πάτρια πράσσων, οὐδ' αὐτὸ τοῦτο ἐπιτηδεύων φαίνεσθαι, τὸ τὰ πάτρια φυλάσσειν.

7 Ἔτι δὲ τὸ μὴ εὐμετακίνητον καὶ ῥιπταστ-ικόν, ἀλλὰ καὶ τόποις, καὶ πράγμασι τοῖς αὐτοῖς ἐνδιατριπτικόν· καὶ τὸ μετὰ τοὺς παρ-οξυσμοὺς τῆς κεφαλαλγίας νεαρὸν εὐθὺς καὶ ἀκμαῖον πρὸς τὰ συνήθη ἔργα· καὶ τὸ μὴ εἶναι αὐτῷ πολλὰ τὰ ἀπόρρητα, ἀλλὰ ὀλίγιστα καὶ σπανιώτατα, καὶ ταῦτα ὑπὲρ τῶν κοινῶν μόνον· καὶ τὸ ἔμφρον καὶ μεμετρημένον ἔν τε θεωριῶν ἐπιτελέσει καὶ ἔργων κατασκευαῖς καὶ διανομαῖς καὶ τοῖς τοιούτοις, <ἃ> ἀνθρώπου [1] πρὸς αὐτὸ τὸ

---

[1] ἀνθρώποις PAD : ἃ ἀνθρώπου Schenkl.

---

[1] Julian calls Marcus τετράγωνος—"a man foursquare."

BOOK I

complete,[1] deaf to flattery, able to preside over his own affairs and those of others.

Besides this also was his high appreciation of all true philosophers without any upbraiding of the others, and at the same time without any undue subservience to them; then again his easiness of access and his graciousness that yet had nothing fulsome about it; and his reasonable attention to his bodily requirements, not as one too fond of life, or vain of his outward appearance,[2] nor yet as one who neglected it, but so as by his own carefulness to need but very seldom the skill of the leech or medicines and outward applications.

But most of all a readiness to acknowledge without jealousy the claims of those who were endowed with any especial gift, such as eloquence or knowledge of law or ethics or any other subject, and to give them active support, that each might gain the honour to which his individual eminence entitled him; and his loyalty to constitutional precedent without any parade of the fact that it was according to precedent.

Furthermore he was not prone to change or vacillation, but attached to the same places and the same things; and after his spasms of violent headache he would come back at once to his usual employments with renewed vigour; and his secrets were not many but very few and at very rare intervals, and then only political secrets; and he shewed good sense and moderation in his management of public spectacles, and in the construction of public works, and in congiaria[3] and the like, as a man who

[2] Capit. (*Vit. Pii* xiii. 1) says he wore stays to keep himself upright in old age.

[3] lit. "*distributions.*" *cp.* Capit. *Vit. Pii* iv. 9; viii. 11.

δέον πραχθῆναι δεδορκότος, οὐ πρὸς τὴν ἐπὶ τοῖς
πραχθεῖσιν εὐδοξίαν.

8 Οὐκ [ἐν] ἀωρὶ λούστης, οὐχὶ φιλοικοδόμος,
οὐ περὶ τὰς ἐδωδὰς ἐπινοητής, οὐ περὶ ἐσθήτων
ὑφὰς καὶ χρόας, οὐ περὶ σωμάτων ὥρας. †ἡ ἀπὸ
Λωρίου στολὴ ἀνάγουσα ἀπὸ τῆς κάτω ἐπαύλεως,
καὶ τῶν ἐν Λανουβίῳ τὰ πολλά.† τῷ τελώνῃ
ἐν Τούσκλοις παραιτουμένῳ ὡς ἐχρήσατο, καὶ
πᾶς ὁ τοιοῦτος τρόπος.

9 Οὐδὲν ἀπηνὲς οὐδὲ μὴν ἀδυσώπητον οὐδὲ
λάβρον οὐδὲ ὡς ἄν τινα εἰπεῖν ποτε " ἕως
ἱδρῶτος·" ἀλλὰ πάντα διειλημμένα λελογίσθαι,
ὡς ἐπὶ σχολῆς, ἀταράχως, τεταγμένως, ἐρρωμένως, συμφώνως ἑαυτοῖς. ἐφαρμόσειε δ' ἂν
αὐτῷ τὸ περὶ τοῦ Σωκράτους μνημονευόμενον,
ὅτι καὶ ἀπέχεσθαι καὶ ἀπολαύειν ἐδύνατο τούτων,
ὧν πολλοὶ πρός τε τὰς ἀποχὰς ἀσθενῶς καὶ
πρὸς τὰς ἀπολαύσεις ἐνδοτικῶς ἔχουσιν. τὸ δὲ
ἰσχύειν καὶ ἐπικαρτερεῖν[1] καὶ ἐννήφειν ἑκατέρῳ
ἀνδρός ἐστιν ἄρτιον καὶ ἀήττητον ψυχὴν ἔχοντος,
οἷον ἐν τῇ νόσῳ τῇ Μαξίμου.

ιζ. Παρὰ τῶν θεῶν, τὸ ἀγαθοὺς πάππους,
ἀγαθοὺς γονέας, ἀγαθὴν ἀδελφήν, ἀγαθοὺς δι-
δασκάλους, ἀγαθοὺς οἰκείους, συγγενεῖς, φίλους,
σχεδὸν ἅπαντας ἔχειν· καὶ ὅτι περὶ οὐδένα αὐτῶν
προέπεσον πλημμελῆσαί τι καίτοι διάθεσιν ἔχων
τοιαύτην, ἀφ' ἧς, εἰ ἔτυχε, κἂν ἔπραξά τι τοιοῦτο·

---

[1] ἔτι καρτερεῖν PA : ἐπικαρτερεῖν Cas.

---

[1] Xen. *Mem.* I. 3, § 15. πολλοί would here seem = οἱ πολλοί.
[2] The Greek may also mean "To be strong and to persist
without excess in each case is characteristic," and ἑκατέρῳ
suits this better.

18

had an eye to what had to be done and not to the credit to be gained thereby.

He did not bathe at all hours; he did not build for the love of building; he gave no thought to his food, or to the texture and colour of his clothes, or the comeliness of his slaves. His robe came up from Lorium, his country-seat in the plains, and Lanuvium supplied his wants for the most part. Think of how he dealt with the customs' officer at Tusculum when the latter apologized, and it was a type of his usual conduct.

There was nothing rude in him, nor yet overbearing or violent nor carried, as the phrase goes, " to the sweating state"; but everything was considered separately, as by a man of ample leisure, calmly, methodically, manfully, consistently. One might apply to him what is told of Socrates,[1] that he was able to abstain from or enjoy those things that many are not strong enough to refrain from and too much inclined to enjoy. But to have the strength to persist in the one case and be abstemious in the other[2] is characteristic of a man who has a perfect and indomitable soul, as was seen in the illness of Maximus.

17. FROM THE GODS, to have good grandfathers,[3] good parents, a good sister, good teachers, good companions, kinsmen, friends—nearly all of them; and that I fell into no trespass against any of them, and yet I had a disposition that way inclined, such as might have led me into something of the sort,[4] had

---

[3] i e. M. Annius Verus, three times consul (Dio 69. 21, § 1) and *praef. urbi* (Capit. i. 2), who died 138, and P. Calvisius Tullus, cons. suff. 109. See Capit. i. 3; Fronto, *ad Caes.* iii. 2. [4] *cp.* i. 17, § 6; xi. 18, § 4.

τῶν θεῶν δὲ εὐποιΐα τὸ μηδεμίαν συνδρομὴν
πραγμάτων γενέσθαι, ἥτις ἔμελλέ με ἐλέγξειν.

2 Καὶ τὸ μὴ ἐπὶ πλέον τραφῆναι παρὰ τῇ παλλακῇ
τοῦ πάππου· καὶ τὸ τὴν ὥραν διασῶσαι· καὶ τὸ
μὴ πρὸ ὥρας ἀνδρωθῆναι, ἀλλ' ἔτι καὶ ἐπιλαβεῖν
τοῦ χρόνου.

3 Τὸ ἄρχοντι καὶ πατρὶ ὑποταχθῆναι, ὃς ἔμελλε
πάντα τὸν τῦφον ἀφαιρήσειν μου, καὶ εἰς ἔννοιαν
ἄξειν τοῦ ὅτι δυνατόν ἐστιν ἐν αὐλῇ βιοῦντα
μήτε δορυφορήσεων χρῄζειν μήτε ἐσθήτων
σημειωδῶν μήτε λαμπάδων καὶ ἀνδριάντων
[τοιῶνδέ τινων] καὶ τοῦ ὁμοίου κόμπου· ἀλλ'
ἔξεστιν ἐγγυτάτω ἰδιώτου συστέλλειν ἑαυτόν, καὶ
μὴ διὰ τοῦτο ταπεινότερον ἢ ῥᾳθυμότερον ἔχειν
πρὸς τὰ ὑπὲρ τῶν κοινῶν ἡγεμονικῶς πραχθῆναι
δέοντα.

4 Τὸ ἀδελφοῦ τοιούτου τυχεῖν δυναμένου μὲν
διὰ ἤθους ἐπεγεῖραί με πρὸς ἐπιμέλειαν ἐμαυτοῦ,
ἅμα δὲ καὶ τιμῇ καὶ στοργῇ εὐφραίνοντός με·
τὸ παιδία μοι ἀφυῆ μὴ γενέσθαι μηδὲ κατὰ
τὸ σωμάτιον διάστροφα· τὸ μὴ ἐπὶ πλέον με
προκόψαι ἐν ῥητορικῇ καὶ ποιητικῇ καὶ τοῖς
ἄλλοις ἐπιτηδεύμασιν, ἐν οἷς ἴσως ἂν κατεσχέθην,
εἰ ᾐσθόμην ἐμαυτὸν εὐόδως προϊόντα. τὸ φθάσαι
τοὺς τροφέας ἐν ἀξιώματι καταστῆσαι, οὗ δὴ

---

[1] *cp.* ix. 21. After his father's death Marcus was
brought up at his grandfather's house (Capit. i. 7). Capit.
(v. 3) says he migrated *de maternis hortis* much against his
will to the imperial palace when adopted by Hadrian. It
is possible but not likely that "grandfather" here means
Hadrian.

[2] L. Verus, whose character was more of a warning than
an example, as Lucian *Nigr.* 19 calls Rome for its wickedness

it so chanced; but by the grace of God there was no such coincidence of circumstances as was likely to put me to the test.

And that I was not brought up any longer with my grandfather's[1] concubine, and that I kept unstained the flower of my youth; and that I did not make trial of my manhood before the due time, but even postponed it.

That I was subordinated to a ruler and a father capable of ridding me of all conceit, and of bringing me to recognize that it is possible to live in a Court and yet do without body-guards and gorgeous garments and linkmen and statues and the like pomp; and that it is in such a man's power to reduce himself very nearly to the condition of a private individual and yet not on this account to be more paltry or more remiss in dealing with what the interests of the state require to be done in imperial fashion.

That it was my lot to have such a brother,[2] capable by his character of stimulating me to watchful care over myself, and at the same time delighting me by his deference[3] and affection: that my children have not been devoid of intelligence nor physically deformed. That I did not make more progress in rhetoric[4] and poetry[5] and my other studies, in which I should perhaps have been engrossed, had I felt myself making good way in them. That I lost no time in promoting my tutors to such posts of

γυμνάσιον ἀρετῆς, see Epict. iii. 20, § 11. Marcus seems to have been genuinely fond of him, see Fronto, *ad Ver.* ii. 1; *ad Caes.* ii. 17; and cp. Aristides, *Paneg. in Cyz.* § 425 (Jebb).

[3] Capit. *Vit. Ver.* viii. 5.   [4] i. 7.

[5] I. 7. cp. Fronto, *ad Caes.* i. 8; *ad Ant.* i. 2 (Nab. p. 96); *de Eloq.* 3 (Nab. p. 150).

ἐδόκουν μοι ἐπιθυμεῖν, καὶ μὴ ἀναβαλέσθαι ἐλπίδι
τοῦ με,[1] ἐπεὶ νέοι ἔτι ἦσαν, ὕστερον αὐτὸ πράξειν.
τὸ γνῶναι Ἀπολλώνιον, Ῥουστικόν, Μάξιμον.

5 Τὸ φαντασθῆναι περὶ τοῦ κατὰ φύσιν βίου
ἐναργῶς καὶ πολλάκις, οἷός τίς ἐστι· ὥστε, ὅσον
ἐπὶ τοῖς θεοῖς καὶ ταῖς ἐκεῖθεν διαδόσεσι καὶ
συλλήψεσι καὶ ἐπινοίαις, μηδὲν κωλύειν ἤδη
κατὰ φύσιν ζῆν με, ἀπολείπεσθαι δὲ ἔτι τούτου
παρὰ τὴν ἐμὴν αἰτίαν, καὶ παρὰ τὸ μὴ διατηρεῖν
τὰς ἐκ τῶν θεῶν ὑπομνήσεις καὶ μονονουχὶ
διδασκαλίας.

6 Τὸ ἀντισχεῖν μοι τὸ σῶμα ἐπὶ τοσοῦτον ἐν
τοιούτῳ βίῳ· τὸ μήτε Βενεδίκτης ἅψασθαι μήτε
Θεοδότου, ἀλλὰ καὶ ὕστερον ἐν ἐρωτικοῖς πάθεσι
γενόμενον ὑγιᾶναι· τὸ χαλεπήναντα πολλάκις
Ῥουστίκῳ μηδὲν πλέον πρᾶξαι, ἐφ' ᾧ ἂν μετ-
έγνων· τὸ μέλλουσαν νέαν τελευτᾶν τὴν τεκοῦσαν
ὅμως οἰκῆσαι μετ' ἐμοῦ τὰ τελευταῖα ἔτη.

7 Τὸ ὁσάκις ἐβουλήθην ἐπικουρῆσαί τινι πενο-
μένῳ ἢ εἰς ἄλλο τι χρήζοντι, μηδέποτε ἀκοῦσαί
με, ὅτι οὐκ ἔστι μοι χρήματα, ὅθεν γένηται· καὶ
τὸ αὐτῷ ἐμοὶ χρείαν ὁμοίαν, ὡς παρ' ἑτέρου
μεταλαβεῖν, μὴ συμπεσεῖν· τὸ τὴν γυναῖκα
τοιαύτην εἶναι, οὕτωσὶ μὲν πειθήνιον, οὕτω δὲ
φιλόστοργον, οὕτω δὲ ἀφελῆ· τὸ ἐπιτηδείων
τροφέων εἰς τὰ παιδία εὐπορῆσαι.

---

[1] τοῦ μὴ PA : με Cas.

---

[1] e.g. Rusticus, cons. ii. in 162, and praef. urbi ; Pro-
culus, see Capit. ii. 5.
[2] i. 9.   [3] Dio 71. 36, § 3.
[4] Domitia Lucilla, dau. of P. Calvisius Tullus. She died
in 156, aged about 50. For her see above i. 3 ; viii. 25 ;

BOOK I

honour [1] as they seemed to desire, and that I did not put them off with the hope that I would do this later on since they were still young. That I got to know Apollonius, Rusticus, Maximus.

That I had clear and frequent conceptions as to the true meaning of a life according to Nature,[2] so that as far as the Gods were concerned and their blessings and assistance and intention, there was nothing to prevent me from beginning at once to live in accordance with Nature, though I still come short of this ideal by my own fault, and by not attending to the reminders, nay, almost the instructions, of the Gods.

That my body holds out so long in such a life as mine [3]; that I did not touch Benedicta or Theodotus, but that even afterwards, when I did give way to amatory passions, I was cured of them; that, though often offended with Rusticus, I never went so far as to do anything for which I should have been sorry; that my mother,[4] though she was to die young, yet spent her last years with me.

That as often as I had the inclination to help any-one, who was in pecuniary distress or needing any other assistance, I was never told that there was no money available for the purpose; and that I was never under any similar need of accepting help from another. That I have been blessed with a wife so docile,[5] so affectionate, so unaffected; [6] that I had no lack of suitable tutors for my children.

Fronto, *ad Caes.* iv. 6 ; Capit. vi. 9. Her head appears on a coin of Nicaea in Bithynia.   [5] *cp.* Fronto, *ad Caes.* v. 11.
   [6] *cp.* Fronto, *ad Pium* 2, *ad fin.* for Pius' opinion of his daughter. The coiffure of the younger Faustina as seen on coins is much simpler than that of her mother. She was with Marcus in Pannonia for a time at least.

8 Τὸ δι' ὀνειράτων βοηθήματα δοθῆναι ἄλλα
τε καὶ ὡς μὴ πτύειν αἷμα καὶ μὴ ἰλιγγιᾶν, καὶ
τὸ τοῦ ἐν[1] Καιήτῃ †"ὥσπερ χρήσῃ"† ὅπως τε
ἐπεθύμησα φιλοσοφίας, μὴ ἐμπεσεῖν εἴς τινα σοφ-
ιστήν, μηδὲ ἀποκαθίσαι ἐπὶ τοὺς συγγραφεῖς,†[2]
ἢ συλλογισμοὺς ἀναλύειν, ἢ περὶ τὰ μετεωρο-
λογικὰ καταγίνεσθαι. πάντα γὰρ ταῦτα ' θεῶν
βοηθῶν καὶ τύχης δεῖταί <τινος>.[3] '

Τὰ ἐν Κονάδοις πρὸς τῷ Γρανούᾳ. α'[4]

[1] τούτου PA : τὸ τοῦ ἐν Καιήτῃ " ὥσπερ χρήσῃ " Lofft.
[2] τοὺς συγγραφεῖς PA: τὸ συγγράφειν Reiske: ἐπὶ τοῦ
γρίφους (*riddles*) Schenkl.
[3] I have added τινὸς to complete the apparent senarius,
the source of which is not known.
[4] It is not clear what this numeral (= 1) represents.

[1] *cp.* Fronto, *ad Caes.* iii. 9, and below, ix. 27. Artemidorus,
De Somniis iv. 24, and Pliny *N.H.* xxv. 6. Marcus
himself became a dream-giver after his death, see Capit.
xviii. 7. Dreams were the recognised method by which the

BOOK I

That by the agency of dreams [1] I was given antidotes both of other kinds and against the spitting of blood and vertigo; and there is that response also at Caieta, "*as thou shalt use it.*" And that, when I had set my heart on philosophy, I did not fall into the hands of a sophist, nor sat down at the author's desk, or became a solver of syllogisms, nor busied myself with physical phenomena. For all the above *the Gods as helpers and good fortune need.*

Written among the Quadi on the Gran.[2]

God of healing communicated his prescriptions. Belief in them was universal, and shared by the atheist Pliny, the sceptic Lucian, Aristides the devotee, Galen the scientist, Dio the historian and man of affairs. It is not unknown to Christians. Yet there have been found writers to gird at Marcus for his "superstitious" belief in dreams!

[2] These words may be intended either to conclude the first book or, more likely, head the second. In the former case, as Gataker points out, τάδε would have been usual, not τά.

ΒΙΒΛΙΟΝ Β[1]

αʹ. Ἕωθεν προλέγειν ἑαυτῷ· συντεύξομαι περι-
έργῳ, ἀχαρίστῳ, ὑβριστῇ, δολερῷ, βασκάνῳ,
ἀκοινωνήτῳ. πάντα ταῦτα συμβέβηκεν ἐκείνοις
παρὰ τὴν ἄγνοιαν τῶν ἀγαθῶν καὶ κακῶν. ἐγὼ
δὲ τεθεωρηκὼς τὴν φύσιν τοῦ ἀγαθοῦ, ὅτι καλόν,
καὶ τοῦ κακοῦ, ὅτι αἰσχρόν, καὶ τὴν αὐτοῦ τοῦ
ἁμαρτάνοντος φύσιν, ὅτι μοι συγγενής, οὐχὶ
αἵματος ἢ σπέρματος τοῦ αὐτοῦ, ἀλλὰ νοῦ καὶ
θείας ἀπομοίρας[2] μέτοχος, οὔτε βλαβῆναι ὑπό
τινος αὐτῶν δύναμαι· αἰσχρῷ γάρ με οὐδεὶς
περιβαλεῖ· οὔτε ὀργίζεσθαι τῷ συγγενεῖ δύναμαι
οὔτε ἀπέχθεσθαι αὐτῷ. γεγόναμεν γὰρ πρὸς
συνεργίαν, ὡς πόδες, ὡς χεῖρες, ὡς βλέφαρα, ὡς
οἱ στοῖχοι τῶν ἄνω καὶ κάτω ὀδόντων. τὸ οὖν
ἀντιπράσσειν ἀλλήλοις παρὰ φύσιν· ἀντιπρακτ-
ικὸν δὲ τὸ ἀγανακτεῖν καὶ ἀποστρέφεσθαι.

βʹ. Ὅ τί ποτε τοῦτό εἰμι, σαρκία ἐστὶ καὶ
πνευμάτιον καὶ τὸ ἡγεμονικόν. ἄφες τὰ βιβλία·
μηκέτι σπῶ· οὐ δέδοται. ἀλλ' ὡς ἤδη ἀποθνῄσκων τῶν μὲν σαρκίων καταφρόνησον· λύθρος καὶ
ὀστάρια καὶ κροκύφαντος ἐκ νεύρων, φλεβίων,
ἀρτηριῶν πλεγμάτιον. θέασαι δὲ καὶ τὸ πνεῦμα,

---

[1] <τοῦ αὐτοῦ Μάρκου· ἄντικρυς ἐπικτητίζει> D.
[2] ἀπόρροια (cp. ii. 4) "efflux from," Corssen.

BOOK II

1. Say to thyself at daybreak : [1] I shall come across the busy-body, the thankless, the overbearing, the treacherous, the envious, the unneighbourly. [2] All this has befallen them because they know not good from evil. But I, in that I have comprehended the nature of the Good that it is beautiful, and the nature of Evil that it is ugly, and the nature of the wrong-doer himself that it is akin to me, not as partaker of the same blood and seed but of intelligence and a morsel of the Divine, can neither be injured by any of them—for no one can involve me in what is debasing—nor can I be wroth with my kinsman and hate him. For we have come into being for co-operation, as have the feet, the hands, the eyelids, the rows of upper and lower teeth. Therefore to thwart one another is against Nature ; and we do thwart one another by shewing resentment and aversion.

2. This that I am, whatever it be, is mere flesh and a little breath and the ruling Reason. Away with thy books [3] ! Be no longer drawn aside by them : it is not allowed. But as one already dying disdain the flesh : it is naught but gore and bones and a network compact of nerves and veins and arteries. Look at the breath too, what sort of thing it is ; air :

[1] v. l.   [2] *cp.* Sen. *de Ira* ii. 10.   [3] *cp.* ii. 3.

ὁποῖόν τί ἐστιν· ἄνεμος· οὐδὲ ἀεὶ τὸ αὐτό, ἀλλὰ
πάσης ὥρας ἐξεμούμενον καὶ πάλιν ῥοφούμενον.
τρίτον οὖν ἐστὶ τὸ ἡγεμονικόν. ὧδε [1] ἐπινοήθητι·
γέρων εἶ· μηκέτι τοῦτο ἐάσῃς δουλεῦσαι, μηκέτι
καθ᾽ ὁρμὴν ἀκοινώνητον νευροσπαστηθῆναι, μηκέτι
τὸ εἱμαρμένον ἢ παρὸν δυσχερᾶναι ἢ μέλλον
ἀποδύρεσθαι.[2]

γ΄. Τὰ τῶν θεῶν προνοίας μεστά, τὰ τῆς τύχης
οὐκ ἄνευ φύσεως ἢ συγκλώσεως καὶ ἐπιπλοκῆς
τῶν προνοίᾳ διοικουμένων. πάντα ἐκεῖθεν ῥεῖ·
πρόσεστι δὲ τὸ ἀναγκαῖον, καὶ τὸ τῷ ὅλῳ κόσμῳ
συμφέρον, οὗ μέρος εἶ. παντὶ δὲ φύσεως μέρει
ἀγαθόν, ὃ φέρει ἡ τοῦ ὅλου φύσις, καὶ ὃ ἐκείνης
ἐστὶ σωστικόν. σώζουσι δὲ κόσμον, ὥσπερ αἱ
τῶν στοιχείων, οὕτως καὶ αἱ τῶν συγκριμάτων
μεταβολαί. ταῦτά σοι ἀρκείτω, εἰ δόγματά ἐστι.[3]
τὴν δὲ τῶν βιβλίων δίψαν ῥῖψον, ἵνα μὴ γογγύζων
ἀποθάνῃς, ἀλλὰ ἵλεως, ἀληθῶς, καὶ ἀπὸ καρδίας
εὐχάριστος τοῖς θεοῖς.

δ΄. Μέμνησο, ἐκ πόσου ταῦτα ἀναβάλλῃ, καὶ
ὁποσάκις προθεσμίας λαβὼν παρὰ τῶν θεῶν οὐ
χρᾷ αὐταῖς. δεῖ δὲ ἤδη ποτὲ αἰσθέσθαι, τίνος
κόσμου μέρος εἶ, καὶ τίνος διοικοῦντος τὸν κόσμον
ἀπόρροια ὑπέστης· καὶ ὅτι ὅρος ἐστί σοι περιγε-
γραμμένος τοῦ χρόνου, ᾧ ἐὰν εἰς τὸ ἀπαιθριάσαι

---

[1] ᾧ δὴ ADC : ᾡδὶ Wilam.: ἀπονοήθητι PADC.
[2] ἀποδύεσθαι AD : ὑποδύεσθαι P : ἀποδύρεσθαι (ὑποδύρ. Lofft)
Rend.
[3] εἰ δόγματά ἐστι AD : ἀεὶ . . . ἔστω PC.

---

[1] cp. ii. 6 ; i. 17, § 6 ; Dio 71. 24, § 4. Marcus would be
a little over 50. Contrast i. 17, § 6, and note. Cromwell
when 51 writing from Dunbar says, " I grow an old man."

BOOK II

and not even that always the same, but every minute belched forth and again gulped down. Then, thirdly, there is the ruling Reason. Put thy thought thus : thou art an old man [1]; let this be a thrall no longer, no more a puppet [2] pulled aside by every selfish impulse ; nor let it grumble any longer at what is allotted to it in the present or dread it in the future.

3. Full of Providence are the works of the Gods, nor are Fortune's works independent of Nature or of the woven texture and interlacement of all that is under the control of Providence. Thence [3] are all things derived [4]; but Necessity too plays its part and the Welfare of the whole Universe of which thou art a portion. But good for every part of Nature is that which the Nature of the Whole brings about, and which goes to preserve it. Now it is the changes not only of the elements but of the things compounded of them that preserve the Universe. Let these reflections suffice thee, if thou hold them as principles. But away with thy thirst for books,[5] that thou mayest die not murmuring but with a good grace, truly and from thy heart grateful to the Gods.

4. Call to mind how long thou deferrest these things, and how many times thou hast received from the Gods grace [6] of the appointed day and thou usest it not. Yet now, if never before, shouldest thou realize of what Universe thou art a part, and as an emanation from what Controller of that Universe thou dost subsist ; and that a limit has been set to thy time, which if thou use not to let daylight

[2] iii. 16 ; vi. 16, 28 ; vii. 3, 29 ; xii. 19. *cp*. Clem. Alex. *Strom.* ii. 3 ; iv. 11. [3] vi. 36 ; xii. 26.
[4] Referred to by Arethas on Dio Chrys. *Orat.* 32. 15 as πάντα ἄνωθεν ῥεῖ. *cp*. St. James, Ep. i. 17. [5] ii. 2.
[6] προθεσμία *lit.* "a time-limit for enforcement of claims after which they lapsed."

29

μὴ χρήσῃ, οἰχήσεται, καὶ οἰχήσῃ, καὶ αὖθις οὐκ
ἔξεσται.[1]

ε΄. Πάσης ὥρας φρόντιζε στιβαρῶς, ὡς Ῥωμ-
αῖος καὶ ἄρρην, τὸ ἐν χερσὶ μετὰ τῆς ἀκριβοῦς
καὶ ἀπλάστου σεμνότητος καὶ φιλοστοργίας καὶ
ἐλευθερίας καὶ δικαιότητος πράσσειν· καὶ σχολὴν
σαυτῷ ἀπὸ πασῶν τῶν ἄλλων φαντασιῶν
πορίζειν. ποριεῖς δέ, ἂν ὡς ἐσχάτην τοῦ βίου
ἑκάστην πρᾶξιν ἐνεργῇς ἀπηλλαγμένην πάσης
εἰκαιότητος καὶ ἐμπαθοῦς ἀποστροφῆς ἀπὸ τοῦ
αἱροῦντος λόγου καὶ ὑποκρίσεως καὶ φιλαυτίας
καὶ δυσαρεστήσεως πρὸς τὰ συμμεμοιραμένα.
ὁρᾷς, πῶς ὀλίγα ἐστίν, ὧν κρατήσας τις δύναται
εὔρουν καὶ θεουδῆ βιῶσαι βίον· καὶ γὰρ οἱ
θεοὶ πλέον οὐδὲν ἀπαιτήσουσι παρὰ τοῦ ταῦτα
φυλάσσοντος.

ϛ΄. Ὕβριζε, ὕβριζε[2] αὐτήν, ὦ ψυχή· τοῦ δὲ
τιμῆσαι σεαυτὴν οὐκέτι καιρὸν ἕξεις· εἷς[3] † γὰρ
ὁ βίος ἑκάστῳ· οὗτος δέ σοι σχεδὸν διήνυσται
μὴ αἰδουμένῃ σεαυτήν, ἀλλ' ἐν ταῖς ἄλλων ψυχαῖς
τιθεμένῃ τὴν σὴν εὐμοιρίαν.

ζ΄. Περισπᾷ τί σε τὰ ἔξωθεν ἐμπίπτοντα;
καὶ σχολὴν πάρεχε σεαυτῷ τοῦ προσμανθάνειν
ἀγαθόν τι, καὶ παῦσαι ῥεμβόμενος. ἤδη δὲ καὶ
τὴν ἑτέραν περιφορὰν φυλακτέον. ληροῦσι γὰρ
καὶ διὰ πράξεων οἱ κεκμηκότες τῷ βίῳ καὶ μὴ
ἔχοντες σκοπόν, ἐφ' ὃν πᾶσαν ὁρμὴν καὶ καθάπαξ
φαντασίαν ἀπευθύνουσιν.

---

[1] ἥξεται P : ἔξεσται AD.   [2] ὑβρίζεις Gat. (cp. §16).
[3] οὐ A : εὖ P : βραχὺς (cp. iv. 26) D : εἶς Boot.

---

[1] § 11 ; vii. 69 ; Sen. *Ep.* xii   [2] §§ 16, 17 ; iv. 2.

into thy soul, it will be gone—and thou!—and never again shall the chance be thine.

5. Every hour make up thy mind sturdily as a Roman and a man to do what thou hast in hand with scrupulous and unaffected dignity and love of thy kind and independence and justice; and to give thyself rest from all other impressions. And thou wilt give thyself this, if thou dost execute every act of thy life as though it were thy last,[1] divesting thyself of all aimlessness[2] and all passionate antipathy to the convictions of reason, and all hypocrisy and self-love and dissatisfaction with thy allotted share. Thou seest how few are the things, by mastering which a man may lead a life of tranquillity and godlikeness; for the Gods also will ask no more from him who keeps these precepts.

6. Wrong thyself,[3] wrong thyself, O my Soul! But the time for honouring thyself will have gone by; for a man has but one life, and this for thee is well-nigh closed,[4] and yet thou dost not hold thyself in reverence, but settest thy well-being in the souls of others.

7. Do those things draw thee at all away, which befall thee from without? Make then leisure for thyself for the learning of some good thing more, and cease being carried aside hither and thither. But therewith must thou take heed of the other error. For they too are triflers, who by their activities have worn themselves out in life without even having an aim whereto they can direct every impulse, aye and even every thought.

[3] Apparently a sarcastic apostrophe, which is not in Marcus' usual manner.
[4] ii. 2.

η'. Παρὰ μὲν τὸ μὴ ἐφιστάνειν, τί ἐν τῇ ἄλλου ψυχῇ γίνεται, οὐ ῥαδίως τις ὤφθη κακοδαιμονῶν· τοὺς δὲ τοῖς τῆς ἰδίας ψυχῆς κινήμασι μὴ παρακολουθοῦντας ἀνάγκη κακοδαιμονεῖν.

θ'. Τούτων ἀεὶ δεῖ μεμνῆσθαι, τίς ἡ τῶν ὅλων φύσις, καὶ τίς ἡ ἐμή, καὶ πῶς αὕτη πρὸς ἐκείνην ἔχουσα, καὶ ὁποῖόν τι μέρος ὁποίου τοῦ ὅλου οὖσα· καὶ ὅτι οὐδεὶς ὁ κωλύων τὰ ἀκόλουθα τῇ φύσει, ἧς μέρος εἶ, πράσσειν τε ἀεὶ καὶ λέγειν.

ι'. Φιλοσόφως ὁ Θεόφραστος, ἐν τῇ συγκρίσει τῶν ἁμαρτημάτων, ὡς ἄν τις κοινότερον τὰ τοιαῦτα συγκρίνειε, φησὶ βαρύτερα εἶναι τὰ κατ' ἐπιθυμίαν πλημμελούμενα τῶν κατὰ θυμόν. ὁ γὰρ θυμούμενος μετά τινος λύπης καὶ λεληθυίας συστολῆς φαίνεται τὸν λόγον ἀποστρεφόμενος· ὁ δὲ κατ' ἐπιθυμίαν ἁμαρτάνων, ὑφ' ἡδονῆς ἡττώμενος, ἀκολαστότερός πως φαίνεται καὶ θηλύτερος ἐν ταῖς ἁμαρτίαις. ὀρθῶς οὖν καὶ φιλοσοφίας ἀξίως ἔφη, μείζονος ἐγκλήματος ἔχεσθαι τὸ μεθ' ἡδονῆς ἁμαρτανόμενον ἤπερ τὸ μετὰ λύπης· ὅλως τε ὁ μὲν προηδικημένῳ μᾶλλον ἔοικε καὶ διὰ λύπης ἠναγκασμένῳ θυμωθῆναι· ὁ δὲ αὐτόθεν πρὸς τὸ ἀδικεῖν ὥρμηται, φερόμενος ἐπὶ τὸ πρᾶξαί τι κατ' ἐπιθυμίαν.

ια'. Ὡς ἤδη δυνατοῦ ὄντος ἐξιέναι τοῦ βίου, οὕτως ἕκαστα ποιεῖν καὶ λέγειν καὶ διανοεῖσθαι. τὸ δὲ ἐξ ἀνθρώπων ἀπελθεῖν, εἰ μὲν θεοὶ εἰσίν,

---

[1] Here Marcus deviates from the strict Stoic doctrine, which allowed no degrees in faults.

[2] For συστολή cp. Diog. Laert. (*Zeno*) 63, ἔλεος εἶναι πάθος καὶ συστολὴν ἄλογον.   [3] *above*, § 5.

BOOK II

8. Not easily is a man found to be unhappy by reason of his not regarding what is going on in another man's soul; but those who do not attend closely to the motions of their own souls must inevitably be unhappy.

9. This must always be borne in mind, what is the Nature of the whole Universe, and what mine, and how this stands in relation to that, being too what sort of a part of what sort of a whole; and that no one can prevent thee from doing and saying always what is in keeping with the Nature of which thou art a part.

10. Theophrastus in his comparison of wrong-doings—for, speaking in a somewhat popular way, such comparison may be made—says in the true philosophical spirit that the offences which are due to lust are more heinous than those which are due to anger.[1] For the man who is moved with anger seems to turn his back upon reason with some pain and unconscious compunction[2]; but he that does wrong from lust, being mastered by pleasure, seems in some sort to be more incontinent and more unmanly in his wrong-doing. Rightly then, and not unworthily of a philosopher, he said that the wrong-doing which is allied with pleasure calls for a severer condemnation than that which is allied with pain; and, speaking generally, that the one wrong-doer is more like a man, who, being sinned against first, has been driven by pain to be angry, while the other, being led by lust to do some act, has of his own motion been impelled to do evil.

11. Let thine every deed and word and thought be those of a man who can depart from life this moment.[3] But to go away from among men, if

οὐδὲν δεινόν· κακῷ γάρ σε οὐκ ἂν περιβάλοιεν· εἰ δὲ ἤτοι οὐκ εἰσίν, ἢ οὐ μέλει αὐτοῖς τῶν ἀνθρωπείων, τί μοι ζῆν ἐν κόσμῳ κενῷ θεῶν ἢ προνοίας κενῷ ; ἀλλὰ καὶ εἰσί, καὶ μέλει αὐτοῖς τῶν ἀνθρωπείων· καὶ τοῖς μὲν κατ' ἀλήθειαν κακοῖς ἵνα μὴ περιπίπτῃ ὁ ἄνθρωπος, ἐπ' αὐτῷ τὸ πᾶν ἔθεντο· τῶν δὲ λοιπῶν εἴ τι κακὸν ἦν, καὶ τοῦτο ἂν προείδοντο, ἵνα ἐπὶ παντὶ ᾖ τὸ μὴ περιπίπτειν αὐτῷ. ὃ δὲ χείρω μὴ ποιεῖ ἄνθρωπον, πῶς ἂν τοῦτο βίον ἀνθρώπου χείρω ποιήσειεν; οὔτε δὲ κατ' ἄγνοιαν οὔτε εἰδυῖα μέν, μὴ δυναμένη δὲ προφυλάξασθαι ἢ διορθώσασθαι ταῦτα, ἡ τῶν ὅλων φύσις παρεῖδεν ἄν· οὔτε ἂν τηλικοῦτον ἥμαρτεν ἤτοι παρ' ἀδυναμίαν ἢ παρ' ἀτεχνίαν, ἵνα τὰ ἀγαθὰ καὶ τὰ κακὰ ἐπίσης τοῖς τε ἀγαθοῖς ἀνθρώποις καὶ τοῖς κακοῖς πεφυρμένως συμβαίνῃ. θάνατος δέ γε καὶ ζωή, δόξα καὶ ἀδοξία, πόνος καὶ ἡδονή, πλοῦτος καὶ πενία, πάντα ταῦτα ἐπίσης συμβαίνει ἀνθρώπων τοῖς τε ἀγαθοῖς καὶ τοῖς κακοῖς οὔτε καλὰ ὄντα οὔτε αἰσχρά. οὔτ' ἄρ' ἀγαθὰ οὔτε κακά ἐστιν.

ιβ'. Πῶς πάντα ταχέως ἐναφανίζεται, τῷ μὲν κόσμῳ αὐτὰ τὰ σώματα, τῷ δὲ αἰῶνι αἱ μνῆμαι αὐτῶν· οἷά ἐστι τὰ αἰσθητὰ πάντα καὶ μάλιστα τὰ ἡδονῇ δελεάζοντα ἢ τῷ πόνῳ φοβοῦντα ἢ τῷ τύφῳ διαβεβοημένα, πῶς εὐτελῆ καὶ εὐκαταφρόνητα καὶ ῥυπαρὰ καὶ εὔφθαρτα καὶ νεκρά, νοερᾶς δυνάμεως ἐφιστάναι. τί εἰσιν οὗτοι, ὧν αἱ ὑπολήψεις καὶ αἱ φωναὶ τὴν εὐδοξίαν <παρ-

---

[1] cp. Fronto, de Nep. Nab. p. 233.   [2] iv. 8.

there are Gods, is nothing dreadful; for they would not involve thee in evil. But if indeed there are no Gods, or if they do not concern themselves with the affairs of men, what boots it for me to live in a Universe empty of Gods or empty of Providence? Nay, but there *are* Gods, and they *do* concern themselves with human things;[1] and they have put it wholly in man's power not to fall into evils that are truly such. And had there been any evil in what lies beyond, for this too would they have made provision, that it should be in every man's power not to fall into it. But how can that make a man's life worse which does not make the man worse?[2] Yet the Nature of the Whole could not have been guilty of an oversight from ignorance or, while cognizant of these things, through lack of power to guard against or amend them; nor could it have gone so far amiss either from inability or unskilfulness, as to allow good and evil to fall without any discrimination alike upon the evil and the good. Still it is a fact that death and life, honour and dishonour, pain and pleasure, riches and penury, do among men one and all betide the Good and the Evil alike, being in themselves neither honourable nor shameful. Consequently they are neither good nor evil.

12. How quickly all things vanish away, in the Universe their actual bodies, and the remembrance of them in Eternity, and of what character are all objects of sense, and particularly those that entice us with pleasure or terrify us with pain or are acclaimed by vanity—how worthless and despicable and unclean and ephemeral and dead!—this is for our faculty of intelligence to apprehend; as also what they really are whose conceptions and whose voices award

ἔχουσι>.¹ τί ἐστι τὸ ἀποθανεῖν, καὶ ὅτι, ἐάν τις αὐτὸ μόνον ἴδῃ καὶ τῷ μερισμῷ τῆς ἐννοίας δια·λύσῃ τὰ ἐμφανταζόμενα αὐτῷ, οὐκέτι ἄλλο τι ὑπολήψεται αὐτὸ εἶναι ἢ φύσεως ἔργον· φύσεως δὲ ἔργον εἴ τις φοβεῖται, παιδίον ἐστίν· τοῦτο μέντοι οὐ μόνον φύσεως ἔργον ἐστίν, ἀλλὰ καὶ συμφέρον αὐτῇ. πῶς ἅπτεται θεοῦ ἄνθρωπος, καὶ κατὰ τί ἑαυτοῦ μέρος, καὶ †ὅταν πῶς [ἔχῃ] διακέηται†² τὸ τοῦ ἀνθρώπου τοῦτο μόριον.

ιγ΄. Οὐδὲν ἀθλιώτερον τοῦ πάντα κύκλῳ ἐκπερι·ερχομένου, καὶ "τὰ νέρθεν γᾶς," φησίν, "ἐρευνῶν·τος," καὶ τὰ ἐν ταῖς ψυχαῖς τῶν πλησίον διὰ τεκμάρσεως ζητοῦντος, μὴ αἰσθομένου δέ, ὅτι ἀρκεῖ πρὸς μόνῳ τῷ ἔνδον ἑαυτοῦ δαίμονι εἶναι καὶ τοῦτον γνησίως θεραπεύειν. θεραπεία δὲ αὐτοῦ, καθαρὸν πάθους διατηρεῖν καὶ εἰκαιότητος καὶ δυσ·αρεστήσεως τῆς πρὸς τὰ ἐκ θεῶν καὶ ἀνθρώπων γινόμενα. τὰ μὲν γὰρ ἐκ θεῶν αἰδέσιμα δι' ἀρετήν· τὰ δὲ ἐξ ἀνθρώπων φίλα διὰ συγγένειαν, ἔστι δὲ ὅτε καὶ τρόπον τινὰ ἐλεεινὰ δι' ἄγνοιαν ἀγαθῶν καὶ κακῶν· οὐκ ἐλάττων ἡ πήρωσις αὕτη τῆς στερισκούσης τοῦ διακρίνειν τὰ λευκὰ καὶ μέλανα.

ιδ΄. Κἂν τρισχίλια ἔτη βιώσεσθαι μέλλῃς, καὶ τοσαυτάκις μύρια, ὅμως μέμνησο ὅτι οὐδεὶς ἄλλον

---

¹ <παρέχουσι> Gat.
² τις ἔχῃ διακαίηται A : ἔχῃ ἢ διακ. Cor. : ποσαχῇ Rader·macher.

---

¹ Pindar, *Frag.* (see Plato, *Theaet.* 173 E).
² § 17; iii. 6, 16.   *cp.* Shaks. *Temp.* ii. 1. 275 : "Con·science, this deity in my bosom," Ant. and Cleo. ii. 3. 19. The δαιμόνιον of Socrates is well known.

renown; what it is to die, and that if a man look at
death in itself, and with the analysis of reason strip
it of its phantom terrors, no longer will he conceive
it to be aught but a function of Nature,—but if a
man be frightened by a function of Nature, he is
childish; and this is not only Nature's function but
her welfare;—and how man is in touch with God
and with what part of himself, and in what disposition of this portion of the man.

13. Nothing can be more miserable than the
man who goes through the whole round of things,
and, as the poet[1] says, *pries into the things beneath
the earth*, and would fain guess the thoughts in
his neighbour's heart, while having no conception
that he needs but to associate himself with the
divine 'genius' in his bosom,[2] and to serve it
truly. And service of it is to keep it pure from
passion and aimlessness and discontent with anything that proceeds from Gods or men. For that
which proceeds from the Gods is worthy of reverence in that it is excellent; and that which proceeds
from men, of love, in that they are akin, and, at
times and in a manner,[3] of compassion, in that they
are ignorant of good and evil—a defect this no less
than the loss of power to distinguish between white
and black.

14. Even if thy life is to last three thousand years
or for the matter of that thirty thousand, yet bear in
mind that no one ever parts with any other life than

---

[3] Marcus qualifies his departure from the strict Stoic view,
for which see Seneca *de Clem.* ii. 4–6, where he calls pity
pusillanimity, and says *sapiens non miserebitur sed succurret.*
Marcus was far from a Stoic in this, see Herodian i. 4, § 2.
See above, p. xiii.

ἀποβάλλει βίον ἢ τοῦτον ὃν ζῇ· οὐδὲ ἄλλον ζῇ ἢ ὃν
ἀποβάλλει. εἰς ταὐτὸ οὖν καθίσταται τὸ μήκιστ-
ον τῷ βραχυτάτῳ. τὸ γὰρ παρὸν πᾶσιν ἴσον, καὶ
τὸ ἀπολλύμενον οὐκ ἴδιον[1] καὶ τὸ ἀποβαλλόμενον
οὕτως ἀκαριαῖον ἀναφαίνεται. οὔτε γὰρ τὸ παρῳχηκὸς οὔτε τὸ μέλλον ἀποβάλλοι ἄν τις. ὃ γὰρ
οὐκ ἔχει, πῶς ἂν τοῦτό τις αὐτοῦ ἀφέλοιτο;
τούτων οὖν τῶν δύο δεῖ μεμνῆσθαι· ἑνὸς μέν, ὅτι
πάντα ἐξ ἀιδίου ὁμοειδῆ καὶ ἀνακυκλούμενα, καὶ
οὐδὲν διαφέρει πότερον ἐν ἑκατὸν ἔτεσιν ἢ ἐν δια-
κοσίοις ἢ ἐν τῷ ἀπείρῳ χρόνῳ τὰ αὐτά τις ὄψεται·
ἑτέρου δέ, ὅτι καὶ ὁ πολυχρονιώτατος καὶ ὁ τάχιστα τεθνηξόμενος τὸ ἴσον ἀποβάλλει. τὸ γὰρ
παρὸν ἐστὶ μόνον, οὗ στερίσκεσθαι μέλλει, εἴπερ
γε ἔχει καὶ τοῦτο μόνον καί, ὃ μὴ ἔχει τις, οὐκ
ἀποβάλλει.

ιέ. Ὅτι πάνθ᾽[2] ὑπόληψις. δῆλα μὲν γὰρ τὰ πρὸς
τὸν Κυνικὸν Μόνιμον λεγόμενα· δῆλον δὲ καὶ τὸ
χρήσιμον τοῦ λεγομένου, ἐάν τις αὐτοῦ τὸ νόστ-
ιμον μέχρι τοῦ ἀληθοῦς δέχηται.

ιϛ. Ὑβρίζει ἑαυτὴν ἡ τοῦ ἀνθρώπου ψυχή,
μάλιστα μέν, ὅταν ἀπόστημα καὶ οἷον φῦμα τοῦ
κόσμου, ὅσον ἐφ᾽ ἑαυτῇ, γένηται. τὸ γὰρ δυσχεραίνειν τινὶ τῶν γινομένων ἀπόστασίς ἐστι τῆς
φύσεως, ἧς ἐν μέρει <αἱ> ἑκάστου τῶν λοιπῶν
φύσεις περιέχονται· ἔπειτα δέ, ὅταν ἄνθρωπόν
τινα ἀποστραφῇ, ἢ καὶ ἐναντία φέρηται, ὡς

[1] οὐκ PA : οὖν Gat. : ἴσον PAD : ἴδιον Schenkl.
[2] Kronenberg for πᾶν.

[1] iii. 10.   [2] Sen. Nat. Q. vi. 32 ad fin.   [3] xii. 36.
[4] τῦφον εἶναι τὰ πάντα, Menander, Frag. 249, Kock (Diog.

the one he is now living,[1] nor lives any other than that which he now parts with. The longest life, then, and the shortest amount but to the same. For the present time is of equal duration for all, while that which we lose is not ours;[2] and consequently what is parted with is obviously a mere moment. No man can part with either the past or the future. For how can a man be deprived of what he does not possess? These two things, then, must needs be remembered: the one, that all things from time everlasting have been cast in the same mould and repeated cycle after cycle, and so it makes no difference whether a man see the same things recur through a hundred years or two hundred,[3] or through eternity: the other, that the longest liver and he whose time to die comes soonest part with no more the one than the other. For it is but the present that a man can be deprived of, if, as is the fact, it is this alone that he has, and what he has not a man cannot part with.

15. Remember that everything is but what we think it. For obvious indeed is the saying fathered on Monimus the Cynic, obvious too the utility of what was said,[4] if one accept the gist of it as far as it is true.

16. The soul of man does wrong to itself then most of all, when it makes itself, as far as it can do so, an imposthume and as it were a malignant growth in the Universe. For to grumble at anything that happens is a rebellion against Nature, in some part of which are bound up the natures of all other things. And the soul wrongs itself then again, when it turns away from any man or even opposes him with

Laert. vi. 3, § 2); Sext. Empir. (*Adv. Log.* ii. 1) attributes the saying to Monimus.

βλάψουσα, οἷαί εἰσιν αἱ τῶν ὀργιζομένων. τρίτον
ὑβρίζει ἑαυτήν, ὅταν ἡσσᾶται ἡδονῆς ἢ πόνου.
τέταρτον, ὅταν ὑποκρίνηται καὶ ἐπιπλάστως καὶ
ἀναλήθως τι ποιῇ ἢ λέγῃ. πέμπτον, ὅταν πρᾶξίν
τινα ἑαυτῆς καὶ ὁρμὴν ἐπ᾽ οὐδένα σκοπὸν ἀφιῇ,
ἀλλὰ εἰκῇ καὶ ἀπαρακολουθήτως ὁτιοῦν ἐνεργῇ,
δέον καὶ τὰ μικρότατα κατὰ τὴν ἐπὶ τὸ τέλος
ἀναφορὰν γίνεσθαι· τέλος δὲ λογικῶν ζῴων,
τὸ ἕπεσθαι τῷ τῆς πόλεως καὶ πολιτείας τῆς
πρεσβυτάτης λόγῳ καὶ θεσμῷ.

ιζ. Τοῦ ἀνθρωπίνου βίου ὁ μὲν χρόνος,
στιγμή, ἡ δὲ οὐσία ῥέουσα, ἡ δὲ αἴσθησις
ἀμυδρά, ἡ δὲ ὅλου τοῦ σώματος σύγκρισις
εὔσηπτος, ἡ δὲ ψυχὴ ῥόμβος, ἡ δὲ τύχη
δυστέκμαρτον, ἡ δὲ φήμη ἄκριτον· συνελόντι
δὲ εἰπεῖν, πάντα τὰ μὲν τοῦ σώματος ποταμός,
τὰ δὲ τῆς ψυχῆς ὄνειρος καὶ τῦφος· ὁ δὲ βίος
πόλεμος καὶ ξένου ἐπιδημία· ἡ δὲ ὑστεροφημία
λήθη. τί οὖν τὸ παραπέμψαι δυνάμενον; ἓν
καὶ μόνον φιλοσοφία. τοῦτο δὲ ἐν τῷ τηρεῖν
τὸν ἔνδον δαίμονα ἀνύβριστον καὶ ἀσινῆ, ἡδονῶν
καὶ πόνων κρείσσονα, μηδὲν εἰκῇ ποιοῦντα μηδὲ
διεψευσμένως καὶ μεθ᾽ ὑποκρίσεως, ἀνενδεῆ τοῦ
ἄλλον ποιῆσαί τι ἢ μὴ ποιῆσαι· ἔτι δὲ τὰ συμβαίνοντα καὶ ἀπονεμόμενα δεχόμενον, ὡς ἐκεῖθέν
ποθεν ἐρχόμενα ὅθεν αὐτὸς ἦλθεν· ἐπὶ πᾶσι δὲ
τὸν θάνατον ἵλεῳ τῇ γνώμῃ περιμένοντα, ὡς
οὐδὲν ἄλλο ἢ λύσιν τῶν στοιχείων ἐξ ὧν ἕκαστον
ζῷον συγκρίνεται. εἰ δὲ αὐτοῖς τοῖς στοιχείοις

---

[1] cp. Eur. *Frag.* 107 : ὅταν γλυκείας ἡδονῆς ἥσσων τις ᾖ.
[2] Aristides *Paneg. ad Cyzic.* § 427 (Jebb), ὁ γὰρ λογισμὸς

BOOK II

intent to do him harm, as is the case with those who are angry. It does wrong to itself, thirdly, when it is overcome by pleasure [1] or pain. Fourthly, when it assumes a mask, and in act or word is insincere or untruthful. Fifthly, when it directs some act or desire of its own towards no mark, and expends its energy on any thing whatever aimlessly and unadvisedly, whereas even the most trifling things should be done with reference to the end in view. Now the end for rational beings is to submit themselves to the reason and law of that archetypal city and polity [2]—the Universe.

17. Of the life of man the duration is but a point,[3] its substance streaming away, its perception dim, the fabric of the entire body prone to decay, and the soul a vortex, and fortune incalculable, and fame uncertain. In a word all the things of the body are as a river, and the things of the soul as a dream and a vapour; and life is a warfare and a pilgrim's sojourn, and fame after death is only forgetfulness. What then is it that can help us on our way? One thing and one alone—Philosophy; and this consists in keeping the divine 'genius' within pure [4] and unwronged, lord of all pleasures and pains, doing nothing aimlessly [5] or with deliberate falsehood and hypocrisy, independent of another's action or inaction; and furthermore welcoming what happens and is allotted, as issuing from the same source, whatever it be, from which the man himself has issued; and above all waiting for death with a good grace as being but a setting free of the elements of which every thing living is made up. But if there

αὐτῶν (Marcus and Lucius) θεῖος καὶ ὡς ἀληθῶς ἄνωθεν ἔχων τὸ παράδειγμα, καὶ πρὸς ἐκείνην ὁρῶν τὴν πολιτείαν.
[3] Plut. *Consol.* 31.   [4] § 13.   [5] § 5, 16.

μηδὲν δεινὸν ἐν τῷ ἕκαστον διηνεκῶς εἰς ἕτερον μεταβάλλειν, διὰ τί ὑπίδηταί τις τὴν πάντων μεταβολὴν καὶ διάλυσιν; κατὰ φύσιν γάρ· οὐδὲν δὲ κακὸν κατὰ φύσιν.

Τὰ ἐν Καρνούντῳ.[1]

[1] These words may very possibly be intended as a heading for Book III.

be nothing terrible in each thing being continuously changed into another thing, why should a man look askance at the change and dissolution of all things? For it is in the way of Nature, and in the way of Nature there can be no evil.

Written at Carnuntum.[1]

[1] Now Haimburg in Hungary.

ΒΙΒΛΙΟΝ Γ

α΄. Οὐχὶ τοῦτο μόνον δεῖ λογίζεσθαι ὅτι καθ᾽
ἑκάστην ἡμέραν ἀπαναλίσκεται ὁ βίος καὶ μέρος
ἔλαττον αὐτοῦ καταλείπεται· ἀλλὰ κἀκεῖνο λογισ-
τέον ὅτι, εἰ ἐπὶ πλέον βιώῃ τις, ἐκεῖνό γε
ἄδηλον, εἰ ἐξαρκέσει ὁμοία αὖθις ἡ διάνοια πρὸς
τὴν σύνεσιν τῶν πραγμάτων καὶ τῆς θεωρίας
τῆς συντεινούσης εἰς τὴν ἐμπειρίαν τῶν τε θείων
καὶ τῶν ἀνθρωπείων. ἐὰν γὰρ παραληρεῖν
ἄρξηται, τὸ μὲν διαπνεῖσθαι καὶ τρέφεσθαι καὶ
φαντάζεσθαι καὶ ὁρμᾶν καὶ ὅσα ἄλλα τοιαῦτα
οὐκ ἐνδεήσει· τὸ δὲ ἑαυτῷ χρῆσθαι, καὶ τοὺς τοῦ
καθήκοντος ἀριθμοὺς ἀκριβοῦν, καὶ τὰ προφαιν-
όμενα διαρθροῦν, καὶ περὶ αὐτοῦ τοῦ, εἰ ἤδη
ἐξακτέον αὐτόν, ἐφιστάνειν, καὶ ὅσα τοιαῦτα
λογισμοῦ συγγεγυμνασμένου πάνυ χρῄζει, προ-
αποσβέννυται. χρὴ οὖν ἐπείγεσθαι, οὐ μόνον τῷ

---

[1] vi. 16. Arist. *Probl.* i. 21 ὅπερ ἐν τῷ θώρακι ἀναπνοή, τοῦτο
ἐν τῷ σώματι διαπνοή διὰ τῶν ἀρτηριῶν (arterial breathing).

[2] *cp.* Sen. *Ep.* 60 *vivit is qui se utitur.*   [3] vi. 26.

[4] x. 8, § 3. The right of suicide was part of the Stoic
creed (Zeno and Cleanthes both took their own lives). Marcus
allows it when circumstances make it impossible for a man
to live his true life (v. 29 ; viii. 47 ; x. 8. *cp.* Epict.
i. 24, § 20 ; i. 25, § 18). Hadrian (*Digest* 28. 3. 6, § 7)

BOOK III

1. We ought not to think only upon the fact that our life each day is waning away, what is left of it being ever less, but this also should be a subject for thought, that even if life be prolonged, yet is it uncertain whether the mind will remain equally fitted in the future for the understanding of facts and for that contemplation which strains after the knowledge of things divine and human. For if a man has entered upon his dotage, there will still be his the power of breathing,[1] and digestion, and thought, and desire, and all such-like faculties; but the full use of himself,[2] the accurate appreciation of the items[3] of duty, the nice discrimination of what presents itself to the senses, and a clear judgment on the question whether it is time for him to end his own life,[4] and all such decisions, as above all require well-trained powers of reasoning— these are already flickering out in him.[5] It needs, then, that we should press onwards, not only because

enumerates as causes of suicide *taedium vitae, valetudinis adversae impatientia, iactatio* (in the case of certain philosophers). Marcus himself, if Dio (71. 30, § 2) is to be trusted, threatened, in a letter to the Senate, to commit suicide, and according to Capitolinus (xxviii. 3) actually hastened his own death by abstaining from food. *cp.* Shaks. *All's Well* i. 2. 58 : "Let me not live after my flame lacks oil."

ἐγγυτέρω τοῦ θανάτου ἑκάστοτε γίνεσθαι, ἀλλὰ
καὶ διὰ τὸ τὴν ἐννόησιν τῶν πραγμάτων καὶ τὴν
παρακολούθησιν προαπολήγειν.

β΄. Χρὴ καὶ τὰ τοιαῦτα παραφυλάσσειν, ὅτι
καὶ τὰ ἐπιγινόμενα τοῖς φύσει γινομένοις ἔχει τι
εὔχαρι καὶ ἐπαγωγόν. οἷον ἄρτου ὀπτωμένου
παραρρήγνυταί τινα μέρη, καὶ ταῦτα οὖν τὰ
διέχοντα οὕτως, καὶ τρόπον τινὰ παρὰ τὸ ἐπάγ-
γελμα τῆς ἀρτοποιίας ἔχοντα, ἐπιπρέπει πως καὶ
προθυμίαν πρὸς τὴν τροφὴν ἰδίως ἀνακινεῖ. πάλιν
τε τὰ σῦκα, ὁπότε ὡραιότατά ἐστι, κέχηνεν. καὶ
ἐν ταῖς δρυπεπέσιν ἐλαίαις αὐτὸ τὸ ἐγγὺς τῇ
σήψει ἴδιόν τι κάλλος τῷ καρπῷ προστίθησιν.
καὶ οἱ στάχυες κάτω νεύοντες, καὶ τὸ τοῦ λέοντος
ἐπισκύνιον, καὶ ὁ τῶν συῶν ἐκ τοῦ στόματος ῥέων
ἀφρός, καὶ πολλὰ ἕτερα, κατ᾽ ἰδίαν εἴ τις σκοπ-
οίη, πόρρω ὄντα τοῦ εὐειδοῦς, ὅμως διὰ τὸ τοῖς
φύσει γινομένοις ἐπακολουθεῖν συνεπικοσμεῖ καὶ
ψυχαγωγεῖ.

2   Ὥστε, εἴ τις ἔχει πάθος καὶ ἔννοιαν βαθυτέραν
πρὸς τὰ ἐν τῷ ὅλῳ γινόμενα, σχεδὸν οὐδὲν
οὐχὶ δόξει αὐτῷ καὶ τῶν κατ᾽ ἐπακολούθησιν
συμβαινόντων ἡδέως πως ἰδίᾳ συνίστασθαι.[1]
οὗτος δὲ καὶ θηρίων ἀληθῆ χάσματα οὐχ ἧσσον
ἡδέως ὄψεται ἢ ὅσα γραφεῖς καὶ πλάσται μιμού-
μενοι δεικνύουσιν· καὶ γραὸς καὶ γέροντος ἀκμήν
τινα καὶ ὥραν καὶ τὸ ἐν παισὶν ἐπαφρόδιτον

---

[1] Lofft for διασυνίστασθαι PA.

---

[1] A very fine early medallion shows Marcus in full chase
after a wild boar (Grueber, Plate xviii.).   cp. Dio 71. 36, § 2,
σῦς ἀγρίους ἐν θήρᾳ κατέβαλεν ἀπὸ ἵππου; Fronto, ad Cæs.
iii. 20 ; iv. 5 ; Capit. iv. 9.

BOOK III

we come each moment nearer to death, but also because our insight into facts and our close touch of them is gradually ceasing even before we die.

2. Such things as this also we ought to note with care, that the accessories too of natural operations have a charm and attractiveness of their own. For instance, when bread is in the baking, some of the parts split open, and these very fissures, though in a sense thwarting the bread-maker's design, have an appropriateness of their own and in a peculiar way stimulate the desire for food. Again when figs are at their ripest, they gape open; and in olives that are ready to fall their very approach to over-ripeness gives a peculiar beauty to the fruit. And the full ears of corn bending downwards, and the lion's beetling brows, and the foam dripping from the jaws of the wild-boar,[1] and many other things, though, if looked at apart from their setting, they are far from being comely, yet, as resultants from the operations of Nature, lend them an added charm and entice our admiration.

And so, if a man has sensibility and a deeper insight into the workings of the Universe, scarcely anything, though it exist only as a secondary consequence to something else, but will seem to him to form in its own peculiar way a pleasing adjunct to the whole. And he will look on the actual gaping jaws[2] of wild beasts[3] with no less pleasure than the representations of them by limners and modellers; and he will be able to see in the aged of either sex a mature prime and comely ripeness, and gaze with chaste eyes

[2] iv. 36.

[3] Such are the things Marcus noticed in the amphitheatre, and not the bloodshed which his soul abhorred (Dio 71. 29, § 3).

τοῖς ἑαυτοῦ σώφροσιν ὀφθαλμοῖς ὁρᾶν δυνήσεται·
καὶ πολλὰ τοιαῦτα οὐ παντὶ πιθανά, μόνῳ δὲ
τῷ πρὸς τὴν φύσιν καὶ τὰ ταύτης ἔργα γνησίως
ᾠκειωμένῳ προσπεσεῖται.

γ΄. Ἱπποκράτης πολλὰς νόσους ἰασάμενος
αὐτὸς νοσήσας ἀπέθανεν. οἱ Χαλδαῖοι πολλῶν
θανάτους προηγόρευσαν, εἶτα καὶ αὐτοὺς τὸ
πεπρωμένον κατέλαβεν. Ἀλέξανδρος καὶ Πομπήϊος καὶ Γάϊος Καῖσαρ ὅλας πόλεις ἄρδην
τοσαυτάκις ἀνελόντες καὶ ἐν παρατάξει πολλὰς
μυριάδας ἱππέων καὶ πεζῶν κατακόψαντες καὶ
αὐτοί ποτε ἐξῆλθον τοῦ βίου. Ἡράκλειτος περὶ
τῆς τοῦ κόσμου ἐκπυρώσεως τοσαῦτα φυσιολογή-
σας ὕδατος τὰ ἐντὸς πληρωθεὶς βολβίτῳ κατα-
κεχρισμένος ἀπέθανεν. Δημόκριτον δὲ οἱ φθεῖρες,
Σωκράτην δὲ ἄλλοι φθεῖρες ἀπέκτειναν.

2 Τί ταῦτα; ἐνέβης, ἔπλευσας, κατήχθης· ἔκβηθι.
εἰ μὲν ἐφ' ἕτερον βίον, οὐδὲν θεῶν κενὸν οὐδὲ ἐκεῖ·
εἰ δὲ ἐν ἀναισθησίᾳ, παύσῃ πόνων καὶ ἡδονῶν
ἀνεχόμενος καὶ λατρεύων τοσούτῳ χείρονι τῷ
ἀγγείῳ †ἥπερ ἐστὶ†[1] τὸ ὑπηρετοῦν· τὸ μὲν γὰρ
νοῦς καὶ δαίμων, τὸ δὲ γῆ καὶ λύθρος.

δ΄. Μὴ κατατρίψῃς τὸ ὑπολειπόμενον τοῦ
βίου μέρος ἐν ταῖς περὶ ἑτέρων φαντασίαις,
ὁπόταν μὴ τὴν ἀναφορὰν ἐπί τι κοινωφελὲς ποιῇ.
ἤτοι γὰρ ἄλλου ἔργου στέρῃ, τουτέστι φανταζό-

---

[1] ἢ (ἢ A) περίεστι PC : ἢ πέρ ἐστι D.

---

[1] iv. 48.
[2] Told of Pherecydes (Diog. Laert. *Pher.* v, viii.), of
Speusippus (*Speus.* ix.), and even of Plato (*Plato* xxix.),
but not elsewhere of Democritus. Lucian (?), *Macrob.* 15,
says Democritus died of starvation aged 104.

upon the alluring loveliness of the young. And many
such things there are which do not appeal to everyone,
but will come home to him alone who is genuinely
intimate with Nature and her works.

3. Hippocrates, after healing many a sick man,
fell sick himself and died. Many a death have
Chaldaeans foretold, and then their own fate has
overtaken them also.[1] Alexander, Pompeius and
Gaius Caesar times without number utterly destroyed
whole cities, and cut to pieces many myriads of horse
and foot on the field of battle, yet the day came
when they too departed this life. Heraclitus, after
endless speculations on the destruction of the world
by fire, came to be filled internally with water, and
died beplastered with cowdung. And lice caused the
death of Democritus,[2] and other vermin of Socrates.

What of this? Thou hast gone aboard, thou hast
set sail, thou hast touched land;[3] go ashore; if
indeed for another life, there is nothing even there
void of Gods; but if to a state of non-sensation,[4] thou
shalt cease being at the mercy of pleasure and pain
and lackeying the bodily vessel[5] which is so much
baser than that which ministers to it. For the one
is intelligence and a divine ' genius,' the other
dust and putrescence.

4. Fritter not away what is left of thy life in
thoughts about others, unless thou canst bring these
thoughts into relation with some common interest.
For verily thou dost hereby cut thyself off from
other work, that is, by thinking what so and so is

[3] An ancient Egyptian euphemism for "dying." "If thou
landest, thou livest again."
[4] cp. Justin, Apol. i. §§ 18, 57.
[5] So vas animi Cic. Tusc. i. 22, § 52. cp. St. Paul, 1 Thess.
iv. 4 (σκεῦος); Dio Chrys. Or. xii. 404 R. ἀνθρώπινον σῶμα ὡς
ἀγγεῖον φρονήσεως καὶ λόγου.

μενος τί ὁ δεῖνα πράσσει καὶ τίνος ἕνεκεν καὶ τί
λέγει καὶ τί ἐνθυμεῖται καὶ τί τεχνάζεται καὶ
ὅσα τοιαῦτα ποιεῖ ἀπορρέμβεσθαι τῆς τοῦ ἰδίου
ἡγεμονικοῦ παρατηρήσεως.

2   Χρὴ μὲν οὖν καὶ τὸ εἰκῇ καὶ μάτην ἐν τῷ
εἱρμῷ τῶν φαντασιῶν περιίστασθαι, πολὺ δὲ
μάλιστα τὸ περίεργον καὶ κακόηθες· καὶ ἐθιστέον
ἑαυτὸν μόνα φαντάζεσθαι, περὶ ὧν εἴ τις ἄφνω
ἐπανέροιτο· "Τί νῦν διανοῇ;" μετὰ παρρησίας
παραχρῆμα ἂν ἀποκρίναιο, ὅτι τὸ καὶ τό· ὡς
ἐξ αὐτῶν εὐθὺς δῆλα εἶναι, ὅτι πάντα ἁπλᾶ καὶ
εὐμενῆ, καὶ ζῴου κοινωνικοῦ καὶ ἀμελοῦντος
ἡδονικῶν ἢ καθάπαξ ἀπολαυστικῶν φαντασμάτων
ἢ φιλονεικίας τινὸς ἢ βασκανίας καὶ ὑποψίας ἢ
ἄλλου τινὸς ἐφ᾽ ᾧ ἂν ἐρυθριάσειας ἐξηγούμενος,
ὅτι ἐν νῷ αὐτὸ εἶχες.

3   Ὁ γάρ τοι ἀνὴρ ὁ τοιοῦτος, οὐκ ἔτι ὑπερ-
τιθέμενος τὸ ὡς ἐν ἀρίστοις ἤδη εἶναι, ἱερεύς
τίς ἐστι καὶ ὑπουργὸς θεῶν, χρώμενος καὶ τῷ
ἔνδον ἱδρυμένῳ αὐτῷ, ὃ παρέχεται τὸν ἄνθρωπον
ἄχραντον ἡδονῶν, ἄτρωτον ὑπὸ παντὸς πόνου,
πάσης ὕβρεως ἀνέπαφον, πάσης ἀναίσθητον
πονηρίας, ἀθλητὴν ἄθλου τοῦ μεγίστου, τοῦ ὑπὸ
μηδενὸς πάθους καταβληθῆναι, δικαιοσύνῃ βε-
βαμμένον εἰς βάθος, ἀσπαζόμενον μὲν ἐξ ὅλης
τῆς ψυχῆς τὰ συμβαίνοντα καὶ ἀπονεμόμενα
πάντα, μὴ πολλάκις δὲ μηδὲ χωρὶς μεγάλης
καὶ κοινωφελοῦς ἀνάγκης φανταζόμενον, τί ποτε
ἄλλος λέγει ἢ πράσσει ἢ διανοεῖται. μόνα γὰρ

---

[1] ii. 5.
[2] cp. Fronto, ad Am. i. 12: *nullum est factum meum
dictumve quod clam ceteris esse velim : quia cuius rei mihimet*

doing and why, what he is saying, having what in mind, contriving what, and all the many like things such as whirl thee aside from keeping close watch over thine own ruling Reason.

We ought therefore to eschew the aimless[1] and the unprofitable in the chain of our thoughts, still more all that is over-curious and ill-natured, and a man should accustom himself to think only of those things about which, if one were to ask on a sudden, *What is now in thy thoughts?* thou couldest quite frankly answer at once, *This or that*; so that thine answer should immediately make manifest that all that is in thee is simple and kindly and worthy of a living being that is social and has no thought for pleasures or for the entire range of sensual images, or for any rivalry, envy, suspicion, or anything else, whereat thou wouldest blush to admit that thou hadst it in thy mind.[2]

For in truth such a man, one who no longer puts off being reckoned now, if never before, among the best, is in some sort a priest and minister of the Gods, putting to use also that which, enthroned within him,[3] keeps the man unstained by pleasures, invulnerable to all pain, beyond the touch of any wrong, proof against all evil, a champion in the highest of championships—that of never being overthrown by any passion—dyed in grain with justice, welcoming with all his soul everything that befalls and is allotted him, and seldom, nor yet without a great and a general necessity, concerning himself with the words or deeds or thoughts of another.

ipse conscius sim, ceteros quoque omnes iuxta mecum scire velim.
[3] ii. 13. 17 ; iii. 6. 16.

τὰ ἑαυτοῦ πρὸς ἐνέργειαν ἔχει,[1] καὶ τὰ ἑαυτῷ ἐκ
τῶν ὅλων συγκλωθόμενα διηνεκῶς ἐννοεῖ· κἀκεῖνα
μὲν καλὰ παρέχεται, ταῦτα δὲ ἀγαθὰ εἶναι πέ-
πεισται. ἡ γὰρ ἑκάστῳ νεμομένη μοῖρα συνεμ-
φέρεταί τε καὶ συνεμφέρει.

4   Μέμνηται δὲ καὶ ὅτι συγγενὲς πᾶν τὸ λογικόν,
καὶ ὅτι κήδεσθαι μὲν πάντων ἀνθρώπων κατὰ
τὴν τοῦ ἀνθρώπου φύσιν ἐστί· δόξης δὲ οὐχὶ τῆς
παρὰ πάντων ἀνθεκτέον ἀλλὰ τῶν ὁμολογουμένως
τῇ φύσει βιούντων μόνων. οἱ δὲ μὴ οὕτως βιοῦντες,
ὁποῖοί τινες οἴκοι τε καὶ ἔξω τῆς οἰκίας, καὶ
νύκτωρ καὶ μεθ' ἡμέραν, οἷοι μεθ' οἵων φύρονται,
μεμνημένος διατελεῖ. οὐ τοίνυν οὐδὲ τὸν παρὰ
τῶν τοιούτων ἔπαινον ἐν λόγῳ τίθεται, οἵγε οὐδὲ
αὐτοὶ ἑαυτοῖς ἀρέσκονται.

έ.   Μήτε ἀκούσιος ἐνέργει μήτε ἀκοινώνητος
μήτε ἀνεξέταστος μήτε ἀνθελκόμενος· μήτε
κομψεία τὴν διάνοιάν σου καλλωπιζέτω· μήτε
πολυρρήμων μήτε πολυπράγμων ἔσο. ἔτι δὲ ὁ ἐν
σοὶ θεὸς ἔστω προστάτης ζῴου ἄρρενος, καὶ
πρεσβύτου καὶ πολιτικοῦ καὶ Ῥωμαίου καὶ
ἄρχοντος ἀνατεταχότος ἑαυτόν, οἷος ἂν εἴη τις
περιμένων τὸ ἀνακλητικὸν ἐκ τοῦ βίου εὔλυτος,
μήτε ὅρκου δεόμενος μήτε ἀνθρώπου τινὸς μάρτ-
υρος. ἐν δὲ τὸ φαιδρὸν[2] καὶ τὸ ἀπροσδεὲς ἔξωθεν
ὑπηρεσίας καὶ τὸ ἀπροσδεὲς ἡσυχίας, ἣν ἄλλοι
παρέχουσιν. ὀρθὸν οὖν εἶναι χρή, οὐχὶ ὀρθού-
μενον.

----

[1] ἕξει ADC.   [2] ἐν δὲ τὸ φαινόμενον AD : ἔτι Morus.

BOOK III

For it is only the things which relate to himself that
he brings within the scope of his activities, and he
never ceases to ponder over what is being spun for
him as his share in the fabric of the Universe, and he
sees to it that the former are worthy, and is assured
that the latter is good. For the fate which is
allotted to each man is swept along with him in the
Universe as well as sweeps him along with it.[1]

And he bears in mind that all that is rational is
akin, and that it is in man's nature to care for all
men, and that we should not embrace the opinion of
all, but of those alone who live in conscious agreement with Nature. But what sort of men they,
whose life is not after this pattern, are at home and
abroad, by night and in the day, in what vices they
wallow and with whom—of this he is ever mindful.
Consequently he takes no account of praise from such
men, who in fact cannot even win their own approval.

5. Do that thou doest neither unwillingly nor
selfishly nor without examination nor against the
grain. Dress not thy thought in too fine a garb. Be
not a man of superfluous words or superfluous deeds.
Moreover let the god that is in thee [2] be lord of a
living creature, that is manly, and of full age, and
concerned with statecraft, and a Roman, and a ruler,
who hath taken his post as one who awaits the signal
of recall from life in all readiness, needing no oath
nor any man as his voucher. Be thine the cheery
face and independence of help [3] from without and
independence of such ease as others can give. It
needs then to stand, and not be set, upright.[4]

---

[1] Or, more abstractly, *is conditioned no less than conditions.*   [2] ii. 13. 17 ; iii. 6.
[3] But see vii. 7.   [4] i. 15, § 3 ; vii. 12.

ϛʹ. Εἰ μὲν κρεῖττον εὑρίσκεις ἐν τῷ ἀν-
θρωπίνῳ βίῳ δικαιοσύνης, ἀληθείας, σωφροσύνης,
ἀνδρείας, καὶ καθάπαξ τοῦ ἀρκεῖσθαι ἑαυτῇ τὴν
διάνοιάν σου ἐν οἷς κατὰ τὸν λόγον τὸν ὀρθὸν
πράσσοντά σε παρέχεται, καὶ τῇ εἱμαρμένῃ ἐν
τοῖς ἀπροαιρέτως ἀπονεμομένοις—εἰ τούτου, φημί,
κρεῖττόν τι ὁρᾷς, ἐπ᾽ ἐκεῖνο ἐξ ὅλης τῆς ψυχῆς
τραπόμενος τοῦ ἀρίστου εὑρισκομένου ἀπόλαυε.

2 Εἰ δὲ μηδὲν κρεῖττον φαίνεται αὐτοῦ τοῦ ἐνιδρυ-
μένου ἐν σοὶ δαίμονος, τάς τε ἰδίας ὁρμὰς
ὑποτεταχότος ἑαυτῷ, καὶ τὰς φαντασίας ἐξ-
ετάζοντος, καὶ τῶν αἰσθητικῶν πείσεων, ὡς ὁ
Σωκράτης ἔλεγεν, ἑαυτὸν ἀφειλκυκότος, καὶ τοῖς
θεοῖς ὑποτεταχότος ἑαυτόν, καὶ τῶν ἀνθρώπων
προκηδομένου — εἰ τούτου πάντα τὰ ἄλλα
μικρότερα καὶ εὐτελέστερα εὑρίσκεις, μηδενὶ
χώραν δίδου ἑτέρῳ, πρὸς ὃ ῥέψας ἅπαξ καὶ ἀπο-
κλίνας οὐκ ἔτι ἀπερισπάστως τὸ ἀγαθὸν ἐκεῖνο
τὸ ἴδιον καὶ τὸ σὸν προτιμᾶν δυνήσῃ· ἀντικαθ-
ῆσθαι γὰρ τῷ λογικῷ καὶ πολιτικῷ[1] ἀγαθῷ οὐ
θέμις οὐδ᾽ ὁτιοῦν ἑτερογενές, οἷον τὸν παρὰ τῶν
πολλῶν ἔπαινον ἢ ἀρχὰς ἢ πλοῦτον ἢ ἀπολαύσεις
ἡδονῶν. πάντα ταῦτα, κἂν πρὸς ὀλίγον ἐναρ-
μόζειν δόξῃ, κατεκράτησεν ἄφνω καὶ παρήνεγκεν.

3 Σὺ δέ, φημί, ἁπλῶς καὶ ἐλευθέρως ἑλοῦ τὸ
κρεῖττον καὶ τούτου ἀντέχου· "Κρεῖττον δὲ τὸ
συμφέρον." εἰ μὲν τὸ ὡς λογικῷ, τοῦτο τήρει· εἰ
δὲ τὸ ὡς ζῴῳ, ἀπόφηναι καὶ ἀτύφως φύλασσε

---

[1] ποιητικῷ PA: πολιτικῷ Gat.

---

[1] iii. 4, § 3, 12, 16, or good ʻgenius,ʼ but *cp.* iii. 5, θεός.

BOOK III

6. If indeed thou findest in the life of **man a** better thing than justice, than truth, than temperance, than manliness, and, in a word, than thy mind's satisfaction with itself in things wherein it shews thee acting according to the true dictates of reason, and with destiny in what is allotted thee apart from thy choice—if, I say, thou seest anything better than this, turn to it with all thy soul and take thy fill of the best, as thou findest it.

But if there appears nothing better than the very deity [1] enthroned in thee, which has brought into subjection to itself all individual desires, which scrutinizes the thoughts, and, in the words of Socrates, has withdrawn itself from all the enticements of the senses, and brought itself into subjection to the Gods, and cherishes a fellow-feeling for men—if thou findest everything else pettier and of less account than this, give place to nought else, to which if thou art but once plucked aside, and incline thereto, never more shalt thou be able without distraction to give paramount honour to that good which is thine own peculiar heritage. For it is not right that any extraneous thing at all, such as the praise of the many, or office, or wealth, or indulgence in pleasure, should avail against that good which is identical with reason and a civic spirit. All these things, even if they seem for a little to fit smoothly into our lives, on a sudden overpower us and sweep us away.

But do thou, I say, simply and freely choose the better and hold fast to it. *But that is the better which is to my interest.* If it is to thy interest as a rational creature, hold that fast ; but if as a mere animal, declare it boldly and maintain thy judgment without

τὴν κρίσιν· μόνον ὅπως ἀσφαλῶς τὴν ἐξέτασιν
ποιήσῃ.

ζ'. Μὴ τιμήσῃς ποτὲ ὡς συμφέρον σεαυτοῦ,
ὃ ἀναγκάσει σέ ποτε τὴν πίστιν παραβῆναι, τὴν
αἰδῶ ἐγκαταλιπεῖν, μισῆσαί τινα, ὑποπτεῦσαι,
καταράσασθαι, ὑποκρίνασθαι, ἐπιθυμῆσαί τινος
τοίχων καὶ παραπετασμάτων δεομένου. ὁ γὰρ
τὸν ἑαυτοῦ νοῦν καὶ δαίμονα καὶ τὰ ὄργια τῆς
τούτου ἀρετῆς προελόμενος, τραγῳδίαν οὐ ποιεῖ,
οὐ στενάζει, οὐκ ἐρημίας, οὐ πολυπληθείας
δεήσεται· τὸ μέγιστον, ζήσει μήτε διώκων
μήτε φεύγων· πότερον δὲ ἐπὶ πλέον διάστημα
χρόνου τῷ σώματι περιεχομένῃ τῇ ψυχῇ ἢ
ἐπ᾽ ἔλασσον χρήσεται, οὐδ᾽ ὁτιοῦν αὐτῷ μέλει·
κἂν γὰρ ἤδη ἀπαλλάσσεσθαι δέῃ, οὕτως
εὐλύτως ἄπεισιν, ὡς ἄλλο τι τῶν αἰδημόνως καὶ
κοσμίως ἐνεργεῖσθαι δυναμένων ἐνεργησείων,[1] τοῦτο μόνον παρ᾽ ὅλον τὸν βίον εὐλαβούμενος, τὸ τὴν
διάνοιαν ἔν τινι ἀνοικείῳ νοεροῦ <καὶ> πολιτικοῦ
ζῴου τροπῇ γενέσθαι.

η'. Οὐδὲν ἂν ἐν τῇ διανοίᾳ τοῦ κεκολασμένου
καὶ ἐκκεκαθαρμένου πυῶδες οὐδὲ μὴν μεμολυσ-
μένον οὐδὲ ὕπουλον εὕροις. οὐδὲ ἀσυντελῆ τὸν
βίον αὐτοῦ ἡ πεπρωμένη καταλαμβάνει, ὡς ἄν
τις εἴποι τὸν τραγῳδὸν πρὸ τοῦ τελέσαι καὶ
διαδραματίσαι ἀπαλλάσσεσθαι. ἔτι δὲ οὐδὲν
δοῦλον οὐδὲ κομψόν, οὐδὲ προσδεδεμένον οὐδὲ
ἀπεσχισμένον, οὐδὲ ὑπεύθυνον οὐδὲ ἐμφωλεῦν.

θ'. Τὴν ὑποληπτικὴν δύναμιν σέβε. ἐν ταύτῃ

---

[1] ἐνεργήσεων P : ἐνεργήσειν A : ἐνεργησείων Radermacher.

[1] iii. 16 ; Epict. iii. 22, § 16. *cp.* Plutarch, *Sympos.* vii. 5.

arrogance. Only see to it that thou hast made thy enquiry without error.

7. Prize not anything as being to thine interest that shall ever force thee to break thy troth, to surrender thine honour, to hate, suspect, or curse anyone, to play the hypocrite, to lust after anything that needs walls and curtains.[1] For he that has chosen before all else his own intelligence and good 'genius,' and to be a devotee of its supreme worth, does not strike a tragic attitude or whine, nor will he ask for either a wilderness or a concourse of men; above all he will live neither chasing anything nor shunning it. And he recks not at all whether he is to have his soul overlaid with his body for a longer or a shorter span of time,[2] for even if he must take his departure at once, he will go as willingly as if he were to discharge any other function that can be discharged with decency and orderliness, making sure through life of this one thing, that his thoughts should not in any case assume a character out of keeping with a rational and civic creature.

8. In the mind of the man that has been chastened and thoroughly cleansed thou wilt find no foul abscess or gangrene or hidden sore. Nor is his life cut short, when the day of destiny overtakes him, as we might say of a tragedian's part, who leaves the stage before finishing his speech and playing out the piece.[3] Furthermore there is nothing there slavish or affected, no dependence on others or severance from them,[4] no sense of accountability or skulking to avoid it.

9. Hold sacred thy capacity for forming opinions.

[2] Sen. *N.Q.* vi. 32, *ad fin.*   [3] xii. 36; Sen. *Ep.* 77.
[4] viii. 34.

τὸ πᾶν, ἵνα ὑπόληψις τῷ ἡγεμονικῷ σου μηκέτι
ἐγγένηται ἀνακόλουθος τῇ φύσει καὶ τῇ τοῦ
λογικοῦ ζῴου κατασκευῇ. αὕτη δὲ ἐπαγγέλλεται
ἀπροπτωσίαν καὶ τὴν πρὸς ἀνθρώπους οἰκείωσιν
καὶ τὴν τοῖς θεοῖς ἀκολουθίαν.

ι΄. Πάντα οὖν ῥίψας, ταῦτα μόνα τὰ ὀλίγα
σύνεχε· καὶ ἔτι συμμνημόνευε, ὅτι μόνον ζῇ
ἕκαστος τὸ παρὸν τοῦτο τὸ ἀκαριαῖον· τὰ δὲ
ἄλλα ἢ βεβίωται ἢ ἐν ἀδήλῳ. μικρὸν μὲν οὖν ὃ
ζῇ ἕκαστος, μικρὸν δὲ τὸ τῆς γῆς γωνίδιον ὅπου
ζῇ· μικρὸν δὲ καὶ ἡ μηκίστη ὑστεροφημία, καὶ
αὕτη δὲ κατὰ διαδοχὴν ἀνθρωπαρίων τάχιστα
τεθνηξομένων καὶ οὐκ εἰδότων οὐδὲ ἑαυτούς, οὔτιγε
τὸν πρόπαλαι τεθνηκότα.

ια΄. Τοῖς δὲ εἰρημένοις παραστήμασιν ἓν ἔτι
προσέστω, τὸ ὅρον ἢ ὑπογραφὴν ἀεὶ ποιεῖσθαι
τοῦ ὑποπίπτοντος φανταστοῦ, ὥστε αὐτὸ ὁποῖόν
ἐστι κατ᾽ οὐσίαν γυμνὸν ὅλον δι᾽ ὅλων διῃρη-
μένως βλέπειν, καὶ τὸ ἴδιον ὄνομα αὐτοῦ καὶ τὰ
ὀνόματα ἐκείνων, ἐξ ὧν συνεκρίθη καὶ εἰς ἃ
ἀναλυθήσεται, λέγειν παρ᾽ ἑαυτῷ.

2   Οὐδὲν γὰρ οὕτως μεγαλοφροσύνης ποιητικόν,
ὡς τὸ ἐλέγχειν ὁδῷ καὶ ἀληθείᾳ ἕκαστον τῶν
⟨ἐν⟩ τῷ βίῳ ὑποπιπτόντων δύνασθαι καὶ τὸ ἀεὶ
οὕτως εἰς αὐτὰ ὁρᾶν, ὥστε συνεπιβάλλειν, ὁποίῳ
τινὶ τῷ κόσμῳ ὁποίαν τινὰ τοῦτο χρείαν παρεχ-
όμενον τίνα μὲν ἔχει ἀξίαν ὡς πρὸς τὸ ὅλον, τίνα
δὲ ὡς πρὸς τὸν ἄνθρωπον, πολίτην ὄντα πόλεως
τῆς ἀνωτάτης, ἧς αἱ λοιπαὶ πόλεις ὥσπερ οἰκίαι
εἰσίν· τί ἐστι, καὶ ἐκ τίνων συγκέκριται, καὶ

----

¹ ii. 14.   ² iv 3, § 3 ; viii. 21.
³ xii. 10. 18.

BOOK III

With that it rests wholly that thy ruling Reason
should never admit any opinion out of harmony
with Nature, and with the constitution of a rational
creature. This ensures due deliberation and fellowship
with mankind and fealty to the Gods.

10. Jettison everything else, then, and lay hold
of these things only, few as they are ; and remember
withal that it is only this present,[1] a moment of
time, that a man lives : all the rest either has been
lived or may never be.   Little indeed, then, is
a man's life, and little the nook of earth [2] whereon
he lives, and little even the longest after-fame,
and that too handed on through a succession of
manikins, each one of them very soon to be dead,
with no knowledge even of themselves, let alone
of a man who has died long since.

11. To the stand-bys mentioned add yet another,
that a definition or delineation should be made of
every object that presents itself, so that we may
see what sort of thing it is in its essence [3] stripped
of its adjuncts, a separate whole taken as such,
and tell over with ourselves both its particular
designation and the names of the elements that
compose it and into which it will be disintegrated.

For nothing is so conducive to greatness of mind
as the ability to examine systematically and honestly
everything that meets us in life, and to regard
these things always in such a way as to form a
conception of the kind of Universe they belong
to, and of the use which the thing in question
subserves in it ; what value it has for the whole
Universe and what for man, citizen as he is of
the highest state, of which all other states are
but as households ; what it actually is, and com-

πόσον χρόνον πέφυκε παραμένειν τοῦτο, τὸ τὴν
φαντασίαν μοι νῦν ποιοῦν· καὶ τίνος ἀρετῆς πρὸς
αὐτὸ χρεία, οἷον ἡμερότητος, ἀνδρείας, ἀληθείας,
πίστεως, ἀφελείας, αὐταρκείας, τῶν λοιπῶν.

3   Διὸ δεῖ ἐφ᾽ ἑκάστου λέγειν, τοῦτο μὲν παρὰ
θεοῦ ἥκει· τοῦτο δὲ κατὰ τὴν σύλληξιν καὶ τὴν
συμμηρυομένην σύγκλωσιν καὶ τὴν τοιαύτην
σύντευξίν τε καὶ τύχην· τοῦτο δὲ παρὰ τοῦ
συμφύλου καὶ συγγενοῦς καὶ κοινωνοῦ, ἀγνοοῦντος
μέντοι ὅ τι αὐτῷ κατὰ φύσιν ἐστίν. ἀλλ᾽ ἐγὼ οὐκ
ἀγνοῶ· διὰ τοῦτο χρῶμαι αὐτῷ κατὰ τὸν τῆς
κοινωνίας φυσικὸν νόμον εὔνως καὶ δικαίως· ἅμα
μέντοι τοῦ κατ᾽ ἀξίαν ἐν τοῖς μέσοις συστοχάζομαι.

ιβ΄. Ἐὰν τὸ παρὸν ἐνεργῇς ἑπόμενος τῷ
ὀρθῷ λόγῳ ἐσπουδασμένως, ἐρρωμένως, εὐμενῶς,
καὶ μηδὲν παρεμπόρευμα,[1] ἀλλὰ τὸν ἑαυτοῦ
δαίμονα καθαρὸν ἑστῶτα τηρῇς, ὡς εἰ καὶ ἤδη
ἀποδοῦναι δέοι· ἐὰν τοῦτο συνάπτῃς μηδὲν περιμένων μηδὲ φεύγων, ἀλλὰ τῇ παρούσῃ κατὰ
φύσιν ἐνεργείᾳ καὶ τῇ, ὧν λέγεις καὶ φθέγγῃ,
ἡρωϊκῇ ἀληθείᾳ ἀρκούμενος, εὐζωήσεις. ἔστι δὲ
οὐδεὶς ὁ τοῦτο κωλῦσαι δυνάμενος.

ιγ΄. Ὥσπερ οἱ ἰατροὶ ἀεὶ τὰ ὄργανα καὶ
σιδήρια πρόχειρα ἔχουσι πρὸς τὰ αἰφνίδια τῶν
θεραπευμάτων, οὕτω τὰ δόγματα σὺ ἔτοιμα ἔχε
πρὸς τὸ τὰ θεῖα καὶ ἀνθρώπινα εἰδέναι, καὶ πᾶν

---

[1] παρεμπορεύῃ Gat.: Perhaps ἐν παρεμπορεύματι.

[1] Notice the fondness of Marcus for compounds of συν- and
his use here of alliteration, cp. xii. 14.

pounded of what elements, and likely to last how long—namely this that now gives me the impression in question; and what virtue it calls for from me, such as gentleness, manly courage, truth, fidelity, guilelessness, independence, and the rest.

In each case therefore must thou say: *This has come from God; and this is due to the conjunction of fate and the contexture of the world's web and some such coincidence and chance;* [1] *while that comes from a clansman and a kinsman and a neighbour, albeit one who is ignorant of what is really in accordance with his nature. But I am not ignorant, therefore I treat him kindly and justly, in accordance with the natural law of neighbourliness; at the same time, of things that are neither good nor bad, my aim is to hit their true worth.*

12. If in obedience to right reason thou doest the thing that thy hand findeth to do earnestly, manfully, graciously, and in no sense as a by-work, [2] and keepest that divine ' genius ' [3] of thine in its virgin state, just as if even now thou wert called upon to restore it to the Giver—if thou grapple this to thee, looking for nothing, shrinking from nothing, but content with a present sphere of activity such as Nature allows, and with chivalrous truth in every word and utterance of thy tongue, thou shalt be happy in thy life. And there is no one that is able to prevent this.

13. Just as physicians always keep their lancets and instruments ready to their hands for emergency operations, so also do thou keep thine axioms ready for the diagnosis of things human and divine, and

---

[2] *cp.* Dio 71. 6, § 2 (of Marcus), οὐδὲν ἐν παρέργῳ οὔτε ἔλεγεν οὔτε ἔγραψεν οὔτε ἐποίει.

[3] iii. 6, § 2.

καὶ τὸ μικρότατον οὕτω ποιεῖν, ὡς τῆς ἀμφοτερων
πρὸς ἄλληλα συνδέσεως μεμνημένον. οὔτε γὰρ
ἀνθρώπινόν τι ἄνευ τῆς ἐπὶ τὰ θεῖα συναναφορᾶς
εὖ πράξεις οὔτε ἔμπαλιν.

ιδ΄. Μηκέτι πλανῶ· οὔτε γὰρ τὰ ὑπομνημάτιά
σου μέλλεις ἀναγινώσκειν, οὔτε τὰς τῶν ἀρχαίων
Ῥωμαίων καὶ Ἑλλήνων πράξεις, καὶ τὰς ἐκ τῶν
συγγραμμάτων ἐκλογάς, ἃς εἰς τὸ γῆρας σαυτῷ
ἀπετίθεσο. σπεῦδε οὖν εἰς τέλος,[1] καὶ τὰς κενὰς
ἐλπίδας ἀφεὶς σαυτῷ βοήθει, εἴ τί σοι μέλει
σεαυτοῦ, ἕως ἔξεστιν.

ιε΄. Οὐκ ἴσασι πόσα σημαίνει τὸ κλέπτειν,[2] τὸ
σπείρειν, τὸ ὠνεῖσθαι,[3] τὸ ἡσυχάζειν, τὸ ὁρᾶν τὰ
πρακτέα, ὃ οὐκ ὀφθαλμοῖς γίνεται ἀλλ' ἑτέρᾳ
τινὶ ὄψει.

ις΄. Σῶμα, ψυχή, νοῦς· σώματος αἰσθήσεις,
ψυχῆς ὁρμαί, νοῦ δόγματα. τὸ μὲν τυποῦσθαι
φανταστικῶς καὶ τῶν βοσκημάτων, τὸ δὲ
νευροσπαστεῖσθαι ὁρμητικῶς καὶ τῶν θηρίων
καὶ τῶν ἀνδρογύνων καὶ Φαλάριδος καὶ Νέρ-
ωνος· τὸ δὲ τὸν νοῦν ἡγεμόνα ἔχειν ἐπὶ τὰ
φαινόμενα καθήκοντα, καὶ τῶν θεοὺς μὴ νομιζόν-
των καὶ τῶν τὴν πατρίδα ἐγκαταλειπόντων καὶ
τῶν <πᾶν[4]> ποιούντων, ἐπειδὰν κλείσωσι τὰς
θύρας.

2   Εἰ οὖν τὰ λοιπὰ[5] κοινά ἐστι πρὸς τὰ εἰρημένα,

---

[1] εἰς τέλος P : εἰ θέλεις AC.
[2] σκάπτειν "to delve" Polak.   [3] κινεῖσθαι Richards.
[4] <πᾶν> Cor. <ποῖ οὐ> Bury.
[5] For τὰ λοιπὰ I would prefer τοιαῦτα.

---

[1] i.e. the human and the divine.
[2] It is not clear whether Marcus refers to the present book.
He uses a similar word for the discourses of Epictetus (i. 7).

for the performing of every act, even the pettiest, with the fullest consciousness of the mutual ties between these two.[1] For thou shalt never carry out well any human duty unless thou correlate it to the divine, nor the reverse.

14. Go astray no more ; for thou art not likely to read thy little *Memoranda*,[2] or the *Acts of the Romans and the Greeks of Old Time*,[3] and the extracts [4] from their writings which thou wast laying up against thine old age. Haste then to the consummation and, casting away all empty hopes, if thou carest aught for thy welfare, come to thine own rescue, while it is allowed thee.

15. They know not how full of meaning are—to thieve,[5] to sow, to buy, to be at peace, to see what needs doing, and this is not a matter for the eye but for another sort of sight.

16. *Body, Soul, Intelligence :* for the body sensations, for the soul desires, for the intelligence axioms. To receive impressions by way of the senses is not denied even to cattle ; to be as puppets [6] pulled by the strings of desire is common to wild beasts and to pathics and to a Phalaris and a Nero. Yet to have the intelligence a guide to what they deem their duty is an attribute of those also who do not believe in Gods and those who fail their country in its need and those who do their deeds behind closed doors.[7]

If then all else is the common property of the

---

[3] ii. 2. Some have seen here a reference to a history written by Marcus himself. See p. xv.

[4] See Fronto, *ad Caes.* ii. 10, *excerpta ex libris sexaginta in quinque tomis.*   [5] xi. 3.   [6] ii. 2.

[7] Must undoubtedly refer to the Christians, who were accused precisely of these three things—atheism, want of patriotism, and secret orgies. *cp.* also, i. 6 ; vii. 68 ; viii. 48, 51 ; and see note pp. 381 ff.

λοιπὸν τὸ ἴδιόν ἐστι τοῦ ἀγαθοῦ φιλεῖν
μὲν καὶ ἀσπάζεσθαι τὰ συμβαίνοντα καὶ συγκλωθόμενα αὐτῷ· τὸν δὲ ἔνδον ἐν τῷ στήθει
ἱδρυμένον δαίμονα μὴ φύρειν μηδὲ θορυβεῖν ὄχλῳ
φαντασιῶν, ἀλλὰ ἵλεων διατηρεῖν, κοσμίως ἑπόμενον θεῷ, μήτε φθεγγόμενόν τι παρὰ τὰ ἀληθῆ
μήτε ἐνεργοῦντα παρὰ τὰ δίκαια. εἰ δὲ ἀπιστοῦ-
σιν αὐτῷ πάντες ἄνθρωποι, ὅτι ἁπλῶς καὶ αἰδημόνως καὶ εὐθύμως βιοῖ, οὔτε χαλεπαίνει τινὶ
τούτων, οὔτε παρατρέπεται τῆς ὁδοῦ τῆς ἀγούσης
ἐπὶ τὸ τέλος τοῦ βίου, ἐφ᾽ ὃ δεῖ ἐλθεῖν καθαρόν,
ἡσύχιον, εὔλυτον, ἀβιάστως τῇ ἑαυτοῦ μοίρᾳ
συνηρμοσμένον.

classes mentioned, there is left as the characteristic of the good man to delight in and to welcome what befalls and what is being spun for him by destiny; and not to sully the divine ' genius ' that is enthroned in his bosom,[1] nor yet to perplex it with a multitude of impressions, but to maintain it to the end in a gracious serenity, in orderly obedience to God, uttering no word that is not true and doing no deed that is not just. But if all men disbelieve in his living a simple and modest and cheerful life, he is not wroth with any of them, nor swerves from the path which leads to his life's goal, whither he must go pure, peaceful, ready for release, needing no force to bring him into accord with his lot.

[1] iii. 6, § 2 ; St. Paul, 1 Cor. iii. 16.

D

ΒΙΒΛΙΟΝ Δ

α΄. Τὸ ἔνδον κυριεῦον, ὅταν κατὰ φύσιν ἔχῃ, οὕτως ἔστηκε πρὸς τὰ συμβαίνοντα, ὥστε ἀεὶ πρὸς τὸ δυνατὸν καὶ διδόμενον μετατίθεσθαι ῥᾳδίως. ὕλην γὰρ ἀποτεταγμένην οὐδεμίαν φιλεῖ, ἀλλὰ ὁρμᾷ μὲν πρὸς τὰ <προ>ηγούμενα[1] μεθ' ὑπεξαιρέσεως· τὸ δὲ ἀντεισαγόμενον ὕλην ἑαυτῷ ποιεῖ, ὥσπερ τὸ πῦρ, ὅταν ἐπικρατῇ τῶν ἐπεμπιπτόντων, ὑφ' ὧν ἂν μικρός τις λύχνος ἐσβέσθη· τὸ δὲ λαμπρὸν πῦρ τάχιστα ἐξῳκείωσεν ἑαυτῷ τὰ ἐπιφορούμενα καὶ κατηνάλωσεν καὶ ἐξ αὐτῶν ἐκείνων ἐπὶ μεῖζον ἤρθη.

β΄. Μηδὲν ἐνέργημα εἰκῇ μηδὲ ἄλλως ἢ κατὰ θεώρημα συμπληρωτικὸν τῆς τέχνης ἐνεργείσθω.

γ΄. Ἀναχωρήσεις αὑτοῖς ζητοῦσιν, ἀγροικίας καὶ αἰγιαλοὺς καὶ ὄρη· εἴωθας δὲ καὶ σὺ τὰ τοιαῦτα μάλιστα ποθεῖν. ὅλον δὲ τοῦτο ἰδιωτικώτατόν ἐστιν, ἐξὸν ἧς ἂν ὥρας ἐθελήσῃς εἰς ἑαυτὸν ἀναχωρεῖν. οὐδαμοῦ γὰρ οὔτε ἡσυχιώτερον οὔτε

---

[1] <προ> Gat.

---

[1] iii. 6, § 2, etc. *cp.* Lucian, *Somn.* 10, ἡ ψυχή, ὅπερ σου κυριώτατόν ἐστιν.

[2] *i.e.* conditionally or as far as circumstances will allow, vi. 50. *cp.* St. James, Ep. iv. 15.

[3] v. 20; vi. 50; Sen. *de Prov.* 2.   [4] ii. 5 etc.

BOOK IV

1. THAT which holds the mastery[1] within us, when it is in accordance with Nature, is so disposed towards what befalls, that it can always adapt itself with ease to what is possible and granted us. For it is wedded to no definite material, but, though in the pursuit of its high aims it works under reservations,[2] yet it converts into material for itself any obstacle that it meets with, just as fire[3] when it gets the mastery of what is thrown in upon it. A little flame would have been stifled by it, but the blazing fire instantly assimilates what is cast upon it and, consuming it, leaps the higher in consequence.

2. Take no act in hand aimlessly[4] or otherwise than in accordance with the true principles perfective of the art.

3. Men seek out retreats for themselves in the country, by the seaside, on the mountains, and thou too art wont to long above all for such things.[5] But all this is unphilosophical to the last degree, when thou canst at a moment's notice retire into thyself.[6] For nowhere can a man find a retreat more full of

[5] e.g. Lorium, Lanuvium, Alsium, Centumcellae, Praeneste, Baiae, Caieta, all holiday resorts of Marcus; see especially Fronto de Fer. Als. Nab. p. 223 ff. cp. x. 15, 23.

[6] cp. Arethas on Dio Chrys. xx. 8, μὴ οὖν βελτίστη καὶ λυσιτελεστάτη πασῶν ἡ εἰς αὐτὸν ἀναχώρησις. See below iv. 3, § 4 ; vii. 28.

ἀπραγμονέστερον ἄνθρωπος ἀναχωρεῖ ἢ εἰς τὴν
ἑαυτοῦ ψυχήν· μάλισθ᾽ ὅστις ἔχει ἔνδον τοιαῦτα,
εἰς ἃ ἐγκύψας ἐν πάσῃ εὐμαρείᾳ εὐθὺς γίνεται·
τὴν δὲ εὐμάρειαν οὐδὲν ἄλλο λέγω ἢ εὐκοσμίαν.
συνεχῶς οὖν δίδου σεαυτῷ ταύτην τὴν ἀναχώρ-
ησιν, καὶ ἀνανέου σεαυτόν· βραχέα δὲ ἔστω
καὶ στοιχειώδη, ἃ εὐθὺς ἀπαντήσαντα ἀρκέσει
εἰς τὸ πᾶσαν †ἀνίαν ἀποκλύσαι†,[1] καὶ ἀπο-
πέμψαι σε μὴ δυσχεραίνοντα ἐκείνοις, ἐφ᾽ ἃ
ἐπανέρχῃ.

2   Τίνι γὰρ δυσχεραίνεις; τῇ τῶν ἀνθρώπων κακίᾳ;
ἀναλογισάμενος τὸ κρίμα, ὅτι τὰ λογικὰ ζῷα
ἀλλήλων ἕνεκεν γέγονε, καὶ ὅτι τὸ ἀνέχεσθαι
μέρος τῆς δικαιοσύνης, καὶ ὅτι ἄκοντες ἁμαρτάνουσι, καὶ πόσοι ἤδη διεχθρεύσαντες, ὑποπτεύ-
σαντες, μισήσαντες, διαδορατισθέντες ἐκτέτανται,
τετέφρωνται, παύου ποτέ. ἀλλὰ καὶ τοῖς ἐκ τῶν
ὅλων ἀπονεμομένοις δυσχεραίνεις; ἀνανεωσά-
μενος τὸ διεζευγμένον· "᾽Ήτοι πρόνοια, ἢ ἄτομοι,"
καὶ ἐξ ὅσων ἀπεδείχθη, ὅτι ὁ κόσμος ὡσανεὶ
πόλις. ἀλλὰ τὰ σωματικά σου ἅψεταί ἔτι;
ἐννοήσας ὅτι οὐκ ἐπιμίγνυται λείως ἢ τραχέως
κινουμένῳ πνεύματι ἡ διάνοια, ἐπειδὰν ἅπαξ
ἑαυτὴν ἀπολάβῃ καὶ γνωρίσῃ τὴν ἰδίαν ἐξουσίαν·
καὶ λοιπὸν ὅσα περὶ πόνου καὶ ἡδονῆς ἀκήκοας
καὶ συγκατέθου.

3   ᾽Αλλὰ τὸ δοξάριόν σε περισπάσει; ἀπιδὼν εἰς
τὸ τάχος τῆς πάντων λήθης, καὶ τὸ χάος τοῦ ἐφ᾽

---

[1] πᾶσαν αὐτὴν ἀποκλύσαι PC : ἀποκλεῖσαι AD : λύπην Reiske,
ἀνίαν Gat., αὐλήν Lofft.   Many accept the last, but it does
not suit the next clause and would also require <τὴν>.

---

¹ For ἐγκύψας cp. St. James, Ep. i. 25, παρακύψας.
² vii. 22, 63 ; xi. 18, § 3.   ³ viii. 17 ; ix. 28, 39.

peace or more free from care than his own soul—
above all if he have that within him, a steadfast
look[1] at which and he is at once in all good ease,
and by good ease I mean nothing other than good
order. Make use then of this retirement continually
and regenerate thyself. Let thy axioms be short
and elemental, such as when set before thee will
at once rid thee of all trouble, and send thee away
with no discontent at those things to which thou art
returning.

Why with what art thou discontented? The
wickedness of men? Take this conclusion to heart,
that rational creatures have been made for one
another; that forbearance is part of justice; that
wrong-doing is involuntary;[2] and think how many
ere now, after passing their lives in implacable
enmity, suspicion, hatred, and at daggers drawn
with one another, have been laid out and burnt to
ashes—think of this, I say, and at last stay thy
fretting. But art thou discontented with thy share
in the whole? Recall the alternative: *Either
Providence or Atoms!*[3] and the abundant proofs
there are that the Universe is as it were a state.[4]
But is it the affections of the body that shall still
lay hold on thee? Bethink thee that the Intelligence, when it has once abstracted itself and learnt
its own power,[5] has nothing to do with the motions
smooth or rough of the vital breath. Bethink thee
too of all that thou hast heard and subscribed to
about pleasure and pain.

But will that paltry thing, Fame, pluck thee aside?
Look at the swift approach of complete forgetfulness,

---

[4] ii. 16 *ad fin.*; iv. 4; x. 15; xii. 36. St. Paul, Philip-
pians iii. 20.   [5] v. 14.

ἑκάτερα ἀπείρου αἰῶνος, καὶ τὸ κενὸν τῆς
ἀπηχήσεως, καὶ τὸ εὐμετάβολον καὶ ἄκριτον
τῶν εὐφημεῖν [1] δοκούντων, καὶ τὸ στενὸν τοῦ
τόπου, ἐν ᾧ περιγράφεται. ὅλη τε γὰρ ἡ γῆ
στιγμή, καὶ ταύτης πόστον γωνίδιον ἡ κατοίκησις
αὕτη; καὶ ἐνταῦθα πόσοι καὶ οἷοί τινες οἱ
ἐπαινεσόμενοι;

4   Λοιπὸν οὖν μέμνησο τῆς ὑποχωρήσεως τῆς
εἰς τοῦτο τὸ ἀγρίδιον ἑαυτοῦ· καὶ πρὸ παντὸς
μὴ σπῶ μηδὲ κατεντείνου, ἀλλὰ ἐλεύθερος ἔσο
καὶ ὅρα τὰ πράγματα ὡς ἀνήρ, ὡς ἄνθρωπος,
ὡς πολίτης, ὡς θνητὸν ζῷον. ἐν δὲ τοῖς
προχειροτάτοις, εἰς ἃ ἐγκύψεις, ταῦτα ἔστω
τὰ δύο. ἐν μέν, ὅτι τὰ πράγματα οὐχ
ἅπτεται τῆς ψυχῆς, ἀλλ' ἔξω ἕστηκεν ἀτρεμ-
οῦντα· αἱ δὲ ὀχλήσεις ἐκ μόνης τῆς ἔνδον
ὑπολήψεως. ἕτερον δέ, ὅτι πάντα ταῦτα ὅσα
ὁρᾷς ὅσον οὐδέπω μεταβάλλει καὶ οὐκ ἔτι
ἔσται· καὶ ὅσων ἤδη μεταβολαῖς αὐτὸς παρα-
τετύχηκας, συνεχῶς διανοοῦ. 'ὁ κόσμος,
ἀλλοίωσις· ὁ βίος, ὑπόληψις.'

δ'. Εἰ τὸ νοερὸν ἡμῖν κοινόν, καὶ ὁ λόγος, καθ'
ὃν λογικοί ἐσμεν, κοινός· εἰ τοῦτο, καὶ ὁ προσ-
τακτικὸς τῶν ποιητέων ἢ μὴ λόγος κοινός· εἰ
τοῦτο, καὶ ὁ νόμος κοινός· εἰ τοῦτο, πολῖταί ἐσμεν·
εἰ τοῦτο, πολιτεύματός τινος μετέχομεν· εἰ τοῦτο,
ὁ κόσμος ὡσανεὶ πόλις ἐστί. τίνος γὰρ ἄλλου

---

[1] ἐφ' ἡμῖν PADC: εὐφημεῖν Gat.: perhaps ἐφ' ἡμῶν
εὐφημεῖν.

[1] iii. 10; viii. 21.

[2] ii. 15; iv. 7; xii. 22. A maxim of Democrates, a Pytha-
gorean; cp. Shak. *Hamlet* ii. 2. 256, "There is nothing
either good or bad but thinking makes it so"; Tennyson:

and the void of infinite time on this side of us and on that, and the empty echo of acclamation, and the fickleness and uncritical judgment of those who claim to speak well of us, and the narrowness of the arena to which all this is confined. For the whole earth is but a point, and how tiny a corner[1] of it is this the place of our sojourning! and how many therein and of what sort are the men who shall praise thee!

From now therefore bethink thee of the retreat into this little plot that is thyself. Above all distract not thyself, be not too eager, but be thine own master, and look upon life as a man, as a human being, as a citizen, as a mortal creature. But among the principles readiest to thine hand, upon which thou shalt pore, let there be these two. One, that objective things do not lay hold of the soul, but stand quiescent without; while disturbances are but the outcome of that opinion which is within us. A second, that all this visible world changes in a moment, and will be no more; and continually bethink thee to the changes of how many things thou hast already been a witness. 'The Universe—mutation: Life—opinion.'[2]

4. If the intellectual capacity is common to us all, common too is the reason, which makes us rational creatures. If so, that reason also is common which tells us to do or not to do. If so, law[3] also is common. If so, we are citizens. If so, we are fellow-members of an organised community. If so, the Universe is as it were a state[4]—for of what

"All things are, as they seem, to all." Some have been found to say that even matter has no objective existence.

[3] vii. 9. *cp.* Aur. Vict. *Epit.* xvi. 4, *Mundi lex seu Natura.*

[4] iv. 3, § 2.

φήσει τις τὸ τῶν ἀνθρώπων πᾶν γένος κοινοῦ
πολιτεύματος μετέχειν; ἐκεῖθεν δέ, ἐκ τῆς κοινῆς
ταύτης πόλεως, καὶ αὐτὸ τὸ νοερὸν καὶ λογικὸν
καὶ νομικὸν ἡμῖν· ἢ πόθεν; ὥσπερ γὰρ τὸ γεῶδές
μοι ἀπό τινος γῆς ἀπομεμέρισται, καὶ τὸ ὑγρὸν
ἀφ' ἑτέρου στοιχείου καὶ τὸ πνευματικὸν ἀπὸ
πηγῆς¹ τινος καὶ τὸ θερμὸν καὶ πυρῶδες ἔκ τινος
ἰδίας πηγῆς (οὐδὲν γὰρ ἐκ τοῦ μηδενὸς ἔρχεται,
ὥσπερ μηδ' εἰς τὸ οὐκ ὂν ἀπέρχεται), οὕτω δὴ
καὶ τὸ νοερὸν ἥκει ποθέν.

ε΄. Ὁ θάνατος τοιοῦτος, οἷον γένεσις, φύσεως
μυστήριον, σύγκρισις ἐκ τῶν αὐτῶν στοιχείων,
<διάκρισις>² εἰς ταὐτά· ὅλως δὲ οὐκ ἐφ' ᾧ ἄν τις
αἰσχυνθείη· οὐ γὰρ παρὰ τὸ ἑξῆς τῷ νοερῷ ζῴῳ
οὐδὲ παρὰ τὸν λόγον τῆς παρασκευῆς.³

ϛ΄. Ταῦτα οὕτως ὑπὸ τῶν τοιούτων πέφυκε
γίνεσθαι ἐξ ἀνάγκης· ὁ δὲ τοῦτο μὴ θέλων
θέλει τὴν συκῆν ὀπὸν μὴ ἔχειν. ὅλως δ' ἐκεῖνο
μέμνησο, ὅτι ἐντὸς ὀλιγίστου χρόνου καὶ σὺ καὶ
οὗτος τεθνήξεσθε, μετὰ βραχὺ δὲ οὐδὲ ὄνομα
ὑμῶν ὑπολειφθήσεται.

ζ΄. Ἆρον τὴν ὑπόληψιν, ἦρται τὸ βέβλαμμαι·
ἆρον τὸ "βέβλαμμαι," ἦρται ἡ βλάβη.

η΄. Ὁ χείρω αὐτὸν ἑαυτοῦ ἄνθρωπον οὐ ποιεῖ,
τοῦτο οὐδὲ τὸν βίον αὐτοῦ χείρω ποιεῖ, οὐδὲ
βλάπτει οὔτε ἔξωθεν οὔτε ἔνδοθεν.

θ΄. Ἠνάγκασται ἡ τοῦ συμφέροντος φύσις
τοῦτο ποιεῖν.

---

¹ πηγῆς PC : γῆς AD : πνοῆς Schenkl.   ² <διάκρισις> or
<διάλυσις> Gat.   ³ We should expect κατασκευῆς.

---

¹ Lit. *the pneumatic*, here = τὸ ἀερῶδες (x. 7, § 2).
² vii. 64.   ³ v. 17.

other single polity can the whole race of mankind be said to be fellow-members?—and from it, this common State, we get the intellectual, the rational, and the legal instinct, or whence do we get them? For just as the earthy part has been portioned off for me from some earth, and the watery from another element, and the aerial [1] from some source, and the hot and fiery from some source of its own—for nothing comes from the non-existent, any more than it disappears into nothingness—so also the intellect has undoubtedly come from somewhere.

5. Death like birth is a secret of Nature—a combination of the same elements, a breaking up into the same—and not at all a thing in fact for any to be ashamed of,[2] for it is not out of keeping with an intellectual creature or the reason of his equipment.

6. Given such men, it was in the nature of the case inevitable that their conduct should be of this kind.[3] To wish it otherwise, is to wish that the fig-tree had no acrid juice.[4] As a general conclusion call this to mind, that within a very short time both thou and he will be dead, and a little later not even your names will be left behind you.

7. Efface the opinion, *I am harmed,* and at once the feeling of being harmed disappears; efface the feeling, and the harm disappears at once.[5]

8. That which does not make a man himself worse than before cannot make his life worse [6] either, nor injure it whether from without or within.

9. The nature of the general good could not but have acted so.

---

[4] xii. 16.   *cp.* Bacon, *On Revenge.*
[5] iv. 3, § 4; vii. 14, 29; ix. 7; xii. 25.   [6] ii. 11; vii. 64.

ι΄. Ὅτι πᾶν τὸ συμβαῖνον δικαίως συμβαίνει· ὅ, ἐὰν ἀκριβῶς παραφυλάσσῃς, εὑρήσεις· οὐ λέγω μόνον κατὰ τὸ ἑξῆς, ἀλλ' ὅτι κατὰ τὸ δίκαιον καὶ ὡς ἂν ὑπό τινος ἀπονέμοντος τὸ κατ' ἀξίαν. παραφύλασσε οὖν, ὡς ἤρξω· καί, ὅ τι ἂν ποιῇς, σὺν τούτῳ ποίει, σὺν τῷ ἀγαθὸς εἶναι, καθ' ὃ νενόηται ἰδίως ὁ ἀγαθός. τοῦτο ἐπὶ πάσης ἐνεργείας σῶζε.

ια΄. Μὴ τοιαῦτα ὑπολάμβανε, οἷα ὁ ὑβρίζων κρίνει ἢ οἷά σε κρίνειν βούλεται· ἀλλ' ἴδε αὐτά, ὁποῖα κατ' ἀλήθειάν ἐστιν.

ιβ΄. Δύο ταύτας ἑτοιμότητας ἔχειν ἀεὶ δεῖ· τὴν μέν, πρὸς τὸ πρᾶξαι μόνον, ὅπερ ἂν ὁ τῆς βασιλικῆς καὶ νομοθετικῆς λόγος ὑποβάλλῃ, ἐπ' ὠφελείᾳ ἀνθρώπων· τὴν δέ, πρὸς τὸ μεταθέσθαι, ἐὰν ἄρα τις παρῇ διορθῶν καὶ μετάγων ἀπό τινος οἰήσεως. τὴν μέντοι μεταγωγὴν ἀεὶ ἀπό τινος πιθανότητος ὡς δικαίου ἢ κοινωφελοῦς γίνεσθαι, καὶ τὰ παραπλήσια†[1] τοιαῦτα μόνον εἶναι δεῖ, οὐχ ὅτι ἡδὺ ἢ ἔνδοξον ἐφάνη.

ιγ΄. Λόγον ἔχεις; "ἔχω." τί οὖν οὐ χρᾷ; τούτου γὰρ τὸ ἑαυτοῦ ποιοῦντος τί ἄλλο θέλεις;

ιδ΄. Ἐνυπέστης ὡς μέρος. ἐναφανισθήσῃ τῷ γεννήσαντι· μᾶλλον δὲ ἀναληφθήσῃ εἰς τὸν λόγον αὐτοῦ τὸν σπερματικὸν κατὰ μεταβολήν.

ιε΄. Πολλὰ λιβανωτοῦ βωλάρια ἐπὶ τοῦ αὐτοῦ βωμοῦ· τὸ μὲν προκατέπεσεν, τὸ δὲ ὕστερον· διαφέρει δ' οὐδέν.

---

[1] παραπαίονα A.

---

[1] x. 25. [2] cp. Capit. xxii. 4.
[3] vii. 73; ix. 42 ad fin. [4] ii. 3.
[5] The primal Fire and the eternal Reason are one and the

74

BOOK IV

10. Note that all that befalls befalleth justly. Keep close watch and thou wilt find this true, I do not say, as a matter of sequence merely but as a matter of justice also, and as would be expected from One whose dispensation is based on desert.[1] Keep close watch, then, as thou hast begun, and whatsoever thou doest, do it as only a good man should in the strictest sense of that word. In every sphere of activity safeguard this.

11. Harbour no such opinions as he holds who does thee violence, or as he would have thee hold. See things in all their naked reality.

12. Thou shouldest have these two readinesses always at hand; the one which prompts thee to do only what thy reason in its royal and law-making capacity shall suggest for the good of mankind; the other to change thy mind,[2] if one be near to set thee right, and convert thee from some vain conceit. But this conversion should be the outcome of a persuasion in every case that the thing is just or to the common interest—and some such cause should be the only one—not because it is seemingly pleasant or popular.

13. Hast thou reason? *I have.* Why then not use it? For if this performs its part, what else[3] wouldest thou have?

14. Thou hast subsisted as part of the Whole.[4] Thou shalt vanish into that which begat thee, or rather thou shalt be taken again into its Seminal Reason[5] by a process of change.

15. Many little pellets of frankincense fall upon the same altar, some are cast on it sooner, some later : but it makes no difference.

same, and held to contain the seed of all things. *cp.* Just. *Apol.* ii. 8, 13 for λόγος σπερματικὸς used of Christ.

ιϛ'. Ἐντὸς δέκα ἡμερῶν θεὸς αὐτοῖς δόξεις, οἷς νῦν θηρίον καὶ πίθηκος, ἐὰν ἀνακάμψῃς ἐπὶ τὰ δόγματα καὶ τὸν σεβασμὸν τοῦ λόγου.

ιζ. Μὴ ὡς μύρια μέλλων ἔτη ζῆν. τὸ χρεὼν ἐπήρτηται· ἕως ζῇς, ἕως ἔξεστιν, ἀγαθὸς γενοῦ.

ιη'. Ὅσην εὐσχολίαν[1] κερδαίνει ὁ μὴ βλέπων τί ὁ πλησίον εἶπεν ἢ ἔπραξεν ἢ διενοήθη, ἀλλὰ μόνον τί αὐτὸς ποιεῖ, ἵνα αὐτὸ τοῦτο δίκαιον ἢ καὶ ὅσιον· †ἢ[2] κατὰ τὸν ἀγαθὸν μὴ μέλαν† ἦθος περιβλέπεσθαι, ἀλλ' 'ἐπὶ τῆς γραμμῆς τρέχειν ὀρθόν, μὴ διερριμμένον.'

ιθ'. Ὁ περὶ τὴν ὑστεροφημίαν ἐπτοημένος οὐ φαντάζεται, ὅτι ἕκαστος τῶν μεμνημένων αὐτοῦ τάχιστα καὶ αὐτὸς[3] ἀποθανεῖται· εἶτα πάλιν [καὶ αὐτὸς] ὁ ἐκεῖνον διαδεξάμενος, μέχρι καὶ πᾶσα ἡ μνήμη ἀποσβῇ διὰ ἁπτομένων[4] καὶ σβεννυμένων προϊοῦσα. ὑπόθου δ', ὅτι καὶ ἀθάνατοι μὲν οἱ μεμνησόμενοι, ἀθάνατος δ' ἡ μνήμη· τί οὖν τοῦτο πρὸς σέ; καὶ οὐ λέγω, ὅτι οὐδὲν πρὸς τὸν τεθνηκότα· ἀλλὰ πρὸς τὸν ζῶντα τί ὁ ἔπαινος; πλὴν ἄρα δι' οἰκονομίαν τινά· παρίῃς †[5] γὰρ νῦν ἀκαίρως τὴν φυσικὴν δόσιν, ἄλλου τινὸς ἐχόμενος λόγου λοιπόν.†

[1] εὐσχολίαν Gat.: ἀσχολίαν PA.
[2] ἢ I have written this for ἢ PA: Ἀγαθῶνα Xyl.: δεῖ γὰρ τὸν ἀγαθὸν Morus: ἄλλων for μέλαν Stich. Perhaps μέλαν <ἄλλων>. μὴ is not easy to explain.   [3] <καὶ αὐτὸς> P.

[4] ἐπτοημένων PA: ἁπτομένων Schultz.

[5] ἁπτομένων καὶ σβεννυμένων is derived directly from Heracleitus fr. lxxvii.   [6] παρίῃς ... ἐχόμενος Gat.: παρὲς PA: ἐχόμενον P: ἐχομένην AD.

---

[1] There was a Greek proverb: ἢ θεὸς ἢ θηρίον (Arist. *Pol.* i, 2, *Eth.* vii. 1). Plut. *Stoic. Parad.* speaks of conversion by philosophy from a θηρίον to a θεός. See Justin's clever application of this proverb, *Apol.* i. 24.

16. Ere ten days are past, thou shalt rank as a god with them that hold thee now a wild-beast or an ape,[1] if thou but turn back to thy axioms and thy reverence of reason.

17. Behave not as though thou hadst ten thousand years to live. Thy doom hangs over thee. While thou livest, while thou mayest, become good.

18. What richness of leisure doth he gain who has no eye for his neighbour's words or deeds or thoughts,[2] but only for his own doings, that they be just and righteous ! Verily it is not for the good man to peer about into the blackness of another's heart,[3] but to 'run straight for the goal with never a glance aside.'

19. He whose heart flutters for after-fame[4] does not reflect that very soon every one of those who remember him, and he himself, will be dead, and their successors again after them, until at last the entire recollection of the man will be extinct, handed on as it is by links that flare up and are quenched. But put the case that those who are to remember are even immortal,[5] and the remembrance immortal, what then is that to thee? To the dead man, I need scarcely say, the praise is nothing, but what is it to the living, except, indeed, in a subsidiary way?[6] For thou dost reject the bounty of nature unseasonably in the present, and clingest to what others shall say of thee hereafter.[7]

---

[2] iii. 4 *ad init.*   [3] iv. 28.

[4] ii. 17 ; iii. 10 ; viii. 44 ; x. 34.   [5] iv. 33.

[6] iv. 19, 51 ; xi. 18, § 5. The Greek word covers the meanings *expediency, management,* or *means to an end.* We use it in a sort of double sense in the expression *economy of truth.*

[7] Marcus is perhaps finding real fault with himself for caring so much what people said of him ; see Capit. xx. 5 ; xxix. 5. But the reading is doubtful.

κ'. Πᾶν τὸ καὶ ὁπωσοῦν καλὸν ἐξ ἑαυτοῦ
καλόν ἐστι, καὶ ἐφ' ἑαυτὸ καταλήγει, οὐκ ἔχον
μέρος ἑαυτοῦ τὸν ἔπαινον. οὔτε γοῦν χεῖρον ἢ
κρεῖττον γίνεται τὸ ἐπαινούμενον. τοῦτό φημι
καὶ ἐπὶ τῶν κοινότερον καλῶν λεγομένων· οἷον
ἐπὶ τῶν ὑλικῶν καὶ ἐπὶ τῶν τεχνικῶν κατα-
σκευασμάτων· τό γε δὴ ὄντως καλὸν τίνος χρείαν
ἔχει; οὐ μᾶλλον ἢ νόμος, οὐ μᾶλλον ἢ ἀλήθεια,
οὐ μᾶλλον ἢ εὔνοια, ἢ αἰδώς. τί τούτων διὰ τὸ
ἐπαινεῖσθαι καλόν ἐστιν, ἢ ψεγόμενον φθείρεται;
σμαράγδιον γὰρ ἑαυτοῦ χεῖρον γίνεται, ἐὰν μὴ
ἐπαινῆται; τί δὲ χρυσός, ἐλέφας, πορφύρα, λύρα,
μαχαίριον, ἀνθύλλιον, δενδρύφιον;

κα'. Εἰ διαμένουσιν αἱ ψυχαί, πῶς αὐτὰς ἐξ
ἀϊδίου χωρεῖ ὁ ἀήρ; Πῶς δὲ ἡ γῆ χωρεῖ τὰ τῶν
ἐκ τοσούτου αἰῶνος θαπτομένων σώματα; ὥσπερ
γὰρ ἐνθάδε ἡ τούτων <μετὰ> ποσήν τινα [1] ἐπι-
διαμονὴν μεταβολὴ καὶ διάλυσις χώραν ἄλλοις
νεκροῖς ποιεῖ, οὕτως αἱ εἰς τὸν ἀέρα μεθιστάμεναι
ψυχαί, ἐπὶ ποσὸν συμμείνασαι, μεταβάλλουσι
καὶ χέονται καὶ ἐξάπτονται εἰς τὸν τῶν ὅλων
σπερματικὸν λόγον ἀναλαμβανόμεναι, καὶ τοῦτον
τὸν τρόπον χώραν ταῖς προσσυνοικιζομέναις
παρέχουσιν. τοῦτο δ' ἄν τις ἀποκρίναιτο ἐφ' ὑπο-
θέσει τοῦ τὰς ψυχὰς διαμένειν.

2   Χρὴ δὲ μὴ μόνον ἐνθυμεῖσθαι τὸ πλῆθος τῶν
θαπτομένων οὑτωσὶ σωμάτων, ἀλλὰ καὶ τὸ τῶν
ἑκάστης ἡμέρας ἐσθιομένων ζῴων ὑφ' ἡμῶν τε

---

[1] πρὸς ἥντινα PA : ἐπὶ ποσὴν Rend. : <μετὰ> Cas.

[1] vii. 15.   [2] cp. Tzetz. *Chil.* vii. 806.
[3] iii. 3 ; vi. 24 ; vii. 32, 50 ; viii. 25, 58 ; xii. 5. The Stoic
doctrine on this point was not very definite, but it was

BOOK IV

20. Everything, which has any sort of beauty of its own, is beautiful of itself, and looks no further than itself, not counting praise as part of itself. For indeed that which is praised is made neither better nor worse thereby. This is true also of the things that in common parlance are called beautiful, such as material things and works of art. Does, then, the truly beautiful need anything beyond? Nay, no more than law, than truth, than kindness, than modesty. Which of these owes its beauty to being praised, or loses it by being blamed? What! Does an emerald[1] forfeit its excellence by not being praised? Does gold, ivory, purple, a lyre, a poniard, a floweret, a shrub?

21. If souls outlive their bodies, how does the air contain them[2] from times beyond ken? How does the earth contain the bodies of those who have been buried in it for such endless ages? For just as on earth the change of these bodies, after continuance for a certain indefinite time, followed by dissolution, makes room for other dead bodies, so souls, when transferred into the air, after lasting for a certain time,[3] suffer change and are diffused and become fire, being taken again into the Seminal Reason of the Whole, and so allow room for those that subsequently take up their abode there. This would be the answer one would give on the assumption that souls outlive their bodies.

But not only must the multitude of bodies thus constantly being buried be taken into account, but also that of the creatures devoured daily by ourselves

mostly held that souls might exist till the next cyclical conflagration, when they became merged into the λόγος σπερματικός. Marcus wavers in his belief.

καὶ τῶν ἄλλων ζῴων. ὅσος γὰρ ἀριθμὸς κατ-
αναλίσκεται καὶ οὑτωσί πως θάπτεται ἐν τοῖς
τῶν τρεφομένων σώμασι· καὶ ὅμως δέχεται ἡ
χώρα αὐτὰ διὰ τὰς ἐξαιματώσεις, διὰ τὰς εἰς τὸ
ἀερῶδες ἢ πυρῶδες ἀλλοιώσεις.

3   Τίς ἐπὶ τούτου ἡ ἱστορία τῆς ἀληθείας; διαίρε-
σις εἰς τὸ ὑλικὸν καὶ εἰς τὸ αἰτιῶδες.

κβʹ. Μὴ ἀπορρέμβεσθαι· ἀλλ' ἐπὶ πάσης
ὁρμῆς τὸ δίκαιον ἀποδιδόναι καὶ ἐπὶ πάσης
φαντασίας σώζειν τὸ καταληπτικόν.

κγʹ. Πᾶν μοι συναρμόζει, ὃ σοὶ εὐάρμοστον
ἐστιν, ὦ κόσμε. οὐδέν μοι πρόωρον οὐδὲ ὄψιμον
τὸ σοὶ εὔκαιρον. πᾶν μοι καρπός, ὃ φέρουσιν αἱ
σαὶ ὧραι, ὦ φύσις· ἐκ σοῦ πάντα, ἐν σοὶ πάντα,
εἰς σὲ πάντα. ἐκεῖνος μέν φησι, "Πόλι φίλη
Κέκροπος." σὺ δὲ οὐκ ἐρεῖς, "Ὦ πόλι φίλη Διός;"

κδʹ. "Ὀλίγα πρῆσσε," φησίν, "εἰ μέλλεις εὐ-
θυμήσειν·" μήποτε ἄμεινον τἀναγκαῖα πράσσειν,
καὶ ὅσα ὁ τοῦ φύσει πολιτικοῦ ζῴου λόγος αἱρεῖ
καὶ ὡς αἱρεῖ; τοῦτο γὰρ οὐ μόνον τὴν ἀπὸ τοῦ
καλῶς πράσσειν εὐθυμίαν φέρει, ἀλλὰ καὶ τὴν
ἀπὸ τοῦ ὀλίγα πράσσειν. τὰ πλεῖστα γάρ, ὧν
λέγομεν καὶ πράσσομεν οὐκ ἀναγκαῖα ὄντα ἐάν τις
περιέλῃ, εὐσχολώτερος καὶ ἀταρακτότερος ἔσται.
ὅθεν δεῖ καὶ παρ' ἕκαστα ἑαυτὸν ὑπομιμνήσκειν,
μή τι τοῦτο οὐ τῶν ἀναγκαίων; δεῖ δὲ μὴ μόνον
πράξεις τὰς μὴ ἀναγκαίας περιαιρεῖν ἀλλὰ καὶ

---

[1] cp. Fronto, ad Caes. i. 6 ; Athenag. Apol. 36. Apuleius
(Met. iv. ad init.) calls beasts the living tombs of condemned
criminals. Longinus (de Subl. iii.) inveighs against the trope,
as used by Gorgias of Leontini. Spenser F.Q ii. 8. 16.
[2] vii. 29.   [3] Nature, God, and the Universe were
identical in the Stoic creed ; see Sen. N.Q. ii. 45.

and the other animals. How great is the number consumed and thus in a way buried [1] in the bodies of those who feed upon them! And yet room is made for them all by their conversion into blood, by their transmutation into air or fire.

Where in this case lies the way of search for the truth? In a separation of the Material from the Causal.[2]

22. Be not whirled aside; but in every impulse fulfil the claims of justice, and in every impression safeguard certainty.

23. All that is in tune with thee, O Universe,[3] is in tune with me! Nothing that is in due time for thee is too early or too late for me! All that thy seasons bring, O Nature, is fruit for me! All things come from thee, subsist in thee, go back to thee.[4] There is one who says *Dear City of Cecrops*[5]! Wilt thou not say *O dear City of Zeus*?

24. *If thou wouldest be tranquil in heart,* says the Sage,[6] *do not many things.* Is not this a better maxim? do but what is needful, and what the reason of a living creature born for a civic life demands, and as it demands. For this brings the tranquillity which comes of doing few things no less than of doing them well. For nine-tenths of our words and deeds being unnecessary, if a man retrench there, he will have more abundant leisure and fret the less. Wherefore forget not on every occasion to ask thyself, *Is this one of the unnecessary things?* But we must retrench not only actions but thoughts which are

---

[4] St. Paul, Rom. xi. 36, ἐξ αὐτοῦ δι' αὐτοῦ εἰς αὐτὸν τὰ πάντα.

[5] Seemingly a Fragment from Aristophanes.

[6] Democritus (Stob. i. 100), τὸν εὐθυμεῖσθαι μέλλοντα χρὴ μὴ πολλὰ πρήσσειν; iii. 5; Sen. *de Tran.* 12, *Hanc stabilem animi sedem Graeci* εὐθυμίαν *vocant, de qua Democriti volumen egregium est: ego Tranquillitatem voco.*

φαντασίας· οὕτως γὰρ οὐδὲ πράξεις παρέλκουσαι ἐπακολουθήσουσιν.

κε΄. Πείρασον πῶς σοι χωρεῖ καὶ ὁ τοῦ ἀγαθοῦ ἀνθρώπου βίος τοῦ ἀρεσκομένου μὲν τοῖς ἐκ τῶν ὅλων ἀπονεμομένοις, ἀρκουμένου δὲ τῇ ἰδίᾳ πράξει δικαίᾳ καὶ διαθέσει εὐμενεῖ.

κϛ΄. Ἑώρακας ἐκεῖνα; ἴδε καὶ ταῦτα. σεαυτὸν μὴ τάρασσε· ἅπλωσον σεαυτόν. ἁμαρτάνει τις; ἑαυτῷ ἁμαρτάνει. συμβέβηκέ σοί τι; καλῶς· ἐκ τῶν ὅλων ἀπ' ἀρχῆς σοι συγκαθείμαρτο καὶ συνεκλώθετο πᾶν τὸ συμβαῖνον. τὸ δ' ὅλον, βραχὺς ὁ βίος· κερδαντέον τὸ παρὸν σὺν εὐλογιστίᾳ καὶ δίκῃ. νῆφε ἀνειμένος.[1]

κζ΄. Ἤτοι κόσμος διατεταγμένος ἢ κυκεὼν † συμπεφορημένος [2] μέν, ἀλλὰ κόσμος.† ἢ ἐν σοὶ μέν τις κόσμος ὑφίστασθαι δύναται, ἐν δὲ τῷ παντὶ ἀκοσμία, καὶ ταῦτα οὕτως πάντων διακεκριμένων καὶ διακεχυμένων καὶ συμπαθῶν;

κη΄. Μέλαν ἦθος, θῆλυ ἦθος, περισκελὲς ἦθος, θηριῶδες, βοσκηματῶδες, παιδαριῶδες, βλακικόν, κίβδηλον, βωμολόχον, καπηλικόν, τυραννικόν.

κθ΄. Εἰ ξένος κόσμου ὁ μὴ γνωρίζων τὰ ἐν αὐτῷ ὄντα, οὐχ ἧττον ξένος καὶ ὁ μὴ γνωρίζων τὰ γινόμενα. φυγάς, ὁ φεύγων τὸν πολιτικὸν λόγον·

---

[1] ἀνειμέρως A.
[2] συμπεφυρμένος Schultz, but cp. Plato, Phaed. 253 E: Rendall reads ἀλλὰ μὴν κόσμος ἢ.

---

[1] iv. 37 ; ix. 37. Dio (71. 34 §§ 4, 5) says of Marcus οὐδὲν προσποίητον εἶχε, and he is a far better authority than Capit. xxix. 6 and xx. 1–4.　　[2] ix. 4, 38.　　[3] iii. 11 ; iv. 34.

unnecessary, for then neither will superfluous actions follow.

25. Try living the life of the good man who is more than content with what is allotted to him out of the whole, and is satisfied with his own acts as just and his own disposition as kindly: see how that answers.

26. Hast thou looked on that side of the picture? Look now on this! Fret not thyself; study to be simple.[1] Does a man do wrong? The wrong rests with him.[2] Has something befallen thee? It is well. Everything that befalls was from the beginning destined and spun[3] for thee as thy share out of the Whole. To sum up, life is short.[4] Make profit of the present by right reasoning and justice. In thy relaxation be sober.

27. Either there is a well-arranged Order of things, or a maze,[5] indeed, but not without a plan. Or can a sort of order subsist in thee, while in the Universe there is no order, and that too when all things, though separated and dispersed, are still in sympathetic connexion?

28. A black character,[6] an unmanly character, an obstinate character, inhuman, animal, childish, stupid, counterfeit, cringing, mercenary, tyrannical.[7]

29. If he is an alien in the Universe who has no cognizance of the things that are in it, no less is he an alien[8] who has no cognizance of what is happening in it. He is an exile, who exiles himself from civic

---

[4] iv. 17. [5] vi. 10. [6] iv. 18.

[7] Marcus here in his vehemence seems to violate his own gentle precepts. He must be thinking of some monster of iniquity, such as Nero.

[8] iv. 46. *cp.* 1 St. Peter, iv. 12.

τυφλός, ὁ καταμύων τῷ νοερῷ ὄμματι· πτωχός, ι
ἐνδεὴς ἑτέρου καὶ μὴ πάντα ἔχων παρ᾽ ἑαυτοῦ τὰ
εἰς τὸν βίον χρήσιμα· ἀπόστημα κόσμου, ὁ
ἀφιστάμενος καὶ χωρίζων ἑαυτὸν τοῦ τῆς κοινῆς
φύσεως λόγου διὰ τοῦ δυσαρεστεῖν τοῖς συμ-
βαίνουσιν· ἐκείνη γὰρ φέρει τοῦτο, ἢ καὶ σὲ
ἤνεγκεν· ἀπόσχισμα πόλεως, ὁ τὴν ἰδίαν ψυχὴν
τῆς τῶν λογικῶν ἀποσχίζων, μιᾶς οὔσης.

λ΄. Ὁ μὲν χωρὶς χιτῶνος φιλοσοφεῖ, ὁ δὲ
χωρὶς βιβλίου· ἄλλος οὗτος ἡμίγυμνος, "᾽Άρτους
οὐκ ἔχω," φησί, "καὶ ἐμμένω τῷ λόγῳ." ἐγὼ δὲ
τροφὰς τὰς ἐκ τῶν μαθημάτων οὐκ ἔχω, καὶ
ἐμμένω.

λα΄. Τὸ τεχνίον, ὃ ἔμαθες, φίλει, τούτῳ προσ-
αναπαύου· τὸ δὲ ὑπόλοιπον τοῦ βίου διέξελθε,
ὡς θεοῖς μὲν ἐπιτετροφὼς τὰ σεαυτοῦ πάντα ἐξ
ὅλης τῆς ψυχῆς, ἀνθρώπων δὲ μηδενὸς μήτε
τύραννον μήτε δοῦλον σεαυτὸν καθιστάς.

λβ΄. Ἐπινόησον λόγου χάριν τοὺς ἐπὶ Οὐεσ-
πασιανοῦ καιρούς, ὄψει ταῦτα πάντα· γαμοῦν-
τας, παιδοτροφοῦντας, νοσοῦντας, ἀποθνήσκοντας,
πολεμοῦντας, ἑορτάζοντας, ἐμπορευομένους, γεωρ-
γοῦντας, κολακεύοντας, αὐθαδιζομένους, ὑποπτεύ-
οντας, ἐπιβουλεύοντας, ἀποθανεῖν τινας εὐχο-
μένους, γογγύζοντας ἐπὶ τοῖς παροῦσιν, ἐρῶντας,
θησαυρίζοντας, ὑπατείας, βασιλείας ἐπιθυμ-
οῦντας. οὐκοῦν ἐκεῖνος μὲν ὁ τούτων βίος οὐκ
ἔτι οὐδαμοῦ.

2 Πάλιν ἐπὶ τοὺς καιροὺς τοὺς Τραϊανοῦ μετάβηθι·
πάλιν τὰ αὐτὰ πάντα· τέθνηκε κἀκεῖνος ὁ βίος.

---

[1] St. Matt. xiii. 15.   [2] ii. 16.
[3] viii. 34. cp. St. Paul, Rom. xii. 5 ; 1 Cor. xii. 20 f.

reason ; blind, he who will not see with the eyes of his understanding [1] ; a beggar, he who is dependent on another, and cannot draw from his own resources all that his life requires ; an imposthume [2] on the Universe, he who renounces, and severs himself from, the reason of our common Nature, because he is ill pleased at what happens – for the same Nature brings this into being, that also brought thee ; a limb cut off from the community, [3] he who cuts off his own soul from the soul of all rational things, which is but one.

30. One philosopher goes without a shirt, a second without a book, a third yonder half-naked : says he, *I am starving for bread, yet cleave I fast to Reason ;* and I too : I get no fruit of my learning, yet cleave I to her.

31. Cherish the art, though humble, that thou hast learned, and take thy rest therein ; and pass through the remainder of thy days as one that with his whole soul has given all that is his in trust to the Gods, and has made of himself neither a tyrant nor a slave to any man.

32. Think by way of illustration upon the times of Vespasian, and thou shalt see all these things : mankind marrying, rearing children, sickening, dying, warring, making holiday, trafficking, tilling, flattering others, vaunting themselves, suspecting, scheming, praying for the death of others, [4] murmuring at their own lot, loving, hoarding, coveting a consulate, coveting a kingdom. Not a vestige of that life of theirs is left anywhere any longer.

Change the scene again to the times of Trajan. Again it is all the same ; that life too is dead. In like

---

[4] See a characteristic anecdote of Marcus' mother, Capit. vi. 9.

ὁμοίως καὶ τὰς ἄλλας ἐπιγραφὰς χρόνων καὶ
ὅλων ἐθνῶν ἐπιθεώρει, καὶ βλέπε πόσοι κατεν-
ταθέντες μετὰ μικρὸν ἔπεσον καὶ ἀνελύθησαν εἰς
τὰ στοιχεῖα. μάλιστα δὲ ἀναπολητέον ἐκείνους,
οὓς αὐτὸς ἔγνως κενὰ σπωμένους, ἀφέντας ποιεῖν
τὸ κατὰ τὴν ἰδίαν κατασκευὴν καὶ τούτου ἀπρὶξ
ἔχεσθαι καὶ τούτῳ ἀρκεῖσθαι. ἀναγκαῖον δὲ
ὧδε τὸ μεμνῆσθαι, ὅτι καὶ ἡ ἐπιστροφὴ καθ'
ἑκάστην πρᾶξιν ἰδίαν ἀξίαν ἔχει καὶ συμμετρίαν.
οὕτως γὰρ οὐκ ἀποδυσπετήσεις, ἐὰν μὴ ἐπὶ
πλέον ἢ προσῆκε περὶ τὰ ἐλάσσω καταγίνῃ.

λγ΄. Αἱ πάλαι συνήθεις λέξεις γλωσσήματα
νῦν. οὕτως οὖν καὶ τὰ ὀνόματα τῶν πάλαι
πολυυμνήτων νῦν τρόπον τινὰ γλωσσήματά ἐστι,
Κάμιλλος, Καίσων, Οὐόλεσος, Δέντατος,[1] κατ'
ὀλίγον δὲ καὶ Σκιπίων, καὶ Κάτων, εἶτα καὶ
Αὔγουστος, εἶτα καὶ Ἁδριανὸς καὶ Ἀντωνῖνος.
ἐξίτηλα γὰρ πάντα καὶ μυθώδη ταχὺ γίνεται·
ταχὺ δὲ καὶ παντελὴς λήθη κατέχωσεν. καὶ
ταῦτα λέγω ἐπὶ τῶν θαυμαστῶς πως λαμψάντων.
οἱ γὰρ λοιποὶ ἅμα τῷ ἐκπνεῦσαι "ἄιστοι,
ἄπυστοι." τί δὲ καὶ ἔστιν ὅλως τὸ ἀείμνηστον;
ὅλον κενόν. τί οὖν ἔστι, περὶ ὃ δεῖ σπουδὴν
εἰσφέρεσθαι; ἓν τοῦτο, διάνοια δικαία καὶ
πράξεις κοινωνικαὶ καὶ λόγος οἷος μήποτε
διαψεύσασθαι καὶ διάθεσις ἀσπαζομένη πᾶν τὸ
συμβαῖνον ὡς ἀναγκαῖον, ὡς γνώριμον, ὡς ἀπ'
ἀρχῆς τοιαύτης καὶ πηγῆς ῥέον.

[1] Οὐόλεσος PA: Οὐολόγεσος Mo[2]: Λεοννάτος PA: Δέντατος Wyse.

---

[1] iii. 11 ad fin. [2] vii. 6.

BOOK IV

manner contemplate all the other records of past time and of entire nations, and see how many after all their high-strung efforts sank down so soon in death and were resolved into the elements. But above all must thou dwell in thought upon those whom thou hast thyself known, who, following after vanity, neglected to do the things that accorded with their own constitution and, cleaving steadfastly thereto, to be content with them. And here it is essential to remember that a due sense of value [1] and proportion should regulate the care bestowed on every action. For thus wilt thou never give over in disgust, if thou busy not thyself beyond what is right with the lesser things.

33. Expressions once in use are now obsolete. So also the names of those much be-sung [2] heroes of old are in some sense obsolete, Camillus, Caeso, Volesus,[3] Dentatus, and a little later Scipio and Cato, then also Augustus, and then Hadrianus and Antoninus. For all things quickly fade away and become legendary, and soon absolute oblivion encairns them. And here I speak of those who made an extraordinary blaze in the world. For the rest, as soon as the breath is out of their bodies, it is, *Out of sight, out of mind.*[4] But what, when all is said, is even everlasting remembrance [5]? Wholly vanity. What then is it that calls for our devotion? This one thing: justice in thought, in act unselfishness and a tongue that cannot lie and a disposition ready to welcome all that befalls as unavoidable, as familiar,[6] as issuing from a like origin and fountain-head.

[3] Volesus, or Volusus, was the family name of the Valerii. Valerius Poplicola must be meant, the obsolete name adding to the point.   [4] Hom. *Od.* i. 242.   [5] iv. 19.   [6] iv. 44.

λδ΄. Ἑκὼν σεαυτὸν τῇ Κλωθοῖ συνεπιδίδου, παρέχων συννῆσαι οἷστισί ποτε πράγμασι βούλεται.

λε΄. Πᾶν ἐφήμερον, καὶ τὸ μνημονεῦον καὶ τὸ μνημονευόμενον.

λϛ΄. Θεώρει διηνεκῶς πάντα κατὰ μεταβολὴν γινόμενα καὶ ἐθίζου ἐννοεῖν, ὅτι οὐδὲν οὕτως φιλεῖ ἡ τῶν ὅλων φύσις ὡς τὸ τὰ ὄντα μεταβάλλειν, καὶ ποιεῖν νέα ὅμοια. σπέρμα γὰρ τρόπον τινὰ πᾶν τὸ ὂν τοῦ ἐξ αὐτοῦ ἐσομένου. σὺ δὲ μόνα σπέρματα φαντάζῃ τὰ εἰς γῆν ἢ μήτραν καταβαλλόμενα· τοῦτο δὲ λίαν ἰδιωτικόν.

λζ΄. Ἤδη τεθνήξῃ, καὶ οὔπω οὔτε ἁπλοῦς, οὔτε ἀτάραχος, οὔτε ἀνύποπτος τοῦ βλαβῆναι ἂν ἔξωθεν, οὔτε ἵλεως πρὸς πάντας, οὔτε τὸ φρονεῖν ἐν μόνῳ τῷ δικαιοπραγεῖν τιθέμενος.

λη΄. Τὰ ἡγεμονικὰ αὐτῶν διάβλεπε, καὶ τοὺς φρονίμους, οἷα μὲν φεύγουσιν, οἷα δὲ διώκουσιν.

λθ΄. Ἐν ἀλλοτρίῳ ἡγεμονικῷ κακὸν σὸν οὐχ ὑφίσταται· οὐδὲ μὴν ἔν τινι τροπῇ καὶ ἑτεροιώσει τοῦ περιέχοντος. ποῦ οὖν; ὅπου τὸ περὶ κακῶν ὑπολαμβάνον σοί ἐστι. τοῦτο οὖν μὴ ὑπολαμβανέτω, καὶ πάντα εὖ ἔχει. κἂν τὸ ἐγγυτάτω αὐτοῦ, τὸ σωμάτιον, τέμνηται, καίηται, διαπυΐσκηται, σήπηται, ὅμως τὸ ὑπολαμβάνον περὶ τούτων μόριον ἡσυχαζέτω· τουτέστι, κρινέτω μήτε κακόν τι εἶναι μήτε ἀγαθόν, ὃ ἐπίσης δύναται κακῷ ἀνδρὶ καὶ ἀγαθῷ συμβαίνειν. ὃ γὰρ <καὶ τῷ παρὰ φύσιν>[1] καὶ τῷ κατὰ φύσιν

---

[1] <καὶ τῷ παρὰ φύσιν> Cas. Gat.

---

[1] cp. Herodian (i. 2, § 4) of Marcus, τοὺς προσιόντας δεξιούμενος, and Aristides, ad Reg. § 112 (Jebb).

BOOK IV

34. Offer thyself whole-heartedly to Clotho, letting her spin thy thread to serve what purpose soever she will.

35. Ephemeral all of them, the rememberer as well as the remembered!

36. Unceasingly contemplate the generation of all things through change, and accustom thyself to the thought that the Nature of the Universe delights above all in changing the things that exist and making new ones of the same pattern. For in a manner everything that exists is the seed of that which shall come out of it. But thou imaginest that only to be seed that is deposited in the earth or the womb, a view beyond measure unphilosophical.

37. A moment and thou wilt be dead; and not even yet art thou simple, nor unperturbed, nor free from all suspicion that thou canst be injured by externals, nor gracious [1] to all, nor convinced that wisdom and just dealing are but one.

38. Consider narrowly their ruling Reason, and see what wise men avoid and what they seek after. [2]

39. Harm to thee cannot depend on another's ruling Reason, nor yet on any vagary or phase of thy environment. On what then? On the power that is thine of judging what is evil. Let this, then, pass no judgment, and all is well. Even if its closest associate, the poor body, be cut, be burnt, fester, gangrene, yet let the part which forms a judgment [3] about these things hold its peace, that is, let it assume nothing to be either good or bad, which can befall a good man or a bad indifferently. [4] For that which befalls alike the man who lives by the

---

[2] cp. iii. 4 ad init. This precept does not really contradict what is said in iii. 4 etc.   [3] xi. 16.   [4] ii. 11 ad med.

βιοῦντι ἐπίσης συμβαίνει, τοῦτο οὔτε κατὰ φύσιν
ἐστὶν οὔτε παρὰ φύσιν.

μ΄. Ὡς ἓν ζῷον τὸν κόσμον μίαν οὐσίαν καὶ
ψυχὴν μίαν ἐπέχον συνεχῶς ἐπινοεῖν· καὶ πῶς
εἰς αἴσθησιν μίαν τὴν τούτου πάντα ἀναδίδοται·
καὶ πῶς ὁρμῇ μιᾷ πάντα πράσσει· καὶ πῶς
πάντα πάντων τῶν γινομένων συναίτια· καὶ οἵα
τις ἡ σύννησις καὶ συμμήρυσις.

μα΄. "Ψυχάριον εἶ βαστάζον νεκρόν," ὡς Ἐπίκτητος ἔλεγεν.

μβ΄. Οὐδέν ἐστι κακὸν τοῖς ἐν μεταβολῇ
γινομένοις· ὡς οὐδὲ ἀγαθὸν <τοῖς> ἐκ μεταβολῆς
ὑφισταμένοις.

μγ΄. Ποταμός τις ἐκ τῶν γινομένων καὶ ῥεῦμα
βίαιον ὁ αἰών· ἅμα τε γὰρ ὤφθη ἕκαστον καὶ
παρενήνεκται, καὶ ἄλλο παραφέρεται, τὸ δὲ
ἐνεχθήσεται.

μδ΄. Πᾶν τὸ συμβαῖνον οὕτως σύνηθες καὶ
γνώριμον, ὡς τὸ ῥόδον ἐν τῷ ἔαρι καὶ ὀπώρα
ἐν τῷ θέρει· τοιοῦτον γὰρ καὶ νόσος καὶ θάνατος
καὶ βλασφημία καὶ ἐπιβουλὴ καὶ ὅσα τοὺς
μωροὺς εὐφραίνει ἢ λυπεῖ.

με΄. Τὰ ἑξῆς ἀεὶ τοῖς προηγησαμένοις οἰκείως
ἐπιγίνεται· οὐ γὰρ οἷον καταρίθμησίς τίς ἐστιν
ἀπηρτημένως[1] καὶ μόνον τὸ κατηναγκασμένον
ἔχουσα, ἀλλὰ συνάφεια εὔλογος· καὶ ὥσπερ
συντέτακται συνηρμοσμένως τὰ ὄντα, οὕτως τὰ

---

[1] ἀπηρτημένων Gat.

---

[1] A Stoic doctrine, Diog. Laert. Zeno. 36.
[2] For ἀναδίδοσθαι, cp. v. 26.   [3] iii. 11.
[4] Not now found in his works. Swinburne has " A little

rule and the man who lives contrary to the rule of
Nature, is neither in accordance with Nature nor
contrary to it.

40. Cease not to think of the Universe as one living
Being,[1] possessed of a single Substance and a single
Soul; and how all things trace back to its single
sentience;[2] and how it does all things by a
single impulse; and how all existing things are joint
causes of all things that come into existence; and
how intertwined in the fabric is the thread and how
closely woven the web.[3]

41. Thou art a *little soul bearing up a corpse*, as
Epictetus said.[4]

42. Nothing is evil to that which is subject to
change, even as there is no good for that which
exists as the result of change.

43. As a river[5] consisting of all things that come
into being, aye, a rushing torrent, is Time. No
sooner is a thing sighted than it is carried past, and
lo, another is passing, and it too will be carried away.

44. Everything that happens is as usual and
familiar,[6] as the rose in spring and the fruit in
summer. The same applies to disease and death
and slander and treachery and all that gladdens the
foolish or saddens them.

45. That which comes after always has a close
relationship to what has gone before. For it is not
like some enumeration of items separately taken and
following a mere hard and fast sequence, but there
is a rational connection; and just as existing things
have been combined in a harmonious order, so also

soul for a little bears up this corpse which is man" (*Hymn
to Proserpine*). cp. Ignat. *ad Smyrn.* 5 νεκροφόρος.
[5] ii. 17; v. 23; vi. 15 (Heraclitus).   [6] iv. 33.

γινόμενα οὐ διαδοχὴν ψιλὴν ἀλλὰ θαυμαστήν
τινα οἰκειότητα ἐμφαίνει.

μϛ΄. Ἀεὶ τοῦ Ἡρακλειτείου μεμνῆσθαι· ὅτι
"γῆς θάνατος ὕδωρ" γενέσθαι, καὶ "ὕδατος
θάνατος ἀέρα" γενέσθαι, καὶ "ἀέρος πῦρ," καὶ
ἔμπαλιν. μεμνῆσθαι δὲ καὶ "τοῦ ἐπιλανθανο-
μένου, ᾗ ἡ ὁδὸς ἄγει" καὶ ὅτι "ᾧ μάλιστα διηνεκῶς ὁμιλοῦσι," λόγῳ τῷ τὰ ὅλα διοικοῦντι, "τούτῳ
διαφέρονται·" καὶ "οἷς καθ᾽ ἡμέραν ἐγκυροῦσι,
ταῦτα αὐτοῖς ξένα φαίνεται·" καὶ ὅτι οὐ δεῖ
"ὥσπερ καθεύδοντας ποιεῖν καὶ λέγειν" καὶ
γὰρ καὶ τότε δοκοῦμεν ποιεῖν καὶ λέγειν· καὶ
ὅτι οὐ δεῖ "παῖδας τοκεώνων,"[1] τουτέστι κατὰ
ψιλόν, "καθότι παρειλήφαμεν."

μζ΄. Ὥσπερ εἴ τίς σοι θεῶν εἶπεν, ὅτι αὔριον
τεθνήξῃ ἢ πάντως γε εἰς τρίτην, οὐκ ἔτ᾽ ἂν
παρὰ μέγα ἐποιοῦ τὸ εἰς τρίτην μᾶλλον ἢ
αὔριον, εἴ γε μὴ ἐσχάτως ἀγεννὴς εἶ· πόσον γάρ
ἐστι τὸ μεταξύ; οὕτως καὶ τὸ εἰς πολλοστὸν
ἔτος μᾶλλον ἢ αὔριον μηδὲν μέγα εἶναι νόμιζε.

μη΄. Ἐννοεῖν συνεχῶς πόσοι μὲν ἰατροὶ
ἀποτεθνήκασι πολλάκις τὰς ὀφρῦς ὑπὲρ τῶν
ἀρρώστων συσπάσαντες· πόσοι δὲ μαθηματικοὶ
ἄλλων θανάτους ὥς τι μέγα προειπόντες· πόσοι
δὲ φιλόσοφοι, περὶ θανάτου ἢ ἀθανασίας μυρία
διατεινάμενοι· πόσοι δὲ ἀριστεῖς πολλοὺς ἀπο-
κτείναντες· πόσοι δὲ τύραννοι ἐξουσίᾳ ψυχῶν

---

[1] τοκέων ὦν PAD : τοκεώνων Rend. This Ionic word was
recovered for Meleager by Headlam (*Anth. Pal.* vii. 79).

---

[1] vi. 38 ; vii. 9.
[2] A favourite with Marcus, see Index II.   [3] vi. 42.

BOOK IV

all that comes into being bears the stamp not of a mere succession but of a wonderful relationship.[1]

46. Always bear in mind what Heraclitus [2] said: *The death of earth is to pass into water, and the death of water to pass into air, and of air to pass into fire,* and so back again. Bear in mind too *the wayfarer who forgets the trend of his way,* and that *men are at variance with the one thing with which they are in the most unbroken communion,* the Reason that administers the whole Universe; and that *what they encounter every day, this they deem strange*; and that we must not *act and speak like men asleep,*[3]—for in fact even in sleep we seem to act and speak;—and that there should be nothing of the *children from parents* style, that is, no mere perfunctory *what our fathers have told us.*

47. Just as, if a God had told thee,[4] *Thou shalt die to-morrow or in any case the day after,* thou wouldest no longer count it of any consequence whether it were the day after to-morrow or to-morrow, unless thou art in the last degree mean-spirited,[5] for how little is the difference![6]—so also deem it but a trifling thing that thou shouldest die after ever so many years rather than to-morrow.

48. Cease not to bear in mind how many physicians are dead after puckering up their brows so often over their patients; and how many astrologers after making a great parade of predicting the death of others;[7] and how many philosophers after endless disquisitions on death and immortality; how many great captains after butchering thousands[8]; how many tyrants after exercising with revolting insolence

---

[4] *cp.* the story of Mycerinus (Herod. ii. 129), and M. Arnold's poem.   [5] Sen. *N.Q.* ii. 59 *ad med.*
[6] Or *interval, cp.* iv. 50.   [7] iii. 3. Epict. iii. 10, 15.   [8] *ibid.*

μετὰ δεινοῦ φρυάγματος ὡς ἀθάνατοι κεχρημένοι·
πόσαι δὲ πόλεις ὅλαι, ἵν᾽ οὕτως εἴπω, τεθνή-
κασιν, Ἑλίκη καὶ Πομπήιοι καὶ Ἡρκλάνον¹ καὶ
ἄλλαι ἀναρίθμητοι.

2   Ἔπιθι δὲ καὶ ὅσους οἶδας, ἄλλον ἐπ᾽ ἄλλῳ· ὁ
μὲν τοῦτον κηδεύσας εἶτα ἐξετάθη, ὁ δὲ ἐκεῖνον·
πάντα δὲ ἐν βραχεῖ. τὸ γὰρ ὅλον, κατιδεῖν ἀεὶ τὰ
ἀνθρώπινα ὡς ἐφήμερα καὶ εὐτελῆ, καὶ ἐχθὲς μὲν
μυξάριον, αὔριον δὲ τάριχος ἢ τέφρα. τὸ ἀκαριαῖον
οὖν τούτου τοῦ χρόνου κατὰ φύσιν διελθεῖν,
καὶ ἵλεως καταλῦσαι, ὡς ἂν εἰ ἐλαία πέπειρος
γενομένη ἔπιπτεν εὐφημοῦσα τὴν ἐνεγκοῦσαν
καὶ χάριν εἰδυῖα τῷ φύσαντι δένδρῳ.

μθ´.   Ὅμοιον εἶναι τῇ ἄκρᾳ, ᾗ διηνεκῶς τὰ
κύματα προσρήσσεται· ἡ δὲ ἕστηκε, καὶ περὶ
αὐτὴν κοιμίζεται τὰ φλεγμήναντα τοῦ ὕδατος.

2   "Ἀτυχὴς ἐγώ, ὅτι τοῦτό μοι συνέβη." οὐμενοῦν
ἀλλ᾽ "εὐτυχὴς ἐγώ, ὅτι τούτου μοι συμβεβη-
κότος ἄλυπος διατελῶ οὔτε ὑπὸ <τοῦ> παρόντος
θραυόμενος οὔτε <τὸ> ἐπιὸν φοβούμενος."
συμβῆναι μὲν γὰρ τὸ τοιοῦτο παντὶ ἐδύνατο·
ἄλυπος δὲ οὐ πᾶς ἐπὶ τούτῳ ἂν διετέλεσεν. διὰ
τί οὖν ἐκεῖνο μᾶλλον ἀτύχημα ἢ τοῦτο εὐτύχημα;
λέγεις δὲ ὅλως ἀτύχημα ἀνθρώπου, ὃ οὐκ ἔστιν
ἀπότευγμα τῆς φύσεως τοῦ ἀνθρώπου; ἀπότευγμα δὲ τῆς φύσεως τοῦ ἀνθρώπου εἶναι δοκεῖ
σοι, ὃ μὴ παρὰ τὸ βούλημα τῆς φύσεως αὐτοῦ
ἐστιν; τί οὖν; τὸ βούλημα μεμάθηκας· μή τι
οὖν τὸ συμβεβηκὸς τοῦτο κωλύει σε δίκαιον

---

¹ Lucian uses it, *Charon* 23.
² x. 34. This is invariably referred to ὁ μέν, "another
closed *his* eyes," but it must surely answer to τοῦτον.

their power of life and death, as though themselves immortal; and how many entire cities are, if I may use the expression, dead,[1] Helice and Pompeii and Herculaneum, and others without number.

Turn also to all, one after another, that come within thine own knowledge. One closed a friend's eyes and was then himself laid out, and the friend who closed his,[2] he too was laid out—and all this in a few short years. In a word, fail not to note how short-lived are all mortal things, and how paltry— yesterday a little mucus,[3] to-morrow a mummy or burnt ash. Pass then through this tiny span of time in accordance with Nature, and come to thy journey's end with a good grace, just as an olive falls when it is fully ripe, praising the earth that bare it and grateful to the tree that gave it growth.

49. Be like a headland of rock on which the waves break incessantly; but it stands fast and around it the seething of the waters sinks to rest.

Ah, unlucky am I, that this has befallen me ! Nay, but rather, lucky am I that, though this has befallen me, yet am I still unhurt, neither crushed by the present nor dreading the future. For something of the kind could have befallen everyone, but everyone would not have remained unhurt in spite of it. Why then count that rather a misfortune than this a good fortune? And in any case dost thou reckon that a misfortune for a man which is not a miscarriage from his nature? And wouldst thou have that to be an aberration from a man's nature, which does not contravene the will of his nature! What then? This will thou hast learnt to know. Does what has befallen thee hinder thee one whit from being just,

[3] vi. 13.

εἶναι, μεγαλόψυχον, σώφρονα, ἔμφρονα, ἀπρόπτ
ωτον, ἀδιάψευστον, αἰδήμονα, ἐλεύθερον, τἆλλα,
ὧν παρόντων ἡ φύσις ἡ τοῦ ἀνθρώπου ἀπέχει
τὰ ἴδια; μέμνησο λοιπὸν ἐπὶ παντὸς τοῦ εἰς
λύπην σε προαγομένου, τούτῳ χρῆσθαι τῷ
δόγματι· "Οὐχ ὅτι τοῦτο ἀτύχημα, ἀλλὰ τὸ
φέρειν αὐτὸ γενναίως εὐτύχημα."

ν΄. Ἰδιωτικὸν μέν, ὅμως δὲ ἀνυστικὸν βοήθημα
πρὸς θανάτου καταφρόνησιν ἡ ἀναπόλησις τῶν
γλίσχρως ἐνδιατριψάντων τῷ ζῆν. τί οὖν αὐτοῖς
πλέον ἢ τοῖς ἀώροις; πάντως πού ποτε κεῖνται,
Καδικιανός, Φάβιος, Ἰουλιανός, Λέπιδος, ἢ εἴ
τις τοιοῦτος, οἳ πολλοὺς ἐξήνεγκαν, εἶτα ἐξηνέχθ
ησαν· ὅλον, μικρόν ἐστι τὸ διάστημα, καὶ
τοῦτο δι᾽ ὅσων καὶ μεθ᾽ οἵων ἐξαντλούμενον καὶ
ἐν οἵῳ σωματίῳ; μὴ οὖν ὡς πρᾶγμα. βλέπε
γὰρ ὀπίσω τὸ ἀχανὲς τοῦ αἰῶνος, καὶ τὸ πρόσω
ἄλλο ἄπειρον. ἐν δὴ τούτῳ, τί διαφέρει ὁ τρι
ήμερος τοῦ τριγερηνίου;

να΄. Ἐπὶ τὴν σύντομον ἀεὶ τρέχε· σύντομος δὲ
ἡ κατὰ φύσιν, ὥστε κατὰ τὸ ὑγιέστατον πᾶν
λέγειν καὶ πράσσειν. ἀπαλλάσσει γὰρ ἡ
τοιαύτη πρόθεσις κόπων καὶ στρατείας,[1] καὶ
πάσης οἰκονομίας καὶ κομψείας.

---

[1] στραγγείας (*vacillation*) Stephan. But Pollux in his Onomasticon, dedicated to Commodus in Marcus' lifetime, rejects
the word.

---

[1] iv. 48, § 2.   [2] iv. 47.

[3] τριγερήνιος, a clever conflation between τριγέρων and
Γερήνιος, an epithet of Nestor from a town in Messenia.

high-minded, chaste, sensible, deliberate, straight-forward, modest, free, and from possessing all the other qualities, the presence of which enables a man's nature to come fully into its own? Forget not in future, when anything would lead thee to feel hurt, to take thy stand upon this axiom: *This is no misfortune, but to bear it nobly is good fortune.*

50. An unphilosophical but none the less an effective help to the contemning of death is to tell over the names of those who have clung long and tenaciously to life. How are they better off than those who were cut off before their time? After all, they lie buried somewhere at last, Cadicianus, Fabius, Julianus, Lepidus, and any others like them, who after carrying many to their graves were at last carried to their own.[1] Small, in any point of view, is the difference [2] in length, and that too lived out to the dregs amid what great cares and with what sort of companions and in what kind of a body! Count it then of no consequence. For look at the yawning gulf of Time behind thee, and before thee at another Infinity to come. In this Eternity the life of a baby of three days and the life of a Nestor of three centuries [3] are as one.[4]

51. Run ever the short way; and the short way is the way of Nature, that leads to all that is most sound in speech and act. For a resolve such as this is a release from troubles and strife, from all mental reservation [5] and affectation.

[4] *cp.* Ecclesiasticus, xli. 4.   [5] iv. 19.

E

ΒΙΒΛΙΟΝ Ε

α΄. Ὄρθρου ὅταν δυσόκνως ἐξεγείρῃ, πρόχειρον
ἔστω, ὅτι "ἐπὶ ἀνθρώπου ἔργον ἐγείρομαι" ἔτι
οὖν [1] δυσκολαίνω, εἰ πορεύομαι ἐπὶ τὸ ποιεῖν, ὧν
ἕνεκεν γέγονα, καὶ ὧν χάριν προῆγμαι εἰς τὸν
κόσμον; ἢ ἐπὶ τοῦτο κατεσκεύασμαι, ἵνα κατακεί-
μενος ἐν στρωματίοις ἐμαυτὸν θάλπω; "Ἀλλὰ τοῦτο
ἥδιον." πρὸς τὸ ἥδεσθαι οὖν γέγονας; ὅλως δὲ
σὺ [2] πρὸς πεῖσιν,[3] ἢ πρὸς ἐνέργειαν; οὐ βλέπεις
τὰ φυτάρια, τὰ στρουθάρια, τοὺς μύρμηκας, τοὺς
ἀράχνας, τὰς μελίσσας τὸ ἴδιον ποιούσας, τὸ [4]
καθ' αὑτὰς συγκροτούσας κόσμον; ἔπειτα σὺ οὐ
θέλεις τὰ ἀνθρωπικὰ ποιεῖν; οὐ τρέχεις ἐπὶ τὸ
κατὰ τὴν σὴν φύσιν; "Ἀλλὰ δεῖ καὶ ἀναπαύ-
εσθαι." φημὶ κἀγώ· ἔδωκε μέντοι καὶ τούτου
μέτρα ἡ φύσις· ἔδωκε μέντοι καὶ τοῦ ἐσθίειν καὶ
πίνειν· καὶ ὅμως σὺ ὑπὲρ τὰ μέτρα, ὑπὲρ τὰ
ἀρκοῦντα προχωρεῖς· ἐν δὲ ταῖς πράξεσιν οὐκ ἔτι,
ἀλλ' ἐντὸς τοῦ δυνατοῦ.

[1] τί οὖν Menag. [2] οὐ PAD: σὺ Schmidt.
[3] ποιεῖν P: <τὸ> ποιεῖν Cor.: ποίησιν Wilam.
[4] τὸν PD: συγκοσμούσας P.

---

[1] ii. 1.
[2] Marcus in younger days was an early riser, getting up
even at 3 o'clock (Fronto, *ad Caes.* iv. 5) or 5 o'clock (*ibid.*

BOOK V

1. At daybreak,[1] when loth to rise,[2] have this thought ready in thy mind : *I am rising for a man's work.* Am I then still peevish that I am going to do that for which I was born and for the sake of which I came into the world ? Or was I made for this, that I should nuzzle under the bed-clothes and keep myself warm ? *But this is pleasanter.* Hast thou been made then for pleasure ? In a word, I ask thee, to be acted upon or to act ? Consider each tiny plant, each little bird, the ant, the spider, the bee, how they go about their own work and do each his part for the building up of an orderly Universe. Dost *thou* then refuse to do the work of a man ? Dost thou not hasten to do what Nature bids thee. *But some rest, too, is necessary.* I do not deny it. Howbeit Nature has set limits to this, and no less so to eating and drinking. Yet thou exceedest these limits and exceedest sufficiency. But in acts it is no longer so ; *there* thou comest short of the possibility.

iv. 6). He admits sleepiness of habit (*ibid.* i. 4 ; v. 59), but says it is so cold in his bedroom that he can scarcely put his hands outside his bedclothes. Fronto constantly urges him to take more sleep (*ibid.* ii. 5 ; v. 1, 2 ; *de Fer. Als.* 2, Nab. p. 227) : *sleep as much as a free man should!* At the last he suffered dreadfully from insomnia, see Galen xiv. 3 (Kühn) ; Dio 71. 24, § 4.

2 Οὐ γὰρ φιλεῖς σεαυτόν· ἐπεί τοι καὶ τὴν
φύσιν ἄν σου καὶ τὸ βούλημα ταύτης ἐφίλεις.
ἄλλοι δὲ τὰς τέχνας ἑαυτῶν φιλοῦντες συγ-
κατατήκονται τοῖς κατ᾽ αὐτὰς ἔργοις ἄλουτοι
καὶ ἄσιτοι· σὺ τὴν φύσιν τὴν σεαυτοῦ ἔλασσον
τιμᾷς ἢ ὁ τορευτὴς τὴν τορευτικήν, ἢ ὁ ὀρχηστὴς
τὴν ὀρχηστικήν, ἢ ὁ φιλάργυρος τὸ ἀργύριον,
ἢ ὁ κενόδοξος τὸ δοξάριον. καὶ οὗτοι, ὅταν
προσπαθῶσιν, οὔτε φαγεῖν οὔτε κοιμηθῆναι
θέλουσι μᾶλλον ἢ ταῦτα συναύξειν, πρὸς ἃ
διαφέρονται· σοὶ δὲ αἱ κοινωνικαὶ πράξεις εὐ-
τελέστεραι φαίνονται καὶ ἥσσονος σπουδῆς ἄξιαι;

β΄. Ὡς εὔκολον ἀπώσασθαι καὶ ἀπαλεῖψαι
πᾶσαν φαντασίαν [τὴν] ὀχληρὰν ἢ ἀνοίκειον καὶ
εὐθὺς ἐν πάσῃ γαλήνῃ εἶναι.

γ΄. Ἄξιον ἑαυτὸν κρῖνε παντὸς λόγου καὶ
ἔργου τοῦ κατὰ φύσιν· καὶ μή σε περισπάτω[1] ἡ
ἐπακολουθοῦσά τινων μέμψις ἢ λόγος, ἀλλά, εἰ
καλὸν πεπρᾶχθαι ἢ εἰρῆσθαι, μὴ σεαυτὸν ἀπ-
αξίου. ἐκεῖνοι μὲν γὰρ ἴδιον ἡγεμονικὸν ἔχουσι καὶ
ἰδίᾳ ὁρμῇ χρῶνται· ἃ σὺ μὴ περιβλέπου, ἀλλ᾽
εὐθεῖαν πέραινε ἀκολουθῶν τῇ φύσει τῇ ἰδίᾳ καὶ
τῇ κοινῇ· μία δὲ ἀμφοτέρων τούτων ἡ ὁδός.

δ΄. Πορεύομαι διὰ τῶν κατὰ φύσιν, μέχρι
πεσὼν ἀναπαύσομαι, ἐναποπνεύσας μὲν τούτῳ, ἐξ
οὗ καθ᾽ ἡμέραν ἀναπνέω, πεσὼν δὲ ἐπὶ τούτῳ, ἐξ
οὗ καὶ τὸ σπερμάτιον ὁ πατήρ μου συνέλεξε καὶ
τὸ αἱμάτιον ἡ μήτηρ καὶ τὸ γαλάκτιον ἡ τροφός·

---

[1] Cor. for παρειπάτω.

---

[1] cp. of Marcus himself καμάτοις καὶ φροντίσι τετρυχωμένος
(*Herodian* i. 3, § 1) and Julian, *Conviv.* 407. See Plutarch's

For thou lovest not thyself, else surely hadst thou loved thy nature also and to do her will. But others who love their own art wear themselves to a shadow with their labours over it, forgetting to wash or take food.[1] But thou holdest thine own nature in less honour than the chaser of metal his art of chasing, than the dancer his dancing, than the miser his money-bags, than the popularity-hunter his little applause. And these, when they are exceptionally in earnest, are ready to forgo food and sleep, so that they forward the things in which they are interested. But dost thou deem the acts of a social being of less worth and less deserving of attention?

2. How easy a thing it is to put away and blot out every impression[2] that is disturbing or alien, and to be at once in perfect peace.

3. Deem no word or deed that is in accord with Nature to be unworthy of thee, and be not plucked aside by the consequent censure of others or what they say,[3] but if a thing is good to do or say, judge not thyself unworthy of it. For those others have their own ruling Reason and follow their own bent. Do not thou turn thine eyes aside, but keep to the straight path, following thy own and the universal Nature; and the path of these twain is one.[4]

4. I fare forth through all that Nature wills until the day when I shall sink down and rest from my labours, breathing forth my last breath into the air whence I daily draw it in, and falling upon that earth, whence also my father gathered the seed, and my mother the blood, and my nurse the milk; whence

___

story of Nikias the painter (*de Sene Polit.* 4; *Non posse suav. vivere sec. Epicur.* 11). *cp.* Archimedes.   [2] vii. 29; viii. 47.   [3] x. 11. *cp.* 1 St. Peter, ii. 20.   [4] iv. 29

ἐξ οὗ καθ' ἡμέραν τοσούτοις ἔτεσι βόσκομαι, καὶ
ἀρδεύομαι, ὃ φέρει με πατοῦντα, καὶ εἰς τοσαῦτα
ἀποχρώμενον αὐτῷ.

ε΄. Δριμύτητά σου οὐκ ἔχουσι θαυμάσαι.
ἔστω· ἀλλὰ ἕτερα πολλά, ἐφ' ὧν οὐκ ἔχεις
εἰπεῖν "Οὐ γὰρ πέφυκα." ἐκεῖνα οὖν παρέχου,
ἅπερ ὅλα ἐστὶν ἐπὶ σοί, τὸ ἀκίβδηλον, τὸ σεμνόν,
τὸ φερέπονον, τὸ ἀφιλήδονον, τὸ ἀμεμψίμοιρον,
τὸ ὀλιγοδεές, τὸ εὐμενές, τὸ ἐλεύθερον, τὸ ἀπέρισσ-
ον, τὸ ἀφλύαρον, τὸ μεγαλεῖον.[1] οὐκ αἰσθάνῃ
πόσα ἤδη παρέχεσθαι δυνάμενος, ἐφ' ὧν οὐδεμία
ἀφυΐας καὶ ἀνεπιτηδειότητος πρόφασις, ὅμως ἔτι
κάτω μένεις ἑκών; ἢ καὶ γογγύζειν, καὶ γλισχρεύεσθαι, καὶ κολακεύειν, καὶ τὸ σωμάτιον κατ-
αιτιᾶσθαι, καὶ ἀρεσκεύεσθαι, καὶ περπερεύεσθαι,
καὶ τοσαῦτα ῥιπτάζεσθαι τῇ ψυχῇ διὰ τὸ ἀφυῶς
κατεσκευάσθαι ἀναγκάζῃ; οὔ, μὰ τοὺς θεούς·
ἀλλὰ τούτων μὲν πάλαι ἀπηλλάχθαι ἐδύνασο·
μόνον δέ, εἰ ἄρα, ὡς βραδύτερος καὶ δυσπαρ-
ακολουθητότερος καταγινώσκεσθαι· καὶ τοῦτο δὲ
ἀσκητέον μὴ παρενθυμουμένῳ μηδὲ ἐμφιληδοῦντι
τῇ νωθείᾳ.

ϛ΄. Ὁ μέν τίς ἐστιν, ὅταν τι δεξιὸν περί τινα
πράξῃ, πρόχειρος καὶ λογίσασθαι αὐτῷ τὴν χάριν.
ὁ δὲ πρὸς τοῦτο μὲν οὐ πρόχειρος, ἄλλως μέντοι
παρ' ἑαυτῷ, ὡς περὶ χρεώστου διανοεῖται καὶ
οἶδεν, ὃ πεποίηκεν. ὁ δέ τις τρόπον τινὰ οὐδὲ

---

[1] ἀμεγαλεῖον Rend.

[1] vii. 67 ; *cp.* Fronto, *ad Ant.* i. 2.
[2] *cp.* Hor. *Ep.* i. 1. 28–32.   [3] *cp.* i. 5.
[4] *cp.* Aristides, *ad Reg.* § 114 (Jebb) of Marcus, οὐδεμίας
ἡδονῆς ἡττημένος ; and Fronto, *de Fer. Als.* Nab. p. 225,
volpem facilius quis tibi quam voluptatem conciliaverit.

daily for so many years I am fed and watered; which bears me as I tread it under foot and make full use of it in a thousand ways.

5. Sharpness of wit men cannot praise thee for.[1] Granted! Yet there are many other qualities of which thou canst not say: *I had not that by nature*.[2] Well then, display those which are wholly in thy power, sterling sincerity, dignity, endurance of toil,[3] abstinence from pleasure.[4] Grumble not at thy lot, be content with little,[5] be kindly, independent, frugal, serious, high-minded.[6] Seest thou not how many virtues it is in thy power to display now, in respect of which thou canst plead no natural incapacity or incompatibility, and yet thou art content still with a lower standard? Or art thou forced to be discontented, to be grasping, to flatter, to inveigh against the body, to play the toady and the braggart, and to be so unstable in thy soul, because forsooth thou hast no natural gifts? By the Gods, *No!* but long ere now couldest thou have shaken thyself free from all this and have lain under the imputation only, if it must be so, of being somewhat slow and dull of apprehension. And this too thou must amend with training and not ignore thy dulness or be in love with it.

6. One man, when he has done another a kindness, is ready also to reckon on a return.[7] A second is not ready to do this, but yet in his heart of hearts ranks the other as a debtor, and he is conscious of what he has done[8] But a third is in a manner not

---

[5] *cp.* i. 5; Julian, *Conviv.* 427.
[6] Or *humble*, if we read ἀμεγαλεῖον, but *cp.* v. 9.
[7] St. Luke vi. 34; xiv. 12.
[8] Sen. *de Benef.* ii. 6. But see the speech of Marcus to his soldiers (as reported by Dio, 71. 26, §2) on the revolt of Cassius.

οἶδεν, ὃ πεποίηκεν, ἀλλὰ ὅμοιός ἐστιν ἀμπέλῳ
βότρυν ἐνεγκούσῃ καὶ μηδὲν ἄλλο προσεπι-
ζητούσῃ μετὰ τὸ ἅπαξ τὸν ἴδιον καρπὸν ἐνηνοχ-
έναι, ὡς ἵππος δραμών, κύων ἰχνεύσας, μέλισσα
μέλι ποιήσασα. ἄνθρωπος δ᾽ <ἐν>[1] εὖ ποιήσας
οὐκ ἐπιβοᾶται,[2] ἀλλὰ μεταβαίνει ἐφ᾽ ἕτερον, ὡς
ἄμπελος ἐπὶ τὸ πάλιν ἐν τῇ ὥρᾳ τὸν βότρυν
ἐνεγκεῖν.

2 "Ἐν τούτοις οὖν δεῖ εἶναι τοῖς τρόπον τινὰ
ἀπαρακολουθήτως αὐτὸ ποιοῦσι;" ναί· ἀλλ᾽
αὐτὸ τοῦτο δεῖ παρακολουθεῖν· ἴδιον γὰρ
φησὶ τοῦ κοινωνικοῦ τὸ αἰσθάνεσθαι, ὅτι
κοινωνικῶς ἐνεργεῖ. "καὶ νὴ Δία βούλεσθαι καὶ
τὸν κοινωνὸν αἰσθέσθαι." ἀληθὲς μέν ἐστιν, ὃ
λέγεις, τὸ δὲ νῦν λεγόμενον παρεκδέχῃ· διὰ
τοῦτο ἔσῃ εἷς ἐκείνων, ὧν πρότερον ἐπεμνήσθην·
καὶ γὰρ ἐκεῖνοι λογικῇ τινι πιθανότητι παράγον-
ται. ἐὰν δὲ θελήσῃς συνεῖναι, τί ποτέ ἐστι τὸ
λεγόμενον, μὴ φοβοῦ, μὴ παρὰ τοῦτο παραλίπῃς
τι ἔργον κοινωνικόν.

ζ. Εὐχὴ Ἀθηναίων· "Ὗσον, ὗσον, ὦ φίλε
Ζεῦ, κατὰ τῆς ἀρούρας τῆς Ἀθηναίων καὶ τῶν
πεδίων." ἤτοι οὐ δεῖ εὔχεσθαι ἢ οὕτως ἁπλῶς
καὶ ἐλευθέρως.

η΄. Ὁποῖόν τί ἐστι τὸ λεγόμενον, ὅτι "συν-
έταξεν ὁ Ἀσκληπιὸς τούτῳ ἱππασίαν, ἢ ψυχρο-
λουσίαν, ἢ ἀνυποδησίαν·" τοιοῦτόν ἐστι καὶ τὸ
συνέταξε τούτῳ ἡ τῶν ὅλων φύσις νόσον, ἢ

---

¹ <ἐν> cp. x. 8.   ² ἐπισπᾶται AD.

---

¹ vii. 73; ix. 42, § 4. cp. Fronto, de Nep. 2 ad fin. Seneca
Ep. 81 (Montaigne ii. 16.).   ² xi. 4; xii. 29.
³ e.g. a man who acts on the precept, "Let not thy left

conscious of it, but is like the vine that has borne a cluster of grapes, and when it has once borne its due fruit looks for no reward beyond,[1] as it is with a steed when it has run its course, a hound when it has singled out the trail, a bee when she hath made her comb. And so a man when he hath done one thing well, does not cry it abroad, but betakes himself to a second,[2] as a vine to bear afresh her clusters in due season.

A man then must be of those who act thus as it were unconsciously? Yes; but he must be conscious of the fact, for it is, we are told, the peculiar characteristic of the man of true neighbourly instincts to be aware that he puts such instincts into practice. *And by heaven to wish that his neighbour also should be aware of it.* What thou sayest is true; but thou misconceivest what is now said: consequently thou wilt be one of those whom I mentioned before, for in fact they are led astray by a certain plausibility of reasoning. But if thou thinkest it worth while to understand what has been said, fear not that thou wilt be led thereby to neglect any social act.

7. A prayer of the Athenians: *Rain, Rain, O dear Zeus, upon the corn-land of the Athenians*[4] *and their meads.* Either pray not at all, or in this simple and frank fashion.

8. We have all heard, *Aesculapius has prescribed for so and so riding exercise, or cold baths,*[5] *or walking barefoot.* Precisely so it may be said that the Universal Nature has prescribed for so and so sickness or

---

hand know what thy right hand doeth," must act so designedly.

[4] *cp.* Pausan. i. 24, § 3.

[5] See the amazing story of an icy bathe prescribed so to Aristides (*Sacr. Serm.* ii. 529, Jebb ff.).

πήρωσιν, ἢ ἀποβολὴν ἢ ἄλλο τι τῶν τοιούτων.
καὶ γὰρ ἐκεῖ τὸ "συνέταξε" τοιοῦτόν τι σημαίνει·
ἔταξε τούτῳ τοῦτο ὡς κατάλληλον πρὸς ὑγίειαν·
καὶ ἐνταῦθα τὸ συμβαῖνον ἑκάστῳ τέτακταί πως
αὐτῷ κατάλληλον πρὸς τὴν εἱμαρμένην. οὕτως
γὰρ καὶ "συμβαίνειν" αὐτὰ ἡμῖν λέγομεν, ὡς καὶ
τοὺς τετραγώνους λίθους ἐν τοῖς τείχεσιν ἢ ἐν
ταῖς πυραμίσι, 'συμβαίνειν' οἱ τεχνῖται λέγουσι,
συναρμόζοντες ἀλλήλοις τῇ ποιᾷ συνθέσει. ὅλως
γὰρ ἁρμονία ἐστὶ μία, καὶ ὥσπερ ἐκ πάντων τῶν
σωμάτων ὁ κόσμος τοιοῦτον σῶμα συμπληροῦται,
οὕτως ἐκ πάντων τῶν αἰτίων ἡ εἱμαρμένη τοιαύτη
αἰτία συμπληροῦται. νοοῦσι δέ, ὃ λέγω, καὶ οἱ
τέλεον ἰδιῶται· φασὶ γάρ, "Τοῦτο ἔφερεν αὐτῷ."
οὐκοῦν τοῦτο τούτῳ ἐφέρετο, καὶ τοῦτο τούτῳ
συνετάττετο.   δεχώμεθα οὖν αὐτά, ὡς ἐκεῖνα,
ἃ ὁ Ἀσκληπιὸς συντάττει.   πολλὰ γοῦν καὶ ἐν
ἐκείνοις ἐστὶ τραχέα· ἀλλὰ ἀσπαζόμεθα τῇ
ἐλπίδι τῆς ὑγιείας.

2   Τοιοῦτόν τί σοι δοκείτω, ἄνυσις καὶ συντέλεια
τῶν τῇ κοινῇ φύσει δοκούντων, οἷον ἡ σὴ ὑγίεια·
καὶ οὕτως ἀσπάζου πᾶν τὸ γινόμενον, κἂν ἀπηνέστ-
ερον δοκῇ, διὰ τὸ ἐκεῖσε ἄγειν, ἐπὶ τὴν τοῦ κόσμου
ὑγίειαν, καὶ τὴν τοῦ Διὸς εὐοδίαν καὶ εὐπραγίαν.
οὐ γὰρ ἂν τοῦτό τινι ἔφερεν, εἰ μὴ τῷ ὅλῳ συν-
έφερεν.   οὐδὲ γὰρ ἡ τυχοῦσα φύσις φέρει τι, ὃ
μὴ τῷ διοικουμένῳ ὑπ' αὐτῆς κατάλληλόν ἐστιν.

3   Οὐκοῦν κατὰ δύο λόγους στέργειν χρὴ τὸ
συμβαῖνόν σοι· καθ' ἕνα μέν, ὅτι σοὶ ἐγίνετο,

maim or loss or what not of the same kind. For, in the former case, *prescribed* has some such meaning as this : He ordained this for so and so as conducive to his health ; while in the latter what befalls each man has been ordained in some way as conducive to his destiny. For we say that things *fall to* us, as the masons too say that the huge squared stones in walls and pyramids *fall into* their places, adjusting themselves harmoniously to one another in a sort of structural unity. For, in fine, there is one harmony of all things, and just as from all bodies the Universe is made up into such a body as it is, so from all causes is Destiny made up into such a Cause. This is recognized by the most unthinking, for they say : *Fate brought this on him.* So then this was brought on this man, and this prescribed for this man. Let us then accept our fate, as we accept the prescriptions of Aesculapius. And in fact in these, too, there are many "bitter pills," but we welcome them in hope of health.

Take much the same view of the accomplishment and consummation of what Nature approves as of thy health, and so welcome whatever happens, should it even be somewhat distasteful, because it contributes to the health of the Universe and the well-faring and well-doing of Zeus himself. For he had not brought this on a man, unless it had brought welfare to the Whole. For take any nature thou wilt, it never brings upon that which is under its control anything that does not conduce to its interests.

For two reasons then it behoves thee to acquiesce in what befalls : one, that it was for thee it took

καὶ σοὶ συνετάττετο, καὶ πρὸς σέ πως εἶχεν,
ἄνωθεν ἐκ τῶν πρεσβυτάτων αἰτίων συγ-
κλωθόμενον· καθ' ἕτερον δέ, ὅτι τῷ τὸ ὅλον
διοικοῦντι τῆς εὐοδίας καὶ τῆς συντελείας
καὶ νὴ Δία τῆς συμμονῆς αὐτῆς καὶ τὸ ἰδίᾳ
εἰς ἕκαστον ἧκον αἴτιόν ἐστιν. πηροῦται γὰρ
τὸ ὁλόκληρον, ἐὰν καὶ ὁτιοῦν διακόψῃς τῆς συν-
αφείας καὶ συνεχείας, ὥσπερ τῶν μορίων, οὕτω
δὴ καὶ τῶν αἰτίων. διακόπτεις δέ, ὅσον ἐπὶ σοί,
ὅταν δυσαρεστῇς, καὶ τρόπον τινὰ ἀναιρεῖς.[1]

θ'. Μὴ σικχαίνειν μηδὲ ἀπαυδᾶν μηδὲ ἀπο-
δυσπετεῖν, εἰ μὴ καταπυκνοῦταί σοι τὸ ἀπὸ
δογμάτων ὀρθῶν ἕκαστα πράσσειν· ἀλλὰ ἐκ-
κρουσθέντα πάλιν ἐπανιέναι καὶ ἀσμενίζειν, εἰ τὰ
πλείω ἀνθρωπικώτερα, καὶ φιλεῖν τοῦτο, ἐφ' ὃ
ἐπανέρχῃ· καὶ μὴ ὡς πρὸς παιδαγωγὸν τὴν
φιλοσοφίαν ἐπανιέναι· ἀλλ' ὡς οἱ ὀφθαλμιῶντες
πρὸς τὸ σπογγάριον καὶ τὸ ᾠόν, ὡς ἄλλος πρὸς
κατάπλασμα, ὡς πρὸς καταιόνησιν. οὕτως γὰρ
οὐδὲν ἐπιδείξῃ τὸ πειθαρχεῖν τῷ λόγῳ, ἀλλὰ
προσαναπαύσῃ αὐτῷ. μέμνησο δέ, ὅτι φιλοσοφία μόνα θέλει, ἃ ἡ φύσις σου θέλει· σὺ δὲ
ἄλλο ἤθελες οὐ κατὰ φύσιν. "Τί γὰρ τούτων
προσηνέστερον;" ἡ γὰρ ἡδονὴ οὐχὶ διὰ τοῦτο
σφάλλει; ἀλλὰ θέασαι, εἰ προσηνέστερον μεγαλο-
ψυχία, ἐλευθερία, ἁπλότης, εὐγνωμοσύνη,
ὁσιότης. αὐτῆς γὰρ φρονήσεως τί προσηνέστερ-

[1] ἀναιρῇς PA.

---

[1] Or, *from above.*   [2] cp. Sen. *Ep.* 74.

place, and was prescribed for thee, and had reference in some sort to thee, being a thread of destiny spun from the first [1] for thee from the most ancient causes; the other, that even what befalls each individual is the cause of the well-faring, of the consummation [2] and by heaven of the very permanence of that which controls the Universe. For the perfection of the Whole is impaired, if thou cuttest off ever so little of the coherence and continuance of the Causes no less than of the parts. And thou dost cut them off, as far as lies with thee, and bring them to an end, when thou murmurest.

9. Do not feel qualms [3] or despondency or discomfiture if thou dost not invariably succeed in acting from right principles; but when thou art foiled,[4] come back again to them, and rejoice if on the whole thy conduct is worthy of a man, and love the course to which thou returnest. Come not back to Philosophy as to a schoolmaster, but as the sore-eyed to their sponges and their white of egg,[5] as this patient to his plaster and that to his fomentations. Thus wilt thou rest satisfied with Reason, yet make no parade of obeying her. And forget not that Philosophy wishes but what thy nature wishes, whereas thy wish was for something else that accords not with Nature. *Yes, for it would have been the acme of delight.* Ah, is not that the very reason why pleasure trips us up? Nay, see if these be not more delightful still: high-mindedness, independence, simplicity, tenderness of heart,[6] sanctity of life. Why what is more delightful than wisdom herself,

---

[3] Lit. *be nauseated* (cp. viii. 24).   [4] v. 36.

[5] Shaks. *Lear* iii. 7. 109.

[6] Galen xii. 17 (Kühn) calls Marcus εὐγνώμων, μέτριος, ἥμερος, πρᾶος.

ον; ὅταν τὸ ἄπταιστον, καὶ εὔρουν ἐν πᾶσι τῆς
παρακολουθητικῆς καὶ ἐπιστημονικῆς δυνάμεως
ἐνθυμηθῇς.

ιʹ. Τὰ μὲν πράγματα ἐν τοιαύτῃ τρόπον τινὰ
ἐγκαλύψει ἐστίν, ὥστε φιλοσόφοις οὐκ ὀλίγοις
οὐδὲ τοῖς τυχοῦσιν ἔδοξε παντάπασιν ἀκατά-
ληπτα εἶναι· πλὴν αὐτοῖς γε τοῖς Στωικοῖς
δυσκατάληπτα δοκεῖ· καὶ πᾶσα ἡ ἡμετέρα συγκατάθεσις μεταπτωτή· ποῦ γὰρ ὁ ἀμετάπτωτος;
μέτιθι τοίνυν ἐπ' αὐτὰ τὰ ὑποκείμενα, ὡς ὀλιγό-
χρονα καὶ εὐτελῆ καὶ δυνάμενα ἐν κτήσει
κιναίδου ἢ πόρνης ἢ λῃστοῦ εἶναι. μετὰ τοῦτο
ἔπιθι ἐπὶ τὰ τῶν συμβιούντων ἤθη, ὧν μόλις
ἐστὶ καὶ τοῦ χαριεστάτου ἀνασχέσθαι, ἵνα μὴ
λέγω, ὅτι καὶ ἑαυτόν τις μόγις ὑπομένει.

2   Ἐν τοιούτῳ οὖν ζόφῳ καὶ ῥύπῳ καὶ τοσαύτῃ
ῥύσει τῆς τε οὐσίας καὶ τοῦ χρόνου, καὶ τῆς
κινήσεως καὶ τῶν κινουμένων, τί ποτ' ἐστὶ
τὸ ἐκτιμηθῆναι ἢ τὸ ὅλως σπουδασθῆναι
δυνάμενον, οὐδ' ἐπινοῶ. τοὐναντίον γὰρ δεῖ
παραμυθούμενον ἑαυτὸν περιμένειν τὴν φυσικὴν
λύσιν, καὶ μὴ ἀσχάλλειν τῇ διατριβῇ, ἀλλὰ
τούτοις μόνοις προσαναπαύεσθαι· ἑνὶ μὲν τῷ,
ὅτι οὐδὲν συμβήσεταί μοι, ὃ οὐχὶ κατὰ τὴν
τῶν ὅλων φύσιν ἐστίν· ἑτέρῳ δέ, ὅτι ἔξεστί μοι
μηδὲν πράσσειν παρὰ τὸν ἐμὸν θεὸν καὶ δαίμονα.
οὐδεὶς γὰρ ὁ ἀναγκάσων τοῦτον παραβῆναι.

ιαʹ. "Πρὸς τί ποτε ἄρα νῦν χρῶμαι τῇ ἐμαυτοῦ
ψυχῇ;" παρ' ἕκαστα τοῦτο ἐπανερωτᾶν ἑαυτόν,

---

[1] vi. 34. *cp.* Sen. *Ep.* 81.
[2] iv. 50; ix. 3. For a qualifying picture to this very
pessimistic view see vi. 48.

when thou thinkest how sure and smooth in all
its workings is the faculty of understanding and
knowledge?

10. Things are in a sense so wrapped up in mystery
that not a few philosophers, and they no ordinary
ones, have concluded that they are wholly beyond
our comprehension : nay, even the Stoics themselves
find them hard to comprehend. Indeed every
assent we give to the impressions of our senses is
liable to error, for where is the man who never errs?
Pass on then to the objective things themselves, how
transitory they are, how worthless, the property,
quite possibly, of a boy-minion, a harlot, or a brigand.[1]
After that turn to the characters of thine associates,
even the most refined of whom it is difficult to put up
with, let alone the fact that a man has enough to do
to endure himself.[2]

What then there can be amid such murk and
nastiness, and in so ceaseless an ebbing of substance
and of time, of movement and things moved, that
deserves to be greatly valued or to excite our ambition
in the least, I cannot even conceive. On the
contrary, a man should take heart of grace to await his
natural dissolution, and without any chafing at delay
comfort [3] himself with these twin thoughts alone : the
one, that nothing will befall me that is not in accord
with the Nature of the Universe ; the other, that it
is in my power to do nothing contrary to the God
and the 'genius' [4] within me. For no one can force
me to disobey that.

11. *To what use then am I putting my soul?* Never
fail to ask thyself this question and to cross-examine

[3] A favourite word. *cp.* **iv.** 31 ; **v.** 9 = " to take rest in."
[4] **ii.** 13 ; **iii.** 5 etc.

καὶ ἐξετάζειν, τί μοί ἐστι νῦν ἐν τούτῳ τῷ μορίῳ,
ὃ δὴ ἡγεμονικὸν καλοῦσι· καὶ τίνος ἄρα νῦν ἔχω
ψυχήν; μήτι παιδίου; μήτι μειρακίου; μήτι
γυναικαρίου; μήτι τυράννου; μήτι κτήνους;
μήτι θηρίου;

ιβʹ. Ὁποῖά τινά ἐστι τὰ τοῖς πολλοῖς
δοκοῦντα ἀγαθά, κἂν ἐντεῦθεν λάβοις. εἰ γάρ
τις ἐπινοήσειεν ὑπάρχοντά τινα ὡς ἀληθῶς
ἀγαθά, οἷον φρόνησιν, σωφροσύνην, δικαιοσύνην,
ἀνδρίαν, οὐκ ἂν ταῦτα προεπινοήσας ἔτι ἀκοῦσαι
δυνηθείη τὸ "ὑπὸ τῶν ἀγαθῶν."[1] οὐ γὰρ ἐφαρ-
μόσει. τὰ δέ γε τοῖς πολλοῖς φαινόμενα ἀγαθὰ
προεπινοήσας τις, ἐξακούσεται καὶ ῥᾳδίως δέξεται,
ὡς οἰκείως ἐπιλεγόμενον τὸ ὑπὸ τοῦ κωμικοῦ
εἰρημένον. οὕτως καὶ οἱ πολλοὶ φαντάζονται τὴν
διαφοράν. οὐ γὰρ ἂν τοῦτο μὲν οὖν[2] προσ-
έκοπτε καὶ ἀπηξιοῦτο· τὸ δὲ ἐπὶ τοῦ πλούτου
καὶ τῶν πρὸς τρυφὴν ἢ δόξαν εὐκληρημάτων
παρεδεχόμεθα ὡς ἱκνουμένως καὶ ἀστείως εἰρημένον. πρόιθι οὖν καὶ ἐρώτα, εἰ τιμητέον καὶ
ἀγαθὰ ὑποληπτέον τὰ τοιαῦτα, ὧν προεπινοη-
θέντων οἰκείως ἂν ἐπιφέροιτο τὸ τὸν κεκτημένον
αὐτὰ "ὑπὸ τῆς εὐπορίας οὐκ ἔχειν, ὅποι χέσῃ."

ιγʹ. Ἐξ αἰτιώδους καὶ ὑλικοῦ συνέστηκα·
οὐδέτερον δὲ τούτων εἰς τὸ μὴ ὂν φθαρήσεται,

---

[1] τὶ ὑπὸ τῷ ἀγαθῷ : τὸ Morus : τῶν ἀγαθῶν Nauck.
[2] οὖν Lofft for οὐ : Rendall keeps οὐ and translates
"would not fail to shock."

---

[1] sc. as in the case of things really good.
[2] From Menander Frag. 530 (Kock). The substitution of
πτύσῃ for χέσῃ would mitigate the coarseness of the phrase,

thyself thus : What relation have I to this part of
me which they call the ruling Reason? And whose
Soul anyhow have I got now? The Soul of a child?
Of a youth? Of a woman? Of a tyrant? Of a
domestic animal? Of a wild beast?

12. What are counted as good things in the estim-
ation of the many thou canst gather even from this.
For if a man fix his mind upon certain things as really
and unquestionably good, such as wisdom, temperance, justice, manliness, with this preconception in
his mind he could no longer bear to listen to the
poet's, *By reason of his wealth of goods*—; for it
would not apply. But, if a man first fix his mind
upon the things which appear good to the multitude, he will listen and readily accept as aptly
added the quotation from the Comic Poet. In
this way even the multitude have a perception of
the difference. For otherwise this jest would
not[1] offend and be repudiated, while we accept
it as appropriately and wittily said of wealth and
of the advantages which wait upon luxury and
popularity. Go on, then, and ask whether we should
prize and count as good those things, with which
first fixed in our mind we might germanely quote
of their possessor, that *for his very wealth of goods
he has no place to ease himself in.*[2]

13. I am made up of the Causal[3] and the Material,
and neither of these disappears into nothing, just

and we might then *cp.* Diog. Laert. *Diog.* 6 and *Arist.* 4,
passages in which we are told that the philosopher being taken
to a magnificent house where spitting was forbidden spat in
his host's face, explaining that he could find no other place.

[3] The Efficient, or Formal, or Formative principle, here
the Soul, but the Soul itself consists of a causal element
(νοῦς) and a material (τὸ πνευμάτιον).

ὥσπερ οὐδὲ ἐκ τοῦ μὴ ὄντος ὑπέστη. οὐκοῦν
καταταχθήσεται πᾶν μέρος ἐμὸν κατὰ μεταβολὴν
εἰς μέρος τι τοῦ κόσμου, καὶ πάλιν ἐκεῖνο εἰς
ἕτερον μέρος τι τοῦ κόσμου μεταβαλεῖ, καὶ ἤδη
εἰς ἄπειρον. κατὰ τοιαύτην δὲ μεταβολὴν κἀγὼ
ὑπέστην καὶ οἱ ἐμὲ γεννήσαντες, καὶ ἐπανιόντι
εἰς ἄλλο ἄπειρον. οὐδὲν γὰρ κωλύει οὕτως
φάναι, κἂν κατὰ περιόδους πεπερασμένας ὁ
κόσμος διοικῆται.

ιδ΄. Ὁ λόγος καὶ ἡ λογικὴ τέχνη δυνάμεις
εἰσὶν ἑαυταῖς ἀρκούμεναι καὶ τοῖς καθ᾽ ἑαυτὰς
ἔργοις· ὁρμῶνται μὲν οὖν ἀπὸ τῆς οἰκείας
ἀρχῆς, ὁδεύουσι δὲ εἰς τὸ προκείμενον τέλος·
καθ᾽ ὃ κατορθώσεις αἱ τοιαῦται πράξεις ὀνομάζ-
ονται τὴν ὀρθότητα τῆς ὁδοῦ σημαίνουσαι.

ιε΄. Οὐδὲν τούτων ῥητέον ἀνθρώπου, ἃ ἀνθρώπῳ, καθὸ ἄνθρωπός ἐστιν, οὐκ ἐπιβάλλει.
οὐκ ἔστιν ἀπαιτήματα ἀνθρώπου, οὐδὲ ἐπαγγέλλεται αὐτὰ ἡ τοῦ ἀνθρώπου φύσις, οὐδὲ τελειό-
τητές εἰσι τῆς τοῦ ἀνθρώπου φύσεως. οὐ τοίνυν
οὐδὲ τὸ τέλος ἐν αὐτοῖς ἐστι τῷ ἀνθρώπῳ κείμενον, οὐδέ γε τὸ συμπληρωτικὸν τοῦ τέλους, τὸ
ἀγαθόν. ἔτι εἴ τι τούτων ἦν ἐπιβάλλον τῷ
ἀνθρώπῳ, οὐκ ἂν τὸ ὑπερφρονεῖν αὐτῶν καὶ κατ-
εξανίστασθαι ἐπιβάλλον ἦν, οὐδὲ ἐπαινετὸς ἦν
ὁ ἀπροσδεῆ τούτων ἑαυτὸν παρεχόμενος· οὐδ᾽ ἂν
ὁ ἐλαττωτικὸς ἑαυτοῦ ἔν τινι τούτων ἀγαθὸς ἦν,
εἴπερ ταῦτα ἀγαθὰ ἦν. νῦν δέ, ὅσῳπερ πλείω
τις ἀφαιρῶν ἑαυτοῦ τούτων ἢ τοιούτων ἑτέρων
ἢ καὶ ἀφαιρούμενός τι τούτων ἀνέχηται, τοσῷδε
μᾶλλον ἀγαθός ἐστιν.

ιϛ΄. Οἷα ἂν πολλάκις φαντασθῇς, τοιαύτη σοι

as neither did it come into existence out of nothing. So shall my every part by change be told off[1] to form some part of the Universe, and that again be changed into another part of it, and so on to infinity. It was by such process of change that I too came into being and my parents, and so backwards into a second infinity. And the statement is quite legitimate, even if the Universe be arranged according to completed cycles.[2]

14. Reason and the art of reasoning are in themselves and in their own proper acts self-sufficing faculties. Starting from a principle peculiar to them, they journey on to the end set before them. Wherefore such actions are termed *right acts*, as signifying that they follow the right way.

15. Call none of those things a man's that do not fall to him as man. They cannot be claimed of a man; man's nature does not guarantee them; they are no consummations of that nature. Consequently neither is the end for which man lives placed in these things, nor yet that which is perfective of the end, namely The Good. Moreover, if any of these things did fall to a man, it would not fall to him to contemn them and set his face against them, nor would a man be commendable who shewed himself still lacking in these things, nor yet would he be a good man who came short of himself in any of them, if so be these things were good. But as it is, the more a man can cut himself free, or even be set free, from these and other such things with equanimity, by so much the more is he good.

16. The character of thy mind will be such as is

---

[1] viii. 25.   [2] v. 32; xi. 1. See Index III. ($\pi\epsilon\rho\iota o\delta o\iota$).

ἔσται ἡ διάνοια· βάπτεται γὰρ ὑπὸ τῶν φαντασιῶν ἡ ψυχή. βάπτε οὖν αὐτὴν τῇ συνεχείᾳ
τῶν τοιούτων φαντασιῶν· οἷον ὅτι, ὅπου ζῆν
ἐστιν, ἐκεῖ καὶ εὖ ζῆν· ἐν αὐλῇ δὲ ζῆν ἐστιν·
ἔστιν ἄρα καὶ εὖ ζῆν ἐν αὐλῇ. καὶ πάλιν ὅτι
οὗπερ ἕνεκεν ἕκαστον κατεσκεύασται, [πρὸς ὃ
δὲ κατεσκεύασται,¹] πρὸς τοῦτο φέρεται· πρὸς
ὃ φέρεται δέ, ἐν τούτῳ τὸ τέλος αὐτοῦ· ὅπου δὲ
τὸ τέλος, ἐκεῖ καὶ τὸ συμφέρον καὶ τἀγαθὸν
ἑκάστου· τὸ ἄρα ἀγαθὸν τοῦ λογικοῦ ζῴου
κοινωνία. ὅτι γὰρ πρὸς κοινωνίαν γεγόναμεν,
πάλαι δέδεικται. ἢ οὐκ ἦν ἐναργὲς ὅτι τὰ
χείρω τῶν κρειττόνων ἕνεκεν, τὰ δὲ κρείττω
ἀλλήλων; κρείττω δὲ τῶν μὲν ἀψύχων τὰ
ἔμψυχα, τῶν δὲ ἐμψύχων τὰ λογικά.

ιζ΄. Τὸ τὰ ἀδύνατα διώκειν μανικόν· ἀδύνατον δὲ τὸ τοὺς φαύλους μὴ τοιαῦτά τινα ποιεῖν.

ιη΄. Οὐδὲν οὐδενὶ συμβαίνει, ὃ οὐχὶ πέφυκε
φέρειν. ἄλλῳ τὰ αὐτὰ συμβαίνει καὶ ἤτοι
ἀγνοῶν, ὅτι συμβέβηκεν, ἢ ἐπιδεικνύμενος μεγαλο-
φροσύνην εὐσταθεῖ καὶ ἀκάκωτος μένει. δεινὸν
οὖν ἄγνοιαν καὶ ἀρέσκειαν ἰσχυροτέρας εἶναι
φρονήσεως.

ιθ΄. Τὰ πράγματα αὐτὰ οὐδ᾽ ὁπωστιοῦν
ψυχῆς ἅπτεται, οὐδὲ ἔχει εἴσοδον πρὸς ψυχήν,
οὐδὲ τρέψαι οὐδὲ κινῆσαι ψυχὴν δύναται· τρέπει

---

¹ The words in brackets omitted by A, which however adds
δὲ after τοῦτο. After the first κατεσκ. Gat. inserts πρὸς τοῦτο
κατεσκεύασται.

---

¹ vii. 3 ; Sen. *Ep.* 95.   ² viii. 9. *cp.* Sen. *Ep.* 28.
³ ii. 1 ; iii. 4, § 1.
⁴ ii. 1. But Marcus does not necessarily refer to his own
book.   ⁵ vii. 55 ; xi. 18, § 1 ; Sen. *Ep.* 65 *ad fin.*

BOOK V

the character of thy frequent thoughts,[1] for the soul takes its dye from the thoughts. Dye her then with a continuous succession of such thoughts as these : Where life is possible, there it is possible also to live well.—*But the life is life in a Court.*[2] Well, in a Court too it is possible to live well. And again : A thing is drawn towards that for the sake of which it has been made, and its end lies in that towards which it is drawn and, where its end lies, there lie also its interest and its good. The Good, then, for a rational creature is fellowship with others.[3] For it has been made clear long ago[4] that we were constituted for fellowship. Or was it not obvious that the lower were for the sake of the higher[5] and the higher for the sake of one another? And living things are higher than lifeless,[6] and those that have reason than those that have life only.

17. To crave impossibilities is lunacy ; but it is impossible for the wicked to act otherwise.[7]

18. Nothing befalls anyone that he is not fitted by nature to bear.[8] Others experience the same things as thou, but either from ignorance that anything has befallen them, or to manifest their greatness of mind, they stand firm and get no hurt. A strange thing indeed that ignorance and vanity should prove stronger than wisdom ![9]

19. Things of themselves cannot take the least hold of the Soul, nor have any access to her, nor deflect or move her ; but the Soul alone deflects

---

[6] cp. Chrysippus : τὸ ζῷον τοῦ μὴ ζῴου κρεῖττον.
[7] iv. 6 ; vii. 71 ; xi. 18 *ad fin* ; Sen *de Ira* ii. 31.
[8] viii. 46 ; x. 3 ; St. Paul, 1 Cor. x. 13
[9] cp. Sen. *Ep. 36 ad fin.* : *turpissimum si eam securitatem nobis ratio non praestat, ad quam stultitia perducit.*

δὲ καὶ κινεῖ αὐτὴ ἑαυτὴν μόνη, καὶ οἵων ἂν
κριμάτων καταξιώσῃ ἑαυτήν, τοιαῦτα ἑαυτῇ ποιεῖ
τὰ προσυφεστῶτα.

κ΄. Καθ᾽ ἕτερον μὲν λόγον ἡμῖν ἐστιν οἰκειό-
τατον ἄνθρωπος, καθ᾽ ὅσον εὖ ποιητέον αὐτοὺς[1]
καὶ ἀνεκτέον· καθ᾽ ὅσον δὲ ἐνίστανταί τινες εἰς
τὰ οἰκεῖα ἔργα, ἕν τι τῶν ἀδιαφόρων μοι γίνεται
ὁ ἄνθρωπος οὐχ ἧσσον ἢ ἥλιος ἢ ἄνεμος ἢ
θηρίον. ὑπὸ τούτων δὲ ἐνέργεια μέν τις ἐμποδ-
ισθείη ἄν· ὁρμῆς δὲ καὶ διαθέσεως οὐ γίνεται
ἐμπόδια διὰ τὴν ὑπεξαίρεσιν καὶ τὴν περι-
τροπήν. περιτρέπει γὰρ καὶ μεθίστησι πᾶν τὸ
τῆς ἐνεργείας κώλυμα ἡ διάνοια εἰς τὸ προ-
ηγούμενον· καὶ πρὸ ἔργου γίνεται τὸ τοῦ ἔργου
τούτου ἐφεκτικόν· καὶ πρὸ ὁδοῦ τὸ τῆς ὁδοῦ
ταύτης ἐνστατικόν.

κα΄. Τῶν ἐν τῷ κόσμῳ τὸ κράτιστον τίμα·
ἔστι δὲ τοῦτο τὸ πᾶσι χρώμενον καὶ πάντα
διέπον. ὁμοίως δὲ καὶ τῶν ἐν σοὶ τὸ κράτιστον
τίμα· ἔστι δὲ τοῦτο τὸ ἐκείνῳ ὁμογενές. καὶ γὰρ
ἐπὶ σοῦ τὸ τοῖς ἄλλοις χρώμενον τοῦτό ἐστι, καὶ
ὁ σὸς βίος ὑπὸ τούτου διοικεῖται.

κβ΄. Ὁ τῇ πόλει οὐκ ἔστι βλαβερόν, οὐδὲ
τὸν πολίτην βλάπτει. ἐπὶ πάσης τῆς τοῦ
βεβλάφθαι φαντασίας τοῦτον ἔπαγε τὸν κανόνα·
εἰ ἡ πόλις ὑπὸ τούτου μὴ βλάπτεται, οὐδὲ ἐγὼ
βέβλαμμαι· εἰ δὲ ἡ πόλις βλάπτεται, οὐκ
ὀργιστέον τῷ βλάπτοντι τὴν πόλιν. τί τὸ
παρορώμενον;[2]

---

[1] More correctly αὐτόν. [2] sc. ἀλλὰ δεικτέον before τί Gat.

---

[1] vi. 8.   [2] xi. 16.   [3] iv. 1 ; vi. 50.

and moves herself,[1] and whatever judgments she deems it right to form, in conformity with them she fashions for herself the things that submit themselves to her from without.[2]

20. In one respect a man is of very close concern to us, in so far as we must do him good and forbear; but in so far as any stand in the way of those acts which concern us closely, then man becomes for me as much one of things indifferent as the sun, as the wind, as a wild-beast. Though a man may in some sort fetter my activity, yet on my own initiative and mental attitude no fetters can be put because of the power they possess of conditional action[3] and of adaptation to circumstances. For everything that stands in the way of its activity is adapted and transmuted by the mind into a furtherance of it,[4] and that which is a check on this action is converted into a help to it, and that which is a hindrance in our path goes but to make it easier.

21. Prize the most excellent thing in the Universe; and this is that which utilizes all things and controls all things. Prize in like manner the most excellent thing in thyself;[5] and this is that which is akin to the other. For this, which utilizes all else is in thee too, and by it thy life is governed.

22. That which is not hurtful to the community cannot hurt the individual.[6] Test every case of apparent hurt by this rule: if the community be not hurt by this, neither am I hurt; but if the community be hurt, there is no need to be angry with him that hath done the hurt,[7] but to enquire, In what hath he seen amiss?[8]

---

[4] iv. 1; x. 31 *ad fin.*   [5] vi. 16 *ad fin.*
[6] v. 35; vi. 54.   [7] v. **35.**   [8] xi. 13.

κγ΄. Πολλάκις ἐνθυμοῦ τὸ τάχος τῆς παραφορᾶς καὶ ὑπεξαγωγῆς τῶν ὄντων καὶ γινομένων. ἥ τε γὰρ οὐσία οἷον ποταμὸς ἐν διηνεκεῖ ῥύσει· καὶ αἱ ἐνέργειαι ἐν συνεχέσι μεταβολαῖς, καὶ τὰ αἴτια ἐν μυρίαις τροπαῖς, καὶ σχεδὸν οὐδὲν ἑστώς, καὶ † τὸ πάρεγγυς τόδε ἄπειρον τοῦ[1] παρῳχηκότος † καὶ μέλλοντος ἀχανές, ᾧ πάντα ἐναφανίζεται. πῶς οὖν οὐ μωρὸς ὁ ἐν τούτοις φυσώμενος ἢ σπώμενος ἢ σχετλιάζων † ὡς ἔν τινι χρόνῳ καὶ ἐπὶ μακρὸν <ἂν> ἐνοχλήσαντι; †[2]

κδ΄. Μέμνησο τῆς συμπάσης οὐσίας, ἧς ὀλίγιστον μετέχεις· καὶ τοῦ σύμπαντος αἰῶνος, οὗ βραχὺ καὶ ἀκαριαῖόν σοι διάστημα ἀφώρισται· καὶ τῆς εἱμαρμένης, ἧς πόστον εἶ μέρος;

κε΄. Ἄλλος ἁμαρτάνει τι εἰς ἐμέ; ὄψεται· ἰδίαν ἔχει διάθεσιν, ἰδίαν ἐνέργειαν. ἐγὼ νῦν ἔχω, ὅ με θέλει νῦν ἔχειν ἡ κοινὴ φύσις, καὶ πράσσω, ὅ με νῦν πράσσειν θέλει ἡ ἐμὴ φύσις.

κϛ΄. Τὸ ἡγεμονικὸν καὶ κυριεῦον τῆς ψυχῆς σου μέρος ἄτρεπτον ἔστω ὑπὸ τῆς ἐν τῇ σαρκὶ λείας ἢ τραχείας κινήσεως· καὶ μὴ συγκρινέσθω, ἀλλὰ περιγραφέτω ἑαυτὸ καὶ περιοριζέτω τὰς πείσεις ἐκείνας ἐν τοῖς μορίοις. ὅταν δὲ ἀναδιδῶνται κατὰ τὴν ἑτέραν †[3] συμπάθειαν εἰς τὴν διάνοιαν, ὡς ἐν σώματι ἡνωμένῳ, τότε πρὸς μὲν τὴν αἴσθησιν φυσικὴν οὖσαν οὐ πειρατέον ἀντιβαίνειν, τὴν δὲ ὑπόληψιν τὴν ὡς περὶ ἀγαθοῦ ἢ κακοῦ μὴ προστιθέτω τὸ ἡγεμονικὸν ἐξ ἑαυτοῦ.

[1] τοῦ τε PA.

[2] μικρὸν P: ἐνοχλήσοντι Lofft: ἐνοχλῆσάν τι Fournier. The future sense seems required.

[3] ἑτέρων <ἑτέροις> Schenkl: μερῶν Rend. (cp. Sext. Emp. adv. Math. ix. 80): ἡμετέραν Rich.

BOOK V

23. Think often on the swiftness with which the things that exist and that are coming into existence are swept past us and carried out of sight. For all substance[1] is as a river in ceaseless flow,[2] its activities ever changing and its causes subject to countless variations, and scarcely anything stable; and ever beside us is this infinity of the past and yawning abyss of the future, wherein all things are disappearing.[3] Is he not senseless who in such an environment puffs himself up, or is distracted, or frets as over a trouble lasting and far-reaching?

24. Keep in memory the universal Substance, of which thou art a tiny part; and universal Time, of which a brief, nay an almost momentary, span has been allotted thee; and Destiny, in which how fractional thy share?[4]

25. Another does me some wrong? He shall see to it.[5] His disposition is his own, his activities are his own. What the universal Nature wills me to have now, that I now have, and what my nature wills me now to do, that I do.

26. Let the ruling and master Reason of thy soul be proof against any motions in the flesh smooth or rough. Let it not mingle itself with them, but isolate and restrict those tendencies to their true spheres. But when in virtue of that other sympathetic connection these tendencies grow up into the mind as is to be expected in a single organism, then must thou not go about to resist the sensation, natural as it is, but see that thy ruling Reason adds no opinion of its own as to whether such is good or bad.

[1] Or, *Being.*   [2] iv. 43; vii. 19.   [3] xii. 32.
[4] Epict. i. 12, 26.   [5] St. Matt. xii. 4, 24.

κζ'. Συζῆν θεοῖς. συζῇ δὲ θεοῖς ὁ συνεχῶς δεικνὺς αὐτοῖς τὴν ἑαυτοῦ ψυχὴν ἀρεσκομένην μὲν τοῖς ἀπονεμομένοις, ποιοῦσαν δέ, ὅσα βούλεται ὁ δαίμων, ὃν ἑκάστῳ προστάτην καὶ ἡγεμόνα ὁ Ζεὺς ἔδωκεν, ἀπόσπασμα ἑαυτοῦ. οὗτος δέ ἐστιν ὁ ἑκάστου νοῦς καὶ λόγος.

κη'. Τῷ γράσωνι μήτι ὀργίζῃ; μήτι τῷ ὀζο-στόμῳ ὀργίζῃ; τί σοι ποιήσει; τοιοῦτον στόμα ἔχει, τοιαύτας μάλας ἔχει· ἀνάγκη τοιαύτην ἀπο-φορὰν ἀπὸ τοιούτων γίνεσθαι. "'Αλλ' ὁ ἄνθρωπος λόγον ἔχει, φησί,[1] καὶ δύναται συννοεῖν ἐφ-ιστάνων, τί πλημμελεῖ." εὖ σοι γένοιτο· τοιγαρ-οῦν καὶ σὺ λόγον ἔχεις· κίνησον λογικῇ διαθέσει λογικὴν διάθεσιν, δεῖξον, ὑπόμνησον. εἰ γὰρ ἐπαίει, θεραπεύσεις καὶ οὐ χρεία ὀργῆς.

Οὔτε τραγῳδὸς οὔτε πόρνη.

κθ'. Ὡς ἐξελθὼν ζῆν διανοῇ, οὕτως ἐνταῦθα ζῆν ἔξεστιν. ἐὰν δὲ μὴ ἐπιτρέπωσι, τότε καὶ τοῦ ζῆν ἔξιθι· οὕτως μέντοι, ὡς μηδὲν κακὸν πάσχων. "Καπνός, καὶ ἀπέρχομαι." τί αὐτὸ πρᾶγμα δοκεῖς; μέχρι δέ με τοιοῦτον οὐδὲν ἐξάγει, μένω ἐλεύθερος, καὶ οὐδείς με κωλύσει ποιεῖν ἃ θέλω· θέλω δὲ[2] κατὰ φύσιν τοῦ λογικοῦ καὶ κοινωνικοῦ ζῴου.

λ'. Ὁ τοῦ ὅλου νοῦς κοινωνικός. πεποίηκε γοῦν τὰ χείρω τῶν κρειττόνων ἕνεκεν· καὶ τὰ κρείττω ἀλλήλοις συνήρμοσεν. ὁρᾷς, πῶς ὑπέταξε, συνέταξε, καὶ τὸ κατ' ἀξίαν ἀπένειμεν ἑκάστοις

---

[1] φύσει AD.   [2] <τὰ>.

[1] ii. 1, 4; xii. 26, 30.
[2] Epict. i. 14, § 12 ἐπίτροπον ἑκάστῳ παρέστησε (sc. Zeus) τὸν ἑκάστου δαίμονα καὶ παρέδωκε φυλάσσειν αὐτὸν αὐτῷ.

BOOK V

27. Walk with the Gods! And he does walk with the Gods, who lets them see his soul invariably satisfied with its lot and carrying out the will of that 'genius,' a particle [1] of himself, which Zeus has given to every man as his captain and guide [2]—and this is none other than each man's intelligence and reason.

28. If a man's armpits are unpleasant, art thou angry with him? If he has foul breath? What would be the use? The man has such a mouth, he has such armpits. Some such effluvium was bound to come from such a source. *But the man has sense,* quotha! *With a little attention he could see wherein he offends.* I congratulate thee! Well, thou too hast sense. By a rational attitude, then, in thyself evoke a rational attitude in him,[3] enlighten him, admonish him. If he listen, thou shalt cure him,[4] and have no need of anger.

Neither tragedian nor harlot.

29. Thou canst live on earth as thou dost purpose to live when departed. But if men will not have it so, then is it time for thee even to go out of life,[5] yet not as one who is treated ill. *'Tis smoky and I go away.*[6] Why think it a great matter? But while no such cause drives me forth, I remain a free man, and none shall prevent me from doing what I will, and I will what is in accordance with the nature of a rational and social creature.

30. The intelligence of the Universe is social. It hath at any rate made the lower things for the sake of the higher, and it adapted the higher [7] to one another. Thou seest how it hath subordinated, coordinated, and given each its due lot

---

[3] x. 4 ; Epict. ii. 8, § 11.   [4] *cp.* St. Matt. xviii. 15.
[5] See on iii. 1. *cp.* viii. 47.
[6] Epict. i. 25, § 18 ; iv. 10, § 27. Plut. *On Tranquill.* § 27 *ad finem.*   [7] v. 16.

καὶ τὰ κρατιστεύοντα εἰς ὁμόνοιαν ἀλλήλων
συνήγαγεν.

λαʹ. Πῶς προσενήνεξαι μέχρι νῦν θεοῖς, γον-
εῦσιν, ἀδελφοῖς, γυναικί, τέκνοις, διδασκάλοις,
τροφεῦσι, φίλοις, οἰκείοις, οἰκέταις; εἰ πρὸς
πάντας σοι μέχρι νῦν ἐστι τὸ

" Μήτε τινὰ ῥέξαι ἐξαίσιον, μήτε <τι> εἰπεῖν." [1]

ἀναμιμνήσκου δὲ καὶ δι' οἵων διελήλυθας καὶ
οἷα ἤρκεσας ὑπομεῖναι. καὶ ὅτι πλήρης ἤδη σοι
ἡ ἱστορία τοῦ βίου καὶ τελευτᾷ [2] ἡ λειτουργία·
καὶ πόσα ὦπται καλά, καὶ πόσων μὲν ἡδονῶν
καὶ πόνων ὑπερεῖδες, πόσα δὲ ἔνδοξα παρεῖδες,
εἰς ὅσους δὲ ἀγνώμονας εὐγνώμων ἐγένου.

λβʹ. Διὰ τί συγχέουσιν ἄτεχνοι καὶ ἀμαθεῖς
ψυχαὶ ἔντεχνον καὶ ἐπιστήμονα; τίς οὖν ψυχὴ
ἔντεχνος καὶ ἐπιστήμων; ἡ εἰδυῖα ἀρχὴν καὶ
τέλος, καὶ τὸν δι' ὅλης τῆς οὐσίας διήκοντα λόγον
καὶ διὰ παντὸς τοῦ αἰῶνος κατὰ περιόδους τεταγ-
μένας οἰκονομοῦντα τὸ πᾶν.

λγʹ. Ὅσον οὐδέπω σποδὸς ἢ σκελετός, καὶ
ἤτοι ὄνομα ἢ οὐδὲ ὄνομα· τὸ δὲ ὄνομα ψόφος καὶ
ἀπήχημα. τὰ δὲ ἐν τῷ βίῳ πολυτίμητα κενὰ καὶ
σαπρὰ καὶ μικρὰ καὶ κυνίδια διαδακνόμενα καὶ
παιδία φιλόνεικα, γελῶντα, εἶτα εὐθὺς κλαίοντα.
πίστις δὲ καὶ αἰδὼς καὶ δίκη καὶ ἀλήθεια

" Πρὸς Ὄλυμπον ἀπὸ χθονὸς εὐρυοδείης."

---

[1] Marcus quotes this line in a form that does not scan.
cp. vii. 39 if the text is correct.
[2] τελευταία AD : τελεα P : τελευτᾷ Schenkl.

---

[1] Hom. *Od.* iv. 690.
[2] x. 36. There is no Pharisaism here, as some have most un-
warrantably asserted.   [3] *cp.* St. Paul, 1 Cor. i. 27 (*Auth. Vers.*).

BOOK V

and brought the more excellent things into mutual accord.

31. How hast thou borne thyself heretofore towards Gods, parents, brethen, wife, children, teachers, tutors, friends, relations, household? Canst thou say truly of them all to this day,

Doing to no man wrong, nor speaking aught that is evil?[1]

And call to mind all that thou hast passed through, all thou hast found strength to bear; that the story of thy life is now full-told and thy service is ending; and how many beautiful sights thou hast seen, how many pleasures and pains thou hast disregarded, forgone what ambitions, and repaid with kindness how much unkindness.[2]

32. Why do unskilled and ignorant souls confound[3] him who has skill and has knowledge? What soul, then, has skill and knowledge? Even that which knoweth beginning and end, and the reason that informs all Substance, and governs the Whole from ordered cycle to cycle[4] through all eternity.

33. But a little while and thou shalt be burnt ashes or a few dry bones, and possibly a name, possibly not a name even.[5] And a name is but sound and a far off echo. And all that we prize so highly in our lives is empty and corrupt and paltry, and we but as puppies snapping at each other, as quarrelsome children now laughing and anon in tears. But faith and modesty and justice and truth

Up from the wide-wayed Earth have winged their flight to Olympus.[6]

---

[4] v. 13; x. 7.   [5] viii. 25; xii. 27.
[6] Hesiod, *Op.* 197. *cp.* Eur. *Med.* 439 and Lucian, *Nigr.* 16, who, speaking of Rome, says much the same of αἰδώς and ἀρετή and δικαιοσύνη. See also Dio 71, 24, § 2.

τί οὖν ἔτι τὸ ἐνταῦθα κατέχον; εἴγε τὰ μὲν
αἰσθητὰ εὐμετάβλητα καὶ οὐχ ἑστῶτα· τὰ δὲ
αἰσθητήρια ἀμυδρὰ καὶ εὐπαρατύπωτα· αὐτὸ δὲ
τὸ ψυχάριον ἀναθυμίασις ἀφ' αἵματος· τὸ δὲ
εὐδοκιμεῖν παρὰ τοιούτοις κενόν. τί οὖν; περιμενεῖς[1] ἵλεως τὴν εἴτε σβέσιν εἴτε μετάστασιν.
ἕως δὲ ἐκείνης ὁ καιρὸς ἐφίσταται, τί ἀρκεῖ; τί δ'
ἄλλο ἢ θεοὺς μὲν σέβειν καὶ εὐφημεῖν, ἀνθρώπους
δὲ εὖ ποιεῖν, καὶ "ἀνέχεσθαι" αὐτῶν καὶ "ἀπ-
έχεσθαι·" ὅσα δὲ ἐντὸς ὅρων τοῦ κρεᾳδίου καὶ
τοῦ πνευματίου, ταῦτα μεμνῆσθαι μήτε σὰ ὄντα
μήτε ἐπὶ σοί.

λδ'. Δύνασαι ἀεὶ εὐροεῖν, εἴγε καὶ εὐοδεῖν,[2]
εἴγε καὶ ὁδῷ ὑπολαμβάνειν καὶ πράσσειν. δύο
ταῦτα κοινὰ τῇ τε τοῦ θεοῦ καὶ τῇ τοῦ ἀνθρώπου
καὶ παντὸς λογικοῦ ζώου ψυχῇ· τὸ μὴ ἐμποδίζεσθαι ὑπ' ἄλλου· καὶ τὸ ἐν τῇ δικαικῇ διαθέσει
καὶ πράξει ἔχειν τὸ ἀγαθόν, καὶ ἐνταῦθα τὴν
ὄρεξιν ἀπολήγειν.

λε'. Εἰ μήτε κακία ἐστὶ τοῦτο ἐμὴ μήτε
ἐνέργεια κατὰ κακίαν ἐμὴν μήτε τὸ κοινὸν βλάπτεται, τί ὑπὲρ αὐτοῦ διαφέρομαι; τίς δὲ βλάβη
τοῦ κοινοῦ;

λϛ'. Μὴ ὁλοσχερῶς τῇ φαντασίᾳ συναρπάζ-
εσθαι· ἀλλὰ βοηθεῖν μὲν κατὰ δύναμιν καὶ κατ'
ἀξίαν· κἂν εἰς τὰ μέσα ἐλαττῶνται,[3] μὴ μέντοι
βλάβην αὐτὸ φαντάζεσθαι, κακὸν γὰρ ἔθος.
ἀλλ' ὡς ὁ γέρων ἀπελθὼν τὸν τοῦ θρεπτοῦ

---

[1] περιμένεις PA : περιμενεῖς Wilam.
[2] Lofft and Stich. for εὔδειν A, ὁδεύειν P.
[3] ἐλαττῶνται has no subject : ἐλαττοῖ τι Cor.

---

[1] vi. 15. *cp.* Tzetz. *Chil.* vii. 803 ; viii. 223.

BOOK V

What then keeps thee here?—if indeed sensible objects are ever changing and unstable, and our faculties are so feeble and so easily misled; and the poor soul itself is an exhalation from blood [1]; and to be well-thought of in such a world mere vanity. What then remains? To wait with a good grace for the end, whether it be extinction or translation.[2] But till our time for that be come, what sufficeth? What but to reverence the Gods and to praise them, to do good unto men and to *bear with them and forbear*,[3] but, for all else that comes within the compass of this poor flesh and breath, to remember that it is not thine nor under thy control?

34. Thou hast it in thy power that the current of thy life be ever fair, if also 'tis thine to make fair way, if also in ordered way to think and act. The Soul of God and the souls of men and of every rational creature have these two characteristics in common: to suffer no let or hindrance from another, and to find their good in a condition and practice of justice, and to confine their propension to this.

35. If this be no vice of mine nor the outcome of any vice of mine, and if the common interest does not suffer, why concern myself about it? And how can the common interest suffer?[4]

36. Be not carried incontinently away by sense-impressions, but rally to the fight as thou canst and as is due. If there be failure [5] in things indifferent, yet think not there is any great harm done; for that is an evil habit. But as the greybeard (in the play)

[2] Marcus never seems to have made up his mind which it was to be. See iv. 21 ; viii. 25 ; xi. 3.
[3] These two constituted for Epictetus the whole "Law and the Prophets"; see Aulus Gellius xvii. 19=Bear ill and abstain from pleasures.   [4] v. 22 ; vi. 54.   [5] v. 36.

ῥόμβον ἀπῄτει μεμνημένος, ὅτι ῥόμβος, οὕτως οὖν
καὶ ὧδε· †ἐπεί τοι γίνῃ καλῶν[1] ἐπὶ τῶν ἐμβόλων,†
ἄνθρωπε, ἐπελάθου, τί ταῦτα ἦν; " Ναί· ἀλλὰ
τούτοις περισπούδαστα." διὰ τοῦτ' οὖν καὶ σὺ
μωρὸς γένῃ;

2 Ἐγενόμην ποτέ, ὁπουδήποτε καταλειφθείς,
εὔμοιρος ἄνθρωπος· τὸ δὲ "εὔμοιρος," ἀγαθὴν
μοῖραν σεαυτῷ ἀπονείμας· ἀγαθαὶ δὲ μοῖραι
ἀγαθαὶ τροπαὶ ψυχῆς, ἀγαθαὶ ὁρμαί, ἀγαθαὶ
πράξεις.

[1] ἐπεὶ τί γίνεται καλὸν Xyl.: ἐγκαλῶν Cor.   ἔπειτα τί might
be read.

taking his leave reclaimed his foster-child's top, not forgetting that it was but a top, so do thou here also.[1] Since indeed thou art found haranguing on the hustings, O Man, hast thou forgotten what this really means? *Aye, but people will have it.* Must thou too be a fool in consequence?

Time was that wheresoever forsaken[2] I was a man well-portioned; but that *man well-portioned* is he that hath given himself a good portion; and good portions are good tendencies of the soul, good impulses, good actions.

[1] It is not known what Marcus alludes to. The following words are unintelligible.
[2] Or *overtaken* (καταληφθείς).

ΒΙΒΛΙΟΝ ϛ΄

α΄. Ἡ τῶν ὅλων οὐσία εὐπειθὴς καὶ εὐτρεπής· ὁ δὲ ταύτην διοικῶν λόγος οὐδεμίαν ἐν ἑαυτῷ αἰτίαν ἔχει τοῦ κακοποιεῖν· κακίαν γὰρ οὐκ ἔχει οὐδέ τι κακῶς ποιεῖ οὐδὲ βλάπτεταί τι ὑπ' ἐκείνου. πάντα δὲ κατ' ἐκεῖνον γίνεται καὶ περαίνεται.

β΄. Μὴ διαφέρου, πότερον ῥιγῶν ἢ θαλπόμενος τὸ πρέπον ποιεῖς, καὶ πότερον νυστάζων ἢ ἱκανῶς ὕπνου ἔχων, καὶ πότερον κακῶς ἀκούων ἢ εὐφημούμενος, καὶ πότερον ἀποθνήσκων ἢ πράττων τι ἀλλοῖον. μία γὰρ τῶν βιωτικῶν πράξεων καὶ αὕτη ἐστί, καθ' ἣν ἀποθνήσκομεν· ἀρκεῖ οὖν καὶ ἐπὶ ταύτης 'τὸ παρὸν εὖ θέσθαι.'

γ΄. Ἔσω βλέπε· μηδενὸς πράγματος μήτε ἡ ἰδία ποιότης μήτε ἡ ἀξία παρατρεχέτω σε.

δ΄. Πάντα τὰ ὑποκείμενα τάχιστα μεταβαλεῖ, καὶ ἤτοι ἐκθυμιαθήσεται, εἴπερ ἥνωται ἡ οὐσία, ἢ σκεδασθήσεται.

ε΄. Ὁ διοικῶν λόγος οἶδε, πῶς διακείμενος, καὶ τί ποιεῖ καὶ ἐπὶ τίνος ὕλης.

---

[1] Not so all Stoics ; cp. Sen. de Prov. 5: non potest artifex mutare materiem.

[2] vi. 22.

BOOK VI

1. THE Universal Substance is docile [1] and **ductile**; and the Reason that controls it has no motive in itself to do wrong. For it hath no wrongness and doeth no wrong, nor is anything harmed by it. But all things come into being and fulfil their purpose as it directs.

2. Make no difference in doing thy duty [2] whether thou art shivering or warm, drowsy [3] or sleep-satisfied, defamed or extolled, dying or anything else. For the act of dying too is one of the acts of life. [4] So it is enough in this also to *get the work in hand done well.* [5]

3. Look within. Let not the special quality [6] or worth of anything escape thee.

4. All objective things will anon be changed and either etherialized into the Universal Substance, if that indeed be one, or dispersed abroad. [7]

5. The controlling Reason knows its own bent and its work and the medium it works in.

---

[3] Galen (xiv. 3, Kühn) says of Marcus that, owing to the theriac which he prescribed him, συνέβαινεν αὐτῷ νυστάζειν καρωδῶς ἐν ταῖς ὁσημέραις πράξεσιν.

[4] cp. Sen. *Ep.* 77 *ad fin.*: *Unum ex vitae officiis, mori.*

[5] A saying of the "Wise Men." See Suidas. cp. Luc. *Necy.* 21. It was a trait of Marcus, Dio 71. 26, § 4.

[6] = that which makes a thing what it is.

[7] viii. 25 *ad fin.*; x. 7, § 2.

ϛ'. Αριστος τρόπος τοῦ ἀμύνεσθαι τὸ μὴ ἐξομοιοῦσθαι.

ζ'. Ἑνὶ τέρπου καὶ προσαναπαύου, τῷ ἀπὸ πράξεως κοινωνικῆς μεταβαίνειν ἐπὶ πρᾶξιν κοινωνικὴν σὺν μνήμῃ θεοῦ.

η'. Τὸ ἡγεμονικόν ἐστι τὸ ἑαυτὸ ἐγεῖρον καὶ τρέπον καὶ ποιοῦν μὲν ἑαυτό, οἷον ἂν καὶ θέλῃ, ποιοῦν δὲ ἑαυτῷ φαίνεσθαι πᾶν τὸ συμβαῖνον, οἷον αὐτὸ θέλει.

θ'. Κατὰ τὴν τῶν ὅλων φύσιν ἕκαστα περαίνεται, οὐ γὰρ κατ' ἄλλην γέ τινα φύσιν ἤτοι ἔξωθεν περιέχουσαν ἢ ἐμπεριεχομένην ἔνδον ἢ ἔξω ἀπηρτημένην.

ι'. Ἤτοι κυκεὼν καὶ ἀντεμπλοκὴ καὶ σκεδασμός· ἢ ἕνωσις καὶ τάξις καὶ πρόνοια. εἰ μὲν οὖν τὰ πρότερα, τί καὶ ἐπιθυμῶ εἰκαίῳ συγκρίματι καὶ φυρμῷ τοιούτῳ ἐνδιατρίβειν; τί δέ μοι καὶ μέλει ἄλλου τινὸς ἢ τοῦ ὅπως ποτὲ "αἶα γίνεσθαι"; τί δὲ καὶ ταράσσομαι; ἥξει γὰρ ἐπ' ἐμὲ ὁ σκεδασμός, ὅ τι ἂν ποιῶ. εἰ δὲ θάτερά ἐστι, σέβω καὶ εὐσταθῶ καὶ θαρρῶ τῷ διοικοῦντι.

ια'. Ὅταν ἀναγκασθῇς ὑπὸ τῶν περιεστηκότων οἱονεὶ διαταραχθῆναι, ταχέως ἐπάνιθι εἰς ἑαυτὸν καὶ μὴ ὑπὲρ τὰ ἀναγκαῖα ἐξίστασο τοῦ ῥυθμοῦ· ἔσῃ γὰρ ἐγκρατέστερος τῆς ἁρμονίας τῷ συνεχῶς εἰς αὐτὴν ἐπανέρχεσθαι.

ιβ'. Εἰ μητρυιάν τε ἅμα εἶχες καὶ μητέρα,

---

¹ cp. Epict. *Frag.* 130. So Diogenes being asked "How shall I avenge myself of mine enemy?" said, "By behaving like a gentleman," Plut. *de Leg. Poet.* 5.

BOOK VI

6. The best way of avenging thyself is not to do likewise.[1]

7. Delight in this one thing and take thy rest therein—from social act to go on to social act, keeping all thy thoughts on God.

8. The ruling Reason it is that can arouse and deflect itself, make itself whatever it will,[2] and invest everything that befalls with such a semblance as it wills.

9. In accordance with the Nature of the Universe is accomplished each several thing. For surely this cannot be in accordance with any other nature, that either envelops it from without, or is enveloped by it within, or exists in external detachment outside it.

10. Either a medley and a tangled web[3] and a dispersion abroad, or a unity and a plan and a Providence. If the former, why should I even wish to abide in such a random welter and chaos? Why care for anything else than to *turn again to the dust* at last.[4] Why be disquieted? For, do what I will, the dispersion must overtake me. But if the latter, I bow in reverence, my feet are on the rock, and I put my trust in the Power that rules.

11. When forced, as it seems, by thine environment to be utterly disquieted, return with all speed into thy self, staying in discord no longer than thou must. By constant recurrence to the harmony,[5] thou wilt gain more command over it.

12. Hadst thou at once a stepmother and a mother

---

[2] v. 19.   [3] iv. 27 ; vii. 50.
[4] Hom. *Il.* vii. 99 ; *cp.* below, vii. 50. Tobit iii. 6.
[5] *cp.* Dio Chrys. xxxii. 676 R. ἔξω τῆς ἁρμονίας τῆς κατὰ φύσιν.

ἐκείνην τ' ἂν ἐθεράπευες, καὶ ὅμως ἡ ἐπάνοδός
σοι πρὸς τὴν μητέρα συνεχὴς ἐγίνετο. τοῦτό
σοι νῦν ἐστιν ἡ αὐλὴ καὶ ἡ φιλοσοφία· ὧδε
πολλάκις ἐπάνιθι καὶ προσαναπαύου ταύτῃ, δι'
ἣν καὶ τὰ ἐκεῖ σοι ἀνεκτὰ φαίνεται καὶ σὺ ἐν
αὐτοῖς ἀνεκτός.

ιγ'. Οἷον δὴ τὸ φαντασίαν λαμβάνειν ἐπὶ
τῶν ὄψων καὶ τῶν τοιούτων ἐδωδίμων, ὅτι νεκρὸς
οὗτος ἰχθύος, οὗτος δὲ νεκρὸς ὄρνιθος ἢ χοίρου·
καὶ πάλιν ὅτι ὁ Φάλερνος χυλάριόν ἐστι
σταφυλίου, καὶ ἡ περιπόρφυρος τριχία προ-
βατίου αἱματίῳ κόγχης δεδευμένα· καὶ ἐπὶ τῶν
κατὰ τὴν συνουσίαν ἐντερίου παράτριψις καὶ
μετά τινος σπασμοῦ μυξαρίου ἔκκρισις· οἷαι δὴ
αὗταί εἰσιν αἱ φαντασίαι καθικνούμεναι αὐτῶν
τῶν πραγμάτων καὶ διεξιοῦσαι δι' αὐτῶν, ὥστε
ὁρᾶν, οἷά τινά ποτ' ἐστίν· οὕτως δεῖ παρ' ὅλον
τὸν βίον ποιεῖν καί, ὅπου λίαν ἀξιόπιστα τὰ
πράγματα φαντάζεται, ἀπογυμνοῦν αὐτὰ καὶ
τὴν εὐτέλειαν αὐτῶν καθορᾶν καὶ τὴν ἱστορίαν,†
ἐφ' ᾗ σεμνύνεται, περιαιρεῖν. δεινὸς γὰρ ὁ τῦφος
παραλογιστὴς καί, ὅτε δοκεῖς μάλιστα περὶ τὰ
σπουδαῖα καταγίνεσθαι, τότε μάλιστα κατα-
γοητεύει. ὅρα γοῦν, ὁ Κράτης τί περὶ αὐτοῦ
τοῦ Ξενοκράτους λέγει.

ιδ'. Τὰ πλεῖστα, ὧν ἡ πληθὺς θαυμάζει, εἰς
γενικώτατα ἀνάγεται, τὰ ὑπὸ ἕξεως ἢ φύσεως
συνεχόμενα, λίθους, ξύλα, συκᾶς, ἀμπέλους,

---

[1] Sen. *Ep.* 103.
[2] For life in kings' courts see Lucian, *Calumn.* 10, and
Icaro-Men. 16.   [3] *cp.* Lucian. *Dem.* § 41.
[4] *cp.* Tzetz. *Chil.* vii. 801. He reads νευρίου for ἐντερίου.

thou wouldst pay due service to the former, and yet
thy constant recourse would be to thy mother. So
hast thou now the court and philosophy for stepmother and mother. Cease not then to come to the
latter and take thy rest in her,[1] whereby shall both
thy court life seem more tolerable [2] to thee, and thou
to thy court life.

13. As in the case of meat and similar eatables
the thought strikes us, this is the dead body of a fish,
this of a fowl or pig; and again that this Falernian is
merely the juice of a grape-cluster, and this purple-
edged robe is nought but sheep's wool [3] steeped
in the blood of a shell-fish; or, of sexual inter-
course, that it is merely internal attrition and the
spasmodic excretion of mucus [4]—such, I say, as are
these impressions that get to grips with the actual
things and enter into the heart of them, so as to see
them as they really are, thus should it be thy life
through, and where things look to be above measure
convincing, laying them quite bare, behold their
paltriness and strip off their conventional prestige.
For conceit is a past master in fallacies and, when
thou flatterest thyself most that thou art engaged
in worthy tasks, then art thou most of all deluded
by it. At any rate, see what Crates has to say about
none other than Xenocrates.[5]

14. Objects admired by the common sort come
chiefly under things of the most general kind, which
are held together by physical coherence,[6] such as
stones and wood, or by a natural unity, such as figs,

---

[5] It is not known what Marcus here refers to.
[6] cp. Sext. Emp. adv. Math. viii. 2; ix. 81, τὰ μὲν ὑπὸ ψιλῆς
ἕξεως συνέχεται, τὰ δὲ ὑπὸ φύσεως, τὰ δὲ ὑπὸ ψυχῆς· καὶ ἕξεως μὲν
ὡς λίθοι καὶ ξύλα, φύσεως δὲ καθάπερ τὰ φυτά, ψυχῆς δὲ τὰ ζῷα.

ἐλαίας· τὰ δὲ ὑπὸ τῶν ὀλίγῳ μετριωτέρων [1] εἰς
τὰ ὑπὸ ψυχῆς, οἷον ποίμνας, ἀγέλας· τὰ δὲ ὑπὸ
τῶν ἔτι χαριεστέρων εἰς τὰ ὑπὸ λογικῆς ψυχῆς,
οὐ μέντοι καθολικῆς, ἀλλὰ καθὸ τεχνικὴ ἢ
ἄλλως πως ἐντρεχής, ἢ κατὰ ψιλὸν τὸ πλῆθος
ἀνδραπόδων κεκτῆσθαι. ὁ δὲ ψυχὴν λογικὴν
καθολικὴν καὶ πολιτικὴν τιμῶν οὐδὲν ἔτι τῶν
ἄλλων ἐπιστρέφεται, πρὸ ἁπάντων δὲ τὴν ἑαυτοῦ
ψυχὴν λογικῶς καὶ κοινωνικῶς ἔχουσαν καὶ
κινουμένην διασώζει καὶ τῷ ὁμογενεῖ εἰς τοῦτο
συνεργεῖ.

ιε΄. Τὰ μὲν σπεύδει γίνεσθαι, τὰ δὲ σπεύδει
γεγονέναι, καὶ τοῦ γινομένου δὲ ἤδη τι ἀπέσβη·
ῥύσεις καὶ ἀλλοιώσεις ἀνανεοῦσι τὸν κόσμον
διηνεκῶς, ὥσπερ τὸν ἄπειρον αἰῶνα ἡ τοῦ χρόνου
ἀδιάλειπτος φορὰ νέον ἀεὶ παρέχεται. ἐν δὴ
τούτῳ τῷ ποταμῷ τί ἄν τις τούτων τῶν παρα-
θεόντων ἐκτιμήσειεν, ἐφ᾽ οὗ στῆναι οὐκ ἔξεστιν·
ὥσπερ εἴ τίς τι τῶν παραπετομένων στρουθαρίων
φιλεῖν ἄρχοιτο· τὸ δ᾽ ἤδη ἐξ ὀφθαλμῶν ἀπελήλ-
υθεν. τοιοῦτον δή τι καὶ αὐτὴ ἡ ζωὴ ἑκάστου,
οἷον ἡ ἀφ᾽ αἵματος ἀναθυμίασις καὶ ἡ ἐκ τοῦ
ἀέρος ἀνάπνευσις. ὁποῖον γάρ ἐστι τὸ ἅπαξ
ἑλκύσαι τὸν ἀέρα καὶ ἀποδοῦναι, ὅπερ παρ᾽
ἕκαστον ποιοῦμεν, τοιοῦτόν ἐστι καὶ τὸ τὴν πᾶσαν
ἀναπνευστικὴν δύναμιν, ἣν χθὲς καὶ πρώην ἀπο-
τεχθεὶς ἐκτήσω, ἀποδοῦναι ἐκεῖ, ὅθεν τὸ πρῶτον
ἔσπασας.

[1] <θαυμαζόμενα> Mor.

vines, olives; and those which are admired by
persons of a somewhat higher capacity may be
classed as things which are held together by a
conscious life, such as flocks and herds; and those
which are admired by persons still more refined, as
things held together by a rational soul; I do not
mean rational as part of the Universal Reason, but in
the sense of master of an art or expert in some other
way, or merely in so far as to own a host of slaves.
But he that prizes a soul which is rational, universal,
and civic, no longer turns after anything else, but
rather than everything besides keeps his own soul,
in itself and in its activity, rational and social, and
to this end works conjointly with all that is akin to
him.

15. Some things are hastening to be, others to be
no more, while of those that haste into being some
part is already extinct. Fluxes and changes per-
petually renew the world, just as the unbroken
march of time makes ever new the infinity of ages.
In this river of change,[1] which of the things which
swirl past him, whereon no firm foothold is possible,
should a man prize so highly? As well fall in love
with a sparrow[2] that flits past and in a moment is gone
from our eyes. In fact a man's life itself is but as an
exhalation from blood[3] and an inhalation from the
air. For just as it is to draw in the air once into
our lungs and give it back again, as we do every
moment, so is it to give back thither, whence thou
didst draw it first, thy faculty of breathing which
thou didst receive at thy birth yesterday or the day
before.

---

[1] iv. 43; vii. 19.
[2] *cp.* the parable of the sparrow in Bede ii. 13.   [3] v. 33.

ιϛ'. Οὔτε τὸ διαπνεῖσθαι ὡς τὰ φυτὰ τίμιον,
οὔτε τὸ ἀναπνεῖν ὡς τὰ βοσκήματα καὶ τὰ θηρία,
οὔτε τὸ τυποῦσθαι κατὰ φαντασίαν, οὔτε τὸ
νευροσπαστεῖσθαι καθ' ὁρμήν, οὔτε τὸ συναγελάζ-
εσθαι, οὔτε τὸ τρέφεσθαι· τοῦτο γὰρ ὅμοιον
τῷ ἀποκρίνειν τὰ περιττώματα τῆς τροφῆς.

2 Τί οὖν τίμιον; τὸ κροτεῖσθαι; οὐχί. οὐκοῦν οὐδὲ
τὸ ὑπὸ γλωσσῶν κροτεῖσθαι· αἱ γὰρ παρὰ τῶν
πολλῶν εὐφημίαι κρότος γλωσσῶν. ἀφῆκας οὖν
καὶ τὸ δοξάριον· τί καταλείπεται τίμιον; δοκῶ
μὲν τὸ κατὰ τὴν ἰδίαν κατασκευὴν κινεῖσθαι
καὶ ἴσχεσθαι, ἐφ' ὃ καὶ αἱ ἐπιμέλειαι ἄγουσι
καὶ αἱ τέχναι. ἥ τε γὰρ τέχνη πᾶσα τοῦτο
στοχάζεται, ἵνα τὸ κατασκευασθὲν ἐπιτηδείως
ἔχῃ πρὸς τὸ ἔργον πρὸς ὃ κατεσκεύασται· ὅ
τε φυτουργὸς ὁ ἐπιμελούμενος τῆς ἀμπέλου καὶ
ὁ πωλοδάμνης καὶ ὁ τοῦ κυνὸς ἐπιμελούμενος,
τοῦτο ζητεῖ. αἱ δὲ παιδαγωγίαι, αἱ δὲ δι-
δασκαλίαι ἐπὶ τὶ[1] σπεύδουσιν. ὧδε οὖν τὸ
τίμιον.

3 Καὶ τοῦτο μὲν ἂν εὖ ἔχῃ, οὐδὲν τῶν ἄλλων
περιποιήσεις σεαυτῷ. οὐ παύσῃ καὶ ἄλλα
πολλὰ τιμῶν; οὔτ' οὖν ἐλεύθερος ἔσῃ οὔτε
αὐτάρκης οὔτε ἀπαθής. ἀνάγκη γὰρ φθονεῖν,
ζηλοτυπεῖν, ὑφορᾶσθαι τοὺς ἀφελέσθαι ἐκεῖνα
δυναμένους, ἐπιβουλεύειν τοῖς ἔχουσι τὸ τιμώ-
μενον ὑπὸ σοῦ· ὅλως πεφύρθαι ἀνάγκη τὸν
ἐκείνων τινὸς ἐνδεῆ· προσέτι δὲ πολλὰ καὶ τοῖς

[1] τὶ P: τί AD: perhaps τουτί,

138

BOOK VI

16. Neither is it an inner respiration,[1] such as that of plants, that we should prize, nor the breathing which we have in common with cattle and wild animals, nor the impressions we receive through our senses, nor that we are pulled by our impulses like marionettes,[2] nor our gregarious instincts, nor our need of nutriment; for that is on a par with the rejection of the waste products of our food.

What then is to be prized? The clapping of hands? No. Then not the clapping of tongues either. For the acclamations of the multitude are but a clapping of tongues. So overboard goes that poor thing Fame also. What is left to be prized? This methinks: to limit our action or inaction to the needs of our own constitution, an end that all occupations and arts set before themselves. For the aim of every art is that the thing constituted should be adapted to the work for which it has been constituted. It is so with the vine-dresser who looks after the vines, the colt-trainer, and the keeper of the kennel. And this is the end which the care of children and the methods of teaching have in view. There then is the thing to be prized!

This once fairly made thine own, thou wilt not seek to gain for thyself any of the other things as well. Wilt thou not cease prizing many other things also? Then thou wilt neither be free nor sufficient unto thyself nor unmoved by passion. For thou must needs be full of envy and jealousy, be suspicious of those that can rob thee of such things, and scheme against those who possess what thou prizest. In fine, a man who needs any of those things cannot but be in complete turmoil, and in many cases find

[1] iii. 1.   [2] ii. 2 etc.

θεοῖς μέμφεσθαι· ἡ δὲ τῆς ἰδίας διανοίας αἰδὼς
καὶ τιμὴ σεαυτῷ τε ἀρεστόν σε ποιήσει καὶ τοῖς
ἀνθρώποις εὐάρμοστον καὶ τοῖς θεοῖς σύμφωνον,
τουτέστιν ἐπαινοῦντα, ὅσα ἐκεῖνοι διανέμουσι καὶ
διατετάχασιν.

ιζ'. Ἄνω, κάτω, κύκλῳ φοραὶ τῶν στοιχείων.
ἡ δὲ τῆς ἀρετῆς κίνησις ἐν οὐδεμιᾷ τούτων, ἀλλὰ
θειότερόν τι καὶ ὁδῷ δυσεπινοήτῳ προϊοῦσα
εὐοδεῖ.

ιη'. Οἷόν ἐστιν, ὃ ποιοῦσι. τοὺς μὲν ἐπὶ τοῦ
αὐτοῦ χρόνου καὶ μεθ' ἑαυτῶν ζῶντας ἀνθρώπους
εὐφημεῖν οὐ θέλουσιν· αὐτοὶ δὲ ὑπὸ τῶν μετα-
γενεστέρων εὐφημηθῆναι, οὓς οὔτε εἶδόν ποτε
οὔτε ὄψονται, περὶ πολλοῦ ποιοῦνται. τοῦτο
δὲ ἐγγύς ἐστι τῷ λυπηθῆναι ἄν, ὅτι οὐχὶ καὶ
οἱ προγενέστεροι περὶ σοῦ λόγους εὐφήμους
ἐποιοῦντο.

ιθ'. Μή, εἴ τι αὐτῷ σοὶ δυσκαταπόνητον,
τοῦτο ἀνθρώπῳ ἀδύνατον ὑπολαμβάνειν· ἀλλ' εἴ
τι ἀνθρώπῳ δυνατὸν καὶ οἰκεῖον, τοῦτο καὶ
σεαυτῷ ἐφικτὸν νόμιζε.

κ'. Ἐν τοῖς γυμνασίοις καὶ ὄνυξι κατέδρυψέ
τις καὶ τῇ κεφαλῇ ἐρραγεὶς πληγὴν ἐποίησεν·
ἀλλ' οὔτε ἐπισημαινόμεθα οὔτε προσκόπτομεν
οὔτε ὑφορώμεθα ὕστερον ὡς ἐπίβουλον· καίτοι
φυλαττόμεθα, οὐ μέντοι ὡς ἐχθρὸν οὐδὲ μεθ'
ὑποψίας, ἀλλ' ἐκκλίσεως εὐμενοῦς. τοιοῦτόν τι
γενέσθω καὶ ἐν τοῖς λοιποῖς μέρεσι τοῦ βίου·
πολλὰ παρενθυμώμεθα τῶν οἷον προσγυμναζο-
μένων. ἔξεστι γάρ, ὡς ἔφην, ἐκκλίνειν, καὶ
μηδὲν ὑποπτεύειν μηδὲ ἀπέχθεσθαι.

κα'. Εἴ τίς με ἐλέγξαι καὶ παραστῆσαί μοι,

fault even with the Gods.[1]   But by reverencing and
prizing thine own mind, thou shalt make thyself
pleasing in thine own sight, in accord with mankind,
and in harmony with the gods, that is, grateful to
them for all that they dispense and have ordained.

17. Up, down,[2] round and round sweep the
elements along.   But the motion of virtue is in none
of these ways.   It is something more divine, and
going forward on a mysterious path fares well upon
its way.[3]

18. What a way to act!   Men are chary of com-
mending their contemporaries and associates, while
they themselves set great store by the commendation
of posterity, whom they have never seen or shall see.
But this is next door to taking it amiss that thy
predecessors also did not commend thee.

19. Because thou findest a thing difficult for thyself
to accomplish do not conceive it to be impracticable
for others; but whatever is possible for a man and in
keeping with his nature consider also attainable by
thyself.

20. Suppose that a competitor in the ring has
gashed us with his nails and butted us violently with
his head, we do not protest or take it amiss or
suspect our opponent in future of foul play.   Still
we do keep an eye on him, not indeed as an enemy,
or from suspicion of him, but with good-humoured
avoidance.   Act much in the same way in all the
other parts of life.   Let us make many allowances
for our fellow-athletes as it were.   Avoidance is
always possible, as I have said, without suspicion
or hatred.

21. If any one can prove and bring home to me

[1] vi. 41.   [2] vi. 17; iv. 46; ix. 28.   [3] vii. 53.

ὅτι οὐκ ὀρθῶς ὑπολαμβάνω ἢ πράσσω, δύναται,
χαίρων μεταθήσομαι· ζητῶ γὰρ τὴν ἀλήθειαν,
ὑφ' ἧς οὐδεὶς πώποτε ἐβλάβη. βλάπτεται δὲ ὁ
ἐπιμένων ἐπὶ τῆς ἑαυτοῦ ἀπάτης καὶ ἀγνοίας.

κβ'. Ἐγὼ τὸ ἐμαυτοῦ καθῆκον ποιῶ· τὰ ἄλλα
με οὐ περισπᾷ· ἤτοι γὰρ ἄψυχα ἢ ἄλογα, ἢ
πεπλανημένα καὶ τὴν ὁδὸν ἀγνοοῦντα.

κγ'. Τοῖς μὲν ἀλόγοις ζῴοις καὶ καθόλου
πράγμασι καὶ ὑποκειμένοις, ὡς λόγον ἔχων λόγον
μὴ ἔχουσι, χρῶ μεγαλοφρόνως καὶ ἐλευθέρως·
τοῖς δὲ ἀνθρώποις, ὡς λόγον ἔχουσι, χρῶ
κοινωνικῶς. ἐφ' ἅπασι δὲ θεοὺς ἐπικαλοῦ· καὶ
μὴ διαφέρου πρὸς τὸ πόσῳ χρόνῳ ταῦτα πράξεις·
ἀρκοῦσι γὰρ καὶ τρεῖς ὧραι τοιαῦται.

κδ'. Ἀλέξανδρος ὁ Μακεδὼν καὶ ὁ ὀρεωκόμος
αὐτοῦ ἀποθανόντες εἰς ταὐτὸ κατέστησαν· ἤτοι
γὰρ <ἂν>ελήφθησαν εἰς τοὺς αὐτοὺς τοῦ κόσμου
σπερματικοὺς λόγους ἢ διεσκεδάσθησαν ὁμοίως
εἰς τὰς ἀτόμους.

κε'. Ἐνθυμήθητι, πόσα κατὰ τὸν αὐτὸν
ἀκαριαῖον χρόνον ἐν ἑκάστῳ ἡμῶν ἅμα γίνεται
σωματικὰ ὁμοῦ καὶ ψυχικά· καὶ οὕτως οὐ θαυμάσεις, εἰ πολὺ πλείω, μᾶλλον δὲ πάντα τὰ
γινόμενα[1] ἐν τῷ ἑνί τε καὶ σύμπαντι, ὃ δὴ κόσμον
ὀνομάζομεν, ἅμα ἐνυφίσταται.

κϛ'. Ἐάν τίς σοι προβάλῃ, "πῶς γράφεται τὸ
Ἀντωνίνου ὄνομα," μήτι κατεντεινόμενος προοίσῃ
ἕκαστον τῶν στοιχείων; τί οὖν, ἐὰν ὀργίζωνται,

---

[1] γινόμενα <καὶ γεννητὰ> Schenkl.

---

[1] iv. 12; vi. 30, § 2; viii. 16.   [2] iv. 46.
[3] Usually singular in the Greek. See iv. 14. 21; ix. 1.

142

that a conception or act of mine is wrong, I will amend¹ it, and be thankful. For I seek the truth, whereby no one was ever harmed. But he is harmed who persists in his own self-deception and ignorance.

22. I do my own duty; other things do not distract me. For they are either inanimate or irrational, or such as have gone astray and know not the road.²

23. Conduct thyself with magnanimity and freedom towards irrational creatures and, generally, towards circumstances and objective things, for thou hast reason and they have none. But men have reason, therefore treat them as fellow creatures. And in all cases call upon the Gods, and do not concern thyself with the question, *How long shall I do this?* Three hours are enough so spent.

24. Death reduced to the same condition Alexander the Macedonian and his muleteer, for either they were taken back into the same Seminal Reason³ of the Universe or scattered alike into the atoms.⁴

25. Bear in mind how many things happen to each one of us with respect to our bodies as well as our souls in the same momentary space of time, so wilt thou cease to wonder that many more things—not to say all the things that come into existence in that One and Whole which in fact we call the Universe—subsist in it at one time.

26. If one enquire of thee, *How is the name Antoninus written?* wilt thou with vehemence enunciate each constituent letter? What then? If thy listeners lose their temper, wilt thou lose

---

⁴ Marcus puts the two alternatives (Stoic and Epicurean), though he does not himself admit the second.

μήτι ἀντοργιῇ; οὐκ ἐξαριθμήσῃ πρᾴως προϊὼν
ἕκαστον τῶν γραμμάτων; οὕτως οὖν καὶ ἐνθάδε
μέμνησο, ὅτι πᾶν καθῆκον ἐξ ἀριθμῶν τινῶν
συμπληροῦται. τούτους δεῖ τηροῦντα καὶ μὴ
θορυβούμενον μηδὲ τοῖς δυσχεραίνουσιν ἀντι-
δυσχεραίνοντα περαίνειν ὁδῷ τὸ προκείμενον.

κζ΄. Πῶς ὠμόν ἐστι, μὴ ἐπιτρέπειν τοῖς
ἀνθρώποις ὁρμᾶν ἐπὶ τὰ φαινόμενα αὐτοῖς οἰκεῖα
καὶ συμφέροντα· καίτοι τρόπον τινὰ οὐ συγ-
χωρεῖς αὐτοῖς τοῦτο ποιεῖν, ὅταν ἀγανακτῇς,
ὅτι ἁμαρτάνουσι. φέρονται γὰρ πάντως ὡς
ἐπὶ οἰκεῖα καὶ συμφέροντα αὐτοῖς. "᾿Αλλ᾽ οὐκ
ἔχει οὕτως." οὐκοῦν δίδασκε καὶ δείκνυε μὴ
ἀγανακτῶν.

κη΄. Θάνατος ἀνάπαυλα αἰσθητικῆς ἀντι-
τυπίας καὶ ὁρμητικῆς νευροσπαστίας καὶ δια-
νοητικῆς διεξόδου καὶ τῆς πρὸς τὴν σάρκα
λειτουργίας.

κθ΄. Αἰσχρόν ἐστιν, ἐν ᾧ βίῳ τὸ σῶμά σοι
μὴ ἀπαυδᾷ, ἐν τούτῳ τὴν ψυχὴν προαπαυδᾶν.

λ΄. Ὅρα, μὴ 'ἀποκαισαρωθῇς,' μὴ βαφῇς·
γίνεται γάρ. τήρησον οὖν σεαυτὸν ἁπλοῦν,
ἀγαθόν, ἀκέραιον, σεμνόν, ἄκομψον, τοῦ δικαίου
φίλον, θεοσεβῆ, εὐμενῆ, φιλόστοργον, ἐρρωμένον
πρὸς τὰ πρέποντα ἔργα. ἀγώνισαι, ἵνα τοιοῦτος
συμμείνῃς, οἷόν σε ἠθέλησε ποιῆσαι φιλοσοφία.
αἰδοῦ θεούς, σῷζε ἀνθρώπους. βραχὺς ὁ βίος·

---

[1] iii. 1.   [2] v. 28. The Christians are meant.
[3] viii. 36. So Marcus himself in a letter to Fronto (*ad Caes.*

thine ? Wouldst thou not go on gently to enumerate
each letter ? So recollect that in life too every
duty is the sum of separate items.[1] Of these thou
must take heed, and carry through methodically
what is set before thee, in no wise troubled or shewing
counter-irritation against those who are irritated with
thee.

27. How intolerant it is not to permit men to
cherish an impulse towards what is in their eyes
congenial and advantageous ! Yet in a sense thou
withholdest from them the right to do this, when
thou resentest their wrong-doing. For they are
undoubtedly drawn to what they deem congenial
and advantageous. *But they are mistaken.* Well,
then, teach and enlighten them without any resentment.[2]

28. Death is a release from the impressions of
sense, and from impulses that make us their puppets,
from the vagaries of the mind, and the hard service
of the flesh.

29. It is a disgrace for the soul to be the first to
succumb in that life in which the body does not
succumb.[3]

30. See thou be not *Caesarified,* nor take that
dye,[4] for there is the possibility. So keep thyself a
simple and good man, uncorrupt, dignified, plain, a
friend of justice, god-fearing, gracious, affectionate,
manful in doing thy duty. Strive to be always such
as Philosophy minded to make thee. Revere the
Gods, save mankind. Life is short. This only is the

---

iv. 8) : *Turpe fuerit diutius vitam corporis quam animi
studium ad reciperandam sanitatem posse durare.*

[4] There was also a "philosophic dye"; see Lucian, *Bis
Accus.* 8.

εἰς καρπὸς τῆς ἐπιγείου ζωῆς, διάθεσις ὁσία καὶ
πράξεις κοινωνικαί.

2   Πάντα ὡς ᾿Αντωνίνου μαθητής· τὸ ὑπὲρ τῶν
κατὰ λόγον πρασσομένων εὔτονον ἐκείνου, καὶ
τὸ ὁμαλὲς πανταχοῦ, καὶ τὸ ὅσιον, καὶ τὸ
εὔδιον¹ τοῦ προσώπου, καὶ τὸ μειλίχιον, καὶ τὸ
ἀκενόδοξον, καὶ τὸ περὶ τὴν κατάληψιν τῶν
πραγμάτων φιλότιμον· καὶ ὡς ἐκεῖνος οὐκ ἄν τι
ὅλως παρῆκε, μὴ πρότερον εὖ μάλα κατιδὼν καὶ
σαφῶς νοήσας· καὶ ὡς ἔφερεν ἐκεῖνος τοὺς ἀδίκως
αὐτὸν μεμφομένους μὴ ἀντιμεμφόμενος· καὶ ὡς
ἐπ᾿ οὐδὲν ἔσπευδεν· καὶ ὡς διαβολὰς οὐκ ἐδέχετο·
καὶ ὡς ἀκριβὴς ἦν ἐξεταστὴς ἠθῶν καὶ πράξεων·
καὶ οὐκ ὀνειδιστής, οὐ ψοφοδεής, οὐχ ὑπόπτης,
οὐ σοφιστής· καὶ ὡς ὀλίγοις ἀρκούμενος, οἷον
οἰκήσει, στρωμνῇ, ἐσθῆτι, τροφῇ, ὑπηρεσίᾳ·
καὶ ὡς φιλόπονος καὶ μακρόθυμος· καὶ οἷος
μέν<ειν> ἐν τῷ <αὐτῷ>² μέχρι ἑσπέρας διὰ
τὴν λιτὴν δίαιταν μηδὲ τοῦ ἀποκρίνειν τὰ περιττώματα παρὰ τὴν συνήθη ὥραν χρῄζων· καὶ τὸ
βέβαιον καὶ ὅμοιον ἐν ταῖς φιλίαις αὐτοῦ· καὶ
τὸ ἀνέχεσθαι <τῶν> ἀντιβαινόντων παρρησιαστ-
ικῶς ταῖς γνώμαις αὐτοῦ, καὶ χαίρειν, εἴ τις
δεικνύοι κρεῖττον· καὶ ὡς θεοσεβὴς χωρὶς δεισι-
δαιμονίας· ἵν᾿ οὕτως εὐσυνειδήτῳ σοι ἐπιστῇ ἡ
τελευταία ὥρα, ὡς ἐκείνῳ.

λα΄.   ᾿Ανάνηφε καὶ ἀνακαλοῦ σεαυτόν, καὶ
ἐξυπνισθεὶς πάλιν καὶ ἐννοήσας, ὅτι ὄνειροί σοι

---

¹ εὔδιον Xyl.: εὐόδιον PA.   ² μὲν ἐν τῷ PA : as in text Cas.

harvest of earthly existence, a righteous disposition and social acts.

Do all things as a disciple of Antoninus.[1] Think of his constancy in every act rationally undertaken, his invariable equability, his piety, his serenity of countenance, his sweetness of disposition, his contempt for the bubble of fame, and his zeal for getting a true grasp of affairs. How he would never on any account dismiss a thing until he had first thoroughly scrutinized and clearly conceived it; how he put up with those who found fault with him unfairly, finding no fault with them in return; how he was never in a hurry; how he gave no ear to slander,[2] and with what nicety he tested dispositions and acts; was no imputer of blame, and no craven, not a suspicious man, nor a sophist, what little sufficed him whether for lodging or bed, dress, food, or attendance; how fond he was of work, and how long-suffering; how he would remain the whole day at the same occupation,[3] owing to his spare diet[4] not even requiring to relieve nature except at the customary time; and how loyal he was to his friends and always the same; and his forbearance towards those who openly opposed his views, and his pleasure when anyone pointed out something better[5]; and how god-fearing he was and yet not given to superstition. Take heed to all this, that thy last hour come upon thee as much at peace with thy conscience as he was.

31. Be sober once more and call back thy senses, and being roused again from sleep and realizing that they were but dreams that beset thee, now awake

---

[1] cp. i. 16 throughout.   [2] i. 5.
[3] Or, *in the same place.*   [4] cp. i. 3.   [5] vi. 21; viii. 16.

ἠνώχλουν, πάλιν ἐγρηγορὼς βλέπε ταῦτα, ὡς
ἐκεῖνα ἔβλεπες.

λβ΄. Ἐκ σωματίου εἰμὶ καὶ ψυχῆς. τῷ μὲν
οὖν σωματίῳ πάντα ἀδιάφορα· οὐδὲ γὰρ δύναται
διαφέρεσθαι. τῇ δὲ διανοίᾳ ἀδιάφορα, ὅσα μή
ἐστιν αὐτῆς ἐνεργήματα· ὅσα δέ γε αὐτῆς ἐστιν
ἐνεργήματα, ταῦτα πάντα ἐπ᾽ αὐτῇ ἐστιν. καὶ
τούτων μέντοι περὶ μόνον τὸ παρὸν πραγματ-
εύεται· τὰ γὰρ μέλλοντα καὶ παρῳχηκότα
ἐνεργήματα αὐτῆς καὶ αὐτὰ ἤδη ἀδιάφορα.

λγ΄. Οὐκ ἔστιν ὁ πόνος τῇ χειρὶ οὐδὲ τῷ
ποδὶ παρὰ φύσιν, μέχρις ἂν ποιῇ ὁ ποῦς τὰ τοῦ
ποδὸς καὶ ἡ χεὶρ τὰ τῆς χειρός. οὕτως οὖν οὐδὲ
ἀνθρώπῳ, ὡς ἀνθρώπῳ, παρὰ φύσιν ἐστὶν ὁ
πόνος, μέχρις ἂν ποιῇ τὰ τοῦ ἀνθρώπου. εἰ δὲ
παρὰ φύσιν αὐτῷ οὐκ ἔστιν, οὐδὲ κακόν ἐστιν
αὐτῷ.

λδ΄. Ἡλίκας ἡδονὰς ἤσθησαν λησταί, κίναιδοι,
πατραλοῖαι, τύραννοι.

λε΄. Οὐχ ὁρᾷς, πῶς οἱ βάναυσοι τεχνῖται
ἁρμόζονται μὲν μέχρι τινὸς πρὸς τοὺς ἰδιώτας,
οὐδὲν ἧσσον μέντοι ἀντέχονται τοῦ λόγου τῆς
τέχνης, καὶ τούτου ἀποστῆναι οὐχ ὑπομένουσιν;
οὐ δεινόν, εἰ ὁ ἀρχιτέκτων καὶ ὁ ἰατρὸς μᾶλλον
αἰδέσονται τὸν τῆς ἰδίας τέχνης λόγον ἢ ὁ
ἄνθρωπος τὸν ἑαυτοῦ, ὃς αὐτῷ κοινός ἐστι πρὸς
τοὺς θεούς;

λϛ΄. Ἡ Ἀσία, ἡ Εὐρώπη γωνίαι τοῦ κόσμου·
πᾶν πέλαγος σταγὼν τοῦ κόσμου· Ἄθως βωλά-
ριον τοῦ κόσμου· πᾶν τὸ ἐνεστὼς τοῦ χρόνου
στιγμὴ τοῦ αἰῶνος. πάντα μικρά, εὔτρεπτα,
ἐναφανιζόμενα.

again, look at these realities as thou didst at those thy dreams.

32. I consist of body and soul.[1] To the body indeed all things are indifferent, for it cannot concern itself with them. But to the mind[2] only those things are indifferent which are not its own activities ; and all those things that are its own activities are in its own power. Howbeit, of these it is only concerned with the present ; for as to its activities in the past and the future, these two rank at once among things indifferent.

33. For hand or foot to feel pain is no violation of nature, so long as the foot does its own appointed work, and the hand its own. Similarly pain for a man, as man, is no unnatural thing so long as he does a man's appointed work. But, if not unnatural, then is it not an evil either.

34. The pleasures of the brigand, the pathic, the parricide, the tyrant[3]—just think what they are !

35. Dost thou not see how the mechanic craftsman, though to some extent willing to humour the non-expert, yet holds fast none the less to the principles of his handicraft, and cannot endure to depart from them. Is it not strange that the architect and the physician should hold the rationale of their respective arts in higher reverence than a man his own reason, which he has in common with the Gods?

36. Asia, Europe, corners of the Universe : the whole Ocean a drop in the Universe : Athos but a little clod therein : all the present a point in Eternity :—everything on a tiny scale, so easily changed, so quickly vanished.

---

[1] v. 13. [2] Here διάνοια = ψυχή. [3] v. 10.

2   Πάντα ἐκεῖθεν ἔρχεται, ἀπ᾽ ἐκείνου τοῦ κοινοῦ
ἡγεμονικοῦ ὁρμήσαντα ἢ κατ᾽ ἐπακολούθησιν.
καὶ τὸ χάσμα οὖν τοῦ λέοντος καὶ τὸ δηλητήριον
καὶ πᾶσα κακουργία, ὡς ἄκανθα, ὡς βόρβορος,
ἐκείνων ἐπιγεννήματα τῶν σεμνῶν καὶ καλῶν.
μὴ οὖν αὐτὰ ἀλλότρια τούτου, οὗ σέβεις,
φαντάζου· ἀλλὰ τὴν πάντων πηγὴν ἐπιλογίζου.

λζ΄. Ὁ τὰ νῦν ἰδὼν πάντα ἑώρακεν, ὅσα τε
ἐξ ἀιδίου ἐγένετο καὶ ὅσα εἰς τὸ ἄπειρον ἔσται·
πάντα γὰρ ὁμογενῆ καὶ ὁμοειδῆ.

λη΄. Πολλάκις ἐνθυμοῦ τὴν ἐπισύνδεσιν πάντων τῶν ἐν τῷ κόσμῳ καὶ σχέσιν πρὸς ἄλληλα.
τρόπον γάρ τινα πάντα ἀλλήλοις ἐπιπέπλεκται,
καὶ πάντα κατὰ τοῦτο φίλα ἀλλήλοις ἐστίν· καὶ
γὰρ ἄλλῳ ἄλλο[1] ἑξῆς ἐστι ταῦτα[2] διὰ τὴν
τονικὴν κίνησιν[3] καὶ σύμπνοιαν καὶ τὴν ἕνωσιν
τῆς οὐσίας.

λθ΄. Οἷς συγκεκλήρωσαι πράγμασι, τούτοις
συνάρμοζε σεαυτόν· καὶ οἷς συνείληχας ἀνθρώποις, τούτους φίλει, ἀλλ᾽ ἀληθινῶς.

μ΄. Ὄργανον, ἐργαλεῖον, σκεῦος πᾶν εἰ, πρὸς
ὃ κατεσκεύασται, ποιεῖ, εὖ ἔχει· καίτοι ἐκεῖ ὁ
κατασκευάσας ἐκποδών. ἐπὶ δὲ τῶν ὑπὸ φύσεως
συνεχομένων ἔνδον ἐστὶ καὶ παραμένει ἡ κατα-
σκευάσασα δύναμις· καθὸ καὶ μᾶλλον αἰδεῖσθαι
αὐτὴν δεῖ καὶ νομίζειν, ἐὰν κατὰ τὸ βούλημα

[1] ἄλλῳ ἄλλο Cor.: ἄλλῳ P ἄλλο A.
[2] τοῦτο PA : ταῦτα Schenkl.
[3] τοπικὴν κόνησιν P by an obvious misprint as Xyl. translates *constantem motum.*

[1] ii. 3 ; v. 8, § 5 ; xii. 26.   [2] iii. 2.
[3] ii. 14 ; iv. 32 ; vii. 1, 49 ; xi. Ι ; xii. 24.

All things come from that one source, from that ruling Reason of the Universe,[1] either under a primary impulse from it or by way of consequence. And therefore the gape of the lion's jaws[2] and poison and all noxious things, such as thorns and mire, are but after-results of the grand and the beautiful. Look not then on these as alien to that which thou dost reverence, but turn thy thoughts to the one source of all things.

37. He, who sees what now is, hath seen all that ever hath been from times everlasting, and that shall be to eternity[3]; for all things are of one lineage and one likeness.

38. Meditate often on the intimate union and mutual interdependence of all things in the Universe. For in a manner all things are mutually intertwined, and thus all things have a liking for one another. For these things are consequent one on another by reason of their contracting and expanding[4] motion, the sympathy[5] that breathes through them, and the unity of all substance.

39. Fit thyself to the environment that is thy portion,[6] and love the men among whom thy lot is thrown, but whole-heartedly.[7]

40. Every implement, tool, or vessel is well if it do the work for which it is made, and yet in their case the maker is not at hand. But in the things which owe their organic unity to Nature, the Power that made is within them and abides there. Wherefore also must thou reverence it the more, and

---

[4] τονικήν ; see Index III.
[5] cp. Diog. Laert. Zeno 70 : τὴν τῶν οὐρανίων πρὸς τὰ ἐπίγεια συμπνοίαν καὶ συντονίαν. [6] vii. 57.
[7] vi. 48; viii. 22. cp. 1 St. Peter, i. 22.

ταύτης σαυτὸν¹ ἔχῃς καὶ² διεξάγῃς, ἔχειν σοι
πάντα κατὰ νοῦν. ἔχει δὲ οὕτως καὶ τῷ παντὶ
κατὰ νοῦν τὰ ἑαυτοῦ.

μαʹ. Ὅ τι ἂν τῶν ἀπροαιρέτων ὑποστήσῃς
σαυτῷ ἀγαθὸν ἢ κακόν, ἀνάγκη κατὰ τὴν περί-
πτωσιν τοῦ τοιούτου κακοῦ ἢ τὴν ἀπότευξιν τοῦ
τοιούτου ἀγαθοῦ, μέμψασθαί σε θεοῖς, καὶ
ἀνθρώπους δὲ μισῆσαι τοὺς αἰτίους ὄντας ἢ
ὑποπτευομένους ἔσεσθαι τῆς ἀποτεύξεως ἢ τῆς
περιπτώσεως· καὶ ἀδικοῦμεν δὴ πολλὰ διὰ τὴν
πρὸς ταῦτα διαφοράν. ἐὰν δὲ μόνα τὰ ἐφ᾽ ἡμῖν
ἀγαθὰ καὶ κακὰ κρίνωμεν, οὐδεμία αἰτία καταλείπεται οὔτε θεῷ ἐγκαλέσαι οὔτε πρὸς ἄνθρωπον
στῆναι στάσιν πολεμίου.

μβʹ. Πάντες εἰς ἓν ἀποτέλεσμα συνεργοῦμεν,
οἱ μὲν εἰδότως καὶ παρακολουθητικῶς, οἱ δὲ
ἀνεπιστάτως· ὥσπερ καὶ "τοὺς καθεύδοντας,"
οἶμαι, ὁ Ἡράκλειτος "ἐργάτας εἶναι" λέγει, καὶ
συνεργοὺς τῶν ἐν τῷ κόσμῳ γινομένων. ἄλλος
δὲ κατ᾽ ἄλλο συνεργεῖ· ἐκ περιουσίας δὲ καὶ
ὁ μεμφόμενος καὶ ὁ ἀντιβαίνειν πειρώμενος
καὶ ἀναιρεῖν τὰ γινόμενα. καὶ γὰρ τοῦ τοιούτου
ἔχρῃζεν ὁ κόσμος. λοιπὸν οὖν σύνες, εἰς τίνας
σεαυτὸν κατατάσσεις· ἐκεῖνος μὲν γὰρ πάντως
σοι καλῶς χρήσεται ὁ τὰ ὅλα διοικῶν, καὶ παρα-
δέξεταί σε εἰς μέρος τι τῶν συνεργῶν καὶ συν-
εργητικῶν. ἀλλὰ σὺ μὴ τοιοῦτο μέρος γένῃ, οἷος

¹ αὐτὸν A : omit P : σαυτὸν Cor. : αὐτὸς Schenkl.
² ἔχῃς καὶ P : omit A.

realize that if thou keep and conduct thyself ever according to its will, all is to thy mind. So also to its mind are the things of the Universe.

41. If thou regardest anything not in thine own choice as good or evil for thyself, it is inevitable that, on the incidence of such an evil or the miscarriage of such a good, thou shouldst upbraid the Gods,[1] aye, and hate men as the actual or supposed cause of the one or the other; and in fact many are the wrong-doings we commit by setting a value on such things.[2] But if we discriminate as good and evil only the things in our power, there is no occasion left for accusing the Gods [3] or taking the stand of an enemy towards men.

42. We are all fellow-workers towards the ful-filment of one object, some of us knowingly and intelligently, others blindly; just as Heraclitus, I think, says that *even when they sleep men are workers* and fellow-agents in all that goes on in the world.[4] One is a co-agent in this, another in that, and in abundant measure also he that murmurs and seeks to hinder or disannul what occurs. For the Universe had need of such men also. It remains then for thee to decide with whom thou art ranging thyself. For He that controls the Universe will in any case put thee to a good use and admit thee to a place among his fellow-workers and coadjutors. But see that thou fill no such place as the paltry

---

[1] vi. 16 § 3; ix. 1 *ad med.* cp. Epict. i. 27 § 13.
[2] *i.e.* treating as important things which are ἀδιάφορα, or of no consequence either way.   [3] vi. 16 § 3.
[4] *cp.* iv. 46. But Plutarch in his treatise *On Superstition* cites a saying of Heraclitus to the effect that sleepers live in a world of their own.

ὁ εὐτελὴς καὶ γελοῖος στίχος ἐν τῷ δράματι,
οὗ Χρύσιππος μέμνηται.

μγ΄. Μήτι ὁ ἥλιος τὰ τοῦ ὑετοῦ ἀξιοῖ ποιεῖν;
μή τι ὁ Ἀσκληπιὸς τὰ τῆς Καρποφόρου; τί δὲ
τῶν ἄστρων ἕκαστον; οὐχὶ διάφορα μέν, συνεργὰ
δὲ πρὸς ταυτόν;

μδ΄. Εἰ μὲν οὖν ἐβουλεύσαντο περὶ ἐμοῦ καὶ
τῶν ἐμοὶ συμβῆναι ὀφειλόντων οἱ θεοί, καλῶς
ἐβουλεύσαντο· ἄβουλον γὰρ θεὸν οὐδὲ ἐπινοῆσαι
ῥᾴδιον· κακοποιῆσαι δέ με διὰ τίνα αἰτίαν
ἔμελλον ὁρμᾶν; τί γὰρ αὐτοῖς ἢ τῷ κοινῷ, οὗ
μάλιστα προνοοῦνται, ἐκ τούτου περιεγένετο;
εἰ δὲ μὴ ἐβουλεύσαντο κατ' ἰδίαν περὶ ἐμοῦ,
περί γε τῶν κοινῶν πάντως ἐβουλεύσαντο, οἷς
κατ' ἐπακολούθησιν καὶ ταῦτα συμβαίνοντα
ἀσπάζεσθαι καὶ στέργειν ὀφείλω. εἰ δ' ἄρα περὶ
μηδενὸς βουλεύονται (πιστεύειν μὲν οὐχ ὅσιον),
ἢ μηδὲ θύωμεν μηδὲ εὐχώμεθα μηδὲ ὀμνύωμεν
μηδὲ τὰ ἄλλα πράσσωμεν, ἅπερ ἕκαστα ὡς πρὸς
παρόντας καὶ συμβιοῦντας τοὺς θεοὺς πράσσομεν. εἰ δὲ ἄρα περὶ μηδενὸς τῶν καθ' ἡμᾶς
βουλεύονται, ἐμοὶ μὲν ἔξεστι περὶ ἐμαυτοῦ
βουλεύεσθαι· ἐμοὶ δέ ἐστι σκέψις περὶ τοῦ
συμφέροντος. συμφέρει δὲ ἑκάστῳ, τὸ κατὰ τὴν
ἑαυτοῦ κατασκευὴν καὶ φύσιν· ἡ δὲ ἐμὴ φύσις
λογικὴ καὶ πολιτική· πόλις καὶ πατρὶς ὡς μὲν

---

[1] Plutarch (*adv. Stoic.* §§ 13, 14) vigorously denounces this
sophism, as he counts it, of Chrysippus that what is evil in
itself has a value as a foil to the good. He quotes Chrysippus
(*Frag. Phys.* 1181 Arnim):

ὥσπερ γὰρ αἱ κωμῳδίαι ἐπιγράμματα γελοῖα φέρουσιν ἃ καθ'
ἑαυτὰ μέν ἐστι φαῦλα, τῷ δὲ ὅλῳ ποιήματι χάριν τινὰ προστίθησιν,

and ridiculous line in the play which Chrysippus mentions.[1]

43. Does the sun take upon himself to discharge the functions of the rain? or Asclepius of the Fruit-bearer[2]? And what of each particular star? Do they not differ in glory yet co-operate to one end?

44. If the Gods have taken counsel about me and the things to befall me, doubtless they have taken good counsel. For it is not easy even to imagine a God without wisdom. And what motive could they have impelling them to do me evil? For what advantage could thereby accrue to them or to the Universe which is their special care? But if the Gods have taken no counsel for me individually, yet they have in any case done so for the interests of the Universe, and I am bound to welcome and make the best of[3] those things also that befall as a necessary corollary to those interests. But if so be they take counsel about nothing at all—an impious belief—in good sooth let us have no more of sacrifices and prayers and oaths, nor do any other of these things every one of which is a recognition of the Gods as if they were at our side and dwelling amongst us—but if so be, I say, they do not take counsel about any of our concerns, it is still in my power to take counsel about myself, and it is for me to consider my own interest. And that is to every man's interest which is agreeable to his own constitution and nature. But my nature is rational and civic; my city and country,

οὕτως ψέξειας ἂν αὐτὴν ἐφ' ἑαυτῆς τὴν κακίαν· τοῖς δὲ ἄλλοις οὐκ ἄχρηστός ἐστιν.

[2] That is, the Earth, or possibly Demeter.

[3] v. 8 § 3; x. 6, 11.

'Αντωνίνῳ μοι ἡ Ῥώμη, ὡς δὲ ἀνθρώπῳ ὁ κόσμος. τὰ ταῖς πόλεσιν οὖν ταύταις ὠφέλιμα μόνα ἐστί μοι ἀγαθά.

με΄. Ὅσα ἑκάστῳ συμβαίνει, ταῦτα τῷ ὅλῳ συμφέρει· ἤρκει τοῦτο. ἀλλ' ἔτι ἐκεῖνο ὡς ἐπίπαν ὄψει παραφυλάξας, ὅσα ἀνθρώπῳ, καὶ ἑτέροις ἀνθρώποις. κοινότερον δὲ νῦν τὸ συμφέρον ἐπὶ τῶν μέσων λαμβανέσθω.

μϛ΄. Ὥσπερ προσίσταταί σοι τὰ ἐν τῷ ἀμφι- θεάτρῳ καὶ τοῖς τοιούτοις χωρίοις, ὡς ἀεὶ τὰ αὐτὰ ὁρώμενα, καὶ τὸ ὁμοειδὲς προσκορῆ τὴν θέαν ποιεῖ· τοῦτο καὶ ἐπὶ ὅλου τοῦ βίου πάσχειν· πάντα γὰρ ἄνω κάτω τὰ αὐτὰ καὶ ἐκ τῶν αὐτῶν. μέχρι τίνος οὖν;

μζ΄. Ἐννόει συνεχῶς παντοίους ἀνθρώπους καὶ παντοίων μὲν ἐπιτηδευμάτων, παντοδαπῶν δὲ ἐθνῶν, τεθνεῶτας· ὥστε κατιέναι τοῦτο μέχρι Φιλιστίωνος καὶ Φοίβου καὶ Ὀριγανίωνος. μέτιθι νῦν ἐπὶ τὰ ἄλλα φῦλα. ἐκεῖ δὴ μετα- βαλεῖν ἡμᾶς δεῖ, ὅπου τοσοῦτοι μὲν δεινοὶ ῥήτορες, τοσοῦτοι δὲ σεμνοὶ φιλόσοφοι, Ἡρά- κλειτος, Πυθαγόρας, Σωκράτης· τοσοῦτοι δὲ ἥρωες πρότερον, τοσοῦτοι δὲ ὕστερον στρατηγοί, τύραννοι· ἐπὶ τούτοις δὲ Εὔδοξος, Ἵππαρχος, Ἀρχιμήδης, ἄλλαι φύσεις ὀξεῖαι, μεγαλόφρονες, φιλόπονοι, πανοῦργοι, αὐθάδεις, αὐτῆς τῆς ἐπικήρ-

---

[1] v. 8; x. 6 etc.
[2] i.e. indifferent, neither good nor bad.
[3] A personal touch. See Fronto, *ad Caes.* iv. 12 : *theatro libros lectitabas* ; ii. 6, *idem theatrum, idem odium* (*v.l.* otium) ; *cp.* ii. 10; Naber, p. 34 ; *cp.* Capit. xv. § 1.
[4] A Cynic philosopher of Gadara. His Syrian compatriot, Lucian, the prince of mockers, was yet alive and mocking.

BOOK VI

as Antoninus, is Rome; as a man, the world. The things then that are of advantage to these communities, these, and no other, are good for me.

45. All that befalls the Individual is to the interest of the Whole also.[1] So far, so good. But further careful observation will shew thee that, as a general rule, what is to the interest of one man is also to the interest of other men. But in this case the word *interest* must be taken in a more general sense as it applies to intermediate[2] things.

46. As the shows in the amphitheatre and such places grate upon thee[3] as being an everlasting repetition of the same sight, and the similarity makes the spectacle pall, such must be the effect of the whole of life. For everything up and down is ever the same and the result of the same things. How long then?

47. Never lose sight of the fact that men of all kinds, of all sorts of vocations and of every race under heaven, are dead; and so carry thy thought down even to Philistion and Phoebus and Origanion. Now turn to all other folk. We must pass at last to the same bourne whither so many wonderful orators have gone, so many grave philosophers, Heraclitus, Pythagoras, Socrates: so many heroes of old time, and so many warriors, so many tyrants of later days: and besides them, Eudoxus, Hipparchus, Archimedes, and other acute natures, men of large minds, lovers of toil, men of versatile powers, men of strong will, mockers, like Menippus[4]

cp. Luc. *Pisc.* 26, where the Scholiast (Arethas) refers to this passage. Diog. Laert. mentions a Meleager, the contemporary of Menippus, as a writer of similar character.

ου καὶ ἐφημέρου τῶν ἀνθρώπων ζωῆς χλευασταί,
οἷον Μένιππος καὶ ὅσοι τοιοῦτοι. περὶ πάντων
τούτων ἐννόει, ὅτι πάλαι κεῖνται. τί οὖν τοῦτο
δεινὸν αὐτοῖς; τί δαὶ τοῖς μηδ᾽ ὀνομαζομένοις
ὅλως; Ἕν ᾧδε πολλοῦ ἄξιον, τὸ μετ᾽ ἀληθείας
καὶ δικαιοσύνης εὐμενῆ τοῖς ψεύσταις καὶ ἀδίκοις
διαβιοῦν.

μη΄. Ὅταν εὐφρᾶναι σεαυτὸν θέλῃς, ἐνθυμοῦ
τὰ προτερήματα τῶν συμβιούντων· οἷον τοῦ μὲν
τὸ δραστήριον, τοῦ δὲ τὸ αἰδῆμον, τοῦ δὲ τὸ
εὐμετάδοτον, ἄλλου δὲ ἄλλο τι. οὐδὲν γὰρ
οὕτως εὐφραίνει, ὡς τὰ ὁμοιώματα τῶν ἀρετῶν
ἐμφαινόμενα τοῖς ἤθεσι τῶν συζώντων καὶ ἀθρόα
ὡς οἷόν τε συμπίπτοντα. διὸ καὶ πρόχειρα αὐτὰ
ἑκτέον.

μθ΄. Μήτι δυσχεραίνεις, ὅτι τοσῶνδέ τινων
λιτρῶν εἶ καὶ οὐ τριακοσίων; οὕτω δὲ καὶ
ὅτι μέχρι τοσῶνδε ἐτῶν βιωτέον σοι καὶ οὐ
μέχρι πλείονος· ὥσπερ γὰρ τῆς οὐσίας ὅσον
ἀφώρισταί σοι στέργεις, οὕτως καὶ ἐπὶ τοῦ
χρόνου.

ν΄. Πειρῶ μὲν πείθειν αὐτούς, πρᾶττε δὲ καὶ
ἀκόντων,[1] ὅταν τῆς δικαιοσύνης ὁ λόγος οὕτως
ἄγῃ. ἐὰν μέντοι βίᾳ τις προσχρώμενος ἐνίστη-
ται, μετάβαινε ἐπὶ τὸ εὐάρεστον καὶ ἄλυπον,
καὶ συγχρῶ εἰς ἄλλην ἀρετὴν τῇ κωλύσει·
καὶ μέμνησο, ὅτι μεθ᾽ ὑπεξαιρέσεως ὥρμας, ὅτι
καὶ τῶν ἀδυνάτων οὐκ ὠρέγου. τίνος οὖν;

---

[1] τῶν ἀκόντων P: αὐτῶν ἀκ. Menag.

and many another such, of man's perishable and transitory life itself. About all these reflect that they have long since been in their graves. What terrible thing then is this for them? What pray for those whose very names are unknown? One thing on earth is worth much—to live out our lives in truth and justice, and in charity with liars and unjust men.

48. When thou wouldst cheer thine heart, think upon the good qualities of thy associates[1]; as for instance, this one's energy, that one's modesty, the generosity of a third, and some other trait of a fourth. For nothing is so cheering as the images of the virtues mirrored in the characters of those who live with us, and presenting themselves in as great a throng as possible. Have these images then ever before thine eyes.

49. Thou art not aggrieved, art thou, at being so many pounds in weight and not three hundred? Then why be aggrieved if thou hast only so many years to live and no more? For as thou art content with the amount of matter allotted thee, so be content also with the time.

50. Try persuasion first, but even though men would say thee nay, act when the principles of justice so direct. Should any one however withstand thee by force, take refuge in being well-content and unhurt, and utilize the obstacle for the display of some other virtue. Recollect that the impulse thou hadst was conditioned[2] by circumstances,[3] and thine aim was not to do impossibilities. What then was it?

---

[1] But *cp.* v. 10.   [2] iv. 1 ; v. 20.
[3] Lit. *was with a reservation, i.e.* "should circumstances allow." *cp.* iv. 1 ; viii. 41.

τῆς τοιᾶσδέ τινος ὁρμῆς. τούτου δὲ τυγχάνεις·
ἐφ' οἷς προήχθημεν, ταῦτα γίνεται.

να'. Ὁ μὲν φιλόδοξος ἀλλοτρίαν ἐνέργειαν
ἴδιον ἀγαθὸν ὑπολαμβάνει, ὁ δὲ φιλήδονος ἰδίαν
πεῖσιν· ὁ δὲ νοῦν ἔχων ἰδίαν πρᾶξιν.

νβ'. Ἔξεστι περὶ τούτου μηδὲν ὑπολαμβάνειν καὶ μὴ ὀχλεῖσθαι τῇ ψυχῇ· αὐτὰ γὰρ τὰ
πράγματα οὐκ ἔχει φύσιν ποιητικὴν τῶν ἡμετέρων
κρίσεων.

νγ'. Ἔθισον σεαυτὸν πρὸς τῷ ὑφ' ἑτέρου
λεγομένῳ γίνεσθαι ἀπαρενθυμήτως καὶ ὡς οἷόν
τε ἐν τῇ ψυχῇ τοῦ λέγοντος γίνου.

νδ'. Τὸ τῷ σμήνει μὴ συμφέρον οὐδὲ τῇ
μελίσσῃ συμφέρει.

νε'. Εἰ κυβερνῶντα οἱ ναῦται ἢ ἰατρεύοντα
οἱ κάμνοντες κακῶς ἔλεγον, ἄλλῳ τινὶ ἂν
προσεῖχον[1] ἢ πῶς αὐτὸς ἐνεργοίη τὸ τοῖς ἐμπλέ-
ουσι σωτήριον ἢ τὸ τοῖς θεραπευομένοις
ὑγιεινόν;

νϛ'. Πόσοι, μεθ' ὧν εἰσῆλθον εἰς τὸν κόσμον,
ἤδη ἀπεληλύθασιν.

νζ'. Ἰκτεριῶσι τὸ μέλι πικρὸν φαίνεται· καὶ
λυσσοδήκτοις τὸ ὕδωρ φοβερόν· καὶ παιδίοις τὸ
σφαιρίον καλόν. τί οὖν ὀργίζομαι; ἢ δοκεῖ σοι
ἔλασσον ἰσχύειν τὸ διεψευσμένον ἢ τὸ χόλιον τῷ
ἰκτεριῶντι καὶ ὁ ἰὸς τῷ λυσσοδήκτῳ;

νη'. Κατὰ τὸν λόγον τῆς σῆς φύσεως βιοῦν σε

---

[1] If προσεῖχον is 1st pers. sing. we must with Richards
read ἐνεργοίην and understand ἐμὲ with κυβερνῶντα: πῶς
ἄν τις Schenkl.

BOOK VI

To feel some such impulse as thou didst. In that thou art successful. That which alone was in the sphere of our choice [1] is realized.

51. The lover of glory conceives his own good to consist in another's action, the lover of pleasure in his own feelings, but the possessor of understanding in his own actions.

52. We need not form any opinion about the thing in question or be harassed in soul, for Nature gives the thing itself no power to compel our judgments.

53. Train thyself to pay careful attention to what is being said [2] by another and as far as possible enter into his soul.

54. That which is not in the interests of the hive cannot be in the interests of the bee.[3]

55. If the sailors spoke ill of a steersman or the sick of a physician, what else would they have in mind but how the man should best effect the safety of the crew or the health of his patients?

56. How many have already left the world who came into it with me!

57. To the jaundiced honey tastes bitter; and the victim of hydrophobia has a horror of water; and to little children their ball is a treasure. Why then be angry? Or dost thou think that error is a less potent factor than bile in the jaundiced and virus in the victim of rabies?

58. From living according to the reason of thy nature no one can prevent thee: contrary to the

---

[1] Casaubon translates "that for which we were brought into the world," but can προάγω mean this?
[2] Obviously no contradiction of iv. 18 etc. See also vii. 4. 30.   [3] v. 22.

οὐδεὶς κωλύσει· παρὰ τὸν λόγον τῆς κοινῆς
φύσεως οὐδέν σοι συμβήσεται.

νθ΄. Οἷοί εἰσιν, οἷς θέλουσιν ἀρέσκειν, καὶ δι᾿
οἷα περιγινόμενα, καὶ δι᾿ οἵων ἐνεργειῶν. ὡς
ταχέως ὁ αἰὼν πάντα καλύψει· καὶ ὅσα ἐκάλυψεν
ἤδη.

reason of the Universal Nature nothing shall befall thee.

59. The persons men wish to please,[1] the objects they wish to gain, the means they employ—think of the character of all these! How soon will Time hide all things! How many a thing has it already hidden!

[1] vii. 62.

ΒΙΒΛΙΟΝ Ζ

αʹ. Τί ἐστὶ κακία; τοῦτ' ἔστιν, ὃ πολλάκις εἶδες. καὶ ἐπὶ παντὸς δὲ τοῦ συμβαίνοντος πρόχειρον ἔχε, ὅτι τοῦτό ἐστιν, ὃ πολλάκις εἶδες. ὅλως ἄνω κάτω τὰ αὐτὰ εὑρήσεις, ὧν μεσταὶ αἱ ἱστορίαι αἱ παλαιαί, αἱ μέσαι, αἱ ὑπόγυιοι· ὧν νῦν μεσταὶ αἱ πόλεις καὶ <αἱ>[1] οἰκίαι. οὐδὲν καινόν· πάντα καὶ συνήθη καὶ ὀλιγοχρόνια.

βʹ. Ἢ[2] τὰ δόγματα πῶς ἄλλως δύναται νεκρωθῆναι, ἐὰν μὴ αἱ κατάλληλοι αὐτοῖς φαντασίαι σβεσθῶσιν; ἃς διηνεκῶς ἀναζωπυρεῖν ἐπὶ σοί ἐστι. δύναμαι περὶ τούτου, ὃ δεῖ, ὑπολαμβάνειν· εἰ δ' ἄρα[3] δύναμαι, τί ταράσσομαι; τὰ ἔξω τῆς ἐμῆς διανοίας οὐδὲν ὅλως πρὸς τὴν ἐμὴν διάνοιαν. τοῦτο μάθε καὶ ὀρθὸς εἶ.

2 Ἀναβιῶναι σοι ἔξεστιν· ἴδε πάλιν τὰ πράγματα, ὡς ἑώρας· ἐν τούτῳ γὰρ τὸ ἀναβιῶναι.

γʹ. Πομπῆς κενοσπουδία, ἐπὶ σκηνῆς δράματα ποίμνια, ἀγέλαι, διαδορατισμοί,[4] κυνιδίοις ὀστάριον ἐρριμμένον, ψωμίον εἰς τὰς τῶν ἰχθύων δεξαμενάς, μυρμήκων ταλαιπωρίαι καὶ ἀχθοφορίαι

---

[1] <αἱ> Cor.

[2] ἢ A: ἦ Schenkl: omit. P: πῶς γὰρ A omit. P: πῶς γ Schenkl.   [3] γὰρ A: δ' ἄρα Schenkl.

[4] After διαδορατισμοὶ Lofft ingeniously inserts τί εἰσι μοι τί ἐμοί; Schenkl.

164

BOOK VII

1. WHAT is vice? A familiar sight enough. So in everything that befalls have the thought ready: *This is a familiar sight*. Look up, look down, everywhere thou wilt find the same things, whereof histories ancient, medieval, and modern are full; and full of them at this day are cities and houses. There is no new thing under the sun.[1] Everything is familiar, everything fleeting.

2. How else can thy axioms be made dead than by the extinction of the ideas that answer to them? And these it lies with thee ever to kindle anew into flame. I am competent to form the true conception of a thing. If so, why am I harassed? What is outside the scope of my mind has absolutely no concern with my mind. Learn this lesson and thou standest erect.

Thou canst begin a new life! See but things afresh as thou usedst to see them; for in this consists the new life.

3. Empty love of pageantry, stage-plays, flocks and herds, sham-fights, a bone thrown to lap-dogs, crumbs cast in a fish-pond, painful travail of ants and their bearing of burdens, skurryings of scared little

---

[1] Eccles. i. 9 *cp.* also Justin's *Apol.* i. 57, addressed to Pius and Marcus.

μυιδίων ἐπτοημένων διαδρομαί, σιγιλλάρια νευρο-
σπαστούμενα. χρὴ οὖν ἐν τούτοις εὐμενῶς μὲν καὶ
μὴ καταφρυαττόμενον ἑστάναι· παρακολουθεῖν
μέντοι, ὅτι τοσούτου ἄξιος ἕκαστός ἐστιν, ὅσου
ἄξιά ἐστι ταῦτα, περὶ ἃ ἐσπούδακεν.

δ΄. Δεῖ κατὰ λέξιν παρακολουθεῖν τοῖς λεγο-
μένοις, καὶ καθ᾽ ἑκάστην ὁρμὴν τοῖς γινομένοις.
καὶ ἐπὶ μὲν τοῦ ἑτέρου εὐθὺς ὁρᾶν, ἐπὶ τίνα
σκοπὸν ἡ ἀναφορά· ἐπὶ δὲ τοῦ ἑτέρου παραφυλάσσειν, τί τὸ σημαινόμενον.

ε΄. Πότερον ἐξαρκεῖ ἡ διάνοιά μου πρὸς τοῦτο
ἢ οὔ; εἰ μὲν ἐξαρκεῖ, χρῶμαι αὐτῇ πρὸς τὸ ἔργον,
ὡς ὀργάνῳ παρὰ τῆς τῶν ὅλων φύσεως δοθέντι.
εἰ δὲ μὴ ἐξαρκεῖ, ἤτοι παραχωρῶ τοῦ ἔργου τῷ
δυναμένῳ κρεῖττον ἐπιτελέσαι, ἐὰν ἄλλως τοῦτο
μὴ καθήκῃ, ἢ πράσσω, ὡς δύναμαι, προσπαρα-
λαβὼν τὸν δυνάμενον κατὰ πρόσχρησιν τοῦ ἐμοῦ
ἡγεμονικοῦ ποιῆσαι τὸ εἰς τὴν κοινωνίαν νῦν
καίριον καὶ χρήσιμον. ὅ τι γὰρ ἂν δι᾽ ἐμαυτοῦ
ἢ σὺν ἄλλῳ ποιῶ, ὧδε μόνον χρὴ συντείνειν, εἰς
τὸ κοινῇ χρήσιμον καὶ εὐάρμοστον.

ϛ΄. Ὅσοι μὲν πολυύμνητοι γενόμενοι ἤδη
λήθῃ παραδέδονται· ὅσοι δὲ τούτους ὑμνήσαντες
πάλαι ἐκποδών.

ζ΄. Μὴ αἰσχύνου βοηθούμενος· πρόκειται γάρ
σοι ἐνεργεῖν τὸ ἐπιβάλλον ὡς στρατιώτῃ ἐν
τειχομαχίᾳ. τί οὖν, ἐὰν σὺ μὲν χωλαίνων ἐπὶ
τὴν ἔπαλξιν ἀναβῆναι μόνος μὴ δύνῃ, σὺν ἄλλῳ
δὲ δυνατὸν ᾖ τοῦτο;

---

[1] ii. 2 etc.   [2] cp. ix. 41 (Epicurus).
[3] v. 16. cp. Dem. Olynth. iii. 32: ἅττα γὰρ ἂν τὰ ἐπιτηδ-

mice, puppets moved by strings[1]: amid such environment therefore thou must take thy place graciously and not 'snorting defiance,'[2] nay thou must keep abreast of the fact that everyone is worth just so much as those things are worth in which he is interested.[3]

4. In conversation keep abreast of what is being said,[4] and, in every effort, of what is being done. In the latter see from the first to what end it has reference, and in the former be careful to catch the meaning.

5. Is my mind competent for this or not? If competent, I apply it to the task as an instrument given me by the Universal Nature. If not competent, I either withdraw from the work in favour of someone who can accomplish it better, unless for other reasons duty forbids; or I do the best I can, taking to assist me any one that can utilize my ruling Reason to effect what is at the moment seasonable and useful for the common welfare. For in whatsoever I do either by myself or with another I must direct my energies to this alone, that it shall conduce to the common interest[5] and be in harmony with it.

6. How many much-lauded heroes have already been given as a prey unto forgetfulness,[6] and how many that lauded them have long ago disappeared!

7. Blush not to be helped[7]; for thou art bound to carry out the task that is laid upon thee as a soldier to storm the breach. What then, if for very lameness thou canst not mount the ramparts unaided, but canst do this with another's help?

εύματα τῶν ἀνθρώπων ᾖ, τοιοῦτον ἀνάγκη καὶ τὸ φρόνημα ἔχειν.
cp. Clem. Alex. *Strom.* iv. 23.   [4] vi. 53.   [5] iv. 12.
[6] iii. 10; iv. 33; viii. 21.   [7] x. 12.   See saying of Marcus, Capit. xxii. 4, quoted below, p. 360.

η΄. Τὰ μέλλοντα μὴ ταρασσέτω· ἥξεις γὰρ ἐπ'
αὐτά, ἐὰν δεήσῃ, φέρων τὸν αὐτὸν λόγον, ᾧ νῦν
πρὸς τὰ παρόντα χρᾷ.

θ΄. Πάντα ἀλλήλοις ἐπιπλέκεται καὶ ἡ σύνδεσις
ἱερά, καὶ σχεδόν τι οὐδὲν ἀλλότριον ἄλλο ἄλλῳ.
συγκατατέτακται γὰρ καὶ συγκοσμεῖ τὸν αὐτὸν
κόσμον. κόσμος τε γὰρ εἷς ἐξ ἁπάντων, καὶ θεὸς
εἷς διὰ πάντων, καὶ οὐσία μία, καὶ νόμος εἷς,
λόγος κοινὸς πάντων τῶν νοερῶν ζῴων, καὶ
ἀλήθεια μία· εἴγε καὶ τελειότης μία τῶν ὁμογενῶν καὶ τοῦ αὐτοῦ λόγου μετεχόντων ζῴων.

ι΄. Πᾶν τὸ ἔνυλον ἐναφανίζεται τάχιστα τῇ
τῶν ὅλων οὐσίᾳ· καὶ πᾶν αἴτιον εἰς τὸν τῶν ὅλων
λόγον τάχιστα ἀναλαμβάνεται· καὶ παντὸς
μνήμη τάχιστα ἐγκαταχώννυται τῷ αἰῶνι.

ια΄. Τῷ λογικῷ ζῴῳ ἡ αὐτὴ πρᾶξις κατὰ
φύσιν ἐστὶ καὶ κατὰ λόγον.

ιβ΄. Ὀρθὸς ἢ [1] ὀρθούμενος.

ιγ΄. Οἷόν ἐστιν ἐν ἡνωμένοις τὰ μέλη τοῦ
σώματος, τοῦτον ἔχει τὸν λόγον ἐν διεστῶσι τὰ
λογικὰ πρὸς μίαν τινὰ συνεργίαν κατεσκευασ-
μένα. μᾶλλον δέ σοι ἡ τούτου νόησις προσπεσεῖται, ἐὰν πρὸς ἑαυτὸν πολλάκις λέγῃς, ὅτι ‘μέλος’
εἰμὶ τοῦ ἐκ τῶν λογικῶν συστήματος. ἐὰν δὲ [διὰ
τοῦ ῥῶ στοιχείου] ‘μέρος’ εἶναι ἑαυτὸν λέγῃς,
οὔπω ἀπὸ καρδίας φιλεῖς τοὺς ἀνθρώπους, οὔπω
σε καταληκτικῶς [2] εὐφραίνει τὸ εὐεργετεῖν· ἔτι [3] ὡς

[1] μὴ Cas.; but *cp.* § 7.
[2] καταληπτικῶς (“assured delight”) PA: em. Gat.
[3] ἔτι εἰ ὡς A.

---

[1] vi. 38.   [2] iv. 45.   [3] iv. 4.
[4] ii. 12.   [5] Sen. *de Vit. Beat.* 8.

8. Be not disquieted about the future. If thou must come thither, thou wilt come armed with the same reason which thou appliest now to the present.

9. All things are mutually intertwined,[1] and the tie is sacred, and scarcely anything is alien the one to the other. For all things have been ranged side by side,[2] and together help to order one ordered Universe. For there is both one Universe, made up of all things, and one God immanent in all things, and one Substance, and one Law, one Reason common to all intelligent creatures,[3] and one Truth: if indeed there is also one perfecting of living creatures that have the same origin and share the same reason.

10. A very little while and all that is material is lost to sight in the Substance of the Universe,[4] a little while and all Cause is taken back into the Reason of the Universe, a little while and the remembrance of everything is encairned in Eternity.

11. To the rational creature the same act is at once according to nature and according to reason.[5]

12. Upright, or made upright.[6]

13. The principle which obtains where limbs and body unite to form one organism, holds good also for rational things with their separate individualities, constituted as they are to work in conjunction. But the perception of this shall come more home to thee, if thou sayest to thyself, I am a *limb* of the organized body of rational things. But if [using the letter *R*] thou sayest thou art but a *part*,[7] not yet dost thou love mankind from the heart, nor yet does well-doing delight thee for its own sake.[8] Thou

---

[6] cp. vii. 7 ; but see iii. 5.

[7] The pun may be kept by *limb—rim*.   [8] cp. iv. 20.

πρέπον αὐτὸ ψιλὸν ποιεῖς· οὔπω ὡς σαυτὸν εὖ ποιῶν.

ιδ'. ὃ θέλει, ἔξωθεν προσπιπτέτω τοῖς παθεῖν ἐκ τῆς προσπτώσεως ταύτης δυναμένοις. ἐκεῖνα γάρ, ἐὰν θελήσῃ, μέμψεται τὰ παθόντα· ἐγὼ δέ, ἐὰν μὴ ὑπολάβω, ὅτι κακὸν τὸ συμβεβηκός, οὔπω βέβλαμμαι. ἔξεστι δέ μοι μὴ ὑπολαβεῖν.

ιε'. "Ο τι ἄν τις ποιῇ ἢ λέγῃ, ἐμὲ δεῖ ἀγαθὸν εἶναι· ὡς ἂν εἰ ὁ χρυσὸς ἢ ὁ σμάραγδος ἢ ἡ πορφύρα τοῦτο ἀεὶ ἔλεγεν, "Ο τι ἄν τις ποιῇ ἢ λέγῃ, ἐμὲ δεῖ σμάραγδον εἶναι καὶ τὸ ἐμαυτοῦ χρῶμα ἔχειν."

ις'. Τὸ ἡγεμονικὸν αὐτὸ ἑαυτῷ οὐκ ἐνοχλεῖ, οἷον λέγω, οὐ φορεῖ †[1] ἑαυτὸ εἰς ἐπιθυμίαν. εἰ δέ τις ἄλλος αὐτὸ φοβῆσαι ἢ λυπῆσαι δύναται, ποιείτω. αὐτὸ γὰρ ἑαυτὸ ὑποληπτικῶς οὐ τρέψει εἰς τοιαύτας τροπάς.

Τὸ σωμάτιον, μὴ πάθῃ τι, αὐτὸ μεριμνάτω, εἰ δύναται, καὶ λεγέτω, εἴ τι πάσχει· τὸ δὲ ψυχάριον τὸ φοβούμενον, τὸ λυπούμενον, τὸ περὶ τούτων ὅλως ὑπολαμβάνον, οὐδὲν μὴ πάθῃ· οὐ γὰρ ἕξις αὐτῷ[2] εἰς κρίσιν τοιαύτην.

Ἀπροσδεές ἐστιν, ὅσον ἐφ' ἑαυτῷ, τὸ ἡγεμονικόν, ἐὰν μὴ ἑαυτῷ ἔνδειαν ποιῇ· κατὰ ταῦτα δὲ καὶ ἀτάραχον καὶ ἀνεμπόδιστον, ἐὰν μὴ ἑαυτὸ ταράσσῃ καὶ ἐμποδίζῃ.

ιζ'. Εὐδαιμονία ἐστὶ δαίμων ἀγαθὸς ἢ <ἡγεμονικὸν>[3] ἀγαθόν. τί οὖν ὧδε ποιεῖς,

---

[1] φοβεῖ PA : σοβεῖ Schenkl : I suggest φορεῖ or τρέπει.
[2] ἕξεις αὐτὸ PA : ἕξις αὐτῷ Schenkl : ἕλξεις Schultz.
[3] <ἡγεμονικὸν> Gat.

dost practise it still as a bare duty, not yet as a boon
to thyself.

14. Let any external thing, that will, be incident
to whatever is able to feel this incidence. For that
which feels can, if it please, complain.[1]   But I,
if I do not consider what has befallen me to be
an evil,[2] am still unhurt. And I *can* refuse so to
consider it.

15. Let any say or do what he will, I cannot but
for my part be good. So might the emerald—or gold
or purple—never tire of repeating, *Whatever any one
shall do or say, I cannot but be an emerald and keep my
colour.*

16. The ruling Reason is never the disturber of
its own peace, never, for instance, hurries itself into
lust.   But if another can cause it fear or pain, let
it do so. For it will not let its own assumptions
lead it into such aberrations.

Let the body take thought for itself, if it may,
that it suffer no hurt and, if it do so suffer, let it
proclaim the fact.[3] But the soul that has the faculty
of fear, the faculty of pain, and alone can assume
that these exist, can never suffer; for it is not given
to making any such admission.[4]

In itself the ruling Reason wants for nothing
unless it create its own needs, and in like manner
nothing can disturb it, nothing impede it, unless the
disturbance or impediment come from itself.

17. Well-being[5] is a good Being, or a ruling
Reason that is good. What then doest thou here,

---

[1] vii. 33; viii. 28   [2] iv. 7, 39.   [3] vii. 14, 33.
[4] vi. 52; vii. 14, 33; viii. 40 etc.
[5] Defined by Chrysippus as "harmony of our δαιμων with
God's will."

ὦ φαντασία ; ἀπέρχου, τοὺς θεούς σοι, ὡς ἦλθες·
οὐ γὰρ χρῄζω σου. ἐλήλυθας δὲ κατὰ τὸ
ἀρχαῖον ἔθος. οὐκ ὀργίζομαί σοι· μόνον ἄπιθι.

ιη΄. Φοβεῖταί τις μεταβολήν ; τί γὰρ δύναται
χωρὶς μεταβολῆς γενέσθαι; τί δὲ φίλτερον ἢ
οἰκειότερον τῇ τῶν ὅλων φύσει ; σὺ δὲ αὐτὸς
λούσασθαι δύνασαι, ἐὰν μὴ τὰ ξύλα μεταβάλῃ ;
τραφῆναι δὲ δύνασαι, ἐὰν μὴ τὰ ἐδώδιμα
μεταβάλῃ; ἄλλο δέ τι τῶν χρησίμων δύναται
συντελεσθῆναι χωρὶς μεταβολῆς ; οὐχ ὁρᾷς οὖν,
ὅτι καὶ αὐτὸ τὸ σὲ μεταβαλεῖν ὅμοιόν ἐστι καὶ
ὁμοίως ἀναγκαῖον τῇ τῶν ὅλων φύσει ;

ιθ΄. Διὰ τῆς τῶν ὅλων οὐσίας ὡς διὰ χειμάρ-
ρου, διεκπορεύεται πάντα τὰ σώματα, τῷ ὅλῳ
συμφυῆ καὶ συνεργά, ὡς τὰ ἡμέτερα μέρη ἀλλήλοις.

Πόσους ἤδη ὁ αἰὼν Χρυσίππους, πόσους
Σωκράτεις, πόσους Ἐπικτήτους καταπέπωκεν;
τὸ δ᾽ αὐτὸ καὶ ἐπὶ παντὸς οὑτινοσοῦν σοι
ἀνθρώπου τε καὶ πράγματος προσπιπτέτω.

κ΄. Ἐμὲ ἓν μόνον περισπᾷ, μή τι αὐτὸς
ποιήσω, ὃ ἡ κατασκευὴ τοῦ ἀνθρώπου οὐ θέλει, ἢ
ὡς οὐ θέλει, ἢ ὃ νῦν οὐ θέλει.

κα΄. Ἐγγὺς μὲν ἡ σὴ περὶ πάντων λήθη·
ἐγγὺς δὲ ἡ πάντων περὶ σοῦ λήθη.

κβ΄. Ἴδιον ἀνθρώπου φιλεῖν καὶ τοὺς πταί-
οντας. τοῦτο δὲ γίνεται, ἐὰν συμπροσπίπτῃ σοι,

---

[1] vii. 29 ; *cp.* Ecclesiasticus, xxxvii. 3, *i.e.* opinion we form
of a thing. [2] iv. 43 ; v. 23 ; vi. 15.

[3] Referred by some (see Zeller, *Stoics*, p. 158, Engl. trans.)
to the theory that at each cyclical regeneration of the world
the same persons and events repeat themselves. But see
x. 31.

[4] Aul. Gellius ii. 18 speaks of Epict. as recently dead ;

O Imagination? [1]   Avaunt, in God's name, as thou camest, for I desire thee not!   But thou art come according to thine ancient wont.   I bear thee no malice ; only depart from me!

18. Does a man shrink from change?   Why, what can come into being save by change?   What be nearer or dearer to the Nature of the Universe? Canst thou take a hot bath unless the wood for the furnace suffer a change?   Couldst thou be fed, if thy food suffered no change, and can any of the needs of life be provided for apart from change? Seest thou not that a personal change is similar, and similarly necessary to the Nature of the Universe?

19. Through the universal Substance as through a rushing torrent [2] all bodies pass on their way, united with the Whole in nature and activity, as our members are with one another.

How many a Chrysippus,[3] how many a Socrates, how many an Epictetus [4] hath Time already devoured !   Whatsoever man thou hast to do with and whatsoever thing, let the same thought strike thee.

20. I am concerned about one thing only, that I of myself do not what man's constitution does not will, or wills not now, or in a way that it wills not.

21. A little while and thou wilt have forgotten everything, a little while and everything will have forgotten thee.

22. It is a man's especial privilege [5] to love even those who stumble.   And this love follows as soon as

Them. *Or.* v. p. 63 D. implies that he was alive under the Antonines.   Lucian, *adv. Ind.* 13 speaks of his earthenware lamp having been bought by an admirer for 3,000 drachmas.
   [5] Fronto, *ad Ver.* ii. 2: *Hominis maxime proprium ignoscere.*   cp. St. Matt. v. 44 ; Dio 71. 26, § 2.

ὅτι καὶ συγγενεῖς καὶ δι' ἄγνοιαν καὶ ἄκοντες
ἁμαρτάνουσι, καὶ ὡς μετ' ὀλίγον ἀμφότεροι
τεθνήξεσθε, καὶ πρὸ πάντων, ὅτι οὐκ ἔβλαψέ σε·
οὐ γὰρ τὸ ἡγεμονικόν σου χεῖρον ἐποίησεν, ἢ
πρόσθεν ἦν.

κγ'. Ἡ τῶν ὅλων φύσις ἐκ τῆς ὅλης οὐσίας,
ὡς κηροῦ, νῦν μὲν ἱππάριον ἔπλασε, συγχέασα δὲ
τοῦτο εἰς δενδρύφιον[1] συνεχρήσατο τῇ ὕλῃ αὐτοῦ,
εἶτα εἰς ἀνθρωπάριον, εἶτα εἰς ἄλλο τι· ἕκαστον
δὲ τούτων πρὸς ὀλίγιστον ὑπέστη. δεινὸν δὲ
οὐδὲν τὸ διαλυθῆναι τῷ κιβωτίῳ, ὥσπερ οὐδὲ τὸ
συμπαγῆναι.[2]

κδ'. Τὸ ἐπίκοτον τοῦ προσώπου λίαν παρὰ
φύσιν. <ὃ> ὅταν πολλάκις † ἐνῇ, ἀποθνήσκει δὴ
πρόσχημα,[3] ἢ τὸ τελευταῖον ἀπεσβέσθη, ὥστε
ὅλως ἐξαφθῆναι μὴ δύνασθαι. αὐτῷ γε τούτῳ
παρακολουθεῖν πειρῶ, ὅτι παρὰ τὸν λόγον. εἰ
γὰρ καὶ ἡ συναίσθησις τοῦ ἁμαρτάνειν οἰχήσεται,
τίς ἔτι τοῦ ζῆν αἰτία;

κε'. Πάντα, ὅσα ὁρᾷς, ὅσον οὔπω μεταβαλεῖ
ἡ τὰ ὅλα διοικοῦσα φύσις, καὶ ἄλλα ἐκ τῆς οὐσίας
αὐτῶν ποιήσει, καὶ πάλιν ἄλλα ἐκ τῆς ἐκείνων
οὐσίας, ἵνα ἀεὶ νεαρὸς ᾖ ὁ κόσμος.

κϛ'. Ὅταν τις ἁμάρτῃ τι εἰς σέ, εὐθὺς ἐνθυμοῦ,
τί ἀγαθὸν ἢ κακὸν ὑπολαβὼν ἥμαρτεν. τοῦτο γὰρ
ἰδὼν ἐλεήσεις αὐτόν, καὶ οὔτε θαυμάσεις, οὔτε

---

[1] δένδρου φύσιν PA : δενδρύφιον Nauck.
[2] <ἀγαθὸν> after συμπαγῆναι Kronenberg.
[3] ὅταν πολλάκις ἐναποθνήσκειν ἢ πρόσχημα PA : ὅθεν πολλάκις
ἐναποθνήσκει τὸ πρόσχημα Fournier : I have patched up this
incurable passage, as above. Possibly ἤδη would be better
than δή.

thou reflectest that they are of kin to thee and
that they do wrong involuntarily and through
ignorance,[1] and that within a little while both
they and thou will be dead[2]; and this, above all,
that the man has done thee no hurt[3]; for he has
not made thy ruling Reason worse than it was
before.

23. The Nature of the Whole out of the Substance
of the Whole,[4] as out of wax, moulds at one time
a horse, and breaking up the mould kneads the
material up again into a tree, then into a man,
and then into something else; and every one of
these subsists but for a moment. It is no more a
hardship for the coffer to be broken up than it
was for it to be fitted together.

24. An angry scowl on the face is beyond measure
unnatural, and when it is often seen there, all
comeliness begins at once to die away, and in the end
is so utterly extinguished that it can never be re-
kindled at all. From this very fact try to reach the
conclusion that it is contrary to reason. The consciousness of wrong-doing once lost, what motive is
left for living any more?

25. Everything that thou seest will the Nature
that controls the Universe change, no one knows
how soon, and out of its substance make other
compounds,[5] and again others out of theirs, that the
world may ever renew its youth.

26. Does a man do thee wrong? Go to and mark
what notion of good and evil was his that did the
wrong. Once perceive that and thou wilt feel

---

[1] cp. St. Luke xxiii. 34.
[2] iv. 6.   [3] ii. 1; ix. 38.
[4] vii. 25. cp. St. Paul, Rom. ix. 20.   [5] vii. 23.

ὀργισθήσῃ. ἤτοι γὰρ καὶ αὐτὸς τὸ αὐτὸ ἐκείνῳ
ἀγαθὸν ἔτι ὑπολαμβάνεις ἢ ἄλλο ὁμοειδές. δεῖ
οὖν συγγινώσκειν. εἰ δὲ μηκέτι ὑπολαμβάνεις τὰ
τοιαῦτα ἀγαθὰ καὶ κακά, ῥᾷον εὐμενὴς ἔσῃ τῷ
παρορῶντι.

κζʹ. Μὴ τὰ ἀπόντα ἐννοεῖν, ὡς ἤδη[1] ὄντα· ἀλλὰ
τῶν παρόντων τὰ δεξιώτατα ἐκλογίζεσθαι καὶ
τούτων χάριν ὑπομιμνήσκεσθαι, πῶς ἂν ἐπεζητ-
εῖτο, εἰ μὴ παρῆν. ἅμα μέντοι φυλάσσου, μὴ
διὰ τοῦ οὕτως ἀσμενίζειν αὐτοῖς ἐθίσῃς ἐκτιμᾶν
αὐτά, ὥστε, ἐάν ποτε μὴ παρῇ, ταραχθήσεσθαι.

κηʹ. Εἰς σαυτὸν συνειλοῦ. φύσιν ἔχει τὸ
λογικὸν ἡγεμονικόν, ἑαυτῷ ἀρκεῖσθαι δικαιο-
πραγοῦντι καὶ παρ' αὐτὸ τοῦτο γαλήνην ἔχοντι.

κθʹ. Ἐξάλειψον τὴν φαντασίαν. στῆσον τὴν
νευροσπαστίαν. περίγραψον τὸ ἐνεστὼς τοῦ
χρόνου. γνώρισον τὸ συμβαῖνον ἢ σοὶ ἢ ἄλλῳ.
δίελε καὶ μέρισον τὸ ὑποκείμενον εἰς τὸ αἰτιῶδες
καὶ ὑλικόν. ἐννόησον τὴν ἐσχάτην ὥραν. τὸ
ἐκείνῳ ἁμαρτηθὲν ἐκεῖ κατάλιπε, ὅπου ἡ ἁμαρτία
ὑπέστη.

λʹ. Συμπαρεκτείνειν τὴν νόησιν τοῖς λεγομέν-
οις. εἰσδύεσθαι τὸν νοῦν εἰς τὰ γινόμενα καὶ
ποιοῦντα.

λαʹ. Φαίδρυνον σεαυτὸν ἁπλότητι καὶ αἰδοῖ
καὶ τῇ πρὸς τὸ ἀνὰ μέσον ἀρετῆς καὶ κακίας
ἀδιαφορίᾳ. φίλησον τὸ ἀνθρώπινον γένος. ἀκολ-

---

[1] ἡδέα (ἡδίω Rend.) Schultz.

---

[1] cp. ii. 13 ; x. 30 ; Herodian i. 4, § 2 ; Dio 71. 10, § 4.
[2] xi. 18, § 4.   [3] Epict. Frag. 129.   [4] cp. Hor. Ep. i. 10, 31.
[5] iv. 3 ad init. ; viii. 48.   [6] vii. 17 ; viii. 29 ; ix. 7.

compassion,[1] not surprise or anger. For thou hast still thyself either the same notion of good and evil as he or another not unlike. Thou needs must forgive him then.[2] But if thy notions of good and evil are no longer such, all the more easily shalt thou be gracious to him that sees awry.

27. Dream not of that which thou hast not as though already thine, but of what thou hast pick out the choicest blessings, and do not forget in respect of them how eagerly thou wouldst have coveted them, had they not been thine.[3] Albeit beware that thou do not inure thyself, by reason of this thy delight in them, to prize them so highly as to be distressed if at any time they are lost to thee.[4]

28. Gather thyself into thyself.[5] It is characteristic of the rational Ruling Faculty to be satisfied with its own righteous dealing and the peace which that brings.

29. Efface imagination![6] Cease to be pulled as a puppet by thy passions.[7] Isolate the present. Recognize what befalls either thee or another. Dissect and analyze all that comes under thy ken into the Causal and the Material. Meditate on thy last hour.[8] Let the wrong thy neighbour does thee rest with him that did the wrong.[9]

30. Do thy utmost to keep up with what is said.[10] Let thy mind enter into the things that are done and the things that are doing them.

31. Make thy face to shine with simplicity and modesty and disregard of all that lies between virtue and vice. Love human-kind. Follow God.[11] Says

---

[7] ii. 2 etc.   [8] ii. 5.   [9] ix. 20, 38.   [10] vii. 4.
[11] 1 St. Peter, ii. 17. *cp.* Sen. *de Vit. Beat.* 15 : *Deum sequere.* Dio Chrys. ii. 98 R.

οὔθησον θεῷ. ἐκεῖνος μέν φησιν, ὅτι "πάντα
νομιστί, †ἐτεῇ¹ δὲ μόνα†² τὰ στοιχεῖα." ἀρκεῖ δὲ
μεμνῆσθαι, ὅτι τὰ πάντα νομιστὶ ἔχει. ἤδη λίαν
ὀλίγα.†

λβ′. Περὶ θανάτου· ἢ σκεδασμός, εἰ ἄτομοι·
ἢ <εἰ> ἕνωσις,³ ἤτοι σβέσις ἢ μετάστασις.

λγ′. Περὶ πόνου· "τὸ μὲν ἀφόρητον ἐξάγει· τὸ
δὲ χρονίζον, φορητόν." καὶ ἡ διάνοια τὴν ἑαυτῆς
γαλήνην κατὰ ἀπόληψιν διατηρεῖ, καὶ οὐ χεῖρον
τὸ ἡγεμονικὸν γέγονεν. τὰ δὲ κακούμενα μέρη
ὑπὸ τοῦ πόνου, εἴ τι δύναται, περὶ αὐτοῦ
ἀποφηνάσθω.

λδ′. Περὶ δόξης· ἴδε τὰς διανοίας αὐτῶν, οἷαι,
καὶ οἷα μὲν φεύγουσαι, οἷα δὲ διώκουσαι. καὶ
ὅτι, ὡς αἱ θῖνες ἄλλαι ἐπ᾿ ἄλλαις ἐπιφορούμεναι
κρύπτουσι τὰς προτέρας, οὕτως ἐν τῷ βίῳ τὰ
πρότερα ὑπὸ τῶν ἐπενεχθέντων τάχιστα
ἐκαλύφθη.

λε′. [Πλατωνικόν.]⁴ "Ἦι οὖν ὑπάρχει διανοίᾳ
μεγαλοπρέπεια καὶ θεωρία παντὸς μὲν χρόνου,
πάσης δὲ οὐσίας, ἆρα οἴει τούτῳ μέγα τι δοκεῖν
εἶναι τὸν ἀνθρώπινον βίον; ἀδύνατον, ἦ δ᾿ ὅς.
οὐκοῦν καὶ θάνατον οὐ δεινόν τι ἡγήσεται ὁ
τοιοῦτος; ἥκιστά γε."

---

¹ ἐτεῇ Usener : ἐτὶ εἰ P : ἔτι ἢ A.
² δαίμονα PA : δὲ μόνα Cor. : δαιμόνια Xyl.
³ εἰ ἕνωσις Cas., Schenkl : ἢ PA : κένωσις P.
⁴ <Πλατωνικὸν> P : so <᾿Αντισθενικὸν> § 36, and <Πλα-
τωνικὰ> § 44.

the Sage: *All things by Law, but in very truth only elements.* But it suffices to remember that all things *are* by law: there thou hast it briefly enough.[1]

32. OF DEATH: Either dispersion if atoms; or, if a single Whole, either extinction or a change of state.[2]

33. OF PAIN: *When unbearable it destroys us, when lasting, it is bearable,*[3] and the mind safeguards its own calm by withdrawing itself, and the ruling Reason takes no hurt. As to the parts that are impaired by the pain, let them say their say about it as they can.[4]

34. OF GLORY: Look at the minds of its votaries, their characteristics, ambitions, antipathies.[5] Remember too that, as the sands of the sea drifting one upon the other bury the earlier deposits, so in life the earlier things are very soon hidden under what comes after.

35. [From Plato.][6] *Dost thou think that the life of man can seem any great matter to him who has true grandeur of soul and a comprehensive outlook on all Time and all Substance? " It cannot seem so," said he. Will such a man then deem death a terrible thing? " Not in the least."*

---

[1] The reading and meaning are uncertain. The Sage is Democritus, and we should expect *atoms* rather than *elements* to be mentioned. Leopold aptly quotes Sext. Emp. vii. 35: νόμῳ γλυκὺ καὶ νόμῳ πικρόν, νόμῳ θερμὸν νόμῳ ψυχρόν . . . ἐτεῇ δὲ ἄτομα καὶ κένον. Fournier cleverly makes a hexameter of the words πάντα νομίστ᾽, ἐτεῇ δὲ μόνα στοιχεῖα <κένον τε>.

[2] Sen. *Ep.* 65 *ad fin.* : *Mors aut finis aut transitus.*

[3] vii. 16, 64. *cp.* Aesch. *Frag.* 310 : θάρσει· πόνου γὰρ ἄκρον οὐκ ἔχει χρόνον ; Diog. Laert. *Epicurus* xxxi. 4. Tert. *Apol.* 45.   [4] vii. 14 ; viii. 40.   [5] vi. 59.   [6] *Rep.* 486 A.

λϛ΄. ['Αντισθενικόν.] "Βασιλικὸν μὲν εὖ πράττειν, κακῶς δὲ ἀκούειν."

λζ΄. Αἰσχρόν ἐστι τὸ μὲν πρόσωπον ὑπήκοον εἶναι καὶ σχηματίζεσθαι καὶ κατακοσμεῖσθαι, ὡς κελεύει ἡ διάνοια, αὐτὴν δ᾽ ὑφ᾽ ἑαυτῆς μὴ σχηματίζεσθαι καὶ κατακοσμεῖσθαι.

λη΄. "Τοῖς πράγμασιν γὰρ οὐχὶ θυμοῦσθαι χρεών·
μέλει γὰρ αὐτοῖς οὐδέν."

λθ΄. "'Αθανάτοις τε θεοῖς καὶ ἡμῖν χάρματα δοίης."

μ΄. "Βίον θερίζειν, ὥστε κάρπιμον στάχυν,
καὶ τὸν μὲν εἶναι, τὸν δὲ μή."

μα΄. "Εἰ δ᾽ ἠμελήθην ἐκ θεῶν καὶ παῖδ᾽ ἐμώ,
ἔχει λόγον καὶ τοῦτο."

μβ΄. "Τὸ γὰρ εὖ μετ᾽ ἐμοῦ καὶ τὸ δίκαιον."

μγ΄. "Μὴ συνεπιθρηνεῖν, μὴ σφύζειν."

μδ΄. [Πλατωνικά.] "'Εγὼ δὲ τούτῳ δίκαιον ἂν λόγον ἀντείποιμι· ὅτι οὐ καλῶς λέγεις, ὦ ἄνθρωπε, εἰ οἴει δεῖν κίνδυνον ὑπολογίζεσθαι τοῦ ζῆν ἢ τεθνάναι ἄνδρα, ὅτου τι καὶ σμικρὸν ὄφελος· ἀλλ᾽ οὐκ ἐκεῖνο μόνον σκοπεῖν, ὅταν πράττῃ, πότερον δίκαια ἢ ἄδικα πράττει καὶ ἀνδρὸς ἀγαθοῦ <ἔργα>[1] ἢ κακοῦ."

με΄. "Οὕτω γὰρ ἔχει, ὦ ἄνδρες 'Αθηναῖοι, τῇ ἀληθείᾳ· οὗ ἄν τις αὐτὸν τάξῃ ἡγησάμενος

---

[1] <ἔργα> from Plato, Gat.: so δεῖ below.

---

[1] cp. Epict. iv. 6, § 20; 1 St. Peter, ii. 20. See Diog. Laert. *Antisthenes* § 4. Plutarch attributes the saying to Alexander. [2] vii. 60.

[3] Eur. *Bellerophon*, Frag. 289; xi. 6. Twice quoted by Plutarch. [4] Unknown.

BOOK VII

36. [From Antisthenes.] *'Tis royal to do well and be ill spoken of.* [1]

37. It is a shame that while the countenance [2] is subject to the mind, taking its cast and livery from it, the mind cannot take its cast and its livery from itself.

38. *It nought availeth to be wroth with things,*
      For they reck not of it. [3]

39. *Unto the deathless Gods and to us give cause for rejoicing.* [4]

40. *Our lives are reaped like the ripe ears of corn,*
      And as one falls, another still is born. [5]

41. *Though me and both my sons the Gods have*
      spurned,
      For this too there is reason. [6]

42. *For justice and good luck shall bide with me.* [7]

43. *No chorus of loud dirges, no hysteria.* [8]

44. [Citations from Plato]:

I might fairly answer such a questioner : Thou art mistaken if thou thinkest that a man, who is worth anything at all, ought to let considerations of life and death weigh with him rather than in all that he does consider but this, whether it is just or unjust and the work of a good man or a bad. [9]

45. *This, O men of Athens, is the true state of the case : Wherever a man has stationed himself, deeming*

---

[5] Eur. *Hypsipyle*, Frag. 757 ; xi. 6.   Cic. *Tusc.* iii. 25, § 59 *Vita omnibus metenda, ut fruges.* Epict. ii. 6. 14. *cp.* Job v. 26.

[6] Eur. *Antiope*, Frag. 207 ; xi. 6.

[7] *sc.* σύμμαχον ἔσται Eur. *Frag.* 910. Twice quoted by Cicero *ad Att.* vi. 1, § 8 ; viii. 8, § 2). *cp.* Arist *Ach.* 661.

[8] Unknown.

[9] Plato, *Apol.* 28 B.   Socrates is answering a question whether he is not ashamed of risking his life in a vocation such as his.

βέλτιστον εἶναι ἢ ὑπ' ἄρχοντος ταχθῇ, ἐνταῦθα
<δεῖ>, ὡς ἐμοὶ δοκεῖ, μένοντα κινδυνεύειν, μηδὲν
ὑπολογιζόμενον μήτε θάνατον μήτε ἄλλο μηδὲν
πρὸ τοῦ αἰσχροῦ."

μϚ'. "'Αλλ', ὦ μακάριε, ὅρα, μὴ ἄλλο τι τὸ
γενναῖον καὶ τὸ ἀγαθὸν ἢ τὸ σώζειν τε καὶ
σώζεσθαι· μὴ γὰρ τοῦτο μέν, τὸ ζῆν ὁποσονδὴ
χρόνον, τόν γε ὡς ἀληθῶς ἄνδρα, ἐατέον ἐστί, καὶ
οὐ φιλοψυχητέον, ἀλλ' ἐπιτρέψαντα περὶ τούτων
τῷ θεῷ καὶ πιστεύσαντα ταῖς γυναιξίν, ὅτι 'τὴν
εἱμαρμένην οὐδ' ἂν εἷς ἐκφύγοι,' τὸ ἐπὶ τούτῳ
σκεπτέον, τίνα ἂν τρόπον τοῦτον, ὃν μέλλει
χρόνον βιῶναι, ὡς ἄριστα βιῴη."

μζ'. Περισκοπεῖν ἄστρων δρόμους ὥσπερ
συμπεριθέοντα· καὶ τὰς τῶν στοιχείων εἰς
ἄλληλα μεταβολὰς συνεχῶς ἐννοεῖν· ἀποκαθαίρ-
ουσι γὰρ αἱ τούτων φαντασίαι τὸν ῥύπον τοῦ
χαμαὶ βίου.

μή. Καλὸν τὸ τοῦ Πλάτωνος. καὶ δὴ περὶ
ἀνθρώπων τοὺς λόγους ποιούμενον ἐπισκοπεῖν
δεῖ καὶ τὰ ἐπίγεια, ὥσπερ ποθὲν ἄνωθεν, κατὰ [1]
ἀγέλας, στρατεύματα, γεώργια, γάμους, δια-
λύσεις, γενέσεις, θανάτους, δικαστηρίων θόρυβον,
ἐρήμους χώρας, βαρβάρων ἔθνη ποικίλα, ἑορτάς,
θρήνους, ἀγοράς, τὸ παμμιγὲς καὶ τὸ ἐκ τῶν
ἐναντίων συγκοσμούμενον.

μθ'. Τὰ προγεγονότα ἀναθεωρεῖν, τὰς τοσ-

[1] κάτω Cas.

---

[1] Plato, *Apol.* 28 E.   [2] Plato, *Gorgias*, 512 DE.
[3] What follows is obviously not a saying of Plato. We
must therefore refer back to what precedes, or suppose that
Plato's words have dropped out.

it the best for him, or has been stationed by his commander, there methinks he ought to stay and run every risk, taking into account neither death nor any thing else save dishonour.[1]

46. *But, my good sir, see whether nobility and goodness do not mean something other than to save and be saved; for surely a man worthy of the name must waive aside the question of the duration of life however extended, and must not cling basely to life, but leaving these things in the hands of God pin his faith to the women's adage, 'his destiny no man can flee,' and thereafter consider in what way he may best live for such time as he has to live.[2]*

47. Watch the stars in their courses as one that runneth about with them therein; and think constantly upon the reciprocal changes of the elements, for thoughts on these things cleanse away the mire of our earthly life.

48. Noble is this saying of Plato's.[3] Moreover he who discourses of men should, as if from some vantage-point [4] above, take a bird's-eye view of the things of earth, in its gatherings,[5] armies, husbandry, its marriages and separations,[6] its births and deaths, the din of the law-court and the silence of the desert, barbarous races manifold, its feasts and mournings and markets, the medley of it all and its orderly conjunction of contraries.

49. Pass in review the far-off things of the past

---

[4] ix. 30. *cp.* Lucian, *Char.* § 15; *Icaro-Men.* § 12.

[5] If κατὰ ἀγέλας be read, it will mean literally, *drove by drove, i.e. in its aggregations*; if κάτω, ἀγέλας, the latter word must refer to gatherings of *men*.

[6] This might mean *treaties of peace*, but there seems to be a system of contrasted pairs.

αὑτας τῶν ἡγεμονιῶν μεταβολάς.[1] ἔξεστι καὶ
τὰ ἐσόμενα προεφορᾶν. ὁμοειδῆ γὰρ πάντως
ἔσται, καὶ οὐχ οἷόν τε ἐκβῆναι τοῦ ῥυθμοῦ τῶν
νῦν γινομένων· ὅθεν καὶ ἴσον τὸ τεσσαράκοντα
ἔτεσιν ἱστορῆσαι τὸν ἀνθρώπινον βίον τῷ ἐπὶ ἔτη
μύρια. τί γὰρ πλέον ὄψει;

ν′.   "Καὶ τὰ μὲν ἐκ γῆς
φύντ᾽ εἰς γαῖαν, τὰ δ᾽ ἀπ᾽ αἰθερίου
βλαστόντα γονῆς εἰς οὐράνιον
πόλον ἦλθε πάλιν·"

ἢ τοῦτο διάλυσις τῶν ἐν ταῖς ἀτόμοις ἀντεμ-
πλοκῶν καὶ τοιοῦτός τις σκορπισμὸς τῶν ἀπαθῶν
στοιχείων.

να′. Καὶ

"Σίτοισι καὶ ποτοῖσι καὶ μαγεύμασι
παρεκτρέποντες ὀχετόν, ὥστε μὴ θανεῖν."

2   "Θεόθεν δὲ πνέοντ᾽ οὖρον ἀνάγκη
τλῆναι καμάτοις ἀνοδύρτοις."

νβ′.[2] "Καββαλικώτερος," ἀλλ᾽ οὐχὶ κοινων-
ικώτερος οὐδὲ αἰδημονέστερος οὐδ᾽ εὐτακτότερος
ἐπὶ τοῖς συμβαίνουσιν οὐδὲ εὐμενέστερος πρὸς τὰ
τῶν πλησίον παροράματα.

νγ′. "Οπου ἔργον ἐπιτελεῖσθαι δύναται κατὰ
τὸν κοινὸν θεοῖς καὶ ἀνθρώποις λόγον, ἐκεῖ οὐδὲν
δεινόν· ὅπου γὰρ ὠφελείας τυχεῖν ἔξεστι διὰ τῆς

---

[1] τὰς . . . μεταβολὰς seems out of place, and Jackson
would put the words after ποικίλα, in previous section.

[2] Here P has a note, οὐκ ἔστιν ἀρχὴ τοῦτο, ἀλλ᾽ < ἐκ >
τῶν ἀνωτέρω τῶν πρὸ τῶν Πλατονικῶν συναφές.

and its succession of sovranties without number.
Thou canst look forward and see the future also.
For it will most surely be of the same character,[1]
and it cannot but carry on the rhythm of existing
things. Consequently it is all one, whether we
witness human life for forty years or ten thousand.
For what more shalt thou see?

50. *All that is earth-born gravitates earthwards,*
   Dust unto dust ; and all that from ether
   Grows, speeds swiftly back again heavenward ; [2]

that is, either there is a breaking up of the closely-
linked atoms or, what is much the same, a scattering
of the impassive elements.

51. Again :

   With meats and drinks and curious sorceries
   Side-track the stream, so be they may not die.[3]

   When a storm from the Gods beats down on our
      bark,
   At our oars then we needs must toil and complain
      not.[4]

52. *Better at the cross-buttock,*[5] may be, but not at
shewing public spirit or modesty, or being readier for
every contingency or more gracious to our neighbour
if he sees awry.

53. A work that can be accomplished in obedience
to that reason which we share with the Gods is
attended with no fear. For no harm need be
anticipated, where by an activity that follows the

---

[1] vi. 37.
[2] Eur. *Chrys.* Frag. 836. Constantly quoted. *cp.* Lucr.
ii. 991 ; Genesis iii. 19: γῆ εἶ καὶ ἐς γῆν ἀπελεύσῃ ; Ecclesiasticus xl. 11 ; Plut. *Consol.* 15.
[3] Eur. *Suppl.* 1110.   [4] Unknown.
[5] Plutarch, *Apophth.* 2. 206 E.

εὐοδούσης καὶ κατὰ τὴν κατασκευὴν προιούσης
ἐνεργείας, ἐκεῖ οὐδεμίαν βλάβην ὑφορατέον.

νδʹ. Πανταχοῦ καὶ διηνεκῶς ἐπὶ σοί ἐστι καὶ
τῇ παρούσῃ συμβάσει θεοσεβῶς εὐαρεστεῖν, καὶ
τοῖς παροῦσιν ἀνθρώποις κατὰ δικαιοσύνην
προσφέρεσθαι, καὶ τῇ παρούσῃ φαντασίᾳ ἐμφιλοτεχνεῖν, ἵνα μή τι ἀκατάληπτον παρεισρυῇ.

νεʹ. Μὴ περιβλέπου ἀλλότρια ἡγεμονικά,
ἀλλ' ἐκεῖ βλέπε κατ' εὐθύ, ἐπὶ τί σε ἡ φύσις
ὁδηγεῖ, ἥ τε τοῦ ὅλου διὰ τῶν συμβαινόντων σοι
καὶ ἡ σὴ διὰ τῶν πρακτέων ὑπὸ σοῦ. πρακτέον
δὲ ἑκάστῳ τὸ ἑξῆς τῇ κατασκευῇ· κατεσκεύασται
δὲ τὰ μὲν λοιπὰ τῶν λογικῶν ἕνεκεν, ὥσπερ καὶ
ἐπὶ παντὸς ἄλλου τὰ χείρω τῶν κρειττόνων
ἕνεκεν, τὰ δὲ λογικὰ ἀλλήλων ἕνεκεν.

2   Τὸ μὲν οὖν προηγούμενον ἐν τῇ τοῦ ἀνθρώπου
κατασκευῇ τὸ κοινωνικόν ἐστι· δεύτερον δὲ τὸ
ἀνένδοτον πρὸς τὰς σωματικὰς πείσεις· λογικῆς
γὰρ καὶ νοερᾶς κινήσεως ἴδιον περιορίζειν ἑαυτὴν
καὶ μήποτε ἡττᾶσθαι μήτε αἰσθητικῆς μήτε ὁρμητικῆς κινήσεως· ζῳώδεις γὰρ ἑκάτεραι· ἡ δὲ νοερὰ
ἐθέλει πρωτιστεύειν καὶ μὴ κατακρατεῖσθαι ὑπ'
ἐκείνων. δικαίως γε· πέφυκε γὰρ χρηστικὴ
πᾶσιν ἐκείνοις. τρίτον ἐν τῇ λογικῇ κατασκευῇ
τὸ ἀπρόπτωτον καὶ ἀνεξαπάτητον. τούτων οὖν
ἐχόμενον τὸ ἡγεμονικὸν εὐθεῖαν[1] περαινέτω, καὶ
ἔχει τὰ ἑαυτοῦ.

νϛʹ. Ὡς ἀποτεθνηκότα δεῖ, καὶ μέχρι νῦν

---

[1] εὐθείᾳ Schenkl : εὐθέα PA : εὐθεῖαν Cor. (cp. x. 11).

right road, and satisfies the demands of our constitution, we can ensure our own weal.

54. At all times and in all places it rests with thee both to be content with thy present lot as a worshipper of the Gods, and to deal righteously with thy present neighbours, and to labour lovingly at thy present thoughts, that nothing unverified should steal into them.

55. Look not about thee at the ruling Reason of others, but look with straight eyes at this, *To what is Nature guiding thee?*—both the Nature of the Universe, by means of what befalls thee and thy nature by means of the acts thou hast to do. But everyone must do what follows from his own constitution; and all other things have been constituted for the sake of rational beings—just as in every other case the lower are for the sake of the higher [1]— but the rational for their own sake.

Social obligation then is the leading feature in the constitution of man and, coming second to it, an uncompromising resistance to bodily inclinations. For it is the privilege of a rational and intelligent motion to isolate itself, and never to be overcome by the motions of sense or desire; for either kind is animal-like. But the motion of the Intelligence claims ever to have the pre-eminence and never to be mastered by them. And rightly so, for it is its nature to put all those to its own use. Thirdly, the rational constitution is free from precipitancy and cannot be misled. Let the ruling Reason then, clinging to these characteristics, accomplish a straight course and then it comes into its own.

56. As one that is dead, and his life till now lived

[1] v. 16, 30; xi. 10.

βεβιωκότα,[1] τὸ λοιπὸν ἐκ τοῦ περιόντος ζῆσαι κατὰ τὴν φύσιν.

νζ. Μόνον φιλεῖν τὸ ἑαυτῷ συμβαῖνον καὶ συγκλωθόμενον. τί γὰρ ἁρμοδιώτερον;

νή. Ἐφ' ἑκάστου συμβάματος ἐκείνους πρὸ ὀμμάτων ἔχειν, οἷς τὰ αὐτὰ συνέβαινεν, ἔπειτα ἤχθοντο, ἐξενίζοντο, ἐμέμφοντο· νῦν οὖν ἐκεῖνοι ποῦ; οὐδαμοῦ· τί οὖν; καὶ σὺ θέλεις ὁμοίως; οὐχὶ δὲ τὰς μὲν ἀλλοτρίας τροπὰς καταλιπεῖν τοῖς τρέπουσι καὶ τρεπομένοις; αὐτὸς δὲ περὶ τὸ πῶς χρῆσθαι αὐτοῖς ὅλος γίνεσθαι; χρήσῃ γὰρ καλῶς, καὶ ὕλη σου ἔσται· μόνον πρόσεχε καὶ θέλε σεαυτῷ καλὸς [2] εἶναι ἐπὶ παντός, οὗ πράσσεις· καὶ μέμνησο† <ἐπ'> [3] ἀμφοτέρων, ὅτι καὶ διάφορον† ἐφ' οὗ ἡ πρᾶξις.

νθ'. Ἔνδον σκέπε.[4] ἔνδον ἡ πηγὴ τοῦ ἀγαθοῦ καὶ ἀεὶ ἀναβλύειν δυναμένη, ἐὰν ἀεὶ σκάπτῃς·

ξ'. Δεῖ καὶ τὸ σῶμα πεπηγέναι καὶ μὴ διερρῖφθαι μήτε ἐν κινήσει μήτε ἐν σχέσει. οἷον γάρ τι ἐπὶ τοῦ προσώπου παρέχεται ἡ διάνοια, συνετὸν [5] αὐτὸ καὶ εὔσχημον συντηροῦσα,[6] τοιοῦτο καὶ ἐπὶ ὅλου τοῦ σώματος ἀπαιτητέον. πάντα δὲ ταῦτα σὺν τῷ ἀνεπιτηδεύτῳ φυλακτέα.

ξα'. Ἡ βιωτικὴ τῇ παλαιστικῇ ὁμοιοτέρα ἤπερ τῇ ὀρχηστικῇ κατὰ τὸ πρὸς τὰ ἐμπίπτοντα καὶ οὐ προεγνωσμένα ἔτοιμος καὶ ἀπτῶς ἑστάναι.

---

[1] <οὐ> Reiske. [2] καλῶς A.
[3] <ἐπ'> Gat.: κἀδιάφορον Kron.: Schultz and Schenkl mark a lacuna after ὅτι.
[4] βλέπε P: σκοπεῖ D: σκάπτε Schultz.
[5] συνεστὸς Cor.
[6] καὶ συντηροῦσα A: ἀεὶ for καὶ Schenkl.

and gone, thou must live the rest of thy days as so much to the good,[1] and live according to Nature.

57. Love only what befalls thee and is spun for thee by fate. For what can be more befitting for thee?

58. In every contingency keep before thine eyes those who, when these same things befell them, were straightway aggrieved, estranged,[2] rebellious. Where are they now? Nowhere! What then? Wouldst thou too be like them? Why not leave those alien deflections to what deflects and is deflected by them, and devote thyself wholly to the question how to turn these contingencies to the best advantage? For then wilt thou make a noble use of them, and they shall be thy raw material. Only in thought and will take heed to be beautiful to thyself in all that thou doest. And remember, in rejecting the one and using the other, that the thing which matters is the aim of the action.

59. Look within. Within is the fountain of Good,[3] ready always to well forth if thou wilt alway delve.

60. The body too should be firmly set and suffer no distortion in movement or bearing. For what the mind effects in the face,[4] by keeping it composed and well-favoured, should be looked for similarly in the whole body. But all this must be secured without conscious effort.

61. The business of life is more akin to wrestling [5] than dancing, for it requires of us to stand ready and unshakeable against every assault however unforeseen.

---

[1] *cp.* Sen. *Ep.* 12 *ad fin. Quisquis dixit* " Vixi," *quotidie ad lucrum surgit.*   [2] Or, *taken by surprise. cp.* viii. 15.
[3] St. John iv. 14.   [4] vii. 37. *cp.* vii. 24.
[5] St. Paul, Eph. vi. 12.

ξβ΄. Συνεχῶς ἐφιστάναι, τίνες εἰσὶν οὗτοι, ὑφ'
ὧν μαρτυρεῖσθαι θέλεις, καὶ τίνα ἡγεμονικὰ
ἔχουσιν. οὔτε γὰρ μέμψῃ τοῖς ἀκουσίως πταί-
ουσιν, οὔτε ἐπιμαρτυρήσεως δεήσῃ, ἐμβλέπων εἰς
τὰς πηγὰς τῆς ὑπολήψεως καὶ ὁρμῆς αὐτῶν.

ξγ΄. "Πᾶσα ψυχή," φησίν, "ἄκουσα στέρεται
ἀληθείας·" οὕτως οὖν καὶ δικαιοσύνης καὶ
σωφροσύνης καὶ εὐμενείας καὶ παντὸς τοῦ
τοιούτου. ἀναγκαιότατον δὲ τὸ διηνεκῶς τούτου
μεμνῆσθαι· ἔσῃ γὰρ πρὸς πάντας πρᾳότερος.

ξδ΄. Ἐπὶ μὲν παντὸς πόνου πρόχειρον ἔστω,
ὅτι οὐκ αἰσχρόν, οὐδὲ τὴν διάνοιαν τὴν κυβερν-
ῶσαν χείρω ποιεῖ· οὔτε γὰρ καθὸ λογική[1] ἐστιν
οὔτε καθὸ κοινωνικὴ διαφθείρει αὐτήν· ἐπὶ
μέντοι τῶν πλείστων πόνων καὶ τὸ τοῦ Ἐπικού-
ρου σοι βοηθείτω, ὅτι "οὔτε ἀφόρητον οὔτε αἰών-
ιον," ἐὰν τῶν ὅρων μνημονεύῃς καὶ μὴ προσ-
δοξάζῃς. κἀκείνου δὲ μέμνησο, ὅτι πολλά, πόνῳ
τὰ αὐτὰ ὄντα, λανθάνει δυσχεραινόμενα· οἷον τὸ
νυστάζειν καὶ τὸ καυματίζεσθαι καὶ τὸ ἀν-
ορεκτεῖν· ὅταν οὖν τινι τούτων δυσαρεστῇς,
λέγε ἑαυτῷ, ὅτι πόνῳ ἐνδίδως.

ξε΄. Ὅρα, μήποτέ <τι> τοιοῦτον πάθῃς πρὸς
τοὺς ἀπανθρώπους, οἷον οἱ <ἀπ>άνθρωποι[2] πρὸς
τοὺς ἀνθρώπους.

ξϛ΄. Πόθεν ἴσμεν, εἰ μὴ Τηλαύγης Σωκράτους τὴν διάθεσιν κρείσσων ἦν; οὐ γὰρ ἀρκεῖ,

[1] καθὸ ὑλική P Mo 2 : καθολική A : καθὸ λογική Cas.
[2] <ἀπ>άνθρωποι Cas.

---

[1] vi. 5ʒ; vii. 34.
[2] Quoted by Epictetus (i. 63, 28 § 4) as from Plato (see
Plato, *Soph.* 238 C ; *Rep.* iii. 412); viii. 14 ; x. 30 ; xi. 18, § 3.
= No soul is deprived wittingly.

62. Continually reflect, who they are whose favourable testimony thou desirest,[1] and what their ruling Reason; for thus wilt thou not find fault with those who unintentionally offend, nor wilt thou want their testimony, when thou lookest into the inner springs of their opinions and desires.

63. *Every soul*, says Plato, *is bereft of truth against its will.*[2] Therefore it is the same also with justice and temperance and lovingkindness and every like quality. It is essential to keep this ever in mind, for it will make thee gentler towards all.[3]

64. Whenever thou art in pain, have this reflection ready, that this is nothing to be ashamed of, nor can it make worse the mind that holds the helm. For it cannot impair it in so far as it is rational or in so far as it is social. In most pains, however, call to thy rescue even Epicurus when he says that a pain is *never unbearable*[4] *or interminable*, so that thou remember its limitations and add nothing to it in imagination.[5] Recollect this too that many of our every-day discomforts are really pain in disguise, such as drowsiness,[6] a high temperature, want of appetite. When inclined to be vexed at any of these, say to thyself : *I am giving in to pain.*[7]

65. See that thou never have for the inhuman the feeling which the inhuman have for human kind.

66. How do we know that Telauges[8] may not have excelled Socrates in character? For it is not enough

[3] The same word is used of Marcus by Galen (xii. 17 Kühn) ; by Athenag. *Apol.* 1. 1 ; by Lucian, *Peregr.* 17 ; and by Aristides, *ad Reg.* §§ 105, 112.
[4] vii. 33.   [5] viii. 49.
[6] vi. 2.   [7] *cp.* vi. 29.
[8] Son of Pythagoras. See Diog. Laert. *Pyth.* 22. 26.

εἰ Σωκράτης ἐνδοξότερον ἀπέθανε, καὶ ἐντρεχέσ-
τερον τοῖς σοφισταῖς διελέγετο, καὶ καρτερικώ-
τερον ἐν τῷ πάγῳ διενυκτέρευεν, καὶ τὸν Σαλαμί-
νιον κελευσθεὶς ἄγειν γεννικώτερον ἔδοξεν
ἀντιβῆναι, καὶ " ἐν ταῖς ὁδοῖς ἐβρενθύετο" περὶ
οὗ καὶ μάλιστ' ἄν τις ἐπιστήσειεν,[1] εἴπερ ἀληθὲς
ἦν· ἀλλ' ἐκεῖνο δεῖ σκοπεῖν, ποίαν τινὰ τὴν
ψυχὴν εἶχε Σωκράτης, καὶ εἰ ἐδύνατο ἀρκεῖσθαι
τῷ δίκαιος εἶναι τὰ πρὸς ἀνθρώπους καὶ ὅσιος
τὰ πρὸς θεοὺς μήτε ἐκεῖ[2] πρὸς τὴν κακίαν
ἀγανακτῶν μηδὲ μὴν δουλεύων τινὸς ἀγνοίᾳ μήτε
τῶν ἀπονεμομένων ἐκ τοῦ ὅλου ὡς ξένον τι
δεχόμενος ἢ ὡς ἀφόρητον ὑπομένων μήτε τοῖς
τοῦ σαρκιδίου πάθεσιν ἐμπαρέχων συμπαθῆ τὸν
νοῦν.

ξζ. Ἡ φύσις οὐχ οὕτως συνεκέρασε τῷ
συγκρίματι, ὡς μὴ ἐφεῖσθαι περιορίζειν ἑαυτὸν
καὶ τὰ ἑαυτοῦ ὑφ' ἑαυτῷ ποιεῖσθαι· λίαν γὰρ
ἐνδέχεται θεῖον ἄνδρα γενέσθαι καὶ ὑπὸ μηδενὸς
γνωρισθῆναι. τούτου μέμνησο ἀεί, καὶ ἔτι
ἐκείνου, ὅτι ἐν ὀλιγίστοις κεῖται τὸ εὐδαιμόνως
βιῶσαι· καὶ μή, ὅτι ἀπήλπισας διαλεκτικὸς καὶ
φυσικὸς ἔσεσθαι, διὰ τοῦτο ἀπογνῷς καὶ ἐλεύθερος καὶ αἰδήμων καὶ κοινωνικὸς καὶ εὐπειθὴς
θεῷ.

ξη. Ἀβιάστως διαζῆσαι ἐν πλείστῃ θυμηδίᾳ,
κἂν πάντες καταβοῶσιν ἅτινα βούλονται, κἂν

---

[1] ἀπιστήσειεν Gat. : dubitari potest Xyl.
[2] εἰκῇ P : ἐκείνων Schenkl.

---

[1] Plato, Apol. 20 C ; Epict. iv. 7 § 30.
[2] Or γενναιότερον, more honourable.

that Socrates died a more glorious death, and disputed more deftly with the Sophists, and with more hardihood braved whole nights in the frost, and, when called upon to fetch the Salaminian,[1] deemed it more spirited[2] to disobey, and that he *carried his head high as he walked*[3]—and about the truth of this one can easily judge—; but the point to elucidate is this: what sort of soul had Socrates,[4] and could he rest satisfied with being just in his dealings with men and religious in his attitude towards the Gods, neither resentful at the wickedness of others nor yet lackeying the ignorance of anyone, nor regarding as alien to himself anything allotted to him from the Whole, nor bearing it as a burden intolerable, nor letting his intelligence be swayed sympathetically by the affections of the flesh?

67. Nature did not make so intimate a blend in the compound as not to allow a man to isolate himself and keep his own things in his own power. For it is very possible to be a godlike man and yet not to be recognized by any.[5] Never forget this; nor that the happy life depends on the fewest possible things[6]; nor because thou hast been baulked in the hope of becoming skilled in dialectics and physics,[7] needest thou despair of being free and modest and unselfish and obedient to God.

68. Thou mayest live out thy life with none to constrain thee in the utmost peace of mind even though the whole world cry out against thee what

[3] Arist. *Nub.* 363 ; Plato, *Symp.* 221 B. The meaning of the parenthesis is not clear. [4] cp. Dio *Orat.* iii. *ad init.*
[5] Sen. (*Ep.* 79) instances Democritus, Socrates, and Cato.
[6] Julian, *Conviv.* 427. 21, where Marcus, asked in what consists the imitation of the Gods, says δεῖσθαι τῶν ἐλαχίστων. cp. Lucian, *Cynic.* 12 : οἱ δ' ἔγγιστοι θεοῖς ἐλαχίστων δέονται. Diog. Laert. *Socr.* 11.   [7] i. 17, § 8 ; cp. v. 5 ; viii. 1.

H

τὰ θηρία διασπᾷ τὰ μελύδρια τοῦ περιτεθραμμένου τούτου φυράματος. τί γὰρ κωλύει ἐν
πᾶσι τούτοις τὴν διάνοιαν σώζειν ἑαυτὴν ἐν
γαλήνῃ, καὶ κρίσει [τῇ] περὶ τῶν περιεστηκότων
ἀληθεῖ, καὶ χρήσει τῶν ὑποβεβλημένων ἑτοίμῃ;
ὥστε τὴν μὲν κρίσιν λέγειν τῷ προσπίπτοντι·
"Τοῦτο ὑπάρχεις κατ᾽ οὐσίαν, κἂν κατὰ δόξαν
ἀλλοῖον φαίνῃ," τὴν δὲ χρῆσιν λέγειν τῷ ὑποπίπτ-
οντι· "Σὲ ἐζήτουν." ἀεὶ γάρ μοι τὸ παρὸν ὕλη
ἀρετῆς λογικῆς καὶ πολιτικῆς καὶ τὸ σύνολον
τέχνης ἀνθρώπου ἢ θεοῦ. πᾶν γὰρ τὸ συμβαῖνον θεῷ ἢ ἀνθρώπῳ ἐξοικειοῦται καὶ οὔτε
καινὸν οὔτε δυσμεταχείριστον, ἀλλὰ γνώριμον
καὶ εὐεργές.

ξθ´. Τοῦτο ἔχει ἡ τελειότης τοῦ ἤθους, τὸ
πᾶσαν ἡμέραν ὡς τελευταίαν διεξάγειν καὶ μήτε
σφύζειν μήτε ναρκᾶν μήτε ὑποκρίνεσθαι.

ο´. Οἱ θεοί, ἀθάνατοι ὄντες, οὐ δυσχεραίνουσιν, ὅτι ἐν τοσούτῳ αἰῶνι δεήσει αὐτοὺς
πάντως ἀεὶ τοιούτων ὄντων καὶ τοσούτων φαύλων
ἀνέχεσθαι· προσέτι δὲ καὶ κήδονται αὐτῶν
παντοίως. σὺ δὲ ὅσον οὐδέπω λήγειν μέλλων
ἀπαυδᾷς, καὶ ταῦτα, εἰς ὢν τῶν φαύλων;

οα´. Γελοῖόν ἐστι τὴν μὲν ἰδίαν κακίαν μὴ
φεύγειν, ὃ καὶ δυνατόν ἐστι· τὴν δὲ τῶν ἄλλων
φεύγειν, ὅπερ ἀδύνατον.

οβ´. Ὅ ἂν ἡ λογικὴ καὶ πολιτικὴ δύναμις
εὑρίσκῃ μήτε νοερὸν μήτε κοινωνικόν, εὐλόγως
καταδεέστερον ἑαυτῆς κρίνει.

---

[1] xi. 3. Applies accurately to the Christians.   cp. i. 6;
iii. 16; viii. 48, 51, § 2.   [2] iv. 1.

they will, even though beasts tear limb from limb this plastic clay that has encased thee with its growth.[1] For what in all this debars the mind from keeping itself in calmness, in a right judgment as to its environment, and in readiness to use all that is put at its disposal? so that the judgment can say to that which meets it: *In essential substance thou art this, whatever else the common fame would have thee be.* And the use can say to the object presented to it: *Thee was I seeking.* For the thing in hand is for me ever material for the exercise of rational and civic virtue,[2] and in a word for the art of a man or of God. For everything that befalls is intimately connected with God or man, and is not new or difficult to deal with, but familiar and feasible.

69. This is the mark of a perfect character, to pass through each day as if it were the last,[3] without agitation, without torpor, without pretence.

70. The Gods—and they are immortal—do not take it amiss that for a time so long they must inevitably and always put up with worthless men who are what they are and so many[4]; nay they even care for them in all manner of ways. But thou, though destined to die so soon, criest off, and that too though thou art one of the worthless ones thyself.

71. It is absurd not to eschew our own wickedness, which is possible, but to eschew that of others, which is not possible.[5]

72. Whatever thy rational and civic faculty discovers to be neither intelligent nor social, it judges with good reason to fall short of its own standard.

[3] ii. 5. [4] St. Matt. v. 45.
[5] v. 17 ; ix. 42.

ογ΄. Ὅταν σὺ εὖ πεποιηκὼς ᾖς καὶ ἄλλος εὖ πεπονθώς, τί ἐπιζητεῖς τρίτον παρὰ ταῦτα, ὥσπερ οἱ μωροί, τὸ καὶ δόξαι εὖ πεποιηκέναι ἢ τὸ ἀμοιβῆς τυχεῖν;

οδ΄. Οὐδεὶς κάμνει ὠφελούμενος. ὠφέλεια δὲ πρᾶξις κατὰ φύσιν· μὴ οὖν κάμνε ὠφελούμενος, ἐν ᾧ ὠφελεῖς.

οε΄. Ἡ τοῦ ὅλου φύσις ἐπὶ τὴν κοσμοποιίαν ὥρμησε· νῦν δὲ ἤτοι πᾶν τὸ γινόμενον κατ᾽ ἐπακολούθησιν γίνεται, ἢ ἀλόγιστα καὶ τὰ κυριώτατά ἐστιν, ἐφ᾽ ἃ ποιεῖται ἰδίαν ὁρμὴν τὸ τοῦ κόσμου ἡγεμονικόν. εἰς πολλά σε γαληνότερον ποιήσει τοῦτο μνημονευόμενον.

73. When thou hast done well to another and another has fared well at thy hands, why go on like the foolish to look for a third thing besides, that is, the credit also of having done well or a return for the same [1]?

74. No one wearies of benefits received; and to act by the law of Nature is its own benefit. Weary not then of being benefited therein, wherein thou dost benefit others.[2]

75. The Nature of the Whole felt impelled to the creation of a Universe; but now either all that comes into being does so by a natural sequence,[3] or even the most paramount things, towards which the ruling Reason of the Universe feels an impulse of its own, are devoid of intelligence. Recollect this [4] and thou wilt face many an ill with more serenity.

[1] v. 6 ; ix. 42. *cp.* Fronto, *de Nep. ad fin.*
[2] *cp.* St. Paul, Gal. vi. 9; 2 Thess. iii. 13. For the Stoic view see Stob. *Ecl.* ii. 188.
[3] iv. 45 ; ix. 28.
[4] Marcus means that we must consider the second alternative given above as incredible.

α . Καὶ τοῦτο πρὸς τὸ ἀκενόδοξον φέρει, ὅτι οὐκ
ἔτι δύνασαι τὸν βίον ὅλον ἢ τόν γε ἀπὸ νεότητος
φιλόσοφον βεβιωκέναι· ἀλλὰ πολλοῖς τε ἄλλοις
καὶ αὐτὸς σεαυτῷ δῆλος γέγονας πόρρω φιλοσοφίας ὤν. πέφυρσαι οὖν· ὥστε τὴν μὲν δόξαν
τὴν τοῦ φιλοσόφου κτήσασθαι οὐκ ἔτι σοι
ῥᾴδιον· ἀνταγωνίζεται δὲ καὶ ἡ ὑπόθεσις. εἴπερ
οὖν ἀληθῶς ἑώρακας, ποῦ κεῖται τὸ πρᾶγμα,
τὸ μέν, τί δόξεις, ἄφες, ἀρκέσθητι δέ, εἰ κᾂν
τὸ λοιπὸν τοῦ βίου ὅσον δήποτε, <ὡς>¹ ἡ σὴ
φύσις θέλει, βιώσῃ. κατανόησον οὖν, τί θέλει,
καὶ μηδὲν ἄλλο σε περισπάτω· πεπείρασαι γάρ,
περὶ πόσα πλανηθείς, οὐδαμοῦ εὗρες τὸ εὖ ζῆν·
οὐκ ἐν συλλογισμοῖς, οὐκ ἐν πλούτῳ, οὐκ ἐν δόξῃ,
οὐκ ἐν ἀπολαύσει, οὐδαμοῦ. ποῦ οὖν ἐστιν; ἐν
τῷ ποιεῖν ἃ ἐπιζητεῖ ἡ τοῦ ἀνθρώπου φύσις· πῶς
οὖν ταῦτα ποιήσει; ἐὰν δόγματα ἔχῃ, ἀφ᾽ ὧν
αἱ ὁρμαὶ καὶ αἱ πράξεις. τίνα δόγματα; τὰ
περὶ ἀγαθῶν καὶ κακῶν, ὡς οὐδενὸς μὲν ἀγαθοῦ
ὄντος ἀνθρώπῳ, ὃ οὐχὶ ποιεῖ δίκαιον, σώφρονα,

¹ <ὡς> Gat.

BOOK VIII

1. THIS too serves as a corrective to vain-gloriousness, that thou art no longer able to have lived thy life wholly, or even from thy youth up, as a philosopher. Thou canst clearly perceive, and many others can see it too, that thou art far from Philosophy. So then thy life is a chaos,[1] and no longer is it easy for thee to win the credit of being a philosopher; and the facts of thy life too war against it. If then thine eyes have verily seen where the truth lies, care no more what men shall think of thee, but be content if the rest of thy life, whether long or short, be lived as thy nature wills. Make sure then what that will is, and let nothing else draw thee aside. For past experience tells thee in how much thou hast gone astray, nor anywhere lighted upon the true life; no, not in the subtleties of logic,[2] or in wealth or fame or enjoyment, or *anywhere*. Where then is it to be found? In doing that which is the quest of man's nature. How then shall a man do this? By having axioms as the source of his impulses and actions. What axioms? On the nature of Good and Evil, shewing that nothing is for a man's good save what makes him just, temperate, manly, free; nor any

---

[1] Or, *thou hast been besmirched*, but *cp.* vi. 16, § 3.
[2] i. 17 *ad fin.*; vii. 67.

ἀνδρεῖον, ἐλεύθερον, οὐδενὸς δὲ κακοῦ, ὃ οὐχὶ
ποιεῖ τἀναντία τοῖς εἰρημένοις.

β'. Καθ' ἑκάστην πρᾶξιν ἐρώτα σεαυτόν·
" Πῶς μοι αὕτη ἔχει; μὴ μετανοήσω ἐπ' αὐτῇ; "
μικρὸν καὶ τέθνηκα καὶ πάντ' ἐκ μέσου. τί πλέον
ἐπιζητῶ, εἰ τὸ παρὸν ἔργον ζῴου νοεροῦ καὶ
κοινωνικοῦ καὶ ἰσονόμου θεῷ;

γ'. Ἀλέξανδρος [δὲ] καὶ Γάϊος καὶ Πομπήϊος,
τί πρὸς Διογένη καὶ Ἡράκλειτον καὶ Σωκράτην;
οἱ μὲν γὰρ εἶδον τὰ πράγματα καὶ τὰς αἰτίας καὶ
τὰς ὕλας, καὶ τὰ ἡγεμονικὰ ἦν αὐτῶν αὐτά· †[1]
ἐκεῖ δὲ ὅσων πρόνοια καὶ δουλεία πόσων.

δ'. Ὅτι οὐδὲν ἧττον τὰ αὐτὰ ποιήσουσι, κἂν
σὺ διαρραγῇς.

ε'. Τὸ πρῶτον μὴ ταράσσου· πάντα γὰρ κατὰ
τὴν τοῦ ὅλου φύσιν· καὶ ὀλίγου χρόνου οὐδεὶς
οὐδαμοῦ ἔσῃ· ὥσπερ οὐδὲ Ἀδριανός, οὐδὲ Αὔγουστος. ἔπειτα ἀτενίσας εἰς τὸ πρᾶγμα ἴδε αὐτὸ
καὶ συμμνημονεύσας, ὅτι ἀγαθόν σε ἄνθρωπον
εἶναι δεῖ, καὶ τί τοῦ ἀνθρώπου ἡ φύσις ἀπαιτεῖ,
πρᾶξον τοῦτο ἀμεταστρεπτὶ καὶ εἰπέ, ὡς
δικαιότατον φαίνεταί σοι, μόνον εὐμενῶς καὶ
αἰδημόνως καὶ ἀνυποκρίτως.

ς'. Ἡ τῶν ὅλων φύσις τοῦτο ἔργον ἔχει, τὰ
ὧδε ὄντα ἐκεῖ μετατιθέναι, μεταβάλλειν, αἴρειν
ἔνθεν καὶ ἐκεῖ φέρειν. πάντα τροπαί, οὐχ ὥστε

---

[1] αὐτὰ A : ταὐτά P : ταῦτα Cas. : αὐτάρκη Schenkl.

---

[1] Justin (*Apol.* i. 46) mentions Heraclitus and Socrates
and others like them as "living with the divine Logos." And

BOOK VIII

thing for his ill that makes him not the reverse of these.

2. In every action ask thyself, *How does this affect me? Shall I regret it?* But a little and I am dead and all is past and gone. What more do I ask for, as long as my present work is that of a living creature, intelligent, social, and under one law with God?

3. What are Alexander and Gaius and Pompeius to Diogenes and Heraclitus[1] and Socrates? For these latter had their eyes opened to things and to the causes and the material substance of things, and their ruling Reason was their very own. But those—what a host of cares, what a world of slavery!

4. Thou mayst burst thyself with rage, but they will go on doing the same things none the less.

5. Firstly, fret not thyself, for all things are as the Nature of the Universe would have them, and within a little thou shalt be non-existent, and nowhere, like Hadrianus and Augustus. Secondly, look steadfastly at the thing, and see it as it is and, remembering withal that thou must be a good man, and what the Nature of man calls for, do this without swerving, and speak as seemeth to thee most just, only be it graciously, modestly, and without feigning.[2]

6. The Nature of the Universe is charged with this task, to transfer yonder the things which are here, to interchange them, to take them hence and convey them thither. All things are but phases of

in *Apol.* ii. 8 Heraclitus and Musonius are spoken of as hated and slain for their opinions. Gaius is Caesar.

[2] The word here used by Marcus occurs only in Christian writings.

MARCUS AURELIUS

φοβηθῆναι, μή τι καινόν· πάντα συνήθη· ἀλλὰ
καὶ ἴσαι αἱ ἀπονεμήσεις.

ζ. Ἀρκεῖται πᾶσα φύσις ἑαυτῇ εὐοδούσῃ·
φύσις δὲ λογικὴ εὐοδεῖ ἐν μὲν φαντασίαις μήτε
ψευδεῖ μήτε ἀδήλῳ συγκατατιθεμένη, τὰς ὁρμὰς
δὲ ἐπὶ τὰ κοινωνικὰ ἔργα μόνα ἀπευθύνουσα, τὰς
ὀρέξεις δὲ καὶ τὰς ἐκκλίσεις τῶν ἐφ᾽ ἡμῖν μόνων
πεποιημένη, τὸ δὲ ὑπὸ τῆς κοινῆς φύσεως ἀπονεμόμενον πᾶν ἀσπαζομένη. μέρος γὰρ αὐτῆς
ἐστιν, ὡς ἡ τοῦ φύλλου φύσις τῆς τοῦ φυτοῦ
φύσεως· πλὴν ὅτι ἐκεῖ μὲν ἡ τοῦ φύλλου φύσις
μέρος ἐστὶ φύσεως καὶ ἀναισθήτου καὶ ἀλόγου
καὶ ἐμποδίζεσθαι δυναμένης, ἡ δὲ τοῦ ἀνθρώπου
φύσις μέρος ἐστὶν ἀνεμποδίστου φύσεως καὶ
νοερᾶς καὶ δικαίας, εἴγε ἴσους καὶ κατ᾽ ἀξίαν τοὺς
μερισμοὺς χρόνων, οὐσίας, αἰτίου, ἐνεργείας, συμ-
βάσεως, ἑκάστοις ποιεῖται. σκόπει δέ, μὴ εἰ τὸ
<ἓν> πρὸς τὸ ἓν ἴσον εὑρήσεις ἐπὶ παντός, ἀλλὰ
εἰ συλλήβδην τὰ πάντα τοῦδε πρὸς ἀθρόα τὰ τοῦ
ἑτέρου.

η. " Ἀναγινώσκειν οὐκ ἔξεστιν." ἀλλὰ ὕβριν
ἀνείργειν ἔξεστιν· ἀλλὰ ἡδονῶν καὶ πόνων καθ-
υπερτερεῖν ἔξεστιν· ἀλλὰ τοῦ δοξαρίου ὑπεράνω
εἶναι ἔξεστιν· ἀλλὰ ἀναισθήτοις καὶ ἀχαρίστοις
μὴ θυμοῦσθαι, προσέτι κήδεσθαι αὐτῶν ἔξεστιν.

θ. Μηκέτι σου μηδεὶς ἀκούσῃ καταμεμφο-
μένου τὸν ἐν αὐλῇ βίον, μηδὲ σὺ σεαυτοῦ.

ι. Ἡ μετάνοιά ἐστιν ἐπίληψίς τις ἑαυτοῦ, ὡς
χρήσιμόν τι παρεικότος· τὸ δὲ ἀγαθὸν χρήσιμόν
τι δεῖ εἶναι, καὶ ἐπιμελητέον αὐτοῦ τῷ καλῷ καὶ

---

[1] ii. 14; iv. 32; vii. 1 etc.

change, but nothing new-fangled need be feared ; all things are of the wonted type,[1] nay, their distributions also are alike.

7. Every nature is content with itself when it speeds well on its way ; and a rational nature speeds well on its way, when in its impressions it gives assent to nothing that is false or obscure, and directs its impulses towards none but social acts, and limits its inclinations and its aversions only to things that are in its power, and welcomes all that the Universal Nature allots it. For it is a part of that, as the nature of the leaf is of the plant-nature ; with the difference however, that in the case of the plant the nature of the leaf is part of a nature void both of sentience and reason, and liable to be thwarted, while a man's nature is part of a nature unthwartable and intelligent and just, if indeed it divides up equally and in due measure to every one his quotas of time, substance, cause, activity, circumstance. And consider, not whether thou shalt find one thing in every case equal to one thing, but whether, collectively, the whole of this equal to the aggregate of that.

8. *Thou canst not be a student.* But thou canst refrain from insolence ; but thou canst rise superior to pleasures and pains ; but thou canst tread under thy feet the love of glory ; but thou canst forbear to be angry with the unfeeling and the thankless,[2] aye and even care for them.

9. Let no one hear thee any more grumbling at life in a Court,[3] nay let not thine own ears hear thee.

10. Repentance is a sort of self-reproach at some useful thing passed by ; but the good must needs be a useful thing, and ever to be cultivated by the true

---

[2] St. Luke vi. 35.   [3] v. 16.

ἀγαθῷ ἀνδρί· οὐδεὶς δ' ἂν καλὸς καὶ ἀγαθὸς ἀνὴρ μετανοήσειεν ἐπὶ τῷ ἡδονήν τινα παρεικέναι· οὔτε ἄρα χρήσιμον οὔτε ἀγαθὸν ἡδονή.

ιαʹ. Τοῦτο τί ἐστιν αὐτὸ καθ' ἑαυτὸ τῇ ἰδίᾳ κατασκευῇ; τί μὲν τὸ οὐσιῶδες αὐτοῦ καὶ ὑλικόν; τί δὲ τὸ αἰτιῶδες; τί δὲ ποιεῖ ἐν τῷ κόσμῳ; πόσον δὲ χρόνον ὑφίσταται;

ιβʹ. Ὅταν ἐξ ὕπνου δυσχερῶς ἐγείρῃ, ἀναμιμνήσκου, ὅτι κατὰ τὴν κατασκευήν σου ἐστὶ καὶ κατὰ τὴν ἀνθρωπικὴν φύσιν τὸ πράξεις κοινωνικὰς ἀποδιδόναι, τὸ δὲ καθεύδειν κοινὸν καὶ τῶν ἀλόγων ζῴων· ὃ δὲ κατὰ φύσιν ἑκάστῳ, τοῦτο οἰκειότερον καὶ προσφυέστερον καὶ δὴ καὶ προσηνέστερον.

ιγʹ. Διηνεκῶς καὶ ἐπὶ πάσης, εἰ οἷόν τε, φαντασίας φυσιολογεῖν, παθολογεῖν, διαλεκτικεύεσθαι.

ιδʹ. Ὧι ἂν ἐντυγχάνῃς, εὐθὺς σαυτῷ πρόλεγε· οὗτος τίνα δόγματα ἔχει περὶ ἀγαθῶν καὶ κακῶν; εἰ γὰρ περὶ ἡδονῆς καὶ πόνου καὶ τῶν ποιητικῶν ἑκατέρου καὶ περὶ δόξης, ἀδοξίας, θανάτου, ζωῆς τοιάδε τινὰ δόγματα ἔχει, οὐδὲν θαυμαστὸν ἢ ξένον μοι δόξει, ἐὰν τάδε τινὰ ποιῇ· καὶ μεμνήσομαι, ὅτι ἀναγκάζεται οὕτως ποιεῖν.

ιεʹ. Μέμνησο, ὅτι, ὥσπερ αἰσχρόν ἐστι ξενίζεσθαι, εἰ ἡ συκῆ σῦκα φέρει, οὕτως, εἰ ὁ κόσμος τάδε τινὰ φέρει, ὧν ἐστι φορός· καὶ ἰατρῷ δὲ καὶ κυβερνήτῃ αἰσχρὸν ξενίζεσθαι, εἰ πεπύρεχεν οὗτος ἢ εἰ ἀντίπνοια γέγονεν.

---

[1] Or, formative.   [2] v. 1.   [3] Or, axioms.
[4] v. 17; vii. 71; xi. 18, § 3.   [5] 1 St. Peter, iv. 12.

good **man** ; but the true good man would never regret having passed a pleasure by. Pleasure therefore is neither a useful thing nor a good.

11. What of itself is the thing in question as individually constituted? What is the substance and material of it? What the causal[1] part? What doeth it in the Universe? How long doth it subsist?

12. When thou art loth to get up,[2] call to mind that the due discharge of social duties is in accordance with thy constitution and in accordance with man's nature, while even irrational animals share with us the faculty of sleep; but what is in accordance with the nature of the individual is more congenial, more closely akin to him, aye and more attractive.

13. Persistently and, if possible, in every case test thy impressions by the rules of physics, ethics, logic.

14. Whatever man thou meetest, put to thyself at once this question: *What are this man's convictions* [3] *about good and evil?* For if they are such and such about pleasure and pain and what is productive of them, about good report and ill report, about death and life, it will be in no way strange or surprising to me if he does such and such things. So I will remember that he is constrained to act as he does.[4]

15. Remember that, as it is monstrous to be surprised at a fig-tree bearing figs, so also is it to be surprised at the Universe bearing its own particular crop. Likewise it is monstrous for a physician or a steersman to be surprised[5] that a patient has fever or that a contrary wind has sprung up.

ιϛ'. Μέμνησο, ὅτι καὶ τὸ μετατίθεσθαι καὶ ἕπεσθαι τῷ διορθοῦντι ὁμοίως ἐλεύθερόν ἐστιν. σὴ γὰρ ἐνέργεια κατὰ τὴν σὴν ὁρμὴν καὶ κρίσιν καὶ δὴ καὶ κατὰ νοῦν τὸν σὸν περαινομένη.

ιζ'. Εἰ μὲν ἐπὶ σοί, τί αὐτὸ ποιεῖς; εἰ δὲ ἐπ' ἄλλῳ, τίνι μέμφῃ; ταῖς ἀτόμοις ἢ τοῖς θεοῖς; ἀμφότερα μανιώδη. οὐδενὶ μεμπτέον. εἰ μὲν γὰρ δύνασαι, διόρθωσον· εἰ δὲ τοῦτο μὴ δύνασαι, τό γε πρᾶγμα αὐτό· εἰ δὲ μηδὲ τοῦτο, πρὸς τί ἔτι σοι φέρει τὸ μέμψασθαι; εἰκῇ γὰρ οὐδὲν ποιητέον.

ιη'. Ἔξω τοῦ κόσμου τὸ ἀποθανὸν οὐ πίπτει. εἰ ὧδε μένει, καὶ μεταβάλλει ὧδε καὶ διαλύεται εἰς τὰ ἴδια, ἃ στοιχεῖά ἐστι τοῦ κόσμου καὶ σά. καὶ αὐτὰ δὲ μεταβάλλει καὶ οὐ γογγύζει.

ιθ'. Ἕκαστον πρός τι γέγονεν, ἵππος, ἄμπελος· τί θαυμάζεις; καὶ ὁ Ἥλιος ἐρεῖ, "πρός τι ἔργον γέγονα," καὶ οἱ λοιποὶ θεοί. σὺ οὖν πρὸς τί; τὸ ἥδεσθαι; ἴδε, εἰ ἀνέχεται ἡ ἔννοια.

κ'. Ἡ φύσις ἐστόχασται ἑκάστου οὐδέν τι ἔλασσον τῆς ἀπολήξεως ἢ τῆς ἀρχῆς τε καὶ διεξαγωγῆς, ὡς ὁ ἀναβάλλων τὴν σφαῖραν· τί οὖν ἢ ἀγαθὸν τῷ σφαιρίῳ ἀναφερομένῳ ἢ κακὸν καταφερομένῳ ἢ καὶ πεπτωκότι; τί δὲ ἀγαθὸν τῇ πομφόλυγι συνεστώσῃ ἢ κακὸν διαλυθείσῃ; τὰ ὅμοια δὲ καὶ ἐπὶ λύχνου.

---

[1] *cp.* vi. 30; vii. 7. *cp.* Capit. xxii. 4: "Aequius est ut ego tot talium amicorum consilium sequar, quam ut tot tales amici meam unius voluntatem sequantur"; *Digest.* 37. 14. 17.

[2] Annius Verus, grandfather of Marcus, was the best ball-player of his day, see *Wilmanns Inscr.* 574. Marcus himself was an adept at the ball-game, Capit. iv. 9.

BOOK VIII

16. Remember that neither a change of mind nor a willingness to be set right by others[1] is inconsistent with true freedom of will. For thine alone is the active effort that effects its purpose in accordance with thy impulse and judgment, aye and thy intelligence also.

17. If the choice rests with thee, why do the thing? if with another, whom dost thou blame? Atoms or Gods? To do either would be crazy folly. No one is to blame. For if thou canst, set the offender right. Failing that, at least set the thing itself right. If that too be impracticable, what purpose is served by imputing blame? For without a purpose nothing should be done.

18. That which dies is not cast out of the Universe. As it remains here, it also suffers change here and is dissolved into its own constituents, which are the elements of the Universe and thy own. Yes, and they too suffer change and murmur not.

19. Every thing, be it a horse, be it a vine, has come into being for some end. Why wonder? Helios himself will say: *I exist to do some work*; and so of all the other Gods. For what then dost thou exist? For pleasure? Surely it is not to be thought of.

20. Nature has included in its aim in every case the ceasing to be no less than the beginning and the duration, just as the man who tosses up his ball.[2] But what good does the ball gain while tossed upwards, or harm as it comes down, or finally when it reaches the ground? Or what good accrues to the bubble while it coheres, or harm in its bursting? And the same holds good with the lamp-flame.

κα΄. Ἔκστρεψον καὶ θέασαι, οἷόν ἐστι, γηράσαν δὲ οἷον γίνεται, νοσῆσαν δέ, ἀποπνεῦσαν δέ.†[1]

2 Βραχύβιον καὶ ὁ ἐπαινῶν καὶ ὁ ἐπαινούμενος, καὶ ὁ μνημονεύων καὶ ὁ μνημονευόμενος. προσέτι δὲ καὶ ἐν γωνίᾳ τούτου τοῦ κλίματος, καὶ οὐδὲ ἐνταῦθα πάντες συμφωνοῦσι, καὶ οὐδὲ αὐτός τις ἑαυτῷ· καὶ ὅλη δὲ ἡ γῆ στιγμή.

κβ΄. Πρόσεχε τῷ ὑποκειμένῳ ἢ τῇ ἐνεργείᾳ ἢ τῷ δόγματι[2] ἢ τῷ σημαινομένῳ.

2 Δικαίως ταῦτα πάσχεις· μᾶλλον δὲ θέλεις ἀγαθὸς αὔριον γενέσθαι ἢ σήμερον εἶναι.

κγ΄. Πράσσω τι; πράσσω ἐπ᾽ ἀνθρώπων εὐποιίαν ἀναφέρων· συμβαίνει τί μοι; δέχομαι ἐπὶ τοὺς θεοὺς ἀναφέρων καὶ τὴν πάντων πηγήν, ἀφ᾽ ἧς πάντα τὰ γινόμενα συμμηρύεται.

κδ΄. Ὁποῖόν σοι φαίνεται τὸ λούεσθαι· ἔλαιον, ἱδρώς, ῥύπος, ὕδωρ γλοιῶδες, πάντα σικχαντά· τοιοῦτον πᾶν μέρος τοῦ βίου καὶ πᾶν ὑποκείμενον.

κε΄. Λούκιλλα Οὐῆρον, εἶτα Λούκιλλα· Σέκουνδα Μάξιμον, εἶτα Σέκουνδα· Ἐπιτύγχανος Διότιμον, εἶτα Ἐπιτύγχανος· Φαυστῖναν Ἀντωνῖνος, εἶτα Ἀντωνῖνος. τοιαῦτα πάντα· Κέλερ Ἀδριανόν, εἶτα Κέλερ.[3] οἱ δὲ δριμεῖς ἐκεῖνοι ἢ προγνωστικοὶ ἢ τετυφωμένοι, ποῦ; οἷον δριμεῖς μὲν Χάραξ καὶ Δημήτριος [ὁ Πλατωνικός][4] καὶ

---

[1] πορνεῦσαν P: πορνεύσας δὲ A: διαπυῆσαν Leopold: ἀποπνεῦσαν Gat.

[2] ἢ τῷ δόγματι ἢ τῇ ἐνεργείᾳ P.

[3] Stich would transfer Κέλερ . . . Κέλερ to the beginning of the paragraph.

[4] ὁ Πλατωνικὸς possibly a wrong gloss.

BOOK VIII

21. Turn it[1] inside out and see what it is like, what it comes to be when old, when sickly, when carrion.

They endure but for a short season, both praiser and praised, rememberer and remembered.[2] All this too in a tiny corner of this continent, and not even there are all in accord, no nor a man with himself; and the whole earth is itself a point.[3]

22. Fix thy attention on the subject-matter or the act or the principle or the thing signified.

Rightly served! Thou wouldst rather become a good man to-morrow than be one to-day.

23. Am I doing some thing? I do it with reference to the well-being of mankind. Does something befall me? I accept it with a reference to the Gods and to the Source of all things from which issue, linked together, the things that come into being.

24. What bathing is when thou thinkest of it—oil, sweat, filth, greasy water, everything revolting—such is every part of life and every object we meet with.

25. Lucilla[4] buried Verus, then Lucilla was buried; Secunda Maximus,[5] then Secunda; Epitynchanus Diotimus, then Epitynchanus; Antoninus Faustina, then Antoninus. The same tale always: Celer[6] buried Hadrianus and then Celer was buried. And those acute wits, men renowned for their prescience or their pride, where are they? Such acute wits, for instance, as Charax and Demetrius [the Platonist[7]]

---

[1] *i.e.* the body.　[2] iii. 10; iv. 3, § 3.　[3] iv. 3, § 3; vi. 36.
[4] The mother of Marcus, not as Gataker, Long, etc. the daughter.　[5] i. 15.　[6] See Index II.
[7] Arethas on Lucian, *de Salt.* § 63, alludes to this passage, but Lucian's Demetrius is the Cynic whom in *Demon.* § 3 he couples with Epictetus. (*cp.* also *adv. Ind.* § 19.) See Index II.

Εὐδαίμων καὶ εἴ τις τοιοῦτος. πάντα ἐφήμερα, τεθνηκότα πάλαι· ἔνιοι μὲν οὐδὲ ἐπ' ὀλίγον μνημονευθέντες· οἱ δὲ εἰς μύθους μεταβαλόντες· οἱ δὲ ἤδη καὶ ἐκ μύθων ἐξίτηλοι. τούτων οὖν μεμνῆσθαι, ὅτι δεήσει ἤτοι σκεδασθῆναι τὸ συγκριμάτιόν σου, ἢ σβεσθῆναι τὸ πνευμάτιον, ἢ μεταστῆναι καὶ ἀλλαχοῦ καταταχθῆναι.[1]

κϛ'. Εὐφροσύνη ἀνθρώπου ποιεῖν τὰ ἴδια ἀνθρώπου. ἴδιον δὲ ἀνθρώπου εὔνοια πρὸς τὸ ὁμόφυλον, ὑπερόρασις τῶν αἰσθητικῶν κινήσεων, διάκρισις τῶν πιθανῶν φαντασιῶν, ἐπιθεώρησις τῆς τῶν ὅλων φύσεως καὶ τῶν κατ' αὐτὴν γινομένων.

κζ'. Τρεῖς σχέσεις· ἡ μὲν πρὸς τὸ ἀγγεῖον[2] τὸ περικείμενον· ἡ δὲ πρὸς τὴν θείαν αἰτίαν, ἀφ' ἧς συμβαίνει πᾶσι πάντα· ἡ δὲ πρὸς τοὺς συμβιοῦντας.

κη'. Ὁ πόνος ἤτοι τῷ σώματι κακόν· οὐκοῦν ἀποφαινέσθω· ἢ τῇ ψυχῇ· ἀλλ' ἔξεστιν αὐτῇ, τὴν ἰδίαν αἰθρίαν καὶ γαλήνην διαφυλάσσειν καὶ μὴ ὑπολαμβάνειν, ὅτι κακόν. πᾶσα γὰρ κρίσις καὶ ὁρμή καὶ ὄρεξις καὶ ἔκκλισις ἔνδον, καὶ οὐδὲν[3] ὧδε ἀναβαίνει.

κθ'. Ἐξάλειφε τὰς φαντασίας συνεχῶς σεαυτῷ λέγων· "Νῦν ἐπ' ἐμοί ἐστιν, ἵνα ἐν ταύτῃ τῇ ψυχῇ μηδεμία πονηρία ἢ μηδὲ ἐπιθυμία μηδὲ ὅλως ταραχή τις· ἀλλὰ βλέπων πάντα, ὁποῖά ἐστι, χρῶμαι ἑκάστῳ κατ' ἀξίαν." μέμνησο ταύτης τῆς ἐξουσίας κατὰ φύσιν.

---

[1] καταχθῆναι A.
[2] αἴτιον PA: ἀγγεῖον (cp. iii. 3, xii. 2) Valckenaer: σωμάτιον Cor.   [3] <κακὸν> P, but cp. viii. 49.

and Eudaemon, and others like them. All creatures of a day, dead long ago!—some not remembered even for a while, others transformed into legends,[1] and yet others from legends faded into nothingness! Bear then in mind that either this thy composite self must be scattered abroad, or thy vital breath be quenched, or be transferred[2] and set elsewhere.

26. It brings gladness to a man to do a man's true work. And a man's true work is to shew goodwill to his own kind, to disdain the motions of the senses, to diagnose specious impressions, to take a comprehensive view of the Nature of the Universe and all that is done at her bidding.

27. Thou hast three relationships—the first to the vessel thou art contained in; the second to the divine Cause wherefrom issue all things to all; and the third to those that dwell with thee.[3]

28. Pain is an evil either to the body—let the body then denounce it[4]—or to the Soul; but the Soul can ensure her own fair weather and her own calm sea,[5] and refuse to account it an evil. For every conviction and impulse and desire and aversion is from within,[6] and nothing climbs in thither.

29. Efface thy impressions,[7] saying ever to thyself: *Now lies it with me that this soul should harbour no wickedness nor lust nor any disturbing element at all; but that, seeing the true nature of all things,[8] I should deal with each as is its due.* Bethink thee of this power that Nature gives thee.

---

[1] xii. 27.   [2] Or, *leave thee*; but *cp.* v. 33.
[3] i. 12; v. 10, 48; ix. 3 *ad fin.*   [4] vii. 33.   [5] xii. 22.
[6] v. 19; St. Matt. xv. 18.   [7] vii. 17, 29; ix. 7.   [8] iii. 11.

λ'. Λαλεῖν καὶ ἐν συγκλήτῳ καὶ πρὸς πάνθ' ὁντινοῦν κοσμίως, μὴ περιτράνως· Ὑγιεῖ λόγῳ χρῆσθαι.

λα'. Αὐλὴ Αὐγούστου, γυνή, θυγάτηρ, ἔγγονοι, πρόγονοι, ἀδελφή, Ἀγρίππας, συγγενεῖς, οἰκεῖοι, φίλοι, Ἄρειος, Μαικήνας, ἰατροί, θύται· ὅλης αὐλῆς θάνατος. εἶτα ἔπιθι τὰς ἄλλας <καταστροφὰς>[1] μὴ καθ' ἑνὸς ἀνθρώπου θάνατον, οἷον Πομπηίων. κἀκεῖνο δὲ τὸ ἐπιγραφόμενον τοῖς μνήμασιν, "Ἔσχατος τοῦ ἰδίου γένους," ἐπιλογίζεσθαι, πόσα ἐσπάσθησαν οἱ πρὸ αὐτῶν, ἵνα διάδοχόν τινα καταλίπωσιν· εἶτα ἀνάγκη ἔσχατόν τινα γενέσθαι· πάλιν ὧδε ὅλου γένους θάνατον.

λβ'. Συντιθέναι δεῖ τὸν βίον κατὰ μίαν πρᾶξιν, καὶ εἰ ἑκάστη τὸ ἑαυτῆς παρέχει,[2] ὡς οἷόν τε, ἀρκεῖσθαι· ἵνα δὲ τὸ ἑαυτῆς παρέχῃ,[3] οὐδὲ εἷς σε κωλῦσαι δύναται. "Ἀλλ' ἐνστήσεταί τι ἔξωθεν." οὐδὲν εἴς γε τὸ δικαίως[4] καὶ σωφρόνως καὶ εὐλογίστως· "Ἄλλο δέ τι ἴσως ἐνεργητικὸν κωλυθήσεται;" ἀλλὰ τῇ πρὸς αὐτὸ τὸ κώλυμα εὐαρεστήσει καὶ τῇ ἐπὶ τὸ διδόμενον εὐγνώμονι μεταβάσει εὐθὺς ἄλλη πρᾶξις ἀντικαθίσταται ἐναρμόσουσα εἰς τὴν σύνθεσιν, περὶ ἧς ὁ λόγος.

λγ'. Ἀτύφως μὲν λαβεῖν, εὐλύτως δὲ ἀφεῖναι.

---

[1] <ἐπιγραφὰς> Breithaupt : Schenkl supplies αὐλὰς with a lacuna after : perhaps τὸν ὅλης φυλῆς with Lofft's μηκέθ' ἑνὸς would give the meaning.

[2] πάσχει A : παρέχει P : ἀπέχει Schenkl.

[3] ἀπέχῃ PA : παρέχῃ Morus.

[4] A verb is missing, e.g. <διακεῖσθαι> Rend., <πράττειν> Morus.

BOOK VIII

30. Say thy say in the Senate or to any person whatsoever becomingly and naturally.[1] Use sound speech.

31. The court of Augustus—wife, daughter, descendants, ancestors, sister, Agrippa, kinsfolk, household, friends, Areius,[2] Maecenas, physicians, diviners—dead, the whole court of them! Pass on then to other records and the death not of individuals but of a clan, as of the Pompeii. And that well-known epitaph, *Last of his race*—think over it and the anxiety shewn by the man's ancestors that they might leave a successor. But after all some one must be the last of the line—here again the death of a whole race!

32. Act by act thou must build up thy life, and be content, if each act as far as may be fulfils its end.[3] And there is never a man that can prevent it doing this. *But there will be some impediment from without.* There can be none to thy behaving justly, soberly, wisely. *But what if some other exercise of activity be hindered?* Well, a cheerful acceptance of the hindrance and a tactful transition to what is allowed will enable another action to be substituted that will be in keeping with the built-up life of which we are speaking.

33. Accept without arrogance, surrender without reluctance.

---

[1] Dr. Bigg does not scruple to say that Marcus spoke in such a pedantic jargon as to be *unintelligible to his hearers!* This is pitiable nonsense. See Fronto, *ad Ant.* i. 1 : *quanto studio quantoque favore et voluptate dicentem te audit senatus populusque Romanus* ; cp. *ad Caes.* iii. 1.

[2] Domestic philosopher to Augustus, as Rusticus was to Marcus. See Them. *Orat.* v. 63 d ; xiii. 173 c ; Sen. *ad Marciam*, § 4.

[3] Or, *receives its due reward* (ἀπέχει).

λδʹ. Εἴ ποτε εἶδες χεῖρα ἀποκεκομμένην ἢ
πόδα, ἢ κεφαλὴν ἀποτετμημένην χωρίς πού
ποτε ἀπὸ τοῦ λοιποῦ σώματος κειμένην· τοιοῦτον
ἑαυτὸν ποιεῖ, ὅσον ἐφ᾽ ἑαυτῷ, ὁ μὴ θέλων τὸ
συμβαῖνον καὶ ἀποσχίζων ἑαυτὸν ἢ ὁ ἀκοινώνη-
τόν τι πράσσων. ἀπέρριψαί πού ποτε ἀπὸ
τῆς κατὰ φύσιν ἑνώσεως· ἐπεφύκεις γὰρ μέρος·
νῦν <δὲ> σεαυτὸν ἀπέκοψας. ἀλλ᾽ ὧδε κομψὸν
ἐκεῖνο, ὅτι ἔξεστί σοι πάλιν ἑνῶσαι σεαυτόν.
τοῦτο ἄλλῳ μέρει οὐδενὶ θεὸς ἐπέτρεψεν, χωρισ-
θέντι καὶ διακοπέντι πάλιν συνελθεῖν. ἀλλὰ
σκέψαι τὴν χρηστότητα, ᾗ τετίμηκε τὸν ἄνθρω-
πον· καὶ γὰρ ἵνα τὴν ἀρχὴν μὴ ἀπορραγῇ ἀπὸ
τοῦ ὅλου, ἐπ᾽ αὐτῷ ἐποίησεν· καὶ ἀπορραγέντι
πάλιν ἐπανελθεῖν καὶ συμφῦναι καὶ τὴν τοῦ
μέρους τάξιν ἀπολαβεῖν ἐποίησεν.

λεʹ. Ὥσπερ τὰς ἄλλας δυνάμεις ἑκάστῳ[1] τῶν
λογικῶν† σχεδὸν ὅσον†[2] ἡ τῶν λογικῶν φύσις,
οὕτως καὶ ταύτην παρ᾽ αὐτῆς εἰλήφαμεν. ὃν
τρόπον γὰρ ἐκείνη πᾶν τὸ ἐνιστάμενον καὶ ἀντι-
βαῖνον ἐπιπεριτρέπει καὶ κατατάσσει εἰς τὴν
εἱμαρμένην, καὶ μέρος ἑαυτῆς ποιεῖ, οὕτως καὶ τὸ
λογικὸν ζῷον δύναται πᾶν κώλυμα ὕλην ἑαυτοῦ
ποιεῖν, καὶ χρῆσθαι αὐτῷ, ἐφ᾽ οἷον ἂν καὶ
ὥρμησεν.

λϛʹ. Μή σε συγχείτω ἡ τοῦ ὅλου βίου φαντασία. μὴ συμπερινόει, ἐπίπονα οἷα καὶ ὅσα
πιθανὸν ἐπιγεγενῆσθαι, ἀλλὰ καθ᾽ ἕκαστον τῶν
παρόντων ἐπερώτα σεαυτόν· τί τοῦ ἔργου τὸ
ἀφόρητον καὶ ἀνύποιστον; αἰσχυνθήσῃ γὰρ

---

[1] ἕκαστος P.
[2] σχεδὸν ὅσον : ἐσκέδασεν Cor. : <ἔδωκεν> Schultz.

34. Thou hast seen a hand cut off or a foot, or a head severed from the trunk, and lying at some distance from the rest of the body. Just so does the man treat himself, as far as he may, who wills not what befalls and severs himself from mankind or acts unsocially. Say thou hast been torn away in some sort from the unity of Nature; for by the law of thy birth thou wast a part; but now thou hast cut thyself off. Yet here comes in that exquisite provision, that thou canst return again to thy unity.[1] To no other part has God granted this, to come together again, when once separated and cleft asunder. Aye, behold His goodness, wherewith He hath glorified man! For He hath let it rest with a man that he be never rent away from the Whole, and if he do rend himself away, to return again and grow on to the rest and take up his position again as part.

35. Just as the Nature of rational things has given each rational being almost all his other powers, so also have we received this one from it; that, as this Nature moulds to its purpose whatever interference or opposition it meets, and gives it a place in the destined order of things, and makes it a part of itself, so also can the rational creature convert every hindrance into material for itself[2] and utilize it for its own purposes.

36. Let not the mental picture of life as a whole confound thee. Fill not thy thoughts with what and how many ills may conceivably await thee, but in every present case ask thyself: *What is there in this experience so crushing, so insupportable?* Thou wilt blush

---

[1] Sen. *Ep.* 98: *licet in integrum restitui* (a legal phrase for a restoration to all rights). *cp.* xi. 8.

[2] iv. 1; v. 20; vi. 50.

ὁμολογῆσαι. ἔπειτα ἀναμίμνησκε σεαυτόν, ὅτι
οὔτε τὸ μέλλον οὔτε τὸ παρῳχηκὸς βαρεῖ σε
ἀλλὰ ἀεὶ τὸ παρόν. τοῦτο δὲ κατασμικρύνεται,
ἐὰν αὐτὸ μόνον περιορίσῃς καὶ ἀπελέγχῃς τὴν
διάνοιαν, εἰ πρὸς τοῦτο ψιλὸν ἀντέχειν μὴ
δύναται.

λζʹ. Μήτι νῦν παρακάθηται τῇ τοῦ κυρίου[1]
σορῷ Πάνθεια ἢ Πέργαμος; τί δὲ; τῇ Ἀδριανοῦ
Χαβρίας ἢ Διότιμος; γελοῖον. τί δέ; εἰ παρεκά-
θηντο, ἔμελλον αἰσθάνεσθαι; τί δέ, εἰ ἠσθάνοντο,
ἔμελλον ἡσθήσεσθαι; τί δέ, εἰ ἥδοντο, ἔμελλον
οὗτοι ἀθάνατοι εἶναι; οὐ καὶ τούτους πρῶτον μὲν
γραίας καὶ γέροντας γενέσθαι οὕτως εἵμαρτο,
εἶτα ἀποθανεῖν; τί οὖν ὕστερον ἔμελλον ἐκεῖνοι
ποιεῖν, τούτων ἀποθανόντων; γράσος πᾶν τοῦτο
καὶ λύθρον ἐν θυλάκῳ.

ληʹ. Εἰ δύνασαι ὀξὺ βλέπειν, βλέπε,† " κρίνων," φησί, " σοφώτατα."†[2]

λθʹ. Δικαιοσύνης κατεξαναστατικὴν ἀρετὴν
οὐχ ὁρῶ ἐν τῇ τοῦ λογικοῦ ζῴου κατασκευῇ·
ἡδονῆς δὲ ὁρῶ τὴν ἐγκράτειαν.

μʹ. Ἐὰν ἀφέλῃς τὴν σὴν ὑπόληψιν περὶ τοῦ
λυπεῖν σε δοκοῦντος, αὐτὸς ἐν τῷ ἀσφαλεστάτῳ
ἔστηκας. "Τίς αὐτός;" ὁ λόγος. "Ἀλλ' οὐκ
εἰμὶ λόγος." ἔστω. οὐκοῦν ὁ μὲν λόγος αὐτὸς
ἑαυτὸν μὴ λυπείτω. εἰ δέ τι ἄλλο σοι κακῶς
ἔχει, ὑπολαβέτω αὐτὸ περὶ αὐτοῦ.

---

[1] τοῦ κυρίου P: τοῦ κυροῦ A: [τοῦ] Οὐήρου Salm., but
Marcus does not speak of Lucius as Verus.
[2] σοφωτάτοις P: σοφωτάτης (with δικαιοσύνης, § 39) A:
σοφώτατα Xyl.

---

[1] See on vi. 29.
[2] Lucian (?) (*Imag.* §§ 10, 22), mentions Pantheia as the

to confess. Remind thyself further that it is not the
future nor the past but the present always that
brings thee its burden. But this is reduced to in-
significance if thou isolate it, and take thy mind to
task[1] if it cannot hold out against this mere trifle.

37. Does Pantheia[2] now watch by the urn of her
lord, or Pergamus? What, does Chabrias or Diotimus
by Hadrian's? Absurd! What then? Had they sat
there till now, would the dead have been aware of it?
and, if aware of it, would they have been pleased?
and, if pleased, would that have made the mourners
immortal? Was it not destined that these like
others should become old women and old men
and then die? What then, when they were dead,
would be left for those whom they had mourned
to do? It is all stench and foul corruption 'in
a sack of skin.'[3]

38. Hast thou keenness of sight? Use it *with
judgment ever so wisely*, as the saying goes.

39. In the constitution of the rational creature I
see no virtue incompatible with justice, but incompatible with pleasure I see—continence.

40. Take away thy opinion[4] as to any imagined
pain, and thou thyself art set in surest safety.
What is 'thyself'? Reason. *But I am not reason.*
Be it so. At all events let the Reason not cause
itself pain, but if any part in thee is amiss, let it
form its own opinion about itself.[5]

matchless concubine τῷ μεγάλῳ βασιλεῖ χρήστῳ καὶ ἡμέρῳ
ὄντι (meaning apparently Lucius Verus). Lucian (*Nigr.*
§ 31) speaks of οἱ κελεύοντες καὶ παραμένειν τινὰς οἰκέτας τοῖς
τάφοις.
³ Epict. *Frag.* 94. *cp.* Diog. Laert. *Anaxarchus*, § 2 ;
Zeno Eleat. § 5. Howell, *Familiar Letters*, viii. 2, 50, speaks
of "this small skinful or bagful of bones."
⁴ vii. 16 ; viii. 47.   ⁵ vii. 33.

μα΄. Ἐμποδισμὸς αἰσθήσεως κακὸν ζωτικῆς φύσεως· ἐμποδισμὸς ὁρμῆς ὁμοίως κακὸν ζωτικῆς φύσεως. ἔστι δέ τι ἄλλο ὁμοίως ἐμποδιστικὸν καὶ κακὸν τῆς φυτικῆς κατασκευῆς. οὕτως τοίνυν ἐμποδισμὸς νοῦ κακὸν νοερᾶς φύσεως. πάντα δὴ ταῦτα ἐπὶ σεαυτὸν μετάφερε. πόνος <ἢ> ἡδονὴ ἅπτεταί σου; ὄψεται ἡ αἴσθησις. ὁρμήσαντι ἔνστημα ἐγένετο; εἰ μὲν ἀνυπεξαιρέτως ὁρμᾷς, ἤδη ὡς λογικοῦ κακόν. εἰ δὲ τὸ κοινὸν λαμβάνεις, οὔπω βέβλαψαι οὐδὲ ἐμπεπόδισαι. τὰ μέντοι τοῦ νοῦ ἴδια οὐδεὶς ἄλλος εἴωθεν ἐμποδίζειν· τούτου γὰρ οὐ πῦρ, οὐ σίδηρος, οὐ τύραννος, οὐ βλασφημία, οὐχ ὁτιοῦν ἅπτεται· "ὅταν γένηται σφαῖρος, κυκλοτερὴς μένει.†"[1]

μβ΄. Οὐκ εἰμὶ ἄξιος ἐμαυτὸν λυπεῖν· οὐδὲ γὰρ ἄλλον πώποτε ἑκὼν ἐλύπησα.

μγ΄. Εὐφραίνει ἄλλον ἄλλο· ἐμὲ δέ, ἐὰν ὑγιὲς ἔχω τὸ ἡγεμονικόν, μὴ ἀποστρεφόμενον μήτε ἄνθρωπόν τινα μήτε <τι> τῶν ἀνθρώποις συμβαινόντων· ἀλλὰ πᾶν εὐμενέσιν ὀφθαλμοῖς ὁρῶν τε καὶ δεχόμενον καὶ χρώμενον ἑκάστῳ κατ᾽ ἀξίαν.

μδ΄. Τοῦτον[2] ἰδοὺ τὸν χρόνον σεαυτῷ χάρισαι. οἱ τὴν ὑστεροφημίαν μᾶλλον διώκοντες οὐ λογίζονται, ὅτι ἄλλοι τοιοῦτοι μέλλουσιν ἐκεῖνοι εἶναι, οἷοί εἰσιν οὗτοι, οὓς βαροῦνται· κἀκεῖνοι

---

[1] μονίη Rend. (cp. xii. 3) : by changing σφαῖρος to σφαῖρα (xi. 12) we get a senarius.　　[2] τουτονὶ δὴ Leop.

BOOK VIII

41. To the animal nature a thwarting of sense-perception is an evil, as is also to the same nature the thwarting of impulse. There is similarly some other thing that can thwart the constitution of plants and is an evil to them. Thus then the thwarting of intelligence is an evil to the intelligent nature. Transfer the application of all this to thyself. Does pain, does pleasure take hold of thee? The senses shall look to it. Wast thou impelled to a thing and wast thwarted? If thy impulse counts on an unconditional fulfilment, failure at once becomes an evil to thee as a rational creature. But accept the universal limitation, and thou hast so far received no hurt nor even been thwarted.[1] Indeed no one else is in a way to thwart the inner purposes of the mind. For it no fire can touch, nor steel, nor tyrant, nor obloquy,[2] nor any thing soever: *a sphere*[3] *once formed continues round and true.*

42. It were not right that I should pain myself for not even another have I ever knowingly pained.[4]

43. One thing delights one, another thing another. To me it is a delight if I keep my ruling Reason sound, not looking askance at man or anything that befalls man, but regarding all things with kindly eyes, accepting and using everything for its intrinsic worth.

44. See thou dower thyself with this present time. Those that yearn rather for after-fame do not realize that their successors are sure to be very much the same as the contemporaries whom they find such a

---

[1] vi. 50.   [2] vii. 68; Epict. iii. 22. 43.   [3] xi. 12; xii. 3.
[4] *cp.* Them. *Orat.* xv. p. 191 B, quoted App. ii.; *cp.* Diog. Laert. *Zeno* 64.

δὲ θνητοί. τί δὲ ὅλως πρὸς σέ, ἂν ἐκεῖνοι φωναῖς
τοιαύταις ἀπηχῶσιν ἢ ὑπόληψιν τοιαύτην περὶ
σοῦ ἔχωσιν;

μέ. Ἆρόν με καὶ βάλε, ὅπου θέλεις. ἐκεῖ[1] γὰρ
ἔξω τὸν ἐμὸν δαίμονα ἵλεων, τουτέστιν ἀρκού-
μενον, εἰ ἔχοι καὶ ἐνεργοίη κατὰ τὸ ἑξῆς τῇ ἰδίᾳ
κατασκευῇ.

2 Ἆρα τοῦτο ἄξιον, ἵνα δι᾽ αὐτὸ κακῶς μοι ἔχῃ
ἡ ψυχὴ καὶ χείρων ἑαυτῆς ᾖ ταπεινουμένη,
ὀρεγομένη, συνδυομένη,[2]† πτυρομένη; καὶ τί
εὑρήσεις τούτου ἄξιον;

μϛ. Ἀνθρώπῳ οὐδενὶ συμβαίνειν τι δύναται, ὃ
οὐκ ἔστιν ἀνθρωπικὸν σύμπτωμα· οὐδὲ βοΐ, ὃ οὐκ
ἔστι βοϊκόν· οὐδὲ ἀμπέλῳ, ὃ οὐκ ἔστιν ἀμπελικόν·
οὐδὲ λίθῳ, ὃ οὐκ ἔστι λίθου ἴδιον. εἰ οὖν
ἑκάστῳ συμβαίνει, ὃ καὶ εἴωθε καὶ πέφυκε, τί ἂν
δυσχεραίνοις; οὐ γὰρ ἀφόρητόν σοι ἔφερεν ἡ
κοινὴ φύσις.

μζ. Εἰ μὲν διά τι τῶν ἐκτὸς λυπῇ, οὐκ
ἐκεῖνό σοι ἐνοχλεῖ, ἀλλὰ τὸ σὸν περὶ αὐτοῦ
κρῖμα. τοῦτο δὲ ἤδη ἐξαλεῖψαι ἐπὶ σοί ἐστιν. εἰ
δὲ λυπεῖ σέ τι τῶν ἐν τῇ σῇ διαθέσει, τίς ὁ
κωλύων διορθῶσαι τὸ δόγμα; ὅμως δὲ καὶ εἰ
λυπῇ, ὅτι οὐχὶ τόδε τι ἐνεργεῖς ὑγιές σοι
φαινόμενον, τί οὐχὶ μᾶλλον ἐνεργεῖς ἢ λυπῇ;
" Ἀλλὰ ἰσχυρότερόν τι ἐνίσταται." μὴ οὖν λυποῦ·
οὐ γὰρ παρὰ σὲ ἡ αἰτία τοῦ μὴ ἐνεργεῖσθαι.
" Ἀλλὰ οὐκ ἄξιον ζῆν μὴ ἐνεργουμένου τούτου."

[1] κἀκεῖ Kron.   [2] συνδεομένη Gat.

burden, and no less mortal. What is it anyway to thee if there be this or that far-off echo of their voices, or if they have this or that opinion about thee?

45. Take me up and cast me where thou wilt. For even there will I keep my 'genius' gracious, that is, content if in itself and in its activity it follow the laws of its own constitution.

Is this worth while, that on its account my soul should be ill at ease and fall below itself, grovelling, grasping, floundering, affrighted? What *could* make it worth while?

46. Nothing can befall a man that is not a contingency natural to man; nor befall an ox, that is not natural to oxen, nor a vine, that is not natural to a vine, nor to a stone that is not proper to it. If therefore only what is natural and customary befalls each, why be aggrieved? For the common Nature brings thee nothing that thou canst not bear.[1]

47. When thou art vexed at some external cross, it is not the thing itself that troubles thee,[2] but thy judgment on it. And this thou canst annul in a moment. But if thou art vexed at something in thine own character, who can prevent thee from rectifying the principle that is to blame?[3] So also if thou art vexed[4] at not undertaking that which seems to thee a sound act, why not rather undertake it than be vexed? *But there is a lion in the path!* Be not vexed then, for the blame of inaction rests not with thee. *But life is not worth living, this left undone.* Depart

---

[1] *cp.* St. Paul, 1 Cor. x. 13.
[2] *cp.* Epict. *Man.* 5.
[3] viii. 40.
[4] v. 9, 36; viii. 10; xi. 19.

ἄπιθι οὖν ἐκ τοῦ ζῆν εὐμενής, ἦ καὶ ὁ ἐνεργῶν
ἀποθνήσκει, ἅμα ἵλεως τοῖς ἐνισταμένοις.

μη΄. Μέμνησο, ὅτι ἀκαταμάχητον γίνεται τὸ
ἡγεμονικόν, ὅταν εἰς ἑαυτὸ συστραφὲν ἀρκεσθῇ
ἑαυτῷ μὴ ποιοῦντι, ὃ μὴ θέλει, κἂν ἀλόγως
παρατάξηται. τί οὖν, ὅταν καὶ μετὰ λόγου
<καὶ> περιεσκεμμένως κρίνῃ περί τινος; διὰ τοῦτο
ἀκρόπολίς ἐστιν ἡ ἐλευθέρα παθῶν διάνοια·
οὐδὲν γὰρ ὀχυρώτερον ἔχει ἄνθρωπος, ἐφ᾽ ὃ κατα-
φυγὼν ἀνάλωτος λοιπὸν ἂν εἴη. ὁ μὲν οὖν μὴ
ἑωρακὼς τοῦτο ἀμαθής· ὁ δὲ ἑωρακὼς καὶ μὴ
καταφεύγων ἀτυχής.

μθ΄. Μηδὲν πλέον σαυτῷ λέγε, ὧν αἱ προ-
ηγούμεναι φαντασίαι ἀναγγέλλουσιν. ἤγγελται,
ὅτι ὁ δεῖνά σε κακῶς λέγει. ἤγγελται τοῦτο· τὸ
δέ, ὅτι βέβλαψαι, οὐκ ἤγγελται. βλέπω ὅτι
νοσεῖ τὸ παιδίον. βλέπω· ὅτι δὲ κινδυνεύει οὐ
βλέπω. οὕτως οὖν μένε ἀεὶ ἐπὶ τῶν πρώτων
φαντασιῶν, καὶ μηδὲν αὐτὸς ἔνδοθεν ἐπίλεγε, καὶ
οὐδέν σοι γίνεται· μᾶλλον δὲ ἐπίλεγε, ὡς γνωρίζων ἕκαστα τῶν ἐν τῷ κόσμῳ συμβαινόντων.

ν΄. "Σίκυος πικρός." ἄφες. "Βάτοι ἐν τῇ ὁδῷ."
ἔκκλινον. ἀρκεῖ. μὴ προσεπείπῃς· "Τί δὲ καὶ
ἐγίνετο ταῦτα ἐν τῷ κόσμῳ;" ἐπεὶ καταγελασθήσῃ
ὑπὸ ἀνθρώπου φυσιολόγου, ὡς ἂν καὶ ὑπὸ
τέκτονος καὶ σκυτέως γελασθείης καταγινώσκων,
ὅτι ἐν τῷ ἐργαστηρίῳ ξέσματα καὶ περιτμήματα

---

[1] iii. 1 ; v. 29 ; Epict. i. 24, § 20.   [2] vii. 28.

[3] xi. 3. In both places Marcus seems to have the Christians in mind.

[4] cp. Fronto, ad Ver. ii. 1 (of Marcus) : *arcem munitam et
invictam et inexpugnabilem quae in fratris tui pectore sita est.*
cp. Epict. iv. 5. 26.

then from life,[1] dying with the same kindly feelings as he who effects his purpose, and accepting with a good grace the obstacles that thwart thee.

48. Never forget that the ruling Reason shews itself unconquerable when, concentrated in itself,[2] it is content with itself, so it do nothing that it doth not will, even if it refuse from mere opposition [3] and not from reason—much, more, then, if it judge of a thing on reasonable grounds and advisedly. Therefore the Mind, unmastered by passions, is a very citadel, for a man has no fortress more impregnable [4] wherein to find refuge and be untaken for ever. He indeed who hath not seen this is ignorant, but he that hath seen it and takes not refuge therein is luckless.

49. Say no more to thyself than what the initial impressions report.[5] This has been told thee, that so and so speaks ill of thee. This *has* been told thee, but it has not been told thee that thou art harmed.[6] I see that my child is ailing. I see it, but I do not see that he is in danger. Keep then ever to first impressions and supplement them not on thy part from within, and nothing [7] happens to thee. And yet do supplement them with this, that thou art familiar with every possible contingency in the world.

50. *The gherkin is bitter.* Toss it away. *There are briars in the path.* Turn aside. That suffices, and thou needest not to add *Why are such things found in the world?* For thou wouldst be a laughing stock to any student of nature; just as thou wouldst be laughed at by a carpenter and a cobbler if thou tookest them to task because in their shops are seen sawdust and parings from what they are

---

[5] iv. 7 etc.   [6] Yet Capit. (xx. § 5) says that Marcus was *suae curiosissimus famae, cp. ibid.* xxii. § 6 ; xxiii. § 7, 9 ; xxix. § 5   [7] *cp.* viii. 28.

τῶν κατασκευαζομένων ὁρᾷς. καίτοι ἐκεῖνοί γε
ἔχουσι, ποῦ αὐτὰ ῥίψωσιν· ἡ δὲ τῶν ὅλων φύσις
ἔξω οὐδὲν ἔχει· ἀλλὰ τὸ θαυμαστὸν τῆς τέχνης
ταύτης ἐστίν, ὅτι περιορίσασα ἑαυτὴν πᾶν τὸ
ἔνδον διαφθείρεσθαι καὶ γηράσκειν καὶ ἄχρηστον
εἶναι δοκοῦν, εἰς ἑαυτὴν μεταβάλλει, καὶ ὅτι
πάλιν ἄλλα νεαρὰ ἐκ τούτων αὐτῶν ποιεῖ· ἵνα
μήτε οὐσίας ἔξωθεν χρῄζῃ μήτε, ὅπου ἐκβάλῃ τὰ
σαπρότερα, προσδέηται. ἀρκεῖται οὖν καὶ χώρᾳ
τῇ ἑαυτῆς καὶ ὕλῃ τῇ ἑαυτῆς καὶ τέχνῃ τῇ ἰδίᾳ.

να΄. Μήτε ἐν ταῖς πράξεσιν ἐπισύρειν μήτε
ἐν ταῖς ὁμιλίαις φύρειν μήτε ἐν ταῖς φαντασίαις
ἀλᾶσθαι· μήτε τῇ ψυχῇ καθάπαξ συνέλκεσθαι
ἢ ἐκθόρνυσθαι· μήτε ἐν τῷ βίῳ ἀσχολεῖσθαι.

2 "Κτείνουσι, κρεανομοῦσι, κατάραις ἐλαύνουσι."
τί οὖν ταῦτα πρὸς τὸ τὴν διάνοιαν μένειν
καθαράν, φρενήρη, σώφρονα, δικαίαν; οἷον εἴ τις
παραστὰς πηγῇ διαυγεῖ καὶ γλυκείᾳ βλασφημοίη
αὐτήν, ἡ δὲ οὐ παύεται πότιμον ἀναβλύζουσα·
κἂν πηλὸν ἐμβάλῃ, κἂν κοπρίαν, τάχιστα
διασκεδάσει αὐτὰ καὶ ἐκκλύσει καὶ οὐδαμῶς
βαφήσεται. πῶς οὖν πηγὴν ἀέναον ἕξεις καὶ μὴ
φρέαρ[1]; ἂν φυλάσσῃς σεαυτὸν πάσης ὥρας εἰς
ἐλευθερίαν μετὰ τοῦ εὐμενῶς καὶ ἁπλῶς καὶ
αἰδημόνως.

νβ΄. Ὁ μὲν μὴ εἰδώς, ὅ τι ἐστὶ κόσμος, οὐκ
οἶδεν, ὅπου ἐστίν. ὁ δὲ μὴ εἰδὼς πρὸς ὅ τι
πέφυκεν, οὐκ οἶδεν ὅστις ἐστίν, οὐδὲ τί ἐστι
κόσμος. ὁ δὲ ἕν τι τούτων ἀπολιπὼν οὐδὲ πρὸς

---

[1] καὶ μὴ φρέαρ omit AD ; ἂν φυλάσσῃς AD ; φύου P.

---

[1] Or, *for space, material, craftsmanship she is content with
herself alone.*

224

making. And yet *they* have space for the disposal of their fragments; while the Universal Nature has nothing outside herself; but the marvel of her craftsmanship is that, though she is limited to herself, she transmutes into her own substance all that within her seems to be perishing and decrepit and useless, and again from these very things produces other new ones; whereby she shews that she neither wants any substance outside herself nor needs a corner where she may cast her decaying matter. Her own space, her own material, her own proper craftsmanship is all that she requires.[1]

51. Be not dilatory in doing, nor confused in conversation, nor vague in thought; let not thy soul be wholly concentred in itself nor uncontrollably agitated; leave thyself leisure in thy life.

They kill us, they cut us limb from limb, they hunt us with execrations![2] How does that prevent thy mind being still pure, sane, sober, just? Imagine a man to stand by a crystal-clear spring of sweet water, and to rail at it; yet it fails not to bubble up with wholesome water. Throw in mud or even filth and it will quickly winnow them away and purge itself of them and take never a stain. How then possess thyself of a living fountain and no mere well?[3] By guiding thyself carefully every hour into freedom with kindliness, simplicity, and modesty.

52. He that knoweth not what the Universe is knoweth not where he is. He that knoweth not the end of its being knoweth not who he is or what the Universe is.[4] But he that is wanting in the knowledge of any

---

[2] Marcus must be thinking of the Christians. *cp.* vii 68. See Appendix.   [3] St. John, iv. 14-16.
[4] *cp.* Epict. ii. 24, § 19.

I

ὅ τι αὐτὸς πέφυκεν εἴποι. τίς οὖν φαίνεταί σοι
ὁ τὸν τῶν κροτούντων ἔπαινον φεύγων ἢ διώκων,†[1]
οἳ οὔθ᾽ ὅπου εἰσὶν οὔτε οἵτινές εἰσι γινώσκουσιν;

νγ΄. Ἐπαινεῖσθαι θέλεις ὑπὸ ἀνθρώπου τρὶς
τῆς ὥρας ἑαυτῷ καταρωμένου; ἀρέσκειν θέλεις
ἀνθρώπῳ, ὃς οὐκ ἀρέσκει ἑαυτῷ; ἀρέσκει ἑαυτῷ
ὁ μετανοῶν ἐφ᾽ ἅπασι σχεδόν, οἷς πράσσει;

νδ΄. Μηκέτι μόνον συμπνεῖν τῷ περιέχοντι
ἀέρι, ἀλλ᾽ ἤδη καὶ συμφρονεῖν τῷ περιέχοντι
πάντα νοερῷ. οὐ γὰρ ἧττον ἡ νοερὰ δύναμις πάντῃ
κέχυται καὶ διαπεφοίτηκε τῷ σπάσαι δυναμένῳ,
ἤπερ ἡ ἀερώδης τῷ ἀναπνεῦσαι δυναμένῳ.

νε΄. Γενικῶς μὲν ἡ κακία οὐδὲν βλάπτει τὸν
κόσμον, ἡ δὲ κατὰ μέρος οὐδὲν βλάπτει τὸν
ἕτερον. μόνῳ δὲ βλαβερά ἐστι τούτῳ, ᾧ ἐπι-
τέτραπται καὶ ἀπηλλάχθαι αὐτῆς, ὁπόταν πρῶτον
οὗτος θελήσῃ.

νϛ΄. Τῷ ἐμῷ προαιρετικῷ τὸ τοῦ πλησίον
προαιρετικὸν ἐπίσης ἀδιάφορόν ἐστιν, ὡς καὶ τὸ
πνευμάτιον αὐτοῦ καὶ τὸ σαρκίδιον. καὶ γὰρ εἰ
ὅτι μάλιστα ἀλλήλων ἕνεκεν γεγόναμεν, ὅμως τὰ
ἡγεμονικὰ ἡμῶν ἕκαστον τὴν ἰδίαν κυρίαν ἔχει·
ἐπεί τοι ἔμελλεν ἡ τοῦ πλησίον κακία ἐμοῦ κακὸν
εἶναι· ὅπερ οὐκ ἔδοξε τῷ θεῷ, ἵνα μὴ ἐπ᾽ ἄλλῳ ᾖ
τὸ ἐμὲ ἀτυχεῖν.

νζ΄. Ὁ ἥλιος κατακεχύσθαι δοκεῖ, καὶ πάντη
γε κέχυται, οὐ μὴν ἐκκέχυται. ἡ γὰρ χύσις αὕτη

---

[1] ἢ δίων (δίω A) ἢ P: διώκων Cas.: ἢ ψόγον φεύγων ἢ ἔπαινον
διώκων Gat.

of these things could not tell what is the end of his own being. What then must we think of those that court or eschew the verdict of the clappers, who have no conception where or who they are?

53. Carest thou to be praised by a man who execrates himself thrice within the hour? Carest thou to win the approval of a man who wins not his own? Can he be said to win his own approval who regrets almost every thing he does?

54. Be no longer content merely to breathe in unison with the all-embracing air, but from this moment think also in unison with the all-embracing Intelligence. For that intelligent faculty is everywhere diffused and offers itself on every side to him that can take it in no less than the aerial to him that can breathe.

55. Taken generically, wickedness does no harm to the Universe,[1] and the particular wickedness does no harm to others. It is harmful to the one individual alone, and he has been given the option of being quit of it the first moment he pleases.

56. To my power of choice[2] the power of choice of my neighbour is as much a matter of indifference as is his vital breath and his flesh. For however much we may have been made for one another, yet our ruling Reason is in each case master in its own house. Else might my neighbour's wickedness become my bane; and this was not God's will, that another might not have my unhappiness in his keeping.[3]

57. The sun's light is diffused down, as it seems, yes, and in every direction, yet it does not diffuse itself away. For this diffusion is an extension. At any

---

[1] v. 35. [2] Not distinguishable from the 'ruling Reason.'
[3] Sen. *Ep.* 70 *ad med.* : *nemo nisi vitio suo miser est.*

τάσις ἐστίν. "ἀκτῖνες" γοῦν αἱ αὐγαὶ αὐτοῦ
ἀπὸ τοῦ "ἐκτείνεσθαι" λέγονται. ὁποῖον δέ
τι ἐστὶν ἀκτίς, ἴδοις ἄν, εἰ διά τινος στενοῦ εἰς
ἐσκιασμένον οἶκον τὸ ἀφ᾽ ἡλίου φῶς εἰσδυόμενον
θεάσαιο· τείνεται¹ γὰρ κατ᾽ εὐθύ, καὶ ὥσπερ
διερείδεται² πρὸς τὸ στερέμνιον, ὅ τι ἂν ἀπαντ-
ήσῃ, διεῖργον τὸν ἐπέκεινα ἀέρα· ἐνταῦθα δὲ
ἔστη καὶ οὐ κατώλισθεν οὐδὲ ἔπεσεν. τοιαύτην
οὖν τὴν χύσιν καὶ διάχυσιν τῆς διανοίας εἶναι
χρή, μηδαμῶς ἔκχυσιν ἀλλὰ τάσιν καὶ πρὸς
τὰ ἀπαντῶντα κωλύματα μὴ βίαιον μηδὲ ῥαγ-
δαίαν τὴν ἐπέρεισιν ποιεῖσθαι· μηδὲ μὴν κατα-
πίπτειν, ἀλλὰ ἵστασθαι καὶ ἐπιλάμπειν τὸ
δεχόμενον. αὐτὸ γὰρ ἑαυτὸ στερήσει τῆς αὐγῆς
τὸ μὴ παραπέμπον αὐτήν.

νη΄. Ὁ τὸν θάνατον φοβούμενος ἤτοι ἀναισθ-
ησίαν φοβεῖται ἢ αἴσθησιν ἑτεροίαν. ἀλλ᾽
εἴτε οὐκέτι αἴσθησιν οὐδὲ κακοῦ τινος αἰσθήσῃ·
εἴτε ἀλλοιοτέραν αἴσθησιν κτήσῃ, ἀλλοῖον ζῷον
ἔσῃ καὶ τοῦ ζῆν οὐ παύσῃ.

νθ΄. Οἱ ἄνθρωποι γεγόνασιν ἀλλήλων ἕνεκεν.
ἢ δίδασκε οὖν ἢ φέρε.

ξ΄. Ἄλλως βέλος, ἄλλως νοῦς φέρεται· ὁ
μέντοι νοῦς, καὶ ὅταν εὐλαβῆται καὶ ὅταν περὶ
τὴν σκέψιν στρέφηται, φέρεται κατ᾽ εὐθὺ οὐδὲν
ἧττον καὶ ἐπὶ τὸ προκείμενον.

ξα΄. Εἰσιέναι εἰς τὸ ἡγεμονικὸν ἑκάστου·
παρέχειν δὲ καὶ ἑτέρῳ παντὶ εἰσιέναι εἰς τὸ
ἑαυτοῦ ἡγεμονικόν.

---

¹ τείνεται Cor. for γίνεται.   ² διερείδεται Reiske ; διαιρεῖται PA.

---

¹ A false etymology. The derivation may be from ἀίσσω
or ἄγνυμι. cp. Tert. Apol. 21.

rate the beams of the Sun are called *Extensions*, because they have an *extension* in space.[1] And what a ray is you may easily see, if you observe the sun's light entering through a narrow chink into a darkened room, for it extends straight on, and is as it were brought up against[2] any solid body it encounters that cuts off the air beyond. There the ray comes to a standstill, neither slipping off nor sinking down. Such then should be the diffusion and circumfusion of the mind, never a diffusing away but extension, and it should never make a violent or uncontrollable impact against any obstacle it meets with, no, nor collapse, but stand firm and illuminate what receives it. For that which conducts it not on its way will deprive itself wilfully of its beams.

58. Dread of death is a dread of non-sensation or new sensation.[3] But either thou wilt feel no sensation, and so no sensation of any evil; or a different kind of sensation will be thine, and so the life of a different creature, but still a life.

59. Mankind have been created for the sake of one another.[4] Either instruct therefore or endure.[5]

60. One is the way of an arrow, another of the mind. Howbeit the mind, both when it cautiously examines its ground and when it is engaged in its enquiry, is none the less moving straight forward and towards its goal.

61. Enter into every man's ruling Reason, and give every one else an opportunity to enter into thine.[6]

---

[2] διαιρεῖται (mss.) would mean apparently *cut* or *broken*.
[3] cp. Justin, *Apol.* i. § 57, addressed to Pius and Marcus.
[4] ix. 1 *ad init.*   [5] v. 28 ; ix. 11.
[6] iv. 38. *cp.* vii. 55 ; Epict. iii. 9, § 12.

ΒΙΒΛΙΟΝ Θ

α΄. Ὁ ἀδικῶν ἀσεβεῖ. τῆς γὰρ τῶν ὅλων φύσεως κατεσκευακυίας τὰ λογικὰ ζῷα ἕνεκεν ἀλλήλων, ὥστε ὠφελεῖν μὲν ἄλληλα κατ᾽ ἀξίαν, βλάπτειν δὲ μηδαμῶς, ὁ τὸ βούλημα ταύτης παραβαίνων ἀσεβεῖ δηλονότι εἰς τὴν πρεσβυτάτην τῶν θεῶν.

2 Καὶ ὁ ψευδόμενος δὲ ἀσεβεῖ περὶ τὴν αὐτὴν θεόν. ἡ γὰρ τῶν ὅλων φύσις ὄντων ἐστὶ φύσις. τὰ δέ γε ὄντα πρὸς τὰ ὑπάρχοντα πάντα οἰκείως ἔχει. ἔτι δὲ καὶ ἀλήθεια αὕτη ὀνομάζεται καὶ τῶν ἀληθῶν ἁπάντων πρώτη αἰτία ἐστίν. ὁ μὲν οὖν ἑκὼν ψευδόμενος ἀσεβεῖ, καθόσον ἐξαπατῶν ἀδικεῖ· ὁ δὲ ἄκων, καθόσον διαφωνεῖ τῇ τῶν ὅλων φύσει, καὶ καθόσον ἀκοσμεῖ μαχόμενος τῇ τοῦ κόσμου φύσει· μάχεται γὰρ ὁ ἐπὶ τἀναντία τοῖς ἀληθέσι φερόμενος παρ᾽ ἑαυτόν· ἀφορμὰς γὰρ προειλήφει παρὰ τῆς φύσεως, ὧν ἀμελήσας οὐχ οἷός τέ ἐστι νῦν διακρίνειν τὰ ψευδῆ ἀπὸ τῶν ἀληθῶν.

3 Καὶ μὴν ὁ τὰς ἡδονὰς ὡς ἀγαθὰ διώκων τοὺς δὲ πόνους ὡς κακὰ φεύγων ἀσεβεῖ. ἀνάγκη

BOOK IX

1. INJUSTICE is impiety. For in that the Nature of the Universe has fashioned rational creatures for the sake of one another[1] with a view to mutual benefit based upon worth, but by no means for harm, the transgressor of her will acts with obvious impiety against the most venerable of Deities.

And the liar too acts impiously with respect to the same Goddess. For the Nature of the Universe is the Nature of the things that are. And the things that are have an intimate connexion with all the things that have ever been. Moreover this Nature is named Truth, and is the primary cause of all that is true. The willing liar then is impious in so far as his deceit is a wrong-doing; and the unwilling liar too, for he is out of tune with the Nature of the Whole, and an element of disorder by being in conflict with the Nature of an orderly Universe; for he is in conflict who allows himself, as far as his conduct goes, to be carried into opposition to what is true. And whereas he had previously been endowed by nature with the means of distinguishing false from true, by neglecting to use them he has lost the power.[2]

Again he acts impiously who seeks after pleasure as a good thing and eschews pain as an evil. For

---

[1] v. 30; viii. 59.   [2] vii. 2.

γὰρ τὸν τοιοῦτον μέμφεσθαι πολλάκις τῇ κοινῇ
φύσει, ὡς παρ' ἀξίαν τι ἀπονεμούσῃ τοῖς φαύλοις
καὶ τοῖς σπουδαίοις, διὰ τὸ πολλάκις τοὺς μὲν
φαύλους ἐν ἡδοναῖς εἶναι καὶ τὰ ποιητικὰ τούτων
κτᾶσθαι, τοὺς δὲ σπουδαίους πόνῳ καὶ τοῖς
ποιητικοῖς τούτου περιπίπτειν. ἔτι δὲ ὁ φοβούμενος τοὺς πόνους, φοβηθήσεταί ποτε καὶ τῶν
ἐσομένων τι ἐν τῷ κόσμῳ· τοῦτο δὲ ἤδη ἀσεβές.
ὅ τε διώκων τὰς ἡδονὰς οὐκ ἀφέξεται τοῦ ἀδικεῖν·
τοῦτο δὲ ἐναργῶς ἀσεβές.

4   Χρὴ δέ, πρὸς ἃ ἡ κοινὴ φύσις ἐπίσης ἔχει (οὐ
γὰρ ἂν ἀμφότερα ἐποίει, εἰ μὴ πρὸς ἀμφότερα
ἐπίσης εἶχε), πρὸς ταῦτα καὶ τοὺς τῇ φύσει
βουλομένους ἔπεσθαι ὁμογνώμονας ὄντας ἐπίσης
διακεῖσθαι· ὅστις οὖν πρὸς πόνον καὶ ἡδονὴν ἢ
θάνατον καὶ ζωὴν ἢ δόξαν καὶ ἀδοξίαν, οἷς
ἐπίσης ἡ τῶν ὅλων φύσις χρῆται, αὐτὸς οὐκ
ἐπίσης ἔχει, δῆλον ὡς ἀσεβεῖ. λέγω δὲ τὸ
χρῆσθαι τούτοις ἐπίσης τὴν κοινὴν φύσιν, ἀντὶ
τοῦ πάντα [1] συμβαίνειν ἐπίσης κατὰ τὸ ἑξῆς τοῖς
γινομένοις καὶ ἐπιγινομένοις ὁρμῇ τινι ἀρχαίᾳ τῆς
προνοίας, καθ' ἣν ἀπό τινος ἀρχῆς ὥρμησεν ἐπὶ
τήνδε τὴν διακόσμησιν συλλαβοῦσά τινας λόγους
τῶν ἐσομένων καὶ δυνάμεις γονίμους ἀφορίσασα
ὑποστάσεών τε καὶ μεταβολῶν καὶ διαδοχῶν
τοιούτων.

β΄. Χαριεστέρου μὲν ἦν ἀνδρὸς ἄγευστον
ψευδολογίας καὶ πάσης ὑποκρίσεως καὶ τρυφῆς

---

[1] τοῦ κατὰ τὸ P : em. Schenkl.

such a man must inevitably find frequent fault with the Universal Nature[1] as unfair in its apportionments to the worthless and the worthy, since the worthless are often lapped in pleasures and possess the things that make for pleasure, while the worthy meet with pain and the things that make for pain. Moreover he that dreads pain will some day be in dread of something that must be in the world. And there we have impiety at once. And he that hunts after pleasures will not hold his hand from injustice. And this is palpable impiety.

But those, who are of one mind with Nature and would walk in her ways, must hold a neutral attitude[2] towards those things towards which the Universal Nature is neutral—for she would not be the Maker of both were she not neutral towards both. So he clearly acts with impiety who is not himself neutral towards pain and pleasure, death and life, good report and ill report, things which the Nature of the Universe treats with neutrality. And by the Universal Nature treating these with neutrality I mean that all things happen neutrally in a chain of sequence[3] to things that come into being and to their after products[4] by some primeval impulse of Providence,[5] in accordance with which She was impelled by some primal impulse to this making of an ordered Universe, when She had conceived certain principles for all that was to be, and allocated the powers generative of substances and changes and successions such as we see.

2. It were more graceful doubtless for a man to depart from mankind untainted with falsehood and

---

[1] vi. 16 *ad fin.* 41.   *cp.* Epict. i. 6, § 39.
[2] Or, *attitude of indifference.*   [3] viii. 75.
[4] Or, *that are consequent upon some primeval impulse.*
Providence here = κοινὴ φύσις.   [5] ix. 28.

καὶ τύφου γενόμενον ἐξ ἀνθρώπων ἀπελθεῖν· τὸ
δ᾽ οὖν κορεσθέντα γε τούτων ἀποπνεῦσαι 'δεύτ-
ερος πλοῦς.' ἢ προῄρησαι προσκαθῆσθαι τῇ
κακίᾳ, καὶ οὔπω σε οὐδὲ ἡ πεῖρα πείθει φεύγειν
ἐκ τοῦ λοιμοῦ; λοιμὸς γὰρ διαφθορὰ διανοίας
πολλῷ γε μᾶλλον ἤπερ ἡ τοῦ περικεχυμένου
τούτου πνεύματος τοιάδε τις δυσκρασία καὶ
τροπή. αὕτη μὲν γὰρ ζῴων λοιμός, καθὸ ζῷά
ἐστιν· ἐκείνη δὲ ἀνθρώπων, καθὸ ἄνθρωποί
εἰσιν.

γʹ. Μὴ καταφρόνει θανάτου, ἀλλὰ εὐαρέστει
αὐτῷ ὡς καὶ τούτου ἑνὸς ὄντος, ὧν ἡ φύσις
ἐθέλει. οἷον γάρ ἐστι τὸ νεάσαι, καὶ τὸ γηρᾶσαι,
καὶ τὸ αὐξῆσαι, καὶ τὸ ἀκμάσαι, καὶ ὀδόντας
καὶ γένειον καὶ πολιὰς ἐνεγκεῖν, καὶ σπεῖραι,
καὶ κυοφορῆσαι, καὶ ἀποκυῆσαι, καὶ τὰ ἄλλα
τὰ φυσικὰ ἐνεργήματα, ὅσα αἱ τοῦ σοῦ βίου
ὧραι φέρουσι, τοιοῦτο καὶ τὸ διαλυθῆναι.
τοῦτο μὲν οὖν κατὰ ἄνθρωπόν ἐστι λελογισμένον,
μὴ ὁλοσχερῶς μηδὲ ὡστικῶς μηδὲ ὑπερηφάνως
πρὸς τὸν θάνατον ἔχειν, ἀλλὰ περιμένειν ὡς
μίαν τῶν φυσικῶν ἐνεργειῶν. καὶ ὡς νῦν
περιμένεις, πότε ἔμβρυον ἐκ τῆς γαστρὸς τῆς
γυναικός σου ἐξέλθῃ, οὕτως ἐκδέχεσθαι τὴν ὥραν
ἐν ᾗ τὸ ψυχάριόν σου τοῦ ἐλύτρου τούτου
ἐκπεσεῖται.

2   Εἰ δὲ καὶ ἰδιωτικὸν παράπηγμα ἀψικάρδιον
ἐθέλεις, μάλιστά σε εὔκολον πρὸς τὸν θάνατον
ποιήσει ἡ ἐπίστασις ἡ ἐπὶ τὰ ὑποκείμενα, ὧν
μέλλεις ἀφίστασθαι, καὶ μεθ᾽ οἵων ἠθῶν οὐκέτι

---

¹ But cp. Capit. xxviii. § 4 (of Marcus): *mortem contemnens.*   ² x. 36, § 2.

BOOK IX

all dissimulation and luxury and arrogance; failing that, however, the 'next best course' is to breathe out his life when his gorge has risen at these things. Or is it thy choice to throw in thy lot with vice, and does not even thy taste of it yet persuade thee to fly from the pestilence? For the corruption of the mind is a pest far worse than any such miasma and vitiation of the air which we breathe around us. The latter is a pestilence for living creatures and affects their life, the former for human beings and affects their humanity.

3. Despise not death,[1] but welcome it, for Nature wills it like all else. For dissolution is but one of the processes of Nature,[2] associated with thy life's various seasons, such as to be young, to be old, to wax to our prime and to reach it, to grow teeth and beard and gray hairs, to beget, conceive and bring forth. A man then that has reasoned the matter out should not take up towards death the attitude of indifference, eagerness, or scorn, but await it as one of the processes of Nature.[3] Look for the hour when thy soul shall emerge from this its sheath, as now thou awaitest the moment when the child she carries shall come forth from thy wife's womb.[4]

But if thou desirest a commonplace solace too that will appeal to the heart, nothing will enable thee to meet death with equanimity better than to observe the environment thou art leaving and the sort of characters with whom thy soul shall no longer be

---

[3] *cp.* Montaigne i. 19 (Florio's version): "The same way you came from death to life, returne without passion or amazement from life to death. Your death is but a piece of the world's order, and but a parcel of the world's life."

[4] Hardly a personal touch, as Vibia Aurelia, Faustina's last child, was born in 166. Besides, ἔμβρυον has no article.

ἔσται ἡ <σὴ ψυχὴ> συμπεφυρμένη. προσκόπτ-
εσθαι μὲν γὰρ αὐτοῖς ἥκιστα δεῖ, ἀλλὰ καὶ
κήδεσθαι καὶ πρᾴως φέρειν, μεμνῆσθαι μέντοι,
ὅτι οὐκ ἀπ᾽ ἀνθρώπων ὁμοδογματούντων σοι ἡ
ἀπαλλαγὴ ἔσται. τοῦτο γὰρ μόνον, εἴπερ ἄρα,
ἀνθεῖλκεν ἂν καὶ κατεῖχεν ἐν τῷ ζῆν, εἰ συζῆν
ἐφεῖτο τοῖς τὰ αὐτὰ δόγματα περιπεποιημένοις.
νῦν δὲ ὁρᾷς, ὅσος ὁ κόπος ἐν τῇ διαφωνίᾳ
τῆς συμβιώσεως, ὥστε εἰπεῖν, " Θᾶττον ἔλθοις,
ὦ θάνατε, μή που καὶ αὐτὸς ἐπιλάθωμαι
ἐμαυτοῦ."

δ'. Ὁ ἁμαρτάνων ἑαυτῷ ἁμαρτάνει· ὁ ἀδικῶν
ἑαυτὸν ἀδικεῖ[1] κακὸν ἑαυτὸν ποιῶν.

ε'. Ἀδικεῖ πολλάκις ὁ μὴ ποιῶν τι, οὐ μόνον
ὁ ποιῶν τι.

ϛ'. Ἀρκεῖ ἡ παροῦσα ὑπόληψις καταληπτική,
καὶ ἡ παροῦσα πρᾶξις κοινωνική, καὶ ἡ παροῦσα
διάθεσις εὐαρεστικὴ πρὸς πᾶν τὸ παρὰ τῆς ἐκτὸς[2]
αἰτίας συμβαῖνον.

ζ'. Ἐξαλεῖψαι φαντασίαν· στῆσαι ὁρμήν·
σβέσαι ὄρεξιν· ἐφ᾽ ἑαυτῷ ἔχειν τὸ ἡγεμονικόν.

η'. Εἰς μὲν τὰ ἄλογα ζῷα μία ψυχὴ διῄρηται·
εἰς δὲ τὰ λογικὰ μία νοερὰ ψυχὴ μεμέρισται.
ὥσπερ καὶ μία γῆ ἐστιν ἁπάντων τῶν γεωδῶν,

---

[1] ἀδικεῖ Cor.: κακοῖ P : ἑαυτὸν κακὸν Leop.
[2] τὸ ἐκ τῆς PAD : τῆς ἐκτὸς Reiske (cp. ix. 31).

---

[1] x. 36 ; Plato, *Phaed.* 66 B.
[2] As Marcus himself often was. *cp.* v. 10; vi. 12 ; viii. 8.
[3] x. 4.
[4] *cp.* the despairing echo of these words by General Gordon,
who was a reader of Marcus, from Khartum : " There is
nothing left for me to prevent me speaking evil of everyone
and distrusting my dear Lord but death."

BOOK IX

mixed up.[1] For while it is very far from right to fall foul of them,[2] but rather even to care for and deal gently with them,[3] yet it is well to remember that not from men of like principles with thine will thy release be. For this alone, if anything, could draw us back and bind us to life, if it were but permitted us to live with those who have possessed themselves of the same principles as ours. But now thou seest how thou art driven by sheer weariness at the jarring discord of thy life with them to say : *Tarry not, O Death, lest peradventure I too forget myself.*[4]

4. He that does wrong, does wrong to himself.[5] The unjust man is unjust to himself, for he makes himself bad.[6]

5. There is often an injustice of omission as well as of commission.

6. The present assumption rightly apprehended, the present act socially enacted, the present disposition satisfied with all that befalls it from the Cause external to it—these will suffice.

7. Efface imagination.[7] Restrain impulse. Quench desire. Keep the ruling Reason in thine own power.

8. Among irrational creatures one life is distributed, and among the rational one intellectual soul has been parcelled out. Just as also there is one earth for all the things that are of the earth ; and

[5] iv. 26 ; ix. 38. Epict. ii. 10, § 26.
[6] Or, *does himself harm.* Plutarch (*Stoic. Contrad.* 12) shews that Chrysippus contradicts himself on this point. Justin (*Apol.* i. 3), speaking of persecution to Pius and Marcus, turns the tables on the latter, saying that in injuring innocent Christians they injured themselves. Epict. iv. 5. 10.
[7] vii. 29 ; viii. 29, 49 ; xii. 25.

καὶ ἑνὶ φωτὶ ὁρῶμεν, καὶ ἕνα ἀέρα ἀναπνέομεν,
ὅσα ὁρατικὰ καὶ ἔμψυχα πάντα.

θ΄. Ὅσα κοινοῦ τινος μετέχει, πρὸς τὸ
ὁμογενὲς σπεύδει. τὸ γεῶδες πᾶν ῥέπει ἐπὶ
γῆν, τὸ ὑγρὸν πᾶν σύρρουν, τὸ ἀερῶδες ὁμοίως·
ὥστε χρῄζειν τῶν διειργόντων καὶ βίας. τὸ πῦρ
ἀνωφερὲς μὲν διὰ τὸ στοιχειῶδες πῦρ· παντὶ δὲ
πυρὶ ἐνταῦθα πρὸς τὸ συνεξάπτεσθαι ἕτοιμον
οὕτως, ὥστε καὶ πᾶν τὸ ὑλικὸν τὸ ὀλίγῳ ξηρό-
τερον εὐέξαπτον εἶναι, διὰ τὸ ἔλαττον ἐγκεκρᾶσθαι
αὐτῷ τὸ κωλυτικὸν πρὸς ἔξαψιν. καὶ τοίνυν
πᾶν τὸ κοινῆς [μὲν]¹ νοερᾶς φύσεως μέτοχον
πρὸς τὸ συγγενὲς ὁμοίως σπεύδει ἢ καὶ μᾶλλον.
ὅσῳ γάρ ἐστι κρεῖττον παρὰ τὰ ἄλλα, τοσούτῳ
καὶ πρὸς τὸ συγκιρνᾶσθαι τῷ οἰκείῳ καὶ συγ-
χεῖσθαι ἑτοιμότερον.

2   Εὐθὺς γοῦν ἐπὶ μὲν τῶν ἀλόγων εὑρέθη σμήνη
καὶ ἀγέλαι καὶ νεοσσοτροφίαι καὶ οἷον ἔρωτες·
ψυχαὶ γὰρ ἤδη ἦσαν ἐνταῦθα, καὶ τὸ συναγωγὸν
ἐν τῷ κρείττονι ἐπιτεινόμενον εὑρίσκετο, οἷον
οὔτε ἐπὶ φυτῶν ἦν οὔτε ἐπὶ λίθων ἢ ξύλων.
ἐπὶ δὲ τῶν λογικῶν ζώων πολιτεῖαι καὶ φιλίαι
καὶ οἶκοι καὶ σύλλογοι καὶ ἐν πολέμοις συνθῆκαι
καὶ ἀνοχαί. ἐπὶ δὲ τῶν ἔτι κρειττόνων, καὶ
διεστηκότων τρόπον τινὰ ἕνωσις ὑπέστη, οἵα ἐπὶ
τῶν ἄστρων. οὕτως ἡ ἐπὶ τὸ κρεῖττον ἐπανά-
βασις, συμπάθειαν καὶ ἐν διεστῶσιν ἐργάσασθαι
δύναται.

¹ omit P.

one is the light whereby we see,[1] and one the air we all breathe that have sight and life.

9. All that share in a common element have an affinity for their own kind. The trend of all that is earthy is to earth; fluids all run together; it is the same with the aerial; so that only interposing obstacles and force can keep them apart. Fire indeed has a tendency to rise by reason of the elemental fire, but is so quick to be kindled in sympathy with all fire here below that every sort of matter, a whit drier than usual, is easily kindled owing to its having fewer constituents calculated to offer resistance to its kindling. So then all that shares in the Universal Intelligent Nature has as strong an affinity towards what is akin, aye even a stronger. For the measure of its superiority to all other things is the measure of its readiness to blend and coalesce with that which is akin to it.

At any rate to begin with among irrational creatures we find swarms and herds and bird-colonies and, as it were, love-associations.[2] For already at that stage there are souls, and the bond of affinity shews itself in the higher form to a degree of intensity not found in plants or stones or timber. But among rational creatures are found political communities and friendships and house-holds and gatherings, and in wars treaties and armistices. But in things still higher a sort of unity in separation even exists, as in the stars. Thus the ascent to the higher form is able to effect a sympathetic connexion [3] even among things which are separate.

---

[1] xii. 30. [2] cp. Aesch. *Prom. Vin.* 492: στέργηθρα.
[3] cp. Epict. i. 14 *ad init.*

3 Ὅρα οὖν τὸ νῦν γινόμενον· μόνα γὰρ τὰ νοερὰ
νῦν ἐπιλέλησται τῆς πρὸς ἄλληλα σπουδῆς καὶ
συννεύσεως, καὶ τὸ σύρρουν ὧδε μόνον οὐ βλέπ-
εται. ἀλλ᾿ ὅμως καίτοι φεύγοντες περικαταλαμ-
βάνονται· κρατεῖ γὰρ ἡ φύσις. ὄψει δέ, ὃ λέγω,
παραφυλάσσων. θᾶσσον γοῦν εὕροι τις ἂν
γεῶδές τι μηδενὸς γεώδους προσαπτόμενον ἤπερ
ἄνθρωπον ἀνθρώπου ἀπεσχισμένον.

ι´. Φέρει καρπὸν καὶ ἄνθρωπος καὶ θεὸς καὶ
ὁ κόσμος· ἐν ταῖς οἰκείαις ὥραις ἕκαστα φέρει.
εἰ δὲ ἡ συνήθεια κυρίως τέτριφεν ἐπὶ ἀμπέλου
καὶ τῶν ὁμοίων, οὐδὲν τοῦτο. ὁ λόγος δὲ καὶ
κοινὸν καὶ ἴδιον καρπὸν ἔχει· καὶ γίνεται ἐξ
αὐτοῦ τοιαῦθ᾿ ἕτερα, ὁποῖόν τι αὐτός ἐστιν ὁ
λόγος.

ια´. Εἰ μὲν δύνασαι, μεταδίδασκε· εἰ δὲ μή,
μέμνησο, ὅτι πρὸς τοῦτο ἡ εὐμένειά σοι δέδοται.
καὶ οἱ θεοὶ δὲ εὐμενεῖς τοῖς τοιούτοις εἰσίν· εἰς
ἔνια δὲ καὶ συνεργοῦσιν, εἰς ὑγίειαν, εἰς πλοῦτον,
εἰς δόξαν· οὕτως εἰσὶ χρηστοί. ἔξεστι δὲ καὶ
σοί· ἢ εἰπέ, τίς ὁ κωλύων;

ιβ´. Πόνει, μὴ ὡς ἄθλιος μηδὲ ὡς ἐλεεῖσθαι
ἢ θαυμάζεσθαι θέλων· ἀλλὰ μόνον ἓν θέλε,
κινεῖσθαι καὶ ἴσχεσθαι, ὡς ὁ πολιτικὸς λόγος
ἀξιοῖ.

ιγ´. Σήμερον ἐξῆλθον πάσης περιστάσεως·
μᾶλλον δὲ ἐξέβαλον πᾶσαν περίστασιν· ἔξω γὰρ
οὐκ ἦν, ἀλλὰ ἔνδον ἐν ταῖς ὑπολήψεσι.

---

[1] St. Paul, Gal. v. 22.   [2] v. 28; viii. 59.

[3] *cp.* Fronto, Naber, p. 86 : *Benignitas ingenita quam omnibus ex more tuo tribuis.*   [4] ix. 27.

[5] v. 2; viii. 40; xii. 22. *cp.* Montaigne, i. 40 (Florio's
version) : "Men, saith an ancient Greek sentence, are

BOOK IX

See then what actually happens at the present time ; for at the present time it is only the intelligent creatures that have forgotten their mutual affinity and attraction, and here alone there is no sign of like flowing to like. Yet flee as they will, they are nevertheless caught in the toils, for Nature will have her way. Watch closely and thou wilt see 'tis so. Easier at any rate were it to find an earthy thing in touch with nothing earthy than a man wholly severed from mankind.

10. They all bear fruit—Man and God and the Universe : each in its due season bears. It matters nought that in customary parlance such a term is strictly applicable only to the vine and such things. Reason too hath its fruit both for all and for itself, and there issue from it other things such as is Reason itself.[1]

11. If thou art able, convert the wrong-doer.[2] If not, bear in mind that kindliness was given thee to meet just such a case.[3] The Gods too are kindly to such persons and even co-operate with them for certain ends—for health, to wit, and wealth and fame, so benignant are they.[4] Thou too canst be the same ; or say who is there that prevents thee.

12. Do thy work not as a drudge, nor as desirous of pity or praise. Desire one thing only, to act or not to act as civic reason directs.

13. This day have I got me out of all trouble, or rather have I cast out all trouble, for it was not from without, but within, in my own imagination.[5]

tormented by the opinions they have of things and not the things themselves. . . . If evil have no entrance into us but by our judgment, it seemeth that it lieth in our power either to contemne or turn them to our good. . . . If that which we call evil and torment be neither torment nor evil, but that our fancy only gives it that quality, it is in us to change it."

241

ιδ′. Πάντα ταῦτα συνήθη μὲν τῇ πείρᾳ, ἐφήμερα δὲ τῷ χρόνῳ, ῥυπαρὰ δὲ τῇ ὕλῃ. πάντα νῦν, οἷα ἐπ᾽ ἐκείνων, οὓς κατεθάψαμεν.

ιε′. Τὰ πράγματα ἔξω θυρῶν ἕστηκεν αὐτὰ ἐφ᾽ ἑαυτῶν μηδὲν μήτε εἰδότα περὶ αὑτῶν μήτε ἀποφαινόμενα. τί οὖν ἀποφαίνεται περὶ αὐτῶν; τὸ ἡγεμονικόν.

ιϛ′. Οὐκ ἐν πείσει, ἀλλ᾽ ἐνεργείᾳ τὸ τοῦ λογικοῦ <καὶ> πολιτικοῦ ζῴου κακὸν καὶ ἀγαθόν, ὥσπερ οὐδὲ ἡ ἀρετὴ καὶ κακία αὐτοῦ ἐν πείσει, ἀλλὰ ἐνεργείᾳ.

ιζ′. Τῷ ἀναρριφέντι λίθῳ οὐδὲν κακὸν τὸ κατενεχθῆναι οὐδὲ ἀγαθὸν τὸ ἀνενεχθῆναι.

ιη′. Δίελθε ἔσω εἰς τὰ ἡγεμονικὰ αὐτῶν, καὶ ὄψει, τίνας κριτὰς φοβῇ, οἵους καὶ περὶ αὑτῶν ὄντας κριτάς.

ιθ′. Πάντα ἐν μεταβολῇ· καὶ αὐτὸς σὺ ἐν διηνεκεῖ ἀλλοιώσει καὶ κατά τι φθορᾷ· καὶ ὁ κόσμος δὲ ὅλος.

κ′. Τὸ ἄλλου ἁμάρτημα ἐκεῖ δεῖ καταλιπεῖν.

κα′. Ἐνεργείας ἀπόληξις, ὁρμῆς,[1] ὑπολήψεως παῦλα καὶ οἷον θάνατος, οὐδὲν κακόν. μέτιθι νῦν ἐπὶ ἡλικίαν, οἷον τὴν παιδικήν, τὴν τοῦ μειρακίου, τὴν νεότητα, τὸ γῆρας· καὶ γὰρ τούτων πᾶσα μεταβολὴ θάνατος. μήτι δεινόν; μέτιθι νῦν ἐπὶ βίον τὸν ὑπὸ τῷ πάππῳ, εἶτα τὸν ὑπὸ τῇ μητρί, εἶτα τὸν ὑπὸ τῷ πατρί· καὶ ἄλλας

---

[1] ὁρμῆς requires a substantive like ἀπόληψις or ἡσυχὴ to balance the sentence.

---

[1] iv. 44. [2] iv. 35.
[3] ii. 4 ; iv. 32. [4] viii. 20.

BOOK IX

14. All these are things of familiar experience [1]; in their duration ephemeral,[2] in their material sordid. Everything is now as it was in the days of those whom we have buried.[3]

15. Objective things stand outside the door, keeping themselves to themselves, without knowledge of or message about themselves.   What then has for us a message about them ?   The ruling Reason.

16. Not in being acted upon but in activity lies the evil and the good of the rational and civic creature, just as his virtue too and his vice lie in activity and not in being acted upon.

17. The stone that is thrown into the air is none the worse for falling down, or the better for being carried upwards.[4]

18. Find the way within into their ruling Reason, and thou shalt see what these judges are whom thou fearest and what their judgment of themselves is worth.[5]

19. Change is the universal experience.[6]   Thou art thyself undergoing a perpetual transformation and, in some sort, decay [7] : aye and the whole Universe as well.

20. Another's wrong-doing should be left with him.[8]

21. A cessation of activity, a quiescence from impulse and opinion and, as it were, their death, is no evil.   Turn now to consider the stages of thy life—childhood, boyhood, manhood, old age—each step in the ladder of change a death.   Is there anything terrible here?   Pass on now to thy life under thy grandfather, then under thy mother, then under thy

[5] iv. 38 ; vii. 34.   [6] v. 23 ; vii. 18.
[7] iv. 3 *ad fin.* ; vii. 25.   [8] vii. 29 ; ix. 38.

δὲ πολλὰς διαφορὰς [1] καὶ μεταβολὰς καὶ ἀπο-
λήξεις εὑρίσκων, ἐπερώτα σεαυτόν· "Μήτι
δεινόν;" οὕτως τοίνυν οὐδὲ ἡ τοῦ ὅλου βίου
λῆξις καὶ παῦλα καὶ μεταβολή.

κβ΄. Τρέχε ἐπὶ τὸ σεαυτοῦ ἡγεμονικὸν καὶ τὸ
τοῦ ὅλου, καὶ τὸ τούτου. τὸ μὲν σεαυτοῦ, ἵνα
νοῦν [2] δικαῖκὸν αὐτὸ ποιήσῃς· τὸ δὲ τοῦ ὅλου,
ἵνα συμμνημονεύσῃς, τίνος μέρος εἶ· τὸ δὲ τούτου,
ἵνα ἐπιστήσῃς, πότερον ἄγνοια ἢ γνώμη, καὶ
ἅμα λογίσῃ, ὅτι συγγενές.

κγ΄. Ὥσπερ αὐτὸς σὺ πολιτικοῦ συστήματος
συμπληρωτικὸς εἶ, οὕτως καὶ πᾶσα πρᾶξίς σου
συμπληρωτικὴ ἔστω ζωῆς πολιτικῆς. ἥτις ἐὰν
οὖν πρᾶξίς σου μὴ ἔχῃ τὴν ἀναφορὰν εἴτε
προσεχῶς εἴτε πόρρωθεν ἐπὶ τὸ κοινωνικὸν
τέλος, αὕτη διασπᾷ τὸν βίον καὶ οὐκ ἐᾷ ἕνα
εἶναι καὶ στασιώδης ἐστίν, ὥσπερ ἐν δήμῳ ὁ τὸ
καθ᾽ αὑτὸν μέρος διιστάμενος ἀπὸ τῆς τοιαύτης
συμφωνίας.

κδ΄. Παιδίων ὀργαὶ καὶ παίγνια, καὶ "πνευμ-
άτια νεκροὺς βαστάζοντα," ὥστε ἐναργέστερον
προσπεσεῖν τὸ τῆς Νεκυίας.

κε΄. Ἴθι ἐπὶ τὴν ποιότητα τοῦ αἰτίου, καὶ ἀπὸ
τοῦ ὑλικοῦ αὐτὸ περιγράψας θέασαι· εἶτα καὶ
τὸν χρόνον περιόρισον, ὅσον πλεῖστον ὑφίστασθαι
πέφυκε τοῦτο τὸ ἰδίως ποιόν.

---

[1] διαφθοράς AD.
[2] νῦν Rend.: γοῦν Cor.

---

[1] Pius. See on i. 17, § 3.
[2] cp. Lucian, de Luct. 15.
[3] iv. 41 πνευμάτιον = ψυχάριον.

father,[1] and finding there many other alterations, changes, and cessations, ask thyself: *Is there anything terrible here?* No, nor any in the ending and quiescence and change of the whole of life.[2]

22. Speed to the ruling Reason of thyself, and of the Universe, and of thy neighbour: of thine own, that thou mayest make it just; of that of the Universe, that thou mayest therewithal remember of what thou art a part; of thy neighbour, that thou mayest learn whether it was ignorance with him or understanding, and reflect at the same time that it is akin to thee.

23. As thou thyself art a part perfective of a civic organism, let also thine every act be a part perfective of civic life. Every act of thine then that has no relation direct or indirect to this social end, tears thy life asunder and destroys its unity, and creates a schism, just as in a commonwealth does the man who, as far as in him lies, stands aloof from such a concord of his fellows.

24. Children's squabbles and make-believe, and *little souls bearing up corpses* [3]—the Invocation of the Dead [4] might strike one as a more vivid reality!

25. Go straight to that which makes a thing what it is, its formative cause,[5] and, isolating it from the material, regard it so. Then mark off the utmost time for which the individual object so qualified is calculated to subsist.

[4] Possibly refers to the Νέκυια of Homer (*Od.* xi.). Menippus (Diog. Laert. *Men.* 6) also wrote a Νέκυια (*cp. above*, vi.47). But it was a term for the invocation of the dead, see Just. *Ap.* i. 18.

[5] To the Formative, or Efficient Cause, of things is due not only that they exist, but that they are what they are. To translate the words here literally by *the quality of the Cause* conveys no meaning. *cp.* vi. 3.

κϛ΄. Ἀνέτλης μύρια διὰ τὸ μὴ ἀρκεῖσθαι τῷ
σῷ ἡγεμονικῷ ποιοῦντι ταῦτα, εἰς ἃ κατεσκεύασται. ἀλλὰ ἅλις.

κζ΄. Ὅταν ἄλλος ψέγῃ σε, ἢ μισῇ, ἢ τοιαῦτά
τινα ἐκφωνῶσιν, ἔρχου ἐπὶ τὰ ψυχάρια αὐτῶν,
δίελθε ἔσω καὶ ἴδε, ποῖοί τινές εἰσιν. ὄψει, ὅτι
οὐ δεῖ σε σπᾶσθαι, ἵνα τούτοις τί ποτε περὶ σοῦ
δοκῇ. εὐνοεῖν μέντοι αὐτοῖς δεῖ· φύσει γὰρ φίλοι.
καὶ οἱ θεοὶ δὲ παντοίως αὐτοῖς βοηθοῦσι, δι'
ὀνείρων, διὰ μαντειῶν, πρὸς ταῦτα μέντοι, πρὸς ἃ
ἐκεῖνοι διαφέρονται.

κη΄. Ταῦτά ἐστι τὰ τοῦ κόσμου ἐγκύκλια,
ἄνω κάτω, ἐξ αἰῶνος εἰς αἰῶνα. καὶ ἤτοι ἐφ'
ἕκαστον ὁρμᾷ ἡ τοῦ ὅλου διάνοια· ὅπερ εἰ ἔστιν,
ἀποδέχου τὸ ἐκείνης ὁρμητόν· ἢ ἅπαξ ὥρμησε, τὰ
δὲ λοιπὰ κατ' ἐπακολούθησιν καὶ †τί ἐν τίνι·† [1]
τρόπον γάρ τινα ἄτομοι, †ἢ ἀμερῆ.† τὸ δὲ ὅλον,
εἴτε θεός, εὖ ἔχει πάντα· εἴτε τὸ εἰκῇ, μὴ καὶ σὺ
εἰκῇ.

2   Ἤδη πάντας ἡμᾶς γῆ καλύψει· ἔπειτα καὶ
αὐτὴ μεταβαλεῖ· κἀκεῖνα εἰς ἄπειρον μεταβαλεῖ·
καὶ πάλιν ἐκεῖνα εἰς ἄπειρον. τὰς γὰρ ἐπι-
κυματώσεις τῶν μεταβολῶν καὶ ἀλλοιώσεων
ἐνθυμούμενός τις καὶ τὸ τάχος παντὸς θνητοῦ
καταφρονήσει.

κθ΄. Χειμάρρους ἡ τῶν ὅλων αἰτία·[2] πάντα
φέρει. ὡς εὐτελῆ δὲ καὶ τὰ πολιτικὰ ταῦτα καί,

---

[1] τί ἐν (ἐν A) τίνι P : τί ἐντείνῃ (*Why this striving?*) Cor.
(*cp.* x. 31): τὶ ἐν τινί Stich.   [2] οὐσία Reiske.

---

[1] i. 17 *ad fin.*   [2] ix. 11, 40.
[3] The Heraclitan round of change between the elements;
see iv. 46.   [4] ix. 1, § 4.

BOOK IX

26. By not being content with thy ruling Reason doing the work for which it was constituted, thou hast borne unnumbered ills. Nay, 'tis enough!

27. When men blame or hate thee or give utterance to some such feelings against thee, turn to their souls, enter into them, and see what sort of men they are. Thou wilt perceive that thou needest not be concerned as to what they think of thee. Yet must thou feel kindly towards them, for Nature made them dear to thee. The Gods too lend them aid in divers ways by dreams[1] and oracles, to win those very things on which their hearts are set.[2]

28. The same, upwards, downwards,[3] from cycle to cycle are the revolutions of the Universe. And either the Universal Mind feels an impulse to act in each separate case – and if this be so, accept its impulsion—or it felt this impulse[4] once for all, and all subsequent things follow by way of consequence; and what matters which it be, for if you like to put it so the world is all atoms [or indivisible].[5] But as to the Whole, if God—all is well; if haphazard—be not thou also haphazard.[6]

Presently the earth will cover us all. It too will anon be changed, and the resulting product will go on from change to change, and so for ever and ever. When a man thinks of these successive waves of change and transformation, and their rapidity, he will hold every mortal thing in scorn.[7]

29. The World-Cause is as a torrent, it sweeps everything along. How negligible these manikins

[5] Possibly ἀμερῆ is a gloss, or ὁμοιομερῆ should be read. (cp. Epict. Frag. 175.)

[6] ii. 5 ; iv. 2, etc. τὸ ὅλον may also be taken to mean in fine.

[7] ix. 19 ; xii. 21. cp. Capit. xxviii. 4 of Marcus on his death-bed, ridens res humanas.

ὡς οἴεται, φιλοσόφως πρακτικὰ ἀνθρώπια· μυξῶν
μεστά. ἄνθρωπε, τί ποτε; ποίησον, ὃ νῦν ἡ
φύσις ἀπαιτεῖ. ὅρμησον, ἐὰν διδῶται, καὶ μὴ
περιβλέπου, εἴ τις εἴσεται. μὴ τὴν Πλάτωνος
πολιτείαν ἔλπιζε· ἀλλὰ ἀρκοῦ, εἰ τὸ βραχύτατον
πρόεισι, καὶ τούτου αὐτοῦ τὴν ἔκβασιν, ὡς [1]
μικρόν τί ἐστι, διανοοῦ. δόγμα γὰρ αὐτῶν τίς
μεταβάλλει; χωρὶς δὲ δογμάτων μεταβολῆς τί
ἄλλο ἢ δουλεία στενόντων καὶ πείθεσθαι προσ-
ποιουμένων; ὕπαγε νῦν, καὶ Ἀλέξανδρον καὶ
Φίλιππον καὶ Δημήτριον τὸν Φαληρέα μοι λέγε.
ὄψονται, εἰ εἶδον, τί ἡ κοινὴ φύσις ἤθελεν, καὶ
ἑαυτοὺς ἐπαιδαγώγησαν· εἰ δὲ ἐτραγῴδησαν,
οὐδείς με κατακέκρικε μιμεῖσθαι. ἁπλοῦν ἐστι
καὶ αἰδῆμον τὸ φιλοσοφίας ἔργον· μή με ἄπαγε [2]
ἐπὶ σεμνοτυφίαν.

λ΄. Ἄνωθεν ἐπιθεωρεῖν ἀγέλας μυρίας καὶ
τελετὰς μυρίας καὶ πλοῦν παντοῖον ἐν χειμῶσι
καὶ γαλήναις καὶ διαφορὰς γινομένων, συγγινο-
μένων, ἀπογινομένων. ἐπινόει δὲ καὶ τὸν ὑπ᾽
ἄλλων πάλαι βεβιωμένον βίον, καὶ τὸν μετὰ σὲ
βιωθησόμενον, καὶ τὸν νῦν ἐν τοῖς βαρβάροις
ἔθνεσι βιούμενον· καὶ ὅσοι μὲν οὐδὲ ὄνομά σου
γινώσκουσιν, ὅσοι δὲ τάχιστα ἐπιλήσονται, ὅσοι
δὲ ἐπαινοῦντες ἴσως νῦν σε τάχιστα ψέξουσι·
καὶ ὡς οὔτε ἡ μνήμη ἀξιόλογόν γε οὔτε ἡ δόξα
οὔτε ἄλλο τι τὸ σύμπαν.

λα΄. Ἀταραξία μὲν περὶ τῶν ἀπὸ τῆς ἐκτὸς

---

[1] ὡς οὐ P.   [2] Perhaps ἀπαγέτω.

that busy themselves with civic matters and flatter themselves that they act therein as philosophers! Drivellers all! What then, O Man? Do what Nature asks of thee now. Make the effort if it be given thee to do so and look not about to see if any shall know it.[1] Dream not of Utopias, but be content if the least thing go forward, and count the outcome of the matter in hand as a small thing.[2] For who can alter another's conviction? Failing a change of conviction, we merely get men pretending to be persuaded and chafing like slaves under coercion. Go to now and tell me of Alexander and Philip and Demetrius of Phalerum. Whether they realized the will of Nature and schooled themselves thereto, is their concern. But if they played the tragedy-hero, no one has condemned me to copy them. Simple and modest is the work of Philosophy: lead me not astray into pomposity and pride.

30. Take a bird's-eye view of the world, its endless gatherings [3] and endless ceremonials,[4] voyagings manifold in storm and calm, and the vicissitudes of things coming into being, participating in being, ceasing to be. Reflect too on the life lived long ago by other men, and the life that shall be lived after thee, and is now being lived in barbarous countries; and how many have never even heard thy name, and how many will very soon forget it, and how many who now perhaps acclaim, will very soon blame thee, and that neither memory nor fame nor anything else whatever is worth reckoning.

31. Freedom from perturbance in all that befalls

---

[2] Or, reading οὐ μικρόν: *deem the success of the matter in hand no small thing.*   [3] vii. 3, 48.
[4] nearly = our colloquial "functions."

αἰτίας συμβαινόντων, δικαιότης δὲ ἐν τοῖς παρὰ τὴν ἐκ σοῦ αἰτίαν ἐνεργουμένοις· τουτέστιν ὁρμὴ καὶ πρᾶξις καταλήγουσα ἐπ᾿ αὐτὸ τὸ κοινωνικῶς πρᾶξαι ὡς τοῦτό σοι κατὰ φύσιν ὄν.

λβ΄. Πολλὰ περισσὰ περιελεῖν τῶν ἐνοχλούντων σοι δύνασαι, ὅλα ἐπὶ τῇ ὑπολήψει σου κείμενα· καὶ πολλὴν εὐρυχωρίαν περιποιήσεις ἤδη σεαυτῷ, <τῷ>[1] τὸν ὅλον κόσμον περιειληφέναι τῇ γνώμῃ, καὶ τὸν ἀίδιον αἰῶνα περινοεῖν, καὶ τὴν τῶν κατὰ μέρος ἑκάστου πράγματος ταχεῖαν μεταβολὴν ἐπινοεῖν, ὡς βραχὺ μὲν τὸ ἀπὸ γενέσεως μέχρι διαλύσεως, ἀχανὲς δὲ τὸ πρὸ τῆς γενέσεως, ὡς καὶ τὸ μετὰ τὴν διάλυσιν ὁμοίως ἄπειρον.

λγ΄. Πάντα, ὅσα ὁρᾷς, τάχιστα φθαρήσεται καὶ οἱ φθειρόμενα αὐτὰ ἐπιδόντες τάχιστα καὶ αὐτοὶ φθαρήσονται· καὶ ὁ ἐσχατόγηρως ἀποθανὼν εἰς ἴσον καταστήσεται τῷ προώρῳ.

λδ΄. Τίνα τὰ ἡγεμονικὰ τούτων, καὶ περὶ οἷα ἐσπουδάκασι, καὶ δι᾿ οἷα φιλοῦσι καὶ τιμῶσι. γυμνὰ νόμιζε βλέπειν τὰ ψυχάρια αὐτῶν. ὅτε δοκοῦσι βλάπτειν ψέγοντες ἢ ὠφελεῖν ἐξυμνοῦντες, ὅση οἴησις.

λε΄. Ἡ ἀποβολὴ οὐδὲν ἄλλο ἐστὶν ἢ μεταβολή. τούτῳ δὲ χαίρει ἡ τῶν ὅλων φύσις, καθ᾿ ἣν πάντα, καθὼς[2] γίνεται, ἐξ αἰῶνος ὁμοειδῶς ἐγίνετο, καὶ εἰς ἄπειρον τοιαῦθ᾿ ἕτερα ἔσται. τί οὖν λέγεις, ὅτι ἐγίνετό τε πάντα <κακῶς>[3] καὶ

---

[1] <τῷ> Gat.
[2] καλῶς PA : καθὼς Schenkl.
[3] So Reiske: ὃ καὶ πάντα P : omit A.

from the external Cause, and justice in all that thine own inner Cause prompts thee to do; that is, impulse and action finding fulfilment in the actual performance of social duty as being in accordance with thy nature.

32. It is in thy power to rid thyself of many unnecessary troubles, for they exist wholly in thy imagination. Thou wilt at once set thy feet in a large room by embracing the whole Universe in thy mind and including in thy purview time everlasting, and by observing the rapid change in every part of everything, and the shortness of the span between birth and dissolution, and that the yawning immensity before birth is only matched by the infinity after our dissolution.

33. All that thine eyes behold will soon perish and they, who live to see it perish, will in their turn perish no less quickly; and he who outlives all his contemporaries and he who dies before his time will be as one in the grave.

34. What is the ruling Reason [1] of these men, and about what sort of objects have they been in earnest, and from what motives do they lavish their love and their honour! View with the mind's eye their poor little souls in their nakedness. What immense conceit this of theirs, when they fancy that there is bane in their blame or profit in their praises!

35. Loss and change,[2] they are but one. Therein doth the Universal Nature take pleasure,[3] through whom are all things done now as they have been in like fashion from time everlasting; and to eternity shall other like things be. Why then dost thou say that all things have been evil and will remain evil

---

[1] vii. 34, 62; ix. 18.
[2] The play on the words cannot be kept.   [3] vii. 18.

πάντα ἀεὶ κακῶς ἔσται, καὶ οὐδεμία ἄρα
δύναμις ἐν τοσούτοις θεοῖς ἐξευρέθη ποτὲ ἡ
διορθώσουσα ταῦτα, ἀλλὰ κατακέκριται ὁ κόσμος
ἐν ἀδιαλείπτοις κακοῖς συνέχεσθαι;

λϛ΄. Τὸ σαπρὸν τῆς ἑκάστῳ ὑποκειμένης ὕλης·
ὕδωρ, κόνις, ὀστάρια, γράσος· ἢ πάλιν πῶροι γῆς
τὰ μάρμαρα, καὶ ὑποστάθμαι ὁ χρυσός, ὁ
ἄργυρος, καὶ τριχία ἡ ἐσθής· καὶ αἷμα ἡ
πορφύρα, καὶ τὰ ἄλλα πάντα τοιαῦτα. καὶ τὸ
πνευμάτιον[1] δὲ ἄλλο τοιοῦτον καὶ ἐκ τούτων εἰς
ταῦτα μεταβάλλον.

λζ΄. Ἅλις τοῦ ἀθλίου βίου καὶ γογγυσμοῦ
καὶ πιθηκισμοῦ. τί ταράσσῃ; τί τούτων καινόν;
τί σε ἐξίστησι; τὸ αἴτιον; ἴδε αὐτό. ἀλλ᾽ ἡ
ὕλη; ἴδε αὐτήν. ἔξω δὲ τούτων οὐδέν ἐστιν·
ἀλλὰ καὶ πρὸς τοὺς θεοὺς ἤδη ποτὲ ἁπλούστερος
καὶ χρηστότερος γενοῦ.

2 Ἴσον τὸ ἑκατὸν ἔτεσι καὶ τὸ τρισὶ ταῦτα
ἱστορῆσαι.

λη΄. Εἰ μὲν ἥμαρτεν, ἐκεῖ τὸ κακόν. τάχα δ᾽
οὐχ ἥμαρτεν.

λθ΄. Ἤτοι ἀπὸ μιᾶς πηγῆς νοερᾶς πάντα ὡς
ἑνὶ σώματι ἐπισυμβαίνει, καὶ οὐ δεῖ τὸ μέρος τοῖς
ὑπὲρ τοῦ ὅλου γινομένοις μέμφεσθαι· ἢ ἄτομοι
καὶ οὐδὲν ἄλλο ἢ κυκεὼν καὶ σκεδασμός. τί
οὖν ταράσσῃ; τῷ ἡγεμονικῷ λέγε·[2] "Τέθνηκας,
ἔφθαρσαι, τεθηρίωσαι, ὑποκρίνῃ, συναγελάζῃ,
βόσκῃ."

μ΄. Ἤτοι οὐδὲν δύνανται οἱ θεοὶ ἢ δύνανται.

---

[1] πνευματικὸν Cas.: πνευμάτιον PA.
[2] λέγεις PA : λέγε Cor. Perhaps λέγε σύ.

to the end, and that no help has after all been found in Gods, so many as they be, to right these things, but that the fiat hath gone forth that the Universe should be bound in an unbroken chain of ill?

36. Seeds of decay in the underlying material of everything—water, dust, bones, reek! Again, marble but nodules of earth, and gold and silver but dross, garments merely hair-tufts, and purple only blood. And so with everything else. The soul too another like thing and liable to change from this to that.

37. Have done with this miserable way of life, this grumbling, this apism! Why fret? What is the novelty here? What amazes thee? The Cause? Look fairly at it. What then, the Material? Look fairly at that. Apart from these two, there is nothing. But in regard to the Gods also now even at the eleventh hour show thyself more simple,[1] more worthy.

Whether thy experience of these things lasts three hundred years or three, it is all one.

38. If he did wrong, with him lies the evil. But maybe he did no wrong.[2]

39. Either there is one intelligent source, from which as in one body all after things proceed—and the part ought not to grumble at what is done in the interests of the whole—or there are atoms, and nothing but a medley and a dispersion.[3] Why then be harassed? Say to thy ruling Reason: *Thou art dead! Thou art corrupt! Thou hast become a wild beast! Thou art a hypocrite! Thou art one of the herd! Thou battenest with them!*

40. Either the Gods have no power or they have

[1] iv. 26.   [2] vii. 29.   [3] iv. 27; vi. 10; vii. 32; xii. 14.

εἰ μὲν οὖν μὴ δύνανται, τί εὔχῃ; εἰ δὲ δύνανται,
διὰ τί οὐχὶ μᾶλλον εὔχῃ διδόναι αὐτοὺς τὸ μήτε
φοβεῖσθαί τι τούτων μήτε ἐπιθυμεῖν τινος
τούτων μήτε λυπεῖσθαι ἐπί τινι τούτων μᾶλλον
ἤπερ τὸ μὴ παρεῖναί τι τούτων ἢ τὸ παρεῖναι;
πάντως γάρ, εἰ δύνανται συνεργεῖν ἀνθρώποις,
καὶ εἰς ταῦτα δύνανται συνεργεῖν. ἀλλὰ ἴσως
ἐρεῖς, ὅτι "Ἐπ' ἐμοὶ αὐτὰ οἱ θεοὶ ἐποίησαν."
εἶτα οὐ κρεῖσσον χρῆσθαι τοῖς ἐπὶ σοὶ μετ'
ἐλευθερίας ἢ διαφέρεσθαι πρὸς τὰ μὴ ἐπὶ σοὶ
μετὰ δουλείας καὶ ταπεινότητος; τίς δέ σοι εἶπεν,
ὅτι οὐχὶ καὶ εἰς τὰ ἐφ' ἡμῖν οἱ θεοὶ συλλαμ-
βάνουσιν; ἄρξαι γοῦν περὶ τούτων εὔχεσθαι καὶ
ὄψει. οὗτος εὔχεται· "Πῶς κοιμηθῶ μετ' ἐκείνης."
σύ· "Πῶς μὴ ἐπιθυμήσω τοῦ κοιμηθῆναι μετ'
ἐκείνης." ἄλλος· "Πῶς στερηθῶ ἐκείνου." σύ·
"Πῶς μὴ χρῄζω τοῦ στερηθῆναι." ἄλλος· "Πῶς
μὴ ἀποβάλω τὸ τεκνίον." σύ· "Πῶς μὴ φοβηθῶ
ἀποβαλεῖν." ὅλως ὧδε ἐπίστρεψον τὰς εὐχάς, καὶ
θεώρει, τί γίνεται.

μα΄. Ὁ Ἐπίκουρος λέγει, ὅτι "Ἐν τῇ νόσῳ
οὐκ ἦσάν μοι αἱ ὁμιλίαι περὶ τῶν τοῦ σωματίου
παθῶν οὐδὲ πρὸς τοὺς εἰσιόντας τοιαῦτά τινα,"
φησίν, "ἐλάλουν· ἀλλὰ τὰ προηγούμενα φυσιο-
λογῶν διετέλουν, καὶ πρὸς αὐτῷ τούτῳ ὤν, πῶς
ἡ διάνοια συμμεταλαμβάνουσα τῶν ἐν τῷ σαρκιδίῳ τοιούτων[1] κινήσεων ἀταρακτεῖ, τὸ ἴδιον
ἀγαθὸν τηροῦσα. οὐδὲ τοῖς ἰατροῖς ἐμπαρεῖχον,"
φησί, "καταφρυάττεσθαι, ὡς τι ποιοῦσιν, ἀλλ' ὁ

---

[1] τοιούτων P : ποιούντων A : ποιῶν τινων Schenkl.

---

[1] vi. 44.
[2] ix. 27. St. Paul, Rom. viii. 26 : τὸ πνεῦμα συναντιλαμ-

BOOK IX

power. If they have no power, why pray to them[1]? But if they have power, why not rather pray that they should give thee freedom from fear of any of these things and from lust for any of these things and from grief at any of these things [rather] than that they should grant this or refuse that. For obviously if they can assist men at all, they can assist them in this. But perhaps thou wilt say: *The Gods have put this in my power.* Then is it not better to use what is in thy power like a free man than to concern thyself with what is not in thy power like a slave and an abject? And who told thee that the Gods do not co-operate with us[2] even in the things that are in our power? Begin at any rate with prayers for such things and thou wilt see. One prays: *How may I lie with that woman!*[3] Thou: *How may I not lust to lie with her!* Another: *How may I be quit of that man!* Thou: *How may I not wish to be quit of him!* Another: *How may I not lose my little child!* Thou: *How may I not dread to lose him.*[4] In a word, give thy prayers this turn, and see what comes of it.

41. Listen to Epicurus[5] where he says: *In my illness my talk was not of any bodily feelings, nor did I chatter about such things to those who came to see me, but I went on with my cardinal disquisitions on natural philosophy, dwelling especially on this point, how the mind, having perforce its share in such affections of the flesh, yet remains unperturbed, safeguarding its own proper good. Nor did I—he goes on—let the physicians ride the high horse as if they were doing*

βάνεται. Gataker very aptly quotes Augustine, *de Grat. Christi* i. 15: *Cur petitur quod ad nostram pertinet potestatem, si Deus non adjuvat voluntatem?*

[3] Sen. *Ep.* 10 *ad fin.*; Shak. *Lucr.* 50.

[4] Capit. xxi. § 3.　　　[5] See Diog. Laert. *Epicur.* § 10.

βίος ἤγετο εὖ καὶ καλῶς." ταὐτὰ οὖν ἐκείνῳ ἐν
νόσῳ, ἐὰν νοσῇς, καὶ ἐν ἄλλῃ τινὶ περιστάσει· τὸ
γὰρ μὴ ἀφίστασθαι φιλοσοφίας ἐν οἷς δήποτε τοῖς
προσπίπτουσι μηδὲ [τῷ] ἰδιώτῃ καὶ ἀφυσιολόγῳ[1]
συμφλυαρεῖν πάσης αἱρέσεως κοινόν . . . . πρὸς
μόνῳ δὲ τῷ νῦν πρασσομένῳ εἶναι καὶ τῷ ὀργάνῳ,
δι' οὗ πράσσεις.[2]

μβ'. Ὅταν τινὸς ἀναισχυντίᾳ προσκόπτῃς,
εὐθὺς πυνθάνου σεαυτοῦ· "Δύνανται οὖν ἐν τῷ
κόσμῳ ἀναίσχυντοι μὴ εἶναι;" οὐ δύνανται. μὴ
οὖν ἀπαίτει τὸ ἀδύνατον. εἷς γὰρ καὶ οὗτός
ἐστιν ἐκείνων τῶν ἀναισχύντων, οὓς ἀνάγκη ἐν τῷ
κόσμῳ εἶναι. τὸ δ' αὐτὸ καὶ ἐπὶ τοῦ πανούργου
καὶ ἐπὶ τοῦ ἀπίστου καὶ παντὸς τοῦ ὁτιοῦν
ἁμαρτάνοντος ἔστω σοι πρόχειρον. ἅμα γὰρ
τῷ ὑπομνησθῆναι, ὅτι τὸ γένος τῶν τοιούτων
ἀδύνατόν ἐστι μὴ ὑπάρχειν, εὐμενέστερος ἔσῃ
πρὸς τοὺς καθ' ἕνα. εὔχρηστον δὲ κἀκεῖνο
εὐθὺς ἐννοεῖν, "Τίνα ἔδωκεν ἡ φύσις τῷ
ἀνθρώπῳ ἀρετὴν πρὸς τοῦτο τὸ ἁμάρτημα."
ἔδωκε γάρ, ὡς ἀντιφάρμακον πρὸς μὲν τὸν
ἀγνώμονα τὴν πραότητα, πρὸς δὲ ἄλλον ἄλλην
τινὰ δύναμιν.

2   Ὅλως δὲ ἔξεστί σοι μεταδιδάσκειν τὸν πε-
πλανημένον· πᾶς γὰρ ὁ ἁμαρτάνων ἀφαμαρτάνει
τοῦ προκειμένου καὶ πεπλάνηται. τί δὲ καὶ
βέβλαψαι; εὑρήσεις γὰρ μηδένα τούτων, πρὸς
οὓς παροξύνῃ, πεποιηκότα τι τοιοῦτον, ἐξ οὗ ἡ
διάνοιά σου χείρων ἔμελλε γενήσεσθαι· τὸ δὲ

---

[1] ἀφυσιολόγῳ Gat.: φυσιολόγῳ (natural philosopher) PA.
[2] πράσσει PA. This verb has no subject and Wilam. and
Schenkl mark a lacuna before πρὸς μόνῳ: πράσσεις Reiske.

BOOK IX

grand things, but my life went on well and happily.
Imitate him then in sickness, if thou art sick, and in
any other emergency; for it is a commonplace of
every sect not to renounce Philosophy whatever
difficulties we encounter, nor to consent to babble
as he does that is unenlightened in philosophy and
nature; . . . devote thyself to thy present work
alone and thy instrument for performing it.

42. When thou art offended by shamelessness in
any one, put this question at once to thyself: *Can it be
then that shameless men should not exist in the world?* It
can not be. Then ask not for what can not be.[1]
For this man in question also is one of the shameless
ones that must needs exist in the world. Have the
same reflection ready for the rogue, the deceiver, or
any other wrongdoer whatever. For the remembrance that this class of men cannot but exist will
bring with it kindlier feelings towards individuals of
the class. Right useful too is it to bethink thee at
once of this: *What virtue has Nature given man as
a foil to the wrong-doing in question?* For as an
antidote against the unfeeling man she has given
gentleness,[2] and against another man some other
resource.

In any case it is in thy power to teach the man
that has gone astray the error of his ways. For
every one that doth amiss misses his true mark and
hath gone astray. But what harm hast thou suffered?
Thou wilt find that not one of the persons against
whom thou art exasperated has done anything
capable of making thy mind worse; but it is in

---

[1] v. 17. *cp.* Dio 71. 34, § 4.
[2] Epict. *Man.* 10; St. Paul, Tit. iii. 2: πραότητα πρὸς
πάντας.

κακόν σου καὶ τὸ βλαβερὸν ἐνταῦθα πᾶσαν τὴν
ὑπόστασιν ἔχει.

3 Τί δαὶ κακὸν ἢ ξένον γέγονεν, εἰ ὁ ἀπαίδευτος
τὰ τοῦ ἀπαιδεύτου πράσσει; ὅρα, μὴ σεαυτῷ
μᾶλλον ἐγκαλεῖν ὀφείλῃς, ὅτι οὐ προσεδόκησας
τοῦτον τοῦτο ἁμαρτήσεσθαι. σὺ γὰρ καὶ ἀφορμὰς
ἐκ τοῦ λόγου εἶχες πρὸς τὸ ἐνθυμηθῆναι, ὅτι εἰκός
ἐστι τοῦτον τοῦτο ἁμαρτήσεσθαι, καὶ ὅμως
ἐπιλαθόμενος θαυμάζεις, εἰ ἡμάρτηκε.

4 Μάλιστα δέ, ὅταν ὡς ἀπίστῳ ἢ ἀχαρίστῳ
μέμφῃ, εἰς σεαυτὸν ἐπιστρέφου. προδήλως γὰρ
σὸν τὸ ἁμάρτημα, εἴτε περὶ τοῦ τοιαύτην διάθεσιν ἔχοντος ἐπίστευσας, ὅτι τὴν πίστιν φυλάξει,
εἴτε τὴν χάριν διδοὺς μὴ καταληκτικῶς ἔδωκας,
μηδὲ ὥστε ἐξ αὐτῆς τῆς σῆς πράξεως εὐθὺς
ἀπειληφέναι πάντα τὸν καρπόν.

5 Τί γὰρ πλέον θέλεις εὖ ποιήσας ἄνθρωπον;
οὐκ ἀρκεῖ τοῦτο, ὅτι κατὰ φύσιν τὴν σήν τι
ἔπραξας, ἀλλὰ τούτου μισθὸν ζητεῖς; ὡς εἰ ὁ
ὀφθαλμὸς ἀμοιβὴν ἀπῄτει, ὅτι βλέπει, ἢ οἱ
πόδες, ὅτι βαδίζουσιν. ὥσπερ γὰρ ταῦτα πρὸς
τόδε τι γέγονεν, ἅπερ κατὰ τὴν ἰδίαν κατασκευὴν
ἐνεργοῦντα ἀπέχει τὸ ἴδιον, οὕτως καὶ ὁ ἄνθρωπος εὐεργετικὸς πεφυκώς, ὁπόταν τι εὐεργετικὸν ἢ
ἄλλως εἰς τὰ μέσα συνεργητικὸν πράξῃ, πεποίηκε,
πρὸς ὃ κατεσκεύασται, καὶ ἔχει τὸ ἑαυτοῦ.

---

[1] Lit. *there*, *i.e. in thy mind*.

[2] *cp.* the striking parallel in Dio 71. 24, § 2, τὸ μηδὲν
πιστὸν ἐν ἀνθρώποις εἶναι : *ibid.* 71. 26, § 2, πίστιν καταλύσαντι
πιστὸν διαγενέσθαι, where Marcus is speaking to his soldiers
on the revolt of Cassius ; and 27, § 1, where, writing to the
Senate, he calls Cassius ἀχάριστος. I cannot help thinking

BOOK IX

thy mind[1] that the evil for thee and the harmful have their whole existence.

Where is the harm or the strangeness in the boor acting—like a boor? See whether thou art not thyself the more to blame in not expecting that he would act thus wrongly. For thy reason too could have given thee means for concluding that this would most likely be the case. Nevertheless all this is forgotten, and thou art surprised at his wrongdoing.

But above all, when thou findest fault with a man for faithlessness and ingratitude,[2] turn thy thoughts to thyself. For evidently the fault is thine own, whether thou hadst faith that a man with such a character would keep faith with thee, or if in bestowing a kindness thou didst not bestow it absolutely and as from the very doing of it having at once received the full complete fruit.[3]

For when thou hast done a kindness, what more wouldst thou have? Is not this enough that thou hast done something in accordance with thy nature? Seekest thou a recompense for it? As though the eye should claim a guerdon for seeing, or the feet for walking! For just as these latter were made for their special work, and by carrying this out according to their individual constitution they come fully into their own, so also man, formed as he is by nature for benefiting others, when he has acted as benefactor or as co-factor in any other way for the general weal, has done what he was constituted for, and has what is his.[4]

that this section of the *Thoughts* was written at the time of the rebellion in 175, and that Marcus is here taking himself to task.   [3] v. 6; vii. 73.

[4] iv. 49; xi. 1. *cp.* St. Matt. vi. 2. Marcus was noted for εὐεργεσία, Dio 71. 34, §3; *C.I.Gr.* 2495, 4697ᶜ.

ΒΙΒΛΙΟΝ Ι

α΄. Ἔσῃ ποτὲ ἆρα, ὦ ψυχή, ἀγαθὴ καὶ ‿πλῆ
καὶ μία καὶ γυμνή, φανερωτέρα τοῦ περικειμένου
σοι σώματος; γεύσῃ ποτὲ ἆρα τῆς φιλητικῆς καὶ
στερκτικῆς διαθέσεως; ἔσῃ ποτὲ ἆρα πλήρης
καὶ ἀνενδεὴς καὶ οὐδὲν ἐπιποθοῦσα οὐδὲ ἐπι-
θυμοῦσα οὐδενὸς οὔτε ἐμψύχου οὔτε ἀψύχου
πρὸς ἡδονῶν ἀπολαύσεις; οὐδὲ χρόνου, ἐν ᾧ ἐπὶ
μακρότερον ἀπολαύσεις; οὐδὲ τόπου ἢ χώρας ἢ
ἀέρων εὐκαιρίας οὐδὲ ἀνθρώπων εὐαρμοστίας;
ἀλλὰ ἀρκεσθήσῃ τῇ παρούσῃ καταστάσει καὶ
ἡσθήσῃ τοῖς παροῦσι πᾶσι, καὶ συμπείσεις σεαυτήν, ὅτι πάντα, <ἅ>[1] σοι πάρεστι, παρὰ τῶν
θεῶν πάρεστι καὶ πάντα σοι εὖ ἔχει καὶ εὖ
ἕξει, ὅσα φίλον αὐτοῖς καὶ ὅσα μέλλουσι δώσειν
ἐπὶ σωτηρίᾳ τοῦ τελείου ζῴου, τοῦ ἀγαθοῦ καὶ
δικαίου καὶ καλοῦ καὶ γεννῶντος πάντα καὶ
συνέχοντος καὶ περιέχοντος καὶ περιλαμβάνον-
τος διαλυόμενα εἰς γένεσιν ἑτέρων ὁμοίων; ἔσῃ
ποτὲ ἆρα τοιαύτη, οἵα θεοῖς τε καὶ ἀνθρώποις
οὕτω συμπολιτεύεσθαι, ὡς μήτε μέμφεσθαί τι
αὐτοῖς μήτε καταγινώσκεσθαι ὑπ᾽ αὐτῶν;

---

[1] <ἅ> Lemercier and Schenkl: παρὰ τῶν θεῶν πάρεστι καὶ
transposed by Schenkl from before καὶ εὖ ἕξει P.

BOOK X

1. WILT thou then, O my Soul, ever at last be good and simple and single and naked, shewing thyself more visible than the body that overlies thee? Wilt thou ever taste the sweets of a loving and a tender heart? Ever be full-filled and self-sufficing, longing for nothing, lusting after nothing animate or inanimate, for the enjoyment of pleasures —not time wherein the longer to enjoy them, nor place or country or congenial climes or men nearer to thy liking—but contented with thy present state[1] and delighted with thy present everything, convincing thyself withal that all that is present for thee is present from the Gods,[2] and that everything is and shall be well with thee that is pleasing to them and that they shall hereafter grant for the conservation of that Perfect Being[3] that is good and just and beautiful, the Begetter and Upholder of all things, that embraces and gathers them in, when they are dissolved, to generate therefrom other like things?[4] Wilt thou ever at last fit thyself so to be a fellow-citizen with the Gods and with men as never to find fault with them or incur their condemnation?

[1] ix. 6.   [2] iii. 11, § 3.
[3] *i.e.* Zeus = the Universe = the First Cause = Nature.
[4] vii. 23.

β'. Παρατήρει, τί σου ἡ φύσις ἐπιζητεῖ, ὡς ὑπὸ φύσεως μόνον διοικουμένου· εἶτα ποίει αὐτὸ καὶ προσίεσο, εἰ μὴ χεῖρον μέλλει διατίθεσθαι σου ἡ ὡς ζῴου φύσις. ἑξῆς δὲ παρατηρητέον, τί ἐπιζητεῖ σου ἡ ὡς ζῴου φύσις· καὶ πᾶν τοῦτο παραληπτέον, εἰ μὴ χεῖρον μέλλει διατίθεσθαι ἡ ὡς ζῴου λογικοῦ φύσις· ἔστι δὲ τὸ λογικὸν εὐθὺς καὶ πολιτικόν. τούτοις δὴ κανόσι χρώμενος μηδὲν περιεργάζου.

γ'. Πᾶν τὸ συμβαῖνον ἤτοι οὕτως συμβαίνει, ὡς πέφυκας αὐτὸ φέρειν ἢ ὡς οὐ πέφυκας αὐτὸ φέρειν. εἰ μὲν οὖν συμβαίνει σοι, ὡς πέφυκας φέρειν, μὴ δυσχέραινε· ἀλλ' ὡς πέφυκας, φέρε. εἰ δέ, ὡς μὴ πέφυκας φέρειν, μὴ δυσχέραινε· φθαρήσεται γάρ σε ἀπαναλῶσαν. μέμνησο μέν-τοι, ὅτι πέφυκας φέρειν πᾶν, περὶ οὗ ἐπὶ τῇ ὑπολήψει ἐστὶ τῇ σῇ φορητὸν καὶ ἀνεκτὸν αὐτὸ ποιῆσαι, κατὰ φαντασίαν τοῦ συμφέρειν ἢ καθ-ήκειν σεαυτῷ τοῦτο ποιεῖν.

δ'. Εἰ μὲν σφάλλεται, διδάσκειν εὐμενῶς καὶ τὸ παρορώμενον δεικνύναι· εἰ δὲ ἀδυνατεῖς, σεαυτὸν αἰτιᾶσθαι, ἢ μηδὲ σεαυτόν.

ε'. Ὅ τι ἄν σοι συμβαίνῃ, τοῦτό σοι ἐξ αἰῶνος προκατεσκευάζετο· καὶ ἡ ἐπιπλοκὴ τῶν αἰτίων συνέκλωθε τήν τε σὴν ὑπόστασιν ἐξ ἀιδίου καὶ τὴν τούτου σύμβασιν.

ς'. Εἴτε ἄτομοι εἴτε φύσις, πρῶτον κείσθω, ὅτι μέρος εἰμὶ τοῦ ὅλου, ὑπὸ φύσεως διοικου-μένου· ἔπειτα, ὅτι ἔχω πως οἰκείως πρὸς τὰ

BOOK X

2. Observe what thy nature asks of thee, as one controlled by Nature alone, then do this and with a good grace, if thy nature as a living creature is not to be made worse thereby. Next must thou observe what thy nature as a living creature asks of thee. And this must thou wholly accept, if thy nature as a rational living creature be not made worse thereby. Now the rational is indisputably also the civic. Comply with these rules then and be not needlessly busy about anything.

3. All that befalls either so befalls as thou art fitted by nature to bear it or as thou art not fitted.[1] If the former, take it not amiss, but bear it as thou art fitted to do. If the latter, take not that amiss either, for when it has destroyed thee, it will itself perish. Howbeit be assured that thou art fitted by nature to bear everything which it rests with thine own opinion about it to render bearable and tolerable, according as thou thinkest it thy interest or thy duty to do so.

4. If a man makes a slip, enlighten him with loving-kindness, and shew him wherein he hath seen amiss.[2] Failing that, blame thyself or not even thyself.

5. Whatever befalls thee was set in train for thee from everlasting, and the interplication of causes was from eternity weaving into one fabric thy existence and the coincidence of this event.[3]

6. Whether there be atoms or a Nature, let it be postulated first, that I am a part of the whole Universe controlled by Nature; secondly, that I stand in some intimate connexion with other kindred parts.

---

[1] viii. 46.   [2] viii. 59; xi. 9, 13, 18, § 9.
[3] iii. 11; iv. 26.

ὁμογενῆ μέρη. τούτων γὰρ μεμνημένος, καθότι μὲν
μέρος εἰμί, οὐδενὶ δυσαρεστήσω τῶν ἐκ τοῦ ὅλου
ἀπονεμομένων· οὐδὲν γὰρ βλαβερὸν τῷ μέρει,
ὃ τῷ ὅλῳ συμφέρει. οὐ γὰρ ἔχει τι τὸ ὅλον, ὃ
μὴ συμφέρει ἑαυτῷ· πασῶν μὲν φύσεων κοινὸν
ἐχουσῶν τοῦτο, τῆς δὲ τοῦ κόσμου προσειληφυίας
τὸ μηδὲ ὑπό τινος ἔξωθεν αἰτίας ἀναγκάζεσθαι
βλαβερόν τι ἑαυτῇ γεννᾶν.

2   Κατὰ μὲν δὴ τὸ μεμνῆσθαι, ὅτι μέρος εἰμὶ ὅλου
τοῦ τοιούτου, εὐαρεστήσω παντὶ τῷ ἀποβαίνοντι.
καθόσον δὲ ἔχω πως οἰκείως πρὸς τὰ ὁμογενῆ
μέρη, οὐδὲν πράξω ἀκοινώνητον, μᾶλλον δὲ
στοχάσομαι τῶν ὁμογενῶν καὶ πρὸς τὸ κοινῇ
συμφέρον πᾶσαν ὁρμὴν ἐμαυτοῦ ἄξω καὶ ἀπὸ
τοὐναντίου ἀπάξω. τούτων δὲ οὕτω περαινο-
μένων ἀνάγκη τὸν βίον εὐροεῖν, ὡς ἂν καὶ πολίτ-
ου βίον εὔρουν ἐπινοήσειας προϊόντος διὰ
πράξεων τοῖς πολίταις λυσιτελῶν καί, ὅπερ ἂν
ἡ πόλις ἀπονέμῃ, τοῦτο ἀσπαζομένου.

ζ΄.   Τοῖς μέρεσι τοῦ ὅλου, ὅσα φύσει περιέχε-
ται ὑπὸ τοῦ κόσμου, ἀνάγκη φθείρεσθαι· λεγέσθω
δὲ τοῦτο σημαντικῶς τοῦ ἀλλοιοῦσθαι· εἰ δὲ
φύσει κακόν τε καὶ ἀναγκαῖόν ἐστι τοῦτο αὐτοῖς,
οὐκ ἂν τὸ ὅλον καλῶς διεξάγοιτο, τῶν μερῶν εἰς
ἀλλοτρίωσιν ἰόντων, καὶ πρὸς τὸ φθείρεσθαι δια-
φόρως κατεσκευασμένων. πότερον γὰρ ἐπεχείρ-
ησεν ἡ φύσις αὐτὴ τὰ ἑαυτῆς μέρη κακοῦν καὶ
περιπτωτικὰ τῷ κακῷ καὶ ἐξ ἀνάγκης ἔμπτωτα

---

¹ vi. 54 ; x. 33, § 4.
² ix. 22.
³ These words can also be translated : *parts of herself that*

264

BOOK X

For bearing this in mind, as I am a part, I shall not be displeased with anything allotted me from the Whole. For what is advantageous to the whole can in no wise be injurious to the part.[1] For the Whole contains nothing that is not advantageous to itself; and all natures have this in common, but the Universal Nature is endowed with the additional attribute of never being forced by any external cause to engender anything hurtful to itself.

As long then as I remember that I am a part of such a whole, I shall be well pleased with all that happens; and in so far as I am in intimate connexion with the parts that are akin to myself, I shall be guilty of no unsocial act, but I shall devote my attention rather to the parts that are akin to myself,[2] and direct every impulse of mine to the common interest and withhold it from the reverse of this. That being done, life must needs flow smoothly, as thou mayst see the life flow smoothly of a citizen who goes steadily on in a course of action beneficial to his fellow-citizens and cheerfully accepts whatever is assigned him by the State.

7. The parts of the Whole—all that Nature has comprised in the Universe—must inevitably perish, taking " perish " to mean " be changed." But if this process is by nature for them both evil and inevitable, the Whole could never do its work satisfactorily, its parts ever going as they do from change to change and being constituted to perish in diverse ways. Did Nature herself set her hand to bringing evil upon parts of herself and rendering them not only liable to fall into evil but of necessity fallen into it,[3]

were both liable to fall into such evil and by necessity fell into doing evil.

εἰς τὸ κακὸν ποιεῖν, ἢ ἔλαθεν αὐτὴν τοιάδε τινὰ
γινόμενα; ἀμφότερα γὰρ ἀπίθανα.

2 Εἰ δέ τις καὶ ἀφέμενος τῆς φύσεως κατὰ τὸ
πεφυκέναι ταῦτα ἐξηγοῖτο, καὶ ὡς γελοῖον ἅμα
μὲν φάναι πεφυκέναι τὰ μέρη τοῦ ὅλου μεταβάλλειν, ἅμα δὲ ὡς ἐπί τινι τῶν παρὰ φύσιν συμβαινόντων θαυμάζειν ἢ δυσχεραίνειν, ἄλλως τε
καὶ τῆς διαλύσεως εἰς ταῦτα γινομένης, ἐξ ὧν
ἕκαστον συνίσταται. ἤτοι γὰρ σκεδασμὸς στοιχείων ἐξ ὧν συνεκρίθην, ἢ τροπὴ τοῦ μὲν
στερεμνίου εἰς τὸ γεῶδες, τοῦ δὲ πνευματικοῦ
εἰς τὸ ἀερῶδες· ὥστε καὶ ταῦτα ἀναληφθῆναι
εἰς τὸν τοῦ ὅλου λόγον, εἴτε κατὰ περίοδον
ἐκπυρουμένου εἴτε ἀιδίοις ἀμοιβαῖς ἀνανεου-
μένου.

3 Καὶ τὸ στερέμνιον δὲ καὶ τὸ πνευματικὸν μὴ
φαντάζου τὸ ἀπὸ τῆς πρώτης γενέσεως. πᾶν γὰρ
τοῦτο ἐχθὲς καὶ τρίτην ἡμέραν ἐκ τῶν σιτίων
καὶ τοῦ ἑλκομένου ἀέρος τὴν ἐπιρροὴν ἔλαβεν.
τοῦτο οὖν, ὃ ἔλαβεν, μεταβάλλει, οὐχ ὃ ἡ μήτηρ
ἔτεκεν. ὑπόθου δ', ὅτι ἐκείνῳ σε λίαν προσπλέκει [1] τῷ ἰδίως ποιῷ, οὐδὲν ὄντι οἶμαι πρὸς τὸ
νῦν λεγόμενον.

η'. Ὀνόματα θέμενος σαυτῷ ταῦτα, ἀγαθός,
αἰδήμων, ἀληθής, ἔμφρων, σύμφρων, ὑπέρφρων,

---

[1] σέ τι Fournier : σὺ λίαν προσπλέκῃ Rend.

---

[1] vii. 32.
[2] iv. 4. Lit. *the pneumatic or breath element.* See Index iii.
[3] iii. 3. Justin, *Apol.* i. 20; ii. 7, contrasts the Christian
theory of the destruction of the world by fire with the Stoic.
[4] προσπλέκει has no subject. ἐκείνῳ must be taken
separately from τῷ ἰδίως ποιῷ and refer to τοῦτο ὃ ἔλαβεν.

BOOK X

or was she not aware that such was the case? Both alternatives are incredible.

But supposing that we even put Nature as an agent out of the question and explain that these things are "naturally" so, even then it would be absurd to assert that the parts of the whole are naturally subject to change, and at the same time to be astonished at a thing or take it amiss as though it befell contrary to nature, and that though things dissolve into the very constituents out of which they are composed. For either there is a scattering of the elements[1] out of which I have been built up, or a transmutation of the solid into the earthy and of the spiritual[2] into the aerial; so that these too are taken back into the Reason of the Universe, whether cycle by cycle it be consumed with fire[3] or renew itself by everlasting permutations.

Aye and so then do not be under the impression that the solid and the spiritual date from the moment of birth. For it was but yesterday or the day before that all this took in its increment from the food eaten and the air breathed. It is then this, that it took in, which changes, not the product of thy mother's womb. But granted that thou art ever so closely bound up[4] with that by thy individuality, this, I take it, has no bearing upon the present argument.

8. Assuming for thyself the appellations, a good man,[5] a modest man,[6] a truthteller,[7] wise of heart,

---

[5] See on x. 16.

[6] Capitolinus and Ammianus call Marcus *verecundus*.

[7] Only two kings have had the honourable cognomen of *Truthteller*, Marcus and Alfred the Great. The former was given *Verissimus* as a pet name by Hadrian when a child, and the town of Tyras in Scythia stamped it on its coins and Justin and Syncellus use it to designate Marcus.

πρόσεχε, μήποτε μετονομάζῃ· καὶ <εἰ>[1] ἀπολλύεις
ταῦτα τὰ ὀνόματα, καὶ ταχέως ἐπάνιε ἐπ' αὐτά.
μέμνησο δέ, ὅτι τὸ μὲν "ἔμφρων" ἐβούλετό σοι
σημαίνειν τὴν ἐφ' ἕκαστα διαληπτικὴν ἐπίστασιν
καὶ τὸ ἀπαρενθύμητον· τὸ δὲ "σύμφρων," τὴν
ἑκούσιον ἀπόδεξιν τῶν ὑπὸ τῆς κοινῆς φύσεως
ἀπονεμομένων· τὸ δὲ "ὑπέρφρων," τὴν ὑπέρτασιν
τοῦ φρονοῦντος μορίου ὑπὲρ λείας ἢ τραχείας
κινήσεις[2] τῆς σαρκὸς καὶ τὸ δοξάριον καὶ τὸν
θάνατον καὶ ὅσα τοιαῦτα. ἐὰν οὖν διατηρῇς
σεαυτὸν ἐν τούτοις τοῖς ὀνόμασι μὴ γλιχόμενος
τοῦ ὑπ' ἄλλων κατὰ ταῦτα ὀνομάζεσθαι, ἔσῃ
ἕτερος, καὶ εἰς βίον εἰσελεύσῃ ἕτερον. τὸ γὰρ
ἔτι τοιοῦτον εἶναι, οἷος μέχρι νῦν γέγονας, καὶ ἐν
βίῳ τοιούτῳ σπαράσσεσθαι καὶ μολύνεσθαι, λίαν
ἐστὶν ἀναισθήτου καὶ φιλοψύχου, καὶ ὁμοίου τοῖς
ἡμιβρώτοις θηριομάχοις, οἵτινες μεστοὶ τραυμά-
των καὶ λύθρου παρακαλοῦσιν ὅμως εἰς τὴν
αὔριον φυλαχθῆναι, παραβληθησόμενοι τοιοῦτοι
τοῖς αὐτοῖς ὄνυξι καὶ δήγμασιν.

2   Ἐμβίβασον οὖν σαυτὸν εἰς τὰ ὀλίγα ταῦτα
ὀνόματα· κἂν μὲν ἐπ' αὐτῶν μένειν δύνῃ, μένε,
ὥσπερ εἰς μακάρων τινὰς νήσους μετῳκισμένος·
ἐὰν δὲ αἴσθῃ, ὅτι ἐκπίπτεις, καὶ οὐ περικρατεῖς,
ἄπιθι θαρρῶν εἰς γωνίαν τινά, ὅπου κρατήσεις, ἢ
καὶ παντάπασιν ἔξιθι τοῦ βίου μὴ ὀργιζόμενος
ἀλλὰ ἁπλῶς καὶ ἐλευθέρως καὶ αἰδημόνως εὖ[3]

---

[1] <εἰ> Schenkl.
[2] κινήσεις Schenkl : κινήσεως A : κίνησιν P.
[3] I have written εὖ for ἐν PA.

---

[1] For Marcus' views on suicide see iii. 1 ; v. 29 ; viii. 47
ad fin. ; ix. 2 ; x. 22, 32. He permits it when external condi-

sympathetic of heart, great of heart, take heed thou be not new-named. And if thou shouldst forfeit these titles, e'en make haste to get back to them. And bear in mind that *wise of heart* was meant to signify for thee a discerning consideration of every object and a thoroughness of thought; *sympathetic of heart,* a willing acceptance of all that the Universal Nature allots thee; *great of heart* an uplifting of our mental part above the motions smooth or rough of the flesh, above the love of empty fame, the fear of death, and all other like things. Only keep thyself entitled to these appellations, not itching to receive them from others, and thou wilt be a new man and enter on a new life. For to be still such as thou hast been till now, and to submit to the rendings and defilements of such a life, is worthy of a man that shews beyond measure a dull senselessness and a clinging to life, and is on a level with the wild-beast fighters that are half-devoured in the arena, who, though a mass of wounds and gore, beg to be kept till the next day, only to be thrown again, torn as they are, to the same teeth and talons.

Take ship then on these few attributions, and if thou canst abide therein, so abide as one who has migrated to some Isles of the Blest. But if thou feelest thyself adrift, and canst not win thy way, betake thyself with a good heart to some nook where thou shalt prevail, or even depart altogether from life,[1] not in wrath but in simplicity, independence, and modesty, having at least done this

tions render the life of virtue impossible, or when a man finds in himself a failure to live the true life (*cp.* St. Augustine's "Let me die lest I die").

γε τοῦτο μόνον πράξας ἐν τῷ βίῳ, τὸ οὕτως
ἐξελθεῖν. πρὸς μέντοι τὸ μεμνῆσθαι τῶν ὀνομ-
άτων μεγάλως συλλήψεταί σοι τὸ μεμνῆσθαι
θεῶν, καὶ ὅτιπερ οὐ κολακεύεσθαι οὗτοι θέλουσιν,
ἀλλὰ ἐξομοιοῦσθαι ἑαυτοῖς τὰ λογικὰ πάντα·
καὶ εἶναι τὴν μὲν συκῆν τὰ συκῆς ποιοῦσαν, τὸν
δὲ κύνα τὰ κυνός, τὴν δὲ μέλισσαν τὰ μελίσσης,
τὸν δὲ ἄνθρωπον τὰ ἀνθρώπου.

θ΄. Μῖμος, πόλεμος, πτοία, νάρκα, δουλεία,
καθ᾽ ἡμέραν ἀπαλείψεταί σου τὰ ἱερὰ ἐκεῖνα
δόγματα, ὁπόσα ὁ φυσιολογητὸς[1] φαντάζῃ καὶ
παραπέμπεις. δεῖ δὲ πᾶν οὕτω βλέπειν καὶ
πράσσειν, ὥστε καὶ τὸ περιστατικὸν[2] ἅμα συν-
τελεῖσθαι καὶ ἅμα τὸ θεωρητικὸν ἐνεργεῖσθαι,
καὶ τὸ ἐκ τῆς περὶ ἑκάστων ἐπιστήμης αὔθαδες
σῴζεσθαι λανθάνον, οὐχὶ κρυπτόμενον.

2 Πότε γὰρ ἁπλότητος ἀπολαύσεις; πότε δὲ
σεμνότητος; πότε δὲ τῆς ἐφ᾽ ἑκάστου γνωρίσεως,
τί τε ἐστὶ κατ᾽ οὐσίαν, καὶ τίνα χώραν ἔχει ἐν τῷ
κόσμῳ, καὶ ἐπὶ πόσον πέφυκεν ὑφίστασθαι, καὶ
ἐκ τίνων συγκέκριται, καὶ τίσι δύναται ὑπάρχειν,
καὶ τίνες δύνανται αὐτὸ διδόναι τε καὶ
ἀφαιρεῖσθαι.

ι΄. Ἀράχνιον μυῖαν θηράσαν μέγα φρονεῖ,
ἄλλος δὲ λαγίδιον, ἄλλος δὲ ὑποχῇ ἀφύην, ἄλλος
δὲ συΐδια, ἄλλος δὲ ἄρκτους, ἄλλος Σαρμάτας.
οὗτοι γὰρ οὐ λησταί, ἐὰν τὰ δόγματα ἐξετάζῃς;

---

[1] ἀφυσιολογήτως Gat. (cp. ix. 41).
[2] πρακτικὸν (*what is practicable*) Cor.

---

[1] cp. Diog. Laert. *Plato*, 42 ; Ignat. *Eph.* §§ 1, 10 ; Justin,
Apol. i. 21 ; Diogn. *Ep.* § 10 ; Julian, *Conviv.* 427. 21, puts
similar words in the mouth of Marcus.

one thing well in life, that thou hast quitted it thus. Howbeit, to keep these attributions in mind it will assist thee greatly if thou bear the Gods in mind, and that it is not flattery they crave but for all rational things to be conformed to their likeness,[1] and that man should do a man's work, as the fig tree does the work of a fig-tree, the dog of a dog, and the bee of a bee.

9. Stage-apery, warfare, cowardice, torpor, servility—these will day by day obliterate all those holy principles of thine which, as the student of Nature,[2] thou dost conceive and accept. But thou must regard and do everything in such a way that at one and the same time the present task may be carried through, and full play given to the faculty of pure thought, and that the self-confidence engendered by a knowledge of each individual thing be kept intact, unobtruded yet unconcealed.

When wilt thou find thy delight in simplicity? *When* in dignity? *When* in the knowledge of each separate thing, what it is in its essence, what place it fills in the Universe, how long it is formed by Nature to subsist, what are its component parts, to whom it can pertain, and who can bestow and take it away?

10. A spider prides itself on capturing a fly; one man on catching a hare, another on netting a sprat, another on taking wild boars, another bears, another Sarmatians.[3] Are not these brigands, if thou test their principles?

---

[2] ἀφυσιολογήτως, would mean *without due study of Nature.*
[3] See Domaszewski, *Marcus-Saüle Plates*, 62. 102, for Marcus "taking Sarmatians"; and *cp.* the story of Alexander and the Scythian, Quintus Curtius vii. **8.**

ιαʹ. Πῶς εἰς ἄλληλα πάντα μεταβάλλει, θεωρητικὴν μέθοδον κτῆσαι, καὶ διηνεκῶς πρόσεχε, καὶ συγγυμνάσθητι περὶ τοῦτο τὸ μέρος. οὐδὲν γὰρ οὕτω μεγαλοφροσύνης ποιητικόν. ἐξεδύσατο τὸ σῶμα καὶ ἐννοήσας, ὅτι ὅσον οὐδέπω πάντα ταῦτα καταλιπεῖν ἀπιόντα ἐξ ἀνθρώπων δεήσει, ἀνῆκεν ὅλον ἑαυτὸν δικαιοσύνῃ μὲν εἰς τὰ ὑφ' ἑαυτοῦ ἐνεργούμενα, ἐν δὲ τοῖς ἄλλοις συμβαίνουσι τῇ τῶν ὅλων φύσει. τί δ' ἐρεῖ τις ἢ ὑπολήψεται περὶ αὐτοῦ ἢ πράξει κατ' αὐτοῦ, οὐδ' εἰς νοῦν βάλλεται δύο τούτοις ἀρκούμενος εἰ[1] αὐτὸς δικαιοπραγεῖ τὸ νῦν πρασσόμενον καὶ φιλεῖ τὸ νῦν ἀπονεμόμενον ἑαυτῷ· ἀσχολίας δὲ πάσας καὶ σπουδὰς ἀφῆκε, καὶ οὐδὲν ἄλλο βούλεται, ἢ εὐθεῖαν περαίνειν διὰ τοῦ νόμου καὶ εὐθεῖαν περαίνοντι ἕπεσθαι τῷ θεῷ.

ιβʹ. Τίς ὑπονοίας χρεία, παρὸν σκοπεῖν, τί δεῖ πραχθῆναι; κἂν μὲν συνορᾷς, εὐμενῶς ἀμεταστρεπτὶ ταύτῃ χωρεῖν· ἐὰν δὲ μὴ συνορᾷς, ἐπέχειν καὶ συμβούλοις τοῖς ἀρίστοις χρῆσθαι· ἐὰν δὲ ἕτερά τινα πρὸς ταῦτα ἀντιβαίνῃ, προϊέναι κατὰ τὰς παρούσας ἀφορμὰς λελογισμένως ἐχόμενον τοῦ φαινομένου δικαίου. ἄριστον γὰρ κατατυγχάνειν τούτου, ἐπεί τοι ἥ γε ἀπόπτωσις ἀπὸ τούτου ἐστί.[2]

2 Σχολαῖόν τι καὶ ἅμα εὐκίνητον ἔσται καὶ φαιδρὸν ἅμα καὶ συνεστηκὸς ὁ τῷ λόγῳ κατὰ πᾶν ἑπόμενος.

ιγʹ. Πυνθάνεσθαι ἑαυτοῦ εὐθὺς ἐξ ὕπνου γινόμενον· "Μήτι διοίσει σοι, ἐὰν ὑπὸ ἄλλου

[1] εἰ Jackson : εἶ A : δικαιοπραγεῖν . . . φιλεῖν P.
[2] ἔστω PA : ἔσται Men.

11. Make thy own a scientific system of enquiry into the mutual change of all things, and pay diligent heed to this branch of study and exercise thyself in it. For nothing is so conducive to greatness of mind. Let a man do this and he divests himself of his body and, realizing that he must almost at once relinquish all these things and depart from among men, he gives himself up wholly to just dealing in all his actions, and to the Universal Nature in all that befalls him. What others may say or think about him or do against him he does not even let enter his mind, being well satisfied with these two things—justice in all present acts and contentment with his present lot.[1] And he gives up all engrossing cares and ambitions, and has no other wish than to achieve the straight course through the Law and, by achieving it, to be a follower of God.

12. What need of surmise when it lies with thee to decide what should be done, and if thou canst see thy course, to take it with a good grace and not turn aside; but if thou canst not see it, to hold back and take counsel of the best counsellors; and if any other obstacles arise therein, to go forward as thy present means shall allow with careful deliberation holding to what is clearly just? For to succeed in this is the best thing of all, since in fact to fail in this would be the only failure.

Leisurely without being lethargic and cheerful as well as composed shall he be who follows Reason in everything.

13. Ask thyself as soon as thou art roused from sleep: *Will it make any difference to me if another does*

---

[1] ix. 6 etc.

γένηται[1] τὰ δίκαια καὶ καλῶς ἔχοντα;" οὐ
διοίσει. μήτι ἐπιλέλησαι, ὅτι οὗτοι οἱ ἐν τοῖς
περὶ ἄλλων ἐπαίνοις καὶ ψόγοις φρυαττόμενοι,
τοιοῦτοι μὲν ἐπὶ τῆς κλίνης εἰσί, τοιοῦτοι δὲ ἐπὶ
τῆς τραπέζης, οἷα δὲ ποιοῦσιν, οἷα δὲ φεύγουσιν,
οἷα δὲ διώκουσιν, οἷα δὲ κλέπτουσιν, οἷα δὲ
ἁρπάζουσιν, οὐ χερσὶ καὶ ποσὶν ἀλλὰ τῷ τιμιω-
τάτῳ ἑαυτῶν μέρει, ᾧ γίνεται, ὅταν θέλῃ <τις>,
πίστις, αἰδώς, ἀλήθεια, νόμος, ἀγαθὸς δαίμων;

ιδ΄. Τῇ πάντα διδούσῃ καὶ ἀπολαμβανούσῃ
φύσει ὁ πεπαιδευμένος καὶ αἰδήμων λέγει· "Δὸς
ὃ θέλεις, ἀπόλαβε ὃ θέλεις." λέγει δὲ τοῦτο οὐ
καταθρασυνόμενος, ἀλλὰ πειθαρχῶν μόνον καὶ
εὐνοῶν αὐτῇ.

ιε΄. Ὀλίγον ἐστὶ τὸ ὑπολειπόμενον τοῦτο.
ζῆσον ὡς ἐν ὄρει. οὐδὲν γὰρ διαφέρει, ἐκεῖ ἢ
ὧδε, ἐάν τις πανταχοῦ ὡς ἐν πόλει τῷ κόσμῳ.
ἰδέτωσαν, ἱστορησάτωσαν οἱ ἄνθρωποι ἄνθρωπον
ἀληθινὸν κατὰ φύσιν ζῶντα. εἰ μὴ φέρουσιν,
ἀποκτεινάτωσαν. κρεῖττον γὰρ ἢ οὕτω ζῆν.[2]

ιϛ΄. Μηκέθ᾿ ὅλως περὶ τοῦ, οἷόν τινα εἶναι τὸν
ἀγαθὸν ἄνδρα <δεῖ>, διαλέγεσθαι, ἀλλὰ εἶναι
τοιοῦτον.

ιζ΄. Τοῦ ὅλου αἰῶνος, καὶ τῆς ὅλης οὐσίας
συνεχῶς φαντασία,[3] καὶ ὅτι πάντα τὰ κατὰ μέρος

---

[1] ψέγηται Lofft; but *cp.* viii. 56 for meaning.
[2] ἢ <μὴ> οὕτω ζῆν would seem to make better sense.
[3] φαντασία <ἔστω> Reiske.

---

[1] vii. 3; ix. 41.
[2] iii. 4 *ad fin.*; vi. 59; vii. 62; viii. 52, 53; ix. 34.
[3] vii. 17.   [4] *cp.* Job i. 21.
[5] x. 23   This striking phrase seems from a comparison of
§ 23 to mean : Count your life here in the city and Court, or,

what is just and right? It will make none. Hast thou forgotten that those who play the wanton[1] in their praise and blame of others, are such as they are[2] in their beds, at their board; and what are the things that they do, the things that they avoid or pursue, and how they pilfer and plunder, not with hands and feet but with the most precious part of them, whereby a man calls into being at will faith, modesty, truth, law, and a good ' genius'?[3]

14. Says the well-schooled and humble heart to Nature that gives and takes back all we have; *Give what thou wilt, take back what thou wilt.*[4] But he says it without any bravado of fortitude, in simple obedience and good will to her.

15. Thou has but a short time left to live. Live as on a mountain[5]; for whether it be here or there, matters not provided that, wherever a man live, he live as a citizen of the World-City.[6] Let men look upon thee, cite thee, as a man in very deed that lives according to Nature. If they cannot bear with thee, let them slay thee. For it were better so than to live their life.

16. Put an end once for all to this discussion of what a good man should be, and be one.[7]

17. Continually picture to thyself Time as a whole, and Substance as a whole, and every individual

maybe, camp, as no whit worse than life in the free and health-giving air of a mountain-top with all its serenity and leisure for study and contemplation. It rests with you to make your "little plot within you" what you please. But, taken alone, "Live as on a mountain" might mean "Live in the open light of day under the eyes of God and men in a purer atmosphere above the pettinesses of the world." *cp.* Cyprian, *De Grat. Dei* 6.   [6] iv. 3, § 2.

[7] Dio (71. 34, § 5) says of Marcus ὡς ἀληθῶς ἀγαθὸς ἀνὴρ ἦν.

ὡς μὲν πρὸς οὐσίαν κεγχραμίς, ὡς δὲ πρὸς χρόνον τρυπάνου περιστροφή.

ιη΄. Εἰς ἕκαστον τῶν ὑποκειμένων ἐφιστάντα ἐπινοεῖν αὐτὸ ἤδη διαλυόμενον καὶ ἐν μεταβολῇ καὶ οἷον σήψει ἢ σκεδάσει γινόμενον ἢ καθότι ἕκαστον πέφυκεν ὥσπερ θνήσκειν.

ιθ΄. Οἷοί εἰσιν ἐσθίοντες, καθεύδοντες, ὀχεύοντες, ἀποπατοῦντες, τὰ ἄλλα. εἶτα οἷοι ἀνδρονομούμενοι†[1] καὶ γαυρούμενοι ἢ χαλεπαίνοντες καὶ ἐξ ὑπεροχῆς ἐπιπλήττοντες. πρὸ ὀλίγου δὲ ἐδούλευον πόσοις, καὶ δι᾽ οἷα, καὶ μετ᾽ ὀλίγον ἐν τοιούτοις ἔσονται.

κ΄. Συμφέρει ἑκάστῳ, ὃ φέρει ἑκάστῳ ἡ τῶν ὅλων φύσις· καὶ τότε συμφέρει, ὅτε ἐκείνη φέρει.

κα΄. "Ἐρᾷ μὲν ὄμβρου γαῖα· ἐρᾷ δὲ ὁ σεμνὸς αἰθήρ." ἐρᾷ δὲ ὁ κόσμος ποιῆσαι, ὃ ἂν μέλλῃ γίνεσθαι. λέγω οὖν τῷ κόσμῳ, ὅτι "σοὶ συνερῶ." μήτι δ᾽ οὕτω κἀκεῖνο λέγεται, ὅτι "φιλεῖ τοῦτο γίνεσθαι";

κβ΄. "Ἤτοι ἐνταῦθα ζῇς καὶ ἤδη εἴθικας, ἢ ἔξω ὑπάγεις καὶ τοῦτο ἤθελες, ἢ ἀποθνήσκεις καὶ ἀπελειτούργησας· παρὰ δὲ ταῦτα οὐδέν. οὐκοῦν εὐθύμει.

κγ΄. Ἐναργὲς ἔστω ἀεὶ τό, ὅτι †τοιοῦτο ἐκεῖνο†[2] ὁ ἀγρός ἐστι· καὶ πῶς πάντα ἐστὶ ταὐτὰ ἐνθάδε τοῖς ἐν ἄκρῳ τῷ ὄρει, ἢ ἐπὶ τοῦ αἰγιαλοῦ,

---

[1] ἀνδρονομύμενοι can hardly be right, but ἀνδρογυνούμενοι which at once occurs to one is soon seen to be out of keeping with the other words in the passage : ἀβρυνόμενοι Reiske.

[2] ἐκεῖνος Reiske : τοῦτο ἐκεῖνο Cor.: ταὐτὸ ἐκείνῳ Richards

BOOK X

thing, in respect of substance, as but a fig-seed and, in respect to time, as but a twist of the drill.

18. Regarding attentively every existing thing reflect that it is already disintegrating and changing, and as it were in a state of decomposition and dispersion, or that everything is by nature made but to die.

19. What are they like when eating, sleeping, coupling, evacuating, and the rest! What again when lording it over others, when puffed up with pride, when filled with resentment or rebuking others from a loftier plane! Yet but a moment ago they were lackeying how many and for what ends, and anon will be at their old trade.[1]

20. What the Universal Nature brings to every thing is for the benefit of that thing, and for its benefit then when she brings it.[2]

21. *The earth is in love with showers and the majestic sky is in love.*[3] And the Universe is in love with making whatever has to be. To the Universe then I say: *Together with thee I will be in love.* Is it not a way we have of speaking, to say, *This or that loves to be so?*

22. Either thy life is here and thou art inured to it; or thou goest elsewhere and this with thine own will; or thou diest and hast served out thy service. There is no other alternative. Take heart then.

23. Never lose sight of the fact that a man's 'freehold'[4] is such as I told thee, and how all the conditions are the same here as on the top of a

---

[1] Or, taking Gataker's emendation (ὁποίοις), *in what plight will they be!*   [2] iv. 23.
[3] Eur. *Frag.* 890. After σεμνὸς Eur. has οὐρανὸς πληρούμενος Ὄμβρου πεσεῖν εἰς γαῖαν Ἀφροδίτης ὕπο. *cp.* Aesch. *Dan. Frag.* 41, imitated by Shelley in his *Love's Philosophy.*
[4] v. 3, § 4.

ἢ ὅπου θέλεις. ἄντικρυς γὰρ εὑρήσεις τὰ τοῦ
Πλάτωνος· "Σηκὸν ἐν ὄρει," φησί, "περιβαλλό-
μενος," καὶ [1] †βδάλλων βληχήματα.†

κδ΄. Τί ἐστί μοι τὸ ἡγεμονικόν μου; καὶ ποῖόν
τι ἐγὼ αὐτὸ ποιῶ νῦν; καὶ πρὸς τί ποτε αὐτῷ
νῦν χρῶμαι; μήτι κενὸν νοῦ ἐστι; μήτι ἀπόλυτον
καὶ ἀπεσπασμένον κοινωνίας; μήτι προστετηκὸς
καὶ ἀνακεκραμένον τῷ σαρκιδίῳ, ὥστε τούτῳ
συντρέπεσθαι;

κε΄. Ὁ τὸν κύριον φεύγων δραπέτης· κύριος
δὲ ὁ νόμος καὶ ὁ παρανομῶν δραπέτης. ἀλλὰ
καὶ ὁ λυπούμενος ἢ ὀργιζόμενος ἢ φοβούμενος οὐ [2]
βούλεταί τι γεγονέναι ἢ γίνεσθαι ἢ γενήσεσθαι
τῶν ὑπὸ τοῦ τὰ πάντα διοικοῦντος τεταγμένων,
ὅς ἐστι νόμος νέμων, ὅσα ἑκάστῳ ἐπιβάλλει. ὁ
ἄρα φοβούμενος ἢ λυπούμενος ἢ ὀργιζόμενος
δραπέτης.

κϛ΄. Σπέρμα εἰς μήτραν ἀφεὶς ἀπεχώρησε
καὶ λοιπὸν ἄλλη αἰτία παραλαβοῦσα ἐργάζεται
καὶ ἀποτελεῖ βρέφος, ἐξ οἵου οἷον· πάλιν τροφὴν
διὰ φάρυγγος ἀφῆκε καὶ λοιπὸν ἄλλη αἰτία
παραλαβοῦσα αἴσθησιν καὶ ὁρμὴν καὶ τὸ ὅλον
ζωὴν καὶ ῥώμην καὶ ἄλλα ὅσα καὶ οἷα ποιεῖ.
ταῦτα οὖν [τὰ] ἐν τοιαύτῃ ἐγκαλύψει γινόμενα

---

[1] καὶ, perhaps κἀκεῖ : βδάλλων Cor.: βδάλλειν A : βάλλειν P :
βληχήματα Stich.: βλήχματα A.   [2] οὐ Nauck : ὃ PA.

---

[1] iv. 3 ad init. ; x. 15.
[2] Theaet. 174 D : Ἀγροῖκον καὶ ἀπαίδευτον ἀπὸ ἀσχολίας οὐδὲν
ἧττον τῶν νομέων τὸν τοιοῦτον ἀναγκαῖον γενέσθαι σηκὸν ἐν ὄρει
τὸ τεῖχος περιβεβημένον. It is not easy to see the application of the words here. Marcus seems to mean that the king
in the midst of his royal city is no better off, *ipso facto*, than

BOOK X

mountain [1] or on the sea-shore or wherever thou pleasest. Quite apposite shalt thou find to be the words of Plato [2]: *Compassed about (by the city wall as) by a sheep-fold on the mountain, and milking flocks.*

24. What is my ruling Reason and what am I making of it now? To what use do I now put it? Is it devoid of intelligence? Is it divorced and severed from neighbourliness? Does it so coalesce and blend with the flesh as to be swayed by it?

25. He that flies from his master is a runaway. But the Law is our master,[3] and he that transgresses the Law is a runaway. Now he also, that is moved by grief or wrath or fear, is fain that something should not have happened or be happening or happen in the future of what has been ordained by that which controls the whole Universe, that is by the Law laying down all that falls to a man's lot. He then is a runaway who is moved by fear or grief or wrath.

26. A man passes seed into a womb and goes his way, and anon another cause takes it in hand and works upon it and perfects a babe—what a consummation from what a beginning![4] Again he [5] passes food down the throat, and anon another cause taking up the work creates sensation and impulse and, in fine, life and strength and other things how many and how mysterious! Muse then on these

the shepherd in his mountain fold. It is the little "plot within him," his ruling Reason that makes the difference. The use of ἐν ὄρει twice in this section appears to have a reference to its use in § 15.   [3] ii. 16 *ad fin.*

[4] *cp.* the remarkable parallel in Justin, *Apol.* i. 19.

[5] There is no subject expressed. It is possible to take the child as the subject.

θεωρεῖν καὶ τὴν δύναμιν οὕτως ὁρᾶν, ὡς καὶ τὴν βρίθουσαν καὶ τὴν ἀνωφερῆ ὁρῶμεν, οὐχὶ τοῖς ὀφθαλμοῖς, ἀλλ' οὐχ ἧττον ἐναργῶς.

κζ΄. Συνεχῶς ἐπινοεῖν, πῶς πάντα τοιαῦτα, ὁποῖα νῦν γίνεται, καὶ πρόσθεν ἐγίνετο· καὶ ἐπινοεῖν γενησόμενα. καὶ ὅλα δράματα καὶ σκηνὰς ὁμοειδεῖς, ὅσα ἐκ πείρας τῆς σῆς ἢ τῆς πρεσβυτέρας ἱστορίας ἔγνως, πρὸ ὀμμάτων τίθεσθαι, οἷον αὐλὴν ὅλην Ἀδριανοῦ καὶ αὐλὴν ὅλην Ἀντωνίνου καὶ αὐλὴν ὅλην Φιλίππου, Ἀλεξάνδρου, Κροίσου· πάντα γὰρ ἐκεῖνα τοιαῦτα ἦν, μόνον δι' ἑτέρων.

κη΄. Φαντάζου πάντα τὸν ἐφ' ὡτινιοῦν λυπούμενον ἢ δυσαρεστοῦντα ὅμοιον τῷ θυομένῳ χοιριδίῳ καὶ ἀπολακτίζοντι καὶ κεκραγότι· ὅμοιον καὶ ὁ οἰμώζων ἐπὶ τοῦ κλινιδίου μόνος σιωπῇ τὴν ἔνδεσιν ἡμῶν· καὶ ὅτι μόνῳ τῷ λογικῷ ζώῳ δέδοται τὸ ἑκουσίως ἕπεσθαι τοῖς γινομένοις· τὸ δὲ ἕπεσθαι ψιλὸν πᾶσιν ἀναγκαῖον.

κθ΄. Κατὰ μέρος ἐφ' ἑκάστου, ὧν ποιεῖς, ἐφιστάνων ἐρώτα σεαυτόν, "Εἰ ὁ θάνατος δεινὸν διὰ τὸ τούτου στέρεσθαι."

λ΄. Ὅταν προσκόπτῃς ἐπί τινος ἁμαρτίᾳ, εὐθὺς μεταβὰς ἐπιλογίζου, τί παρόμοιον ἁμαρτάνεις· οἷον ἀργύριον ἀγαθὸν εἶναι κρίνων ⟨ἢ⟩ τὴν ἡδονὴν ἢ τὸ δοξάριον καὶ κατ' εἶδος.

---

¹ vii. 49.   ² viii. 25, 31.
³ cp. Sen. *Ep.* 107 : *ducunt volentem fata nolentem trahunt* ; de *Vit. Beat.* 15 ; Cleanthes, *Hymn to Zeus* : ὡς ἕψομαι γ' ἄοκνος· ἢν δὲ μὴ θέλω κακὸς γενόμενος, οὐδὲν ἧττον ἕψομαι.
⁴ vii. 26 ; xi. 18, § 4. Plutarch, *Anger* 16.
⁵ Marcus had a horror of avarice ; cp. Vulc. Gallic. *Vit.*

280

BOOK X

things that are done in such secrecy, and detect the
efficient force, just as we detect the descensive and
the ascensive none the less clearly that it is not with
our eyes.

27. Bear in mind continually how all such things
as now exist existed also before our day [1] and, be
assured, will exist after us. Set before thine eyes
whole dramas and their stagings, one like another,
all that thine own experience has shewn thee or thou
hast learned from past history, for instance the entire
court of Hadrianus,[2] the entire court of Antoninus,
the entire court of Philip, of Alexander, of Croesus.
For all those scenes were such as we see now, only
the performers being different.

28. Picture to thyself every one that is grieved at
any occurrence whatever or dissatisfied, as being like
the pig which struggles and screams when sacrificed;
like it too him who, alone upon his bed, bewails in
silence the fetters of our fate; and that to the
rational creature alone has it been granted to submit
willingly to what happens, mere submission being
imperative on all.[3]

29. In every act of thine pause at each step and
ask thyself: *Is death to be dreaded for the loss of this?*

30. Does another's wrong-doing shock thee?
Turn incontinently to thyself and bethink thee what
analogous wrong-doing there is of thine own,[4] such
as deeming money to be a good [5] or pleasure [6] or a
little cheap fame [7] and the like. For by marking

Avid. Cass. viii. 5 : *in imperatore avaritiam acerbissimum esse
malum.* Yet he was accused of it and repudiated the charge
(Capit. xxix. 5) ; and he is also exculpated by Dio (71. 32,
§ 3), and in the Oxyr. Papyri (i. p. 62) we find an Egyptian
official expressly calling him ἀφιλάργυρος.
 [6] See on v. 5.   [7] See on iv. 19.

τούτῳ γὰρ ἐπιβάλλων ταχέως ἐπιλήσῃ τῆς
ὀργῆς συμπίπτοντος τοῦ, ὅτι βιάζεται· τί γὰρ
ποιήσει; ἤ, εἰ δύνασαι, ἄφελε αὐτοῦ τὸ βιαζ-
όμενον.

λα΄. Σατύρωνα ἰδὼν Σωκρατικὸν φαντάζου
ἢ Εὐτύχην ἢ Ὑμένα, καὶ Εὐφράτην ἰδὼν
Εὐτυχίωνα ἢ Σιλουανὸν φαντάζου, καὶ Ἀλκί-
φρονα Τροπαιοφόρον φαντάζου, καὶ Σεύηρον[1]
ἰδὼν Κρίτωνα ἢ Ξενοφῶντα φαντάζου, καὶ εἰς
ἑαυτὸν ἀπιδὼν τῶν Καισάρων τινὰ φαντάζου,
καὶ ἐφ᾽ ἑκάστου τὸ ἀνάλογον. εἶτα συμπροσπιπτέτω σοι· "Ποῦ οὖν ἐκεῖνοι;" οὐδαμοῦ ἢ ὁπουδή.
οὕτως γὰρ συνεχῶς θεάσῃ τὰ ἀνθρώπινα καπνὸν
καὶ τὸ μηδέν· μάλιστα ἐὰν συμμνημονεύσῃς, ὅτι
τὸ ἅπαξ μεταβαλὸν οὐκέτι ἔσται ἐν τῷ ἀπείρῳ
χρόνῳ. τί οὖν[2] ἐντείνῃ; τί δ᾽ οὐκ ἀρκεῖ σοι τὸ
βραχὺ τοῦτο κοσμίως διαπερᾶσαι;

2 Οἵαν ὕλην καὶ ὑπόθεσιν φεύγεις; τί γάρ ἐστι
πάντα ταῦτα ἄλλο πλὴν γυμνάσματα λόγου ἑωρ-
ακότος ἀκριβῶς καὶ φυσιολόγως τὰ ἐν τῷ βίῳ;
μένε οὖν, μέχρι ἐξοικειώσῃς σαυτῷ καὶ ταῦτα, ὡς
ὁ ἐρρωμένος στόμαχος πάντα ἐξοικειοῖ, ὡς τὸ
λαμπρὸν πῦρ, ὅ τι ἂν βάλῃς, φλόγα ἐξ αὐτοῦ καὶ
αὐγὴν ποιεῖ.

λβ΄. Μηδενὶ ἐξέστω εἰπεῖν ἀληθεύοντι περὶ
σοῦ, ὅτι οὐχ ἁπλοῦς ἢ ὅτι οὐκ ἀγαθός· ἀλλὰ

---

[1] Leopold transposed Σεύηρον (see i. 14) and Ξενοφῶντα.
[2] σὺ (τί A) οὖν P : ἐν τίνι PA : ἐντείνῃ Cor. (cp. ix. 28).

---

[1] vii. 63.
[2] Xenophon and Crito are well known. Severus was probably the father of Marcus' son-in-law (i. 14). Euphrates

BOOK X

this thou wilt quickly forget thy wrath, with this
reflection too to aid thee, that a man is under
constraint[1]; for what should he do?   Or, if thou art
able, remove the constraint.

31. Let a glance at Satyron call up the image of
Socraticus or Eutyches or Hymen, and a glance at
Euphrates the image of Eutychion or Silvanus, and a
glance at Alciphron Tropaeophorus, and at Severus
Xenophon or Crito.[2] Let a glance at thyself bring to
mind one of the Caesars, and so by analogy in every
case.   Then let the thought strike thee : *Where are
they now*?   Nowhere,[3] or none can say where.   For
thus shalt thou habitually look upon human things
as mere smoke[4] and as naught; and more than ever
so, if thou bethink thee that what has once
changed will exist no more throughout eternity.
Why strive then and strain[5]?   Why not be content
to pass this thy short span of life in becoming
fashion?

What material, what a field for thy work dost
thou forgo !   For what are all these things but objects
for the exercise of a reason that hath surveyed with
accuracy and due inquiry into its nature the whole
sphere of life?   Continue then until thou hast
assimilated these truths also to thyself, as the vigorous
digestion assimilates every food, or the blazing fire
converts into warmth and radiance whatever is cast
into it.[6]

32. Give no one the right to say of thee with
truth that thou art not a sincere, that thou art not a

was the philosopher friend of Pliny and Hadrian.   Nothing
certain is known of the others.   [3] vii. 58.

[4] xii. 33 and verses at end of ms. A.   See Introd. p. 1.

[5] The ms. reading *what then* (or, *thou then*) *in what?* is
unintelligible.   [6] iv. 1.

283

ψευδέσθω, ὅστις τούτων τι περὶ σοῦ ὑπολήψεται.
πᾶν δὲ τοῦτο ἐπὶ σοί. τίς γὰρ ὁ κωλύων ἀγαθὸν
εἶναί σε καὶ ἁπλοῦν; σὺ μόνον κρῖνον μηκέτι ζῆν,
εἰ μὴ τοιοῦτος ἔσῃ. οὐδὲ γὰρ αἱρεῖ λόγος μὴ
τοιοῦτον ὄντα.

λγʹ. Τί ἐστι τὸ ἐπὶ ταύτης τῆς ὕλης δυνάμενον
κατὰ τὸ ὑγιέστατον πραχθῆναι ἢ ῥηθῆναι; ὅ τι
γὰρ ἂν τοῦτο ᾖ, ἔξεστιν αὐτὸ πρᾶξαι ἢ εἰπεῖν·
καὶ μὴ προφασίζου ὡς κωλυόμενος.

2 Οὐ πρότερον παύσῃ στένων, πρὶν ἢ τοῦτο πάθῃς,
ὅτι οἷόν ἐστι τοῖς ἡδυπαθοῦσιν ἡ τρυφή, τοιοῦτό
σοι τὸ ἐπὶ τῆς ὑποβαλλομένης καὶ ὑποπιπτούσης
ὕλης ποιεῖν τὰ οἰκεῖα τῇ τοῦ ἀνθρώπου κατασκευῇ·
ἀπόλαυσιν γὰρ δεῖ ὑπολαμβάνειν πᾶν, ὃ ἔξεστι
κατὰ τὴν ἰδίαν φύσιν ἐνεργεῖν. πανταχοῦ δὲ
ἔξεστι.

3 Τῷ μὲν οὖν κυλίνδρῳ οὐ πανταχοῦ δίδοται
φέρεσθαι τὴν ἰδίαν κίνησιν οὐδὲ τῷ ὕδατι οὐδὲ
πυρὶ οὐδὲ τοῖς ἄλλοις, ὅσα ὑπὸ φύσεως ἢ ψυχῆς
ἀλόγου διοικεῖται· τὰ γὰρ διείργοντα καὶ ἐνιστά-
μενα πολλά. νοῦς δὲ καὶ λόγος διὰ παντὸς τοῦ
ἀντιπίπτοντος οὕτως πορεύεσθαι δύναται, ὡς
πέφυκε καὶ ὡς θέλει. ταύτην τὴν ῥᾳστώνην
πρὸ ὀμμάτων τιθέμενος, καθ᾽ ἣν ἐνεχθήσεται ὁ
λόγος διὰ πάντων, ὡς πῦρ ἄνω, ὡς λίθος κάτω, ὡς
κύλινδρος κατὰ πρανοῦς, μηκέτι μηδὲν ἐπιζήτει·
τὰ γὰρ λοιπὰ ἐγκόμματα ἤτοι τοῦ σωματικοῦ
ἐστι τοῦ νεκροῦ ἢ χωρὶς ὑπολήψεως καὶ τῆς
αὐτοῦ τοῦ λόγου ἐνδόσεως οὐ θραύει οὐδὲ ποιεῖ

---

¹ viii. 32.
² v. 29 ; x. 8, § 2.

good man, but let anyone that shall form any such an
idea of thee be as one that maketh a lie. All this
rests with thee. For who is there to hinder thee
from being good and sincere[1]? Resolve then to
live no longer if thou be not such.[2] For neither
doth Reason in that case insist that thou shouldest.

33. Taking our 'material' into account, what can
be said or done in the soundest way? Be it what it
may, it rests with thee to do or say it. And let
us have no pretence that thou art being hindered.

Never shalt thou cease murmuring until it be so
with thee that the utilizing, in a manner consistent
with the constitution of man, of the material presented to thee and cast in thy way shall be to thee
what indulgence is to the sensual. For everything
must be accounted enjoyment that it is in a man's
power to put into practice in accordance with his
own nature; and it is everywhere in his power.

A cylinder we know has no power given it of
individual motion everywhere, nor has fire or water
or any other thing controlled by Nature or by
an irrational soul. For the interposing and impeding
obstacles are many. But Intelligence and Reason
make their way through every impediment just as
their nature or their will prompts them. Setting
before thine eyes this ease wherewith the Reason
can force its way through every obstacle, as fire
upwards, as a stone downwards, as a cylinder down a
slope,[3] look for nothing beyond. For other hindrances
either concern that veritable corpse, the body,[4] or,
apart from imagination and the surrender of Reason
herself, cannot crush us or work any harm at all.[5]

---

[3] Aul. Gell. vi. 2, § 11 (from Chrysippus).
[4] iv. 41.   [5] iv. 7.

κακὸν οὐδ᾽ ὁτιοῦν· ἐπεί τοι καὶ ὁ πάσχων αὐτὸ
κακὸς ἂν εὐθὺς ἐγίνετο.

4 Ἐπὶ γοῦν τῶν ἄλλων κατασκευασμάτων
πάντων, ὅ τι ἂν κακόν τινι αὐτῶν συμβῇ, παρὰ
τοῦτο χεῖρον γίνεται αὐτὸ τὸ πάσχον· ἐνταῦθα δέ,
εἰ δεῖ εἰπεῖν, καὶ κρείττων γίνεται ὁ ἄνθρωπος
καὶ ἐπαινετώτερος, ὀρθῶς χρώμενος τοῖς προσ-
πίπτουσιν. ὅλως δὲ μέμνησο, ὅτι τὸν φύσει
πολίτην οὐδὲν βλάπτει, ὃ πόλιν οὐ βλάπτει,
οὐδέ γε πόλιν βλάπτει, ὃ νόμον οὐ βλάπτει·
τούτων δὲ τῶν καλουμένων ἀκληρημάτων οὐδὲν
βλάπτει νόμον. ὃ τοίνυν νόμον οὐ βλάπτει, οὔτε
πόλιν οὔτε πολίτην.

λδʹ. Τῷ δεδηγμένῳ ὑπὸ τῶν ἀληθῶν δογμάτων
ἀρκεῖ καὶ τὸ βραχύτατον καὶ ἐν μέσῳ κείμενον
εἰς ὑπόμνησιν ἀλυπίας καὶ ἀφοβίας. οἷον

"Φύλλα τὰ μέν τ᾽ ἄνεμος χαμάδις χέει,
ὡς ἀνδρῶν γενεή."

φυλλάρια δὲ καὶ τὰ τεκνία σου· φυλλάρια δὲ
καὶ ταῦτα τὰ ἐπιβοῶντα ἀξιοπίστως καὶ ἐπευ-
φημοῦντα ἢ ἐκ τῶν ἐναντίων καταρώμενα ἢ ἡσυχῇ
ψέγοντα καὶ χλευάζοντα· φυλλάρια δὲ ὁμοίως καὶ
τὰ διαδεξόμενα τὴν ὑστεροφημίαν. πάντα γὰρ
ταῦτα   "ἔαρος ἐπιγίγνεται ὥρῃ"

εἶτα ἄνεμος καταβέβληκεν· ἔπειθ᾽ ὕλη ἕτερα
ἀντὶ τούτων φύει. τὸ δὲ ὀλιγοχρόνιον κοινὸν
πᾶσιν· ἀλλὰ σὺ πάντα, ὡς αἰώνια ἐσόμενα,

---

¹ vii. 58.   ² x. 6.   ³ Hom. *Il.* vi. 147 ; *cp.* Ecclus. xiv. 18.

Else indeed would their victim at once become bad.

In fact in the case of all other organisms, if any evil happen to any of them, the victim itself becomes the worse for it. But a man so circumstanced becomes, if I may so say, better and more praiseworthy by putting such contingencies to a right use.[1] In fine, remember that nothing that harms not the city can harm him whom Nature has made a citizen[2]; nor yet does that harm a city which harms not law. But not one of the so-called mischances harms law. What does not harm law, then, does no harm to citizen or city.

34. Even an obvious and quite brief aphorism can serve to warn him that is bitten with the true doctrines against giving way to grief and fear; as for instance,

Such are the races of men as the leaves that the wind scatters earthwards.[3]

And thy children too are little leaves. Leaves also they who make an outcry as if they ought to be listened to, and scatter their praises or, contrariwise, their curses, or blame and scoff in secret. Leaves too they that are to hand down our after-fame. For all these things

Burgeon again with the season of spring[4];

anon the wind hath cast them down,[5] and the forest puts forth others in their stead. Transitoriness is the common lot of all things, yet there is none of these that thou huntest not after or shunnest,

---

[4] *Ibid.*   [5] *cp.* Psalm 103. 16.

φεύγεις καὶ διώκεις. μικρὸν καὶ καταμύσεις·
τὸν δὲ ἐξενεγκόντα σε ἤδη ἄλλος θρηνήσει.

λε΄. Τὸν ὑγιαίνοντα ὀφθαλμὸν πάντα ὁρᾶν
δεῖ τὰ ὁρατὰ καὶ μὴ λέγειν, " τὰ χλωρὰ θέλω."
τοῦτο γὰρ ὀφθαλμιῶντός ἐστι. καὶ τὴν ὑγιαίνουσαν ἀκοὴν καὶ ὄσφρησιν εἰς πάντα δεῖ τὰ
ἀκουστὰ καὶ ὀσφραντὰ ἑτοίμην εἶναι. καὶ τὸν
ὑγιαίνοντα στόμαχον πρὸς πάντα τὰ τρόφιμα
ὁμοίως ἔχειν, ὡς μύλην πρὸς πάντα, ὅσα ἀλέσουσα
κατεσκεύασται. καὶ τοίνυν τὴν ὑγιαίνουσαν
διάνοιαν πρὸς πάντα δεῖ τὰ συμβαίνοντα ἑτοίμην
εἶναι· ἡ δὲ λέγουσα, "Τὰ τεκνία σωζέσθω,"
καὶ "πάντες, ὅ τι ἂν πράξω, ἐπαινείτωσαν,"
ὀφθαλμός ἐστι τὰ χλωρὰ ζητῶν ἢ ὀδόντες τὰ
ἁπαλά.

λϛ΄. Οὐδείς ἐστιν οὕτως εὔποτμος, ᾧ ἀπο-
θνῄσκοντι οὐ παρεστήξονταί τινες ἀσπαζόμενοι τὸ
συμβαῖνον κακόν. σπουδαῖος καὶ σοφὸς ἦν· [μὴ]
τὸ πανύστατον ἔσται τις ὁ καθ' αὑτὸν λέγων·
"Ἀναπνεύσομέν ποτε ἀπὸ τούτου τοῦ παιδαγωγοῦ.
χαλεπὸς μὲν οὐδενὶ ἡμῶν ἦν, ἀλλὰ ᾐσθανόμην,
ὅτι ἡσυχῇ καταγινώσκει ἡμῶν." ταῦτα μὲν οὖν
ἐπὶ τοῦ σπουδαίου. ἐφ' ἡμῶν δὲ πόσα ἄλλα ἐστί,
δι' ἃ πολὺς ὁ ἀπαλλακτιῶν ἡμῶν. τοῦτο οὖν
ἐννοήσεις ἀποθνῄσκων καὶ εὐκολώτερον ἐξελεύσῃ
λογιζόμενος· ἐκ τοιούτου βίου ἀπέρχομαι, ἐν ᾧ
αὐτοὶ οἱ κοινωνοί, ὑπὲρ ὧν τὰ τοσαῦτα ἠγωνισάμην,
ηὐξάμην, ἐφρόντισα, αὐτοὶ ἐκεῖνοι ἐθέλουσί με
ὑπάγειν ἄλλην τινὰ τυχὸν ἐκ τούτου ῥᾳστώνην

---

¹ iv. 48.
² i. 8 ; vii. 41 ; viii. 49 ; ix. 40 ; xi. 34.   Marcus was intensely fond of his children.   Galen describes (xiv. 3, Kühn)

as though it were everlasting. A little while and thou shalt close thine eyes; aye, and for him that bore thee to the grave shall another presently raise the dirge.[1]

35. The sound eye should see all there is to be seen, but should not say: *I want what is green only.* For that is characteristic of a disordered eye. And the sound hearing and smell should be equipped for all that is to be heard or smelled. And the sound digestion should act towards all nutriment as a mill towards the grist which it was formed to grind. So should the sound mind be ready for all that befalls. But the mind that says: *Let my children be safe!*[2] *Let all applaud my every act!* is but as an eye that looks for green things or as teeth that look for soft things.

36. There is no one so fortunate as not to have one or two standing by his death-bed who will welcome the evil which is befalling him. Say he was a worthy man and a wise; will there not be some one at the very end to say in his heart, *We can breathe again at last, freed from this schoolmaster,*[3] *not that he was hard on any of us, but I was all along conscious that he tacitly condemned us?* So much for the worthy, but in our own case how many other reasons can be found for which hundreds would be only too glad to be quit of us! Think then upon this when dying, and thy passing from life will be easier if thou reason thus: I am leaving a life in which even my intimates for whom I have so greatly toiled, prayed, and thought,[4] aye even they wish me gone, expecting belike to gain thereby

his anxiety about Commodus; *cp.* also Fronto, *ad Caes.* iv. 12.   [3] *cp.* Vopiscus, *Vit. Aureliani,* 37, §3; Sen. *Ep.* 11.   [4] Herodian, i. 4, § 3. *cp.* Lucian, *Gallus* 25.

ἐλπίζοντες. τι ἂν οὖν τις ἀντέχοιτο τῆς ἐνταῦθα
μακροτέρας διατριβῆς;

2 Μὴ μέντοι διὰ τοῦτο ἔλαττον εὐμενὴς αὐτοῖς
ἄπιθι, ἀλλὰ τὸ ἴδιον ἔθος διασῴζων φίλος καὶ
εὔνους καὶ ἵλεως· καὶ μὴ πάλιν ὡς ἀποσπώμενος,
ἀλλ' ὥσπερ ἐπὶ τοῦ εὐθανατοῦντος εὐκόλως τὸ
ψυχάριον ἀπὸ τοῦ σώματος ἐξειλεῖται, τοιαύτην
καὶ τὴν ἀπὸ τούτων ἀποχώρησιν δεῖ γενέσθαι·
καὶ γὰρ τούτοις ἡ φύσις <σε> συνῆψε καὶ
συνέκρινεν. ἀλλὰ νῦν διαλύει. διαλύομαι ὡς
ἀπὸ οἰκείων μέν, οὐ μὴν ἀνθελκόμενος, ἀλλ'
ἀβιάστως· ἓν γὰρ καὶ τοῦτο τῶν κατὰ φύσιν.

λζ'. Ἔθισον ἐπὶ παντός, ὡς οἷόν τε, τοῦ
πρασσομένου ὑπό τινος ἐπιζητεῖν κατὰ σαυτόν·
"Οὗτος τοῦτο ἐπὶ τί ἀναφέρει;" ἄρχου δὲ ἀπὸ
σαυτοῦ, καὶ σαυτὸν πρῶτον ἐξέταζε.

λη'. Μέμνησο, ὅτι τὸ νευροσπαστοῦν ἐστιν
ἐκεῖνο τὸ ἔνδον ἐγκεκρυμμένον· ἐκεῖνο ῥητορεία,† [1]
ἐκεῖνο ζωή, ἐκεῖνο, εἰ δεῖ εἰπεῖν, ἄνθρωπος.
μηδέποτε συμπεριφαντάζου τὸ περικείμενον ἀγγει-
ῶδες καὶ τὰ ὀργάνια ταῦτα τὰ περιπεπλασμένα.
ὅμοια γάρ ἐστι σκεπάρνῳ, μόνον διαφέροντα,
καθότι προσφυῆ ἐστιν. ἐπεί τοι οὐ μᾶλλόν τι
τούτων ὄφελός ἐστι τῶν μορίων χωρὶς τῆς
κινούσης καὶ ἰσχούσης αὐτὰ αἰτίας ἢ τῆς κερκίδος
τῇ ὑφαντρίᾳ, καὶ τοῦ καλάμου τῷ γράφοντι, καὶ
τοῦ μαστιγίου τῷ ἡνιόχῳ.

---

[1] ῥητορία A.   Perhaps ἱστορία.

some further ease.[1]   Why then should anyone cling
to a longer sojourn here?

Howbeit go away with no less kindliness towards
them on this account, but maintaining thy true characteristics be friendly and goodnatured and gracious;
nor again as though wrenched apart, but rather
should thy withdrawal from them be as that gentle
slipping away of soul from body which we see when
a man makes a peaceful end.   For it was Nature
that knit and kneaded thee with them, and now she
parts the tie.   I am parted as from kinsfolk, not
dragged forcibly away, but going unresistingly.   For
this severance too is a process of Nature.[2]

37. In every act of another habituate thyself as
far as may be to put to thyself the question: *What
end has the man in view?* [3]   But begin with thyself,
cross-examine thyself first.

38. Bear in mind that what pulls the strings is
that Hidden Thing within us: *that* makes our
speech, *that* our life, *that,* one may say, makes the
man.   Never in thy mental picture of it include the
vessel that overlies it [4] nor these organs that are
appurtenances thereof.   They are like the workman's
adze, only differing from it in being naturally
attached to the body.   Since indeed, severed from
the Cause that bids them move and bids them stay,
these parts are as useless as is the shuttle of the
weaver, the pen of the writer, and the whip of the
charioteer.

---

[1] Is he thinking of Commodus?   [2] ix. 3.
[3] ii. 16.   [4] iii. 3 *ad fin.*; xii. 1.

BIBΛION IA

α'. Τὰ ἴδια τῆς λογικῆς ψυχῆς· ἑαυτὴν ὁρᾷ
ἑαυτὴν διαρθροῖ, ἑαυτήν, ὁποίαν ἂν βούληται
ποιεῖ, τὸν καρπὸν ὃν φέρει αὐτὴ καρπούτα,
—τοὺς γὰρ τῶν φυτῶν καρποὺς καὶ τὸ ἀνάλογοι
ἐπὶ τῶν ζώων ἄλλοι καρποῦνται,—τοῦ ἰδίοι
τέλους τυγχάνει, ὅπου ἂν τὸ τοῦ βίου πέρα
ἐπιστῇ. οὐχ' ὥσπερ ἐπὶ ὀρχήσεως καὶ ὑποκρίς
εως, καὶ τῶν τοιούτων, ἀτελὴς γίνεται ἡ ὅλη
πρᾶξις, ἐάν τι ἐγκόψῃ· ἀλλ' ἐπὶ παντὸς μέρους
καὶ ὅπου ἂν καταληφθῇ, πλῆρες καὶ ἀπροσδεὲ
ἑαυτῇ τὸ προτεθὲν ποιεῖ, ὥστε εἰπεῖν, " ἐγὼ
ἀπέχω τὰ ἐμά."

2   Ἔτι δὲ περιέρχεται τὸν ὅλον κόσμον, καὶ τὸ
περὶ αὐτὸν κενόν, καὶ τὸ σχῆμα αὐτοῦ, καὶ εἰ
τὴν ἀπειρίαν τοῦ αἰῶνος ἐκτείνεται, καὶ τὴ
περιοδικὴν παλιγγενεσίαν τῶν ὅλων ἐμπεριλαμ
βάνει καὶ περινοεῖ, καὶ θεωρεῖ ὅτι οὐδὲν νεώ
τερον ὄψονται οἱ μεθ' ἡμᾶς οὐδὲ περιττότερο
εἶδον οἱ πρὸ ἡμῶν· ἀλλὰ τρόπον τινὰ ὁ τεσσαρα
κοντούτης, ἐὰν νοῦν ὁποσονοῦν ἔχῃ, πάντ
τὰ γεγονότα καὶ τὰ ἐσόμενα ἑώρακε κατὰ τ

---

[1] vi. 8; viii. 35.   *cp.* Epict. i. 17, § 1.
[2] *cp.* Epict. i. 19, § 11: γέγονε τὸ ζῷον ὥστε αὐτοῦ ἕνεκ
πάντα ποιεῖν.   [3] xii. 36.

292

BOOK XI

1. THE properties of the Rational Soul are these:
it sees itself, dissects itself, moulds itself to its own
will,[1] itself reaps its own fruits [2]—whereas the fruits
of the vegetable kingdom and the corresponding
produce of animals are reaped by others,—it wins
to its own goal wherever the bounds of life be set.
In dancing and acting and such-like arts, if any
break occurs, the whole action is rendered imperfect;
but the rational soul in every part and wheresoever
taken [3] shews the work set before it fulfilled and all-
sufficient for itself, so that it can say: *I have to the
full what is my own.*

More than this, it goeth about the whole Universe
and the void surrounding it and traces its plan, and
stretches forth into the infinitude of Time, and
comprehends the cyclical Regeneration [4] of all things,
and takes stock of it, and discerns that our children
will see nothing fresh,[5] just as our fathers too never
saw anything more than we.[6] So that in a manner
the man of forty years, if he have a grain of sense,
in view of this sameness has seen all that has been

---

[4] v. 13, 32; x. 7, § 2.   [5] vi. 37; vii. 1 etc.

[6] *cp.* Lucr. ii. 978: *eadem sunt omnia semper*; Florio's
Montaigne, i. 19: "If you have lived one day you have seene
all."

293

ὁμοειδές. ἴδιον δὲ λογικῆς ψυχῆς καὶ τὸ φιλεῖν
τοὺς πλησίον καὶ ἀλήθεια καὶ αἰδὼς καὶ τὸ
μηδὲν ἑαυτῆς προτιμᾶν, ὅπερ ἴδιον καὶ νόμου.
οὕτως ἄρ' οὐδὲν διήνεγκε λόγος ὀρθὸς καὶ λόγος
δικαιοσύνης.

β'. Ὠιδῆς ἐπιτερποῦς καὶ ὀρχήσεως καὶ
παγκρατίου καταφρονήσεις, ἐὰν τὴν μὲν ἐμμελῆ
φωνὴν καταμερίσῃς εἰς ἕκαστον τῶν φθόγγων,
καὶ καθ' ἕνα πύθῃ σεαυτοῦ, " Εἰ τούτου ἥττων εἶ."
διατραπήσῃ γάρ· ἐπὶ δὲ ὀρχήσεως τὸ ἀνάλογον
ποιήσας καθ' ἑκάστην κίνησιν ἢ σχέσιν· τὸ δ'
αὐτὸ καὶ ἐπὶ τοῦ παγκρατίου. ὅλως οὖν, χωρὶς
ἀρετῆς καὶ τῶν ἀπ' ἀρετῆς, μέμνησο ἐπὶ τὰ κατὰ
μέρος τρέχειν καὶ τῇ διαιρέσει αὐτῶν εἰς
καταφρόνησιν ἰέναι· τὸ δ' αὐτὸ καὶ ἐπὶ τὸν βίον
ὅλον μετάφερε.

γ'. Οἴα ἐστὶν ἡ ψυχὴ ἡ ἕτοιμος, ἐὰν ἤδη
ἀπολυθῆναι δέῃ τοῦ σώματος καὶ ἤτοι σβεσθῆναι
ἢ σκεδασθῆναι ἢ συμμεῖναι. τὸ δὲ ἕτοιμον
τοῦτο, ἵνα ἀπὸ ἰδικῆς κρίσεως ἔρχηται, μὴ κατὰ
ψιλὴν παράταξιν, [ὡς οἱ Χριστιανοί,][1] ἀλλὰ
λελογισμένως καὶ σεμνῶς καὶ, ὥστε καὶ ἄλλον
πεῖσαι, ἀτραγῴδως.

δ'. Πεποίηκά τι κοινωνικῶς; οὐκοῦν ὠφέλημαι.
τοῦτο ἵνα ἀεὶ πρόχειρον ἀπαντᾷ, κᾶι μηδαμοῦ
παύου.

ε'. Τίς σου ἡ τέχνη; "Ἀγαθὸν εἶναι." τοῦτο δὲ

---

[1] ὡς οἱ Χριστιανοί : ungrammatical and pretty certainly a
gloss. See p. 381 ff. Eichstädt *Exercit. Antonin.* iii.

---

[1] St. Mark viii. 36.
[2] A rather brutal combination of boxing and wrestling.
[3] viii. 36. There is surely a fallacy here.

and shall be. Again a property of the Rational Soul is the love of our neighbour, and truthfulness, and modesty, and to prize nothing above itself[1]— a characteristic also of Law. In this way then the Reason that is right reason and the Reason that is justice are one.

2. Thou wilt think but meanly of charming song and dance and the pancratium,[2] if thou analyze the melodious utterance into its several notes and in the case of each ask thyself: *Has this the mastery over me?* For thou wilt recoil from such a confession.[3] So too with the dance, if thou do the like for each movement and posture. The same holds good of the pancratium. In fine, virtue and its sphere of action excepted, remember to turn to the component parts,[4] and by analyzing them come to despise them. Bring the same practice to bear on the whole of life also.

3. What a soul is that which is ready to be released from the body at any requisite moment, and be quenched[5] or dissipated or hold together! But the readiness must spring from a man's inner judgment, and not be the result of mere opposition [as is the case with the Christians].[6] It must be associated with deliberation and dignity and, if others too are to be convinced, with nothing like stage-heroics.

4. Have I done some social act? Well, I am amply rewarded.[7] Keep this truth ever ready to turn to, and in no wise slacken thine efforts.

5. What is thy vocation? *To be a good man.*

---

[4] iii. 11. [5] v. 33; vii. 32.
[6] See p. 382, and *cp.* for philosophers *Digest.* 49. 16. 6. § 7.
[7] vii. 13, 73; ix. 42, § 5; *cp.* Prov. xi. 17: τῇ ψυχῇ αὐτοῦ ἀγαθὸν ποιεῖ ἀνὴρ ἐλεήμων.

πῶς καλῶς γίνεται ἢ ἐκ θεωρημάτων, τῶν μὲν
περὶ τῆς τοῦ ὅλου φύσεως, τῶν δὲ περὶ τῆς ἰδίας
τοῦ ἀνθρώπου κατασκευῆς;

ϛʹ. Πρῶτον αἱ τραγῳδίαι παρήχθησαν ὑπο-
μνηστικαὶ τῶν συμβαινόντων καὶ ὅτι ταῦτα οὕτω
πέφυκε γίνεσθαι καὶ ὅτι, οἷς ἐπὶ τῆς σκηνῆς
ψυχαγωγεῖσθε, τούτοις μὴ ἄχθεσθε ἐπὶ τῆς
μείζονος σκηνῆς. ὁρᾶται γάρ, ὅτι οὕτω δεῖ ταῦτα
περαίνεσθαι καὶ ὅτι φέρουσιν αὐτὰ καὶ οἱ
κεκραγότες, "'Ιὼ Κιθαιρών." καὶ λέγεται δέ
τινα ὑπὸ τῶν τὰ δράματα ποιούντων χρησίμως,
οἷόν ἐστιν ἐκεῖνο μάλιστα·

"Εἰ δ' ἠμελήθην ἐκ θεῶν καὶ παῖδ' ἐμώ,
  ἔχει λόγον καὶ τοῦτο·"
καὶ πάλιν·
"Τοῖς πράγμασιν γὰρ οὐχὶ θυμοῦσθαι <πρέ-
  πον>·"
καὶ
"Βίον θερίζειν ὥστε κάρπιμον στάχυν"
καὶ ὅσα τοιαῦτα.

2   Μετὰ δὲ τὴν τραγῳδίαν ἡ ἀρχαία κωμῳδία
παρήχθη, παιδαγωγικὴν παρρησίαν ἔχουσα, καὶ
τῆς ἀτυφίας οὐκ ἀχρήστως δι' αὐτῆς τῆς εὐθυρ-
ρημοσύνης ὑπομιμνήσκουσα· πρὸς οἷόν τι καὶ
Διογένης ταυτὶ παρελάμβανεν. μετὰ ταύτην[1] <δὲ>
ἡ μέση κωμῳδία, καὶ λοιπὸν ἡ νέα πρὸς τί ποτε
παρείληπται, ἢ κατ' ὀλίγον ἐπὶ τὴν ἐκ μιμήσεως
φιλοτεχνίαν ὑπερρύη, ἐπίστησον. ὅτι μὲν γὰρ

[1] ταύτης A : ταῦτα τις P : ταύτην Stich. : <δὲ> Schenkl.

---

[1] Soph. *Oed. Rex* 1391 ; Epict. i. 24, § 16.   Perhaps Marcus
had in mind the lines of Timocles (Athen. vi. 2) πρὸς ἀλλοτρίῳ
τε ψυχαγωγηθεὶς πάθει Μεθ' ἡδονῆς ἀπῆλθε παιδευθεὶς ἅμα.

BOOK XI

But how be successful in this save by assured conceptions on the one hand of the Universal Nature and on the other of the special constitution of man?

6. Originally tragedies were brought on to remind us of real events, and that such things naturally occur, and that on life's greater stage you must not be vexed at things, which on the stage you find so attractive. For it is seen that these things must be gone through, and they too have to endure them, who cry *Ah, Kithaeron!*[1] Aye, and the dramatic writers contain some serviceable sayings, for example this more especially:

> *Though both my sons and me the gods have spurned,*
> *For this too there is reason;*[2]

and again:

> *It nought availeth to be wroth with things;*[3]

and this:

> *Our lives are reaped like the ripe ears of corn;*[4]

and how many more like them.

And after Tragedy the old Comedy was put on the stage, exercising an educative freedom of speech, and by its very directness of utterance giving us no unserviceable warning against unbridled arrogance. In somewhat similar vein Diogenes[5] also took up this rôle. After this, consider for what purpose the Middle Comedy was introduced, and subsequently the New, which little by little degenerated into ingenious mimicry. For that some serviceable

---

[2] Eur. *Antiope* Frag. 207; vii. 41.
[3] Eur. *Beller.* Frag. 289; vii. 38.
[4] Eur. *Hyps.* Frag. 757; vii. 40.
[5] Diog. Laert. *Diog.* 7; Plut. "On Hearing," 7.

λέγεται καὶ ὑπὸ τούτων τινὰ χρήσιμα, οὐκ
ἀγνοεῖται· ἀλλὰ ἡ ὅλη ἐπιβολὴ τῆς τοιαύτης
ποιήσεως καὶ δραματουργίας πρὸς τίνα ποτὲ
σκοπὸν ἀπέβλεψεν;

ζ΄. Πῶς ἐναργὲς προσπίπτει τὸ μὴ εἶναι
ἄλλην βίου ὑπόθεσιν εἰς τὸ φιλοσοφεῖν οὕτως
ἐπιτήδειον, ὡς ταύτην, ἐν ᾗ νῦν ὢν τυγχάνεις.

η΄. Κλάδος τοῦ προσεχοῦς κλάδου ἀποκοπεὶς
οὐ δύναται μὴ καὶ τοῦ ὅλου φυτοῦ ἀποκεκόφθαι.
οὕτω δὴ καὶ ἄνθρωπος ἑνὸς ἀνθρώπου ἀποσχισθ-
εὶς ὅλης τῆς κοινωνίας ἀποπέπτωκεν. κλάδον
μὲν οὖν ἄλλος ἀποκόπτει· ἄνθρωπος δὲ αὐτὸς
ἑαυτὸν τοῦ πλησίον χωρίζει μισήσας καὶ
ἀποστραφείς· ἀγνοεῖ δέ, ὅτι καὶ τοῦ ὅλου
πολιτεύματος ἅμα ἀποτέτμηκεν ἑαυτόν. πλὴν
ἐκεῖνό γε δῶρον τοῦ συστησαμένου τὴν κοινωνίαν
Διός· ἔξεστι γὰρ πάλιν ἡμῖν συμφῦναι τῷ
προσεχεῖ καὶ πάλιν τοῦ ὅλου συμπληρωτικοῖς
γενέσθαι. πλεονάκις μέντοι γινόμενον τὸ κατὰ
τὴν τοιαύτην διαίρεσιν δυσένωτον καὶ δυσαπο-
κατάστατον <τὸ> ἀποχωροῦν ποιεῖ. ὅλως τε
οὐχ ὅμοιος ὁ κλάδος ὁ ἀπ᾽ ἀρχῆς συμβλαστήσας
καὶ σύμπνους συμμείνας τῷ μετὰ τὴν ἀποκοπὴν
αὖθις ἐγκεντρισθέντι, ὅ τί ποτε λέγουσιν οἱ
φυτουργοί. ὁμοθαμνεῖν μέν, μὴ ὁμοδογματεῖν δέ.

θ΄. Οἱ ἐνιστάμενοι προϊόντι σοι κατὰ τὸν
ὀρθὸν λόγον, ὥσπερ ἀπὸ τῆς ὑγιοῦς πράξεως

---

[1] Lucian, de Salt. 35, says of the Art of Dancing (Panto-
mime) that it requires the acme of culture and even of
philosophy!

[2] cp. Lucan i. 493: "exeat aula qui vult esse pius";

BOOK XI

things are said even by the writers of these is recognized by all. But what end in view had this whole enterprize of such poetical and dramatic composition? [1]

7. How clearly is it borne in on thee that there is no other state of life so fitted to call for the exercise of Philosophy as this in which thou now findest thyself. [2]

8. A branch cut off from its neighbour branch [3] cannot but be cut off from the whole plant. In the very same way a man severed from one man has fallen away from the fellowship of all men. Now a branch is cut off by others, but a man separates himself [4] from his neighbour by his own agency in hating him or turning his back upon him; and is unaware that he has thereby sundered himself from the whole civic community. [5] But mark the gift of Zeus who established the law of fellowship. For it is in our power to grow again to the neighbour branch, and again become perfective of the whole. But such a schism constantly repeated makes it difficult for the seceding part to unite again and resume its former condition. And in general the branch that from the first has shared in the growth of the tree and lived with its life is not like that which has been cut off and afterwards grafted on to it, as the gardeners are apt to tell you. Be of one bush, but not of one mind.

9. As those who withstand thy progress along the path of right reason will never be able to turn thee

---

Montaigne iii. 9 (Florio's version): "Plato saith that who escapes untainted and clean-handed from the managing of the world escapeth by some wonder." See also *above* viii. 1.

[3] St. Paul, Rom. xi. 19.   [4] iv. 29; viii. 34.
[5] ix. 23. Shaks. *Lear*, iv. 2. 34.

ἀποτρέψαι σε οὐ δυνήσονται, οὕτως μηδὲ τῆς
πρὸς αὐτοὺς εὐμενείας ἐκκρουέτωσαν· ἀλλὰ
φύλασσε σεαυτὸν ἐπ' ἀμφοτέρων ὁμοίως, μὴ
μόνον ἐπὶ τῆς εὐσταθοῦς κρίσεως καὶ πράξεως,
ἀλλὰ καὶ ἐπὶ τῆς πρὸς τοὺς κωλύειν ἐπιχειροῦντας
ἢ ἄλλως δυσχεραίνοντας πρᾳότητος. καὶ γὰρ
τοῦτο ἀσθενές, τὸ χαλεπαίνειν αὐτοῖς, ὥσπερ τὸ
ἀποστῆναι τῆς πράξεως καὶ ἐνδοῦναι κατα-
πλαγέντα· ἀμφότεροι γὰρ ἐπίσης λειποτάκται, ὁ
μὲν ὑποτρέσας, ὁ δὲ ἀλλοτριωθεὶς πρὸς τὸν φύσει
συγγενῆ καὶ φίλον.

ι΄. " Οὐκ ἔστι χείρων οὐδεμία φύσις τέχνης." [1]
καὶ γὰρ αἱ τέχναι τὰς φύσεις μιμοῦνται. εἰ δὲ
τοῦτο, ἡ πασῶν τῶν ἄλλων τελεωτάτη καὶ
περιληπτικωτάτη φύσις οὐκ ἂν ἀπολείποιτο
τῆς τεχνικῆς εὐμηχανίας. πᾶσαι δέ γε τέχναι
τῶν κρειττόνων ἕνεκεν τὰ χείρω ποιοῦσιν· οὐκοῦν
καὶ ἡ κοινὴ φύσις. καὶ δὴ ἔνθεν μὲν γένεσις
δικαιοσύνης, ἀπὸ δὲ ταύτης αἱ λοιπαὶ ἀρεταὶ
ὑφίστανται· οὐ γὰρ τηρηθήσεται τὸ δίκαιον, ἐὰν
ἤτοι διαφερώμεθα πρὸς τὰ μέσα ἢ εὐεξαπάτητοι
καὶ προπτωτικοὶ καὶ μεταπτωτικοὶ ὦμεν.

ια΄. †Εἰ μὲν οὖν [2] <μὴ> ἔρχεται† ἐπὶ σὲ τὰ
πράγματα, ὧν αἱ διώξεις καὶ φυγαὶ θορυβοῦσί σε,
ἀλλὰ τρόπον τινὰ αὐτὸς ἐπ' ἐκεῖνα ἔρχῃ, τὸ γοῦν
κρῖμα τὸ περὶ αὐτῶν ἡσυχαζέτω κἀκεῖνα μενεῖ
ἀτρεμοῦντα καὶ οὔτε διώκων οὔτε φεύγων ὀφθήσῃ.

---

[1] Apparently a quotation from some unknown poet.
[2] οὐκ PA : [εἰ μὲν] Οὐκ Leopold.

aside from sound action, so let them not wrest thee from a kindly attitude towards them[1]; but keep a watch over thyself in both directions alike, not only in steadfastness[2] of judgment and action but also in gentleness towards those who endeavour to stand in thy path or be in some other way a thorn in thy side. For in fact it is a sign of weakness to be wroth with them, no less than to shrink from action and be terrified into surrender. For they that do the one or the other are alike deserters of their post,[3] the one as a coward, the other as estranged from a natural kinsman and friend.

10. '*Nature in no case cometh short of art.*' For indeed the arts are copiers of various natures. If this be so, the most consummate and comprehensive Nature of all cannot be outdone by the inventive skill of art. And in every art the lower things are done for the sake of the higher[4]; and this must hold good of the Universal Nature also. Aye and thence is the origin of Justice, and in justice all the other virtues have their root,[5] since justice will not be maintained if we either put a value on things indifferent, or are easily duped and prone to slip and prone to change.

11. If therefore the things, the following after and eschewing of which disturb thee, come not to thee, but thou in a manner dost thyself seek them out, at all events keep thy judgment at rest about them and they will remain quiescent, and thou shalt not be seen following after or eschewing them.

---

[1] x. 36, § 2 etc.   [2] v. 18.   [3] x. 25.
[4] v. 16, 30; vii. 55.
[5] iv. 37; v. 34. *cp.* Theognis, 147: ἐν δὲ δικαιοσύνῃ συλ-λήβδην πᾶσ' ἀρετή 'στιν.

ιβ'. Σφαῖρα ψυχῆς αὐτοειδής,[1] ὅταν μήτε ἐκτείνηται ἐπί τι μήτε ἔσω συντρέχῃ, μήτε σπείρηται †[2] μήτε συνιζάνῃ, ἀλλὰ φωτὶ λάμπηται, ᾧ τὴν ἀλήθειαν ὁρᾷ τὴν πάντων καὶ τὴν ἐν αὑτῇ.

ιγ'. Καταφρονήσει μού τις; ὄψεται· ἐγὼ δὲ ὄψομαι, ἵνα μή τι καταφρονήσεως ἄξιον πράσσων ἢ λέγων εὑρίσκωμαι. μισήσει; ὄψεται· ἀλλὰ ἐγὼ εὐμενὴς καὶ εὔνους παντί, καὶ τούτῳ αὐτῷ ἕτοιμος τὸ παρορώμενον δεῖξαι, οὐκ ὀνειδιστικῶς οὐδὲ ὡς κατεπιδεικνύμενος, ὅτι ἀνέχομαι, ἀλλὰ γνησίως καὶ χρηστῶς, οἷος ὁ Φωκίων ἐκεῖνος, εἴ γε μὴ προσεποιεῖτο. τὰ ἔσω γὰρ δεῖ τοιαῦτα εἶναι, καὶ ὑπὸ τῶν θεῶν βλέπεσθαι ἄνθρωπον πρὸς μηδὲν ἀγανακτικῶς διατιθέμενον μηδὲ δεινοπαθοῦντα. τί γάρ σοι κακόν, εἰ αὐτὸς νῦν ποιεῖς τὸ τῇ φύσει σου οἰκεῖον καὶ δέχῃ τὸ νῦν τῇ τῶν ὅλων φύσει εὔκαιρον, ἄνθρωπος τεταμένος πρὸς τὸ γίνεσθαι δι' ὅτου δὴ τὸ κοινῇ συμφέρον;

ιδ'. Ἀλλήλων καταφρονοῦντες ἀλλήλοις ἀρεσκεύονται καὶ ἀλλήλων ὑπερέχειν θέλοντες ἀλλήλοις ὑποκατακλίνονται.

ιε'. Ὡς σαπρὸς καὶ κίβδηλος ὁ λέγων, "Ἐγὼ προῄρημαι ἁπλῶς σοι προσφέρεσθαι." τί ποιεῖς, ἄνθρωπε; τοῦτο οὐ δεῖ προλέγειν. αὐτοῦ φανήσεται· ἐπὶ τοῦ μετώπου γεγράφθαι ὀφείλει, εὐθὺς

---

[1] αὐτοτελὴς Reiske.   [2] ἐπαίρηται Schenkl.

---

[1] viii. 41 ; xii. 3.   [2] viii. 51.
[3] v. 25 ; Epict. iii. 18, § 9 ; x. 32.   [4] xi. 18, § 9.
[5] Marcus is probably thinking of Phocion's last words, see Aelian xii. 49 μηδὲν Ἀθηναίοις μνησικακήσειν ὑπὲρ τῆς παρ' αὐτῶν φιλοτησίας ἧς νῦν πίνω (*sc.* the cup of hemlock) ; but

12. The soul is 'a sphere truly shaped,'[1] when it neither projects itself towards anything outside nor shrinks together inwardly, neither expands nor contracts,[2] but irradiates a light whereby it sees the reality of all things and the reality that is in itself.

13. What if a man think scorn of me? That will be his affair. But it will be mine not to be found doing or saying anything worthy of scorn. What if he hate me? That will be his affair.[3] But I will be kindly and goodnatured to everyone, and ready to shew even my enemy where he has seen amiss, not by way of rebuke[4] nor with a parade of forbearance, but genuinely and chivalrously like the famous Phocion,[5] unless indeed he was speaking ironically. For such should be the inner springs of a man's heart[6] that the Gods see him not wrathfully disposed at any thing or counting it a hardship. Why, what evil can happen to thee if thou thyself now doest what is congenial to thy nature, and welcomest what the Universal Nature now deems well-timed, thou who art a man intensely eager that what is for the common interest should by one means or another be brought about?

14. Thinking scorn of one another, they yet fawn on one another, and eager to outdo their rivals they grovel one to another.

15. How corrupt is the man, how counterfeit, who proclaims aloud: *I have elected to deal straightforwardly with thee!* Man, what art thou at? There is no need to give this out. The fact will instantly declare itself. It ought to be written on the fore-

Heylbut (*Rhein. Mus.* 39. p. 310) refers to a story in Musonius Rufus, p. 55, Hense.

⁵ *cp.* St. Luke xi. 39 : τὸ ἔσωθεν ὑμῶν—"the inward parts."

ἡ φωνὴ τοιοῦτον ἠχεῖ,[1] εὐθὺς ἐν τοῖς ὄμμασιν
ἐξέχει, ὡς τῶν ἐραστῶν ἐν τῷ βλέμματι πάντα
εὐθὺς γνωρίζει ὁ ἐρώμενος. τοιοῦτον ὅλως δεῖ
τὸν ἁπλοῦν καὶ ἀγαθὸν εἶναι, οἷον γράσωνα, ἵνα ὁ
παραστὰς ἅμα τῷ προσελθεῖν, θέλει οὐ θέλει,
αἴσθηται. ἐπιτήδευσις δὲ ἁπλότητος σκάλμη[2]
ἐστίν. οὐδέν ἐστιν αἴσχιον λυκοφιλίας· πάντων
μάλιστα τοῦτο φεῦγε. ὁ ἀγαθὸς καὶ ἁπλοῦς
καὶ εὐμενὴς ἐν τοῖς ὄμμασιν ἔχουσι ταῦτα καὶ οὐ
λανθάνει.

ιϛʹ. Κάλλιστα διαζῆν, δύναμις αὕτη ἐν τῇ
ψυχῇ, ἐὰν πρὸς τὰ ἀδιάφορά τις ἀδιαφορῇ.
ἀδιαφορήσει δέ, ἐὰν ἕκαστον αὐτῶν θεωρῇ διηρη-
μένως καὶ ὁλικῶς καὶ μεμνημένος, ὅτι οὐδὲν
αὐτῶν ὑπόληψιν περὶ αὑτοῦ ἡμῖν ἐμποιεῖ οὐδὲ
ἔρχεται ἐφ' ἡμᾶς· ἀλλὰ τὰ μὲν ἀτρεμεῖ, ἡμεῖς δέ
ἐσμεν οἱ τὰς περὶ αὐτῶν κρίσεις γεννῶντες καὶ
οἷον γράφοντες ἐν ἑαυτοῖς, ἐξὸν μὲν μὴ γράφειν,
ἐξὸν δέ, κἄν που λάθῃ, εὐθὺς ἐξαλεῖψαι· ὅτι
ὀλίγου χρόνου ἔσται ἡ τοιαύτη προσοχὴ καὶ
λοιπὸν πεπαύσεται ὁ βίος. τί μέντοι δύσκολον
ἄλλως[3] ἔχειν ταῦτα; εἰ μὲν γὰρ κατὰ φύσιν
ἐστί, χαῖρε αὐτοῖς καὶ ῥάδια ἔστω σοι· εἰ δὲ
παρὰ φύσιν, ζήτει, τί ἐστὶ σοὶ κατὰ τὴν σὴν
φύσιν, καὶ ἐπὶ τοῦτο σπεῦδε, κἂν ἄδοξον ᾖ·
παντὶ γὰρ συγγνώμη, τὸ ἴδιον ἀγαθὸν ζητ-
οῦντι.

---

[1] ἔχει PA: ἠχεῖ Reiske.   [2] σκαμβὴ (a bent stick that
can never be made straight) Salm.   [3] καλῶς P.

---

[1] The word is Thracian for a native sword (Pollux x. 38),
as we might say a *kukri*.   Here any concealed weapon to
stab the unsuspecting.

head. There is a ring in the voice that betrays it at once, it flashes out at once from the eyes, just as the loved one can read at a glance every secret in his lover's looks. The simple and good man should in fact be like a man who has a strong smell about him, so that, as soon as ever he comes near, his neighbour is, will-he nill-he, aware of it. A calculated simplicity is a stiletto.[1] There is nothing more hateful than the friendship of the wolf for the lamb. Eschew that above all things. The good man, the kindly, the genuine, betrays these characteristics in his eyes and there is no hiding it.[2]

16. Vested in the soul is the power of living ever the noblest of lives, let a man but be indifferent towards things indifferent. And he will be indifferent, if he examine every one of these things both in its component parts[3] and as a whole, and bear in mind that none of them is the cause in us of any opinion about itself, nor obtrudes itself on us. *They* remain quiescent,[4] and it is we who father these judgments about them and as it were inscribe them on our minds, though it lies with us not to inscribe them and, if they chance to steal in undetected, to erase them at once.[5] Bear in mind too that we shall have but a little while to attend to such things and presently life will be at an end. But why complain of the perversity of things? If they are as Nature wills, delight in them and let them be no hardship to thee. If they contravene Nature, seek then what is in accord with thy nature and speed towards that, even though it bring no fame.[6] For it is pardonable for every man to seek his own good.

[2] *cp.* Ecclesiasticus xix. 29: "A man shall be known by his look."

[3] iii. 11; xii. 18.   [4] xi. 11.   [5] viii. 47.   [6] v. 3; vi. 2.

ιζ'. Πόθεν ἐλήλυθεν ἕκαστον, καὶ ἐκ τίνων
ἕκαστον ὑποκειμένων, καὶ εἰς τί μεταβάλλει,
καὶ οἷον ἔσται μεταβαλόν, καὶ ὡς οὐδὲν κακὸν
πείσεται.

ιη'. Καὶ[1] πρῶτον, τίς ἡ πρὸς ἀνθρώπους μοι
σχέσις· καὶ ὅτι ἀλλήλων ἕνεκεν γεγόναμεν· καὶ
καθ' ἕτερον λόγον προστησόμενος αὐτῶν γέγονα,
ὡς κριὸς ποίμνης ἢ ταῦρος ἀγέλης. ἄνωθεν δὲ
ἔπιθι ἀπὸ τοῦ, εἰ μὴ ἄτομοι, φύσις ἡ τὰ ὅλα
διοικοῦσα· εἰ τοῦτο, τὰ χείρονα τῶν κρειττόνων
ἕνεκεν, ταῦτα δὲ ἀλλήλων.

2 Δεύτερον δέ, ὁποῖοί τινές εἰσιν ἐπὶ τῆς
τραπέζης, ἐν τῷ κλιναρίῳ, τἄλλα· μάλιστα δέ, οἵας
ἀνάγκας δογμάτων κειμένας ἔχουσιν, κα˙ αὐτὰ δὲ
ταῦτα μεθ' οἵου τύφου ποιοῦσιν.

3 Τρίτον, ὅτι, εἰ μὲν ὀρθῶς ταῦτα ποιοῦσιν, οὐ
δεῖ δυσχεραίνειν· εἰ δ' οὐκ ὀρθῶς, δηλονότι
ἄκοντες καὶ ἀγνοοῦντες. πᾶσα γὰρ ψυχὴ ἄκουσα
στέρεται, ὥσπερ τοῦ ἀληθοῦς, οὕτως καὶ τοῦ
κατ' ἀξίαν ἑκάστῳ προσφέρεσθαι. ἄχθονται
γοῦν ἀκούοντες ἄδικοι καὶ ἀγνώμονες καὶ πλεον-
έκται καὶ καθάπαξ ἁμαρτητικοὶ περὶ τοὺς
πλησίον.

4 Τέταρτον, ὅτι καὶ αὐτὸς πολλὰ ἁμαρτάνεις, καὶ
ἄλλος τοιοῦτος εἶ· καὶ εἴ τινων δὲ ἁμαρτημάτων
ἀπέχῃ, ἀλλὰ τήν γε ἕξιν ποιητικὴν[2] ἔχεις, εἰ
καὶ διὰ δειλίαν ἢ δοξοκοπίαν ἢ τοιοῦτό τι κακὸν
ἀπέχῃ τῶν ὁμοίων ἁμαρτημάτων.

---

[1] καὶ PA = κ(εφαλαι)α' Rend., but cp. vii. 51.   [2] ἐποιστικὴν A.

[1] iii. 11.   [2] v. 16, 30 ; viii. 27.   [3] viii. 56, 59.
[4] Dio Chrys. Orat. ii. de Regno, 97 R, ὁ δὲ ταῦρος σαφῶς
πρὸς βασιλέως εἰκόνα πεποίηται.   Epict. i. 2, § 30.

BOOK XI

17. Think whence each thing has come, of what it is built up,[1] into what it changes, what it will be when changed, and that it cannot take any harm.

18. *Firstly:* Consider thy relation[2] to mankind and that we came into the world for the sake of one another[3]; and taking another point of view, that I have come into it to be set over men, as a ram over a flock or a bull over a herd.[4] Start at the beginning from this premiss: If not atoms,[5] then an all-controlling Nature. If the latter, then the lower are for the sake of the higher and the higher for one another.[6]

Secondly: What sort of men they are at board and in bed and elsewhere.[7] Above all how they are the self-made slaves of their principles, and how they pride themselves on the very acts in question.

Thirdly: That if they are acting rightly in this, there is no call for us to be angry. If not rightly, it is obviously against their will and through ignorance.[8] For it is against his will that every soul is deprived, as of truth, so too of the power of dealing with each man as is his due. At any rate, such men resent being called unjust, unfeeling, avaricious, and in a word doers of wrong to their neighbours.

Fourthly: That thou too doest many a wrong thing thyself and art much as others are,[9] and if thou dost refrain from certain wrong-doings, yet hast thou a disposition inclinable thereto[10] even supposing that through cowardice or a regard for thy good name or some such base consideration thou dost not actually commit them.

[5] iv. 3, § 2; viii. 17; ix. 39; x. 6.
[6] ii. 1; v. 16. [7] viii. 14; x. 19.
[8] ii. 1; iv. 3; vii. 22, 63.
[9] vii. 70; x. 30. [10] i. 17 *ad init.*

5 Πέμπτον, ὅτι οὐδέ, εἰ ἁμαρτάνουσι, κατείλ-
ηφας· πολλὰ γὰρ καὶ κατ᾽ οἰκονομίαν γίνεται.
καὶ ὅλως πολλὰ δεῖ πρότερον μαθεῖν, ἵνα τις
περὶ ἀλλοτρίας πράξεως καταληπτικῶς τι
ἀποφήνηται.

6 Ἕκτον, ὅτι, ὅταν λίαν ἀγανακτῇς ἢ καὶ
δυσπαθῇς, ἀκαριαῖος ὁ ἀνθρώπειος βίος καὶ μετ᾽
ὀλίγον πάντες ἐξετάθημεν.

7 Ἕβδομον, ὅτι οὐχ αἱ πράξεις αὐτῶν ἐνοχλοῦσ-
ιν ἡμῖν· ἐκεῖναι γάρ εἰσιν ἐν τοῖς ἐκείνων
ἡγεμονικοῖς· ἀλλὰ αἱ ἡμέτεραι ὑπολήψεις. ἆρον
γοῦν καὶ θέλησον ἀφεῖναι τὴν ὡς περὶ δεινοῦ
κρίσιν, καὶ ἀπῆλθεν ἡ ὀργή. πῶς οὖν ἀρεῖς;
λογισάμενος, ὅτι οὐκ αἰσχρόν· ἐὰν γὰρ μὴ
μόνον ᾖ τὸ αἰσχρὸν κακόν, ἀνάγκη καὶ σὲ
πολλὰ ἁμαρτάνειν καὶ λῃστὴν καὶ παντοῖον
γενέσθαι.

8 Ὄγδοον, ὅσῳ χαλεπώτερα ἐπιφέρουσιν αἱ
ὀργαὶ καὶ λῦπαι αἱ ἐπὶ τοῖς τοιούτοις, ἤπερ
αὐτά ἐστιν, ἐφ᾽ οἷς ὀργιζόμεθα καὶ λυπούμεθα.

9 Ἔννατον, ὅτι τὸ εὐμενὲς ἀνίκητον, ἐὰν γνήσιον
ᾖ καὶ μὴ σεσηρὸς μηδὲ ὑπόκρισις. τί γάρ σοι
ποιήσει ὁ ὑβριστικώτατος, ἐὰν διατελῇς εὐμενὴς
αὐτῷ καί, εἰ οὕτως ἔτυχε, πρᾴως παραινῇς καὶ
μεταδιδάσκῃς εὐσχολῶν παρ᾽ αὐτὸν ἐκεῖνον τὸν
καιρόν, ὅτε κακὰ ποιεῖν σε ἐπιχειρεῖ· "Μή,
τέκνον· πρὸς ἄλλο πεφύκαμεν. ἐγὼ μὲν οὐ μὴ

---

[1] Or, "with an eye to circumstances," "with some further
end in view," knowledge of which would justify the action or
shew its necessity.
[2] ix. 38.   [3] vii. 16 ; viii. 40 ; ix. 13 ; xi. 11, 16.
[4] vii. 16.   [5] x. 10.

BOOK XI

Fifthly: That thou hast not even proved that they are doing wrong, for many things are done even ' by way of policy.' [1] Speaking generally a man must know many things before he can pronounce an adequate opinion on the acts of another.

Sixthly: When thou art above measure angry or even out of patience, bethink thee that man's life is momentary, and in a little while we shall all have been laid out. [2]

Seventhly: That in reality it is not the acts men do that vex us—for they belong to the domain of *their* ruling Reason—but the opinions we form of those acts. [3] Eradicate these, be ready to discard thy conclusion that the act in question is a calamity, and thine anger is at an end. [4] How then eradicate these opinions? By realizing that no act of another debases us. For unless that alone which debases is an evil, thou too must perforce do many a wrong thing and become a brigand [5] or any sort of man.

Eighthly: Bethink thee how much more grievous are the consequences of our anger and vexation at such actions than are the acts themselves which arouse that anger and vexation.

Ninthly: That kindness is irresistible, [6] be it but sincere and no mock smile or a mask assumed. For what can the most unconscionable of men do to thee, if thou persist in being kindly to him, and when a chance is given exhort him mildly and, at the very time when he is trying to do thee harm, quietly teach him a better way [7] thus: *Nay, my child, we have been made for other things. I shall be in*

---

[6] Sen. *de Ben.* vii. 31 : *vincit malos pertinax bonitas.*
[7] v. 28 ; vi. 27 ; viii. 59 ; x. 4 ; xi. 13.

βλαβῶ, σὺ δὲ βλάπτῃ, τέκνον." καὶ δεικνύναι
εὐαφῶς καὶ ὁλικῶς, ὅτι τοῦτο οὕτως ἔχει,
ὅτι οὐδὲ μέλισσαι αὐτὸ ποιοῦσιν οὐδ' ὅσα
συναγελαστικὰ πέφυκεν. δεῖ δὲ μήτε εἰρωνικῶς
αὐτὸ ποιεῖν μήτε ὀνειδιστικῶς, ἀλλὰ φιλο-
στόργως καὶ ἀδήκτως τῇ ψυχῇ· καὶ μὴ ὡς ἐν
σχολῇ, μηδὲ ἵνα ἄλλος παραστὰς θαυμάσῃ· ἀλλ'
ἤτοι[1] πρὸς μόνον, καὶ ἐὰν ἄλλοι τινὲς περιεστήκ-
ωσιν.

10 Τούτων τῶν ἐννέα κεφαλαίων μέμνησο, ὡς
παρὰ τῶν Μουσῶν δῶρα εἰληφώς· καὶ ἄρξαι
ποτὲ ἄνθρωπος εἶναι, ἕως ζῇς. φυλακτέον δὲ
ἐπίσης τῷ ὀργίζεσθαι αὐτοῖς τὸ κολακεύειν
αὐτούς· ἀμφότερα γὰρ ἀκοινώνητα καὶ πρὸς
βλάβην φέρει. πρόχειρον δὲ ἐν ταῖς ὀργαῖς,
ὅτι οὐχὶ τὸ θυμοῦσθαι ἀνδρικόν, ἀλλὰ τὸ πρᾷον
καὶ ἥμερον, ὥσπερ ἀνθρωπικώτερον, οὕτως καὶ
ἀρρενικώτερον, καὶ ἰσχύος καὶ νεύρων καὶ ἀνδρείας τούτῳ μέτεστιν, οὐχὶ τῷ ἀγανακτοῦντι καὶ
δυσαρεστοῦντι. ὅσῳ γὰρ ἀπαθείᾳ τοῦτο οἰκειότερον, τοσούτῳ καὶ δυνάμει. ὥσπερ τε ἡ λύπη
ἀσθενοῦς, οὕτως καὶ ἡ ὀργή. ἀμφότεροι γὰρ
τέτρωνται καὶ ἐνδεδώκασιν.

11 Εἰ δὲ βούλει, καὶ δέκατον παρὰ τοῦ Μουσηγέ-
του δῶρον λάβε, ὅτι τὸ μὴ ἀξιοῦν ἁμαρτάνειν
τοὺς φαύλους μανικόν· ἀδυνάτου γὰρ ἐφίεται.
τὸ δὲ συγχωρεῖν ἄλλοις μὲν εἶναι τοιούτους,
ἀξιοῦν δέ, μὴ εἰς σὲ ἁμαρτάνειν, ἄγνωμον καὶ
τυραννικόν.

---

[1] ἤ τοι Fournier.

[1] ix. 4. [2] xi. 13.
[3] cp. Dio 71. 3, § 4. [4] iv. 31.

no wise harmed, but thou art harming thyself,[1] *my child.* Shew him delicately and without any personal reference that this is so, and that even honey-bees do not act thus nor any creatures of gregarious instincts. But thou must do this not in irony[2] or by way of rebuke, but with kindly affection and without any bitterness at heart, not as from a master's chair, nor yet to impress the bystanders, but as if he were indeed alone even though others are present.

Bethink thee then of these nine heads, taking them as a gift from the Muses, and begin at last to be a *man* while life is thine. But beware of flattering[3] men no less than being angry with them.[4] For both these are non-social and conducive of harm. In temptations to anger a precept ready to thy hand is this : to be wroth is not manly, but a mild and gentle disposition, as it is more human, so it is more masculine. Such a man, and not he who gives way to anger and discontent, is endowed with strength and sinews and manly courage. For the nearer such a mind attains to a passive calm,[5] the nearer is the man to strength. As grief is a weakness, so also is anger. In both it is a case of a wound and a surrender.

But take if thou wilt as a tenth gift from Apollo, the Leader of the Muses, this, that to expect the bad not to do wrong is worthy of a madman ; for that is to wish for impossibilities.[6] But to acquiesce in their wronging others, while expecting them to refrain from wronging thee, is unfeeling and despotic.[7]

---

[5] The Stoic ἀπάθεια. [6] v. 17 ; vii. 71 ; ix. 42.
[7] vi. 27 ; Sen. *de Ira* ii. 31. ἀγνώμον might also be translated *senseless*.

ιθ΄. Τέσσαρας μάλιστα τροπὰς τοῦ ἡγεμονικοῦ
παραφυλακτέον διηνεκῶς καί, ἐπειδὰν φωράσ-
ῃς, ἀπαλειπτέον ἐπιλέγοντα ἐφ᾽ ἑκάστου οὕτως·
"Τοῦτο τὸ φάντασμα οὐκ ἀναγκαῖον· τοῦτο
λυτικὸν κοινωνίας· τοῦτο οὐκ ἀπὸ σαυτοῦ μέλλεις
λέγειν." τὸ γὰρ μὴ ἀφ᾽ ἑαυτοῦ λέγειν ἐν τοῖς
ἀτοπωτάτοις νόμιζε. τέταρτον δέ ἐστι, καθ᾽ ὃ
σεαυτῷ ὀνειδιεῖς, ὅτι τοῦτο ἡττωμένου ἐστὶ καὶ
ὑποκατακλινομένου τοῦ ἐν σοὶ θειοτέρου μέρους τῇ
ἀτιμοτέρᾳ καὶ θνητῇ μοίρᾳ τῇ τοῦ σώματος, καὶ
ταῖς τούτου παχείαις ἰδέαις.[1]

κ΄. Τὸ μὲν πνευμάτιόν[2] σου καὶ τὸ πυρῶδες
πᾶν, ὅσον ἐγκέκραται, καίτοι φύσει ἀνωφερῆ
ὄντα, ὅμως πειθόμενα τῇ τῶν ὅλων διατάξει,
παρακρατεῖται ἐνταῦθα ἐπὶ τοῦ συγκρίματος.
καὶ τὸ γεῶδες δὲ τὸ ἐν σοὶ πᾶν καὶ τὸ ὑγρόν,
καίτοι κατωφερῆ ὄντα, ὅμως ἐγήγερται καὶ
ἔστηκε τὴν οὐχ ἑαυτῶν φυσικὴν στάσιν. οὕτως
ἄρα καὶ τὰ στοιχεῖα ὑπακούει τοῖς ὅλοις,
ἐπειδάν που καταταχθῇ, σὺν βίᾳ μένοντα, μέχρις
ἂν ἐκεῖθεν πάλιν τὸ ἐνδόσιμον τῆς διαλύσεως
σημήνῃ.

2   Οὐ δεινὸν οὖν μόνον τὸ νοερόν σου μέρος
ἀπειθὲς εἶναι καὶ ἀγανακτεῖν τῇ ἑαυτοῦ χώρᾳ;
καίτοι οὐδέν γε βίαιον τούτῳ ἐπιτάσσεται, ἀλλὰ
μόνα ὅσα κατὰ φύσιν ἐστὶν αὐτῷ· οὐ μέντοι
ἀνέχεται, ἀλλὰ τὴν ἐναντίαν φέρεται. ἡ γὰρ ἐπὶ
τὰ ἀδικήματα καὶ τὰ ἀκολαστήματα καὶ τὰς
ὀργὰς καὶ τὰς λύπας καὶ τοὺς φόβους κίνησις
οὐδὲν ἄλλο ἐστὶν ἢ ἀφισταμένου τῆς φύσεως.

---

[1] ἡδοναῖς P.   [2] Perhaps πνευματικόν, cp. iv. 4, see Index iii.

19. Against four perversions of the ruling Reason thou shouldest above all keep unceasing watch, and, once detected, wholly abjure them,[1] saying in each case to thyself: *This thought is not necessary;*[2] *this is destructive of human fellowship; this could be no genuine utterance from the heart.*—And not to speak from the heart, what is it but a contradiction in terms?—The fourth case is that of self-reproach,[3] for that is an admission that the divine part of thee has been worsted by and acknowledges its inferiority to the body, the baser and mortal partner, and to its gross notions.

20. Thy soul and all the fiery part that is blended with thee, though by Nature ascensive, yet in submission to the system of the Universe are held fast here in thy compound personality. And the entire earthy part too in thee and the humid, although naturally descensive, are yet upraised and take up a station not their natural one. Thus indeed we find the elements also in subjection to the Whole and, when set anywhere, remaining there under constraint until the signal sound for their release again therefrom.

Is it not then a paradox that the intelligent part alone of thee should be rebellious and quarrel with its station? Yet is no constraint laid upon it but only so much as is in accordance with its nature. Howbeit it does not comply and takes a contrary course. For every motion towards acts of injustice and licentiousness, towards anger and grief and fear, but betokens one who cuts himself adrift from Nature. Aye

---

[1] xi. 16. [2] iv. 24.
[3] v. 36; viii. 10. *cp.* Fronto, *ad Caes.* iv. 13, where Marcus reproaches himself when 19 years old for backwardness in philosophy.

καὶ ὅταν δέ τινι τῶν συμβαινόντων δυσχεραίνῃ
τὸ ἡγεμονικόν, καταλείπει καὶ τότε τὴν ἑαυτοῦ
χώραν. πρὸς ὁσιότητα[1] γὰρ καὶ θεοσέβειαν
κατεσκεύασται οὐχ ἧττον ἢ πρὸς δικαιοσύνην.
καὶ γὰρ ταῦτα ἐν εἴδει ἐστὶ τῆς εὐκοινωνησίας,
μᾶλλον δὲ πρεσβύτερα τῶν δικαιοπραγημά-
των.

κα΄. Ὧι μὴ εἷς καὶ ὁ αὐτός ἐστιν ἀεὶ τοῦ βίου
σκοπός, οὗτος εἷς καὶ ὁ αὐτὸς δι᾽ ὅλου τοῦ βίου
εἶναι οὐ δύναται. οὐκ ἀρκεῖ <δὲ> τὸ εἰρημένον,
ἐὰν μὴ κἀκεῖνο προσθῇς, ὁποῖον εἶναι δεῖ τοῦτον
τὸν σκοπόν. ὥσπερ γὰρ οὐχ ἡ πάντων τῶν
ὁπωσοῦν <τοῖς> πλείοσι δοκούντων ἀγαθῶν
ὑπόληψις ὁμοία ἐστίν, ἀλλ᾽ ἡ τῶν τοιῶνδέ τινων,
τουτέστι τῶν κοινῶν, οὕτω καὶ τὸν σκοπὸν δεῖ
τὸν κοινωνικὸν καὶ πολιτικὸν ὑποστήσασθαι. ὁ
γὰρ εἰς τοῦτον πάσας τὰς ἰδίας ὁρμὰς ἀπευθύνων
πάσας τὰς πράξεις ὁμοίας ἀποδώσει καὶ κατὰ
τοῦτο ἀεὶ ὁ αὐτὸς ἔσται.

κβ΄. Τὸν μῦν τὸν ὀρεινὸν καὶ τὸν κατοικίδιον[2]
καὶ τὴν πτοίαν τούτου καὶ διασόβησιν.

κγ΄. Σωκράτης καὶ τὰ τῶν πολλῶν δόγματα
Λαμίας ἐκάλει, παιδίων δείματα.

κδ΄. Λακεδαιμόνιοι τοῖς μὲν ξένοις ἐν ταῖς
θεωρίαις ὑπὸ τῇ σκιᾷ τὰ βάθρα ἐτίθεσαν, αὐτοὶ
δέ, οὗ ἔτυχον, ἐκαθέζοντο.

---

[1] ἰσότητα PA: em. Cas.
[2] ὀρεινὸν and κατοικίδιον require transposing to give τούτου
its correct meaning.

---

[1] xi. 9.
[2] xii. 2.   ὁσιότης = δικαιοσύνη πρὸς θεούς, see Stob. Ecl.
ii. 104.   [3] But cp. xi. 10.

and when the ruling Reason in a man is vexed at anything that befalls, at that very moment it deserts its station.[1] For it was not made for justice alone, but also for piety[2] and the service of God. And in fact the latter are included under the idea of a true fellowship, and indeed are prior to the practice of justice.[3]

21. He who has not ever in view one and the same goal of life cannot be throughout his life one and the same.[4] Nor does that which is stated suffice, there needs to be added what that goal should be. For just as opinion as to all the things that in one way or another are held by the mass of men to be good is not uniform, but only as to certain things, such, that is, as affect the common weal, so must we set before ourselves as our goal the common and civic weal. For he who directs all his individual impulses towards this goal will render his actions homogeneous and thereby be ever consistent with himself.[5]

22. Do not forget the story of the town mouse and the country mouse, and the excitement and trepidation of the latter.[6]

23. Socrates used to nickname the opinions of the multitude *Ghouls*,[7] bogies to terrify children.

24. The Spartans at their spectacles assigned to strangers seats in the shade, but themselves took their chance of seats anywhere.

---

[4] *cp.* Dio 71. 34, § 5: ὅμοιος διὰ πάντων ἐγένετο καὶ ἐν οὐδένι ἠλλοιώθη: Aristides *ad Reg.* § 113 (Jebb), says he was ὁ αὐτὸς διὰ τέλους.   [5] i. 8.   [6] Aesop, *Fab.* 297; Hor. *Sat.* ii. 6 ff.   [7] *Lamiae,* or "*vampires,*" "fabulous monsters said to feed on human flesh," Hor. *A.P.* 540; Apul. *Met.* i. 57. *cp.* Epict. ii. 1, § 14: ταῦτα Σωκράτης μορμολυκεῖα ἐκάλει: Philostr. *Vit. Apoll.* iv. 25, whence Keats took his *Lamia.*

κε΄. Τῷ Περδίκκᾳ ὁ Σωκράτης περὶ τοῦ μὴ ἔρχεσθαι παρ' αὐτὸν· "Ἵνα," ἔφη, "μὴ τῷ κακίστῳ ὀλέθρῳ ἀπόλωμαι," τουτέστι, μὴ εὖ παθὼν οὐ δυνηθῶ ἀντευποιῆσαι.

κϛ΄. Ἐν τοῖς τῶν Ἐφεσίων[1] γράμμασι παράγγελμα ἔκειτο συνεχῶς ὑπομιμνήσκεσθαι τῶν παλαιῶν τινος τῶν ἀρετῇ χρησαμένων.

κζ΄. Οἱ Πυθαγόρειοι ἔωθεν εἰς τὸν οὐρανὸν ἀφορᾶν, ἵν' ὑπομιμνησκώμεθα τῶν ἀεὶ κατὰ τὰ αὐτὰ καὶ ὡσαύτως τὸ ἑαυτῶν ἔργον διανυόντων καὶ τῆς τάξεως καὶ τῆς καθαρότητος καὶ τῆς γυμνότητος. οὐδὲν γὰρ προκάλυμμα ἄστρου.

κη΄. Οἷος ὁ Σωκράτης, τὸ κῴδιον ὑπεζωσμένος, ὅτε ἡ Ξανθίππη λαβοῦσα τὸ ἱμάτιον ἔξω προῆλθεν· καὶ ἃ εἶπεν ὁ Σωκράτης τοῖς ἑταίροις αἰδεσθεῖσι καὶ ἀναχωρήσασιν, ὅτε αὐτὸν εἶδον οὕτως ἐσταλμένον.

κθ΄. Ἐν τῷ γράφειν καὶ ἀναγινώσκειν οὐ πρότερον ἄρξεις, πρὶν ἀρχθῇς. τοῦτο πολλῷ μᾶλλον ἐν τῷ βίῳ.

λ΄. "Δοῦλος πέφυκας, οὐ μέτεστί σοι λόγου."

λα΄. "Ἐμὸν δ' ἐγέλασσε φίλον κῆρ."

λβ΄. "Μέμψονται δ' ἀρετὴν χαλεποῖς βάζοντες ἔπεσσιν."

λγ΄. "Σῦκον χειμῶνος ζητεῖν μαινομένου·

---

[1] Ἐπικουρείων Gat. (from Sen. Ep. xi). The only Ἐφεσίων γράμματα known were magical formulae.

---

[1] According to Diog. Laert. Socr. 9 ; Sen. de Ben. v. 6, § 2 ; Arist. Rhet. A. 23, this was Archelaus, son of Perdiccas.

[2] cp. Fronto, ad Appianum, Nab. p. 251.

[3] Sen. Ep. 11, attributes the precept to the Epicureans:

BOOK XI

25. Socrates refused the invitation of Perdiccas[1] to his court, *That I come not*, said he, *to a dishonoured grave*, meaning, that I be not treated with generosity and have no power to return it.[2]

26. In the writings of the Ephesians[3] was laid down the advice to have constantly in remembrance some one of the ancients who lived virtuously.

27. Look, said the Pythagoreans, at the sky in the morning, that we may have in remembrance those hosts of heaven that ever follow the same course and accomplish their work in the same way, and their orderly system, and their purity, and their nakedness; for there is no veil before a star.

28. Think of Socrates with the sheepskin wrapped round him, when Xanthippe had gone off with his coat, and what he said to his friends when they drew back in their embarrassment at seeing him thus accoutred.

29. In reading and writing thou must learn first to follow instruction before thou canst give it. Much more is this true of life.

30. *'Tis not for thee, a slave, to reason[4] why.*

31. *. . . . and within me my heart laughed.*[5]

32. *Virtue they will upbraid and speak harsh words in her hearing.*[6]

33. *Only a madman will look for figs in winter.*

---

aliquis vir bonus nobis eligendus est ac semper ante oculos habendus ut sic tanquam illo spectante vivamus et omnia illo vidente faciamus. Hoc Epicurus praecepit. See, however, Plut. *Symp.* vii. 5 *ad fin.*

[4] It is not clear whether λόγος here means *speech* or *reason* or both. The citation, of which the author is not known, has no obvious application; still less has the following quotation from Homer. [5] Hom. *Od.* ix. 413.

[6] Hes. *Op.* 185, where the reading is ἄρα τοῖς for ἀρετήν.

τοιοῦτος ὁ τὸ παιδίον ζητῶν, ὅτε οὐκ ἔτι δίδοται."

λδ΄. "Καταφιλοῦντα τὸ παιδίον δεῖν," ἔλεγεν ὁ Ἐπίκτητος, "ἔνδον ἐπιφθέγγεσθαι· Αὔριον ἴσως ἀποθανῇ." δύσφημα ταῦτα· "Οὐδὲν δύσφημον," ἔφη, "ἀλλὰ ¹ φυσικοῦ τινος ἔργου σημαντικόν. ἢ καὶ τὸ τοὺς στάχυας θερισθῆναι δύσφημον."

λε΄. Ὄμφαξ, σταφυλή, σταφίς, πάντα μεταβολαί, οὐκ εἰς τὸ μὴ ὄν, ἀλλ᾽ εἰς τὸ νῦν μὴ ὄν.

λϛ΄. "Λῃστὴς προαιρέσεως οὐ γίνεται" τὸ τοῦ Ἐπικτήτου.

λζ΄. "Τέχνην δὲ," ἔφη,² "περὶ τὸ συγκατατίθεσθαι εὑρεῖν, καὶ ἐν τῷ περὶ τὰς ὁρμὰς τόπῳ τὸ προσεκτικὸν φυλάσσειν, ἵνα μεθ᾽ ὑπεξαιρέσεως, ἵνα κοινωνικαί, ἵνα κατ᾽ ἀξίαν· καὶ ὀρέξεως μὲν παντάπασιν ἀπέχεσθαι, ἐκκλίσει δὲ πρὸς μηδὲν τῶν οὐκ ἐφ᾽ ἡμῖν χρῆσθαι."

λη΄. "Οὐ περὶ τοῦ τυχόντος οὖν," ἔφη, "ἐστὶν ὁ ἀγών, ἀλλὰ περὶ τοῦ μαίνεσθαι ἢ μή."

λθ΄. Ὁ Σωκράτης ἔλεγε· "Τί θέλετε; λογικῶν ψυχὰς ἔχειν ἢ ἀλόγων; Λογικῶν. Τίνων λογικῶν; ὑγιῶν ἢ φαύλων; Ὑγιῶν. Τί οὖν οὐ ζητεῖτε; Ὅτι ἔχομεν. Τί οὖν μάχεσθε καὶ διαφέρεσθε;"

---

¹ ἀλλὰ omit P : perhaps ὄνομα from Epict. iii. 24, § 91.
² ἔφη δὲ A : δεῖ Kron.

---

¹ Epict. iii. 24, § 86 quoted, not *verbatim*.
² *ibid.* iii. 24, § 88.   ³ Epict. iii. 24, § 91.
⁴ *ibid.* iii. 22, § 105.

BOOK XI

No better is he who looks for a child when he may no longer have one.[1]

34. *A man while fondly kissing his child,* says Epictetus, *should whisper in his heart*[2]: *'To-morrow peradventure thou wilt die.'* Ill-omened words these! *Nay,* said he, *nothing is ill-omened that signifies a natural process. Or it is ill-omened also to talk of ears of corn being reaped.*

35. The grape unripe, mellow, dried—in every stage we have a change, not into non-existence, but into the not now existent.[3]

36. Hear Epictetus: *no one can rob us of our free choice.*[4]

37. *We must,* says he,[5] *hit upon the true science of assent and in the sphere of our impulses pay good heed that they be subject to proper reservations;*[6] *that they have in view our neighbour's welfare; that they are proportionate to worth. And we must abstain wholly from inordinate desire and shew avoidance in none of the things that are not in our control.*

38. *It is no casual matter, then,* said he, *that is at stake, but whether we are to be sane or no.*[7]

39. Socrates was wont to say:[8] *What would ye have? The souls of reasoning or unreasoning creatures? Of reasoning creatures. Of what kind of reasoning creatures? Sound or vicious? Sound. Why then not make a shift to get them? Because we have them already. Why then fight and wrangle?*

[5] *i.e.* Epictetus. cp. iii. 22, § 105, and *Manual*, ii. 2.
[6] iv. 1; v. 20; vi. 50; *i.e. not unconditionally,* but subject to modification by circumstances.
[7] Epict. i. 22, §§ 17–21; Hor. *Sat.* ii. 3. 43.
[8] Only found here.

BIBΛION IB

α΄. Πάντα ἐκεῖνα, ἐφ᾽ ἃ διὰ περιόδου εὔχῃ
ἐλθεῖν, ἤδη ἔχειν δύνασαι, ἐὰν μὴ σαυτῷ φθονῇς.
τοῦτο δέ ἐστιν, ἐὰν πᾶν τὸ παρελθὸν καταλίπῃς
καὶ τὸ μέλλον ἐπιτρέψῃς τῇ προνοίᾳ καὶ τὸ παρὸν
μόνον ἀπευθύνῃς πρὸς ὁσιότητα καὶ δικαιοσύνην.
ὁσιότητα μέν, ἵνα φιλῇς τὸ ἀπονεμόμενον· σοὶ γὰρ
αὐτὸ ἡ φύσις ἔφερε καὶ σὲ τούτῳ. δικαιοσύνην
δέ, ἵνα ἐλευθέρως καὶ χωρὶς περιπλοκῆς λέγῃς
τε τἀληθῆ καὶ πράσσῃς τὰ κατὰ νόμον καὶ
κατ᾽ ἀξίαν· μὴ ἐμποδίζῃ δέ σε μήτε κακία
ἀλλοτρία μήτε ὑπόληψις μήτε φωνὴ μηδὲ μὴν
αἴσθησις τοῦ περιτεθραμμένου σοι σαρκιδίου·
ὄψεται γὰρ τὸ πάσχον.

2   Ἐὰν οὖν, ὁτεδήποτε πρὸς ἐξόδῳ γένῃ, πάντα
τὰ ἄλλα καταλιπὼν μόνον τὸ ἡγεμονικόν σου
καὶ τὸ ἐν σοὶ θεῖον τιμήσῃς, καὶ μὴ τὸ παύσεσθαί
ποτε <τοῦ> ζῆν φοβηθῇς, ἀλλὰ τό γε μηδέποτε
ἄρξασθαι κατὰ φύσιν ζῆν, ἔσῃ ἄνθρωπος ἄξιος
τοῦ γεννήσαντος κόσμου καὶ παύσῃ ξένος ὢν τῆς
πατρίδος καὶ θαυμάζων ὡς ἀπροσδόκητα τὰ καθ᾽

---

[1] x. 33 ; Hor. *Ep.* i. 11 *ad fin.*

BOOK XII

1. All those things, which thou prayest to attain by a roundabout way, thou canst have at once if thou deny them not to thyself[1]; that is to say, if thou leave all the Past to itself and entrust the Future to Providence,[2] and but direct the Present in the way of piety and justice: piety, that thou mayest love thy lot, for Nature brought it to thee and thee to it; justice, that thou mayest speak the truth freely and without finesse, and have an eye to law and the due worth of things[3] in all that thou doest; and let nothing stand in thy way, not the wickedness of others, nor thine own opinion, nor what men say, nor even the sensations of the flesh that has grown around thee[4]; for the part affected will see to that.

If then, when the time of thy departure is near, abandoning all else thou prize thy ruling Reason alone and that which in thee is divine,[5] and dread the thought, not that thou must one day cease to live, but that thou shouldst never yet have begun to live according to Nature, then shalt thou be a man worthy of the Universe that begat thee, and no longer an alien[6] in thy fatherland, no longer shalt thou marvel at what happens every day as if it

[2] vii. 8; St. Matt. vi. 34.   [3] xi. 37 (Epictetus).
[4] vii. 68.   [5] xii. 26.   [6] iv. 29; xii. 13.

ἡμέραν γινόμενα καὶ κρεμάμενος ἐκ τοῦδε καὶ
τοῦδε.

β΄. Ὁ θεὸς πάντα τὰ ἡγεμονικὰ γυμνὰ τῶν
ὑλικῶν ἀγγείων καὶ φλοιῶν καὶ καθαρμάτων[1]
ὁρᾷ. μόνῳ γὰρ τῷ ἑαυτοῦ νοερῷ μόνων ἅπτεται
τῶν ἐξ ἑαυτοῦ εἰς ταῦτα ἐρρυηκότων καὶ ἀπωχετ-
ευμένων. ἐὰν δὲ καὶ σὺ τοῦτο ἐθίσῃς ποιεῖν,
τὸν πολὺν περισπασμὸν σεαυτοῦ περιαιρήσεις.
ὁ γὰρ μὴ τὰ περικείμενα κρεᾴδια ὁρῶν ἦπου γε
ἐσθῆτα καὶ οἰκίαν καὶ δόξαν καὶ τὴν τοιαύτην
περιβολὴν καὶ σκηνὴν θεώμενος ἀσχολήσεται;

γ΄. Τρία ἐστίν, ἐξ ὧν συνέστηκας· σωμάτιον,
πνευμάτιον, νοῦς. τούτων τἆλλα μέχρι τοῦ
ἐπιμελεῖσθαι δεῖν σά ἐστι· τὸ δὲ τρίτον μόνον
κυρίως σόν. καὶ ἐὰν[2] χωρίσῃς ἀπὸ σεαυτοῦ,
τουτέστιν ἀπὸ τῆς σῆς διανοίας, ὅσα ἄλλοι
ποιοῦσιν ἢ λέγουσιν ἢ ὅσα αὐτὸς ἐποίησας ἢ
εἶπας, καὶ ὅσα ὡς μέλλοντα ταράσσει σε, καὶ ὅσα
τοῦ περικειμένου σοι σωματίου ἢ τοῦ συμφύτου
πνευματίου ἀπροαίρετα πρόσεστιν, καὶ ὅσα ἡ
ἔξωθεν περιρρέουσα δίνη ἑλίσσει, ὥστε τῶν
συνειμαρμένων ἐξηρημένην <καὶ> καθαρὰν τὴν
νοερὰν δύναμιν ἀπόλυτον ἐφ' ἑαυτῆς ζῆν ποιοῦσαν τὰ δίκαια καὶ θέλουσαν τὰ συμβαίνοντα
καὶ λέγουσαν τἀληθῆ—ἐὰν χωρίσῃς, φημί, τοῦ
ἡγεμονικοῦ τούτου τὰ προσηρτημένα ἐκ προσ-
παθείας καὶ τοῦ χρόνου τὰ ἐπέκεινα ἢ

---

[1] I should prefer καλυμμάτων.
[2] διὸ ἐὰν Gat.: καὶ ἐὰν Stich.: ὃ ἐὰν PA.

were unforeseen, and be dependent on this or that.

2. God sees the Ruling Parts of all men stripped of material vessels and husks and sloughs. For only with the Intellectual Part of Himself is He in touch with those emanations only which have welled forth and been drawn off from Himself into them. But if thou also wilt accustom thyself to do this, thou wilt free thyself from the most of thy distracting care. For he that hath no eye for the flesh that envelopes him will not, I trow, waste his time with taking thought for raiment and lodging and popularity and such accessories and frippery.[1]

3. Thou art formed of three things in combination —body, vital breath, intelligence.[2] Of these the first two are indeed thine, in so far as thou must have them in thy keeping, but the third alone is in any true sense thine.[3] Wherefore, if thou cut off from thyself, that is from thy mind, all that others do or say and all that thyself hast done or said, and all that harasses thee in the future, or whatever thou art involved in independently of thy will by the body which envelopes thee and the breath that is twinned with it, and whatever the circumambient rotation outside of thee sweeps along, so that thine intellectual faculty, delivered from the contingencies of destiny, may live pure and undetached by itself, doing what is just, desiring what befalls it, speaking the truth—if, I say, thou strip from this ruling Reason all that cleaves to it from the bodily influences and the things that lie beyond in time and

---

[1] Lit. *stage-scenery;* cp. Sen. *ad Marc.* 10.
[2] ii. 2; iii. 16. Here $\pi\nu\epsilon\nu\mu\acute{a}\tau\iota\sigma\nu = \psi\upsilon\chi\grave{\eta}$ (soul) in its lower sense, see Index III. [3] x. 38.

τὰ παρῳχηκότα ποιήσῃς τε σεαυτόν, οἷος ὁ
Ἐμπεδόκλειος

"Σφαῖρος κυκλοτερής, μονίῃ¹ περιηγέι γαίων,"

μόνον τε ζῆν ἐκμελετήσῃς, ὃ ζῇς, τουτέστι τὸ
παρόν, δυνήσῃ τό γε μέχρι τοῦ ἀποθανεῖν ὑπολειπόμενον ἀταράκτως καὶ εὐμενῶς² καὶ ἵλεως τῷ
σαυτοῦ δαίμονι διαβιῶναι.

δ΄. Πολλάκις ἐθαύμασα, πῶς ἑαυτὸν μὲν
ἕκαστος μᾶλλον πάντων φιλεῖ, τὴν δὲ ἑαυτοῦ
περὶ αὑτοῦ ὑπόληψιν ἐν ἐλάττονι λόγῳ τίθεται ἢ
τὴν τῶν ἄλλων. ἐὰν γοῦν τινα θεὸς ἐπιστὰς ἢ
διδάσκαλος ἔμφρων κελεύσῃ, μηδὲν καθ᾽ ἑαυτὸν
ἐνθυμεῖσθαι καὶ διανοεῖσθαι, ὃ μὴ ἅμα καὶ
γεγωνίσκων ἐξοίσει, οὐδὲ πρὸς μίαν ἡμέραν
τοῦτο ὑπομενεῖ. οὕτω τοὺς πέλας μᾶλλον
αἰδούμεθα, τί ποτε περὶ ἡμῶν φρονήσουσιν, ἢ
ἑαυτούς.

ε΄. Πῶς ποτε πάντα καλῶς καὶ φιλανθρώπως
διατάξαντες οἱ θεοί, τοῦτο μόνον παρεῖδον, τὸ
ἐνίους τῶν ἀνθρώπων, καὶ πάνυ χρηστοὺς καὶ
πλεῖστα πρὸς τὸ θεῖον ὥσπερ συμβόλαια θεμέ-
νους, καὶ ἐπὶ πλεῖστον δι᾽ ἔργων ὁσίων καὶ
ἱερουργιῶν συνήθεις τῷ θείῳ γενομένους, ἐπειδὰν
ἅπαξ ἀποθάνωσι, μηκέτι αὖθις γίνεσθαι, ἀλλ᾽ εἰς
τὸ παντελὲς ἀπεσβηκέναι; τοῦτο δὲ εἴπερ ἄρα
καὶ οὕτως ἔχει, εὖ ἴσθι, ὅτι, εἰ ὡς ἑτέρως ἔχειν
ἔδει, ἐποίησαν ἄν. εἰ γὰρ δίκαιον ἦν, ἦν ἂν καὶ
δυνατόν, καὶ εἰ κατὰ φύσιν, ἤνεγκεν ἂν αὐτὸ ἡ

_____
¹ μονῇ A : κονῇ P : κώνῃ Cor. : μονίῃ Peyron. : περιηθεῖ PA :
περιηγέι Cor.
² εὐμενῶς Reiske : εὐγενῶς PA.

the things that are past, and if thou fashion thyself
like the Empedoclean

*Sphere to its circle true in its poise well-rounded
rejoicing,*[1]

and school thyself to live that life only which is
thine, namely the present, so shalt thou be able
to pass through the remnant of thy days calmly,
kindly, and at peace with thine own 'genius.'[2]

4. Often have I marvelled how each one of us
loves himself above all men, yet sets less store by his
own opinion of himself than by that of everyone else.
At any rate, if a God or some wise teacher should come
to a man and charge him to admit no thought or
design into his mind that he could not utter aloud
as soon as conceived,[3] he could not endure this
ordinance for a single day. So it is clear that we
pay more deference to the opinion our neighbours
will have of us than to our own.

5. How can the Gods, after disposing all things
well and with good will towards men, ever have overlooked this one thing, that some of mankind, and
they especially good men, who have had as it were the
closest commerce with the Divine, and by devout
conduct and acts of worship have been in the most
intimate fellowship with it, should when once dead
have no second existence but be wholly extinguished?[4]
But if indeed this be haply so, doubt not that
they would have ordained it otherwise, had it needed
to be otherwise. For had it been just, it would
also have been feasible, and had it been in conformity
with Nature, Nature would have brought it about.

[1] viii. 41; xi. 12. *cp.* Hor. *Sat.* ii. 7, 95: *in seipso totus
teres atque rotundus.* [2] ii. 13; iii. 5 etc. [3] iii. 4.
[4] For Marcus' views on Immortality, see Introd.

φύσις. ἐκ δὴ τοῦ μὴ οὕτως ἔχειν, εἴπερ οὐχ
οὕτως ἔχει, πιστούσθω σοι, τὸ μὴ δεῆσαι οὕτω
γίνεσθαι. ὁρᾷς γὰρ καὶ αὐτός, ὅτι τοῦτο
παραζητῶν δικαιολογῇ πρὸς τὸν θεόν· οὐκ ἂν δ᾽
οὕτω διελεγόμεθα τοῖς θεοῖς, εἰ μὴ ἄριστοι καὶ
δικαιότατοί εἰσιν. εἰ δὲ τοῦτο, οὐκ ἄν τι περιεῖδον
ἀδίκως καὶ ἀλόγως ἠμελημένον τῶν ἐν τῇ
διακοσμήσει.

ϛ΄. Ἔθιζε καὶ ὅσα ἀπογινώσκεις. καὶ γὰρ ἡ
χεὶρ ἡ ἀριστερά, πρὸς τὰ ἄλλα διὰ τὸ ἀνέθιστον
ἀργὸς οὖσα, τοῦ χαλινοῦ ἐρρωμενέστερον ἢ ἡ
δεξιὰ κρατεῖ. τοῦτο γὰρ εἴθισται.

ζ΄. Ὁποῖον δεῖ καταληφθῆναι ὑπὸ τοῦ θανάτου
καὶ σώματι καὶ ψυχῇ· τὴν βραχύτητα τοῦ βίου,
τὴν ἀχάνειαν τοῦ ὀπίσω καὶ πρόσω αἰῶνος, τὴν
ἀσθένειαν πάσης ὕλης.

η΄. Γυμνὰ τῶν φλοιῶν θεάσασθαι τὰ αἰτιώδη·
τὰς ἀναφορὰς τῶν πράξεων· τί πόνος· τί ἡδονή·
τί θάνατος· τί δόξα· τίς ὁ ἑαυτῷ ἀσχολίας αἴτιος·
πῶς οὐδεὶς ὑπ᾽ ἄλλου ἐμποδίζεται· ὅτι πάντα
ὑπόληψις.

θ΄. Ὅμοιον δ᾽ εἶναι δεῖ ἐν τῇ τῶν δογμάτων
χρήσει παγκρατιαστῇ, οὐχὶ μονομάχῳ· ὁ μὲν γὰρ
τὸ ξίφος, ᾧ χρῆται, ἀποτίθεται καὶ ἀναιρεῖται· ὁ
δὲ τὴν χεῖρα ἀεὶ ἔχει καὶ οὐδὲν ἄλλο ἢ συσ-
τρέψαι αὐτὴν δεῖ.

---

[1] cp. Job (xiii. 3), *I desire to reason with God*, where a
similar point is argued.

[2] iv. 26.   [3] iv. 50 ; v. 23 ; xii. 32.

Therefore from its not being so, if indeed it is not so, be assured that it ought not to have been so. For even thyself canst see that in this presumptuous enquiry of thine thou art reasoning with God.[1] But we should not thus be arguing with the Gods were they not infinitely good and just. But in that case they could not have overlooked anything being wrongly and irrationally neglected in their thorough Ordering of the Universe.

6. Practise that also wherein thou hast no expectation of success. For even the left hand, which for every other function is inefficient by reason of a want of practice, has yet a firmer grip of the bridle than the right. For it has had practice in this.

7. Reflect on the condition of body and soul befitting a man when overtaken by death, on the shortness of life,[2] on the yawning gulf[3] of the past and of the time to come, on the impotence of all matter.

8. Look at the principles of causation stripped of their husks; at the objective of actions; at what pain is, what pleasure, what death, what fame. See who is to blame for a man's inner unrest; how no one can be thwarted by another[4]; that nothing is but what thinking makes it.[5]

9. In our use of principles of conduct we should imitate the pancratiast not the gladiator.[6] For the latter lays aside the blade which he uses, and takes it up again, but the other always has his hand and needs only to clench it.

[4] v. 34; vii. 16.
[5] v. 2; viii. 40; xii. 22. Shak. *Ham.* ii. 2. 256 (from Montaigne).
[6] Or, *the prize-fighter not the duellist.* Some take ἀναιρεῖται to mean ' *is slain.*'

ι΄. Ποῖα¹ αὐτὰ τὰ πράγματα, ὁρᾶν διαιροῦντα
εἰς ὕλην, αἴτιον, ἀναφοράν.

ια΄. Ἡλίκην² ἐξουσίαν ἔχει ἄνθρωπος μὴ
ποιεῖν ἄλλο ἢ ὅπερ μέλλει ὁ θεὸς ἐπαινεῖν, καὶ
δέχεσθαι πᾶν, ὃ ἂν νέμῃ αὐτῷ ὁ θεός.

ιβ΄. Τὸ ἑξῆς τῇ φύσει μήτε θεοῖς μεμπτέον·
οὐδὲν γὰρ ἑκόντες ἢ ἄκοντες ἁμαρτάνουσιν· μήτε
ἀνθρώποις· οὐδὲν γὰρ οὐχὶ ἄκοντες. ὥστε
οὐδενὶ μεμπτέον.

ιγ΄. Πῶς γελοῖος καὶ ξένος ὁ θαυμάζων ὁτιοῦν
τῶν ἐν τῷ βίῳ γινομένων.

ιδ΄. Ἤτοι ἀνάγκη εἱμαρμένη <καὶ> ἀπαρά-
βατος τάξις, ἢ πρόνοια ἱλάσιμος, ἢ φυρμὸς
εἰκαιότητος ἀπροστάτητος. εἰ μὲν οὖν ἀπαρά-
βατος ἀνάγκη, τί ἀντιτείνεις; εἰ δὲ πρόνοια
ἐπιδεχομένη τὸ ἱλάσκεσθαι ἄξιον σαυτὸν ποίησον τῆς ἐκ τοῦ θείου βοηθείας. εἰ δὲ φυρμὸς
ἀνηγεμόνευτος, ἀσμένιζε, ὅτι ἐν τοιούτῳ [τῷ]
κλύδωνι αὐτὸς ἔχεις ἐν σαυτῷ τινα νοῦν ἡγεμονικόν. κἂν παραφέρῃ σε ὁ κλύδων, παραφερέτω
τὸ σαρκίδιον, τὸ πνευμάτιον, τἄλλα· τὸν γὰρ
νοῦν οὐ παροίσει. (ιε΄.) Ἡ τὸ μὲν τοῦ λύχνου
φῶς, μέχρι σβεσθῇ, φαίνει καὶ τὴν αὐγὴν οὐκ
ἀποβάλλει· ἡ δὲ ἐν σοὶ ἀλήθεια καὶ δικαιοσύνη
καὶ σωφροσύνη προαποσβήσεται;

ις΄. Ἐπὶ τοῦ φαντασίαν παρασχόντος, ὅτι
ἥμαρτεν· "Τί δαὶ οἶδα, εἰ τοῦτο ἁμάρτημα;" εἰ δὲ
καὶ ἥμαρτεν, ὅτι κατέκρινεν αὐτὸς ἑαυτὸν καὶ

¹ Gat. for τοιαῦτα : δεῖ αὐτά Reiske.
² τὸ ὑλικὴν (cp. § 18) A at end of § 10.

BOOK XII

10. See things as they really are, analyzing them into Matter, Cause, Objective.[1]

11. What a capacity Man has to do only what God shall approve and to welcome all that God assigns him!

12. Find no fault with Gods for what is the course of Nature, for they do no wrong[2] voluntarily or involuntarily; nor with men, for they do none save involuntarily.[3] Find fault then with none.[4]

13. How ludicrous is he and out of place who marvels at anything that happens in life.[5]

14. There must be either a predestined Necessity and inviolable plan, or a gracious Providence, or a chaos without design or director. If then there be an inevitable Necessity, why kick against the pricks? If a Providence that is ready to be gracious, render thyself worthy of divine succour. But if a chaos without guide, congratulate thyself that amid such a surging sea thou hast in thyself a guiding Reason. And if the surge sweep thee away, let it sweep away the poor Flesh and Breath with their appurtenances: for the Intelligence it shall never sweep away. (15.) What! shall the truth that is in thee and the justice and the temperance be extinguished ere thou art, whereas the light of a lamp shines forth and keeps its radiance until the flame be quenched?

16. Another has given thee cause to think that he has done wrong: *But how do I know that it is a wrong?*[6] And even if he be guilty, suppose that his

---

[1] viii. 11; xii. 18, 29. [2] ii. 11. [3] vii. 22 etc.
[4] Epict. *Man.* 5. [5] xii. 1. [6] vii. 29; ix. 38.

οὕτως ὅμοιον τοῦτο τῷ καταδρύπτειν τὴν ἑαυτοῦ
ὄψιν.

2 Ὅτι ὁ μὴ θέλων τὸν φαῦλον ἁμαρτάνειν ὅμοιος
τῷ μὴ θέλοντι τὴν συκῆν ὀπὸν ἐν τοῖς σύκοις
φέρειν καὶ τὰ βρέφη κλαυθμυρίζεσθαι καὶ τὸν
ἵππον χρεμετίζειν καὶ ὅσα ἄλλα ἀναγκαῖα. τί
γὰρ πάθῃ τὴν ἕξιν ἔχων τοιαύτην; εἰ οὖν γοργὸς
εἶ, ταύτην θεράπευσον.

ιζ'. Εἰ μὴ καθήκει, μὴ πράξῃς· εἰ μὴ ἀληθές
ἐστι, μὴ εἴπῃς. ἡ γὰρ ὁρμή σου ἔστω <ἐπὶ σοί>.

ιη'. Εἰς τὸ πᾶν ἀεὶ ὁρᾶν, τί ἐστιν αὐτὸ ἐκεῖνο
τὸ τὴν φαντασίαν σοι ποιοῦν, καὶ ἀναπτύσσειν,
διαιροῦντα εἰς τὸ αἴτιον, εἰς τὸ ὑλικόν, εἰς τὴν
ἀναφοράν, εἰς τὸν χρόνον, ἐντὸς οὗ πεπαῦσθαι αὐτὸ
δεήσει.

ιθ'. Αἴσθου ποτέ, ὅτι κρεῖττόν τι καὶ δαιμονιώ-
τερον ἔχεις ἐν σαυτῷ τῶν τὰ πάθη ποιούντων
καὶ καθάπαξ τῶν νευροσπαστούντων σε. τί μου
νῦν ἐστιν ἡ διάνοια; μὴ φόβος; μὴ ὑποψία; μὴ
ἐπιθυμία; μὴ ἄλλο τι τοιοῦτον;

κ'. Πρῶτον, τὸ μὴ εἰκῆ μηδὲ ἄνευ ἀναφορᾶς.
δεύτερον, τὸ μὴ ἐπ' ἄλλο τι ἢ ἐπὶ τὸ κοινωνικὸν
τέλος τὴν ἀναγωγὴν ποιεῖσθαι.

κα'. Ὅτι μετ' οὐ πολὺ οὐδεὶς οὐδαμοῦ ἔσῃ,
οὐδὲ τούτων τι, ἃ νῦν βλέπεις, οὐδὲ τούτων τις
τῶν νῦν βιούντων. ἅπαντα γὰρ μεταβάλλειν
καὶ τρέπεσθαι καὶ φθείρεσθαι πέφυκεν, ἵνα ἕτερα
ἐφεξῆς γίνηται.

κβ'. Ὅτι πάντα ὑπόληψις· καὶ αὕτη ἐπὶ σοί.

---

[1] iv. 6.
[2] xii. 10. Or, *application*.

own heart has condemned him, and so he is as one who wounds his own face?

Note that he who would not have the wicked do wrong is as one who would not have the fig-tree secrete acrid juice[1] in its fruit, would not have babies cry, or the horse neigh, or have any other things be that must be. Why, what else can be expected from such a disposition? If then it chafes thee, cure the disposition.

17. If not meet, do it not: if not true, say it not. For let thine impulse be in thy own power.

18. Ever look to the whole of a thing, what exactly that is which produces the impression on thee, and unfold it, analyzing it into its causes, its matter, its objective,[2] and into its life-span within which it must needs cease to be.

19. Become conscious at last that thou hast in thyself something better and more god-like than that which causes the bodily passions and turns thee into a mere marionette.[3] What is my mind now occupied with[4]? Fear? Suspicion? Concupiscence[5]? Some other like thing?

20. Firstly, eschew action that is aimless and has no objective. Secondly, take as the only goal of conduct what is to the common interest.[6]

21. Bethink thee that thou wilt very soon be no one and nowhere, and so with all that thou now seest and all who are now living. For by Nature's law all things must change, be transformed, and perish, that other things may in their turn come into being.[7]

22. Remember that all is but as thy opinion

---

[3] ii. 2 etc. [4] v. 11. [5] ii. 16; ix. 40.
[6] v. 16; xi. 21. [7] ix. 28, 32.

ἆρον οὖν, ὅτε θέλεις, τὴν ὑπόληψιν, καὶ ὥσπερ
κάμψαντι τὴν ἄκραν, γαλήνη, σταθερὰ πάντα
καὶ κόλπος ἀκύμων.

κγ΄. Μία καὶ ἡτισοῦν ἐνέργεια κατὰ καιρὸν
παυσαμένη οὐδὲν κακὸν πάσχει, καθ᾽ ὃ πέπαυται·
οὐδὲ ὁ πράξας τὴν πρᾶξιν ταύτην κατ᾽ αὐτὸ
τοῦτο, καθ᾽ ὃ πέπαυται, κακόν τι πέπονθεν.
ὁμοίως οὖν τὸ ἐκ πασῶν τῶν πράξεων σύστημα,
ὅπερ ἐστὶν ὁ βίος, ἐὰν ἐν καιρῷ παύσηται, οὐδὲν
κακὸν πάσχει κατ᾽ αὐτὸ τοῦτο, καθ᾽ ὃ πέπαυται·
οὐδὲ ὁ καταπαύσας ἐν καιρῷ τὸν εἱρμὸν τοῦτον
κακῶς διετέθη. τὸν δὲ καιρὸν καὶ τὸν ὅρον
δίδωσιν ἡ φύσις, ποτὲ μὲν καὶ ἡ ἰδία, ὅταν ἐν
γήρᾳ, πάντως δὲ ἡ τῶν ὅλων, ἧς τῶν μερῶν
μεταβαλλόντων νεαρὸς ἀεὶ καὶ ἀκμαῖος ὁ σύμπας
κόσμος διαμένει. καλὸν δὲ ἀεὶ πᾶν καὶ ὡραῖον
τὸ συμφέρον τῷ ὅλῳ. ἡ οὖν κατάπαυσις τοῦ βίου
ἑκάστῳ οὐ κακὸν μέν, ὅτι οὐδὲ αἰσχρόν, εἴπερ καὶ
ἀπροαίρετον καὶ οὐκ ἀκοινώνητον· ἀγαθὸν δέ,
εἴπερ τῷ ὅλῳ καίριον καὶ συμφέρον καὶ συμφερό-
μενον. οὕτω γὰρ καὶ θεοφόρητος ὁ φερόμενος
κατὰ ταὐτὰ θεῷ καὶ ἐπὶ ταὐτὰ τῇ γνώμῃ
φερόμενος.

κδ΄. Τρία ταῦτα δεῖ πρόχειρα ἔχειν· ἐπὶ
μὲν ὧν ποιεῖς, εἰ μήτε εἰκῇ μήτε ἄλλως ἢ ὡς ἂν
ἡ δίκη αὐτὴ ἐνήργησεν· ἐπὶ δὲ τῶν ἔξωθεν συμβαινόντων, ὅτι ἤτοι κατ᾽ ἐπιτυχίαν ἢ κατὰ

---

[1] ii. 15 etc.   [2] cp. Lucian, Scyth. ad fin.   [3] ix. 21.
[4] vii. 25.   [5] ii. 11; iv. 3; viii. 1.   [6] ii. 3; iii. 4.

of it,[1] and that is in thy power. Efface thy opinion then, as thou mayest do at will, and lo, a great calm ! Like a mariner that has turned the headland thou findest all at set-fair and a halcyon sea.[2]

23. Any single form of activity, be it what it may, ceasing in its own due season, suffers no ill because it hath ceased, nor does the agent suffer in that it hath ceased to act.[3] Similarly then if life, that sum total of all our acts, cease in its own good time, it suffers no ill from this very fact, nor is he in an ill plight who has brought this chain of acts to an end in its own due time. The due season and the terminus are fixed by Nature, at times even by our individual nature, as when in old age, but in any case by the Universal Nature, the constant change of whose parts keeps the whole Universe ever youthful [4] and in its prime. All that is advantageous to the Whole is ever fair and in its bloom. The ending of life then is not only no evil to the individual—for it brings him no disgrace,[5] if in fact it be both outside our choice and not inimical to the general weal—but a good, since it is timely for the Universe, bears its share in it and is borne along with it.[6] For then is he, who is borne along on the same path as God, and borne in his judgment towards the same things, indeed a man god-borne.[7]

24. Thou must have these three rules ready for use. *Firstly*, not to do anything, that thou doest, aimlessly,[8] or otherwise than as Justice herself would have acted ; and to realize that all that befalls thee from without is due either to Chance or to Providence,

---

[7] Epict. ii. 16, § 42 : πρὸς τὸν θεὸν ἀναβλέψας εἰπεῖν, ὁμο-
γνωμονῶ σοι.   [8] iv. 2 ; viii. 17 ; ix. 28.

πρόνοιαν· οὔτε δὲ τῇ ἐπιτυχίᾳ μεμπτέον οὔτε τῇ
προνοίᾳ ἐγκλητέον. δεύτερον τό· ὁποῖον ἕκαστον
ἀπὸ σπέρματος[1] μέχρι ψυχώσεως καὶ ἀπὸ
ψυχώσεως μέχρι τοῦ τὴν ψυχὴν ἀποδοῦναι, καὶ
ἐξ οἵων ἡ σύγκρισις καὶ εἰς οἷα ἡ λύσις. τρίτον,
εἰ ἄφνω μετέωρος ἐξαρθεὶς κατασκέψαιο τὰ
ἀνθρώπεια καὶ τὴν πολυτροπίαν, ὅτι καταφρονήσεις συνιδὼν ἅμα καὶ ὅσον τὸ περιοικοῦν
ἐναερίων καὶ ἐναιθερίων· καὶ ὅτι, ὁσάκις ἂν
ἐξαρθῇς, ταῦτα ὄψει, τὸ ὁμοειδές, τὸ ὀλιγοχρόνιον.
ἐπὶ τούτοις ὁ τῦφος.

κέ. Βάλε ἔξω τὴν ὑπόληψιν· σέσωσαι. τίς
οὖν ὁ κωλύων ἐκβαλεῖν;

κϛ΄. Ὅταν δυσφορῇς ἐπί τινι, ἐπελάθου τοῦ,
ὅτι πάντα κατὰ τὴν τῶν ὅλων φύσιν γίνεται, καὶ
τοῦ, ὅτι τὸ ἁμαρτανόμενον ἀλλότριον, καὶ ἐπὶ
τούτοις τοῦ, ὅτι πᾶν τὸ γινόμενον οὕτως ἀεὶ
ἐγίνετο καὶ γενήσεται καὶ νῦν πανταχοῦ γίνεται·
τοῦ, ὅση ἡ συγγένεια ἀνθρώπου πρὸς πᾶν τὸ
ἀνθρώπειον γένος· οὐ γὰρ αἱματίου ἢ σπερματίου,
ἀλλὰ νοῦ κοινωνία. ἐπελάθου δὲ καὶ τοῦ, ὅτι ὁ
ἑκάστου νοῦς θεὸς καὶ ἐκεῖθεν ἐρρύηκε· τοῦ, ὅτι
οὐδὲν ἴδιον οὐδενός, ἀλλὰ καὶ τὸ τεκνίον καὶ τὸ

---

[1] στερήματος PA: σπέρματος Gat.: στηρίγματος Schenkl:
possibly στερεώματος (*solidification*).

---

[1] The living soul was supposed by the Stoics to be received
at birth, see Plut. *de Placit. Phil.* v. 15, and *Stoic. Contr.* 38;
and for a reputed conversation on this subject between
Marcus and the rabbi Jehuda, see Talmud, *Sanh.* 91 b
(*Jewish Encycl.* Funk & Wagnalls, 1902).

[2] vii. 48; ix. 30.

[3] *cp.* Lucian, *Charon* (throughout). What Marcus means
by ἐναέριοι and ἐναιθέριοι (or the neuters of these) is not

nor hast thou any call to blame Chance or to impeach Providence. *Secondly* this: to think what each creature is from conception till it receives a living soul, and from its reception of a living soul till its giving back of the same,[1] and out of what it is built up and into what it is dissolved. *Thirdly*, that if carried suddenly into mid-heaven thou shouldest look down upon human affairs[2] and their infinite diversity, thou wilt indeed despise them,[3] seeing at the same time in one view how great is the host that peoples the air and the aether around thee; and that, however often thou wert lifted up on high, thou wouldst see the same sights, everything identical in kind, everything fleeting. Besides, the vanity of it all!

25. Overboard with opinion[4] and thou art safe ashore. And who is there prevents thee from throwing it overboard?

26. In taking umbrage at anything, thou forgettest this, that everything happens in accordance with the Universal Nature[5]; and this, that the wrong-doing is another's[6]; and this furthermore, that all that happens, always did happen,[7] and will happen so, and is at this moment happening everywhere. And thou forgettest how strong is the kinship between man and mankind, for it is a community not of corpuscles, of seed or blood, but of intelligence.[8] And thou forgettest this too, that each man's intelligence is God[9] and has emanated from Him; and this, that nothing is a man's very own, but that his babe, his

clear. But *cp.* Apul. *de deo Socr.*, *circa med.*, and his disquisition on δαίμονες; and the interesting parallel 2 Kings vi. 17.

[4] iv. 7; vii. 17, 29: viii. 29; ix. 7; xii. 22.
[5] v. 8, 10.   [6] ix. 38.   [7] vii. 1.   [8] ii. 1.
[9] *cp.* Eur. *Frag.* 1007, ὁ νοῦς γὰρ ἡμῶν ἐστιν ἐν ἑκάστῳ θεός: Cic. *Tusc.* i. 26, § 65.

σωμάτιον καὶ αὐτὸ τὸ ψυχάριον ἐκεῖθεν ἐλήλυθεν·
τοῦ, ὅτι πάνθ᾽ ὑπόληψις· τοῦ, ὅτι τὸ παρὸν μόνον
ἕκαστος ζῇ καὶ τοῦτο ἀποβάλλει.

κζ΄. Συνεχῶς ἀναπολεῖν τοὺς ἐπί τινι λίαν
ἀγανακτήσαντας, τοὺς ἐν μεγίσταις δόξαις ἢ
συμφοραῖς ἢ ἔχθραις ἢ ὁποιαισοῦν τύχαις
ἀκμάσαντας· εἶτα ἐφιστάνειν "Ποῦ νῦν πάντα
ἐκεῖνα ;" καπνὸς καὶ σποδὸς καὶ μῦθος ἢ οὐδὲ
μῦθος. συμπροσπιπτέτω δὲ καὶ τὸ τοιοῦτο πᾶν,
οἷον Φάβιος Κατουλλῖνος ἐπ᾽ ἀγροῦ, καὶ Λούσιος
Λοῦπος [1] ἐν τοῖς κήποις, καὶ Στερτίνιος ἐν Βαίαις,
καὶ Τιβέριος ἐν Καπρίαις, καὶ Οὐήλιος Ῥοῦφος,[2]
καὶ ὅλως ἡ πρὸς ὁτιοῦν μετ᾽ οἰήσεως διαφορά·
καὶ ὡς εὐτελὲς πᾶν τὸ κατεντεινόμενον· καὶ
ὅσῳ φιλοσοφώτερον τὸ ἐπὶ τῆς δοθείσης ὕλης
ἑαυτὸν δίκαιον, σώφρονα, θεοῖς ἑπόμενον ἀφελῶς
παρέχειν. ὁ γὰρ ὑπὸ ἀτυφίᾳ τῦφος τυφόμενος
πάντων χαλεπώτατος.

κη΄. Πρὸς τοὺς ἐπιζητοῦντας, "Ποῦ γὰρ ἰδὼν
τοὺς θεοὺς ἢ πόθεν κατειληφώς, ὅτι εἰσίν, οὕτω
σέβεις;" πρῶτον μὲν καὶ ὄψει ὁρατοί εἰσιν· ἔπειτα
μέντοι οὐδὲ τὴν ψυχὴν τὴν ἐμαυτοῦ ἑώρακα, καὶ
ὅμως τιμῶ. οὕτως οὖν καὶ τοὺς θεούς, ἐξ ὧν τῆς
δυνάμεως αὐτῶν ἑκάστοτε πειρῶμαι, ἐκ τούτων,
ὅτι τε εἰσί, καταλαμβάνω καὶ αἰδοῦμαι.

[1] Λούσιος Λοῦπος PA. Perhaps we should read Lucius
Lucullus, who would be a typical instance.
[2] ἐν Οὐηλίᾳ Barberini.

---

[1] ii. 3.   [2] xii. 8, 22 etc.   [3] ii. 14 ; xii. 3.
[4] vi. 47 ; viii. 25 ; x. 31.
[5] cp. Pers. v. 132 : cinis et manes et fabula fies.

body, his very soul came forth from Him[1]; and this, that everything is but opinion[2]; and this, that it is only the present moment that a man lives and the present moment only that he loses.[3]

27. Let thy mind dwell continually on those who have shewn unmeasured resentment at things, who have been conspicuous above others for honours or disasters or enmities or any sort of special lot. Then consider, *Where is all that now?*[4] Smoke and dust and a legend or not a legend even.[5] Take any instance of the kind—Fabius Catullinus in the country, Lusius Lupus in his gardens, Stertinius at Baiae, Tiberius in Capreae, and Velius Rufus—in fact a craze for any thing whatever arrogantly[6] indulged. How worthless is everything so inordinately desired! How much more worthy of a philosopher is it for a man without any artifice to shew himself in the sphere assigned to him just, temperate, and a follower of the Gods. For the conceit that is conceited of its freedom from conceit is the most insufferable of all.[7]

28. If any ask, *Where hast thou seen the Gods or how hast thou satisfied thyself of their existence that thou art so devout a worshipper?*[8] I answer: In the first place, they are even visible to the eyes.[9] In the next, I have not seen my own soul either, yet I honour it.[10] So then from the continual proofs of their power I am assured that Gods also exist and I reverence them.

[6] For οἴησις see Epict. i. 8, § 6.
[7] See the story of Plato and Diogenes, Diog. Laert. vi. 2, § 4.
[8] *cp.* Dio 71. 34 § 2.
[9] The stars were Gods in the Stoic view. *cp. above* viii. 19, and Sen. *de Benef.* iv. 8.
[10] Theoph. *Ad Autol.* i. 2 and 5; Min. Fel. *Oct.* 32, *ad fin.*

κθʹ. Σωτηρία βίου ἕκαστον δι᾽ ὅλου αὐτὸ
τί ἐστιν ὁρᾶν, τί μὲν αὐτοῦ τὸ ὑλικόν, τί δὲ τὸ
αἰτιῶδες· ἐξ ὅλης τῆς ψυχῆς τὰ δίκαια ποιεῖν
καὶ τἀληθῆ λέγειν. τί λοιπὸν ἢ ἀπολαύειν τοῦ
ζῆν συνάπτοντα ἄλλο ἐπ᾽ ἄλλῳ ἀγαθόν, ὥστε
μηδὲ τὸ βραχύτατον διάστημα ἀπολείπειν;

λʹ. Ἕν φῶς ἡλίου, κἂν διείργηται τοίχοις,
ὄρεσιν, ἄλλοις μυρίοις. μία οὐσία κοινή, κἂν
διείργηται ἰδίως ποιοῖς σώμασι μυρίοις. μία
ψυχή, κἂν φύσεσι διείργηται μυρίαις καὶ ἰδίαις
περιγραφαῖς. μία νοερὰ ψυχή, κἂν διακεκρίσθαι
δοκῇ. τὰ μὲν οὖν ἄλλα μέρη τῶν εἰρημένων,
οἷον πνεύματα, καὶ ὑποκείμενα ἀναίσθητα καὶ
ἀνοικείωτα ἀλλήλοις· καίτοι κἀκεῖνα τὸ νοοῦν[1]
συνέχει καὶ τὸ ἐπὶ τὰ αὐτὰ βρῖθον. διάνοια δὲ
ἰδίως ἐπὶ τὸ ὁμόφυλον τείνεται καὶ συνίσταται
καὶ οὐ διείργεται τὸ κοινωνικὸν πάθος.

λαʹ. Τί ἐπιζητεῖς; τὸ διαγίνεσθαι;[2] ἀλλὰ τὸ
αἰσθάνεσθαι; τὸ ὁρμᾶν; τὸ αὔξεσθαι; τὸ λήγειν
αὖθις; τὸ φωνῇ χρῆσθαι; τὸ διανοεῖσθαι; τί
τούτων πόθου σοι ἄξιον δοκεῖ; εἰ δὲ ἕκαστα
εὐκαταφρόνητα, πρόσιθι ἐπὶ τελευταῖον τὸ
ἕπεσθαι τῷ λόγῳ καὶ τῷ θεῷ. ἀλλὰ μάχεται
τὸ τιμᾶν ταῦτα, τὸ ἄχθεσθαι, εἰ διὰ τοῦ τεθνηκέναι
στερήσεταί τις αὐτῶν.

---

[1] τὸ ἐνοῦν Rend. : τὸ νοοῦν Gat.: τὸν νοῦν PA.
[2] διαπνεῖσθαι Leopold.

---

[1] xii. 10, 18 etc.   [2] v. 6 ; ix. 23.
[3] viii. 57.

BOOK XII

29. Salvation in life depends on our seeing every-thing in its entirety and and its reality, in its Matter and its Cause[1]: on our doing what is just and speaking what is true with all our soul. What remains but to get delight of life by dovetailing one good act[2] on to another so as not to leave the smallest gap between?

30. There is one Light of the Sun, even though its continuity be broken by walls, mountains,[3] and countless other things. There is one common Substance, even though it be broken up into countless bodies individually characterized. There is one Soul, though it be broken up among countless natures and with individual limitations. There is one Intelligent Soul, though it seem to be divided. Of the things mentioned, however, all the other parts, such as Breath, are the material Substratum of things,[4] devoid of sensation and the ties of mutual affinity—yet even they are knit together by the faculty of intelligence and the gravitation which draws them together. But the mind is peculiarly impelled towards what is akin to it, and coalesces with it, and there is no break in the feeling of social fellowship.

31. What dost thou ask for? Continued existence? But what of sensation? Of desire? Of growth? Or again of coming to an end? Of the use of speech? The exercise of thought? Which of these, thinkest thou, is a thing to long for? But if these things are each and all of no account, address thyself to a final endeavour to follow Reason and to follow God.[5] But it militates against this to prize such things, and to grieve if death comes to deprive us of them.

---

[4] With an alteration of stops these words may mean *such as Breath and Matter, are devoid of sensation.*

[5] vii. 31; xii. 27.

λβ´. Πόστον μέρος τοῦ ἀπείρου καὶ ἀχανοῦς
αἰῶνος ἀπομεμέρισται ἑκάστῳ; τάχιστα γὰρ
ἐναφανίζεται τῷ ἀϊδίῳ. πόστον δὲ τῆς ὅλης
οὐσίας; πόστον δὲ τῆς ὅλης ψυχῆς; ἐν πόστῳ δὲ
βωλαρίῳ τῆς ὅλης γῆς ἕρπεις; πάντα ταῦτα
ἐνθυμούμενος μηδὲν μέγα φαντάζου ἢ τό, ὡς μὲν ἡ
σὴ φύσις ἄγει, ποιεῖν, πάσχειν δέ, ὡς ἡ κοινὴ
φύσις φέρει.

λγ´. Πῶς ἑαυτῷ χρῆται τὸ ἡγεμονικόν; ἐν
γὰρ τούτῳ τὸ πᾶν ἐστι. τὰ δὲ λοιπά, ἢ προ-
αίρετικά ἐστιν ἢ ἀπροαίρετα, νεκρὰ καὶ καπνός.

λδ´. Πρὸς θανάτου καταφρόνησιν ἐγερτικώ-
τατον, ὅτι καὶ οἱ τὴν ἡδονὴν ἀγαθὸν καὶ τὸν
πόνον κακὸν κρίνοντες ὅμως τούτου κατεφρόν-
ησαν.

λε´. Ὧι τὸ εὔκαιρον μόνον ἀγαθὸν καὶ ᾧ τὸ
πλείους κατὰ λόγον ὀρθὸν πράξεις ἀποδοῦναι τῷ
ὀλιγωτέρας ἐν ἴσῳ ἐστί, καὶ ᾧ τὸν κόσμον θεωρῆσαι
πλείονι ἢ ἐλάσσονι χρόνῳ οὐ διαφέρει, τούτῳ
οὐδὲ ὁ θάνατος φοβερόν.

λϛ´. Ἄνθρωπε, ἐπολιτεύσω ἐν τῇ μεγάλῃ ταύτῃ
πόλει· τί σοι διαφέρει, εἰ πέντε ἔτεσιν <ἢ ἑκατόν>;[1]
τὸ γὰρ κατὰ τοὺς νόμους ἴσον ἑκάστῳ. τί οὖν
δεινόν, εἰ τῆς πόλεως ἀποπέμπει σε οὐ τύραννος
οὐδὲ δικαστὴς ἄδικος, ἀλλ᾽ ἡ φύσις ἡ εἰσαγαγοῦσα;

---

[1] <ἢ τρισὶ> Reiske : I have preferred ἑκατόν.

[1] iv. 50 ; v. 24.
[2] Epict. i. 12 § 26 : οὐκ οἶσθα ἡλίκον μέρος εἶ πρὸς τὰ ὄντα;
[3] iii. 4.   [4] v. 11 ; x. 24.   [5] x. 31.

BOOK XII

32. How tiny a fragment of boundless and abysmal Time has been appointed to each man![1] For in a moment it is lost in eternity. And how tiny a part of the Universal Substance![2] How tiny of the Universal Soul! And on how tiny a clod of the whole Earth dost thou crawl! Keeping all these things in mind, think nothing of moment save to do what thy nature leads thee to do, and to bear what the Universal Nature brings thee.[3]

33. How does the ruling Reason treat itself?[4] That is the gist of the whole matter. All else, be it in thy choice or not, is dead dust and smoke.[5]

34. Most efficacious in instilling a contempt for death is the fact that those who count pleasure a good and pain an evil have nevertheless contemned it.[6]

35. Not even death can bring terror to him who regards that alone as good which comes in due season,[7] and to whom it is all one whether his acts in obedience to right reason are few or many, and a matter of indifference whether he look upon the world for a longer or a shorter time.[8]

36. Man, thou hast been a citizen in this World-City,[9] what matters it to thee if for five years or a hundred? For under its laws equal treatment is meted out to all. What hardship then is there in being banished from the city, not by a tyrant or an unjust judge but by Nature who settled thee in it?

[6] *e.g.* Otho, Petronius, and Epicurus, for whose famous syllogism on death see Aul Gell. ii 8 ; Diog. Laert. *Epic.* xxxi. § 2, and *cp.* Bacon's Essay "On Death." Tert. *ad Mart.* §§ 4, 5. [7] x. 20 : xii. 23.
[8] iii. 7 ; xii. 36. [9] ii. 16 ; iii. 11 ; iv. 4.

οἷον εἰ κωμῳδὸν ἀπολύοι τῆς σκηνῆς ὁ παραλαβὼν
στρατηγός. "Ἀλλ᾽ οὐκ εἶπον τὰ πέντε μέρη, ἀλλὰ
τὰ τρία." καλῶς εἶπας· ἐν μέντοι τῷ βίῳ τὰ τρία
ὅλον τὸ δρᾶμά ἐστιν. τὸ γὰρ τέλειον ἐκεῖνος ὁρίζει
ὁ τότε μὲν τῆς συγκρίσεως, νῦν δὲ τῆς διαλύσεως
αἴτιος· σὺ δὲ ἀναίτιος ἀμφοτέρων. ἄπιθι οὖν
ἵλεως· καὶ γὰρ ὁ ἀπολύων ἵλεως.[1]

[1] Here follow in A the verses translated in the Introduction.

BOOK XII

So might a praetor who commissions a comic actor, dismiss him from the stage. *But I have not played my five acts, but only three.* Very possibly, but in life three acts count as a full play.[1] For he, that is responsible for thy composition originally and thy dissolution now, decides when it is complete. But thou art responsible for neither. Depart then with a good grace, for he also that dismisses thee is gracious.

[1] iii. 8 ; xi. 1 ; Epict. *Man* 17 ; Cic. *de Senect.* 70.

THE SPEECHES OF MARCUS

Cum aliquid pulchrius elocutus sum, placeo mihi,
ideoque eloquentiam fugio.

MARCUS apud FRONTO.

THE SPEECHES OF MARCUS

INTRODUCTION

MARCUS learnt from Rusticus to "eschew rhetoric and fine language" [1] and thanked the Gods that "he had not made more progress in his rhetorical studies," [2] but the Greek in which he clothed his *Thoughts* shews that he had made some progress in them, and Dio says he was "practised in the principles of rhetoric." [3]

Only three speeches, purporting to be by Marcus, have come down to us. It is not certain how far we can accept them as authentic. The first is reported by Dio Cassius, who was twenty at the time of its delivery, and as he lived at Rome, and afterwards held high office in the state, he had ample sources of information. He expressly states that Marcus read this address to the soldiers on the rebellion of Cassius, and being written it was more likely to have been preserved verbatim. It cannot be denied that the speech has touches characteristic of Marcus, but of course these might have been purposely introduced by a skilful forger. On the other hand the style is rather rhetorical and artificial and more in keeping with Dio's known proclivities. Still there is a dignity and restraint, not altogether unworthy of the occasion, noticeable throughout. Unfortunately it only comes to us in the epitome of Xiphilinus, and we do not know how far he has curtailed it, and it certainly seems

---

[1] See above, i. 7 ; Fronto, *De Eloq.* 3.
[2] See above, i. 17, § 4.   [3] Dio, **71**. 35, §1.

too short for such an occasion. In any case it must have been delivered in Latin.

The last remark applies also to the dying speech of Marcus as given by Herodian, another contemporary authority, but one who was fond of composing suitable speeches for his characters when what they had actually said was not recoverable. The shortness of this speech may be said to be in its favour, as the Emperor was in the last stages of his illness. The opening words are perhaps too plaintive and personal, but the remainder is natural and appropriate. The last few words of such a ruler and friend must have impressed his hearers and may well have been taken down at the time. Still it is strange that there is no hint of this speech in the description of the last scene given by Capitolinus.[1]

The third speech, from the "Life of Avidius Cassius" by Gallicanus, is much less likely to be genuine. That particular piece of work is full of suspected material, and Marius Maximus, from whom this speech is probably taken, though a contemporary, is not a trustworthy authority, while the diction and absurd rhetoric of the missive, for it was a speech sent to the Senate and not delivered in it, are decidedly against its genuineness.

---

[1] Who here uses as his authority "The last great historian of Rome"; see *Das Kaiserhaus der Antonine und der Letzte Historiker Roms*, Otto Th. Schulz, p. 128, who thinks the anonymous writer may have been Lollius Urbicus. See Lampr. *Vit. Diadum.* ix. 2.

NOTE

As the Speeches and Sayings cannot definitely be attributed to Marcus Aurelius it was thought advisable to print them in smaller type in order to distinguish them from his authentic work.

MARCUS AURELIUS

Ὁ δὲ δὴ Μάρκος παρὰ τοῦ Οὐήρου [1] τοῦ τῆς Καππαδοκίας ἄρχοντος τὴν ἐπανάστασιν αὐτοῦ μαθὼν τέως μὲν συνέκρυπτεν αὐτά, ἐπεὶ δὲ οἱ στρατιῶται τῇ τε φήμῃ ἰσχυρῶς ταράσσοντο καὶ ἐλογοποίουν πολλά, συνεκάλεσεν αὐτοὺς καὶ ἀνέγνω τοιάδε·

"Οὐκ ἀγανακτήσων, ὦ συστρατιῶται, ἢ ὀδυρούμενος παρελήλυθα. χαλεπαίνειν μὲν γὰρ τί δεῖ πρὸς τὸ δαιμόνιον, ᾧ πάντα ἔξεστιν; ὀλοφύρεσθαι δὲ ἴσως ἀνάγκη τοὺς ἀδίκως δυστυχοῦντας· ὃ καὶ ἐμοὶ νῦν συμβέβηκεν. πῶς γὰρ οὐ δεινὸν πολέμοις ἡμᾶς ἐκ πολέμων συμφέρεσθαι; πῶς δ' οὐκ ἄτοπον καὶ ἐμφυλίῳ συμπλακῆναι; πῶς οὐκ ἀμφότερα καὶ δεινότητι καὶ ἀτοπίᾳ νικᾷ, τὸ μηδὲν πιστὸν ἐν ἀνθρώποις εἶναι,[2] ἀλλ' ἐπιβεβουλεῦσθαί τέ με ὑπὸ τοῦ φιλτάτου καὶ ἐς ἀγῶνα ἀκούσιον καθίστασθαι μήτε τι ἠδικηκότα μήτε πεπλημμεληκότα;[3] τίς μὲν γὰρ ἀρετὴ ἀσφαλής, τίς δὲ φιλία ἔτι νομισθήσεται ἐμοῦ ταῦτα πεπονθότος; πῶς δ' οὐκ ἀπόλωλε μὲν πίστις,[4] ἀπόλωλε δὲ ἐλπὶς ἀγαθή; ἀλλ' εἰ μὲν μόνος ἐγὼ ἐκινδύνευον, παρ' οὐδὲν ἂν τὸ πρᾶγμα ἐποιησάμην· οὐ γάρ που καὶ ἀθάνατος ἐγεννήθην· ἐπεὶ δὲ δημοσία τε ἀπόστασις, μᾶλλον δὲ ἐπανάστασις, γέγονε, καὶ ὁ πόλεμος πάντων ὁμοίως ἡμῶν ἅπτεται, ἐβουλόμην, εἰ οἷόν τε ἦν, προσκαλέσασθαι τὸν Κάσσιον καὶ δικαιολογήσασθαι πρὸς αὐτὸν παρ' ὑμῖν ἢ παρὰ τῇ γερουσίᾳ· καὶ ἡδέως ἂν ἀμαχὶ παρεχώρησα αὐτῷ τῆς ἡγεμονίας, εἰ τοῦτο τῷ κοινῷ συμφέρειν ἐδόκει. ὑπὲρ τοῦ κοινοῦ γὰρ καὶ πονῶν καὶ κινδυνεύων διατελῶ, τοσοῦτόν τε ἐνταυθοῖ χρόνον ἔξω τῆς Ἰταλίας πεποίηκα, ἄνθρω-

---

[1] *i.e.* Martius Verus, see below.

[2] He forgot his own precepts; see *Medit.* ix. 42, unless, as is possible, the speech came first.

[3] Dio 71. 34, § 3, οὔτε ἑκὼν οὔτε ἄκων ἐπλημμέλει. *cp.* Aristides, *Orat. ad Regem*, § 106 (Jebb).

[4] *cp. Medit.* v. 33.

THE SPEECHES OF MARCUS

Speech to the Army on the news of the Revolt of Cassius,
175 A.D.

MARCUS, learning of the revolt from Verus, the Governor of Cappadocia, kept the news secret for a time, but as the soldiers were both greatly perturbed by the rumour and were freely discussing it, he called them together and read the following speech :

"It is not, O fellow soldiers, to give way to resentment or lamentations that I am come before you. For what avails it to be wroth with the Divinity that can do whatever pleaseth Him ? Still, perhaps, they that are undeservedly unfortunate cannot but bewail their lot ; and that is the case with me now. For it is surely a terrible thing for us to be engaged in wars upon wars ; surely it is shocking to be involved even in civil strife, and surely it is more than terrible and more than shocking that there is no faith to be found among men, and that I have been plotted against by one whom I held most dear and, although I had done no wrong and committed no transgression, have been forced into a conflict against my will. For what rectitude shall be held safe, what friendship be any longer deemed secure, seeing that this has befallen me ? Has not Faith utterly perished, and good Hope perished with it ? Yet I had counted it a slight thing, had the danger been mine alone—for assuredly I was not born immortal—but now that there has been a defection, or rather a revolt, in the state, and the war comes home to all of us equally, I would gladly, had it been possible, have invited Cassius to argue the question out before you or before the Senate, and willingly without a contest have made way for him in the supreme power, had that seemed expedient for the common weal. For it is only in the public interest that I continue to incur toil and danger, and have spent so much time here beyond the bounds of Italy, an old man as I now am

πος καὶ γέρων ἤδη[1] καὶ ἀσθενὴς[2] καὶ οὔτε τροφὴν ἄλυπον οὐθ'
ὕπνον ἄφροντιν λαβεῖν δυνάμενος.

"Ἐπεὶ δ' οὐκ ἄν ποτε συγκαθεῖναι ἐς τοῦτο ὁ Κάσσιος ἐθελή-
σειε, πῶς γὰρ ἂν πιστεύσειέ μοι, ἄπιστος οὕτω περὶ ἐμὲ
γεγενημένος; ὑμᾶς γε, ὦ συστρατιῶται, χρὴ θαρρεῖν. οὐ γάρ
που κρείττους Κίλικες καὶ Σύροι καὶ Ἰουδαῖοι καὶ Αἰγύπτιοι
ὑμῶν οὔτε ἐγένοντό ποτε οὔτε ἔσονται, οὐδ' ἂν μυριάκις πλείους
ὑμῶν, ὅσῳ νῦν ἐλάττους εἰσίν, ἀθροισθῶσιν. οὐ μὴν οὐδ'
αὐτὸς ὁ Κάσσιος, εἰ καὶ τὰ μάλιστα καὶ στρατηγικὸς εἶναι
καὶ πολλὰ κατωρθωκέναι δοκεῖ, λόγου τινὸς ἄξιος νῦν ἂν φανείη·
οὔτε γὰρ ἀετὸς κολοιῶν ἢ καὶ λέων νεβρῶν ἡγησάμενος ἀξιό-
μαχος γίνεται, καὶ τὸν Ἀραβικὸν τόν τε Παρθικὸν ἐκεῖνον πόλεμον οὐ Κάσσιος ἀλλ' ὑμεῖς κατειργάσασθε. ἄλλως τε, εἰ
καὶ ἐκεῖνος ἐκ τῶν πρὸς Πάρθους πραχθέντων εὐδόκιμός ἐστιν,
ἔχετε καὶ ὑμεῖς Οὐῆρον,[3] ὃς οὐδὲν ἧττον ἀλλὰ καὶ μᾶλλον αὐτοῦ
καὶ ἐνίκησε πλείω καὶ κατεκτήσατο.

"Ἀλλὰ τάχα μὲν καὶ ἤδη μετανενόηκε, ζῶντά με μεμαθηκὼς·
οὐ γάρ που καὶ ἄλλως ἢ ὡς τετελευτηκότος μου τοῦτ' ἐποίησεν.
ἂν δὲ καὶ ἐπὶ πλεῖον ἀντίσχῃ, ἀλλ' ὅταν γε καὶ προσιόντας
ἡμᾶς πύθηται, πάντως γνωσιμαχήσει, καὶ ὑμᾶς φοβηθεὶς καὶ ἐμὲ
αἰδεσθείς. ἐγὼ γοῦν ἓν μόνον δέδοικα, ὦ συστρατιῶται, εἰρήσεται
γὰρ πᾶσα πρὸς ὑμᾶς ἡ ἀλήθεια, μὴ ἤτοι αὐτὸς ἑαυτὸν ἀποκτείνῃ,
αἰσχυνθεὶς ἐς τὴν ἡμετέραν ὄψιν ἐλθεῖν, ἢ ἕτερος μαθὼν, ὅτι τε
ἥξω καὶ ὅτι ἐπ' αὐτὸν ὁρμῶμαι, τοῦτο ποιήσῃ. μέγα γάρ μου
ἆθλον καὶ τοῦ πολέμου καὶ τῆς νίκης, καὶ ἡλίκον οὐδεὶς πώποτε
ἀνθρώπων ἔλαβεν, ἀφαιρήσεται. τί δὲ τοῦτό ἐστιν; ἀδικήσαντα
ἄνθρωπον ἀφεῖναι, πρὸς φιλίαν ὑπερβάντα φίλον μεῖναι, πίστιν
καταλύσαντι πιστὸν[4] διαγενέσθαι. παράδοξα μὲν ἴσως ταῦθ'
ὑμῖν φαίνεται, ἀλλ' οὐκ ἀπιστεῖν ὑμᾶς αὐτοῖς δεῖ· οὐ γάρ που

---

[1] He was 54. cp. Thoughts, i. 17, § 6; ii. 2, 6.
[2] Yet five years more of this anxious and strenuous life
were to be his. cp. Dio, 71. 22, § 3.
[3] Martius Verus. Suidas credits him with tact, slimness,
and warlike ability. He gave Marcus the first news of
the revolt.   [4] cp. Medit. ix. 42.

and an ailing, unable to take food without pain, or sleep without care.

"But since Cassius would never agree to meet me for this purpose—for what faith could he have in me who kept so ill his faith to me?—you, my fellow soldiers, must in any case be of good cheer. For never, I take it, have Cilicians and Syrians and Jews and Egyptians been a match for you, and never will be, no, not though their muster was as many thousand times more numerous than yours as it is now less. Nor need even Cassius himself, ever so good a commander though he is reputed to be, and credited with many successful campaigns, be held of any great account at the present crisis. For an eagle at the head of daws makes no formidable foe, nor a lion at the head of fawns, and as for the Arabian war and the great Parthian war, it was you, not Cassius, who brought them to a successful end. Moreover, even if he has won distinction by his Parthian campaigns, you too have Verus, who has won not less but even far more victories, and made greater acquisitions than he.

"But perhaps even now, learning that I am alive, he has repented of his action; for surely it was only because he believed me dead, that he acted thus. But if he still maintain his opposition, yet when he learns that we are indeed marching against him, he will doubtless take a different view both from dread of you and from reverence for me. I at any rate, fellow soldiers, have but one fear—for I will tell you the whole truth—that either he should take his own life from very shame of coming into our presence, or that another should slay him, learning both that I shall come and that I am actually setting out against him. For great is the prize of war and of victory—a prize such as no one among men has ever won—of which I shall be deprived. And what is that? To forgive a man who has done wrong, to be still a friend to one who has trodden friendship underfoot, to continue faithful to one who has broken faith. What I say may perhaps seem to you incredible, but you must not disbelieve it;

351

MARCUS AURELIUS

καὶ ἁπλῶς πάντα τὰ ἀγαθὰ ἐκ τῶν ἀνθρώπων ἀπόλωλεν, ἀλλ'
ἔστι καὶ παρ' ἡμῖν ἔτι τῆς ἀρχαίας ἀρετῆς λείψανον. ἂν δέ
που ἀπιστῇ τις, καὶ διὰ τοῦτο μεῖζόν ἐστί μοι τὸ ἐπιθύμημα,
ἵνα, ὃ μηδεὶς ἂν πιστεύσειε γενέσθαι δύνασθαι, τοῦτο ἤδη γενόμενον. ὡς ἔγωγε τοῦτ' ἂν μόνον ἐκ τῶν παρόντων κακῶν
κερδάναιμι, εἰ δυνηθείην καλῶς θέσθαι τὸ πρᾶγμα [1] καὶ δεῖξαι
πᾶσιν ἀνθρώποις ὅτι καὶ ἐμφυλίοις πολέμοις ἔστιν ὀρθῶς
χρήσασθαι."—Dio, 71. 24–26, § 4.

Ex Oratione Marci Antonini (ad Senatum missa).

"Habetis igitur p.c., pro gratulatione victoriae generum
meum consulem, Pompeianum [2] dico, cuius aetas olim
remuneranda fuerat consulatu, nisi viri fortes interven-
issent, quibus reddi debuit, quod a re publica debebatur.
Nunc quod ad defectionem Cassianam pertinet, vos oro
atque obsecro, p.c., ut censura vestra deposita meam
pietatem clementiamque servetis, immo vestram, neque
quemquam unum senatus occidat. Nemo senatorum pun-
iatur, nullius fundatur viri nobilis sanguis, deportati
redeant, proscripti bona recipiant. Utinam possem mul-
tatos etiam ab inferis excitare! Non enim umquam
placet in imperatore vindicta sui doloris, quae si iustior
fuerit, acrior videtur. Quare filiis Avidii Cassii et genero
et uxori veniam dabitis. Et quid dico veniam? Cum illi
nihil fecerint. Vivant igitur securi scientes sub Marco
vivere. Vivant in patrimonio parentum pro parte donato,[3]
auro, argento, vestibus fruantur, sint securi, sint vagi ot

---

[1] cp. Medit. vi. 2.
[2] Incorrect. This Pompeianus was consul in **173**. In 176
Claud. Pompeianus Quintianus, who married the daughter of
Verus and Lucilla (see Dio 72. 4, § 4), was cons. suff. As for
the victory, there had been no battle, but Cassius after "a
three months' dream of empire" was assassinated by one of
his own soldiers. See Czwalina, De Epistularum, etc., fide.

for, I take it, all that is good has not vanished utterly from among men, but there still remains among us a vestige of pristine virtue. But if any be incredulous, the greater even on that account is my desire that he should with his own eyes see actually done that which no man would believe could be done. For this would be the only gain I could get from my present troubles, if I were able to bring the matter to an honourable conclusion, and show to all the world that even civil war can be dealt with on right principles." [1]

From a Speech of Marcus Antoninus (sent to the Senate).

"In return, then, for your congratulations on our victory, Conscript Fathers, you have as consul my son-in-law Pompeianus, whose mature years should long ago have been rewarded with a consulship had not other brave men had prior claims for recognition from the state. Now with regard to the rebellion of Cassius, I beg and beseech you, Conscript Fathers, to lay aside all thoughts of severity and safeguard my or rather your humanity and clemency, and let no single person be put to death by the Senate. Let no Senator be punished, the blood of no man of noble birth be spilt ; let the exiles return, the proscribed recover their goods. Would that I could recall the condemned also from the Shades ! For revenge for his own wrongs never sits well on an emperor ; the more it is deserved, the more vindictive it seems. So you must pardon the children of Avidius Cassius, and his son-in-law, and his wife. But why do I say "pardon," whereas *they* have done no wrong ? Let them live, then, in security, knowing that they live under Marcus. Let them live on their patrimony proportionately divided ; let them enjoy their gold, their silver, their raiment ;

[1] Or, *made a right use of.*

---

[3] Capit. *Vit. Marc.* xxvi. 11, 12 : filii Cassii et amplius media parte acceperunt paterni patrimonii et auro atque argento adiuti.

liberi, et per ora omnium ubique populorum circumferant
meae, circumferant vestrae pietatis exemplum. Nec
magna haec est, p.c., clementia, veniam proscriptorum
liberis et coniugibus dari : ego vero a vobis peto, ut
conscios senatorii ordinis et equestris a caede, a pro-
scriptione, a timore, ab infamia, ab invidia, et postremo
ab omni vindicetis iniuria [1] detisque hoc meis temporibus,
ut in causa tyrannidis qui in tumultu cecidit, probetur
occisus. "—Vulcat. *Vit. Avid. Cass.* xii.

Συγκαλέσας τοὺς φίλους ὅσοι τε παρῆσαν τῶν συγγενῶν καὶ
τὸν παῖδα καταστησάμενος, ἐπειδὴ πάντες συνῆλθον, ἡσυχῆ τοῦ
σκίμποδος κουφίσας ἑαυτὸν τοιούτων λόγων ἤρξατο·

'"Ἄχθεσθαι μὲν ὑμᾶς ἐφ' οἷς ὁρᾶτέ με διακείμενον, θαυμαστὸν
οὐδέν· φύσει τε γὰρ τὸ ἀνθρώπινον ἐλεεινὸν [2] ἐν ταῖς τῶν
ὁμοφύλων συμφοραῖς, τά τε δεινὰ ὑπ' ὄψιν πεσόντα οἶκτον
προκαλεῖται μείζονα. ἐμοὶ δέ τι καὶ πλέον ὑπάρχειν παρ' ὑμῶν
οἴομαι· ἐκ γὰρ ὧν αὐτὸς διάκειμαι πρὸς ὑμᾶς, ἀμοιβαίαν εὔνοιαν
εἰκότως ἤλπικα. νῦν δὲ καιρὸς εὔκαιρος ἐμοί τε αἰσθέσθαι μὴ
μάτην πρὸς ὑμᾶς τοσούτου χρόνου τιμήν τε καὶ σπουδὴν κατα-
τεθεῖσθαι, ὑμῖν τε ἀποδοῦναι χάριν δείξασιν ὅτι ὑπὲρ ὧν ἐτύχετε
οὐκ ἀμνημονεῖτε. ὁρᾶτε δή μοι τὸν υἱόν, ὃν αὐτοὶ ἀνεθρέψασθε,
ἄρτι τῆς μειρακίων ἡλικίας ἐπιβαίνοντα,[3] καὶ δεόμενον ὥσπερ ἐν
χειμῶνι καὶ ζάλῃ τῶν κυβερνησόντων, μή ποι φερόμενος ὑπ'

---

[1] This frigid rhetoric does not savour of Marcus.

[2] Pity was scouted by the sterner Stoics; but see *Medit.*
ii. 13.

[3] Commodus would be nineteen, but μειράκιον means a boy
of fourteen or fifteen. Would ἀποβαίνοντα, unless it clashes
with the metaphor that follows, meet the difficulty ? Dio's

let them be unmolested, let them be free to come and go as they please, and let them bear witness among all peoples everywhere to my humanity and yours. Nor is this any great clemency, O Conscript Fathers, that the children and wives of the proscribed should be pardoned: but what I ask of you is that you should shield all accomplices of Cassius among the Senators or Knights from death, proscription, apprehension, degradation, hatred, and in fact from all injury, and grant this glory to my reign, that in a rebellion against the throne he only should prove to have been slain who fell in the revolt."

The Last Words of Marcus.

Calling together his friends and as many of his relations as were at hand, and setting his son before them, when all had come together, he raised himself gently on his pallet-bed, and began to speak as follows:

"That you should be grieved at seeing me in this state is not surprising, for it is natural to mankind to pity the misfortunes of their kinsfolk, and the calamities which fall under our own eyes call forth greater compassion. But I think that something even more will be forthcoming from you to me; for the consciousness of my feelings towards you has led me to hope for a recompense of good-will from you. But now the time is well-timed both for me to learn that I have not lavished love and esteem upon you in vain for all these years, and for you by showing your gratitude to prove that you are not unmindful of the benefits you have received. You see here my son, whose bringing-up has been in your own hands, just embarking upon the age of manhood and, like a ship amid storm and breakers, in need of those who shall guide the helm, lest in his want of experience of the right course

---

account of the speech (71. 30. 2.) differs (see also John of Antioch *Fragm.* 118). Dio says that several persons of senatorial rank were condemned: *Cod. Just.* iv. 8. 6.

ἀτελοῦς τῆς τῶν δεόντων ἐμπειρίας[1] ἐς φαῦλα ἐπιτηδεύματα
προσαραχθῇ. γένεσθε δὴ οὖν αὐτῷ ὑμεῖς ἀνθ' ἑνὸς ἐμοῦ πατέρες
πολλοί, περιέποντές τε καὶ τὰ ἄριστα συμβουλεύοντες. οὔτε
γὰρ χρημάτων πλῆθος οὐδὲν αὔταρκες πρὸς τυραννίδος ἀκρατ-
ίαν, οὔτε δορυφόρων φρουρὰ ἱκανὴ ῥύεσθαι τὸν ἄρχοντα, εἰ
μὴ προυπάρχει ἡ τῶν ὑπηκόων εὔνοια. μάλιστα δὲ ἐκεῖνοι ἐς
ἀρχῆς μῆκος ἀκινδύνως ἤλασαν,[2] ὅσοι μὴ φόβον ἐξ ὠμότητος,
πόθον δὲ τῆς αὐτῶν χρηστότητος ταῖς τῶν ἀρχομένων ψυχαῖς
ἐνέσταξαν. οὐ γὰρ οἱ ἐξ ἀνάγκης δουλεύοντες ἀλλ' οἱ μετὰ
πειθοῦς ὑπακούοντες ἀνύποπτοι καὶ ἔξω κολακείας προσποιήτου
δρῶντές τε καὶ πάσχοντες διατελοῦσιν, καὶ οὐδέ ποτε ἀφηνιάζ-
ουσιν, ἢν μὴ βίᾳ καὶ ὕβρει ἐπὶ τοῦτο ἄχθωσι. χαλεπὸν δὲ
μετριάσαι τε καὶ ὅρον ἐπιθεῖναι ἐπιθυμίαις ὑπηρετούσης ἐξουσίας. τοιαῦτα δὴ συμβουλεύοντες αὐτῷ, καὶ ὧν ἀκούει παρὼν
ὑπομνήσκοντες, ὑμῖν τε αὐτοῖς καὶ πᾶσιν ἄριστον ἀποδείξετε
βασιλέα, τῇ τε ἐμῇ μνήμῃ χαριεῖσθε τὰ μέγιστα, οὕτω τε
μόνως ἀίδιον[3] αὐτὴν ποιῆσαι δυνήσεσθε."—Herodian, i. 4, § 2.

---

[1] Dio (72. 1. 1) says Commodus was by nature ἄκακος, but
from too great ἁπλότης (cp. 71. 22. 3) and cowardice easily
influenced by his entourage, and was thus by ignorance led
into bad ways. See also Julian, Conviv. 429. 14.

[2] cp. Vulc. Gall. Vit. Cass. viii. 3.

THE SPEECHES OF MARCUS

he should be dashed upon the rock of evil habits. Be ye therefore to him many fathers in the place of me, his one father, taking care of him and giving him the best counsel. For neither can any wealth, however abundant, suffice for the incontinence of a tyranny, nor a bodyguard be strong enough to protect the ruler, unless he has first of all the good-will of the governed. For those rulers complete a long course of sovranty without danger who instil into the hearts of their subjects not fear by their cruelty, but love by their goodness. For it is not those who serve as slaves under compulsion, but those who are obedient from persuasion, that are above suspicion, and continue doing and being done by without any cloak of flattery, and never show restiveness unless driven to it by violence and outrage. And it is difficult to check and put a just limit to our desires when Power is their minister. By giving my son then such advice, and bringing to his memory what he now hears with his own ears, you will render him both for yourselves and all mankind the best of kings, and you will do my memory the greatest of services, and thus alone be enabled to make it immortal."

---

[3] This aspiration does not tally with the repeated denunciations of fame in the *Meditations* iii. 10 ; iv. 19, 33, τί δὲ καί ἐστιν ὅλως τὸ ἀείμνηστον; ὅλον κενόν.

THE SAYINGS OF MARCUS

INTRODUCTION

NOTHING lets us into the secret of a man's character better than little anecdotes about him, and even seemingly trivial sayings uttered by him without any thoughts of a listening posterity. Unfortunately few such reminiscences of Marcus are extant, but the little that remains will be found to throw some light on a character which it has become too much the fashion to accuse of feebleness, criminal complaisance and inefficiency on the one hand, and on the other of harshness and cruelty. No support is given here to either of these mutually destructive views of a personality that was a striking combination of 'sweetness and gravity,'[1] of mildness and tenacity, of justice and mercy. We see a truly religious man who lived up to his creed,[2] a tempered Stoicism.

---

[1] *Medit.* i. 15.
[2] Dio 71. 30, § 2 ; Phil. *Vit. Soph.* ii. 11 (p. 242 Kayser) ; *C.I.L.* ii. 6278 = *Eph. Epigr.* vii. 385.

MARCUS AURELIUS

(1) *Capit. iv. 7.*

Post hoc patrimonium paternum sorori[1] totum con-
cessit, cum eum ad divisionem mater vocaret, respondit-
que "avi bonis se esse contentum," addens "ut et mater,
si vellet, in sororem suum patrimonium conferret, ne
inferior esset soror marito."[2]

(2) *Capit. v. 3, 4.*

Ubi autem comperit se ab Hadriano[3] adoptatum, magis
est deterritus quam laetatus, iussusque in Hadriani priv-
atam domum migrare invitus de maternis hortis[4] recessit.
Cumque ab eo domestici quaererent, cur tristis in adopt-
ionem regiam transiret, disputavit "quae mala in se
contineret imperium."

(3) *Capit. xxvii. 7.*

Sententia Platonis[5] semper in ore illius fuit, "Florere
civitates, si aut philosophi imperarent aut imperantes
philosopharentur."

(4) *Dio* 71. 34, § 4 = *Suidas* sub voce Μάρκος.

Εἰ μέν τις χρηστόν τι ἔπραττεν, ἐπῄνει καὶ ἔχρητο ἐς ἐκεῖνο
αὐτῷ,[6] τῶν δὲ ἑτέρων οὐ προσεποιεῖτο, λέγων ὅτι "ποιῆσαι μέν

---

[1] His only sister Cornificia.   [2] Ummidius Quadratus.

[3] Schulz supplies *Antonino auctore* before Hadriano.

[4] These "Gardens," that is, Lucilla's private residence in
its own private grounds, were probably on the Caelian hill.

[5] Plato, *Rep.* 473 D, quoted also by Cicero in his letter to
his brother Quintus, *de provincia administranda*.

[6] A lesson learnt from Pius; see *above*, i. 16, § 6.

THE SAYINGS OF MARCUS

(1)

AFTER this[1] he gave up to his sister all that he had inherited from his father, though his mother invited him to
share it equally, and replied that *he was content with being
his grandfather's heir*, adding that *his mother too, if she
were willing, should bestow her property upon his sister,
that his sister might be on an equality with her husband.*

(2)

When however he learnt that he had been adopted
by Hadrian, he was more abashed than pleased, and
when bidden to migrate to Hadrian's private house, he
left his mother's mansion with regret. And when the
household asked him why he took his adoption into the
royal house so sadly, he enlarged upon *the evils insepar-
able from sovran power.*

(3)

The sentence of Plato was for ever on his lips: *Well
was it for states, if either philosophers were rulers or rulers
philosophers.*[2]

(4)

If anyone did anything excellent, he praised him and
utilized him for that, but did not expect other things
from him, saying, *It is impossible to make men exactly as*

---

[1] About 136 A.D., when Marcus was 15.
[2] Aur. Victor (*De Caes.* xv. 3) applies the saying to Pius.
Justin was well advised therefore in his Apology (i. 3),
addressed to Pius and Marcus, in quoting the similar
aphorism: ἔφη πού καί τις τῶν παλαίων· ἂν μὴ οἱ ἄρχοντες φιλο-
σοφήσωσι καὶ οἱ ἀρχόμενοι, οὐκ ἂν εἴη τὰς πόλεις εὐδαιμονῆσαι.

τινι ἀνθρώπους ὁποίους βούλεται ἔχειν ἀδύνατόν ἐστι,[1] τοῖς δὲ
δὴ οὖσι προσήκει, ἐς ὅ τι ἄν τις αὐτῶν τῷ κοινῷ χρήσιμος
ᾖ, χρῆσθαι."

(5) *Capit. xxii.* 3, 4.

Semper cum optimatibus non solum bellicas res sed
etiam civiles, priusquam faceret aliquid, contulit. Denique sententia illius praecipua semper haec fuit : "Aequius
est, ut ego tot talium amicorum[2] consilium sequar, quam
ut tot tales amici meam unius voluntatem sequantur."

(6) *Dio*, 71. 29, § 3.

Οὕτω γε πόρρω παντὸς φόνου καθειστήκει ὥστε καὶ λεόντά
τινα δεδιδαγμένον ἀνθρώπους ἐσθίειν ἐκέλευσε μὲν ἐπαχθῆναι
αἰτησαμένου τοῦ δήμου, οὔτε δὲ ἐκεῖνον εἶδεν οὔτε τὸν διδάσκα-
λον αὐτοῦ ἠλευθέρωσε, καίπερ ἐπὶ πολὺ τῶν ἀνθρώπων ἐγκει-
μένων οἵ, ἀλλὰ καὶ κηρυχθῆναι προσέταξεν ὅτι "οὐδὲν ἄξιον
ἐλευθερίας πεποίηκεν."[3]

(7) *Capit. xix.* 8.

De qua (*sc.* Faustina) cum diceretur Antonino Marco,
ut eam repudiaret, si non occideret, dixisse fertur : "Si

---

[1] See *above*, ix. 42, and *cp.* vii. 7.

[2] *Amici* was a usual name for the *Concilium*, or Privy
Council, of the Emperor, a body of advisers first organized
by Hadrian, and they may be meant here. Of a difficult
case, where his own interests were involved, Marcus says to
Fronto (*Ad Caes.* i. 17) : " Duas res animo meo carissimas
secutus sum, rationem veram et sententiam tuam. Di velint,
ut semper quod agam, secundo iudicio tuo agam."

[3] The jurist Paulus (*Dig* xl. 9. 17) tells us that Marcus
"prohibuit ex acclamatione populi manumittere"; *cp.*
Cod. vii. 11. 3. Fronto (*Ad Caes.* i. 8) seems to imply that
Pius was more indulgent in this matter.

*one wishes them to be, but it is our duty to utilize them,
such as they are, for any service in which they can be useful
to the common weal.*

(5)

Not only in military but also in civil affairs, before
doing anything, he always consulted the chief men of
the State. In fact this was ever a favourite saying of
his : *It is fairer that I should follow the advice of Friends
so many and so wise, than that Friends so wise and so
many should follow my single will.*[1]

(6)

So averse from all bloodshed was his disposition that,
though at the people's request he allowed a lion trained
to devour men to be introduced into the arena, yet he
not only refused to look at it himself or to enfranchize its
trainer, in spite of a persistent demonstration of the
audience against him, but even had it proclaimed that
the man had done nothing to deserve freedom.[2]

(7)

When it was said to Marcus Antoninus of his wife,
that he should divorce her, if he did not slay her, he is
reported to have said, *If we dismiss the wife, let us also*

---

[1] *cp.* Capit. xi. 10, where we are told that Marcus
consulted his *praefecti* (i.e. *praetorio*) and relied especially on the jurist Scaevola. In the *Digest* he calls
Rusticus, Volusius Maecianus and Salvius Julianus *amici.*
A maxim of his was *Blush not to be helped* (*Medit.* vii. 7);
cp. also Fronto, *Ad Caes.* i. 17, "post consultationem
amicorum."

[2] Yet his bias towards the enfranchisement of slaves was
notorious. See *Digest*, xxxviii. 4. 3 : "quod videlicet favore
constituit libertatis."

uxorem dimittimus, reddamus et dotem."[1] Dos autem
quid habebatur nisi imperium, quod ille ab socero
volente Hadriano adoptatus acceperat.

(8) *Digest iv. 2. 13 = xlviii. 7. 7 (Callistratus).*

Cum Marcianus diceret, "Vim nullam feci," Caesar
dixit, "Tu vim putas solum si homines vulnerentur? Vis
est et tunc quotiens quis id, quod deberi putat, non per
iudicem reposcit. Non puto autem nec verecundiae nec
dignitati nec pietati tuae convenire quicquam non iure
facere."

(9) *Galen, xiv. 658 (Kühn).*

Τῷ δὲ Πειθολάῳ[2] εἶπεν "ἰατρὸν ἔχειν ἕνα καὶ τοῦτον ἐλεύθερον," πάνυ διετέλει τε περὶ ἐμοῦ λέγων ἀεὶ "τὸν μὲν ἰατρῶν
πρῶτόν <με> εἶναι τῶν δὲ φιλοσόφων μόνον."

(10) *Dio,* 71. 3. 3 = Fragm. *Dind. v. p.* 206.
= Zonaras xii. 2.

Καίτοι δὲ ἰσχυροτάτου ἀγῶνος καὶ λαμπρᾶς νίκης γεγενη-
μένης, ὅμως ὁ αὐτοκράτωρ αἰτηθεὶς παρὰ τῶν στρατιωτῶν οὐκ
ἔδωκε χρήματα, αὐτὸ τοῦτο εἰπὼν ὅτι "ὅσῳ ἂν πλεῖον παρὰ τὸ
καθεστηκὸς λάβωσι, τοῦτο ἐκ τοῦ αἵματος τῶν τε γονέων σφῶν
καὶ τῶν συγγενῶν ἐσπεπράξεται· περὶ γάρ τοι τῆς αὐταρχίας ὁ

---

[1] The same thing had been said long before by Burrhus to
Nero of his wife Octavia, and in that case was applicable,
but it was not so in this, and besides Marcus was devoted to
his wife to the last. See *above,* i. 17, § 7 ; Capit. xxvi. 4 ff. ;
Dio, 71. 30, § 1.

[2] One of the court physicians, who had been utterly wrong
in their diagnosis of the illness of Marcus, while Galen had
accurately divined it by merely feeling the patient's pulse.

surrender the dowry. But what was meant by the dowry if not the Empire, which he had received when adopted by his father-in-law at Hadrian's wish ?[1]

(8)

When Marcianus said, "I have done no violence," Caesar said, *Do you think that violence is shewn only if men are wounded? There is violence then also, whenever a man demands back what he thinks due to him otherwise than by judicial process. But I do not think it consistent with either your modesty or your dignity or your loyalty to the state that you should do anything except legally.*

(9)

And he said to Peitholaus that *he had but one physician and he was a free man,* and he went on to say repeatedly about me that *I was the first of physicians and the only philosopher.*[2]

(10)

And yet, though a most stubborn contest had been followed by a brilliant victory, nevertheless, when petitioned by the soldiers, the Emperor refused to give them a largess, saying only this, that *the more they received beyond their fixed pay, the more would be wrung from the life-blood of their parents and kinsfolk; for in the matter*

---

[1] Marcus did not receive the Empire through Pius, but by Hadrian's direct nomination. The latter arranged for Marcus to marry Fabia, the sister of Lucius Commodus, but Pius broke this arrangement in favour of his own daughter Faustina. She inherited an immense *patrimonium* from her father for Marcus.

[2] Galen was one of the most remarkable men of ancient times. On this occasion he reports some more (unimportant) words of Marcus. Galen twice affirms elsewhere that a good physician is also a philosopher.

MARCUS AURELIUS

Θεὸς μόνον κρίνειν δύναται." [1] οὕτω καὶ σωφρόνως καὶ ἐγκρατ-
ῶς αὐτῶν ἦρχεν ὥστε, καίπερ ἐν τοσούτοις καὶ τηλικούτοις
πολέμοις ὤν, μηδὲν ἔξω τοῦ προσήκοντος μητ' ἐκ κολακείας
εἰπεῖν μητ' ἐκ φόβου ποιῆσαι. [2]

(11) *Philostratus*, Vit. Soph. *ii. 1, p. 242, Kayser.*

Ὑπὸ τούτου δὴ τοῦ πάθους ἔκφρων ὁ Ἡρώδης ἐγένετο καὶ
παρῆλθεν ἐς τὸ βασιλεῖον δικαστήριον [3] οὔτε ἔννους καὶ θανάτου
ἐρῶν. παρελθὼν γὰρ καθίστατο ἐς διαβολὰς τοῦ αὐτοκράτορος
οὐδὲ σχηματίσας τὸν λόγον, ὡς εἰκὸς ἦν ἄνδρα γεγυμνασμένον
τῆς τοιᾶσδε ἰδέας μεταχειρίσασθαι τὴν ἑαυτοῦ χολήν, ἀλλ'
ἀπηγκωνισμένη τῇ γλώττῃ καὶ γυμνῇ διετείνετο λέγων "ταῦτά
μοι ἡ Λουκίου ξενία, ὃν σύ μοι ἔπεμψας· ὅθεν δικάζεις, γυναικί
με καὶ τριετεῖ παιδίῳ καταχαριζόμενος." Βασσαίου δὲ τοῦ
πεπιστευμένου τὸ ξίφος θάνατον αὐτῷ φήσαντος ὁ Ἡρώδης
"ὦ λῷστε," ἔφη, "γέρων ὀλίγα φοβεῖται." ὁ μὲν οὖν ἀπῆλθε
τοῦ δικαστηρίου εἰπὼν ταῦτα καὶ μετέωρον καταλείψας πολὺ
τοῦ ὕδατος, [4] ἡμεῖς δὲ τῶν ἐπιδήλως τῷ Μάρκῳ φιλοσοφη-
θέντων καὶ τὰ περὶ τὴν δίκην ταύτην ἡγώμεθα· οὐ γὰρ ξυνήγαγε

---

[1] The other version has : τὸ δὲ κράτος τῆς αὐταρχίας οὐκ ἐν
τοῖς στρατιώταις ἀλλ' ἐν τῷ Θεῷ κεῖται.

[2] cp. Aristides (*Ad Reg.* § 116, Jebb.) : καὶ μὴν τὰ μὲν πρὸς
πολεμίους ἀνδρείοις πολλοῖς ὑπῆρξε γενέσθαι, ὑπὸ δὲ τῶν σφετέρων
στρατιωτῶν αὐτοὺς ἄρχεσθαι < μᾶλλον > ἢ κρατεῖν· ὁ δὲ οὕτω
ῥαδίως ἐκράτησε καὶ κατεστήσατο, ὥστε πολλῶν μὲν καὶ ἀπείρων
ὄντων τῶν δεδομένων αὐτοῖς, χαλεπῶν δὲ καὶ φοβερῶν εἰ μὴ
τοσαῦτα λαμβάνειν, οὐκ ἐπηύξησε (MS ἐπηῦξε) τὰς ἐπιθυμίας
αὐτῶν κ.τ.λ.

[3] The trial took place at Sirmium in Pannonia about
170 A.D., Herodes being accused of cruel and illegal conduct
at Athens. He had been accused by the same persons of
similar malpractices nearly thirty years before (see Fronto,
Ad Caes. iii. 2–6). This Herodes was an Athenian famous
for his riches, his generosity, and his oratory. He had been
the teacher of Marcus in Greek rhetoric.

[4] The water-clock that timed the speakers in a trial.

indeed of his sovranty God alone could be judge. With such wisdom and self-command did he rule them that, though engaged in so many and such great wars, he never swerved from what was right so as either to say anything from flattery or do anything from fear.[1]

(11)

Herodes was driven frantic by this calamity[2] and came up to the Emperor's seat of judgment no longer in his right mind and in love with death. For coming forward he set himself to rail at the Emperor, and without veiling his meaning or keeping his anger in hand, as might have been expected from one who was practised in such rhetorical devices, but in defiant and unbridled language he gave vent to his passion, saying "This is all that comes of my friendship with Lucius,[3] whom you sent to me, that in judging me you gratify your wife and three-year old child."[4] But when Bassaeus,[5] who had been invested with the power of capital punishment, threatened him with death, Herodes said, "My fine fellow, an old man has little more to fear." Saying this he left the court without availing himself of his full time for speaking. But in our opinion the conduct of Marcus at this trial too was signally in keeping with his philosophical tenets ; for

---

[1] This incident recorded by Dio belongs to the earlier stage of the Marcomannic war, when the Emperor was in great straits for money.

[2] The calamity was the death by lightning of his adopted daughters, the children of Alcimedon.

[3] Lucius Verus, the colleague of Marcus, who had died about a year before. He stayed with Herodes on his way to the East in 162.

[4] Vibia Sabina, the last child of Marcus, who with Faustina, hence called *Mater Castrorum*, was with him at Sirmium.

[5] Bassaeus Rufus, praetorian prefect 168-177.

τὰς ὀφρῦς, οὐδὲ ἔτρεψε τὸ ὄμμα, ὃ κἂν διαιτητής τις ἔπαθεν,
ἀλλ' ἐπιστρέψας ἑαυτὸν ἐς τοὺς 'Αθηναίους " ἀπολογεῖσθε,"
ἔφη, " ὦ 'Αθηναῖοι, εἰ καὶ μὴ ξυγχωρεῖ 'Ηρώδης." καὶ
ἀκούων ἀπολογουμένων ἐπὶ πολλοῖς μὲν ἀφανῶς ἤλγησεν,
ἀναγιγνωσκομένης δὲ αὐτῷ καὶ 'Αθηναίων ἐκκλησίας,[1] ἐν ᾗ
ἐφαίνοντο καθαπτόμενοι τοῦ 'Ηρώδου, ὡς τοὺς ἄρχοντας τῆς
'Ελλάδος ὑποποιουμένου πολλῷ τῷ μέλιτι, καί που καὶ βεβοη-
κότες " ὦ πικροῦ μέλιτος" καὶ πάλιν " μακάριοι οἱ ἐν τῷ λοιμῷ
ἀποθνήσκοντες," οὕτως ἐσείσθη τὴν καρδίαν ὑφ' ὧν ἤκουσεν, ὡς
ἐς δάκρυα φανερὰ ὑπαχθῆναι. τῆς δὲ τῶν 'Αθηναίων ἀπολογίας
ἐχούσης κατηγορίαν τοῦ τε 'Ηρώδου καὶ τῶν ἀπελευθέρων τὴν
ὀργὴν ὁ Μάρκος ἐς τοὺς ἀπελευθέρους ἔτρεψε κολάσει χρησά-
μενος ὡς οἷον ἐπιεικεῖ, οὕτω γὰρ αὐτὸς χαρακτηρίζει τὴν ἑαυτοῦ
κρίσιν, μόνῳ δὲ 'Αλκιμέδοντι τὴν τιμωρίαν ἐπανῆκεν " ἀποχρῶ-
σαν εἶναι οἱ" φήσας "τὴν ἐπὶ τοῖς τέκνοις συμφοράν." ταῦτα
μὲν δὴ ὧδε ἐφιλοσοφεῖτο τῷ Μάρκῳ.

(12) *Themistius*, Orat. 15. 191b.

'Αντωνίνῳ τῷ 'Ρωμαίων αὐτοκράτορι, ᾧ τούτῳ αὐτὸ ἐπώνυμον
" ὁ Εὐσεβὴς" ἦν,[2] τοῦ στρατεύματος ὑπὸ δίψους [αὐτῷ]
πιεζομένου, ἀνασχὼν τὼ χεῖρε ὁ βασιλεὺς πρὸς τὸν οὐρανόν
"ταύτῃ" ἔφη "τῇ χειρὶ προυτρεψάμην σε καὶ ἱκέτευσα τὸν
ζωῆς δοτῆρα, ἣ ζωὴν οὐκ ἀφειλόμην." καὶ οὕτω κατήδεσε τὸν
θεὸν τῇ εὐχῇ ὥστε ἐξ αἰθρίας ἧκον νεφέλαι ὑδροφοροῦσαι τοῖς
στρατιώταις.

---

[1] Perhaps ἐγκλήσεως.
[2] This was the peculiar cognomen of Pius, but Marcus
sometimes receives it even in inscriptions.

he did not frown, **or** so much as turn his eyes, as even an arbitrator might have done, but turning to the Athenians said : *Make your plea, men of Athens, even though Herodes is not for allowing you to do so.* And as he listened to their case, at many points he was secretly grieved, but when the complaint of the Athenian Assembly was being read to him, in which they openly attacked Herodes for trying to win over the Governors of Greece with many honeyed words, and somewhere or other even cried out, "O bitter honey!" and again, "Happy they that perish in the pestilence!" he was so deeply moved by what he heard, that he was brought to tears in the sight of all. But as the case of the Athenians comprised an accusation against his freedmen as well as against Herodes, Marcus diverted his anger on to the freedmen, punishing them however as leniently as possible—for that is how he himself characterizes his sentence,—but to Alcimedon alone he remitted the punishment, alleging that his calamity in respect of his children was punishment enough.[1] In a way then thus worthy of a philosopher did Marcus act on this occasion.

(12)

When the army of Antoninus the Roman Emperor, who also had the cognomen of Pius, was perishing of thirst,[2] the king, raising both his hands to heaven, said, *With this hand, wherewith I have taken away no life, have I implored Thee and besought the Giver of life.* And he so prevailed with God by his prayer that upon a clear sky there came up clouds bringing rain to his soldiers.

---

[1] *cp.* his words in the *Digest*, i. 18. 14 : *his madness is in itself punishment enough.*

[2] At the time of the so-called "miraculous victory" over the Quadi in 174 ; see Dio, 71. 8.

MARCUS AURELIUS

(13) *Ammianus Marcellinus, xxii.* **5.**

Cum Palaestinam transiret Aegyptum petens Judae-
orum foetentium et tumultuantium saepe taedio percitus
dolenter dicitur exclamasse, "O Marcomanni, O Quadi,
O Sarmatae, tandem alios vobis inertiores[1] inveni."

(14) *Dio*, Fragm. *Dind. v. p.* 206.

Ὅτι παρασκευαζομένου τοῦ Μάρκου[2] εἰς τὸν κατὰ Κασσίου
πόλεμον οὐδεμίαν βαρβαρικὴν συμμαχίαν ἐδέξατο καίτοι
πολλῶν συνδραμόντων αὐτῷ, λέγων "μὴ χρῆναι τοῖς βαρβάροις εἰδέναι τὰ μεταξὺ Ῥωμαίων κινούμενα κακά."

(15) *Vulc. Gallicanus*, Vit. Cass. *viii.*

Caput eius ad Antoninum cum delatum esset, ille non
exultavit, non elatus est, sed etiam doluit "ereptam sibi
esse occasionem misericordiae," cum diceret "se vivum
illum voluisse capere, ut illa exprobraret beneficia sua
eumque servaret." Denique cum quidam diceret repre-
hendendum Antoninum, quod tam mitis esset in hostem
suum eiusque liberos et adfectus atque omnes, quos
conscios tyrannidis repperisset, addente illo qui repre-
hendebat "Quid si ille vicisset?" dixisse dicitur: "Non
sic deos coluimus nec sic vivimus, ut ille nos vinceret."
Enumeravit deinde "omnes principes, qui occisi essent,
habuisse causas quibus mererentur occidi nec quemquam
facile bonum vel victum a tyranno vel occisum, dicens

---

[1] This word is doubtful, another reading being *inetiores*.
Suggested emendations are *inquietiores, ineptiores.* *cp.*
Josephus *c. Apion* ii. 14, Dind.
[2] This should be in the nominative case.

(13)

When he was crossing Palestine on his way to Egypt, constantly moved with disgust at the unsavoury and turbulent Jews, he is said to have cried out with a groan, *O Marcomanni, O Quadi, O Sarmatians, at length have I found others more good for nothing than you.*[1]

(14)

When Marcus was making preparations for the war against Cassius he would not accept any aid from barbarians, though many offered him their services, saying that *the barbarians must not know the troubles that were being stirred up between Romans.*[2]

(15)

When the head of Cassius was brought to him, Antoninus shewed no exultation or pride, but even lamented that *he had been robbed of an opportunity for compassion, for he had wished to take him alive,* he said, *that he might reproach him with the benefits he had done him, and then spare his life.* Lastly when one said that Antoninus was to blame for his clemency toward his enemy and his enemy's children and relations and all whom he had found to be accomplices in the usurpation, the man who had imputed the blame going on to say, "What if he had been successful?" Marcus is said to have answered, *My worship of the Gods has not been such, my life is not such, that he could be successful.* He then, enumerating all the Emperors who had been killed, pointed out that *they had deserved their fate, and that no good Emperor had easily been overcome by a usurper or slain, adding that Nero had*

---

[1] Or 'more of a bore.' The date would be 176.

[2] So in the Boer War, in view of the native question in South Africa, England refused to employ her Indian and Maori troops.

meruisse Neronem, debuisse Caligulam, Othonem et
Vitellium non imperare voluisse."[1] Etiam de Galba
paria sentiebat, cum diceret "in imperatore avaritiam
esse acerbissimum malum. Denique non Augustum, non
Traianum, non Hadrianum, non patrem suum a rebellibus
potuisse superari, cum et multi fuerint et ipsis vel invitis
vel insciis exstincti." Ipse autem Antoninus a senatu
petiit, "ne graviter in conscios defectionis animadverte-
retur," eo ipso tempore, quo rogavit, "ne quis senator
temporibus suis capitali supplicio adficeretur," quod illi
maximum amorem conciliavit.

(16) *Philostratus*, Vit. Soph. *ii*. 9, *p*. 252, *Kays*.

Οἰκιστὴν δὲ καὶ τὸν Ἀριστείδην τῆς Σμύρνης εἰπεῖν οὐκ
ἀλάζων ἔπαινος ἀλλὰ δικαιότατός τε καὶ ἀληθέστατος. τὴν γὰρ
πόλιν ταύτην ἀφανισθεῖσαν ὑπὸ σεισμῶν τε καὶ χασμάτων
οὕτω τι ὠλοφύρατο πρὸς τὸν Μάρκον, ὡς τῇ μὲν ἄλλῃ μονῳδίᾳ
θαμὰ ἐπιστενάξαι τὸν βασιλέα, ἐπὶ δὲ τῷ "ζέφυροι δὲ ἐρήμην
καταπνέουσι" καὶ δάκρυα τῷ βιβλίῳ[2] ἐπιστάξαι τὸν βασιλέα,
ξυνοικίαν τε τῇ πόλει ἐκ τῶν τοῦ Ἀριστείδου ἐνδοσίμων[3]
νεῦσαι. ἐτύγχανε δὲ καὶ ξυγγεγονὼς ἤδη τῷ Μάρκῳ ὁ Ἀριστείδης ἐν Ἰωνίᾳ, ὡς γὰρ τοῦ Ἐφεσίου Δαμιανοῦ ἤκουον,
ἐπεδήμει μὲν ὁ αὐτοκράτωρ ἤδη τῇ Σμύρνῃ τρίτην ἡμέραν, τὸν
δὲ Ἀριστείδην οὔπω γιγνώσκων ἤρετο τοὺς Κυντιλίους μὴ ἐν
τῷ τῶν ἀσπαζομένων ὁμίλῳ παρεωραμένος αὐτῷ ὁ ἀνὴρ εἴη,

---

[1] Should be *debuisse* or *meruisse*.
[2] We have the letter, addressed to Marcus and Commodus,
in the works of Aristides (Jebb, § 209). Its date would be
177–180.
[3] Lit. *to the tune set by Aristides*.

*deserved, Caligula had earned his death, Otho and Vitellius
ought never to have reigned.* His opinion of Galba was
similar, for he remarked that *in an Emperor avarice* [1] *was
the most hateful of faults. In a word, rebels had never
been able to overcome either Augustus or Trajan or Hadrian
or his own father, for many as they were, they had been
crushed against the wish or without the knowledge of the
reigning Emperor.* Antoninus himself, however, besought
the Senate *not to proceed with severity against accomplices in the rebellion,* asking at the same time that *no
Senator should in his reign be punished with death;* and
this won for him the greatest love.

(16)

It is no flatterer's praise but the truest and most just
to call Aristides the founder of Smyrna. For he made so
moving a lament to Marcus over the utter destruction of
this city by earthquakes and openings in the ground, that
over the rest of the mournful tale the Emperor sighed
repeatedly, but at the "breezes blowing over a city of
desolation" he even let tears fall upon the writing, and
granted the restoration of the city in accordance with the
suggestions of Aristides. It chanced also that Aristides
had already made the acquaintance of Marcus in Ionia,
for when they were attending the lectures of the Athenian
Damianus, the Emperor who had already been three days
in Smyrna, not yet knowing Aristides personally, re-
quested the Quintilii [2] to see that the man should not be
passed over unnoticed in the imperial levée. They said

---

[1] *cp.* Capit. xxix. 5 : *Nihil magis et timuit et deprecatus
est quam avaritiae famam de qua se multis epistulis purgat.*
Dio, after speaking of his liberality and public benefactions,
says (71. 32, § 3) : ἀφ' οὗπερ καὶ νῦν θαυμάζω τῶν αἰτιωμένων
αὐτὸν ὡς οὐ μεγαλόφρονα γενόμενον.

[2] Two brothers, famed for their character, ability, and
fraternal affection. They exercised conjointly the governor-
ship of Achaia, and later a military command in Pannonia.
They also shared an unjust death at the hands of Commodus.

οἱ δὲ οὐδὲ αὐτοὶ ἔφασαν ἑωρακέναι αὐτόν, οὐ γὰρ παρεῖναι
<ἂν> τὸ μὴ οὐ ξυστῆσαι, καὶ ἀφίκοντο τῆς ὑστεραίας τὸν
Ἀριστείδην ἄμφω δορυφοροῦντες, προσειπὼν δὲ αὐτὸν ὁ αὐτοκράτωρ "διὰ τί σε" ἔφη "βραδέως εἴδομεν;" καὶ ὁ Ἀριστείδης
"θεώρημα," ἔφη, "ὦ βασιλεῦ, ἠσχολεῖ, γνώμη δὲ θεωροῦσα
μὴ ἀποκρεμαννύσθω οὗ ζητεῖ." ὑπερησθεὶς δὲ ὁ αὐτοκράτωρ
τῷ ἤθει τἀνδρὸς ὡς ἁπλοϊκωτάτῳ τε καὶ σχολικωτάτῳ "πότε"
ἔφη "ἀκροάσομαί σου;" καὶ ὁ Ἀριστείδης "τήμερον" εἶπεν
"πρόβαλε καὶ αὔριον ἀκροῶ· οὐ γὰρ ἐσμὲν τῶν ἐμούντων ἀλλὰ
τῶν ἀκριβούντων. ἐξέστω δέ, ὦ βασιλεῦ, καὶ τοὺς γνωρίμους
παρεῖναι τῇ ἀκροάσει." "ἐξέστω," ἦ δ' ὁ Μάρκος, "δημοτι-
κὸν γάρ." εἰπόντος δὲ τοῦ Ἀριστείδου, "διδόσθω δὲ αὐτοῖς,
ὦ βασιλεῦ, καὶ βοᾶν καὶ κροτεῖν, ὁπόσον δύνανται," μειδιάσας
ὁ αὐτοκράτωρ "τοῦτο" ἔφη "ἐπὶ σοὶ κεῖται."

(17) *Dio*, 71. 32, § 1 = Fragm. *Dind. v. p.* 207.

Ἐλθὼν δὲ ἐς τὴν Ῥώμην καὶ πρὸς τὸν δῆμον διαλεγόμενος,
ἐπειδὴ μεταξὺ λέγοντος αὐτοῦ τά τε ἄλλα καὶ ὅτι πολλοῖς
ἔτεσιν ἀποδεδημηκὼς ἦν, ἀνεβόησαν "ὀκτώ," καὶ τοῦτο καὶ
ταῖς χερσίν, ἵνα δὴ καὶ χρυσοὺς τοσούτους ἐς τὸ δεῖπνον[1]
λάβωσι, προσενεδείξαντο, διεμειδίασε καὶ ἔφη καὶ αὐτὸς
"ὀκτώ," καὶ μετὰ ταῦτα ἀνὰ διακοσίας δραχμὰς αὐτοῖς κατ-
ένειμεν, ὅσον οὔπω πρότερον εἰλήφεσαν.

(18) *Dio*, 71. 33, § 2.

Ὁ δὲ Μάρκος καὶ χρήματα ἐκ τοῦ δημοσίου[2] ᾔτησε τὴν
βουλὴν οὐχ ὅτι μὴ ἔκειντο ἐπὶ τῇ τοῦ κρατοῦντος ἐξουσίᾳ, ἀλλ'

---

[1] The *congiarium* was originally a distribution of food by
measure. The largest to soldiers was called *donativum*.

[2] *i.e.* the *aerarium*. The Emperor's privy purse was called
fiscus.

they had not seen him themselves, for they would not have failed to introduce him ; and on the next day they both arrived escorting Aristides, and the Emperor addressing him said, *Why have you been so slow in letting me see you?* And Aristides said, " A professional problem, O King, occupied me, and the mind, when so engaged, must not be detached from the prosecution of its enquiry." The Emperor, charmed by the man's character, his extreme naïveté and studiousness, said, *When shall I hear you?* And Aristides replied, "Suggest a subject to-day and hear me to-morrow ; for I am not of those who 'throw up' what is in their minds but of those who speak with precision. But grant, O King, that my pupils also may be present at the hearing." *Certainly,* said Marcus, *they may, for it is free to all.* And on Aristides saying, "Permit them, O King, to cheer and applaud as loud as they can," the Emperor smiling said, *That depends on yourself.*

(17)

On his return to Rome, when, in addressing the people, he mentioned among other things that he had been absent many years, they shouted "Eight,"[1] and signified this besides with their fingers, of course that they might get so many pieces of gold for a congiarium. The Emperor smiled, and himself said, *Yes, eight,* and afterwards distributed 200 drachmas[2] apiece, a larger sum than they had ever received before.

(18)

Marcus even begged of the Senate money from the public treasury, not that it was not in the ruler's

---

[1] From 169 to 176 A.D.
[2] Seven or eight pounds, the denarius aureus being = 25 silver denarii.

MARCUS AURELIUS

ὅτι ὁ Μάρκος πάντα τῆς βουλῆς καὶ τοῦ δήμου καὶ αὐτὰ καὶ τἆλλα ἔλεγεν εἶναι· "ἡμεῖς γάρ," ἔφη πρὸς τὴν βουλὴν λέγων,[1] "οὕτως οὐδὲν ἴδιον ἔχομεν ὥστε καὶ ἐν τῇ ὑμετέρᾳ οἰκίᾳ οἰκοῦμεν."

(19) *Philostratus*, Vit. Soph. ii. 9, p. 240 Kays.

Λουκίου τούτου κἀκεῖνο θαυμάσιον. ἐσπούδαζε μὲν ὁ αὐτο-κράτωρ Μάρκος περὶ Σέξτον τὸν ἐκ Βοιωτίας φιλόσοφον, θαμίζων αὐτῷ καὶ φοιτῶν ἐπὶ θύρας, ἄρτι δὲ ἥκων ἐς τὴν Ῥώμην ὁ Λούκιος ἥρετο τὸν αὐτοκράτορα προ<σ>ίοντα, ποῖ βαδίζοι καὶ ἐφ' ὅ τι, καὶ ὁ Μάρκος "καλὸν" ἔφη "καὶ γηράσκοντι τὸ μανθάνειν· εἶμι δὴ πρὸς Σέξτον τὸν φιλόσοφον μαθησόμενος, ἃ οὔπω οἶδα." καὶ ὁ Λούκιος ἐξάρας τὴν χεῖρα ἐς τὸν οὐρανόν, "Ὦ Ζεῦ," ἔφη, "ὁ Ῥωμαίων βασιλεὺς γηράσκων ἤδη δέλτον ἐξαψάμενος ἐς διδασκάλου φοιτᾷ, ὁ δὲ ἐμὸς βασιλεὺς Ἀλέξαν-δρος δύο καὶ τριάκοντα ἐτῶν ἀπέθανεν."[2]

(20) *Capit.* xxviii.

Cum aegrotare coepisset, filium[3] advocavit atque ab eo primum petiit ut belli reliquias non contemneret, ne

---

[1] The date would be in 178, just before the Emperor's last departure for the war.

[2] For this anecdote *cp.* Dio, 71. 1, § 2 : λέγεται καὶ αὐτο-κράτωρ ὢν μὴ αἰδεῖσθαι ἐς διδασκάλου φοιτᾶν, ἀλλὰ καὶ Σέξτῳ προσιέναι τῷ ἐκ Βοιωτῶν φιλοσόφῳ καὶ ἐς ἀκρόασιν τῶν ῥητορικῶν Ἑρμογένους λόγων μὴ ὀκνῆσαι παραγενέσθαι. The date is most likely 177-8, before the last departure to the war. At this time Marcus was engaged himself in giving lectures on philosophy. See Aur. Victor, *De Caes.* xvi. 9 ; *cp.* Vulc. Gallicanus, *Vit. Cassii*, iii. 7.

[3] His son Commodus, now 19 years old. He was perhaps more weak than vicious. As a matter of fact Pompeianus and the other *amici* of Marcus persuaded Commodus to remain for six months.

power to demand it, but because Marcus said that every-thing, both money and all else, belonged to the Senate and the people ; for *We*, he said, speaking to the Senate, *so far from having anything of our own, even live in a house that is yours.*[1]

(19)

Of this Lucius[2] another surprising story is told. The Emperor Marcus was an eager disciple of Sextus the Boeotian philosopher,[3] being often in his company and frequenting his house. Lucius, who had just come to Rome, asked the Emperor, whom he met on his way, where he was going to and on what errand, and Marcus answered, *It is good even for an old man to learn ;*[4] *I am now on my way to Sextus the philosopher to learn what I do not yet know.* And Lucius, raising his hand to heaven, said, " O Zeus, the king of the Romans in his old age takes up his tablets and goes to school. But my king Alexander died before he was thirty-two."

(20)

When he began to sicken, he sent for his son, and at first besought him not to neglect the relics of the war,[5]

---

[1] The Emperor, if he said these words, can hardly be acquitted of some affectation, as he had a very large fortune in his own right, inherited from his mother and also through Faustina.   [2] A philosopher friend of Herodes Atticus.

[3] Sextus was grandson of Plutarch and a teacher of Marcus ; see Capit. iii. 2, and Marcus himself (i. 9 and note), from which we see what he learnt " in his old age." He also "shewed off" his philosophy before Sextus ; see Themistius, *Orat.* xi. 145*b*.

[4] In this he was in the good company of our own great Alfred. *cp.* also Seneca, *Ep.* 76 : tamdiu discendum est, quamdiu nescias ; Solon, *Fragm.* 8. Bergk, γηράσκων δ' αἰεὶ πολλὰ διδασκόμενος.

[5] The parallel with our Edward II. is very close.

videretur rem publicam prodere. Et cum filius ei
respondisset cupere se primum sanitatem, ut vellet per-
misit petens tamen ut exspectaret paucos dies, haud
simul proficisceretur. Deinde abstinuit victu potuque
mori cupiens auxitque morbum. Sexta die vocatis
amicis et ridens res humanas, mortem autem contemnens
ad amicos dixit, "Quid de me fletis et non magis de
pestilentia et communi morte cogitatis?" Et cum illi
vellent recedere, ingemiscens ait, "Si iam me dimit-
titis, vale vobis dico vos praecedens." Et cum ab eo
quaereretur, cui filium commendaret, ille respondit:
"Vobis, si dignus fuerit, et dis immortalibus." Septimo
die gravatus est et solum filium admisit. Quem statim
dimisit, ne in eum morbus transiret. Dimisso filio caput
operuit quasi volens dormire sed nocte animam efflavit.

(21ᵃ) *Dio* Fragm. *Dind. v. p.* 206.

Ἐνόσησε σφόδρα ὁ Μάρκος, ὥστε ὀλίγας ἐλπίδας ἐπὶ τῆς
σωτηρίας ἔχειν· καὶ πολλάκις ἐν τῇ νόσῳ ἐπεφώνει τὸ τῆς
τραγῳδίας ἰαμβεῖον,

"τοιαῦτα τλήμων πόλεμος ἐξεργάζεται."[1]

(21ᵇ) *Dio* 71. 33, § 4.

Μέλλων οὖν ἀποθνήσκειν τῷ χιλιάρχῳ τὸ σύνθημα αἰτοῦντι
ἔφη, "ἄπελθε πρὸς τὸν ἀνατέλλοντα, ἐγὼ γὰρ δύομαι."

---

[1] This quotation occurs again in Dio, 71. 22, but with a
different application, as a sarcasm against the rise of Pertinax,
a man of humble birth, to the consulship.

lest he should seem to betray the State. But when his son answered that his first care was for health, he let him do as he would, begging him however to wait a few days and not take his departure at once. Then he abstained from food and drink,[1] wishing to die, and aggravated the disease. On the sixth day he called for his friends, and mocking earthly things, but setting death at naught, he said to them, *Why weep for me and not rather think on the pestilence and the death that awaits all?* And when they made as though to retire he said, sighing, *If you now give me my dismissal, I give you my farewell and lead the way for you.* And when it was asked of him to whom he commended his son, he answered, *To you, if he be worthy, and to the immortal Gods.* On the seventh day he grew worse, and allowed only his son to be admitted, but dismissed him at once that he might not take the infection. After parting from his son he veiled his head as if he would sleep, but in the night he breathed his last.

(21ª)

When Marcus was seriously ill, so as to have little hope of recovery, he would often cry out in his illness this verse from the tragedy,

Such is war's disastrous work.[2]

(21ᵇ)

When near his death, being asked by the tribune for the watchword, he said, *Go to the rising sun, for I am setting.*

---

[1] The latter is not likely. He had long been unable to take solid food ; see Dio (71. 6, § 4), who says positively that he was poisoned by order of Commodus. Others say he died of the pestilence.

[2] Pius in the delirium of his last fever *nihil aliud quam de re publica et de regibus, quibus irascebatur, locutus est* (Capit. *Vit. Pii*, xii. 8). Napoleon's last words were *tête d'armée.*

MARCUS AURELIUS

(22) *Philostratus*, Vit. Soph., *Kayser, p. 231*
(or Loeb Ser. refer.).

Μάρκου δὲ τοῦ αὐτοκράτορος πρὸς αὐτὸν εἰπόντος " Τί σοι
δοκεῖ ¹ ὁ Πολέμων ; " στήσας τοὺς ὀφθαλμοὺς ὁ Ἡρώδης ἔφη
" Ἵππων μ' ὠκυπόδων ἀμφὶ κτύπον οὔατα βάλλει," ² ἐνδεικνύμενος
δὴ τὸ ἐπίκροτον καὶ τὸ ὑψηχὲς τῶν λόγων . . .

"Ηριζεν ἡ Σμύρνα ὑπὲρ τῶν ναῶν ³ καὶ τῶν ἐπ' αὐτοῖς δικαίων
ξύνδικον πεποιημένη τὸν Πολέμωνα ἐς τέρμα ἤδη τοῦ βίου ἥκοντα.
ἐπεὶ δὲ ἐν ὁρμῇ τῆς ὑπὲρ τῶν δικαίων ἀποδημίας ἐτελεύτησεν,
ἐγένετο μὲν ἐπ' ἄλλοις ξυνδίκοις ἡ πόλις· πονηρῶς δὲ αὐτῶν ἐν
τῷ βασιλείῳ δικαστηρίῳ διατιθεμένων τὸν λόγον, βλέψας ὁ
αὐτοκράτωρ ἐς τοὺς τῶν Σμυρναίων ξυνηγόρους "Οὐ Πολέμων"
εἶπεν " τουτουὶ τοῦ ἄγωνος ξύνδικος ὑμῖν ἀπεδέδεικτο ; "
" Ναί " ἔφασαν " εἴ γε τὸν σοφιστὴν λέγεις." καὶ ὁ αὐτοκράτωρ
" ἴσως οὖν " ἔφη " καὶ λόγον τινα ξυνέγραψεν ὑπὲρ τῶν δικαίων,
οἷα δὴ ἐπ' ἐμοῦ τε ἀγωνιούμενος καὶ ὑπὲρ τηλικούτων." "Ἴσως "
ἔφασαν " ὦ βασιλεῦ, οὐ μὴν ἡμῖν γε εἰδέναι." καὶ ἔδωκεν ἀναβολὰς
ὁ αὐτοκράτωρ τῇ δίκῃ, ἔστ' ἂν διακομίσθη ὁ λόγος· ἀναγνωσθέντος
δὲ ἐν τῷ δικαστηρίῳ κατ' αὐτὸν ἐψηφίσατο ὁ βασιλεύς, καὶ
ἀπῆλθεν ἡ Σμύρνα τὰ πρωτεῖα νικῶσα, καὶ τὸν Πολέμωνα
αὐτοῖς ἀναβεβιωκέναι φάσκοντες.

(23) *Capit.*, Vit. Marci, xxix. 4.

Priusquam ad bellum Marcomannicum rediret, in
Capitolio iuravit nullum senatorem se sciente occissum,
quom etiam rebelles dixerit se servaturum fuisse, is
scisset.⁴

¹ For Marcus' own youthful opinion of Polemon see Fronto's
Letters, i. 117, ii. 241ⁿ (Loeb).
² Homer, *Iliad*, **x**. 535.
³ The contest was for the religious primacy of the Province
of Asia with Ephesus and other towns.
⁴ See above, p. 355, and the note there.

THE SAYINGS OF MARCUS

When the Emperor Marcus said to Herodes, "What do you think of Polemon ?" he, fixing his eyes, answered, "Hark ! on my ears there is falling the thunder of galloping chargers," signifying thereby the measured beat and resonance of his words . . .

Smyrna, being engaged in a dispute about the Shrines and the privileges attached to them, had chosen as their advocate Polemon, now come to the end of his life.   But when just about to start on his journey to defend their rights he died, and the city fell into the hands of other advocates ; but when these were putting their case badly in the Emperor's court, the latter, turning to the envoys from Smyrna, said, "Was not Polemon appointed your advocate in this contest ?"   "Yea," they said, "if you mean the Sophist."   "Perhaps, then," said the Emperor, "he had composed some speech in behalf of your rights, as was likely, since he was about to contend before me and for such important issues."   "Possibly so, O King," said they, "but not to our knowledge."   The Emperor then adjourned the case till the speech could be brought over ; and when it had been read in court the Emperor gave his verdict in accordance with it ; and Smyrna went away having gained the primacy, and asserting that Polemon had come to life again for their sake.

(23)

Before setting out again for the Marcomannic War, he took an oath on the Capitol that no senator had been put to death with his knowledge, since he would (he said) have saved even rebels, had he known.

381

NOTE ON THE ATTITUDE OF MARCUS TOWARDS THE CHRISTIANS

WITH

HIS EDICT ADDRESSED TO THE COMMON ASSEMBLY OF ASIA

Marcus and the Christians.
(i. 6, iii. 16, vii. 68, viii. 48. 51, xi. 3.)

NOTHING has done the good name of Marcus so much harm as his supposed uncompromising attitude towards the Christians, and in this connexion great emphasis has been laid upon a passage in the present book where the Christians, according to our accepted text, are mentioned. It will be worth while to examine this and certain other passages in the book and see if they throw any light on Marcus' real sentiments towards the Christians.

Taking xi. 3 first, we note that παράταξις, which is persistently translated *obstinacy* to bring it into line with Pliny's *obstinatio*, does not mean obstinacy at all, but *opposition*.[1] This is clear from the use of the word and its verb elsewhere by Marcus. In iii. 3 it is used in its primary sense of armies opposite one another on the field of battle. The only passage where the verb occurs (viii. 48) is very instructive. "Remember," he says, "that the ruling Reason shows itself unconquerable when, concentrated in itself, it is content with itself, so

---

[1] Since this was written I find that M. A. P. Lemercier (*Les Pensées de Marc-Aurèle*, Introd. p. viii. note 2) quotes with approval E. Havet's similar interpretation. Suidas glosses παράταξις with πόλεμος ἐμπαράσκευος.

it do nothing that it doth not will, even if it refuse from mere unreasoning opposition (κᾶν ἀλόγως παρατάξηται)." Here the word is used in exactly the same connexion as in xi. 3, and by no means in a sense entirely condemnatory. It seems to me quite possible that the Emperor may have had the Christians in mind here as well as in xi. 3. Conduct such as that of the Christians was precisely what Marcus is never tired of recommending, viz., not under any compulsion to transgress the demands of the ruling Reason,[1] and if it were found impossible to act up to the standard of right set by the conscience (τὸ ἔνδον ἱδρύμενον) owing to external causes, then to depart cheerfully from life. It appears to me that Marcus in both these passages is really approving of the resistance.

Again the actual mention of the Christians here requires to be considered. The word itself was taboo with the pagan stylists as a barbarism. Even when they are apparently alluding to Christians, such writers as Epictetus, Dio Chrysostom, Plutarch, Aristides, Apuleius, Dio Cassius, Philostratus, do not use the term—much as an Arnold or a Pater would hesitate to use the word "Salvationist." We do not find it in Fronto's extant works nor Galen's. Lucian, however, employed it in the *Alexander* and the *Peregrinus*, if (which some deny) these works are by him. Marcus would no doubt have used the word, as Trajan, Pliny and Hadrian did, in rescripts and official documents, but it is a question whether his literary purism and the example of his favourite Epictetus would have allowed him to employ it in a Greek philosophical treatise. When we look at the clause, ὡς οἱ Χριστιανοί, as here inserted, we see that it is outside the construction, and in fact ungrammatical. It is in the very form of a marginal note,[2] and has every appearance of being a gloss foisted into the text. But even if the words be omitted, Marcus may still have had the

---

[1] He says (viii. 41) that 'nothing can overbear this Reason, not steel, nor tyrant, nor obloquy.'

[2] I see Lemercier holds the same view.

NOTE ON CHRISTIANS

Christians in mind when he wrote the passage, which only condemns an eagerness to meet death without real justification and without due dignity.[1]

There are other expressions in this book which seem to glance at a body of men who must have been often in Marcus's thoughts. For instance, when he speaks (vii. 68) of those who "can live out their lives in the utmost peace of mind, *even though all the world cry out against them what they choose, and the beasts tear them limb from limb*," he cannot be thinking of criminals in the ordinary sense of the word, for it is evident that innocent people are meant, and if so, what innocent people received such treatment? It is not at all impossible—I think it highly probable—that Marcus looked upon the Christians as misguided enthusiasts, who had to be punished as the law then stood,[2] but whom he no more than Hadrian and Pius[3] wished to punish. Again (vii. 51) he quotes the indignant cry of whom but the Christians? *They kill us, they cut us limb from limb, they execrate us!* Adding the comment: *How does that prevent you from being pure, sane, sober, just?* In yet another place (iii. 16), in words that point still more conclusively to the Christians, he acknowledges that to own the Intelligence as ruler and guide to what is a clear duty is found also among "*those who do not believe in Gods, and those who will not stand by*

---

[1] This is not much more than what Clem. Alex. says, *Stromata*, iv. 4. There were some egregious cases of voluntary martyrdom in Spain under the Moslems (see the present writer's *Christianity and Islam in Spain*, pp. 37 ff.). See also the conduct of Callistus, afterwards Bishop of Rome. Hippolytus, *Refut. Haer.* ix. 12. Nor were philosophers exempt from the reproach of dying *iactationis causa* (see *Digest*, xxvii. 3. 6. 7).

[2] This was the view of Rusticus, his 'domestic philosopher.' (See *Acts of Justin Martyr*.)

[3] This is clear from the joint letter of Marcus and Pius to the Larissaeans, Thessalonicans, Athenians, and all the Greeks against mob-violence towards the Christians; see Melito in Eusebius, iv. 26, § 10).

O

their country, and those who do their deeds behind closed doors." Now all these three were the stock charges against Christians, and who can doubt they are hinted at here ? Lastly there is the reference to exorcism (i. 6),[1] in which Marcus says that Diognetus taught him to disbelieve.

As a matter of fact, Marcus has been condemned as a persecutor of the Christians on purely circumstantial and quite insufficient grounds. The general testimony of contemporary Christian writers is against the supposition. So is the known character of Marcus. His distinguishing characteristic, in which he excelled all recorded rulers, was humanity. His φιλανθρωπία is mentioned by Galen, Dio, Philostratus, Athenagoras (twice), Melito, and Aristides (eleven times) ; and his *humanitas* by the eminent jurist Callistratus.[2] As soon could Alexander have turned his back in the day of battle as Marcus shown cruelty to his subjects, however lowly. "Never," says Marcus in the eighth book of his self-communings, "have I willingly injured another," and Themistius (*Orat.* 15) records how, when penned in by his enemies in a new Caudine Forks, he raised his hands to Heaven and cried, "With this hand wherewith I have shed no blood, I appeal to Thee and beseech the Giver of life."

He had a passion for justice, and was most scrupulous in his observance of law, as Papinian, the greatest of jurists, has told us. That he should have encouraged mob-violence against unoffending persons, ordered the torture of innocent women and boys, and violated the rights of citizenship in his insensate fury, is as inconceivable as that St. Louis should have broken the Christian law or become a Mohammedan. That some Christians suffered for their religion in the reign of Marcus is most

---

[1] On which see note above, and *cp.* Lucian, *Philops.* § 16 (of Christ).

[2] Marcus himself in his laws repeatedly appeals to this principle. Capit. says he was noted for the mildness of his punishments, and see p. 369.

NOTE ON CHRISTIANS

probable, though there is perhaps no single martyrdom attributed to this period of which the date [1] is certain beyond cavil. That there was in any sense a general persecution of the Christians at this time is contrary to all the facts. There were numbers of them in Rome itself, with a Bishop at their head. There were actually Christians in the Emperor's household and probably (*e.g.* Apollonius) in the Senate itself. Of all these Roman Christians we only hear of Justin and his six companions being martyred, one of them being a slave of the Emperor. Other Christian slaves in the royal household survived him. If he wished to put down Christianity, why did he not begin with his own palace and with Rome ? [2]

So far from persecuting them, we know that as subordinate ruler with Pius [3] he was responsible for the letter to the Greek cities forbidding outrages against the Christians. The letter to the Common Assembly of Asia, given below, if authentic, emanated from him in conjunction with Pius or from him alone. Its genuineness in the main has been upheld by Harnack, and is certainly capable of defence.

---

[1] Dr. Abbott has given plausible reasons for doubting the date of the Lyons martyrdom, and some (*e.g.* Havet) deny the authenticity of the letter in Eusebius.

[2] The famous caricature of the Christian religion found in the pages' quarters in the Palatine (see Lanciani, *Ancient Rome* 122) dates from this reign.

[3] Melito says distinctly σοῦ τὰ συμπάντα διοικοῦντος αὐτῷ, Euseb. iv. 26. 10 (? πάντα συνδιοικοῦντος).

MARCUS AURELIUS

Ἀντωνίνου πρὸς τὸ Κοινὸν τῆς Ἀσίας ἐπιστολὴ (περὶ τοῦ
καθ᾽ ἡμᾶς λόγου).

(Eusebius, iv. 13 = Nicephorus iii. 28 ; cp. Justin.
Apol. i. ad fin.)

Αὐτοκράτωρ Καῖσαρ Μάρκος Αὐρήλιος Ἀντωνῖνος Σεβαστὸς
[Ἀρμένιος] ἀρχιερεὺς μέγιστος, δημαρχικῆς ἐξουσίας τὸ πέμπτον
καὶ τὸ δέκατον, ὕπατος τὸ τρίτον, τῷ Κοινῷ τῆς Ἀσίας χαίρειν.[1]
Ἐγὼ μὲν οἶδα[2] ὅτι καὶ τοῖς θεοῖς ἐπιμελές ἐστι μὴ λανθάνειν
τοὺς τοιούτους.   πολὺ γὰρ μᾶλλον ἐκεῖνοι κολάσαιεν[3] ἂν τοὺς
μὴ βουλομένους αὐτοὺς προσκυνεῖν ἢ ὑμεῖς.   οὓς εἰς ταραχὴν
ἐμβάλλετε, βεβαιοῦντες τὴν γνώμην αὐτῶν ἥνπερ ἔχουσιν, ὡς
ἀθέων κατηγοροῦντες.[4]   εἴη δ᾽ ἂν κἀκείνοις αἱρετὸν τὸ δοκεῖν
κατηγορουμένοις τεθνάναι μᾶλλον ἢ ζῆν ὑπὲρ τοῦ οἰκείου θεοῦ.[5]
ὅθεν καὶ νικῶσι, προϊέμενοι τὰς ἑαυτῶν ψυχάς, ἥπερ πειθόμενοι
οἷς ἀξιοῦτε πράττειν αὐτούς.   περὶ δὲ τῶν σεισμῶν τῶν γε-
γονότων καὶ γινομένων οὐκ ἄτοπον ὑμᾶς ὑπομνῆσαι, ἀθυμοῦντας
μὲν ὅταν περ ὦσι, παραβάλλοντας δὲ[6] τὰ ἡμέτερα πρὸς τὰ

---

[1] The version in Justin at the end of *Apol.* i. has the following heading : Αὐτοκ. Καῖσ. Τίτος Αἴλιος Ἀδριανὸς Ἀντων.
Σεβ. Εὐσεβής, ἀρχ. μέγ., δημαρ. ἐξ., ὕπατος τὸ πδ΄, πατὴρ
πατρίδος τὸ κα΄ κ.τ.λ.   The dates are out of place and obviously absurd ; πδ΄ = 84 and κα΄ = 21.   Altered to κδ΄ and δ΄
respectively and placed after ἐξουσίας and ὕπατος they would
give the date 161.   [2] ᾤμην Justin.

[3] ἐκείνους κολάσοιεν, εἴπερ δύναιντο J.

[4] οἷς ταραχὴν ἐμβ., καὶ τὴν . . . . κατηγορεῖτε <καὶ ἕτερά τινα
ἐμβάλλετε, ἅτινα οὐ δυνάμεθα ἀποδεῖξαι> J.

[5] These last seven words omitted J.

[6] οὐκ εἰκὸς ὑπομνῆσαι ὑμᾶς ἀθ., ὅτ. π. ὦσι, παραβάλλοντας τὰ
ὑμ. κ.τ.λ. J.

---

[1] An unusual form for Ἀρμενιακός, a title not given till 163.
[2] Marcus was consul for the third time and renewed his

388

NOTE ON CHRISTIANS

Letter of Antoninus to the Common Assembly of Asia (about our religion).

The Emperor Caesar Marcus Aurelius Antoninus Augustus [Armenius[1]] Pontifex Maximus, in the fifteenth year of his Tribunate, Consul for the third time,[2] to the Common Assembly of Asia greeting.

I am confident[3] that the Gods also look to it that such persons should not escape detection. For it is much more their concern than yours to punish those who refuse to worship them. But you harass these men,[4] and harden them in their conviction, to which they hold fast, by accusing them of being atheists. For indeed they would rather choose to be accused and die for their own God than live. Consequently they even come off victorious, giving up their lives rather than comply with your demands. And with respect to the past and present earthquakes[5] it is not amiss to remind you of them, despondent as you are whenever they occur and yet for ever contrasting our belief and conduct with theirs.[6]

Trib. Pot. for the fifteenth time in 161, in which year he became emperor on 7 March and within a few days associated Lucius Verus in the Empire with himself.

[3] The beginning of the rescript is apparently lost. *cp.* for the opening words the *deorum iniuriae dis curae* of Tacitus.

[4] The Justin text says " charge them with disorder," and adds "and bring other charges against them which we cannot prove."

[5] There were several earthquakes in Asia Minor between 138 and 180, Rhodes, Smyrna, and Cyzicus being destroyed, but the dates are not accurately settled. There was certainly one at Smyrna about 177, but that is too late. There was one at least in the reign of Pius, and the one here mentioned is supposed by some to have occurred about 152, but I think it may possibly be identified with one by which Cyzicus was chiefly affected; see Fronto. *Ad Ant.* i. 12 (A.D. 162).

[6] *cp. Or. ad Graecos*, 26; Fronto *De Elogu.* Naber, p. 147; Dio (*Epit. Xiph.*) Pius 4.

ἐκείνων. οἱ μὲν οὖν εὐπαρρησιαστότεροι γίνονται πρὸς τὸν
θεόν, ὑμεῖς δὲ[1] παρὰ πάντα τὸν χρόνον καθ᾽ ὃν ἀγνοεῖν δοκεῖτε,
τῶν τε θεῶν (καὶ) τῶν ἄλλων ἀμελεῖτε, καὶ τῆς θρησκείας τῆς
περὶ τὸν ἀθάνατον, ὃν δὴ τοὺς Χριστιανοὺς θρησκεύοντας
ἐλαύνετε καὶ διώκετε ἕως θανάτου[2].

Ὑπὲρ δὲ τῶν τοιούτων ἤδη καὶ πολλοὶ[3] τῶν περὶ τῆς ἐπαρχίας
ἡγεμόνων καὶ τῷ θειοτάτῳ ἡμῶν ἔγραψαν πατρί· οἷς καὶ ἀντέ-
γραψε μηδὲν ἐνοχλεῖν τοῖς τοιούτοις, εἰ μὴ φαίνοιντό τι περὶ[4]
τὴν τῶν Ῥωμαίων ἡγεμονίαν ἐγχειροῦντες. καὶ ἐμοὶ δὲ περὶ
τῶν τοιούτων πολλοὶ ἐσήμαναν, οἷς δὴ καὶ ἀντέγραψα κατα-
κολουθῶν τῇ τοῦ πατρὸς γνώμῃ. εἰ δέ τις ἐπιμένοι τινὰ τῶν
τοιούτων εἰς πράγματα φέρων ὡς δὴ τοιοῦτον,[5] ἐκεῖνος ὁ κατα-
φερόμενος ἀπολελύσθω τοῦ ἐγκλήματος καὶ ἐὰν φαίνηται
τοιοῦτος ὤν, ὁ δὲ καταφέρων ἔνοχος ἔσται δίκης.[6]

προετέθη ἐν Ἐφέσῳ ἐν τῷ Κοινῷ τῆς Ἀσίας.

[1] Here Harnack supplies ὅτι.
[2] ὅτι εὐπαρ. ὑμῶν γίν. τὸν πρὸς θεόν. καὶ ὑμεῖς μὲν ἀγν.
δοκεῖτε παρ᾽ ἐκείνων τ. χρ. τοὺς θεούς, καὶ τῶν ἱερῶν ἀμ., θρησκ.
δὲ τὴν π. τὸν θεὸν οὐκ ἐπίστασθε. ὅθεν καὶ τοὺς θρησκεύοντας
ἐζηλώσατε καὶ διώκ. ἕως θ. J.
[3] καὶ ἄλλοι τινὲς without ἤδη J.   [4] ἐπὶ J.
[5] εἰ δέ τις ἔχει πρός τινα τῶν τοι. πρᾶγμα καταφέρειν J.
[6] The parts underlined are those which Harnack (*Texte
und Untersuch. z. Gesch. der Alt-Christ. Liter.* xiii.) con-
siders portions of the genuine edict. Eusebius places it
under the reign of Pius, though he gives the superscription
as above. The version in Justin seems to be an "improved"
form of the text, making it clearer and more emphatic.
It is not known whether the rescript was originally in Greek
or Latin, but almost certainly it was in the former.

NOTE ON CHRISTIANS

They indeed show the more outspoken confidence in their God, while you during the whole time of your apparent ignorance both neglect all the other Gods and the worship of the Ever-living One,[1] whose worshippers, the Christians, you in fact harass and persecute to the death.

And on behalf of such persons many Governors also of provinces have before now both written to our deified father, whose answer in fact was not to molest such persons unless they were shewn to be making some attempt in respect to the Roman Government,[2] and to me also many[3] have given information about such men, to whom indeed I also replied in accordance with my father's view. And if any one persist in bringing any such person into trouble for being what he is, let him, against whom the charge is brought, be acquitted even if the charge be made out, but let him who brings the charge be called to account.[4]

Published at Ephesus in the Common Assembly of Asia.

---

[1] Harnack thinks Δία should be supplied and for the following five words substitutes ἐκεῖνος δέ.

[2] If this edict is by Pius, we should expect to find some such injunction in his "deified father" Hadrian's edict about the Christians (see Euseb. iv. 9), but there is none. On the other hand it may have been in the edict of Pius "to all the Greeks" mentioned by Melito (Euseb. iv. 10).

[3] This is the one word in the document except Ἀρμένιος which does not seem consistent with the date 161, when Marcus had only just become emperor.

[4] This portion of the edict seems too favourable to the Christians for even Marcus to have promulgated.

INDEXES

I.—INDEX OF MATTERS

References are to Book and Section of the " Thoughts," and to pages in the rest of the book.

INDEX OF MATTERS

INDEX OF MATTERS

INDEX OF MATTERS

INDEX OF MATTERS

399

INDEX OF MATTERS

INDEX OF MATTERS

INDEX OF MATTERS

II.—INDEX OF PROPER NAMES AND QUOTATIONS IN THE "THOUGHTS"

(For other names see Index I.)

404

INDEX OF PROPER NAMES, ETC.

405

INDEX OF PROPER NAMES, ETC.

INDEX OF PROPER NAMES, ETC.

INDEX OF PROPER NAMES, ETC.

INDEX OF PROPER NAMES, ETC.

III.—GLOSSARY OF GREEK TERMS

ἀδιάφορα (=μέσα), **V.** 20; **VI.** 32, 41, 45; **VII.** 31; **VIII.** 56; **XI.** 16; things indifferent, *i.e.* neither good nor bad = (1) things absolutely indifferent, such as the number of pebbles on the shore; (2) προηγμένα, things to be chosen as having a relative value, as good health; (3) ἀπροηγμένα, to be rejected, as of less relative value. *cp.* Fronto, *De Eloq.* Nab. p. 143

ἀερῶδες, τό, **IV.** 4, 21; **VIII.** 54; **IX.** 9; **X.** 7, § 2. From a comparison of these we get τὸ στερέμνιον = τὸ γεῶδες (earth), τὸ ὑγρὸν (water), τὸ πνευματικὸν = τὸ ἀερῶδες (**X.** 7, § 2, the spiritual or pneumatic into airy or aerial), τὸ πυρῶδες (fire) = ? τὸ νοερόν, *cp.* **XI.** 20

αἰτία, τὸ αἴτιον, τὸ αἰτιῶδες (*see* Seneca, *Ep.* 65), the Causal, Formal, or Formative Principle which makes a thing what it is, contrasted with ὕλη (matter), **IV.** 21; **VI.** 5; **VII.** 29; **VIII.** 3, 11; **XII.** 8, 10, 18, 29; the Primary Cause, or Nature, or God, **VIII.** 27; **IX.** 29; the Individual Cause in Man, **VIII.** 7; **IX.** 31; **X.** 26; the Quality of the Cause, *i.e.* the power it has of making a thing what it is, **IX.** 25; absorbed into the λόγος of the Universe, **VII.** 10; Destiny, the primal Cause and sum of all lower causes, **V.** 8

ἀκατάληπτος, ἀκαταληψία, impossibility of any certain conviction, **v.** 10; **VII.** 54. It was the main position of the Sceptics that nothing could be really known,

but even Socrates and his successors said similar things. Epictetus stoutly maintains the contrary

ἀκοινώνητος, one who selfishly disregards the common interests and cuts himself adrift from his fellows, **II.** 1, 2; **III.** 5; **VIII.** 34; **X.** 6; **XI.** 18 *ad fin.*; **XII.** 23

ἀναφορά, the reference of a thing to its end or purpose, its relation to its objective, with Cause and Matter making up the whole thing, **XII.** 8, 10, 18, 20

ἀξία, (1) the true value or worth of things, (2) the relative value of things preferential, **III.** 11; **VI.** 3, etc.

ἀπάθεια, the passionless calm of the true Stoic. **I.** 9 (of Sextus); **VI.** 16; **XI.** 18 *ad fin.*; *cp.* ἀταραξία

ἅπαξ λεγόμενα, words only found (it seems) in Marcus are: ἀκύβευτος **I.** 8; †ἀνδρονομεῖσθαι **X.** 19; ἀνθύλλιον **IV.** 20; ἀπαλλακτιᾶν **X.** 36; ἀποκαισαριοῦσθαι **VI.** 30; ἀπορρέμβ- εσθαι **III.** 4; **IV** 22; ἀπροστάτητος **XII.** 14; ἀρεσκευτικός **I.** 16; ἀφυσιολογήτως **X.** 9; ἀψικάρδιος **IX.** 3; γαλάκτιον **V.** 4; γλισχρεύεσθαι **V.** 5; γλώσσημα **IV.** 33; ἐμφιλοτεχνεῖν **VII.** 54; †ἐνεργησείειν **III.** 7; ἐντέριον (?) **VI.** 13; †εὐχαριεντίζεσθαι **I.** 15; καλοήθης **I.** 1; κοινονοημοσύνη **I.** 16; μνίδιον **VII.** 3; μυξάριον **IV.** 48; **VI.** 13; ὁμοδογματεῖν **IX.** 3; **XI.** 8; ὁμοθαμνεῖν **XI.** 8; παραξητεῖν **XII.** 5; περίφορος **I.** 15; προπτωτικὸς **XI.** 10; προσρήσσεσθαι **IV.** 49; ῥιπταστικὸς **I.** 16; σεμνοτυφία **IX.** 29; σμαράγδιον **IV.** 20; στρωμάτιον

411

GLOSSARY OF GREEK TERMS

v. 1; συγκατατήκεσθαι v. 1; συμ-
μηρύεσθαι III. 11; VIII. 23; συμμήρυσις IV. 40; συμπεριφιντάζεσθαι
x. 38; συμπροσπίπτειν VII. 22; x.
31; XII. 27; συννεμφέρειν III. 4;
συννήθειν (?) IV. 34; τριγερήνιος,
IV. 50; ὑπέρτασις, X. 8; φαντασιοπλήκτως, I. 7; χυλάριον VI. 13

ἀπροαίρετα, things not in our choice
or power, XII. 3, 23, 33

ἀρχαί, Zeno recognized θεός (τὸ ποιοῦν) and ὕλη (τὸ πάσχον) as ἀρχαί
or Beginnings

ἀταραξία (cp. ἀπάθεια) IX. 31, freedom from perturbation at external
things

ἄτομοι, IV. 3; VI. 24; VII. 32, 50;
VIII. 17; IX. 28, 39; X. 6; XI. 18.
Indivisible atoms endowed with
motion were, according to Democritus, and after him Epicurus
and Lucretius, the origin of all
things without any First Cause.
Marcus often puts this view, but
only to reject it

ἀφορμή = means. Marcus does not
use the word in its Stoic sense of
"disinclination")(ὁρμή

δαίμων, evil spirit, I. 6; good, X.
13; = εὐδαιμονία, VII. 17; the
"genius" or "daemon" within us,
II. 13, 17; III. 6, 7, 12, 16; VIII. 45;
XII. 3; given by Zeus to us, V. 27;
= θεός, V. 10; = νοῦς, III. 3

διάλυσις, VII. 50, etc.; a breaking up
of things into their component
parts, and the subsequent sifting
out of these into the elements

διάνοια, faculty of thought, or mind,
III. 1; = λογικὴ ψυχή, VI. 32; not
affected by the motions of the
πνεῦμα, IV. 3

διαπνεῖσθαι, to breathe through the
veins and arteries, a medical
theory (see Gataker in loc. for il-
lustrations from Galen), III. 1;
VI. 16

δόγμα, a postulate, axiom, or principle established by reason and
experience; what the sensations
are to the body and impulses to
the soul, δόγματα are to the intelligence, III. 16; called "sacred,"
X. 9. See κρίμα and θεώρημα

εἶδος, only used once (XI. 20) in its
philosophical sense of "general
term," "class," or "species"

εἱμαρμένη, ἡ, destiny, III. 6; v. 8,
etc.; = Clotho, IV. 34; τὰ συγκλωθόμενα, III. 4, 11, 16; IV. 26;
ἡ πεπρωμένη, III. 8; τὸ συμβαῖνον,
IV. 44 etc.

ἔκκλισις, avoidance)(ὄρεξις (q.v.),
VIII. 7; XI. 37. The things that
are "within the man" are κρίσις
judgment, ὁρμὴ impulse, ὄρεξις
propension towards, ἔκκλισις
aversion from, a thing, VIII. 28;
but the latter must be reserved
only for things in our power,
VIII. 7; XI. 37

ἐκπύρωσις, cyclical conflagration of
the Universe, a doctrine of
Heraclitus (q.v.), III. 3. Justin
Apol. ii. 7 points out the difference between the Stoic and
Christian view of this conflagration (2 St. Peter iii. 7, 10)

ἔννοια, conception, thought, or notion not amounting to a conviction (δόγμα), but κοινὴ ἔννοια =
φαντασία καταληπτική, a conclusive
conviction. See πρόληψις

ἐξαγωγή = suicide does not occur,
but see III. 1 (ἐξακτέον)

ἕξις, VI. 14; VII. 16; XI. 18; XII. 16.
Lucian, Conviv. 23, says, τί διαφέρει σχέσις ἕξεως; and in Hermot.
81 he laughs at the jargon of
philosophy with its ἕξεις and
σχέσεις, its καταλήψεις and φαντασίαι. Σχέσις, feature; ἕξις, a
simple essential form or quality
(ποιότης); φύσις, a forming power,
VI. 14

εὐδαιμονία, harmony of man's will
(δαίμων) with God's = εὔροια βίου,
VII. 17

εὔρους, εὐροεῖν (εὔροια, Epict. i. 4. 6),
the calm even flow of the virtuous
life = εὐοδεῖν, v. 34; x. 6; even
of Zeus himself, v. 8; εὔρουν καὶ
θεουδῆ βίον, II. 5

ἐνέργεια, the activity of the ψυχὴ
contrasted with πεῖσις (q.v.) = the
passivity of the body, v. 20, etc.

ἡγεμονικόν, τό (or τὸ κυριεῦον, τὸ
προαιρετικόν, VIII. 56), the Ruling

GLOSSARY OF GREEK TERMS

Reason (*q.v.*) or Principle (or Inner Self, *Rendall*), II. 2; IV. 1; v. 26; XII. 14, etc. = λόγος, φύσις, or even τέχνη λογική, v. 4; VIII. 7 (*cp.* ψυχή, v. 32); διάνοια, VII. 64, 68; νοῦς, IX. 22; III. 16; X. 24; XII. 3; sometimes even of God, VII. 75; IX. 22

θεώρημα, a truth perceived in Science, I. 7, § 4, 8; IV. 2; in Ethics = δόγμα, a principle or conviction; τὸ θεωρητικόν, the faculty of pure thought, X. 9; p. 375

καθῆκον, τό = *officium*, duty. Among τὰ καθήκοντα, duty in the highest sense perfectly performed, is κατόρθωμα (not used by M.). κατορθώσεις, v. 14, are acts that are the outcome of right reason

κατάληψις, VI. 30 (καταλαμβάνειν, καταληπτικός (IX. 6), ἀκατάληπτος, τὸ καταληπτικόν)=that which carries conviction; an important term in the Stoic philosophy meaning a "true comprehension" or "clear perception" of a thing without which no right conduct in life is possible." *See under* συγκατάθεσις

κατόρθωσις, *see* καθῆκον

κίνησις, motion = change, v. 10· in the flesh (Epicurus), IX. 41; of the senses, VIII. 26; of the flesh (smooth or rough), X. 8; to anger, fear, etc., VII. 55; of the mind, VII. 55; of virtue, VI. 17;)(σχέσις, VII. 60; XI. 2; tension (τόνος), VI. 38

κοινὸς and its kindred words occur over eighty times, and Marcus apparently coins the beautiful word κοινονοημοσύνη (I. 16), which deserves to rank with the "loving-kindness" of Coverdale's Bible. *See under* Fellowship

κρῖμα, conviction, almost = δόγμα, IV 3, § 2; judgment, v. 19; VIII. 47; XI. 11; *cp.* κρίσις, VI. 52, etc., the antecedent of ὁρμή, VIII. 16, 28; of the Christians, XI. 3; = ὑπόληψις (φαντασία), XI. 16, 18; § 7

λόγος (λογικός), reason or the reason, I. 8; II. 10; IV. 13, 16, 19, 24, 30, 33; v. 8, 9, 14, 28; VI. 23, 30; VII. 8, 11, 24; VIII. 48; IX. 10, 42; X. 31, 32 (νοῦς καὶ λ.); right reason, (= virtue, Cic. *Tusc.* iv. 15. 34), III. 6, 12; XI. 9; XII. 35; civic reason, IV 29; IX. 12; common to Gods and men, VII. 53; λ. of Nature, IV. 29; v 32; VI. 58; VII. 10; common to all intelligent creatures, IV. 4; VII. 9; =a man's self (τὸ ἡγεμονικόν, *q.v.*), VIII. 40; convincing reason II. 5; IV. 24; σπερματικοὶ λόγοι, of the Universe into which all things are taken back = seminal principles, IV. 14, 21; VI 24; = λόγος only, VII. 10: X. 7; λογικός, applied to ζῷον, ἡγεμονικόν, τέχνη, φύσις, ψυχή

οἴησις, self-conceit or illusion, IV. 12; IX. 34; XII. 27

οἰκονομία, IV. 19, 51; XI. 18, § 5; management, and so policy, expediency, adaptation to circumstances, ulterior end, secondary purpose, and even *finesse*. We keep the double sense of the word in our "economy of truth"

ὄρεξις, propension or inclination towards a thing, of which the result is ὁρμή and the incentive φαντασία, IX. 7: *cp.* VIII. 28.)(ἔκκλισις, VIII 7. *See under* πάθος

ὁρμή = φορὰ ψυχῆς ἐπί τι (Stob. *Ecl.* ii. 160), impulse of the mind towards a thing (*see* ὄρεξις), resulting in a πάθος

ὁσιότης = δικαιοσύνη πρὸς θεόν, piety, sanctity, holiness

οὐσία, Substance or Being, sometimes = ὕλη, matter;)(ψυχή, IV. 40

πάθος, the "affect" resulting through πεῖσις from ὁρμή, the second stage of ὄρεξις, which depends itself on assent (συγκατάθεσις). Stobaeus defines it (*Ecl.* ii. 164) as a motion of the Soul contrary to Nature; παθολογεῖν, VIII. 13, to study the πάθη = Ethics

413

GLOSSARY OF GREEK TERMS

παλιγγενεσία, XI. 1; *cp.* VII. 19. The Stoic theory was that everything repeated itself in periodic cycles, when the world was renewed again after each conflagration (*see* ἐκπύρωσις *and under* Heraclitus); *cp.* Chrysippus, περὶ προνοίας, "there will be another Socrates to live the same life again"; and Seneca, *Ep.* 36. 10, "veniet iterum qui nos in lucem reponat dies." But whether Marcus believed in this dismal theory is very doubtful, *cp.* X. 31.

παράταξις, opposed line in battle, so opposition, not obstinacy (XI. 3) III. 3; VIII. 48. *See also* p. 381.

πεῖσις)(ἐνέργεια, V 1, a passive condition antecedent to a κίνησις in the case of the body, corresponding to an ἐνέργεια of the mind, III. 6; V. 26; VI. 51; VII. 55; IX. 16

περίοδοι, V. 13, 32; X. 7. *See* παλιγγενεσία

πνεῦμα = ἄνεμος, II. 2; the surrounding air, IX. 2; the inferior part of the ψυχή as distinct from νοῦς, IV. 3; it and its motion quite distinct from the διάνοια, IV. 3. Marcus does not seem to use the word in the sense of Atmospheric Current unless XII. 30 affords an instance.

πνεύματα, what remains of things when οὐσία, ψυχή, and νοερὰ ψυχή are subtracted, XII. 30

πνευματικόν, τό, the Soul (= τὸ πνευμάτιον) of which the πνεῦμα or breath element at death goes back into τὸ ἀερῶδες, and the νοῦς into τὸ πυρῶδες, IV. 4; X. 7; XI. 20

πνευμάτιον, τό = (1) ψυχή (Soul) in its lower sense (σῶμα, πνευμάτιον, νοῦς, XII. 14) II. 2; VIII. 56; IX, 36; XII. 3, 14; (2) ψυχὴ in its higher sense, including the νοῦς, V. 26, 33; VI. 14; IX. 8, 34; XII. 30; the enveloping body and the πνευμάτιον that has grown with its growth, XII. 3; the vital breath which will be quenched or transferred elsewhere, VIII. 25; the sphere of it and the body

outside our power, V. 33; unstable like all matter, IX. 36; burdened with the body, IX. 24. *See under* ψύχωσις

ποιότης, τὸ ποιόν, the property, quality, or form of a thing (almost = the Cause which makes it what it is, IX. 25); τὸ ἰδίως ποιόν, separate individuality, VI. 3; IX. 25; X. 7; XII. 30

πολιτικός, mostly = κοινωνικός. *See* κοινός

προαίρεσις, free will or choice. *See under* ἀπροαίρετα

προαιρετικόν, τό (= τὸ ἡγεμονικόν), the faculty of choice, VIII. 56

προηγούμενον, τό, the leading or cardinal thing, VII. 55; VIII. 49; IX. 41. Marcus does not use the Stoic expression τὰ προηγμένα things preferential

πρόληψις = a primary conception possessed by all rational beings, Chrysippus in Diog. Laert. vii 53 (ἔννοια φυσικὴ τῶν καθ' ὅλου). Perceptions (φαντασίαι) resulting from sensation (αἴσθησις) produce impressions (τυπώσεις) which repeated form memory and many memories make experience which gives us conceptions (προλήψεις)

σκεδασμός, σκορπισμός (*cp.* διάλυσις), a disintegration of things into their component atoms (VI. 24; VII. 32; VIII. 25) or elements. *See under* Dispersion and Dissolution

σκοπός (or τέλος, V. 15, 16), the end or objective of life, II. 16; VII. 4; XI. 6, 21; to which every ὁρμή and φαντασία should be directed, II. 7. *See under* Aim, Objective

σπερματικὸς λόγος (*see under* λόγος), IV. 14, 21; VI. 24; IX. 1 *ad fin.* = the Generative Reason, because the Primary Fire or Reason contains in it the Germs of all things. The σπερμ. λόγοι are the creative and forming forces in Nature which have produced (1) the Universe as a whole, and (2) individual things individually. Justin, *Apol.* ii. 8. 13, applies the Stoic term to Christ

GLOSSARY OF GREEK TERMS

στοιχεῖα, τά, the elements, earth, water, air, fire, II. 3, 17; VI. 17; IV. 4; X. 7; XI. 20, etc.; almost= atoms, VI. 17; VII. 31

συγκατάθεσις, the full mental assent required for a convincing impression (φαντασία καταληπτική) before convictions (δόγματα) can be translated into movement and action, but even this is liable to error, V. 10. *See under* παθος

σύγκριμα, συγκριμάτων, the compound—man, VII. 67; VIII. 25; XI. 20; composite things)(στοιχεῖα, II. 3; VI. 10 = κυκεών, the 'farrago' of things; σύγκρισις)(λύσις, XII. 24, 36; the elements comprising the σῶμα, II. 17

συμπάθεια, sympathetic connexion or affinity of the parts in an organic whole, V. 26; IX. 9, § 3; mutual interdependence, IV. 27

συνείδησις, It is curious that Marcus never uses this Stoic equivalent for 'Conscience,' but *see* εὐσυνείδητος, VI. 30 *ad fin.*

σύστημα, an organized body, or organism, the parts of which have a relation to one another

σχέσις, a non-essential quality or feature of a thing,)(κίνησις = rest (Rendall), VII. 60; XI. 2; attitude or relation towards other things, I. 12˙ VI. 38; VIII. 27; XI. 18. Three σχέσεις, (1) towards the body, (2) towards God, (3) towards our neighbour, VIII. 27. *See under* ἕξις, κίνησις

σῶμα, τό [σωμάτιον, σάρξ. σαρκία (plur.), σαρκίδιον, κρεάδιον] a compound of τὸ γεῶδες and τὸ ὑγρόν, together forming τὸ στερέμνιον, IV. 4; X. 7; the vessel or sheath of Soul, III. 3; VIII. 27; IX. 3; that which overlays the Soul, XII. 2, 3

τελος, *see* σκοπός

τόνος (τονικός) = tension imparted to soul by atmospheric substance therein existing (Zeller), the cause of virtues and vices. Zeller also says that the Stoics imagined two sorts of motion, the one (= our

Repulsion) tending outwards and giving rise to the qualities of matter, the other (our *Attraction*) tending inwards and causing condensation. Cleanthes calls τόνος a πληγὴ πυρός

ὕλη, τὸ ὑλικόν, matter on which the αἴτιον (*q.v.*) acts

ὑποκείμενον, τό (or plural), matter not in its primary condition but as formed by the αἴτιον, VII. 29; ἡ ὑποκειμένη ὕλη, IX. 36; all material things and objects, V 10; VI. 4, 23; VIII. 22, 24; IX. 3; X. 18

ὑπεξαίρεσις, IV. 1; V. 20; VI. 50; XI. 37, exception or reservation; *cp.* "sapiens ad omnia *cum exceptione* (μεθ' ὑπεξαιρέσεως) veniet, si nihil inciderit, quod impediat" (Seneca, *De Benef.* iv. 34)

ὑπόληψις, opinion, imagination; all things are merely what we think them to be, II. 15; IV. 3, *ad fin.*; XII. 8, 26; away with opinion! IV. 7; VIII. 40; XI. 18, § 7; XII. 22, 25; leave the fact as it is and add no opinion to it, V. 26; hold the power of forming opinions sacred, III. 9; a ὑπολ καταληπτική (*q.v.*) amounts to a truth, IX. 6. *See under* φαντασία and κρίσις

ὑπόστασις, substance, IX. 1 *ad fin.* subsistence, IX. 42; X. 5

φαντασία, impression, thought, notion: don't go beyond first impressions, VIII. 49; they dye or stamp the soul, V. 16; VI. 16; sift them, VIII. 26; appraise them aright, V. 36; φαντασία καταληπτική, irresistible impression that carries assent, IV. 22; VII. 54; wipe it out, IV. 24; V. 2; VII. 17, 29; VIII. 29; IX. 7. *See under* ὑπόληψις and κρίσις

φυσιολογεῖν, VIII. 13 = Physics; *cp.* IX. 41; X. 9; so of the physiological disquisitions of Heraclitus, III. 3; *cp.* IX. 41 (from Epicurus).

ψυχή, ψυχάριον, Man = σῶμα, ψυχή, νοῦς, III. 16: but the Soul (ψυχή) twofold, (*a*) = πνευμάτιον (πνεῦμα),

4I5

GLOSSARY OF GREEK TERMS

an exhalation from blood (ἀναθυμίασις, V. 33, VI. 15), and an inhalation (ἀνάπνευσις) from the air: (b) ἡ νοερά, λογική, VI. 14, 32; IX. 8; XI. 1; XII. 30; ψυχή = τὸ ἡγεμονικόν, I. 16 ad fin.; IV. 41; V. 26; IX. 3, 27, 34; an emanation from God, XII. 26; imprisoned in the body, III. 7; cp. Int. p. xiv. The natural soul is called ῥομβός, a vortex or current, II. 17, § 1; the rational soul a sphere, XI. 12; its attributes XI. 1 §2. There is a Soul of the Universe, XII. 30, 32, and of God, V. 34, the two being really the same

ψύχωσις. It was a view of the Stoics that the embryo in the womb had only the φυσικὴ ψυχὴ of plants, and that the νοερὰ ψυχὴ came gradually to the child after birth by contact with the (cold) air, XII. 24. It was by the respiration of the atmospheric πνεῦμα that the child received the πνευμάτιον, VI. 15; X. 7

PRINTED IN GREAT BRITAIN BY RICHARD CLAY AND COMPANY, LTD.,
BUNGAY, SUFFOLK

THE LOEB CLASSICAL LIBRARY

1

CICERO : PHILIPPICS. W. C. A. Ker. (3rd Imp. revised)
CICERO : PRO ARCHIA, POST REDITUM, DE DOMO, DE HARUS-
PICUM RESPONSIS, PRO PLANCIO. N. H. Watts. (2nd Imp.)
CICERO : PRO CAECINA, PRO LEGE MANILIA, PRO CLUENTIO,
PRO RABIRIO. H. Grose Hodge. (3rd Imp.)
CICERO : PRO MILONE, IN PISONEM, PRO SCAURO, PRO FONTEIO,
PRO RABIRIO POSTUMO, PRO MARCELLO, PRO LIGARIO, PRO
REGE DEIOTARO. N. H. Watts. (2nd Imp.)
CICERO : PRO QUINCTIO, PRO ROSCIO AMERINO, PRO ROSCIO
COMOEDO, CONTRA RULLUM. J. H. Freese. (2nd Imp.)
CICERO : TUSCULAN DISPUTATIONS. J. E. King. (4th Imp.)
CICERO : VERRINE ORATIONS. L. H. G. Greenwood. 2 Vols.
(Vol. I. 3rd Imp., Vol. II. 2nd Imp.)
CLAUDIAN. M. Platnauer. 2 Vols.
COLUMELLA : DE RE RUSTICA. H. B. Ash. 3 Vols. (Vol. I.
2nd Imp.)
CURTIUS, Q. : HISTORY OF ALEXANDER. J. C. Rolfe. 2 Vols.
FLORUS. E. S. Forster, and CORNELIUS NEPOS. J. C. Rolfe.
(2nd Imp.)
FRONTINUS : STRATAGEMS and AQUEDUCTS. C. E. Bennett and
M. B. McElwain. (2nd Imp.)
FRONTO : CORRESPONDENCE. C. R. Haines. 2 Vols. (2nd Imp.)
GELLIUS. J. C. Rolfe. 3 Vols. (2nd Imp.)
HORACE : ODES and EPODES. C. E. Bennett. (14th Imp. revised.)
HORACE : SATIRES, EPISTLES, ARS POETICA. H. R. Fairclough.
(8th Imp. revised.)
JEROME : SELECTED LETTERS. F. A. Wright. (2nd Imp.)
JUVENAL and PERSIUS. G. G. Ramsay. (7th Imp.)
LIVY. B. O. Foster, F. G. Moore, Evan T. Sage, and A. C.
Schlesinger. 14 Vols. Vols. I.–XIII. (Vol. I. 4th Imp.,
Vols. II.–VI., VII., IX.–XII., 2nd Imp. revised.)
LUCAN. J. D. Duff. (3rd Imp.)
LUCRETIUS. W. H. D. Rouse. (7th Imp. revised.)
MARTIAL, W. G. A. Ker. 2 Vols. (Vol. I. 5th Imp., Vol. II.
4th Imp. revised.)
MINOR LATIN POETS : from PUBLILIUS SYRUS to RUTILIUS
NAMATIANUS, including GRATTIUS, CALPURNIUS SICULUS,
NEMESIANUS, AVIANUS, and others with " Aetna " and the
" Phoenix." J. Wight Duff and Arnold M. Duff. (2nd Imp.)
OVID : THE ART OF LOVE AND OTHER POEMS. J. H. Mozley.
(3rd Imp.)
OVID : FASTI. Sir James G. Frazer. (2nd Imp.)
OVID : HEROIDES and AMORES. Grant Showerman. (5th Imp.)
OVID : METAMORPHOSES. F. J. Miller. 2 Vols. (Vol. I. 9th
Imp., Vol. II. 7th Imp.)
OVID : TRISTIA and EX PONTO. A. L. Wheeler. (3rd Imp.)
PERSIUS. Cf. JUVENAL.
PETRONIUS. M. Heseltine; SENECA : APOCOLOCYNTOSIS.
W. H. D. Rouse. (8th Imp. revised.)
PLAUTUS. Paul Nixon. 5 Vols. (Vols. I. and II. 5th Imp., Vol.
III. 3rd Imp., Vols. IV. and V. 2nd Imp.)

PLINY : LETTERS. Melmoth's Translation revised by W. M. L. Hutchinson. 2 Vols. (Vol. I. 6th *Imp.*, Vol. II. 4th *Imp.*)

PLINY : NATURAL HISTORY. H. Rackham and W. H. S. Jones. 10 Vols. Vols. I.–V. and IX. H. Rackham. Vol. VI. W. H. S. Jones. (Vol. I. 3rd *Imp.*, Vols. II. and IV. 2nd *Imp.*)

PROPERTIUS. H. E. Butler. (6th *Imp.*)

PRUDENTIUS. H. J. Thomson. 2 Vols.

QUINTILIAN. H. E. Butler. 4 Vols. (3rd *Imp.*)

REMAINS OF OLD LATIN. E. H. Warmington. 4 Vols. Vol. I. (ENNIUS AND CAECILIUS.) Vol. II. (LIVIUS, NAEVIUS, PACUVIUS, ACCIUS.) Vol. III. (LUCILIUS and LAWS OF XII TABLES.) Vol. IV. (2nd *Imp.*) (ARCHAIC INSCRIPTIONS.)

SALLUST. J. C. Rolfe. (3rd *Imp. revised.*)

SCRIPTORES HISTORIAE AUGUSTAE. D. Magie. 3 Vols. (Vol. I. 3rd *Imp. revised*, Vol. II. 2nd *Imp.*)

SENECA : APOCOLOCYNTOSIS. Cf. PETRONIUS.

SENECA : EPISTULAE MORALES. R. M. Gummere. 3 Vols. (Vol. I. 3rd *Imp.*, Vols. II. and III. 2nd *Imp. revised.*)

SENECA : MORAL ESSAYS. J. W. Basore. 3 Vols. (Vol. II. 3rd *Imp.*, Vols. I and III. 2nd *Imp. revised.*)

SENECA : TRAGEDIES. F. J. Miller. 2 Vols. (Vol. I. 4th *Imp.*, Vol. II. 3rd *Imp. revised.*)

SIDONIUS : POEMS and LETTERS. W. B. Anderson. 2 Vols. Vol. I.

SILIUS ITALICUS. J. D. Duff. 2 Vols. (Vol. I. 2nd *Imp.*, Vol. II. 3rd *Imp.*)

STATIUS. J. H. Mozley. 2 Vols. (2nd *Imp.*)

SUETONIUS. J. C. Rolfe. 2 Vols. (Vol. I. 7th *Imp.*, Vol. II. 6th *Imp. revised.*)

TACITUS : DIALOGUS. Sir Wm. Peterson. AGRICOLA and GERMANIA. Maurice Hutton. (6th *Imp.*)

TACITUS : HISTORIES and ANNALS. C. H. Moore and J. Jackson. 4 Vols. (Vols. I and II. 3rd *Imp.*, Vols. III. and IV. 2nd *Imp.*)

TERENCE. John Sargeaunt. 2 Vols. (7th *Imp.*)

TERTULLIAN : APOLOGIA and DE SPECTACULIS. T. R. Glover. MINUCIUS FELIX. G. H. Rendall. (2nd *Imp.*)

VALERIUS FLACCUS. J. H. Mozley. (2nd *Imp. revised.*)

VARRO : DE LINGUA LATINA. R. G. Kent. 2 Vols. (2nd *Imp. revised.*)

VELLEIUS PATERCULUS and RES GESTAE DIVI AUGUSTI. F. W Shipley.

VIRGIL. H. R. Fairclough. 2 Vols. (Vol. I. 17th *Imp.*, Vol. II. 13th *Imp. revised.*)

VITRUVIUS : DE ARCHITECTURA. F. Granger. 2 Vols. (Vol. I. 2nd *Imp.*)

Greek Authors

ACHILLES TATIUS. S. Gaselee. (*2nd Imp.*)

AENEAS TACTICUS, ASCLEPIODOTUS and ONASANDER. The Illinois Greek Club. (*2nd Imp.*)

AESCHINES. C. D. Adams. (*2nd Imp.*)

AESCHYLUS. H. Weir Smyth. 2 Vols. (Vol. I. *6th Imp.*, Vol. II. *5th Imp.*)

ALCIPHRON, AELIAN, PHILOSTRATUS LETTERS. A. R. Benner and F. H. Fobes.

ANDOCIDES, ANTIPHON. Cf. MINOR ATTIC ORATORS.

APOLLODORUS. Sir James G. Frazer. 2 Vols. (*2nd Imp.*)

APOLLONIUS RHODIUS. R. C. Seaton. (*4th Imp.*)

THE APOSTOLIC FATHERS. Kirsopp Lake. 2 Vols. (Vol. I. *8th Imp.*, Vol. II. *6th Imp.*)

APPIAN: ROMAN HISTORY. Horace White. 4 Vols. (Vol. I. *3rd Imp.*, Vols. II., III. and IV. *2nd Imp.*)

ARATUS. Cf. CALLIMACHUS.

ARISTOPHANES. Benjamin Bickley Rogers. 3 Vols. Verse trans. (Vols. I. and II. *5th Imp.*, Vol. III. *4th Imp.*)

ARISTOTLE: ART OF RHETORIC. J. H. Freese. (*3rd Imp.*)

ARISTOTLE: ATHENIAN CONSTITUTION, EUDEMIAN ETHICS, VICES AND VIRTUES. H. Rackham. (*3rd Imp.*)

ARISTOTLE: GENERATION OF ANIMALS. A. L. PECK. (*2nd Imp.*)

ARISTOTLE: METAPHYSICS. H. Tredennick. 2 Vols. (*3rd Imp.*)

ARISTOTLE: METEOROLOGICA. H. D. P. Lee.

ARISTOTLE: MINOR WORKS. W. S. Hett. On Colours, On Things Heard, On Physiognomies, On Plants, On Marvellous Things Heard, Mechanical Problems, On Indivisible Lines, On Situations and Names of Winds, On Melissus, Xenophanes, and Gorgias.

ARISTOTLE: NICOMACHEAN ETHICS. H. Rackham. (*5th Imp. revised.*)

ARISTOTLE: OECONOMICA and MAGNA MORALIA. G. C. Armstrong; (with Metaphysics, Vol. II.). (*3rd Imp.*)

ARISTOTLE: ON THE HEAVENS. W. K. C. Guthrie. (*3rd Imp. revised.*)

ARISTOTLE: ON THE SOUL, PARVA NATURALIA, ON BREATH. W. S. Hett. (*2nd Imp. revised.*)

ARISTOTLE: ORGANON. H. P. Cooke and H. Tredennick. 3 Vols. (Vol. I. *2nd Imp.*)

ARISTOTLE: PARTS OF ANIMALS. A. L. Peck; MOTION AND PROGRESSION OF ANIMALS. E. S. Forster. (*3rd Imp. revised.*)

ARISTOTLE: PHYSICS. Rev. P. Wicksteed and F. M. Cornford. 2 Vols. (Vol. I. *2nd Imp.*, Vol. II. *3rd Imp.*)

ARISTOTLE: POETICS and LONGINUS. W. Hamilton Fyfe; DEMETRIUS ON STYLE. W. Rhys Roberts. (*5th Imp. revised.*)

ARISTOTLE: POLITICS. H. Rackham. (*4th Imp. revised.*)

ARISTOTLE: PROBLEMS. W. S. Hett. 2 Vols. (*2nd Imp. revised.*)

4

ARISTOTLE: RHETORICA AD ALEXANDRUM (with PROBLEMS, Vol. II.). H. Rackham.

ARRIAN: HISTORY OF ALEXANDER and INDICA. Rev. E. Iliffe Robson. 2 Vols. (*2nd Imp.*)

ATHENAEUS: DEIPNOSOPHISTAE. C. B. Gulick. 7 Vols. (Vols. I., V., and VI. *2nd Imp.*)

ST. BASIL: LETTERS. R. J. Deferrari. 4 Vols. (*2nd Imp.*)

CALLIMACHUS and LYCOPHRON. A. W. Mair; ARATUS. G. R. Mair. (*2nd Imp.*)

CLEMENT OF ALEXANDRIA. Rev. G. W. Butterworth. (*3rd Imp.*)

COLLUTHUS. Cf. OPPIAN.

DAPHNIS AND CHLOE. Thornley's Translation revised by J. M. Edmonds; and PARTHENIUS. S. Gaselee. (*3rd Imp.*)

DEMOSTHENES I: OLYNTHIACS, PHILIPPICS and MINOR ORATIONS. I.–XVII. AND XX. J. H. Vince. (*2nd Imp.*)

DEMOSTHENES II: DE CORONA and DE FALSA LEGATIONE. C. A. Vince and J. H. Vince. (*3rd Imp. revised.*)

DEMOSTHENES III: MEIDIAS, ANDROTION, ARISTOCRATES, TIMOCRATES and ARISTOGEITON, I. AND II. J. H. Vince.

DEMOSTHENES IV–VI: PRIVATE ORATIONS and IN NEAERAM. A. T. Murray. (Vol. IV. *2nd Imp.*)

DEMONSTHENES VII: FUNERAL SPEECH, EROTIC ESSAY, EXORDIA and LETTERS. N. W. and N. J. DeWitt.

DIO CASSIUS: ROMAN HISTORY. E. Cary. 9 Vols. (Vols. I. and II. *2nd Imp.*)

DIO CHRYSOSTOM. J. W. Cohoon and H. Lamar Crosby. 5 Vols. (Vols. I–III. *2nd Imp.*)

DIODORUS SICULUS. 12 Vols. Vols. I.–VI. C. H. Oldfather. Vol. VII. C. L. Sherman. Vols. IX. and X. R. M. Geer. (Vols. I.–III. *2nd Imp.*)

DIOGENES LAERTIUS. R. D. Hicks. 2 Vols. (Vol. I. *4th Imp.*, Vol. II. *3rd Imp.*)

DIONYSIUS OF HALICARNASSUS: ROMAN ANTIQUITIES. Spelman's translation revised by E. Cary. 7 Vols. (Vols. I–IV. *2nd Imp.*)

EPICTETUS. W. A. Oldfather. 2 Vols. (*2nd Imp.*)

EURIPIDES. A. S. Way. 4 Vols. (Vols. I. and II. *7th Imp.*, III. *5th Imp.*, IV. *6th Imp.*) Verse trans.

EUSEBIUS: ECCLESIASTICAL HISTORY. Kirsopp Lake and J. E. L. Oulton. 2 Vols. (Vol. I. *3rd Imp.*, Vol. II. *4th Imp.*)

GALEN: ON THE NATURAL FACULTIES. A. J. Brock. (*4th Imp.*)

THE GREEK ANTHOLOGY. W. R. Paton. 5 Vols. (Vols. I. and II. *5th Imp.*, Vol. III. *4th Imp.*, Vols. IV. and V. *3rd Imp.*)

GREEK ELEGY AND IAMBUS with the ANACREONTEA. J. M. Edmonds. 2 Vols. (Vol. I. *2nd Imp.*)

THE GREEK BUCOLIC POETS (THEOCRITUS, BION, MOSCHUS). J. M. Edmonds. (*7th Imp. revised.*)

GREEK MATHEMATICAL WORKS. Ivor Thomas. 2 Vols. (*2nd Imp.*)

HERODES. Cf. THEOPHRASTUS : CHARACTERS.

HERODOTUS. A. D. Godley. 4 Vols. (Vols. I.–III. 4*th Imp.*, Vol. IV. 3*rd Imp.*)

HESIOD and THE HOMERIC HYMNS. H. G. Evelyn White. (7*th Imp. revised and enlarged.*)

HIPPOCRATES and the FRAGMENTS OF HERACLEITUS. W. H. S. Jones and E. T. Withington. 4 Vols. (3*rd Imp.*)

HOMER : ILIAD. A. T. Murray. 2 Vols. (6*th Imp.*)

HOMER : ODYSSEY. A. T. Murray. 2 Vols. (7*th Imp.*)

ISAEUS. E. W. Forster. (2*nd Imp.*)

ISOCRATES. George Norlin and LaRue Van Hook. 3 Vols.

ST. JOHN DAMASCENE : BARLAAM AND IOASAPH. Rev. G. R. Woodward and Harold Mattingly. (2*nd Imp. revised.*)

JOSEPHUS. H. St. J. Thackeray and Ralph Marcus. 9 Vols. Vols. I.–VII. (Vol. V. 3*rd Imp.*, Vol. VI. 2*nd Imp.*)

JULIAN. Wilmer Cave Wright. 3 Vols. (Vol. I. 2*nd Imp.*, Vol. II. 3*rd Imp.*)

LUCIAN. A. M. Harmon. 8 Vols. Vols. I.–V. (Vols. I and II. 4*th Imp.*, Vol. III. 3*rd Imp.*, Vol. IV. 2*nd Imp.*)

LYCOPHRON. Cf. CALLIMACHUS.

LYRA GRAECA. J. M. Edmonds. 3 Vols. (Vol. I. 4*th Imp.*, Vol. II. *revised and enlarged*, and III. 3*rd Imp.*)

LYSIAS. W. R. M. Lamb. (2*nd Imp.*)

MANETHO. W. G. Waddell ; PTOLEMY : TETRABIBLOS. F. E. Robbins. (2*nd Imp.*)

MARCUS AURELIUS. C. R. Haines. (4*th Imp. revised.*)

MENANDER. F. G. Allinson. (3*rd Imp. revised.*)

MINOR ATTIC ORATORS (ANTIPHON, ANDOCIDES, DEMADES, DEINARCHUS, HYPEREIDES). K. J. Maidment and J. O. Burrt. 2 Vols. Vol. I. K. J. Maidment. (2*nd Imp.*)

NONNOS : DIONYSIACA. W. H. D. Rouse. 3 Vols. (Vol. III. 2*nd Imp.*)

OPPIAN, COLLUTHUS, TRYPHIODORUS. A. W. Mair.

PAPYRI. NON-LITERARY SELECTIONS. A. S. Hunt and C. C. Edgar. 2 Vols. (Vol. I. 2*nd Imp.*) LITERARY SELECTIONS. Vol. I. (Poetry). D. L. Page. (3*rd Imp.*)

PARTHENIUS. Cf. DAPHNIS AND CHLOE.

PAUSANIAS : DESCRIPTION OF GREECE. W. H. S. Jones. 5 Vols. and Companion Vol. arranged by R. E. Wycherley. (Vols. I. and II. 2*nd Imp.*)

PHILO. 11 Vols. Vols. I.–V.; F. H. Colson and Rev. G. H. Whitaker. Vols. VI.–IX.; F. H. Colson. (Vols. I.–III., V.– IX. 2*nd Imp.*, Vol. IV. 3*rd Imp.*)

PHILO : two supplementary Vols. (*Translation only.*)

PHILOSTRATUS : THE LIFE OF APOLLONIUS OF TYANA. F. C. Conybeare. 2 Vols. (Vol. I. 4*th Imp.*, Vol. II. 3*rd Imp.*)

PHILOSTRATUS : IMAGINES; CALLISTRATUS : DESCRIPTIONS. A. Fairbanks.

PHILOSTRATUS and EUNAPIUS : LIVES OF THE SOPHISTS. Wilmer Cave Wright. (2*nd Imp.*)

PINDAR. Sir J. E. Sandys. (7*th Imp. revised.*)

PLATO : CHARMIDES, ALCIBIADES, HIPPARCHUS, THE LOVERS,
THEAGES, MINOS and EPINOMIS. W. R. M. Lamb. (2nd Imp.)
PLATO : CRATYLUS, PARMENIDES, GREATER HIPPIAS, LESSER
HIPPIAS. H. N. Fowler. (4th Imp.)
PLATO : EUTHYPHRO, APOLOGY, CRITO, PHAEDO, PHAEDRUS.
H. N. Fowler. (9th Imp.)
PLATO : LACHES, PROTAGORAS, MENO, EUTHYDEMUS. W. R. M.
Lamb. (3rd Imp. revised.)
PLATO : LAWS. Rev. R. G. Bury. 2 Vols. (3rd Imp.)
PLATO : LYSIS, SYMPOSIUM, GORGIAS. W. R. M. Lamb. (4th
Imp. revised.)
PLATO : REPUBLIC. Paul Shorey. 2 Vols. (Vol. I. 4th Imp.,
Vol. II. 3rd Imp.)
PLATO : STATESMAN, PHILEBUS. H. N. Fowler; ION. W. R. M.
Lamb. (4th Imp.)
PLATO : THEAETETUS and SOPHIST. H. N. Fowler. (4th Imp.)
PLATO : TIMAEUS, CRITIAS, CLITOPHO, MENEXENUS, EPISTULAE.
Rev. R. G. Bury. (3rd Imp.)
PLUTARCH : MORALIA. 14 Vols. Vols. I.-V. F. C. Babbitt;
Vol. VI. W. C. Helmbold; Vol. X. H. N. Fowler. (Vols. I.,
III., and X. 2nd Imp.)
PLUTARCH : THE PARALLEL LIVES. B. Perrin. 11 Vols.
(Vols. I., II., and VII. 3rd Imp., Vols. III., IV., VI., and VIII.-
XI. 2nd Imp.)
POLYBIUS. W. R. Paton. 6 Vols.
PROCOPIUS : HISTORY OF THE WARS. H. B. Dewing. 7 Vols.
(Vol. I. 2nd Imp.)
PTOLEMY : TETRABIBLOS. Cf. MANETHO.
QUINTUS SMYRNAEUS. A. S. Way. Verse trans. (2nd Imp.)
SEXTUS EMPIRICUS. Rev. R. G. Bury. 4 Vols. (Vol. I. and
III. 2nd Imp.)
SOPHOCLES. F. Storr. 2 Vols. (Vol. I. 9th Imp., Vol. II. 6th
Imp.) Verse trans.
STRABO : GEOGRAPHY. Horace L. Jones. 8 Vols. (Vols. I.
and VIII. 3rd Imp., Vols. II., V., and VI. 2nd Imp.)
THEOPHRASTUS : CHARACTERS. J. M. Edmonds; HERODES,
etc. A. D. Knox. (3rd. Imp.)
THEOPHRASTUS : ENQUIRY INTO PLANTS. Sir Arthur Hort,
Bart. 2 Vols. (2nd Imp.)
THUCYDIDES. C. F. Smith. 4 Vols. (Vol. I. 4th Imp., Vols.
II., III. and IV. 3rd Imp. revised.)
TRYPHIODORUS. Cf. OPPIAN.
XENOPHON : CYROPAEDIA. Walter Miller. 2 Vols. (3rd Imp.)
XENOPHON : HELLENICA, ANABASIS, APOLOGY, and SYMPOSIUM.
C. L. Brownson and O. J. Todd. 3 Vols. (Vols. I. and III.
3rd Imp., Vol. II. 4th Imp.)
XENOPHON : MEMORABILIA and OECONOMICUS. E. C. Marchant.
(2nd Imp.)
XENOPHON : SCRIPTA MINORA. E. C. Marchant. (2nd Imp.)

IN PREPARATION

Greek Authors

ARISTOTLE : DE MUNDO, ETC.   D. Furley and E. M. Forster.
ARISTOTLE : HISTORY OF ANIMALS.   A. L. Peck.
ARISTOTLE : METEOROLOGICA.   H. D. P. Lee.
PLOTINUS : A. H. Armstrong.

Latin Authors

ST. AUGUSTINE : CITY OF GOD.
[CICERO] : AD HERENNIUM.   H. Caplan.
CICERO : PRO SESTIO, IN VATINIUM, PRO CAELIO, DE PROVINCIIS
    CONSULARIBUS, PRO BALBO.   J. H. Freese and R. Gardner.
PHAEDRUS.   Ben E. Perry.

DESCRIPTIVE PROSPECTUS ON APPLICATION

London
Cambridge, Mass.

WILLIAM HEINEMANN LTD
HARVARD UNIVERSITY PRESS